PEACE CAMPING

A HISTORY

This history of British Peace Camps begins with some Peace Camping in the 1930s and then runs from Aldermaston in 1958 to the bombing of Libya by U.S.A.F. aircraft from Upper Heyford in 1986

This copy is signed by the editor with an Upper Heyford Peace Camp pencil

mwaugh

Compiler and Editor

Michael H. M. Waugh

© 2017   Michael H. M. Waugh
Except where ownership is given

ISBN: 978-0-9532305-6-3
Second edition minor changes

Design and layout by:
Compositions by Carn
trishc@compsbycarn.demon.co.uk

First edition published Spring 1997.

TABLE OF CONTENTS

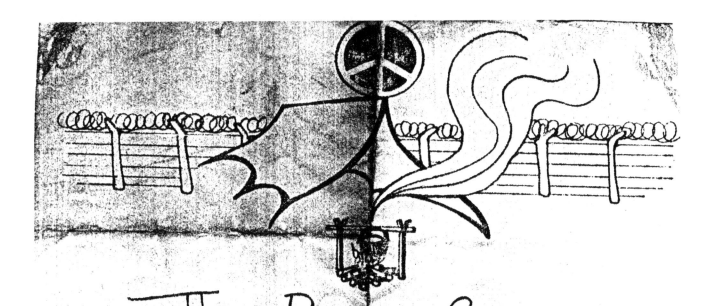

The Peace Camps

are the spearhead of the Peace movement.
    Our presence outside military bases, draws attention to
the mindless escalation of the nuclear arms race, and
constitutes a challenge to the power of the military.
    We must expect reactions from the militarist establishment,
so we need to grow stronger and stronger.
    We need to be more ACTIVE in the great work for Peace.
    Let's come together NOW and focus our energies,
visit and support your nearest Peace Camp.
    We are: Greenham, Burghfield, Molesworth, Waddington,
Upper Heyford, Caerwent, Fairford and Burtonwood. + FASLANE.
    We have only 1 yr. to stop Cruise.
    We must stop the military machine, which threatens all
our lives.
        Peace is a wave which begins in the heart
        and moves outward into the world.

    Have a good festival,

        love and peace xx

BURTONWOOD
DEMO ON
3RD. JULY
    ∇
JOIN US

        BURTONWOOD PEACE CAMPERS
        (Nr. WARRINGTON)   TEL: 061·904·9740.

NORTH

PEACE CAMPS
IN
GREAT BRITAIN

Forss

Lossiemouth

Edsell

Rosyth
Faslane
HOLY
LOCH
Leuchars
Torness
EDINBURGH
GLASGOW

Ouston
Longtown
Hexham

BELFAST
Ballyhoo

Sellafield &
Windscale

Fylingdales
Menwith
Hill
Dovehills
LEEDS
Springfield
LIVERPOOL
DUBLIN
Burtonwood
SHEFFIELD
Styal
Capenhurst
Waddington

Coltishall
DERBY
NOTTINGHAM
Sculthorpe
Cottesmore
Feltwell
Lakenheath &
Mildenhall
Alconbury &
Molesworth
CAMBRIDGE
BIRMINGHAM
Snape & Sizewell
Brawdy
Upper
Heyford
Wethersfield
COLCHESTER
Carmarthen
Fairford
Kemble
Caerwent
Brize Norton
Bridgend
The Chilterns
Foulness
CARDIFF
Welford
Aldermaston
LONDON
BRISTOL
Burghfield
Tilshead &
The Bustard
Greenham Common
Boscombe Down
Petersfield
& Porton
Bramble
BRIGHTON
Eastleigh Hythe
Farm

Luxulyan

St Mawgan

vi

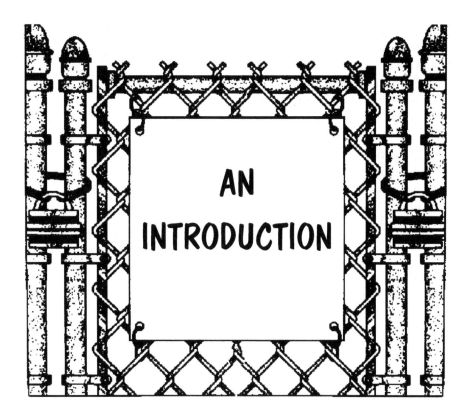

AN INTRODUCTION

I have watched history being made, with the onset of the nuclear age. Its effect on the lives of ordinary folk has led to the rise of a new way of campaigning – the peace camp. Here I have attempted to accurately record the story of the British peace camps, up to January 1987, along with a few notes on camps abroad.

Because of connexions between nuclear power and nuclear weapons, many people campaigned against both. Camps that arose on sites connected with nuclear power were similar to those at nuclear power and nuclear weapons, as well as camps (viz Brighton Beach) protesting at conventional arms.

Peace campers are not a special type of person: they range from wealthy professionals to ex-service personnel and unemployed junkies; they range in age from newborn babies to octogenarians; and they are of both sexes. Some had no home other than the peace camp where they were staying, whereas others had comfortable detached houses.

Between the two World Wars there were several open-air gatherings of pacifists in the English countryside, organised mainly by Quakers. These included the first real peace camps in the Summers of 1935, 1936, 1937, 1938 and 1939. Other camps were organised by the Fellowship of Reconciliation and the Peace Pledge Union. At some of these, people camped overnight, but their camps were not like the peace camps of the latter half of the twentieth century.

The first peace camp after World War II was at Aldermaston, over Easter, 1958. This one used no real NVDA, but at Seabrook, USA, and Torness in Scotland in the seventies, NVDA arose in a big way, setting a trend, which other camps often followed. Camps played key roles in victorious campaigns at Luxulyan, Bridgend in Mid-Glamorgan and on the Larzac in France. At Bridgend the camp kept a twenty-four-hour, seven-day watch on everything the authorities did at the site. Without this, there would have been little, if any, chance of success.

I have lived at Boscombe Down, Faslane, and Upper Heyford, and slept a night at Menwith Hill. I have visited other camps, and the sites where camps have been. I have consulted many people in the peace movement whilst researching this book. Many helped enormously, for which I thank them from the bottom of my heart. Unfortunately, there is only space here to name those who gave most help: the staffs of both *Peace News* and *The Southern Resister* (formerly *The Radiator*) for whom no request was too much; the Faslane peace campers, especially Jane and Phill; the Upper Heyford campers, particularly Margaret and Paul; campers of Greenham Common and Menwith Hill; Sally from Molesworth; Trevor and Julia from Bristol, who helped with Fairford; Sheila Rees of Cardiff; Graham Gavin of Burtonwood; Bob Ward of Barnbow; Brian and Emma from Brambles Farm; Mike Shankland, of Holy Loch Aquarian Peace

Camp; the good folk of Brighton NVDA Network who put me up in Brighton; the Fisher family and the other members of Newport, who did the same in South Wales; Cyril Brown and his family, who put me up, and showed me all the records of the camps at Lakenheath; Peter Emerson, who kindly allowed me to include his two *Peace News* reports of Ballyhoo Peace Camp; Mike Holderness, who permitted me to use his *Peace News* report of Menwith Hill; Rene Gill and the late Richard Kennedy, who allowed me to reproduce their pamphlet *24 Hours at Greenham*, with Richard's brilliant drawings; Lynne Jones, who let me use her piece on the visit of Michael Heseltine to Newbury; Gwen Bagwell, who helped me with information about the 1935-39 Peace Camps, and her sister, Joan Bagwell Lawley, whose essay about these camps I had been allowed to reproduce; and Janey Hulme, whose *New Stateman* reports filled many gaps in my knowledge. Last but not least, Trish Carn, Sandra Horn and George March gave much help.

These people can share any praise that comes my way, but all the blame for errors and omissions must rest with me.

Michael Waugh
Southampton
August 2017

PEACE CAMPS 1935-1939

SOME PEACE CAMPERS FROM THE ISLE OF WIGHT: 1935-1939

and a Memorial to Grace M. Jeffree

In the middle years of the Thirties some young students living in the Isle of Wight started performing 'Peace' plays during the summer vacation. We acted in the open air or in village halls, on Luccombe Common, in Chale Green and Whitwell Methodist Schoolroom, calling ourselves the Isle of Wight Pax Players. We were affiliated to the Pax Players. I remember four of the plays: '*Aftermath*' by H. Quant, '*Brother Sun*', one of the plays of St. Francis by Laurence Housman, '*The White Chateau*' by Reginald Berkeley and' *X = O, A Night in the Trojan War*' by John Drinkwater.

We enjoyed working and playing together in the cause of peace, and in 1935 decided to camp on the mainland and hold open-air meetings every evening for a fortnight at different towns or villages within cycling distance of our encampment. Friends Peace Committee, as it was then, borrowed a bell tent for us, and sent us literature for distribution. We found a second tent ourselves, a literature tent, a camping stove and we all had bicycles. We were seven campers this first year including Grace Jeffree and her brother Edward, three Bagwells, Leslie Lawley and Ben Osborne.

Grace made a diary of the Camp's activities for each of the five years of the Camp. They were her personal record, made from small notebooks. She covered each with paper printed from a lino-cut depicting a tent, a camp fire under a crescent moon and a tree under which stood a speaker with arm outstretched over the heads of his audience. Grace was a biologist whose work in pathological laboratories was, in later years, orientated towards research into cancer. But she also had marked artistic enthusiasms: drawing, painting, sculpture and pottery she enjoyed; and, as I recently discovered, she wrote verse, too. Grace's death on 10 November 1988 was announced in *The Friend*. Inside the cover of the first diary is written the poem:

SALISBURY PLAIN

Peace? when the bagpipes shrill the notes of war,
And stir the depths of passion in the mind,
And, whispering of swords that heroes bore,
The bugle call comes softly on the wind?
Peace? when the planes are flying overhead,
And guns are throbbing through the Summer night,
And our pulse quickens to the sound we dread,
And our hearts share the terror that we fight?
Peace? when the drums are beating, and the Plain
Re-echoes to the sound of marching feet;
When we must long to join the crowd again,
Nor cry alone to the deserted street?
Peace? when our spirits are themselves at strife,
A bitter struggle ere our souls be freed?
We must establish peace within our life
Before we share it with a world in need.

1938 – Leslie speaking at Street, Somerset. Laurence Housman (of Bookshop fame) is standing with folded arms in the audience.

That year we camped in Middle Wallop in the middle of Salisbury Plain, and held meetings at Middle Wallop, Stockbridge, Salisbury, Romsey, Mottisfont, Kings Somborne, Downton Cross, Broughton, East Tytherley, Amesbury, Winchester, Andover and Whitchurch. Each morning we went out in twos or threes. One pair would bill thoroughly the place where that night's meeting was to be held, while others would plan future meetings.

For example, on Thursday, August 15, Grace records:

"Philip and Edward went to Salisbury to arrange Saturday's meeting. Went to Mr. Cowmeadow who sent them to the Editor of the *Salisbury Times*. He offered to include a paragraph about us on Friday. Joan and Leslie to Stockbridge to arrange Friday's meeting. The Vicar seemed sympathetic promised to be Chairman and took them to Mr. Stares who lent us his meadow for the evening. Then on to Romsey where they persuaded the Congregational, Methodist and C. of E. ministers to announce our Sunday's meeting. Gwen, Ben and I tackled the Wallops for the meeting this evening. At Over Wallop we were sent by the Vicar to the caretaker of the village Hall. When we tracked her down we found that all the chairs had been borrowed by the W.I. (There was tank practice through the village that morning). So we got permission to use the Baptist School at Middle Wallop. Gwen and Ben

stayed to distribute handbills while I went back to camp to cook dinner. … there was an audience of four so transferred to the green around the War Memorial. Edward, Gwen, Phil and I spoke to a small audience which included several soldiers. We had keen arguments afterwards. Gwen and I discovered we had tackled a soldier in mufti [mufti is a military word for a soldier in civilian clothes] and at last got back to camp about 10pm.

That day was fairly typical of all our camps. We especially remember Stockbridge, which Phil and

1938 – Preparing handbills in the camp. Benches and tables from the Meeting House. Gwen, Phil, Irene, Elsie and Ronald.

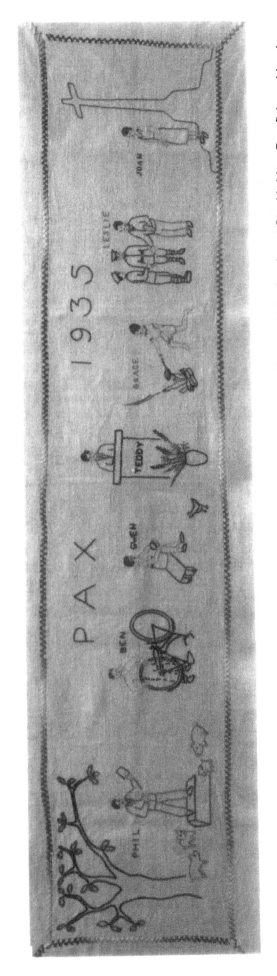

Table runner embroidered by Grace Jeffree showing seven campers: Phil waving his pound note as he speaks to the pigs at Stockbridge, Ben fixing a bicycle puncture, Gwen on a seat listening to Teddy (Edward) speaking from a church pulpit, Grace cooking, Leslie talking to two soldiers, and Joan speaking at a village cross – probably a war memorial. This was embroidered in 1935.

1938 – Long Sutton, with 'The Court House' in the background. Campers, left to right: Leslie, Ben, Gladys, Philip, Joan, Elsie, Irene, Betty, Joseph and Ronald in front.

Grace had billed. They "found one house with a cannon on each gatepost. The evening meeting was poorly attended, (except by the pigs who were very interested), as townsfolk were at the station watching the troops arrive. The Vicar said afterwards that he would not have taken the Chair if he had realised we were pacifists. He had a keen argument with a Baptist, Mr. Hale, who supported us, and afterwards asked us to take the Baptist Service on Sunday. Rode home between machine guns going to a military camp."

We "all went into Stockbridge for the Baptist Service the following Sunday. Leslie took the Service with Joan and Grace reading the lessons. Back to camp for dinner and rested in the afternoon. Roy Moxey joined us this morning for the day and came on to Romsey with us this evening. Had a very good meeting in the Square, catching the churchgoers as they came out."

The next day's meeting was at Mottisfont, a small place, and was held under a tree in front of the smithy. The Vicar took the Chair and though there were only about five women present Grace "felt it was one of our better meetings. Mr. Hale, the Stockbridge Baptist Minister, and some of his friends came to supper that evening and were "very tickled by eating everything off one plate and very good at a sing-song." We had "instituted prayers round camp fire" the very first evening and this night "had prayers before they left. Mr. Hale offered us the Chapel again the next Sunday and invited us to dinner afterwards."

So the following Sunday we took the Baptist Service again in Stockbridge. Edward took the Service this time and "then we split up for dinner with three Baptist families. Met again.afterwards, had our photos taken outside the Chapel, then on to Winchester. There we were joined by Ben Vincent [a teacher at Bembridge School on the Isle of

Wight, Ben had, by 1935, risen to become a headmaster]. Meeting beneath King Alfred's statue. A good crowd, but they would all stay the other side of the road, despite all our efforts to get them over. Cycling back, very weary, were stopped at Stockbridge by Mr. Hale and taken in to supper. Brought his autograph book away with us." The Baptist Minister in Downton, the Rev. Almond was another minister who was very helpful. He took the Chair at our Downton meeting held at the cross. Grace says it was "a good meeting" but she missed most of it as her "head was inside a car having a lengthy argument with the lady who owned it. We parted friends having gone round in circles and got no forrarder." Grace was very good at these conversations, person to person, on the edge of the meeting, or during house to house work. For example at Whitchurch Grace "found a retired Colonel during my house to house work and got him to come along to the meeting."

At Andover the meeting was held in front of the Guildhall "Ran across some Friends in the audience during the speeches and a Communist afterwards, a good chap who took a lot of literature, "to give to his friends. Phil's lamp went phut [out] but he borrowed a torch and got home safely."

When billing Amesbury we were told to "be prepared for a ducking from the military." In the event that day it poured with rain. The three who went to hold the meeting found only two people, so the meeting was abandoned. By contrast again, at Kings Somborne the meeting "was pretty well attended with a scattered crowd of 50 or 60 though there was a large military camp just outside."

"Manoeuvres in this district began yesterday. This morning troops marched down our lane to the accompaniment of bagpipes – a stirring sound – and tonight and last night we were kept awake by planes and anti-aircraft guns "I've always loved aeroplanes till now" comments Grace. "... the meeting at Broughton was badly interrupted by the troops, who clattered past in the middle between Teddy and his audience (they always will stand on the other side of the road)." Friday, August 23, was "again wet, and again just fine enough to hold our meeting at the pump at East Tytherley (with a military notice behind us saying 'Out of Bounds')." On the way home at the end of the Camp, "Passing through Broughton saw our old notice still up: 'There will be a meeting for Peace here this evening at 7.30.' Later passed over a bridge, 'This bridge is demolished.' So much for the military games."

Of course in England in August one is bound to have some rain. One Saturday was hopelessly wet. "The women's tent was so messed up by being lived in all day that we transferred to the Youth Hostel for the night." The nearness of that Youth Hostel was a blessing to us. The day we arrived not only was the bell tent still at the station, but "our luggage in advance had not been heard of." Mr. Roper, the Hostel Warden, not only helped us investigate, but lent us some Hostel blankets meanwhile. Mrs. Almond, the Baptist Minister's wife at Downton invited us all in to supper after our meeting there. We had tea at Mrs. Cowmeadow's "first washing in the canal with Leslie's soap, and being offered another wash directly we got in. We had a very good meeting in the Square at Salisbury. It must have been all that washing!

We met military people, Communists, the Vicar of Mottisfont who took the Chair for us and whose wife had 'Douglas Social Credit' views and was very helpful, and people with Second Advent ideas whom "Ben tackled very effectively and answered very well."

All the notices that we had printed for our meetings were black lettering on a golden yellow paper. In addition we made banners to advertise the Camp as we rode about – Dorothy's was "fastened to the bar of Edward's bike", Leslie's was large enough to be draped round the base of the Cross at Downton while we were speaking, and Grace embroidered the words Peace Camp in black wool on yellow ribbon which we attached to our handlebars.

We learnt a lot, and we were very greatly helped by the folk we met everywhere. It was an amateurish effort of course, but when the next August came round we were off again. In 1936 we were in Sussex based at Herstmonceux, in 1937 in Oxfordshire at Witney by the river Windrush, in 1938 Somersetshire at Long Sutton and in 1939 in Suffolk at Elmsett and near Elmsett Community. and each one of those camps had its unique features, and each needs a chapter to itself. In truth, I would like to publish Grace's diaries as they are, because they not only tell the story of those days but they reveal her ingenuity, artistry and great sense of fun. It was good to work and play with her.

The preceding pages were first typed by one of the peace campers, Joan Bagwell Lawley, and given to me by her sister, Gwen Bagwell, also a peace camper. [Any words in square brackets in the preceding pages were inserted by myself.] I am very grateful to Gwen for searching out and copying this essay, and for searching out photographs, all in good condition and all over fifty years old, and for her most helpful letters. Also I am grateful to her for the photograph of the table runner she had taken for me by Leslie Lawley. The table runner, which shows campers in action, was embroidered by the late Grace Jeffree.

In addition to the four mentioned above, Gwen told me the other most regular campers were: Philip Bagwell, Edward Jeffree, Ben Osborne and Elsie Yates. From time to time others, including Joseph Pickvance and Ronald Davidson, joined them. The group was always well supported by local Friends (Quakers) and the first I heard of these peace camps came from a Salisbury Quaker. Karlin Capper-Johnson, Friends' House Peace Secretary at the time, actively supported the camps and the Friends' Peace Committee also supported the camps.

Philip, when he was speaking to a group, would often pull out a pound note (a lot of money in the 1930s) and tell his audience how much of every pound of taxes was spent on the armed forces and on armaments. He told them twelve shillings in every pound went on war preparations. He didn't need pie charts; that pound note was enough. The photograph shown of him speaking, pound note in hand, in the centre of Burford, Oxfordshire, was published along with a report of the camp there in *Peace News* on 4th September 1937. I, too, hope to see Grace's peace camp diaries published and regret they can't be included here. These diaries require a volume to themselves. How much more effective our peace camp at Boscombe Down would have been if we campers had read these diaries, and used them as training manuals, before camping there!

1938 – Long Sutton. Friends Meeting House is in the background. Campers, left to right: Leslie, Gladys, Ben, Joan, Elsie, Irene. Photo taken by Gwen Bagwell.

1937 – Philip speaking, with the pound note in his hand.

Apart from setting up tents, and doing all the other jobs in camping, these peace campers held lectures, discussions, a concert, and to prevent boredom arising through too much mental activity, some physical sports, including a cricket match.

The highlight of this national gathering came when, on the Sunday evening, a sermon by Canon Morris was broadcast live from Birmingham by the BBC. These words of Christian pacifism gave the campers new energy and confidence. Considering the amount of influence that the arms industry and the armed forces had in 1937, it is surprising that the BBC not only allowed Canon Morris to broadcast, but allowed the whole sermon to go 'on air' without cutting it when they heard what he was saying.

This sermon, the lectures and discussions, good company, good co-operation between campers – including camp leaders and invited speakers – and much better weather than was normal for August, led to folk going away happy and much better informed, with their morale boosted immensely.

Gwen retired from peace camping over fifty years ago, but the last I heard she was still involved in the peace movement as a Quaker and a CND member. She followed in the footsteps of a father who spent two-and-a-half years in jail as a conscientious objector.

Swanwick, Derbyshire 1937

Brigadier-General F. P. Crozier, the distinguished World War I British Army officer turned pacifist, attended the Peace Pledge Union's national gathering at the beginning of August, 1937. So did Dick Sheppard (of course!), Kingsley Martin, Max Plowman and lots of other folk. It was a family affair, and the prizes for the children's events were presented by none other than Gracie Fields (or rather, John Barclay dressed up to look like the most popular singer of that decade).

L. H. Thomas reported in *Peace News* on August 14, 1937, that representatives came "from all quarters of the British Isles, bursting with the desire to make their pacifism a live force in the country" to Swanwick, Derbyshire, where they set up their tents. He didn't call it a peace camp, but it certainly was one.

1936 – Peace Campers at Battle! Battle Abbey is in the background with Edward speaking and Gwen and Leslie talking with passers-by.

ALCONBURY
and
MOLESWORTH

GUIDED TOURS OF ALCONBURY AND FARMING AT MOLESWORTH (December 1981 - December 1984)

An unfenced, grass field of about 650 acres, crossed by a bridleway, and a private, but ungated, road (officially only a public footpath, but used as a public road) where lay a few dilapidated sheds and offices left over from when this was last used as a military airfield in 1957, was RAF Molesworth in 1981: disused and deserted.

Like RAF Alconbury, ten miles to the East, it didn't even have a proper security fence. Alconbury was much bigger: It had a long runway, a collection of buildings, some USAF Phantom fighter-bombers and a Blackbird SR7 spy plane, and was a key link in a microwave radio network.

Her Majesty's Secretary of State for Defence announced Molesworth to be Britain's second base for Ground Launched Cruise Missiles, and Alconbury to be its supply base. This alarmed many Christians. Consequently, some members of the Society of Friends (Quakers), Pax Christi, Christian CND, and the Fellowship of Reconciliation, including Helen Young and Angela Needham, started a peace camp at what is now Peace Corner, on Holy Innocents Day, 18th December, 1981. To begin the camp, a Service of Eucharist was said, with the Bishop of Huntingdon, Gordon Roe, and the Orton Malpas Vicar,

Michael Scott. There was no immediate reaction from the authorities.

By 31st January, 1982, six regular campers were living on the site in Old Weston Road, near Brington. On some nights up to twenty people were sleeping there. Folk were busy getting the camp publicised, surveying the airfield and leafleting local villages.

The camp's first big action was a 'plant-in', which involved both campers and supporters. The police and the airfield commander were informed in advance. They stayed away on the day, 21st March, when ceremonies began with about 250 people attending a service at a shrine built by architecture students who supported the camp. Folk then planted over fifty trees – oak, ash, horse chestnut, apple and pear; seeds of onions, broad beans and lettuce; fruit and rose bushes; herbs and flowers. 21st March was chosen as it was the Spring Equinox.

Over the next few days, as campers tended their gardens, people brought more plants, trees, and manure. The manure may not have been necessary, because RAF Molesworth is said to lie on grade A agricultural land.

Some years before, the RAF had planted ornamental trees and bushes on the airfield, but years of neglect and battering by the wind had left these looking pretty tired.

A worrying moment came when a contractor arrived to plough the gardens and sow grass, but after a discussion, he and his men were happy to leave.

By now the local bobby, Keith, had become a popular caller at the camp. Peter, the Modsquad inspector, also called and made friends. Everything was peaceful.

In the evening of 21st April, a Coca-Cola bottle with a message inside, was thrown into the camp by an unknown person. The message warned campers that the gardens were to be dug up next morning. The telephone tree was activated and supporters came to the camp, but when, on the morning of 22nd April, the police arrived, there were only fourteen activists at the camp. The airfield commander arrived, and campers were asked to remove the plants, which they refused to do. At the bottom of the garden, on MoD land, a tractor with a harrow came out of the mist. Campers ran over and sat in front of it. The tractor then started manoeuvering, and they kept moving and sitting down in front of it. Just as it seemed the fourteen protesters were winning in this strange game, a second machine appeared, making for the herb garden, which was also on MoD land. Campers split their forces so that some could sit in front of it, too, and they were having a hard time keeping the two vehicles occupied to prevent them ripping up the gardens. Once again, they seemed to be winning, but the fifteen police on site then started moving campers out of the way. Realising that they would have to retreat, campers then started to dig up their plants, helped by a policewoman. There were obviously good relations with police here. Protesters were asked to leave, having dug up what they could. They went and lay down on the gardens, singing. Police put them into vans, and took them to Huntingdon Police Station, where seven campers and two supporters were charged with behaviour likely to lead to a breach of the peace, and bailed.

In April, a letter arrived from Cambridgeshire County Council asking the campers to move. They stayed, so on 18th May a full meeting of the whole council voted thirty-five to twenty-eight in favour of court action to evict the camp.

On Thursday, 27th May, the nine defendants of the gardens action appeared in court, and were each fined £15 plus £25 costs. Helen Young and Angela Needham appealed. At least two defendants refused to pay, and were subsequently imprisoned in Holloway from 1st to 5th December.

After the national CND rally in Hyde Park, in June,

1982, some Molesworth campers were arrested at a 'die-in' outside the US Embassy, and held in custody for a day. They were bailed on condition they leave London and live at the peace camp. This unusual condition could have created complications if the camp had been evicted. When they went to court, they were fined £5 each, with the alternative of a day in jail. They chose the latter, and left court free, because they had already spent a day in custody.

On Wednesday, 23rd June, Molesworth was the seventh peace camp visited by Peter Baker on his sponsored hitch-hike. From here he returned home, via London, where he delivered his letters calling for disarmament to the Prime Minister's house at 10 Downing Street.

On 3rd July, the authorities held an open day at RAF Alconbury. Campers held a vigil at the gates, and leafleted the public there.

On American Independence Day, the USAF celebrated on the base. The peace campers read out their own 'Declaration of Independence for Europe' in a ceremony outside the Main Gate.

Hiroshima Day saw the first monthly blockade of Alconbury by Molesworth Peace Campers. It lasted just ten minutes at noon. This blockade was part of a 108-hour vigil they had organised there.

'Tomorrow's Land – Today' was the theme of a festival held at Molesworth Peace Camp on 2nd and 3rd October.

At the monthly blockade of Alconbury on 6th October, twelve people were arrested and charged with obstruction of the highway. On 3rd November they appeared before Huntingdon magistrates and all the cases were adjourned to 7th December.

No arrests were reported at the next blockade of RAF Alconbury on 6th November.

In November Cambridgeshire County Council wrote to inform Molesworth Peace Camp that they intended to apply for an order in possession. The camp decided to fight their eviction attempt.

Another blockade of RAF Alconbury was held on 6th December, and again no arrests were reported.

In Huntingdon Magistrates Court, on 7th December, all twelve of the people arrested on 6th October were fined. Some refused to pay fines, and at least two of these were subsequently jailed for one week (on 18th May, 1983) for not paying.

Many visitors wished the camp luck at its first birth-

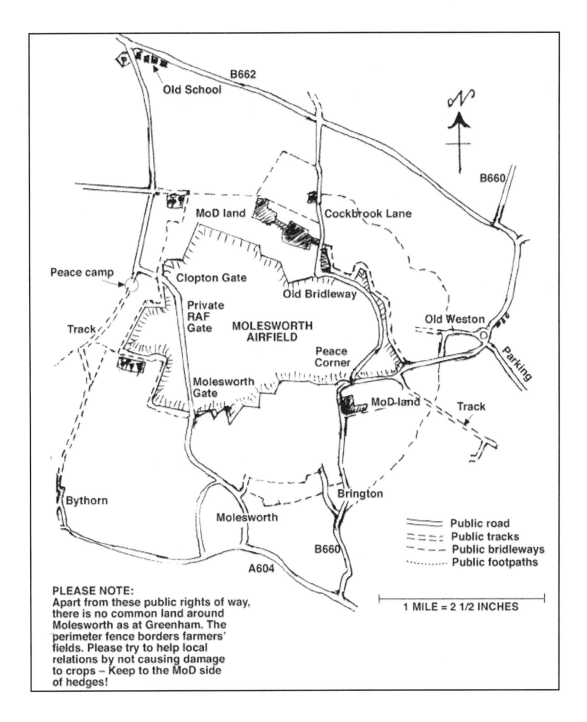

B662

Old School

B660

MoD land

Cockbrook Lane

Peace camp

Clopton Gate

Old Bridleway

Old Weston

Private
RAF
Gate

MOLESWORTH
AIRFIELD

Track

Parking

Peace
Corner

Molesworth
Gate

MoD land

Track

Bythorn

Brington

Molesworth

B660

A604

	Public road
	Public tracks
	Public bridleways
	Public footpaths

1 MILE = 2 1/2 INCHES

PLEASE NOTE:
Apart from these public rights of way,
there is no common land around
Molesworth as at Greenham. The
perimeter fence borders farmers'
fields. Please try to help local
relations by not causing damage
to crops – Keep to the MoD side
of hedges!

day party, held two days early on 26th December, as Boxing Day was a more convenient day for the visitors, it being a Bank Holiday. Campers held a small celebration of their own on 28th December.

In January, the case presented by the peace camp against the High Court granting an order in possession was disallowed. Then, in February, the campers were told that they could, after all, present a case, and that their presentation would be allowed.

RAF Alconbury was again blockaded on 6th January, 6th February (when all the gates were closed successfully for half an hour) and 6th March. Still no arrests were being reported.

Every spring brings new hope, and new growth, especially to those who have prepared their land by ploughing and digging it in the winter, as the Molesworth campers had done. On 3rd April, 1983, they held a second 'Plant-in' on the gardens they had prepared. The authorities apparently let them get on with it.

At about this time, Alconbury Peace Camp Mark I was set up by two unknown peace campers, on the airfield itself. They slept there undisturbed for one night and left in the morning without being discovered by the authorities.

On the 6th April blockade of RAF Alconbury, twelve people blockaded the gates and five sat down inside.

Apparently none of them was charged with any offence.

On 26th April, five campers paid a special visit to Alconbury in the evening and put banners on a 120-foot high water tower in preparation for a visit to the airfield by Michael Heseltine, Secretary of State for Defence, the next day.

At the beginning of June, two former campers were arrested for not paying fines in connexion with Alconbury blockades. The report gave no details, but almost certainly only one blockade – the October one – was involved, and they would have been imprisoned for five days. All through the summer these blockades continued on the sixth of each month, with an extra one on 4th July to commemorate US Independence Day, followed by a vigil until the regular blockade began on 6th July. Whilst this was going on at the Main Gate, three Molesworth campers held a picnic, with a bonfire, on the runway. When they had finished, they strolled over to the Guardroom, to tell the modplods what they had been doing. Again, apparently nobody was charged with any offence.

RAF Alconbury's long-awaited security fences started to be erected in July.

On 26th July, Cambridgeshire County Council at last evicted Molesworth Peace Camp from its Old Weston Road campsite. It will be recalled that, after sending a letter asking the camp to move, the council voted, on 18th May, 1982, to evict it – over fourteen months before the actual eviction! Undoubtedly the legal arguments put up in the courts helped delay the eviction. At the eviction there were four arrests.

Near the Eastern side of Molesworth airfield was an unsurfaced lane – Warren Lane. This was owned jointly by two landlords; the MoD, as landlord of the adjoining farmland, owned the Eastern half, and a farmer owned the Western half. This was a fairly common arrangement in the area for old public rights-of-way that were not maintained by the local council. Warren Lane had side verges – it was over thirty feet from hedge to hedge. Recently, another peace camp had been set up here, mainly by travelling people, and the campers evicted from Peace Corner came across the airfield and joined them.

From 6th to 9th August there was a vigil at Alconbury with daily blockades. No arrests were reported.

By 24th September, the day of Alconbury Air Show, there were two peace camps at Molesworth again: One in Warren Lane off Fay Way, and one near the Peace Corner campsite that had seen the July eviction. Campers from both camps leafleted the air show, and one American camper chained himself to an F1-11 nuclear fighter-bomber. Only the American was charged with any offence, and he was subsequently bound over to keep the peace for one year on 13th October.

Also in October, peace campers were planning a civil court action for damages against the bailiffs at the eviction.

On 10th December 1983 there was a 400-strong march from Alconbury airfield to Peace Corner at Molesworth, followed by a candle-lit vigil and a walk onto the still-unfenced MoD airfield. Some folk then set up camp on the airfield itself. This was the beginning of Rainbow Fields Village.

Christmas, a second birthday party (and here the two newer camps joined in with the reformed Peace Corner Camp's celebration) and the New Year passed peacefully.

On Sunday, 15th January, 1984, the anniversary of the birth of Martin Luther King, Alconbury Peace Camp Mark II was set up when ten people spent the night in a caravan and tents on Cambridgeshire County Council land opposite the main gate to RAF Alconbury. At an opening ceremony the Bishop of Huntingdon blessed the camp.

The very next day council officials told the campers they had twenty-four hours to leave; three hours after this seventy police arrived and sealed off the camp, preventing folk from getting to and from the camp. They then arrested seven people for obstructing the highway and in answer to objections said that for obstruction purposes the highway included the grass verges!

The five campers and two visitors who had been arrested were strip-searched, forcibly fingerprinted and then photographed. After going through this ordeal the two visitors were released without being charged. The five residents were bailed on condition that they stay away from the airfield. There was a one-mile limit on four of them and the fifth, a local villager, had to stay at least half-a-mile away. Complaints against the police were made about the strip-searches, damage to property, refusal of access to solicitors and assault during photography. Needless to say, after the police raid this camp was closed. It had lasted just thirty-two hours and twenty minutes.

On 29th January a vigil was held at RAF Alconbury. During it a schoolgirl was knocked down by a horse ridden by a man. She was not seriously hurt.

Alconbury Peace Camp Mark III was set up with a caravan on British Rail land. It received good publicity in spite of the fact it was only there six hours. Soon after it began British Rail officials accompanied by police came and told campers that if they didn't move before the day was out they would be evicted and charged with the offence of trespass on British Rail land. As they had been interviewed by media people the camp had done some good in publicising their campaign, so the campers decided to leave voluntarily and plan other actions.

Alconbury Peace Camp Mark IV was held on the main runway on 26th February. After setting up camp and making it comfortable the three campers decided to go for a stroll, and pay a courtesy call on the USAF to let them know they were there. They found some US servicemen. The servicemen came to the camp and were very rough when they broke it up. Campers suffered one broken wrist and one badly cut wrist as a result of the use of plastic handcuffs of a type banned in some American states, and not approved for use by any British police force. These injuries led campers to initiate an assault and battery charge against the airfield commander. Up to 30th March, Janey Hulme had estimated that of a total of nineteen arrests so far at Molesworth, nine resulted in charges of obstructing the highway and ten led to releases without charge; whilst of a total of thirty-two arrests at Alconbury, fifteen led to fines for obstructing the highway and the other led to discharges and folk being released without charge. (Janey Hulme's 'Roll Call', *New Statesman*, 30th March, 1984.)

At Easter another 'plant-in' was held at Molesworth and hundreds of people went onto the airfield to plough, dig and plant. Wheat was planted in order that a crop might be grown that could be sent to famine-struck Ethiopia. Paul Rogers and some other activists occupied hangars on the airfield for a time. They were not apparently charged with any offence.

Alconbury Peace Camp Mark V was set up on 29th April. Eviction proceedings started immediately. The campers wisely found an alternative site to occupy when they were evicted. The alternative site was in a field across the road, and should they be evicted from that, a camper's friend owned land nearby and had invited them to camp there. This was a secluded site and campers preferred the Mark V site and the field across the road, because both were easily visible to thousands of people using the Great North Road A1.

The national media ignored Alconbury's new camp

and peace movement journals gave it hardly a mention, which meant that the peace movement outside the local area knew little of its existence. In spite of this, campers were making lots of local friends, especially in Abbot's Ripton village where many folk, already annoyed by aircraft noise, were worried that there would be a great deal more noise when RAF Alconbury became fully operational as the supply base for Molesworth. This helped maintain local media interest, and the camp was getting local publicity. Soon the camp had broken the longevity record of thirty-two hours, twenty minutes set by Alconbury Mark II. The authorities would have found it difficult to block the main road and remove the camp this time because lots of people on the Great North Road would see what was happening and news would soon reach the local supporters of the camp. This camp had much better local support. Understandably the authorities were getting worried. Also the new security fences were proving no real obstacle to campers and security was lax, so they were able to enter the airfield frequently. The authorities were a little upset when a camper told a visiting journalist: "We're giving guided tours of the base to people because it's so easy to get in. Would you like one?"

Modplods were picking up campers on the airfield and asking: "Is this another of those guided tours?" (This story and the two quotations were recalled by Sybilla Snake interviewed as one of the Alconbury Nine in *Peace News*, 31st May 1985). The modplods joked but their bosses were worried.

Also in April, Lanky and Phil were arrested for not paying fines. Terry and Sybilla Snake were arrested trying to stop police taking Phil away. A complaint was lodged because the police had entered the caravan to get Phil with neither just cause nor an arrest warrant.

Meanwhile the county councils were publishing plans for a new road to link A1 and M1. By a happy coincidence (!) this road was planned to pass close to RAF Molesworth, and to have a road junction connecting it to B660, which met the airfield at Peace Corner. B660 was itself to be improved with a bypass for Brington. Obviously this would prove useful to Cruise convoys which could use the road onto the airfield at Peace Corner.

The camp beside Peace Corner was growing, as was Rainbow Fields.

After climbing over the fence onto the airfield, ten people were arrested on the Alconbury runway on 12th or 13th May. A US policewoman strip-searched two of them, and this led to complaints in Parliament. The other eight were strip-searched by the Modsquad.

The bailiffs came and Alconbury Mark V closed after six weeks. The campers simply moved across the road and set up Alconbury Peace Camp Mark VI in the field they had reserved as an alternative site. It was business as usual from the new campsite, with campers continuing to enter the airfield and getting considerable local publicity.

Over the weekend of 8-10th June, 1984, peace campers helped Peterborough nuclear disarmers with a vigil at RAF Alconbury, which was planned to coincide with the Economic Summit Conference in London, and to contrast arms spending with the spending on food for the starving.

Neither the tenant farmer nor the landlord of the field in which Alconbury Mark VI lay applied for an order in possession, so the authorities were denied the pleasure of a conventional eviction at somebody else's expense. The camp was continuing to cause them problems. They felt they had to do something and so, at 06.45 hours on 20th June, 1984, they arrested on private land, six regular campers: Paul Briggs, David Turner, Veronica Dignam, Phil Hudson, Fergus Watts and Paul Rudolf. They were all photographed and fingerprinted. The police confiscated the camp's diary and visitors' book, though the campers did not know these had been taken by the police until they were produced at the final trial.

Shortly afterwards, Roger Oakley was arrested near, but not at, Alconbury Mark VI camp site. The camp, of course, had to close after these arrests.

Doris Mourning spent 20th June in Holloway Prison unaware of what was happening at Alconbury and was surprised when, as she left Holloway at the end of her sentence on 21st June, she was arrested by police, who had come from Huntingdon to London to fetch her.

Within hours, Doris was in Huntingdon Magistrates Court along with the other seven. All were charged with conspiring together and with others unknown to trespass in order to cause criminal damage. The criminal damage on the charge sheets was as defined in the Criminal Law Act, 1977. These were extremely serious charges, and as the death penalty for conspiracy had never been repealed, long prison sentences or even death penalties were possible. The defendants were released on bail with stiff conditions. David Turner was released on condition that he lived at his home in a lo-

cal village and not go within half a mile of the airfield. All the others were forbidden to go within a mile of the airfield. Paul Briggs was bailed on condition he lived at his mother's home in Hereford, where she stood £1,000 surety. Veronica was remanded in Holloway for one week, while police checked her bail surety. Then she, too, was bailed to live in Hereford, but with £500 surety. Paul Rudolf was bound over for twelve months in the sum of £350; fined £500 in £15 weekly instalments starting in August and given a twelve-month suspended prison sentence suspended for two years. Both Rudolf and Paul were unemployed. The next defendant, Paul Briggs, was bound over in the sum of £300, with a sentence of 170 hours of community service. Sybilla was bound over in the sum of £300 and given a community service sentence of 200 hours. Judge Young told Veronica she would have to go to Hereford.

That makes eight; the ninth of the famous Alconbury Nine was Ian Winters, who was arrested in late July or early August. He, too, was charged with conspiracy and released on bail.

All the defendants elected to go to trial and were ordered to appear in Huntingdon Magistrates Court on 18th October.

In July CND National Council met and passed a resolution proposed by Christian CND Vice-Chairperson David Pybus (who also represented the Molesworth and Alconbury Peace Camps) supporting the Alconbury Nine and promising help with legal support and publicity.

On 28th July at 02.45 hours, three Molesworth campers occupied water towers at RAF Alconbury, intending to stay for the 'Air Tattoo '84' show later that day. Modplods and US security police soon found them, however, and tried to persuade them to descend. They would not. A modplod then climbed one tower and knocked the campers' rucksacks containing all their food and drink and warm clothes to the ground. The campers were promised immunity from prosecution but only if they descended immediately. Two descended and were released without charge. The third came down an hour later, was arrested by four modplods and charged.

I visited Molesworth at this time and drove my van across the airfield. I brought back a leaflet, 'Harvest for the Hungry', which, broadly speaking, was about the attempt by Molesworth peace campers to grow food on the airfield and use it to feed the starving of the Third World as well as themselves. This was to lead to loads of food that later left for famine-struck Eritrea. There were really three separate camps working together at Molesworth if one includes the festival as a camp in its own right, which after-knowledge revealed it was. Part of my report written in 1984 for Boscombe Down Peace Camp is relevant here, and illustrates the size of the camps at Molesworth then.

TIME AND LAYOUT

I spent five hours at Molesworth from 14.15 hours to 19.15 hours on 27th August. There was much to see. Molesworth is actually two camps, several miles apart, with an RAF airfield in between them. One is at Warren Lane; the other is at Peace Corner. (Warren Lane was a track off Fay Way. This was the Fay Way Camp. The Peace Corner Camp was at or near the site of the first eviction). A stray caravan and Ford Transit parked at one of the base entrances is not part of the peace camp, so the occupier told me.

WARREN LANE

Mainly residential, this camp has about ten caravans, a tent and a coach converted to a luxury mobile home (for sale at £1,500). There is a wooden cottage under construction here. The camp sprawls along both sides of a bridleway that is owned jointly by two farmers (apparently one was a MoD tenant farmer) who own the adjoining fields about half a mile from the base boundary. One of the farmers has at last succeeded in getting the local council to take out an eviction order on the camp, which is effective from 1st September. Many people who live here appear to work at Peace Corner. Nick and Julia appear to be the people to see if you need information here. There are vegetable plots with crops at two caravans.

PEACE CORNER

This is alongside an old road onto the airfield, and the actual corner is where this road joins the public 'C' road at a 'T' junction. (It is amazing how I drive about without knowing what road I am on! The 'C' road was, of course, Old Weston Road B660). The base road goes for about fifty yards across county council land. On one side you will find the Green Gathering Information Caravan and on the other walled gardens – if you don't believe it, go and see it – wells being dug, and a ditch being infilled. As you cross a non-existent boundary line into the base, you see a peace chapel being built on the right. Its internal measurements are seven and a half metres by five metres approximately and the materials being used include bricks (I helped unload another 1,000 donated while I was there) cement, lumps of stone and concrete and glass. This is on MoD land. Then you see two ploughed fields, ploughed by a hired heavy tractor and plough also on MoD land – actually outlying parts of the airfield. Among the cotoneaster and other shrubs planted by the RAF years ago, fruit trees have been planted by the peace campers. They have loads of tools and a grey Ferguson tractor with hydraulics for light work, but it is not heavy enough to plough the clay soil and thick mat of turf on the airfield.

THE FESTIVAL

Walking onto the airfield, from Peace Corner, I came to the Peace Corner Festival which was like a cross between Southampton Show and Stonehenge. There was an information tent, and here I left one of our own leaflets as I had done at the information caravan and at Warren Lane. I asked them to put a mention of our peace camp in their news-sheet for 28th August and asked if they could include greetings and best wishes from all at Boscombe Down Peace Camp to all at Molesworth. There was music, dancing (both nude and with clothes) circus acts, a clown, literature stalls, an exhibition and countless other attractions. The International Peace Camp Conference was being held there somewhere, but I was unable to find it in the time at my disposal. There were no high fences anywhere on the base.

CONCLUSIONS

It has given me encouragement and shown what can be done by peace campers on MoD and county council land. Our camp is growing and finance should be easier to get now we are established, to which we can put our own money to do things. Perhaps if we provide the labour and collect our wages from DHSS, supporters not living on the camp could provide the bricks, mortar, seeds, tools and machines to build and grow.

That was Molesworth in 1984. The ongoing Peace Corner Festival later became known as Rainbow Fields. The conclusion with its reference to 'our' Boscombe Down Peace Camp shows how ideas spread among the camps.

On 25th August the collection of the harvest of 'Wheat for the Starving' began, in order to send the first load of wheat to Eritrea.

On 31st August there were further conspiracy charges at RAF Alconbury as 300 people blockaded all the gates and charged service people on the base with conspiracy to commit genocide! Legal and cash problems prevented it being done in court. The peace activists served eviction notices on the base, inviting the base commander to a theatrical court case to be held in Huntingdon Market Square where campers were going to apply for a theatrical order in possession for the airfield. About 100 campers were arrested at the blockade and taken to Peterborough.

The three who had been arrested inside the base were detained overnight but the others were released on bail. All appeared in Peterborough Magistrates Court the next day on charges relating to criminal damage, breach of the peace, and obstruction. The thirty-seven who pleaded guilty were dealt with quickly, but sixty-nine pleading not guilty were remanded to two different magistrates courts and several sittings. The dates for Huntingdon were: 1st, 10th, 15th, 24th, 29th and 31st October . The dates for Peterborough were: 8th, 15th, 22nd and 29th October . One report states that eight people pleaded guilty at Peterborough and were fined £25 each. Janey Hulme gives figures of 140 arrested and 119 eventually charged with obstruction. ('Roll Call' *New Statesman*, 30th March, 1984) The other information on these court cases was gleaned from several sources including *Peace News* and the *Molesworth Bulletin*. Unfortunately nobody outside the MoD appears to have made a complete record of these cases.

Meanwhile, a gravel road on Molesworth Airfield was being resurfaced.

The Bishop of Huntingdon returned to Molesworth on 1 September and conducted a service of dedication for the Eirene Peace Chapel, which was still not complete.

The peace camp was still in Warren Lane on 3rd September awaiting its promised eviction.

On 13th and 14th September surveyors attempted to survey Molesworth Airfield, and put in marker posts. They left their posts on the Friday afternoon firmly in the ground. By Monday, 17th September, they had all vanished.

Also about this time, peace campers discovered that Walter Lawrence Construction were to build barracks for 228 Cruise technicians at Alconbury.

The Alconbury Nine appeared before Huntingdon magistrates on Thursday, 17th October. Apparently this was about the eighth appearance before magistrates on these charges for most of them. Here the committal proceedings were adjourned until 11th-14th December.

On 20th October, which the campers called 'Winter Planting Day', a container loaded with wheat was given a big send-off as it left Peace Corner on a lorry bound for the docks and a sea journey to Eritrea. In addition to the wheat the container held clothes and blankets.

Over 100 trees were planted near Eirene in October in memory of Caroline Taylor, killed in a road accident.

Also in October Fergus Watts was arrested and detained in Armley Jail, Leeds. Whilst there he found out that the Alconbury Nine were being watched and their movements monitored by the police.

On 24th November one camper was not charged with any offence when he was ejected from a meeting in Brington called by the local Tory MP to tell local people about the plans for Molesworth.

In November one person was arrested for interfering with surveyors at Molesworth. They were probably surveying a route for the new fence. At about this time the MoD ordered 6,000 concrete fence posts for it. Anybody who deals in fence posts will know that is an enormous order.

Some of the Alconbury Nine addressed the 1984 CND National Conference about their court cases.

On 2nd December, John Parry was arrested at the 'Reclaim Alconbury' action. It was reported that he faced two charges, "the most politically significant of these being the second which reads: 'That you did in this county of Cambridgeshire on 2nd December, 1984, steal a Vibrator, the property of the United States Air Force'. No, it wasn't one of those big mechanical things you use in road building… it was one of the other sort." ['Earwiggings' column, *Peace News*, 25th January 1985]. My research failed to get to the bottom of this intriguing story.

Local people held a public meeting in Old Weston to discuss the government's plans for RAF Molesworth on 12th December, 1984.

At Peterborough Magistrates Court on 11th December, the committal proceedings for the nine were opened. They were all there except for Roger Oakley who was unable to attend as he was recovering from injuries received in a traffic accident. His case was adjourned.

The MoD offered no evidence against David Turner and Ian Winter and their cases were dismissed. Along with the other seven they had been subjected to arrest, bail conditions and police surveillance for eleven months while the MoD were trying to gather evidence to prove them guilty. Even then the MoD did not have enough evidence to send them to trial – let alone to convict them of any crime! Why were they arrested and charged in the first place?

The remaining six faced and cross-examined many witnesses at these proceedings. Squadron Leader

Nelson, the Officer Commanding Alconbury, in answers to the skilful cross-examining, said that there were 3,000 US personnel, 300 civilians, a number of contractors' employees and just one RAF officer on the base. This one officer was really only one quarter of an officer because he had to split his time between Alconbury, Molesworth and two other RAF stations, which he commanded. A modplod described the blue card they were given with instructions on how to deal with protesters and said they had been told to play down the situation so that it did not develop into another Greenham Common.

On Friday 14th December, the magistrates decided there was enough evidence to send the six to trial at Peterborough Crown Court.

Fears of MoD action to evict them were building up among campers at the Rainbow Fields Festival on Molesworth Airfield, when on 17th December a person in civilian clothes claiming to be a Royal Engineers 'mole' told some campers that the Army would be cordoning off part of the airfield either that night or the next. All the camps – Warren Lane, Peace Corner and Rainbow Fields went on full alert. Nothing happened. This may have been a deliberate ploy by the MoD to test the reaction of the campers. A ploy of this sort would be useful if the MoD really were planning an eviction.

At this time there were believed to be 18 USAF F5E jet planes disguised as Russian MiGs stationed at RAF Alconbury.

The Winter Solstice on 21st December was celebrated with a torchlit procession around the perimeter of Molesworth Airfield followed by a sing-song in the big forty feet by forty feet Rainbow Fields Meeting Tent. Mud had been a problem for walkers in the autumn but now it was frozen solid. There were more sing-songs and parties all over the freezing Christmas and New Year, for the three camps by now contained hundreds of protesters and were growing all the time. The surveyors had been seriously delayed and the MoD was not having it all its own way.

At about this time three protesters hindering surveyors were charged with obstructing the highway. One of them, David Turner, announced that he was planning to subpeona Her Majesty's Secretary of State for Defence, Michael Heseltine himself, as a witness. On hearing this the magistrates adjourned to discuss this. Michael Heseltine did not appear on then, but he appeared on Rainbow Fields later.

'TARZAN' HESELTINE INVADES (January - May 1985)

The Molesworth pledge was now becoming well-known. Its aim was to get people and vehicles to RAF Molesworth and keep large numbers of peace campers on the airfield twenty-four hours a day, seven days a week, which would make it virtually impossible for the authorities to evict the three Molesworth Peace Camps. The whole pledge was of most importance in its support of Rainbow Fields Village, which was on MoD land and could be evicted at any time.

The pledge worked in the following manner. The country was divided into regions. Each region was asked to pledge people to attend on a certain day each week with numbers maintained as high as possible throughout the twenty-four hours, so that there would be no low point in their numbers occurring regularly, of which the authorities might take advantage. Pledge forms were issued to all sort of organisations and individuals; everyone was welcome to join. Unfortunately there was no centrally organised transport or even information on how to arrange cheap transport. Regions were left to look after their own and often left it to groups who in turn left it to individuals and families and sometimes it didn't get done at all. Southampton's day was Thursday; we were asked to come every week from midnight Wednesday to midnight Thursday. Southampton CND as a group did not organise a party to come to Molesworth until Thursday, 6th February, 1986. That was over a year late and even then some of us only stayed three hours. We did discuss the pledge in our meetings and decided to go individually. Some were going to visit Molesworth on Sundays because they couldn't manage Thursdays. Nobody came to Molesworth regularly on Thursdays from Southampton. I signed the pledge in Southampton a mere 150 miles from RAF Molesworth without fully realising it would mean leaving home before 20.00 hours every Wednesday and not getting back until 04.00 hours on Friday morning. The distance would again be a problem if I was arrested and charged with anything at Molesworth, for then I would have to attend court in either Peterborough or Huntingdon. Assuming that I could arrange time off work, I would still have to pay travelling expenses and cover any loss of earnings, although if I counted myself as unemployed things would be easier. Many of our group were already committed to Cruise-watch, which was a twenty-four-hour, seven-day commitment and did not want to change. I am sure similar difficulties arose elsewhere.

James Hinton, of CND Projects Committee wrote of the pledge:

> "The scheme helped to provoke Heseltine's invasion (a major own goal for the government) and it has brought visitors to the base every day. Outside a few areas, however, the pledge has not taken off as a mobilising device. Some regions have disregarded it; others have agonised about their inability to get people to the rota scheme." [*Molesworth Bulletin*, July 1985]

In June 1985 for their part CND National Council phased out the rota and the pledge seems to have just faded away.

Some of the Alconbury Nine addressed public meetings to publicise their cases and gain support. These included meetings at Saffron Walden (17th January, 1985) and Cambridge (24th January). The adjourned committal proceedings for Roger Oakley were held on 31st January, and he was committed for trial with the other Alconbury defendants. Some folk thought the reason the authorities were prosecuting these cases with such vigour was to discourage people from signing the Molesworth pledge, for fear of conspiracy charges being brought against pledgers. The matter was raised in Parliament and the Home Secretary had to state that people would not be prosecuted for merely signing the pledge.

At this time, *Peace News* was going to press on alternate Tuesdays. The MoD knew this. They also know the influence this paper had in the peace movement. *Peace News* was the only national newspaper providing regular coverage of the Molesworth Peace Camps and it was sympathetic to them.

On Tuesday, 5th February, *Peace News* went to press reporting that Eirene Peace Chapel was 'nearing completion', and an appeal had been launched to pay for the tiled roof ,which was to be constructed by a work camp working between 30th March and 5th April. It also announced weekend work camps at Molesworth, inviting supporters to camp there for weekends and help with a specific project each weekend, including such things as tree planting and a peace park.

There were rumours of wars and of Army convoys moving all over England on the evening of 5th February. Although cold, the weather was not bad for the time of year and the convoys appeared to be making good progress.

At around 23.00 hours that evening, Ian Hartley, a camper living in the caravan 'Halcyon Spirit' parked

by Peace Corner, saw lights appear on the other side of the airfield. He realised that this was an Army convoy coming to reclaim the airfield for the MoD, jumped into his van, shouted warnings to everybody as he drove through Rainbow Fields, and raced off up the single track road across the airfield along which the convoy was approaching. He then parked his van across the road and sat apparently praying. The convoy was delayed. By the time it was able to continue the Army had lost the element of surprise and the campers were ready for them.

The fences were being built and some campers had already moved off the airfield when Michael Heseltine arrived and toured the site on 6th February, wearing what appeared to be a borrowed Army coat (the famous flak jacket). The television pictures showed a triumphant 'Tarzan' marching with his cohort through a field where soldiers were moving campers. All through that Wednesday Royal Engineers worked with amazing speed, putting fences around the two areas of the airfield. The first area was the airfield itself and the second was a strip of land containing Eirene to the East of the public bridleway. The convoy had come along the bridleway, which by law had to be left for public use. The bridleway remained open for several months before the MoD managed to legally close and gate it.

The Army's timing didn't beat *Peace News*, which managed to insert a stop press page covering the events at the big eviction right up to 14.00 hours on the Wednesday and still came out on the news-stands on time on Friday, 8th February.

Someone very much involved in peace camping is Huw from Faslane. On 5th February, six of his Faslane Peace Camp friends were sentenced to three months imprisonment for an action at the MoD Main Building in London. Huw wrote to me in 1986:

> I also remember ringing the Press Association the night of the sentencing, and being told that umpteen thousand squaddies were en route for Molesworth to evict five hippies and a dog!

Jennifer and Ian Hartley with their dog Robbie were the only people left at Peace Corner by midnight on 6th February. Everyone else there and on Rainbow Fields had been evicted and had either left or was leaving. Gone forever were sixty acres of land prepared for spring planting; gone were four acres of winter wheat (except for one sheaf, harvested by modplods and given to peace campers many months later).

In the first days and weeks after the eviction, the normally sleepy countryside around Molesworth was swarming with pledgers, supporters and evicted campers. There were roadblocks and police checkpoints everywhere, with plans to issue passes to local residents so they could go through easily and not be delayed so much by the checkpoints. White police riot vans were all over the place. Tim and Bridie's home, the Old School House at Clopton, was under twenty-four-hour police surveillance. For no extra charge, British Telecom very decently connected their telephone line to an ansaphone so that callers were told that Tim and Bridie were out and if callers would leave names and addresses or phone numbers they would be contacted when Tim and Bridie returned. Unfortunately, British Telecom neglected to let Tim and Bridie have the phone messages and they knew nothing about the ansaphone until a friend visited and told them!

As soon as the new fences were up, protesters were cutting off tiny pieces of wire and posting them to Ronald Reagan and Michael Heseltine, with notes explaining that if they could do this without being caught, Molesworth did not appear to be a very secure base for nuclear-armed missiles. These actions got national television coverage as did the big eviction. Out of this fence-cutting grew the first Molesworth Snowball, when just three people cut the fence, announced why they did it, and were arrested.

A local paper reported on 7th February that eighteen people had been arrested getting onto Molesworth Airfield. The report didn't say whether they went through the fence or climbed over it.

On 9th February a prayer meeting was held outside the fence by people who could see but not get into Eirene. On the same day at Molesworth, four Peterborough people were arrested and charged with criminal damage. There were also twenty-one arrests on that day of Rainbow Villagers who tried to return to their old campsite on Rainbow Fields.

At about this time, Joan Ruddock, Chairperson of CND, who had been campaigning against Cruise at her local USAF airfield at Greenham Common right from the beginning, announced that CND would support all non-violent action at Molesworth and the Alconbury Nine Defence Committee (A9DC) produced their first Newsletter, the February issue. Of course, the *Molesworth Bulletin* had been in production for some time. Sadly, the eviction ended the production of the daily news-sheet from Rainbow Fields Village as this was produced, edited and duplicated on MoD land.

On 17th February, four people from Brighton were chased by a helicopter, arrested and charged with criminal damage at Molesworth. On the same date four people from Leicester were also arrested and charged with criminal damage here.

When on Ash Wednesday, 20th February, fifteen people from Nottingham and thirty-one from Leicester, helped by other people outside the airfield, got onto the airfield, only three charges for criminal damage were reported and all the others appear to have been released without charge.

Alconbury was not forgotten while all this was happening at Molesworth. On Ash Wednesday, seven members of Christian CND, including a vicar and a dean, held a religious service, scattering ashes on the runway. There were five arrests.

At Molesworth on 22nd February an attempt to reach Eirene was made by three people from Bradford, one of whom, a woman, was arrested when she got in and later released without charge. At Molesworth on 23rd February there were three arrests, on 25th February, two, on 3rd March, one arrest, on 5th March, eight, on 8th March, three and the twenty arrests on 10th March included two at Eirene. These two people had got to the back of the chapel by crawling along inside a coil of razor wire.

With all this activity and much of it publicised, nobody was surprised when the United States Congress expressed doubts about the security of USAF Cruise bases in Britain.

In March three policemen ordered Anne and Dennis to move their caravan within one hour. If it remained, it would be towed away and impounded, they said. The precise location where it stood is not known. A check with the legal support group confirmed that police had the power to order its removal, so it was towed to the Old School House.

Campers now had a legal support group, including real practising lawyers, based at the Celta Shelter in Peterborough. Without them, things would have been much more difficult.

During February and March, inside the 'overnight' fence of coiled razor wire around the main part of the airfield, a new fence was built at Molesworth. The March 1985 edition of the *Molesworth Bulletin* describes it:

> The new 'high security' inner fence is made up of interlocking sections about 8 feet wide by 14 high, with a coil of razor wire along the top. The sections themselves are composed of welded mesh of 1/8-inch diameter galvanised steel at intervals

of 3 inches between vertical strands and with 3/8-inch gaps between horizontals. The 'high security' fence surrounds the land to the West of the bridleway, which runs from Peace Corner to Cockbrook Lane. The land to the East of the bridleway (which includes the chapel and an area where we planted over 100 trees last autumn) is surrounded only by the 'overnight' fence of three coils of razor wire and except on the corner by the chapel is virtually unpoliced most of the time.

'It seems like a good plan (if you can) to get inside a coil of razor wire, either in the outer fence or else on top of the inner fence, and to stay there. That way it's the MoD who have to cut their own fence in order to get you out.'

In spite of its name the 'overnight' fence was actually constructed by Royal Engineers mostly in daylight, on 6th February.

A man from Brighton got through the 'overnight' fence and then climbed into the coil of razor wire atop a section of the weldmesh inner fence that had only recently been erected. This man then proceeded to play a cat-and-mouse game with modplods who tried to coax him down. They even produced a ladder at his request but he stayed up there. Eventually another man went up in the bucket of a mechanical digger, cut the razor wire and brought down the Brighton man. Factory inspectors, trade union officials and many employers take a dim view of people standing in the raised buckets of mechanical diggers. There were safety regulations, codes of practice and laws forbidding this. The police didn't seem to mind, for nobody was prosecuted for it and nobody was prosecuted for cutting the razor wire to get the Brighton man out, either!

During February, cases against four named occupiers of the People's Peace Camp in Warren Lane had been adjourned until 12th March. East Northamptonshire District Council were prosecuting these four campers for establishing dwellings in a rural area without planning permission. If these cases were to succeed the campers would be committing offences under planning laws and could be fined and imprisoned by the magistrates, which would not be the case if they had been evicted by an owner with an order in possession. On 12th March these cases were again adjourned until April.

Barbed wire and razor wire at Molesworth. Courtesy of *Upper Heyford Peace Camp Library.*

On 13th March, a public meeting with slides about Eritrea attracted a big crowd of peace people and local residents. They got enthusiastic and decided to take action to help the starving there; growing food, collecting tools and promoting the idea of 'Molesworth Fields' throughout Britain.

In Huntingdon Magistrates Court on 13th March, four people were found guilty of criminal damage to the new razor wire at Molesworth. The fines and costs totalled from £40 to £70 each. Police applied to the magistrates for permission to photograph and fingerprint the defendants. The magistrates refused on the grounds that photographing and fingerprinting was neither justified nor relevant in these cases, thus proving that the police have no automatic right to photograph or fingerprint defendants, and showing that, even where a guilty verdict is involved, an application for permission to do so will not necessarily succeed.

Since 6th February the Rainbow Villagers had been hounded from place to place, been buzzed by aircraft, been subject to arrest and detention at all times – often without charge – and subjected to the attentions of the police 'A' Team, apparently a band of heavies recruited nationally during the Miners' Strike. They also had to contend with living in cold mobile homes in British winter weather. After leaving Molesworth they were herded by police to a lay-by at Great Barford just over the county boundary in Bedfordshire. The villagers next moved to Graffham Water, Cambridgeshire, and here police stopped half a dozen vehicles from entering and joining the others. They had to go to another lay-by in Bedfordshire and it was a day or two before they were able to rejoin the rest of the convoy. Villagers Mel and Carpenter Jim were charged with assaulting a police officer and obstructing a police officer, respectively, at Graffham Water. Huntingdon magistrates granted a subpoena to Mel to call a television newsreel film that showed Mel being assaulted by police and then dismissed both cases before seeing the rest of Mel and Jim's evidence! They ruled that police had acted illegally in blocking the entrance to Graffham Water without permission from the owners, Anglia Water Board, who had applied for an order in possession, which had not come into effect at the time the vehicles were excluded from this site. When the order took effect, the villagers drove to Desborough Airfield where at the next eviction, the convoy split. Some vehicles went to a lay-by on A6 in Bedfordshire while others made a dash for Molesworth Airfield and pulled up in the bridleway opposite Cockbrook Lane on 22nd March, this being the nearest place to RAF Molesworth they could find to park their mobile homes.

Police acted immediately to move them. Chris Craig, driving his bus with his family on board, was towed off. A contractors' man, lying underneath the bus unhitching the towbar, was accidentally injured (the contractors had been brought in by the police to tow the vehicles). Chris was nearly lynched and then taken straight to prison. His wife and child, along with several other villagers, were left homeless because his bus and five other vehicles were impounded by the police. Chris was threatened with a charge of attempted murder, though when he was finally tried on 14th August, the authorities had to reduce the charge to one of reckless driving in order to secure a conviction.

The remainder of this convoy then went to lay-bys at Allington and on the Great North Road. After a few days they arrived at Polebrook Airfield about seven miles North of Molesworth as the crow flies, where they were joined by the other party of Rainbow Villagers just before Easter.

During the period since Heseltine's eviction, the Rainbow Villagers had always been within a fifteen mile radius of Molesworth. Many of their vehicles had been impounded at one time or another. When some were impounded at Stilton, vandals and thieves did much damage. This gave the police something to do, as they had a legal duty of care in looking after the vehicles, which they had left in the council yard at Stilton. The vehicles were eventually towed out to a lay-by on the Great North Road where police mechanics came and repaired them, and fitted new propshafts. Meanwhile, Criminal Investigation Department officers tracked down the vandals and charged them.

The Rainbow Villagers seemed to be operating in a sensible manner in spite of all their problems. When twenty-five, including a one-month-old baby, were taken to Huntingdon Police Station, their legal observer, Beth, managed to write down everything the police did in her notebook. This was almost certainly a factor in helping the police to decide to release them all, eventually, without charge. They also acted sensibly – and smartly too – when a US Army lorry drove past the lay-by where their vehicles were parked. They ran out and stopped the lorry and a traffic jam began to develop while police extricated the lorry from the instant blockade.

Around the perimeter fence of RAF Molesworth, hardboard boltcutters began appearing. They were absolutely useless for cutting wire, but whenever the police saw them they would come running. The ensuing chaos was a joy for the activists to behold and was sometimes useful to distract attention from real boltcutters cutting the fence elsewhere.

19th March was the last date for objections to the new by-laws for RAF Molesworth, proposed under the provisions of the Military Lands Act 1982. Many objecting letters were sent from all over Britain.

The loss of the airfield as a campsite meant that places to put a camp around Molesworth were now at a premium. Since the MoD had fenced the airfield they were now considering selling off the land to the East of the bridleway and peace campers were working out how to raise funds to buy it.

For the same reason, the ownership of George's Field was of vital importance to peace campers. George, a local farmer, possessed a field of 1·6 acres between B660 and Peace Lane, adjoining Peace Corner. Peace Lane was a piece of old road by-passed when B660 had been improved some years back. George apparently accepted this field in a swap around 1960 and believed he owned it. The MoD wanted this land, probably to give RAF Molesworth better protection from protesters. They discovered that the land was actually owned by the Church of England Diocese of Peterborough and asked the diocese to sell this glebe land to them. Information filtered through that the Bishop of Peterborough, along with his Dean and Chapter, were ready and willing to sell. The Vicar of Orton Malpas, the Rev. Michael Scott, (alias 'Mick the Vic') chained himself to the Bishop's railings in protest. Incidentally, this Rev. Michael Scott is not the Rev. Michael Scott who drove across the Sahara to protest at the French nuclear tests. Rev. Scott then took the Bishop to court. On 18th March Peterborough Diocese was told it could not sell the land until a certain date, because of a complex legal arrangement. That gave Christian CND time to act and they spiked the MoD guns with a higher counter-bid. Subsequently, Peterborough Diocese withdrew its offer to sell to the MoD, but the argument continued for some time as the MoD still wanted to buy the field and the Church of England preferred cash to odd parcels of land.

On April Fool's Day 1985 the new by-laws came into force at RAF Molesworth. It seemed an appropriate date for the introduction of these foolish laws that in time were to create considerable problems for the local police and magistrates.

The by-laws applied to the whole of the airfield and its fences. Anyone getting onto the airfield other than through a gate, or without permission, or by telling a lie would be liable to a fine of up to £100. So would anybody causing or permitting anything (including an aircraft, vehicle or animal) to enter, or to pass through or over, or to be, or to remain on or over the airfield. In addition, persons found guilty were liable to forfeiture of anything found in, upon, or over the airfield to Her Majesty! This only covers the trespass subsection; there were more subsections including one making it an offence to interfere in any way with, or affix anything to any MoD fence on the airfield. Copies of the by-laws were obtainable from the Senior Estates Surveyor of the Department of the Environment in Cambridge.

At 07.15 hours on April Fools' Day the Rainbow Villagers returned to Peace Corner in seven vehicles with a caravan in tow behind one of them. Superintendent Black and Inspector Rogers awaited them, in command of a force of forty-seven police. A police vehicle was blocking the entrance to George's Field where the villagers had hoped to park. They knew George would not mind them being in there, though he was not there to welcome them and they had no letter of invitation from him. The police arrested them all as soon as they stopped at Peace Corner and took them to Thorpe Wood Police Station in Peterborough. Eventually fifteen Rainbow Villagers, a supporter from Milton Keynes and Jerry Hartigan (a family solicitor from Olney) were charged with obstructing Superintendent Black in the execution of his duty. Their trials were to begin on 17th May at Huntingdon.

On Good Friday, 5th April, the Ploughshares Campaign (successor to Wheat for the Starving) loaded the first lorry of 1985 with wheat and gave it a big send-off. The wheat went onto a Band Aid ship for Eritrea. Several more lorries were filled by Ploughshares and sent to the docks where their loads were put on board ship. A total of £25,659.15p – including about £6,000 on Easter Monday alone – was raised; ten tonnes of wheat was donated directly from Oxford; a tonne of soya beans came from Wellingborough; many sacks of rice, lentils, beans, oats, wheat, dried milk and dried fruit were donated; fifty hand-knitted Oxfam-pattern children's jumpers were donated and sent via Oxfam; about fifty sacks of clothing were donated and sent via helpers on the Isle of Sheppey who cleaned and sorted them and nearly 1,500 donated blankets went via Help the Aged to Eritrea. After the Band Aid ship was loaded to the gunwales there was still £10,039.85p in change. This money was sent to Eritrea.

Over Easter, marches came to Molesworth from Leicester, Stevenage and Cambridge. About 25,000 people came. About 600 were on foot and the rest were in an assortment of vehicles. Farmers were expecting crop damage with all these people milling about in the countryside, but when the event was all over only one case of crop damage was alleged to have taken place. This involved an estimated £300 worth of damage to crops planted on a public bridleway. The farmer is believed to have dropped his claim when it was suggested he had illegally ploughed the bridleway.

There were 112 arrests with eighty-one people charged, mainly with highway obstruction and criminal damage and thirty-one released without charge, according to Janey Hulme ('Roll Call', *New Statesman* 31st May, 1985). She estimated there had been a total of 356 arrests to date at Molesworth. Another report gave the number of arrests at Easter as 105. Several sections of the 'overnight' fence were demolished, and at least two people cut the weldmesh fence before being dragged off by police.

One arrest in particular caused anguish. A flying object, believed to have been either a stone or a bottle, hit and knocked cold a modplod. It had come from a person in a group of stone-throwing protesters behind the crowd around the Holy Mackerel affinity group who were fence cutting at the time. Concerned that someone had not been reading the leaflets that had been distributed asking folk to be non-violent, and that someone had been hurt, Holy Mackerel acted to stop the throwing. Police caught the culprit. The modplod was treated for his injury, had some paid sick leave, returned to work, started having blackouts and had to go back on sick leave.

Activists hung many rainbow pennants on the fence and cleared litter from surrounding villages, although some villagers were pleased, Ratepayers Against Molesworth Settlements (RAMS) a local group, whose chairman lived next door to the Old School House, decided the pennants constituted unsightly litter and announced they were going to take them off the fence. Protesters alerted by the announcement removed the pennants before the RAMS got to them. The RAMS then spent an hour trying to scrub off the more permanent messages left on the fence by protesters who had used paint that clung tenaciously to weldmesh. When tidying the villages the protesters did not remove posters the RAMS had flyposted everywhere. The RAMS didn't remove them after Easter either. At least one resident of Leighton Bromswold wrote to his local paper complaining that out-of-date RAMS posters were despoiling the trees, telegraph poles and bridges in his area.

On 10th April, whilst USAF aeroplanes were taking off at RAF Alconbury, twenty Nottingham people entered the airfield. Immediately, a supporter outside telephoned the Air Traffic Control Tower and told the controllers that people were on the airfield. One aircraft delayed take-off even before the group had reached the runway. Flying had to stop completely while the police came out and arrested the activists. They were later released on bail to appear at Huntingdon Police Station on June 5, when they expected to be charged. Apparently the MoD decided not to prosecute in the interest of saving expense and minimising publicity for the action. These arrests included three *Peace News* journalists. Unlike most journalists who were content to stay outside the fence to get their stories, *Peace News*' folk liked to be where the action was!

In April Bridie and Michael published their tape, *Songs for Eirene*, copies of which could be obtained from the Old School House at Clopton.

The High Court ruled on 16th April that Peterborough Diocese was not allowed to sell George's Field without ascertaining the best price offered. Christian CND had, of course, offered more money than the MoD and was also involved in an attempt to buy the land where Eirene stood.

On 21st April, twenty-two people from Cambridge, Colchester and Sutton entered RAF Alconbury and split up. One group walked about a mile along the runway to within 300 yards of a group of parked RAF Canberra bombers. There they set up Alconbury Peace Camp Mark VII, using polythene and bean poles to make tents. They were discovered and nine ran towards the aircraft, past a British guard who shouted: "Stop or I'll shoot!" Luckily, he didn't shoot. The nine climbed onto the wing of a plane and sang peace songs for twenty-five minutes before descending voluntarily and being arrested. The folk who had remained at the camp had already been arrested. Other groups walked round the airfield rearranging signs and painting and decorating various objects for ninety minutes. One group of four surrendered to US servicemen, who threw them to the ground and handcuffed them. Another group went for a stroll and ended up just walking out of the Main Gate without even being challenged by the lone modplod on duty there. All seventeen arrested people were released after about seven hours, except for one woman who was in breach of a bail condition and consequently spent seven days in Holloway Prison. On the same night, another group, the Merseyside Moles, cut down about forty yards of perimeter fence and left without being detected.

In solidarity with the Alconbury Nine, East Midlands Pledge Region organised, with East Anglia CND, a party at Fire Gate on Cockbrook Lane on 23rd April. Over 300 people came to Molesworth for it.

At Alconbury, nine people entered and decorated the runway lights on Monday, 29th April. On the same day, activists demolished forty yards of fence. None of these folk were caught.

When the cases against the four campers in Warren Lane came to court in April, they were adjourned for another month.

The gates to RAF Molesworth were now becoming known by new names. Earth Gate was the one by Peace Corner. The Christian peace camp in Peace Lane was known as Earth Camp. Molesworth Gate was now Air Gate, Fire Gate was on Cockbrook Lane and Clopton Gate was renamed Water Gate.

On May Day a group from Leicester entered RAF Alconbury and six of them, dressed as rabbits, climbed onto a USAF jet aircraft in a peaceful, non-violent hijack. 'Bugs Bunny' took a beautiful photograph, which was subsequently published by *Peace News* on 17th May. All risked prosecution under the Official Secrets Acts in producing and publishing this snapshot but the authorities did not prosecute.

On 4th May, a woman was arrested at Peace Corner apparently in breach of a bail condition that she stay fifteen miles or more away from RAF Molesworth. She may also have had unpaid fines taken into account when, after being remanded in custody in Huntingdon Police Station on 7th May, Huntingdon magistrates sentenced her to thirty days in prison. She was released on 24th May after good conduct remission.

A combined night action at Molesworth and Alconbury on Saturday, 4th May, proved one more time how lax the security at both places can be. At Molesworth an action involving thirty people ended in eleven arrests for trespassing, all under the new by-laws.

One group climbed through a hole they found in the permanent fence and wandered across the base undetected. They climbed the water tower in the centre of the base, the first time anyone has got to the tower since the fence went up. Whilst two sat on top of the tower singing, two others went and reported to the security centre on the base telling them what was happening. All four were arrested, with a further four people arrested in the dog run. Cambridge University Students Union is supporting those who were arrested. Meanwhile thirteen people broke into Alconbury and made it to the runway, occupying planes and singing and dancing. This action was designed to divert police attention away from Molesworth while people were getting there (*Peace News*, 17th May, 1985).

The dog run was the gap between the 'overnight' fence and the permanent weldmesh fence. It got its name because the Modsquad dogs were allowed to run along it.

John Perry of Molesworth Peace Camp was sent to jail for 30 days on Tuesday 7th May for non-payment of fines as a matter of conscience. He was planning to fast during his time there and is cur-

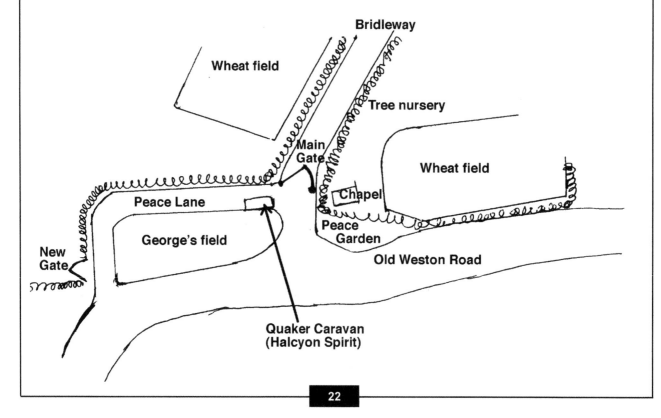

rently being held in Bedford Prison. [*Peace News*, 17th May 1985]

Eleven people from Nottingham got over both fences at Molesworth using ladders, in broad daylight on their last pledge day, 8th May. Five more were arrested in the dog run between the fences.

They took the police completely by surprise, arriving in hired minibuses that just happened to be the same blue as the police vans. By the time the four police in their van at Peace Corner realised what was happening fifty yards down the road, the fence-scaling was well underway, with carpet over the razor wire, a ladder up to the top of the inner fence and more carpet over the razor wire on top. The lone MoD policewoman inside the fence was unable to stop any of the protesters as they jumped down and ran off into the base. When more police arrived they confiscated the ladder and some of the carpet, but it took them twenty minutes to remove all the protesters inside the base from the scaffolding platform they had climbed. The success of the action was due at least in part to thorough preparation at the non-violence training the previous Sunday, where the carpet-ladder sequence was rehearsed several times. The entire action was also filmed by *Diverse Reports* from Channel Four for a TV programme to be shown later that year.

The remaining NVDAers from Nottingham then decided to hold a blockade at the Cockbrook Lane gate, where they held up traffic for several minutes and four more arrests ensued.

> Still not satisfied, the remaining seven went over to Alconbury where they walked through the back gate unnoticed. They were eventually picked up and detained then driven out and dropped near the A1 several miles away. [*Peace News*, 17th May 1985]

Incidentally, police were considering charging Channel Four and *Diverse Reports* with aiding and abetting the trespass, because not only did they film it, but they also used hidden microphones to record the arrest of the Nottingham people.

All but one of the defendants came with lawyers to the Alconbury Nine pre-trial meeting at Peterborough Crown Court. They were given a fortnight to name all the witnesses they wanted to see. When their lists were complete, it was found that some witnesses would have to be brought from the USA as they had returned there after finishing duty at RAF Alconbury.

Judge Christopher Young was to preside over the case.

On 16th May, Andy from the Old School House was

in court charged with trespass under the new by-laws. He had crawled under the razor-wire coils around Eirene and stayed inside the chapel two hours before being arrested. He pleaded not guilty and his case was adjourned to 11th June.

RAINBOW VILLAGE ON TRIAL (March - May 1985)

Rainbow Village on trial: Police Lies and Blind Justice

Brig Oubridge Reports:

> From Friday 17th May until the following Friday, 24th May, the longest Molesworth trial so far took place in front of Huntingdon magistrates. In the six day hearing, eleven Rainbow Villagers and two supporters from Milton Keynes were accused of having obstructed Police Superintendent Blake in the execution of his duty at Peace Corner at 7.15 a.m. on April Fools' Day. Four others failed to appear on the same charge, and hence now face an additional charge of failing to appear, whenever the police may track them down.
>
> The first day of the mammoth trial was almost completely taken up with the evidence of Supt. Blake. He stated that he had been on duty at Peace Corner the previous day, 31st March, and had seen a car, which he knew to be associated with the Rainbow Village, and the occupants appeared to be doing a 'recce'. Knowing the stated intention of the Rainbow Village to return to Molesworth, and it being his duty anyway under a plan agreed with the Asst. Chief Constable to 'secure' Peace Lane (referred to throughout by the prosecution as 'the lay-by'), Blake arranged for forty-seven police officers to be at Peace Corner from 6 a.m. the following morning.
>
> According to Blake's story, seven Rainbow Village vehicles (three coaches, two vans – one towing a caravan – a lorry and a car) all arrived together at 7.15, and stopped, blocking one carriageway of the B660. While a police sergeant spoke to the driver of the leading coach, the other occupants all got out and milled about in the road, which Blake described as a "customary tactic by these people to make things more difficult for the police"! Blake then (so he said) told everyone to get back in their vehicles and move on, and when, after five minutes, they had all refused to do so, he arrested them because he feared a breach of the peace by local villagers.
>
> Cross examined by Neil Davidson, defending most of the accused, Blake said that he could not answer questions on the legality of his actions but that he did "whatever was necessary". He stuck rigidly to his story that he had spent five minutes warning people to go before any arrests were made. Asked

whether 47 police officers might not have been sufficient to prevent local villagers taking matters into their own hands, Blake replied "Not necessarily", although he had earlier stated that his fears of this were based on four such villagers having said in February that such action would take place if the Rainbow Villagers were not removed.

Throughout Blake's evidence and his own preamble, police prosecutor Mr Beale (described by an observer at the trial as "a venomous weasel in half-moon glasses") did his best to bring up (and maliciously misrepresent) any previous incident involving Rainbow Villagers that he could possibly twist into a prejudicial slur against us, answering Neil Davidson's repeated objections with the contention that the court had to take into account Blake's state of mind in deciding whether he was in fact acting reasonably in the execution of his duty. The defendants, on Neil's advice, did their level best throughout to stifle any involuntary reactions of either anger or sheer incredulity at both Blake's version of events and Beale's dubious antics, and were actually congratulated by the chairman of the bench at the end of the first day for their restraint and good behaviour.

The second day of the trial was taken up with a succession of minor police witnesses – one arresting officer for each defendant (although one caused amusement by pointing out the wrong man in court, so that one defendant had apparently been arrested twice and another not at all) a couple of sergeants, and the officers who had taken our statements at Thorpe Wood (Peterborough) Police Station. None of the arresting officers had been able to hear what Supt. Blake had said to us, but they all agreed that he had been talking to us for five minutes before we were put under arrest (even though they were far less clear on when the five minutes began or how long any other portions of the morning's events had taken.) They all agreed that everyone who had been arrested had come quietly and been no trouble at all to deal with and they all maintained that they had no briefing whatsoever before our arrival. One significant fact which emerged from the arresting officers was that neither I nor Mike Johnson Smith could possibly have heard any warning which Supt. Blake gave (even supposing that he gave one), since we had both remained in my van (which had been the last to arrive) out of earshot of Supt. Blake, and that the first thing which any police officer had said to us was "Get out. You're under arrest."

Although we had all declined to answer almost all the questions we were asked at the police station, one thing at least was clear. The one question which we had all immediately answered was "Did you hear Supt. Blake tell you to go?" and the answers ranged from a simple but clear "No", to the more emphatic "That's rubbish, that question! It never happened!"

The morning of the third day, Tuesday, brought us to the last of the prosecution witnesses, Inspector – now – Chief Inspector Rogers, who had been promoted some time after the April 1st incident. Despite his eighteen years in the police, Insp. Rogers was not a very impressive witness; he seemed incapable of looking either at the defendants or the magistrates in the face, and as he muttered at his shoes he looked by far the guiltiest person in the whole court.

Insp. Rogers (referring to the notebook which he had made up with Supt. Blake just after the arrests), was the only police witness who had heard what Blake had said to us, and although he looked exceedingly uncomfortable in doing it, he backed up Blake's version of the events. Although he did slightly vary the by now unconvincingly predictable "five minutes" (he said "four or five minutes"!), he agreed that Blake had warned us all to go, given us time to go, and only then had he arrested us.

At the end of the prosecution case, Neil Davidson made a legal submission that the charges should be dismissed due to there being no case to answer. He and Beale had a lawyers' sparring match citing precedent and counter-precedent on the extent of a police officer's duty, and when police have or do not have the right to block the highway. However there was probably never much chance of Neil's submission being successful, since it would have needed clear legal direction from the clerk to the magistrates in order for them to throw out the case at that point. On the first day of the trial we had had a clerk who looked like he might have been capable of giving such direction, and who had actually been quite sharp in pointing out how far Beale could or could not go. However, from the Monday onwards he had been replaced by a clerk who had been much more content to let Beale get away with whatever he liked and was so much slower to intervene that at times she seemed to be doing the police's job for them.

Nevertheless, when the bench came back in with their decision that the cases against all of the defendants should go on, it was a psychological blow to all of us, not least because we had all been in court already for longer than we had expected, and the strain was beginning to tell. At the end of the day, after the first of the defendants, Rebecca West had given her evidence, another of the defendants, Martin Melville, got to his feet in the dock and announced that he wanted to change his plea. Although Beale was keen for the court to accept a new plea immediately, the magistrates wisely adjourned the case for the night (it was 5 o'clock anyway) in order to give Mel the chance to talk it over with Neil and come back to court in the morning.

Having realised that a guilty plea would not in fact end the ordeal any sooner, since he would still have had to sit through all the rest of the defence case, and that we did still have at least some chance of winning (on appeal, if not immediately), and having had an evening and a night to recover his composure, Mel retracted his change of plea the following morning and the case continued.

By comparison to the police witnesses, the defendants all seemed refreshingly honest. This was probably the most noticeable feature of the defence evidence throughout. All our testimony added up to the same story, told in different ways from a variety of viewpoints, but together making a convincing and consistent whole. We arrived at Peace Corner to find the large police presence and the entrance to George's field blocked off. The lead vehicle stopped, and everyone got out to see what was going on. Blake called everyone into a group, saying that he had something to say to us; when everyone had gathered, he told us we were all under arrest and waved his PCs in to haul us off. No warning to go. No chance to go. No five minutes.

Beccy had been on her way home to Brighton to see her mum, and had gone along to Peace Corner hoping to find some S. E. Region pledgers to get a lift from. She had obeyed Blake's instruction to gather together, and then found herself under arrest. "Are you a Rainbow Warrior?" sneered Mr. Beale at the end of his cross-examination. "Yes," she said firmly.

Postman John had wanted to make tea for people at Easter from George's field, and thought George would not mind. He had gone limp on arrest, and been dragged away, but his arresting officer had already said that he had not been any trouble. He also admitted to being a "Rainbow Warrior".

Roddy tried to explain the Hopi prophesy of the Rainbow Warriors before agreeing to be classified as one. With a flourish, Beale produced a copy of *Peace News* from his inside pocket and attempted to question Roddy about an article by a 'Rainbow Villager'. Neil Davidson had to intervene twice to get a ruling that this was not relevant, since Roddy had not written the article, whatever it said.

Carpenter Jim said that had he been warned by Blake to move on (which he had not), he did not know whether or not he would have done so. He had had charges against him dismissed previously, because the court had ruled that Blake and Co. had been acting illegally in trying to block the entrance to Graffham Water car park.

Mel admitted to being the one who had, according to the police evidence, "urinated into the road" (this incident had been a highlight of the police account of events). He denied that this had been a calculated insult to the police, and pointed out that there had been a bus between him and the policeman who had reported the incident.

Like Roddy, Ben had been still in his sleeping bag, when the buses had arrived at Peace Corner, and had barely had time to find his shoes before being arrested. Like the others, he had simply followed Blake's instructions.

I was the last witness on the Wednesday, and told the court that I had talked with George a couple of days before and felt that George would have been very glad if we had got onto his field, but that it would have put him in a very awkward position to actually ask him and make him an overt conspirator.

Time ran out before I could be cross-examined, and attention shifted to the question of how people could sign on the next day and be expected to be in court in Peterborough (Huntingdon Court would be closed that day) at the earlier time of 9:45. They promised to arrange giros for us in Peterborough.

After court, we went to see George to ask him to be a witness for us. Had he done so, his evidence would have confirmed that he would have been pleased to have us in his field, and would have proved that the police did not have his permission to block the entrance off. But George has been under so much pressure from some of his neighbours and from the police that he didn't want to give evidence, and we didn't want to make him do it against his will.

On Thursday morning we all turned up on time in Peterborough, despite the longer journey. All this time we were under imminent threat of eviction from both our camps at Sharnbrook (outside Bedford) and at the Peace Pagoda in Milton Keynes, and tension was rising as to whether we could finish the case before the bailiffs came in.

Beale's cross-examination of me went on a long time without his quite managing to prove that I was in fact Napoleon! (He had stated before that the fact that I had not got out of my van was irrelevant, since Napoleon would watch a battle from his horse on a hill, but was still responsible!). He did manage to establish that I was some sort of group treasurer and a writer (his emphasis!), as if this automatically made me a prime enemy of the state and therefore guilty by definition!

Jan told how she had had to wait in Jerry's car until Jim came back to help her into her wheelchair and push her, at a run, up to the group around Blake, where she had arrived just in time to be arrested. Mark from Milton Keynes told how he had been asked by Jerry to come along as an independent observer. Like everyone else, he had thought that he was going to find out from Blake what was going on, and simply found out that he was under arrest. Terry, another Rainbow Villager, gave much the same story as everyone else. All were subjected to Beale's relentless and vindictive style of cross-examination, which was by now showing itself to be clearly 'over the top'.

Our star witness that afternoon was Asst. Chief Constable Radcliffe, who had not been mentioned in police evidence, but had shown up at the scene within ten minutes of our arrest. He contradicted Blake's story that the 'securing' of the 'lay-by' had been a plan which he had agreed, but said that, in relation to the CND Easter Demo, "it was my biggest concern, and, if I may say so, CND's biggest concern, that these people would return." When asked about phone taps, he at first hedged, and then resorted to the careful form of words used by successive Home Secretaries to say that there were no authorised phone taps on anyone concerned with Molesworth.

Mike's evidence and that of Jerry Hartigan, a family solicitor and peace activist from Olney, near Milton Keynes, who had come along in response to a late night phone call from Jan to help her move, completed the defence case. Beale seemed to obtain particular enjoyment from grilling a fellow solicitor on Friday morning, trying to cast Jerry in the role of some sort of legal mastermind (which wasn't too convincing).

By that time, the balance of evidence was quite clear to anyone with an unbiased perspective. A journalist who had sat through the whole case agreed that it was obviously a police set-up to round us all up and worry about charges afterwards, and that the police evidence had clearly been a fabrication. However, to return a verdict which would have clearly implied that the police were lying (from Blake down) was something which was beyond the abilities of Huntingdon magistrates. After Neil's closing submission they retired, and in due course came back with the compromise verdict that Mike and I were not guilty, and the other eleven were guilty. It was a verdict with no justice in it, and I felt sick as I walked out of the dock and waited for the others to receive their sentences.

Beale asked for the prosecution costs of £107 per person. The bench fined everyone £25 plus £50 costs, with the exception of Jerry who was charged double. Perhaps it may be reversed on appeal, if people can find the stamina to go for a replay.

We came out of court and headed straight back to Sharnbrook, where a large number of grim and stroppy policemen were helping bailiffs evict the last of our homes from the lay-by. Most of the village had left the previous afternoon for Stratford, en route to Stonehenge, on holiday!!

STOP PRESS: About 100 Rainbow Villagers were among the 500 who were ambushed, beaten up and had their homes destroyed by Stonehenge police.

The entire chapter above, including its title, came from the *Molesworth Bulletin*, No. 7, June, 1985. I am grateful to Brig Oubridge and *Molesworth Bulletin* for publishing this report and allowing me to reprint it.

Later, some of the prosecuted villagers appealed, but, so far as I can ascertain, all lost their appeals.

The STOP PRESS item refers to the stopping by police on 1st June, 1985, of a convoy of vehicles near Parkhouse Corner, en route for a planned festival at Stonehenge. Ironically, this convoy was using A338, a route used by Cruise convoys from Greenham Common, and they had been stopped several times at Parkhouse Corner by cruisewatchers.

MORE ABOUT PERIMETER FENCES, AND THE ALCONBURY NINE CONSPIRACY TRIAL (May – July 1985)

On 22nd May, Molesworth campaigners used a popular old tactic, when they brought some 'big names' to hand leaflets through the perimeter fence. These included Pat Arrowsmith, Bruce Kent, and Peter Tatchell. The leaflets explained the argument that orders to work on Cruise missile bases contravened the Genocide Act, and called on everyone to refuse these illegal orders. These leaflets, produced by a Kent group, were also distributed in nearby villages.

RAF Alconbury was invaded, on 26th May, by six people who climbed the fence.

Groups from East Anglia visited Molesworth on 28th May, cutting the fence in many places. Several small pieces of fence were secretly removed. Altogether twenty people were arrested: eighteen for trespass under the new by-laws, and two for criminal damage. The pieces of fence that had been removed were presented publicly to the US Embassy in London next day.

Jonathon found and picked up a pair of boltcutters, or so he claimed, on Wednesday, 29th May. Police spotted him with them. He was arrested, and charged with going equipped for criminal damage.

On the same date, at 11.30 hours, 230 marchers set off from RAF Alconbury for Fire Gate, which was the main contractors' gate at Molesworth. The sun shone brightly, they walked through beautiful countryside, and were greeted by friendly bystanders. Even the police walking alongside were enjoying it and were friendly. Marchers prepared to participate in NVDA went to the front of the march, so that, if the police got awkward others who were not prepared to be arrested could avoid arrest at the back of the march. The police were not awkward and allowed the march to go right up to Fire Gate without stopping it. More people joined the marchers there, swelling the total number to over 250. A blockade started at 17.00 hours. Soon a party was in full swing with party games, props and 'custard pies' brought by Leicester folk. Many groups from the East Midlands combined to help with this event, which succeeded in diverting and delaying traffic. The other gates were not blockaded.

Huntingdon magistrates found four Welsh Presbyterian churchmen guilty on charges of attempted criminal damage (with blunt tinsnips) and hanging a banner on the fence. They all pleaded guilty and made excellent speeches explaining why they did it. On 30th May each was fined £10 per offence with £7 costs.

On 31st May, after being found guilty of obstructing Cockbrook Lane, the Fire Gate Six were each given a conditional discharge. They had been vigilling at Fire Gate for three days before being arrested, but shortly afterwards five people who had been vigilling there only ten minutes were arrested for obstruction. They were dealt with separately. Also in May, herbicides were sprayed along the ground at the bases of some section of the perimeter fences. Fortunately they were not sprayed on a small garden planted alongside a perimeter fence in memory of Ann Francis, the Greenham woman who was sent to prison for a year in early April 1985 (See 'More Cruise Convoys Outside …' elsewhere in this book). At this time the garden was looking beautiful.

Round the clock vigils had been started at Peace Corner, Fire Gate and Air Gate, so that tabs could be kept on contractors' vehicles entering and leaving RAF Molesworth. Water Gate, which could be observed from the Peoples' Peace Camp, was not then used for contractors' vehicles because it was awkwardly situated.

During May the MoD showed copies of its plans for developing RAF Molesworth to the local parish council.

Also during May an eviction order against some Molesworth peace campers was thrown out of court, and three people arrested and charged under the bylaws for walking and gardening on the airfield were bailed to appear before Huntingdon magistrates on 12th June.

Campers made strenuous efforts to maintain good relations with police and their efforts paid off at Fire Gate, where police gave firewood and cheese rolls to four women encamped there on the night of 9th June. I believe there were several little incidents like this at Molesworth but the others apparently went unrecorded.

In a 'snowball' action at Peace Corner, nineteen people were arrested and charged on 8th June.

Awel Irene from Wales, an admirer of Ann Francis, was arrested at Molesworth by the same modplod who had arrested Ann Francis on Greenham Common! In court Awel spoke with sincerity in her defence referring to an 'inner calling' telling her to act. She was fined £15 with £88 costs. Tom of Peace Corner had spent two hours on the airfield before being discovered and charged with trespass. He was fined £25 with £30 costs. Both these cases were heard by Huntingdon magistrates on 10th June.

Andy was in court again over his trespass charge. The MoD confirmed that he had been arrested outside MoD land. Apparently he had climbed over the perimeter fence at a point where it stood on county council land and he did not cross the actual boundary of the MoD land when he got inside. Both the 'overnight' fence and the weldmesh fence had been erected slightly off course by Peace Corner. They would seem to have constituted an obstruction of the highway, if the precedent, in January 1984, of Alconbury Peace Camp Mark II, is anything to go by. The MoD dropped the charge against Andy and nobody bothered to prosecute them for obstruction, though both fences were later moved back to the true boundary.

A woman was arrested for putting messages on the fence at Peace Corner on 18th June, and on 19th June, Jean Pike was also arrested there for putting a blanket on Earth Gate. Jean was asked her age by arresting officers, and refused to reveal it, as she was legally entitled to do. Both these women were later released without charge.

Local councillors visited the People's Peace Camp in Warren Lane on 21st June and told campers they were to be issued with summonses for living there without planning permission. This could take around two weeks, they said, and if convicted the campers would face heavy fines and possible imprisonment.

> "Have you got application forms so we can apply for permission?"
> "No".

On the next day, a Saturday, seven cyclists arrived at Molesworth Peace Camp after a fortnight-long ride from Barrow-in-Furness, exposing links in the nuclear complex and nuclear bases by visiting them en route.

The 'snowballers' arrested on 8th June appeared before Huntingdon magistrates on 25th June. As the day progressed the court got more and more chaotic, until Gerard, defending himself, was ordered to shut up and refused to do so. He was taken below to the cells to the accompaniment of long and loud applause from the public gallery, which was then cleared. Judith Dawes from Gloucestershire was sentenced to seven days in prison at this same sitting of magistrates because she had not paid fines gathered on the first Molesworth 'snowball'.

Huntingdon CND came to Molesworth on 25th June and released 1,024 balloons, representing the destructive power of an atom bomb of the type used at Hiroshima. Labels were tied to the balloons which explained what they represented and, why they were released, unlike the real radioactive fallout particles they represented which fell from the sky unlabelled and unseen.

At about this time Cambridgeshire County Council Transportation Committee decided to close Peace Lane. Before this could be done their proposal had to be approved by the full county council.

In June students of Sheffield Polytechnic visited Molesworth in the course of making a film about the peace camp.

David Polden of Hornsey CND was sentenced to thirty days in prison in June for not paying fines relating to activities at RAF Molesworth and RAF Alconbury.

Peace campaigners were trying to gather information about a private laboratory that was alleged to carry out tests on animals, Huntingdon Research Centre. It was situated between Molesworth and Alconbury. It was believed that some of the chemical weapons stored at RAF Alconbury may have been tested on animals in this research centre. The regular peace campers do not seem to have got involved in these investigations and I found no further mention of them.

Leicester CND initiated a nationwide day of action against contractors who worked at Molesworth on Wednesday 26th June. The advance notice in the *Molesworth Bulletin* included a map giving the precise location of Blue Circle Cement batching towers beside the main London-Glasgow railway at Syston, which supplied cement to Molesworth contractors. One would have thought that the authorities would

have guarded these towers in case of an action there on the appointed date, but no guard stopped or delayed Leicester CND activists when they climbed one of the towers on 26th June. This event was the talk of the village for many months afterwards. As a result of this and other actions on the nationwide day, twenty-nine members of Nottingham and Leicester CND groups were arrested.

South-East and London Regions of CND combined for a day of action at Molesworth on 1st July. Their blockade didn't succeed in closing the airfield but traffic was delayed and diverted. Considering that only 200 people were there and there appear to have been no arrests, this would seem to have been a good result.

Tim, Bridie, Ian and Jennifer, with John Holten observing, delivered a letter to the Ministry of Defence Main Building asking for assurances that nothing would happen to Eirene until after they had spoken with Michael Heseltine and explained their views to him. They said they would stay in the Main Building until they got a satisfactory reply. Then three civil servants came and discussed the letter with them. They left after receiving assurances that everything would be put before Mr. Heseltine the next morning, and that he would send them a letter during the next week telling them if he was prepared to meet them or not.

We have been forgetting RAF Alconbury. Here, on 9th June, a demonstration of solidarity with the alleged conspirators began with an invasion of the airfield. The message: "People who work on the base are guilty of conspiracy to mass genocide", was left in many places. On 9th and 10th June activists cut down large pieces of fence, painted peace symbols on aircraft, and leafleted service personnel and their families. On the afternoon of 9th June, which was a Sunday, nine people went onto the airfield and were arrested. They were later released without charge. That night, twenty or more climbed over the fence and fourteen of them were arrested. Of these, ten were released without charge and four were held in jail overnight and released on bail to appear in Huntingdon Police Station on 27th June when it was understood they were not charged with any offence. Apparently each of them was let off with a caution.

There were several other solidarity actions for the alleged conspirators all over Britain, with people announcing that they too had conspired to commit criminal damage at Alconbury. In spite of all these confessions nobody else was charged with conspiracy.

The conspiracy trial was held in Northampton County Court. Here at 10.00 hours on Monday 10th June, gathered the seven remaining alleged conspirators: Paul Briggs, Veronica McGuire (formerly Dignam) Phil Hudson, Corrie McUaith (formerly Fergus Watt) Paul Rudolf, Sybilla Snake (formerly Doris Mourning) and Roger Oakley.

Outside the court, Christian CND held a brief service and prayed for the folk on trial. Over 100 supporters had gathered outside with banners. During the course of the morning, they went to the local police station and there confessed to conspiring to cause criminal damage. They were neither arrested nor charged.

All seven defendants pleaded not guilty. They used eighteen of their potential challenges of jury members. Phil and Sybilla, who had not been granted legal aid and had no solicitors, were refused permission to have unqualified advisers ('McKenzie friends') in court.

Judge Christopher Young warned supporters that it was illegal to distribute literature that might influence the jury around the court. This meant leafleting anywhere near the court building was effectively banned.

The prosecution began by showing a video of various parts of the airfield including close-ups of several different sections of the fence. Then they produced the peace camp diary and visitors book from Alconbury Mark VI. The prosecutor made great play of the diary entries and clearly they were to be the cornerstones of his case. He spent all Monday outlining the case and continued on Tuesday. Prosecution witnesses were carefully cross-examined by defendants and their lawyers. To be found guilty, none of the defendants need have committed criminal damage. All the prosecution had to do was to prove that two or more of them had planned or conspired together to criminally damage a specified thing or things. The witnesses gave many instances of criminal damage at RAF Alconbury, some of which took place long before the defendants had got together and set up Alconbury Mark V Peace Camp. Some of this damage was done by peace campers, obviously, but some was done when there were no peace campers around. Although the police knew them all and had 'kept an eye on them', with frequent arrests, none of the peace campers on trial had been charged with any offence of criminal damage. Damage that the police attributed to other causes – even without real proof – was not included in the catalogue of damages presented to the court. Damage done in 1985 was not included. It appeared that drunken American servicemen could

damage things. Oh yes, Corrie had been caught on a water tower with a banner. It took considerable argument to get the prosecutor to admit that as Corrie had been caught with no tools he was neither going to dismantle the tower nor paint and decorate it. The defence submitted that the evidence presented by the prosecuting barrister showed no correlation between the existence of Alconbury Peace Camps Marks V and VI and criminal damage incidents at the airfield, and it had not shown that criminal damage incidents had increased or intensified as a result of the campers being there. Some police in their evidence admitted that they disregarded official guidelines when dealing with the seven defendants on identity parades, but Sybilla couldn't get a policeman to admit he heard her scream when he dragged her face down along the ground. The rough handling of campers on 20th June 1984 – yes, this affair had dragged on for nearly a year already – was played down by police in their evidence and by the prosecution. US personnel appearing in court were under orders not to appear in uniform and one admitted that if life or US property were threatened, they were allowed to shoot intruders. The defendants in the dock with prison warders in charge of them were made to look guilty from the start and the judge was showing no kindness to them. He told Phil and Sybilla who were defending themselves against a professional barrister to consult with the barrister. Then on 27th June the prosecution announced they were calling no more witnesses.

As all this was going on in the court building, the Alconbury Nine supporters were not idle outside. Many supporters visited to watch the trial and among these were nine Londoners who came on 26th June. That night they went to the junction of A1 and A14 in view of RAF Alconbury and set up Alconbury Peace Camp Mark VII. The Londoners stayed there for twelve hours. Although they were under police surveillance the whole time they were not harassed and no attempt to evict them was made. They left of their own accord the next morning, after presenting a visual display of posters and banners to thousands of motorists.

The defence came onto the stage calling no additional witnesses and without videos and books in evidence. The defendants and their lawyers concentrated on pointing out how little evidence existed of agreement on anything at all between the alleged conspirators, and that to have a conspiracy it is necessary to have agreement. Also they again stressed that none of the defendants had ever been convicted of criminal damage. Showing the defendants had no 'form' like this could have been a risky move if one or more of them had criminal records for other offences but this does not seem to have excited the prosecution to display any defendant's criminal record before the court in order to blacken a character. Once again, they stressed the lack of correlation between instances of criminal damage at RAF Alconbury and these peace campers. Phil Hudson wanted to know why he had not been charged with any specific act of criminal damage, if the links between criminal damage and the peace campers were so clear. The prosecutor also brought up this point in his closing speech when he said the correlation between criminal damage and these peace campers was supported by entries in the peace camp diary. On the morning of Wednesday 3rd July the jury retired.

On Thursday morning, the jury were told that majority verdicts would be accepted. At lunch time on Friday, the verdict of acquittal on Corrie was produced. He went free to the obvious displeasure of the prosecution. The jury failed to reach even a majority verdict on Veronica, but they found the others guilty.

The judge sentenced the others on Friday afternoon. Phil Hudson was bound over for two years in the sum of £500; fined £500,which he had to start paying at £15 per week in August; and given a twelve-month prison sentence, suspended for two years. Both Paul Rudolf and Phil were unemployed. The next defendant, Paul Briggs, was bound over in the sum of £350 and sentenced to 150 hours of community service. Roger was bound over in the sum of £300 with a sentence of 200 hours of community service. Judge Young told Veronica she would have to go, at a later date, to Peterborough to discover what the authorities were going to do with her.

When Veronica went to Peterborough she was told her case was to be left on file. That meant that if ever the MoD found any more evidence they could bring her case to court again and may secure a conviction. This has not happened at the time of writing, and it is now extremely unlikely. Even if the MoD did find more evidence, it is unlikely they would prosecute, because they would probably have to bring all those service personnel back from the USA to give evidence and they would have to endure much more publicity and inconvenience.

MORE COURT CASES (July - December 1985)

The campaign to 'Stop the Air Fare' at RAF Alconbury began with unconfirmed rumours of a group entering onto the airfield emptying fuel tanks and painting on the runway.

Police reported about £1,500 worth of fuel missing from a tank drained at Tarmac's Huntingdon deport on the night of 20th/21st July. Plant and vehicles were also painted here. Tarmac was involved in the construction of the weldmesh fence at Molesworth.

Tarmac's Corby depot was picketed by Molesworth activists, members of Corby Trades Council, the Labour Party and the City Council.

In the early hours of 21st July, two women entered RAF Alconbury and painted slogans and peace symbols on an aircraft. They were not caught.

Peace campaigners equated Alconbury Air Fair with warfare rather than funfair, hence their spelling of the work 'Fare' in the name of the campaign. The Air Fair proceeds were going to charity not the MoD. Many 'Stop the Air Fare' campaigners therefore felt it possible to pay £1 per head (£5 per car, £15 per minibus) to go into the base for the Air Fair, though they would rather have given the money directly to charity, I think. Once inside some started leafleting the public. US security personnel with walkie-talkies spotted them and the atmosphere became heavy. The campaigners were followed. There were sixty arrests. Phil Hedgehog was arrested (and later charged with breach of the peace) while photographing other people being arrested. Although the Celta Shelter in Peterborough was open from Saturday 21st July until the following Tuesday morning, there were many reports of arrested people asking the police to inform the Celta Shelter of their arrests and they were not being informed. Police announced that only twenty-three arrests had been made – barely one-third the number recorded by the Celta Shelter when the demonstration ended.

While all this was going on inside, protesters with banners and the Fallout Marching Band picketed the airfield gates.

At its meeting on Monday, 23rd July, Cambridgeshire County Council owing to a split in the Liberal vote in this hung council, voted not to declare the county a NFZ. Councillors did vote, however, to request Her Majesty's Government "to accept full financial responsibility for the adequate policing" of Molesworth and district. They threw out requests from Old Weston, Brington and Molesworth parish councils to remove peace campers from the superseded length of B660 Brington to Old Weston Road by Peace Corner, otherwise known as Peace Lane. The council did, however, take up its highway committee recommendation to close Peace Lane which meant that they would no longer have the expense of maintaining it as a public highway and ownership would be split between the frontagers.

On 27th July a 'snowballing' weekend began which resulted in the arrest of fourteen men, while thirty-two other 'snowballers', including women, were not arrested. These people tried cutting the fence again and even photographed each other doing it, but police would not arrest them. The thirty-two went to Huntingdon Police Station and asked to be arrested. After getting over the initial shock the police treated it as a great joke and still refused to arrest them. Meanwhile some of those charged with cutting the fence had their photographs and fingerprints taken by the police, even though they had withheld consent. They were then bailed to appear before Huntingdon magistrates. It is not certain if the magistrates who were to deal with their cases were the same magistrates who had not so long before, in the same court building, refused police permission to detain Molesworth activists in order to photograph and fingerprint them. Perhaps the police knew they would not get permission if they asked, so they took the photos and the fingerprints while they could and did not bother to ask permission of the magistrates.

According to the *Molesworth Bulletin* on 27th July Mark from Bristol "was arrested for letting air out of the tyres of a police van, placed in the back of the van and hit around the face several times. PC979 of Cambridgeshire Police Force called Mark a 'Wimp' whilst verbally and physically assaulting him." [*Molesworth Bulletin* No.9 August 1985] Mark was released without charge. He had a bleeding nose.

On Sunday 28th July activists held a 'Bye-Bye By-Laws' day, and claimed to have broken every one of the seventeen new by-laws made under the Military Lands Act 1892. Arrest and conviction records are not available, except for an undated *Guardian* report of fifty-six arrests.

When the A-bomb exploded over Hiroshima at 08.15 hours local time on 6th August, 1945 it was 00.15 hours in England. A commemorative service was held outside Eirene Chapel at 00.15 on 6th August, 1985 and at the same time, Reverend Michael Scott and six Christians held a one-minute silence, followed by a service, on the runway of RAF Alconbury. By 01:00 they had been discovered and arrested. They were all released without charge. Michael Scott was arrested on the Alconbury runway again within forty-eight hours and this time was charged with criminal damage. There was also a Hiroshima Day commemorative vigil at Fire Gate, RAF Molesworth.

In Denmark Hiroshima Day was commemorated with a mass trespass at a NATO base. Apparently Tom and Jill from Molesworth knew more about trespassing on military bases than most of the Danes did. The Danish authorities arrested both of them and imprisoned them. After two days Jill was released and deported to England. Tom was released and deported after nine days.

On 8th August a Canberra bomber overshot the runway at RAF Alconbury and burst into flames. The RAF's own fire service extinguished the blaze and a civilian fire engine, which attended, was not needed, so it left.

On 9th August there was another commemorative service outside Eirene at 01.45 hours, the English equivalent of the exact moment that the A-bomb exploded over Nagasaki.

The gate vigils at RAF Molesworth had faded out, but after the Hiroshima Day service a vigil was started again at Fire Gate. Usually it was for daytime only, but sometimes vigillers slept the night there. Police reaction was mixed and sometimes confused. Folk were often left in peace to vigil and sleep but at times police got heavy, kicking sleepers at night and arresting and charging vigillers. One night the vigil moved to a different site, a woman farmer came and asked the vigillers to move off her land. Police offered to move them with threats of violence. In the following week, a MoD fence went up around this farmland.

A logbook of contractors and a collection of photographs of construction work, along with contractors' men and their vehicles, were being made up by people on the vigils.

On 10th August, in a two hour sponsored trespass, two Colchester CND members raised £94 for the 'Molesworth for Life' fund. They were not charged under the by-laws so they had no fines to pay.

On 13th August, 1985, the two-day trial of Chris Craig began. There was no charge of attempted murder. The prosecution reduced the actual charge from grievous bodily harm to reckless driving to improve their chances of getting a conviction. Chris maintained he was driving the bus as instructed by police when the accident happened and was unable to avoid injuring the man. Chris was convicted, sentenced to three months in jail (suspended for two years), fined £350 and banned from driving for twelve months. Since July he had been bailed to an address away from Molesworth, with a condition on his bail that he keep away. Now he was free to return and to move about, provided he was not driving. He was not allowed to drive the bus in which he and his family had lived.

The fourteen 'snowballers' arrested on 27th July appeared in court on 19th August. Most pleaded not guilty and were remanded on bail for an adjournment. The first person to plead guilty was followed by another person standing up in the public gallery pleading guilty to cutting the RAF Molesworth perimeter fence on the same date. He asked to be charged, convicted and sentenced along with his friend in the dock. He was threatened with a contempt of court charge and told to sit down, which he did. Then, one by one, a succession of folk stood up in the public gallery and pleaded guilty to cutting the fence at Molesworth. Some waved photographs showing them doing it. The horrified clerk ordered the court to be cleared and the magistrates adjourned to a back room. The 'snowballers' sat down in the public gallery and refused to leave. Two of the activists then went over to the magistrates in the back room. The two were trying to talk to them, when extra police arrived, dragged them out and charged each of them with wilfully obstructing a police officer in the course of his duty. After about half-an-hour the others walked out, as it was obvious to these self-confessing criminals that they were not going to be arrested.

On August Bank Holiday Monday, Rainbow Village baby Tarot Lorien returned with her mother to celebrate her first birthday at Peace Corner. This was as near as she could be to her birthplace on the airfield. In her first year of life she had been arrested twice – once at Peace Corner and once on her way to Stonehenge in the notorious beanfield on 1st June.

Alconbury Mark VII Peace Camp was set up inside the base beside the runway. After setting it up the three peace campers wandered over the airfield and locked the two main doors to the Detention Centre. Purely by chance they met eight more activists wandering round in a group with pots of paint. The three campers were later arrested, taken out and dumped on the Great North Road without charge. The other eight folk apparently left the airfield without being apprehended.

During August there was a sixty-strong women's gathering, meant to be the first in a series of women's events taking place monthly; Peterborough Nuclear Free Zone City Council announced it was not going to give any contracts to the Tarmac Group of Companies, and Tarmac retaliated by closing its Peterborough office.

Also in August leaflets were produced to draw the attention of trades unionists to Molesworth and Cruise missiles. Two officials of the Union of Construction, Allied Trades and Technicians visited Molesworth. One was their regional organiser for East Anglia. He told campers he used to go into RAF Molesworth and other bases in the course of his trade union work until he spoke out publicly against Cruise. His security clearance and entry passes to these bases were withdrawn and he was no longer allowed to work in them. Campers attended meetings of Peterborough Trades Council and Huntingdon Trades Council in August and asked them to start support groups for the Molesworth Peace camps. An informal meeting was held with Transport and General Workers Union folk, some of whose members worked for Tarmac.

Folk arrested on April Fools Day applied for legal aid to prepare appeals on their charges of obstructing a police officer. The applications were turned down. They then appealed against the legal aid refusals. One was granted aid on appeal but the others were turned down again. Now only this one could start an appeal because of the prohibitive cost of appeals and this would have to be treated as a test case.

Throughout their summer holidays, as in previous years, many students stayed for short periods at the two Molesworth Peace Camps. Brig's van arrived with Jan and Jim's coach, causing police to increase surveillance of the People's Peace Camp where they were parked. Attempts by the authorities to move this camp were increasing.

In summer plans were announced for a new gate to replace Earth Gate. It was to be about fifty yards to the East. Also a new runway was built at Alconbury, and new laws were introduced forbidding camping and loitering near RAF Alconbury. If there was any advance publicity about these laws it did not seem to have been noticed by the residents of Alconbury Weston.

Also during this summer news filtered through Canada and Pensioners for Peace of the 'Ground Defence Plans' for US bases in Britain. These plans were designed to prevent the work of the bases and the Cruise convoys from being disrupted in time of war or national emergency and would in effect put large areas of Britain under martial law, at times decided by the British Government in consultation with the US Government without consulting the British people.

Christine Saltmarshe, an Alconbury Weston villager, asked the USAF and the MoD how these plans would operate in respect of RAF Alconbury and got no answer. She had, like many local folk, made strong friends among the Americans at Alconbury, but when these Americans found out that she was asking about the 'Ground Defence Plans' and supporting the Molesworth Peace Camps, they ostracised her. In June, a RAF helicopter hovered over her house and one of the crew climbed out onto a rope ladder. After a minute or so he climbed back in and the helicopter departed. When she complained through the local police the authorities at first said nothing. When her complaint reached the ear of Lord Jenkins of Putney and Lord Hatch of Luzby the facts came out. The helicopter came from RAF Oakington and the order for the visit had originated from the USAF not the RAF. The pilot was disciplined (for obeying an order?) and ordered to personally apologise to Christine, which he did.

1st September saw the first anniversary of the dedication of Eirene. The MoD again refused a request to hold a service in it so a well-attended service was held outside the wire at Peace Corner.

At Molesworth on 4th September, two Leicester people took a tent onto Molesworth Airfield and erected it in an open area, where it was photographed from outside the perimeter fence. They camped there for eight hours before being arrested by Modplods. *Peace News* published the photograph. Once again *Peace News* and one of its photographers had risked prosecution under the Official Secrets Acts. [*Peace News*, 20th September 1985]

On the same day fifteen people from Nottingham were busy removing roadsigns pointing to RAF Molesworth. Two of them were arrested and charged with criminal damage.

On 10th September Cambridgeshire County Council officially closed Peace Lane, leaving the Church of England's Peterborough Diocese as owner of one side and the MoD as owner of the other. Christians then camped on the church side and challenged the attitude of the Peterborough Diocese to Cruise missiles. Although George had the field the diocese actually owned it and were, therefore, frontagers on one side of Peace Lane.

Also on 10th September RAF Chicksands was invaded by Molesworth Peace Campers in red T-shirts labelled "I'm a Russkie infiltrator". When they had climbed almost to the top of the Air Traffic Control Tower a USAF officer appeared.

"Stay perfectly still, or you'll be shot."

"I've got you covered with my feather duster, and it's armed," an activist carrying a feather duster replied.

There was panic. Things cooled down after modplods arrived and eventually the activists were dumped outside, uninjured and without charge.

East Northamptonshire District Council on 11th September put notices on five vehicles parked in Warren Lane calling for their removal within seven days or the council would tow them off and dispose of them. The owners sent the council a letter threatening legal action if they towed away the vehicles (including one seaworthy boat, two caravans and one car). It seems the district council took no further action but a nasty letter came from Northamptonshire County Council on 18th September telling the People's Peace Camp that they were taking legal action to evict the camp from Warren Lane on the grounds of highway obstruction.

Windows at the London HQ of T. Clark & Son, the electrical contractor whose vans had been seen at Molesworth in July, were covered with posters connecting this firm with construction work at Molesworth and explaining the connexion with nuclear weapons, by eight members of Lambeth Peace Action on Sunday, 15th September.

Some 'snowballers' were in Huntingdon Magistrates Court on 16th September.

Over the weekend of 21st-22nd September more than 200 people visited RAF Molesworth as part of a national 'snowball' being performed at bases all over the United Kingdom. About seventy were arrested. Some were charged with interfering with the perimeter fence, others with criminal damage. There were instances where arrested folk got free inside the base and ran off across the airfield. Some demonstrators attempted to surround 'snowballers' to delay or prevent their arrests. Surprisingly, there were no prosecutions for obstructing or assaulting police officers. Unfortunately, a key organiser of previous Molesworth 'snowballers', Peter Brown, was in prison. Without him, preparation and non-violence training of the unprecedented number of 'snowballers' was difficult.

At last there were sufficient folk at RAF Molesworth to start camps at Fire Gate and Air Gate. The Fire Gate camp set up on Hiroshima Day had closed because of police harassment and lack of numbers. This time the police allowed folk to camp at these two gates and at one the modplods even loaned the campers a brazier. These camps only lasted for the one weekend and did not plan to obstruct the gates on Monday, which may account for the police friendliness.

Some supporters who came from Liverpool organised a party. Everyone appears to have enjoyed the weekend.

During the Sunday night activists entered a high security area of RAF Alconbury and climbed into a watchtower. At 03.00 hours on the Monday morning one left the airfield undetected. At dawn the activists in the watchtower watched Americans doing a military exercise and Sidewinder air-to-air missiles being taken out of bunkers. The peace camper who had left the watchtower was contacting the media. As a result, shortly afterwards local radio and television announced that peace campers were in a watchtower in a high security area of RAF Alconbury. At 09.00 hours, modplods arrived having obviously been alerted by the radio and television publicity. They arrested the five activists, took them to portakabins at Molesworth (now standard practice with arrest at Alconbury) detained them until 17.00 hours and released them on bail with instruction to appear before Peterborough magistrates on 2nd October on charges of trespass under the Military Lands Act 1892.

As well as being very active in the peace movement Rachel Greaves held down a full-time job. Thus one can understand her problems when she was convicted of criminal damage at RAF Molesworth and sent to Holloway Prison for twenty-one days on 23rd September.

Christian peace campers from Earth Camp took over St. Oswald's Chapel in Peterborough Cathedral early in the morning of 27th September. By 1700 hours they had been interviewed by representatives of local and national media and by 20.00 hours a member of the Glebe Committee, which was responsible for diocesan land sales, told them that the sale of George's field, about which they were protesting, had been delayed until January. The protesters at first believed they had gained themselves some time for their campsite at Earth camp, but this hope was shattered on 30th September by letters from the diocesan solicitors telling Earth Camp and the other campers in Peace Lane to move or legal action would be taken to move them. The Diocese of Peterborough had so far received 646 letters about George's field and four bids to buy it. The peace campers in the chapel had been trying to get the Bishop to talk to them about the sale of the field.

One of the visitors to Earth Camp in September, a National Union of Public Employees shop steward, said RAF Molesworth looked like a Nazi concentration camp.

The four Welsh Presbyterians convicted on 30th May of attempted criminal damage and putting a banner on the RAF Molesworth perimeter fence refused to pay their fines. The court refused to imprison them and wanted to serve attachment of earnings orders on them, which would order their employers to deduct fines and court costs from their pay. The Welsh Presbyterian Church did not want to do this and was resisting the imposition of the orders.

In September some Molesworth peace campers were involved in the opposition to the Army exercise 'Brave Defender'.

The High Court turned down the application for an order to evict the People's Camp, which they heard on 2nd October, because Northamptonshire County Council had not prepared their application well enough.

Christians at Earth Camp held a service of worship and erected an enormous wooden cross on 20th October. They also put a smaller cross in St. Oswald's Chapel in Peterborough.

At the CND demonstration in Hyde Park on 26th October there was a Molesworth stall with an enormous banner advertising a blockade planned for 6th February, a whole three-and-a-half months ahead. Already national CND was promoting it and the publicity was going out across the whole United Kingdom. Planning and publicity this far ahead for an action of this kind was exceptional.

The Army did not destroy all the wheat on the four acres on 6th February. Now the remaining wheat had ripened. Peace campers and supporters sent many letters and some petitions to the commander of RAF Molesworth, Flight Lieutenant McDougall, who, at one stage, personally brought round a reply and introduced himself to the campers at Peace Corner. He was asked if peace campers could harvest the wheat, or failing that, if the MoD could harvest it and either send it to Eritrea or give it to the campers so they could send it to Eritrea. The MoD were adamant: It would not be harvested. Then peace campers watched powerless as MoD grass cutters mowed all but a few stalks standing near the chapel.

On 5th October on behalf of the peace camps and the starving Eritreans, Justin Kenrick entered the airfield and attempted to harvest this remnant. His attempt was at first a failure as he was arrested, charged and released on bail with instructions to appear in Huntingdon Magistrates Court on 4th November. He had not been able to cut any wheat before being arrested. As a direct result of his incursion, however, modplods harvested a sheaf of wheat and gave it to Justin.

By now the Ploughshares Campaign and the Tools for Eritrea Project, which were born at Molesworth, were progressing nicely. People were arranging to grow crops (but not on the airfield where it all started) and were collecting tools for Eritrea. There had been rain to break the drought in Eritrea and, with the help of Ploughshares, some crops had been sown there.

Andy and his van moved from the People's Peace Camp to Peace Corner, after Andy was fined £25 for living at the People's Camp in contravention of planning regulations. The prosecution was brought by East Northamptonshire District Council. After adjournments it was finally heard on 8th November, when he was fined £25. For every day after this that he lived there with his van in breach of the regulations he would have to pay a fine of £100. Chris, an ex-serviceman and veteran of the Christmas Island nuclear tests was also sentenced for living at the People's Peace Camp in breach of the planning regulations. He faced a possible prison sentence as he was having difficulties in raising the money to pay his fine.

On the weekend of 9th-10th November there was another 'snowball' at Molesworth. By now about 140 people had taken part in 'snowballs' at RAF Molesworth some more than once.

Northamptonshire County Council's application for an order in possession to evict the remaining campers at The People's Peace Camp was foiled in court twice on 2nd November and 15th November. Campers knew that a third adjournment was very unlikely when the case was due to be heard again on 20th December.

During 1984/5 Carolyne Pybus, Bruce Garrard and Jimmy Johns had represented Molesworth Peace Camp on CND National Council. They gave up their posts at CND National Conference on the weekend of 15th-17th November. Arrangements were made with people on Projects Committee and on National Council to ensure that the Molesworth Peace Camps would still have a voice on National Council. At this time there were still two camps: Earth Camp and its neighbours at Peace Corner, and the People's Peace Camp, much reduced in size, in Warren Lane.

In the early hours of Monday 18th November, campers in Peace Lane were awakened and told to move their tent. A large force of police and contractor's men had gathered with construction equipment at Peace Corner. It looked like 6th February all over again.

The tent was moved and work started on building a new, high weldmesh fence along Peace Lane, marking the start of a new phase in the construction work on the airfield.

Working together North-West Region of CND organised a blockade and Green CND a day of action on Saturday, 23rd November. Traffic going through the gates was delayed. Green CND planted bulbs and saplings alongside the new perimeter fence, on the outside of it. The bridleway across the airfield was now closed, legally, and had been replaced with a bridleway along the outside of the perimeter fence from Fire Gate to Peace Corner. Demonstrators marched along this new route beating the bounds. There were attempts at incursions and several arrests on various charges.

During November the Vicar of Thrapston visited Earth Camp and Halcyon Spirit, the caravan at Peace Corner occupied by Jennifer and Ian Hartley. Though he didn't entirely agree with the peace campers' politics, religions or methods, he seemed sympathetic. Subsequently peace campers went carol singing with his flock in Thrapston, which must have made for good relations with local folk.

John Perry was in court for breach of the planning laws with his tent on 2nd December. He elected to go for a Crown Court trial.

The new fence along Peace Lane was asking to be climbed. It was, on 7th December, by Mark of Peace Corner and four other activists. All were arrested but only three were charged with any offence.

On 17th December Mark, Jerry, the solicitor from Milton Keynes, and five Rainbow Villagers were in Peterborough Crown Court appealing against their convictions for obstructing Superintendent Blake on April Fools Day. The same judge who took the Alconbury Nine trial, Judge Christopher Young took the case. *Molesworth Bulletin* commented:

> After a four-day trial, judge and magistrates took ten minutes to make their decision. In spite of the fact that Superintendent Blake had been seen to lie in court on a previous case involving Rainbow Villagers, the judge chose to believe everything the police said. (*Molesworth Bulletin* 1986. For "magistrates" read "jury". There was an error in the original report.)

Judge Young even tried to insist upon Jane, who was in a wheelchair, standing for him when he entered!

The guilty verdicts were confirmed and £75 extra costs was added to each of the fines, except Jan's, which was left unaltered.

Northamptonshire county Council's application for an order in possession for the site of the People's Peace Camp succeeded when it was presented to a high court judge sitting at Northampton Crown Court on 20th December. The campers negotiated a twenty-eight-day delay on the order so that it would not come into force until after 17th January and, as that was a Friday, eviction was unlikely to occur before Monday, 20th January.

A women-only vigil took place at Air Gate on Friday 21st December. Only one woman appears to have been arrested. Rachel was caught decorating the gate.

On 23rd December, folk were active along the perimeter fence by Peace Corner. Beside Earth Gate, three Christians got through the outer 'overnight' fence of razor wire and two fairies, Twinkle Fairy-Poos and Esmeralda Witchy-Poos from Peace Corner, attempted to climb the weldmesh fence. Both had apparently been celebrating in advance of Christmas and were heavily laden with presents for folk on the other side of the fence. Consequently only Twinkle managed to reach the top and even then she fell down the other side and was greeted by two panic-stricken modplods and a dog. She was arrested and charged with trespass. Twinkle was not allowed to distribute her presents, which the Modsquad kept to produce in court as evidence.

Reverend Michael Scott and three other Christians held a Christmas carol service on the runway at Alconbury in the early hours of Christmas Day. When US servicemen came to investigate, they were offered Christmas presents but would not accept them. The four carol singers were arrested, charged with trespass and bailed to appear before Huntingdon magistrates on 3rd February 1986.

On Boxing Day, three peace campers went for an evening stroll on Alconbury Airfield. They headed for the middle, climbed a water tower, under cover of darkness and spent an hour on top of it singing, playing a harmonica and shouting greetings down to passing cars. They were full of joy tinged with a touch of vertigo.

Despite the loudness of our revelry and the fact that someone scurried from one Detention Centre building to another a mere 100 yards away, we were not discovered. Unprepared to stay there all night we descended from the tower and started walking around the warehouses, when suddenly we came across a 'confidential area' with a figure-regulated lock on the door. While two were trying to work out the combination I noticed a sign saying 'If locked please ring' so we did. A rather bemused American soldier opened the door so we sang him a carol. Patiently he listened till we'd finished, said 'Thank you' and closed the door. As we walked off, amused by his reaction, we saw an American police car, complete with a searchlight pointing in the wrong direction, a few yards from us. Being unnoticed we decided to cross the runway, but were spotted by a truck. Then minutes later we were surrounded by police cars and trucks. With little ceremony they ordered us to lie down on the runway, in which position we were kept until a MoD policeman arrived. We were politely escorted into a truck and taken to the detention Centre. After a short wait we were handcuffed and taken back to Molesworth where we were charged and all released in forty minutes. (Extracted from a report in *Molesworth Bulletin* 1986)

THE BIG BLOCKADE, THE DIGGERS' WALK AND BRAMPTON MEADOW (JANUARY- APRIL 1986)

In early December the publicity was out for the Diggers' Walk to Molesworth at Easter. Wisely it was put out three months in advance to give people time to organise and prepare.

Mentions of the forthcoming blockade were appearing in all sort of odd places by now, and this was an added bonus, which occurred as a result of publicity going out over three months before the event. *Construction News* mentioned the planned blockade in an article about MoD contracts for Molesworth. The MoD was asking for bids for five different contracts running to a total of about £30,000,000 worth of work. Among the firms bidding for the contracts were John Laing, Tarmac, Fairclough, Wimpey, Mowlem, Taylor Woodrow, Alfred McAlpine, French Kier, ARC and Costain. Tarmac had, of course, already been involved in the building of the weldmesh fence so it could be said that this firm had a foot in the door.

After living in Halcyon Spirit for ten-and-a-half months, which included the eviction of 6th February, Jennifer and Ian Hartley went away in December for a well-earned break of six weeks at the WRI Triennial Meeting in India. Their dog also went for a holiday, but only to an address in England. Throughout their time in Halcyon Spirit, Jennifer and Ian had tried to keep up twice-daily services, first in Eirene, then as near to it as they could get after the fence was erected. While they were away, locums on a rota occupied the caravan.

A group from Essex made an incursion into RAF Molesworth and inspected the silos already being built as part of the 'GAMA' project in a high security area. The MoD had processed the tenders and contracts for RAF Molesworth at top speed, hoping to curb protests and direct actions and to speed up the work, but they failed to stop this group. The four members of this group who were arrested were later released without charge. The expedition subsequently gave a detailed report of what they had inspected to the campers at Peace Corner.

A York group planted more trees around the outside of the RAF Molesworth perimeter fence.

New tarmacadam was laid in Cockbrook Lane and peace campers lost no time in painting and decorating it.

There was a short blockade of a quarry near Huntingdon, which was owned by Tarmac and used by vehicles on Molesworth contracts.

On New Year's Eve, Peggie took over from Helen, her dog and cat, at Halcyon Spirit and stayed the night. The weather was fine. There was a party round the campfire at Peace Corner. Campers unsuccessfully tried to offer the modplods some whisky and Christmas pudding. They had more success with the Cambridgeshire Police. Two of them accepted Christmas pudding and two others accepted a tot of whisky each. There followed friendly conversation among police and campers, including German and American women campers. Peggie compared her World War II service in the Women's Auxiliary Air Force with a policeman's service in the miners' strike. Now Peggie was on the outside of the RAF perimeter fence!

A vigil at RAF Alconbury on 19th January marked the second anniversary of weekly vigils there. These were done mainly by local people and Molesworth campers.

Also in January local councillors and officials were briefed by the MoD about their plans in a meeting at RAF Alconbury. At the same time, the gate fifty yards East of Earth Gate and the Brington By-Pass were being built. As yet, construction had not started on the link road from the Great North Road to the M1 Motorway – the A1/M1 Link.

On 18th or 19th January, two people were arrested after 'snowballing' Molesworth with wirecutters.

At the end of January, a caravan resident at Peace Corner had an eviction order thrown out of court because it was made out to him, and it should have been made out to the caravan owner. He was not the owner.

On 3rd February , Michael Scott and the other Christians arrested at the Christmas carol service on Alconbury airfield appeared before Huntingdon magistrates. Michael was fined £25, which he had not paid at the time of writing (Michael was later fined £25 for a Molesworth 'snowballing' and £50 for an Ascension Day Eucharist. All three fines remained unpaid and Michael was under threat of imprisonment on 30th June, 1986.) What happened to the others is not known.

At Peace Corner six people trying to reach Eirene were arrested as soon as they crossed the wire. A diversion at Earth Gate not only failed to distract the police, but also got a seventh person arrested. All these people were charged on 31st January 1986.

On the evening of 5th February, snow began falling steadily and continued until it lay thickly every-

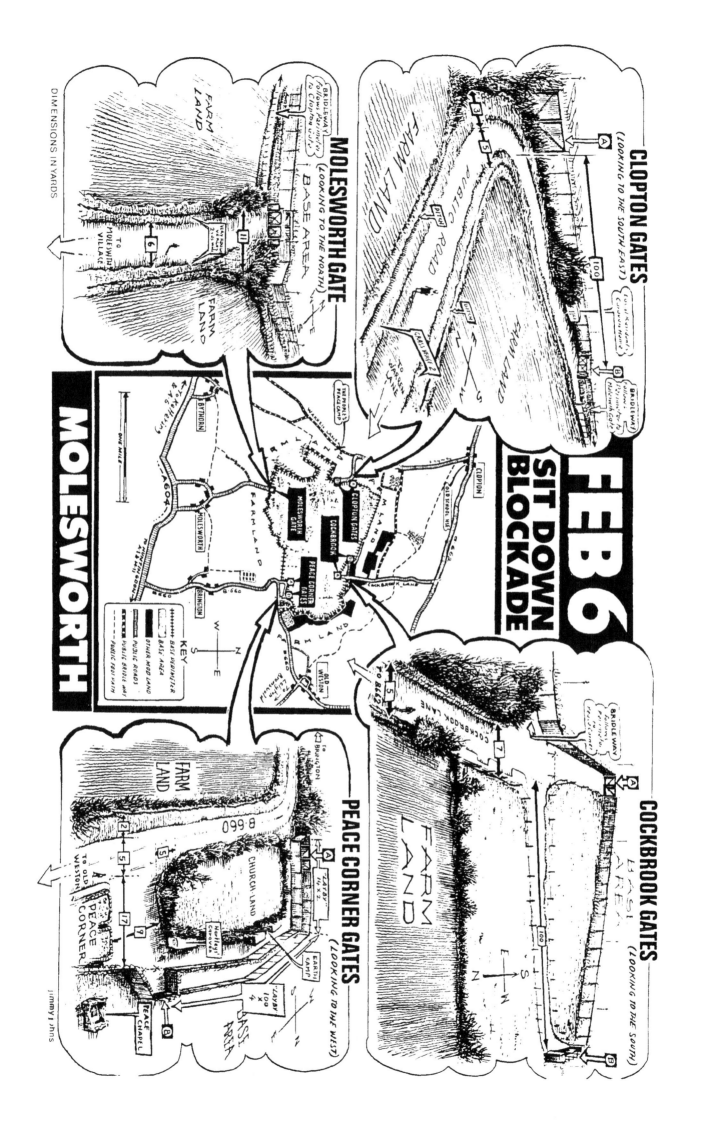

where. Throughout the night and the next morning as the snow spread westward, people came from all over England and Wales to RAF Molesworth.

From Southampton came two minibuses and at least one car. It was pure coincidence that it was a Thursday, and our Molesworth pledge day had been Thursday. We were not there to honour our pledge. We were there to commemorate, with a blockade, the anniversary of the eviction of 6th February 1985. Perhaps if all of us pledgers had honoured our pledges to the letter there would have been no eviction from the airfield. Who knows?

The blockade had been planned in shifts with changes at 09.00 hours and 12.00 so that RAF Molesworth could be kept closed for nine hours continuously throughout the hours of usable daylight. Because of the weather many people arrived late and went home early and the shift system did not work as well as it might have done. Nevertheless, CND organisation coped and the airfield was kept blockaded all day. No traffic passed through the blockade. Workmen already inside at the beginning of the blockade did a little work demolishing a fence near Peace Corner but no outdoor construction work was done. This enabled the MoD to announce that the blockade had not stopped work at Molesworth. Although the weather caused the blockade organisers' difficulties, it caused even greater difficulties to people trying to do construction work. The soil was frozen and water left outside was soon freezing. This meant it was impossible to work with cement or concrete without using gas heaters and screens to keep it warm. On balance the weather favoured us.

On our way to the blockade in our minibus, through falling snow and a motorway traffic jam caused by ice on the road, we were listening to the Radio 4 news broadcasts. Each hourly bulletin gave the latest news from the BBC man at Molesworth: at 07.00 hours there were around 2,000 people at Fire Gate and more at the other gates. After taking over five hours for a three-hour journey, we arrived late at the CND control point in Bythorne. Cheerful, efficient marshals greeted us and directed us to our station at Water Gate. When we got there we saw that our being over two hours late had not prevented the blockade from holding solid and many more people were late.

Ironically, it was from this point that I set off across the airfield on my first visit to Molesworth – there was no gate there then!

Cambridgeshire and Northamptonshire Police were out in force on the roads around Molesworth, but inside, at Water Gate, the guards were London Metropolitan Police in blue overcoats without numbers, and modplods. I saw them arrest two women for trespass in the dog run just to the south of the gate. There was no attempt to move or arrest blockaders and only five people were arrested all day all over the airfield. They were charged under the new by-laws and released on bail with instructions to attend Peterborough Magistrates Court on 17th February.

Something else I saw at Water Gate made me unhappy. A few people were throwing stones over the fence and gate at the police inside, fortunately without hitting anyone. This took place after CND had made abundantly clear in the advance publicity that this was to be a non-violent demonstration and arrests were to be minimised. Already one policeman at Molesworth had been hit and seriously injured by a thrown object at another action. Did we want history to repeat itself? Fortunately the stone-throwing stopped before my horrified brain could think of a way of quietly stopping it.

On a happier note, CND's organisation included radio communication so that ambulances could be called in emergencies in addition to the first aid vehicles that CND had brought along. CND even supplied portaloos for men and women at Water Gate and they worked in spite of the frost, which only lifted for about an hour in the afternoon.

Air Gate was chosen as the women's gate. All the police at Air Gate were women except for the chief inspector in charge. Women blockaders criticised the police for putting a man in charge, although they were pleased to see that otherwise the police had respected the women-only rule.

National CND, peace campers, East Anglian Christians and CND folk spent many thousands of pounds cash and thousands of hours in time organising this blockade. They were rewarded with a turnout of around 5,000 blockaders, all the gates closed all day and local demonstrations in solidarity with the blockade in towns and cities all over Britain involving people who were unable to travel to Molesworth. Also, several groups had taken CND's advice and given their local media statements saying that they would be sending contingents to Molesworth. This meant the blockade received tremendous publicity, not only nationally but also in the local media all over Britain.

On Ash Wednesday, 12th February, Christians held a service of penitence for their sins with ashes at Peace Corner.

On the same day Cambridgeshire County Council workmen blocked both ends of Peace Lane with bollards, while an official served enforcement notices under planning laws telling campers to move from there by 21st March. The notices said they were adversely affecting the 'rural scenic amenity'!

The next day modplods twice moved a tent erected near the MoD fence as a prayer and worship place, because it was on the MoD half of Peace Lane. The third attempt to erect this tent succeeded. It now stood between Dove and Peace Link on the Church of England side of the lane. It was first used by Reverend Michael Scott for a Holy Communion service.

Everyone was out of bed early on Saturday 14th February, at the People's Peace Camp. They had no choice. They were rudely awakened by fifteen bailiffs at 06.00 hours. The East Northamptonshire District Council bailiffs were on overtime rate and did not want to hang about. They gave campers just twenty minutes to leave. There were problems arranging caravan tows at this time on a Saturday and some caravans ended up being towed by bailiffs, with their own vehicles, to a secret place.

Soldiers were already out of bed and participating in a military exercise at 07.00 hours on the same morning in School Lane, a cul-de-sac near RAF Alconbury, when some women arrived with a caravan. The women were not NAAFI tea ladies – they were peace campers setting up camp! They opened the doors of the soldiers' vehicles, greeted the soldiers, chatted to them and interrupted the exercise. It appears that the twenty soldiers in their five vehicles were unable to hold School Lane in the face of a concentrated, non-violent attack by a few women with one car and a caravan. They packed up and left at 10.00 hours leaving the women in sole occupation of School Lane.

At noon police arrived, dragged five women out of the caravan, arrested them and charged them with obstruction of the highway. They were ordered to appear before Huntingdon magistrates on 5th March and released on bail.

Alconbury Mark IX Peace Camp ended a few minutes after the women were arrested, when police towed the caravan out of School Lane. The police did not impound it, which is surprising in view of what had happened to the People's Peace Camp caravans.

Campers returned to Warren Lane and erected tents on 15th February. The bailiffs also returned and evicted them again, with threats of arrest the next time any camper showed his or her face in Warren Lane. This was followed by an attempt to set up a camp at Fire Gate, which failed because campers were arrested. The remaining campers then went to Earth Camp where some settled. Others left the Molesworth area.

During February doubts arose about the ownership of land on the MoD side of Peace Lane, then occupied by the MoD and claimed by them. Peace campers believed that the MoD could not prove ownership and that the scaffolding placed along Peace Lane outside the airfield perimeter fence did not mark the boundary of the land they owned, as they claimed. Peace campers had been climbing over this stretch of fence, pulling down scaffolding and moving scaffolding about, without being charged with any offence – though four people were arrested and charged with obstruction for just hanging around and asking questions near the new gate! Campers wanted to bring the issue of who owned that piece of land and where the MoD boundary really was into court but up to the time of writing they have not been able to do so nor has the MoD been able to buy this land.

On 5th March, the women arrested in School Lane at Alconbury Mark IX Peace Camp appeared before Huntingdon Magistrates. 'Not Guilty' pleas were entered by four and the fifth pleaded guilty to a charge of obstructing the highway. The other four were also charged with highway obstruction. All the charges were adjourned to 22nd April. Rachel pleaded not guilty to an additional charge from Molesworth and that was also adjourned. Apart from Michelle Rivers, who was imprisoned for twenty-eight days for unpaid fines, they were all released on bail.

St. George's Hill near Byfleet, Surrey, is historic because Gerard Winstanley and his followers, the Diggers, occupied common land on this hill and around it in 1649 so that they could sow corn and other crops on which they could live. They believed in love, equality and a God. The land they occupied was wasteland and their occupation bore some similarity with the occupation of the airfield by the peace campers.

At 11.00 hours on Friday 21st March an all-faiths service was held at Weybridge Station and from there the Molesworth Diggers took the tools that had just been blessed, and which had been collected for Eritrea, up St. George's Hill and dipped them in the historic soil. From there they set off on a march right through the centre of London and across the most densely populated corner of Britain to RAF Molesworth, where the tools were again to be dipped ceremonially in the soil before being sent to Eritrea.

The marchers arrived at Molesworth on Easter Monday 31st March. They were joined by another march from Corby, also bringing tools. When an irresistible force meets an immovable object – fifty-seven Molesworth Diggers went over the razor wire and weldmesh fences, dipped their tools in the soil and were arrested. Fortunately their tools were not confiscated as they could have been under the by-laws. By the end of the day a garage had been filled with tools to be despatched to Eritrea.

Cambridgeshire NFZ Action Group had been busy lobbying their county councillors. At the March county council meeting, thanks to the lobbying, the council agreed: (a) to outlaw the dumping of nuclear waste in Cambridgeshire and, (b) to call upon Her Majesty's Government not to waste £3,000,000 on another perimeter fence for RAF Molesworth, but to use this money to upgrade old people's homes. The latter motion was passed by the healthy majority of forty-four Alliance and Labour votes to twenty-four Tory ones.

In the spring of 1986 two of the Alconbury Nine, Phil Hudson and Paul Rudolf, appealed. The judge took into consideration the facts that they remained unemployed and the general situation of high unemployment showed no sign of improving, when he said there was no prospect of them being able to pay and quashed their £500 fines. The suspended sentences stayed.

For some time the Department of Transport had been planning a trunk road to connect the Great North Road to the M1 Motorway. It was planned to run to the South of Molesworth. The new gate at Peace Corner, the Brington By-pass and a new road junction would connect RAF Molesworth with the A1-M1 Link. This would enable cruise convoys to join the network of motorways and dual carriageways quickly. For this reason, many peace campaigners did not want the road to be built.

One strategy that offered some chance of success was to buy a plot of land somewhere along the route and split it into lots of small plots, each individually owned by different people and groups. This strategy had been tried elsewhere with limited success. The land itself could be used by the owners for growing food and peace campers could use it as a rest camp to which they could retreat when overwhelmed by the pressures at RAF Molesworth. When the time came to build the road the government would have to purchase, individually and compulsorily, every plot of land it needed. This would be a tedious and expensive process, which could be lengthened even more by each owner taking the attitude that an Englishman's home (or his plot, at any rate!) is his castle, and no way does he want American Cruise missiles transported over it. Women and corporate bodies, who would also be entitled to own plots and hold on to them just as tenaciously, would not, of course, use the pronoun 'he'! They might just stop the road builders.

The owner of Brampton Meadow and an adjoining field set between A1 on the east, A604 on the south and the River Ouse on the north had recently died. His son, as executor, was charged with selling the land, which lay on the route of the proposed trunk road. Local campaigners discovered this piece of land with a total area of about nine acres, arranged an independent valuation and made an offer. Meanwhile, an appeal was launched for money with which to buy the whole nine acres and, in June 1985, the Molesworth/Alconbury Land Trust was set up. The vendor was happy to sell to the campaigners. Then an event occurred which could make the campaign against the road builders easier. Brampton Meadow was declared a site of special scientific interest because of the plant species that grew in this ancient meadow, especially the Adder's Tongue Fern, whose presence suggested that this land had lain undisturbed since Roman times or earlier. The trustees' names, the location of the land and the names involved in its purchase had to be kept secret so that the authorities could not move in and block the purchase and acquire the land for the Department of Transport quickly.

Over £20,000 was raised from over 1,500 individuals and groups. The money was given to the trust's solicitors for safekeeping. In December 1985, the contract of sale was signed and returned to the vendor's solicitors. The trust itself could not actually buy and sell the land, so a company, the Molesworth/Alconbury Land Company Limited, was formed to buy and sell it.

The offer of £35,000 for the nine acres made through Rapley's property agents of Huntingdon came like a bomb out of the blue in January when the vendor's solicitors told the trust's solicitors about it. The vendor was legally bound, as executor of his late father's estate, to accept the higher bid. As the Molesworth/Alconbury Land Company Limited had not yet paid for the land, the vendor was able to cancel the first sale.

Why a new offerer, believed to be a property developer, would want to pay almost double the independent valuation of the land was a mystery, as was the identity of the new offerer. It was thought that the government was involved but it was impossible to discover who the mystery offerer was. As half the land was a site of special scientific interest, the land would be of very limited value to a developer wishing to build on or even plough it.

The trust had to mail all the people who had given money, asking whether to: (a) wait and see what happened (b) raise the offer to over £35,000 (c) look for another site on the route of the proposed road or (d) to refund folk's money.

That was far as things had got by April 1986.

In spite of the fact that Molesworth Peace Camp and the campaign to stop Cruise missile bases being built at Molesworth and Alconbury had the support of two Anglican bishops (Tony Dumper of Dudley and Gordon Roe of Huntingdon), other clergy of many denominations, eminent people of other faiths and none at all and hundreds of local people, the MoD still went ahead and built the two bases. The authorities cleared eight peace camps at Alconbury and two at Molesworth, including the eviction in February, 1985. They had arrested and charged so many people that the local justices were overwhelmed at times and still the opposition grew.

At the time of writing there is still a peace camp at Molesworth. Its postal address is Molesworth Peace Camp, Peace Corner, outside RAF Molesworth, Old Weston Road, Brington, Huntingdon, Cambridgeshire.

Photo: Keith Ollett.

Cross erected on church land confronting the proposed Cruise missile base. Christian CND's consistent witness, both by direct action and through the courts, prevented the church land from being sold to the MoD to enlarge the base. RAF Molesworth 1986.

A few days before Easter, 1958, the first peace camp was set up near the Falcon Pub in Tadley beside the road that passes the Main Gate of the Atomic Weapons Research Establishment (since renamed the Atomic Weapons Establishment).

AWRE occupied land between the villages of Aldermaston and Tadley. Here the research, development and some of the manufacture of Britain's nuclear weapons took place in great secrecy.

The five or six campers, members of the Direct Action Committee Against Nuclear Weapons Tests, were on a fast and vigil for a week over Easter. They were also leafleting workers going in and out of the establishment. They had just two tents to shelter in during the coldest Easter so far recorded in the twentieth century. On Monday the first Easter March in history passed the camp on its way to Falcon Field. The marchers had braved sleet and snow on the walk from London. This first Aldermaston March, also organised by the Direct Action Committee, achieved international fame, but the peace camp was forgotten by all but a few activists. After the Easter Monday activities had finished the campers packed up and left.

The peace campers returned later that summer and set up a peace camp in a nearby field. For eight weeks they vigilled and leafleted the workers and

visitors to AWRE. As a result, two workers decided to leave and one person was dissuaded from applying to work there. Lorry drivers signed a petition demanding the conversion of the plant to peaceful uses, and one turned back without delivering his load. To do this required courage in those days, when both employers and unions regarded nuclear weapons as a useful part of the British armoury, and their research, development and manufacture as a good source of money. In the ninth week campers occupied the forecourt in front of the Main Gate in a round-the-clock vigil demanding a meeting with the Director, Sir William Penney. They didn't get it and left to be almost forgotten by history.

The third camp here was the Aldermaston Women's Peace Camp set up during the 'Ten Million Women' anti-NATO protest between 20th and 30th September 1984. As in several other actions at Aldermaston around this time, Greenham women were involved.

Neither an eviction nor a single arrest was reported at the three Aldermaston Peace Camps. This has not prevented them from being a valuable part of the campaign against the work being done at Aldermaston. Nuclear disarmers have underestimated their value in that campaign. There have been many other protests at Aldermaston, which fall outside the scope of this book.

SHERGAR AND CHALLENGERS AT BARNBOW

Barnbow Royal Ordnance Factory, Cross Gates, Leeds, Yorkshire manufactured tanks for the British Army.

In 1983 they unveiled a new model, the Challenger, which weighed sixty tons, had a twelve-cylinder Rolls-Royce compression ignition engine, a maximum speed of 35mph or more on surfaced roads, and a 120mm gun with computerised laser sighting. This gun was bigger than the four-inch bore limit imposed on Army ordnance by a peace treaty which Britain signed immediately after World War I. The tank had originally been developed for an overseas customer, the Shah of Iran, who was overthrown. A new government in Iran refused to buy the tanks, so the British Government was left with 250 tanks in the process of manufacture, which would not be paid for by the customer who ordered them. Although the Army had not wanted any Challenger Tanks when asked originally, when the British Government asked them to help by buying the 250 from the cancelled order, they agreed to do so. This new tank would serve alongside the Chieftain, which was the main battle tank of the British Army. The Challenger had several advantages over the Chieftain, the main one being its new Chobham armour, which the MoD claimed to be the best in the world.

One cancelled overseas order was not the only thing expected: Barnbow's Sales and Marketing Manager, Peter McLaughlin, predicted sales of 'around 2,000' overseas though he had not managed to get an over-

Shergar

seas customer to take up the cancelled order for 250!

A public launching for the Challenger was planned, partly so that the public could see what their taxes, through the defence budget, were buying and partly so that foreign defence attaches could inspect what ROF Barnbow could offer them in the way of tanks for sale. The information given to the latter and the answers to their questions were much more detailed than the information given to the British taxpaying public who were footing the bill. This launching called for big names and the ROF wanted the

biggest. Unfortunately, Michael 'Tarzan' Heseltine, Her Majesty's Secretary of State for Defence, was unable to come, so Geoffrey Pattie, the Minister for Defence Procurement, came instead. The army sent no less a person than the Chief of the General Staff, General Sir John Stainier, to head its contingent . Of course Fred Clarke, Chairman and Chief Executive of all the ROFs, was there. About thirty or forty foreign military attaches came to the expenses-paid jamboree. Altogether about 150 bigwigs were ferried to the event in coaches and Army staff cars. A military band played.

About a week before the launching ceremony local peace groups found out for sure what was happening and when it was happening.

There was no time to send letters, convene meetings or visit many people. Bob Ward, Jill Westcott and the other organisers had to use telephones and ran up some pretty big telephone bills.

With only a few days' notice on Sunday 13th March, 1983, a peace camp was set up in an old railway cutting across the road from the factory in the midst of semi-detached suburban houses. There were just seven residents that night but by the morning of Wednesday 16th March, fifty people were at the camp greeting the VIPs and media people as they arrived at the factory. There were also lots of police, who laughed and joked with protestors, and refused to believe that their pantomime horse was the real Shergar (Shergar was a valuable racehorse that had recently gone missing). Some of the people on this peace camp were Greenham women, including

THINK TANK
THINK WAR

MADE IN
G.B.

ARMS SALES
KILL

On Wednesday 16 March, from 9am. — 3pm. officials from the Government, Army and M.O.D., and Arms Sales Experts will be attending the Barnbow Tank Factory in Crossgates, Leeds 15 to see the new "Challenger" Main Battle Tank going through its paces.

Please come along as well.

This extravagant binge is not only to "hand over" the Tank to the British Army, but to sell it to as many foreign armies as possible.

We saw in the Falklands what can happen with such arms sales. In the "peace" since 1945 *over 20 million people have been killed in wars in third world countries* — using weapons sold by countries such as ours.

Stop The Arms Trade!

Invest in Peace

PEACE IS THE REAL CHALLENGER

Leafet advertising the Barnbow demonstration.

Christine Hurst, who had been arrested for obstruction when she had climbed over the fence into RAF Greenham Common just two weeks before.

On arrival the VIPs were driven into the factory past a crowd with placards and banners and a fence decorated with balloons, flowers and streamers. All the demonstrators seemed to have balloons. The band struck up behind the wire and shortly afterwards a dozen women ran onto the car park between the protesting group and the ROF perimeter fence. They whooped, screamed and lay down in a die-in. Within seconds police had hauled them off the car park, but they were not arrested and charged. The campers leafleted passers-by and sang songs while behind the fence a Challenger performed manoeveres to applause from the VIPs sheltering from the rain under a canopy. The campers made do with winter woollies and waterproofs at the gate, with occasional dashes to the peace camp for cups of tea. The kettle was boiled for the tea on a stove made out of an old dustbin and which burned mainly wood.

After the jamboree was over the bigwigs all went home leaving Peter McLaughlin to sort out his export orders. On Thursday 17th March, 1983, the last campers left and the camp was closed.

During the five days the camp had been there nobody had hassled the campers or threatened them with eviction, though they were visited by the police who had asked all sorts of questions.

This peace camp did much good for the peace movement in Leeds and got the issue of arms exports much publicity on local TV and radio and in the local press.

Barnbow Camp site. All photos in this chapter are courtesy of Bob Ward, Leeds CND.

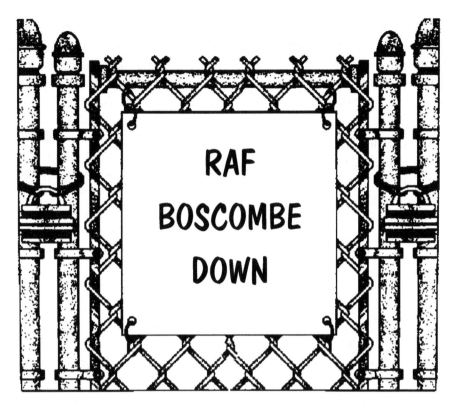

BOSCOMBE DOWN: HOW IT ALL BEGAN

The Home Secretary's ban on marches in the London area prevented CND from holding a national Aldermaston March over Easter 1978, and no other activities were planned for Hampshire, Wiltshire and Berkshire. In this area there were many towns that had forgotten CND and several nuclear bases that needed publicity.

A small but enthusiastic group of nuclear disarmers in Southampton wanted their campaigning to be more effective and were trying out new ideas around this time. This group, to fill the gap left by the lack of planned CND activity here, arranged a series of small actions in the area over that Easter weekend, starting in Portsmouth on Good Friday and culminating in a march from Stroud Green, Newbury, to AWRE Aldermaston on Easter Monday. A programme for the weekend, illustrated with a map showing the likely effects of a nuclear bomb on Berkshire, was printed several months in advance and widely distributed, particularly to the media. Striking 'Dayglo' orange printed posters were also distributed throughout the area.

One of the bases we visited on this 'Close-the-Bases' tour was RAF Boscombe Down. This airbase was about nine-and-a-quarter miles in circumference though the top-secret area inside the security fence was smaller. The outer part of the base on the Amesbury side included the married quarters, a NAAFI shop and barracks. The Modsquad patrolled all of it. In 1985 it was revealed at my trial that there were eleven miles of security fence at RAF Boscombe Down, not counting fences around the houses and gardens on the base. The Aircraft and Armaments Experimental Establishment was here in 1978. Though the A&AEE had handled Britain's first airborne nuclear weapons, the base was unlikely to have held any nuclear weapons in 1978 as none were being actively developed for the RAF at the time. Boscombe Down was, however, a nuclear bomber dispersal airfield and clearly could handle and store every type of weapon the RAF was ever likely to meet.

Historically, there was just a grass airfield here when the A&AEE arrived from Martlesham Heath in East Anglia in 1940. This move was made to get them as far away as possible from the German bombers and spy planes. At the end of World War II the first Meteor jets were still landing and taking-off on grass, but soon afterwards Boscombe Down acquired what was believed to be the longest runway in Europe. Such was the nature of the terrain that it would be easy to extend this runway by over a mile to the old High Post Airfield if necessary, but this was not done.

Thus it was that four nuclear disarmers from Southampton, including myself, arrived on Boscombe Down on Good Friday 1978 for a base visit and held a vigil in a lay-by on the Marlborough Coach Road where it crosses the low security area of the base.

Just one local nuclear disarmer, a Quaker teacher named Janet Cross, joined us. This was only a small affair; we didn't bother to carry our banner the fifty yards or so to the main entrance of the airfield proper, and left before an hour had passed.

The bombshell burst on the front pages of at least two local papers on the following Thursday. *Salisbury Journal*, beside a small item about our base visits in Wiltshire, had a banner headline: 'Boscombe Down to be reinforced against attack'. (*Salisbury Journal*, 30th March, 1978). Beneath it told of the fifty-six acres of farmland, owned by the MoD, that it was going to get back from a farmer who had rented them and was growing crops on them. On it the MoD were going to put thirty-four blast-resistant hangars and other facilities in a big Anglo-American scheme to expand Boscombe Down, and there were plans to draft in US troops and aircraft. *Salisbury Journal* and none of the other papers made any mention of the F1-11 nuclear bombers and the storage of American nuclear weapons at Boscombe Down. These were yet to be revealed.

The news was broken first to a planning committee of Salisbury District Council by Councillor Terry Heffernan, who also happened to be the publicity officer at RAF Boscombe Down. The announcement apparently took Councillor Austin Underwood, who lived well within a mile of the airbase and was a veteran of the pre-CND Operation Gandhi in 1952, by surprise. All he was able to do at the time was call for a public enquiry into the MoD plan.

Security was being tightened. In September 1978 modplods carrying out what was described as a routine search of workers' lockers at A&AEE nearly caused a strike. Another security check at A&AEE in March 1979 actually did cause a strike, when hundreds of workers walked out after Ben Elliot, a craftsman, was stopped and subjected to Modsquad questioning. He collapsed under questioning.

On this second occasion, when telephoned by a reporter, a union official said: "I can't say anything to the press. I have been silenced. I have been told to say nothing about the matter and refer all calls to the MoD in Whitehall."

The reporter contacted the MoD, whose spokesperson said: "I could not speak for the union side." [*Southern Evening Echo* front page, 2nd February, 1979]

It was announced that an outline plan of the forthcoming development on Boscombe Down would be available for public inspection at the offices of Salisbury District Council. An objector from Southampton telephoned their offices and ascertained that the plan was available; the times it was possible to see it, which office it was in and even which file it was in – S/78/137. When that objector went to the correct office, in office hours as advised, having travelled over twenty miles from Southampton, and asked to see the plan, the staff were adamant and refused to let him see it. Once again secrecy rules OK.

In Spring 1979, Southampton CND launched a petition campaigning for the fifty-six acres to be used as a horticultural college and market garden, instead of as a USAF base, and for nuclear armed aircraft to be banned from Boscombe Down.

Southampton CND and Greenpeace held a public meeting at the Southampton Friends' Meeting House on the afternoon of Saturday, 28th April, 1979. A press statement from the meeting, at which the press was not represented, made big stories on the front pages of three local papers. [*Echo* 9th May, 1979; *Salisbury Journal* and *Amesbury Journal* 10th May, 1979] The *Southern Evening Echo* headline proclaimed: 'Uproar at secret air base'. Our press statement neither mentioned an uproar nor that only two people had attended the meeting! Boscombe Down Action Committee (BDAC) was thus born in a blaze of publicity.

BDAC organised its first event, a march from the Greencroft, Salisbury, to Boscombe Down on 9th June 1979. Only about thirty people marched. This march ended not at the main entrance but at a new vehicle gate about half-a-mile south of it. On arrival, plans to dig the land inside the new fence were abandoned because there were so many modplods around that the diggers could not climb over the fence with their tools. Some people told the modplods, in blunt terms, what they thought of the new development.

At this point I want to introduce the commandants of RAF Boscombe Down. Air Commodore John Brownlow, commandant in 1978, was promoted and made commandant of the RAF College, Cranwell, at the beginning of 1980. He was replaced as commandant by Air Commodore Reginald Spiers, CBE, FRAeS, who had already served two tours of duty on Boscombe Down in more junior positions. He moved into the commandant's married quarter in Allington Way and out again four years later, when he was replaced by Air Commodore Graham Williams, AFC, who was replaced, in his turn, by Air Commodore Peter Gover in December 1985.

From time to time the armed forces simulate war

situations with training exercises. While an exercise with USAF F1-11 nuclear fighter-bombers and 500 US troops and airmen was in progress on Boscombe Down, Campaign Atom was demonstrating against USAF F1-11s at RAF Upper Heyford on 17th May 1980. Southampton CND members visited Boscombe Down and Greenham Common on their way to Heyford and met the duty officer on Boscombe Down, Squadron Leader David Bridger. We rode in a coach that belonged to two of our supporters, which turned quite a few heads, being a luxurious retired Bristol single-decker in original 'Wilts & Dorset' livery.

In another, bigger exercise 'Operation Square Leg', held on 22nd September 1980, the first target an enemy missile hit was on Boscombe Down, leaving no doubt of the airfield's importance in government defence planning.

An attempt was made to field a nuclear disarmament candidate, opposed to RAF Boscombe Down in Salisbury, in the 1983 general election, but it failed.

Councillor Austin Underwood had been asking a lot of questions about F1-11s on Boscombe Down. Using information he had gathered, Salisbury CND published *Position Paper No. 4 – Boscombe Down*, which gave much background information about the airbase.

By 1982 CND was growing all over Wessex and groups were forming in every decent-sized town and some villages too. Though all campaigned for nuclear disarmament, not all called themselves CND groups. Stonehenge Activists for Nuclear Disarmament were based on the village of Amesbury immediately to the West of Boscombe Down. SAND organised some of the demonstrations there.

The USAF flew in a 'Starlifter' transport plane, eight or ten F1-11s, and 200 troops and airmen for an exercise on Boscombe Down in September 1983. After hurried preparation on Thursday 8th September, about fifty people assembled for a vigil at the main entrance the next day. There was no gate at the main entrance, just a road that turns off a tarmac stretch of the Marlborough Coach Road at a small roundabout and went between low brick walls towards a bend. Immediately round this bend was a Modsquad station and a barrier across the road out of sight of the entrance by the roundabout. It is at this barrier that the secure part of the airbase, which includes the entire airfield, begins. Demonstrators didn't normally see the main gate as a police cordon would be put across the road into the airbase proper to stop them from going more than about fifteen yards from the

roundabout. At other times civilians could travel up to the barrier unhindered. After a short vigil the demonstrators left peacefully.

Nuclear Disarmers returned to Boscombe Down for a twelve-hour vigil that began at 06.00 hours on Thursday 22nd September and sat down in the main entrance. Some sat at the side, some in the road. Just before 08.00 the modplods asked those sat in the road to move, so that workers waiting in cars and on bikes could enter the base. Some demonstrators moved. David Barnesdale (an anarchist) and Geoff from Christchurch did not move. They were picked up and roughly thrown into a police van by Wiltshire Police. David's glasses were lost. Heather, a local teacher, felt it was her duty to give them support, as the road was about to be opened. She, too, sat down in the road and was thrown into the van. Later she was thrown into a police cell and strip-searched twice. The remaining demonstrators mounted a picket beside the entrance until 18.00 then went home. There were no further arrests. About fifty people had demonstrated.

So far all activity had been concentrated around the main entrance. Even when it had been blocked by a sit-down, the other gates were unaffected, and workers who drove in by the Porton Road Gate, as many did, would not have heard about the demonstration until they got in to work and spoke with colleagues who used the main entrance.

The three people arrested were released on bail and appeared in Salisbury Magistrates Court before the County Bench on the following Tuesday, when their cases were adjourned to 10th October. On their second appearance two were fined £25 each and the third case was adjourned. Heather refused to pay. After some weeks it was made clear to her she would be sent to jail during the school term if she didn't pay. Her employers, the Education Department of Wiltshire County Council, told her if she was jailed during the school term she would lose her job. She paid up on the last possible day. Geoff paid his fine, but David didn't and spent a week in Wormwood Scrubs.

The Greenham Women were taking legal action in the United States of America to try and stop Ground-Launched Cruise Missiles from coming to Britain and Europe. There were vigils and peace camps for up to twenty-four hours, on 8th and 9th November in support of nine of the Greenham women, at military bases with US connexions all over Britain. People were asked to demonstrate at their local bases and Boscombe Down was given as the base for demonstrators from most of Wessex.

The site chosen for the First Boscombe Down Peace Camp, which lasted for twenty-four hours over 8th and 9th November, was a very bad one. SAND had put it on a site about a quarter-mile North of the boundary of the RAF station, beside the Marlborough Coach Road between the RAF boundary and A303. This stretch of A303 was a dangerous fast stretch of dual carriageway with access to the coach road only from the Andover direction. The coach road was only a track here and rarely used. There was a small sign at A303 junction, but the camp was not visible to people using the main road. People approaching from the South either had to use a public footpath along a disused railway and climb a bank to the coach road or cross part of RAF Boscombe Down with no signs to guide them. There were no facilities laid on at the site and we had to bring our own water.

Campers began gathering at the site at 15.00 hours on Tuesday 8th November. Apparently a small group went to the main entrance to hold a vigil as the workers were going home that evening, but the main activity was on the Wednesday when peace campers walked to the main entrance and held a festival there, with music, singing and dancing. There was no sit-down this time. Afterwards some walked down to the A303 flyover and displayed the banner. Motorists passing beneath on A303 more often waved and smiled than showed displeasure. Then police ordered us to move on. They said we might cause an accident by distracting a driver. We didn't think it was worth getting arrested and wanted to go back anyhow, so we complied with their request, though we thought it more likely that we would revive a tired, bored driver and prevent an accident than cause one by distracting a driver. Naturally the police would want as few people as possible to see our banner. Although only about a handful of people stayed the whole period of just over twenty-four hours, there was a total turn-out of a hundred or so people. Beforehand there was national publicity for this event in the peace movement's own papers and afterwards there was more publicity in the local papers and on regional TV. This was all quite good publicity and got news of the developments at Boscombe Down spread further. There were neither arrests nor evictions, the camp ended as planned and people left with the seeds of an idea about a second, permanent camp on a better site on Boscombe Down firmly planted in their minds.

These seeds grew into a plan for a weekend festival leading to a permanent peace camp. Pat Drake and John Fuller in the Andover area; some Salisbury disarmers; Heather, Doug and Austin of SAND and Terry Wynne from Eastleigh were among the people working to make this plan materialise.

CRASH GATE RED AND THE FESTIVAL OF PEACE

The dates set for Boscombe Down Festival of Peace, 15th-17th June, were chosen with great care so as to give a chance of warm weather and not to clash with other events. This festival immediately followed the big CND festival near Glastonbury where it could have been publicised (but apparently wasn't) and preceded by a few days the Summer Solstice at Stonehenge only five miles away where there was another festival. This was convenient for performers who could fit us in time schedules. Also people gathering at Stonehenge could easily visit our festival.

This time with the help of Austin and Doug (whose knowledge of Salisbury Plain was prodigious) an excellent site was found. This had plenty of space for people, tents, stages and vehicles, and could be easily seen and reached from A345. The festival site ran northwards along the grass verges of the Marlborough Coach Road from Low Flying Corner. Although the Coach Road was a track most of the way, it was surfaced for the first fifty yards with tarmac, because off it led a tarmac drive built for vehicles using a double gate in the perimeter fence at the South-Western corner of the airfield. A few yards to the East of this gate was a flimsy red wood and chainlink gate, which could be easily smashed down by a vehicle in an emergency if necessary. This was Crash Gate Red. It led from the airfield onto a wide grass verge with some bushes on it at the junction of Porton Road and the Coach Road. The site for the new peace camp was on this verge. We were told we would risk removal and prosecution for obstruction if we camped in front of Crash Gate Red, but there was plenty of space elsewhere on this wide triangle of land where we could pitch our tents without being evicted. A345 was just 120 yards away down Porton Road. We were in full view of this main road. Because the main runway ended just inside the fence and aircraft using it flew very low overhead, local people had come to watch the aircraft, especially the experimental prototypes, for many years, and had called the place Low Flying Corner.

From here the Coach Road ran Northwards alongside the airfield perimeter fence to pass only about twenty yards from the top secret Ordnance Survey trig point which marked the summit of Boscombe Down. Its approximate height is not hard to guess, as the 400-feet contour line just below it isn't secret and is shown on the Ordnance Survey maps. The new campsite was at an approximate altitude of 390 feet. The Coach Road continued northwards as a track for about a mile, to where a tarmac road curved in to join it from the West and from there is continued as a tarmac C-class road alongside the perimeter fence to the main entrance. It then continued across part of the airbase as an unmarked public footpath, then became a track again just inside the base perimeter, bridged an old railway and headed off northwards past our first campsite. When the expansion first began in 1978 or 1979 somebody illegally dug two trenches across the track just North of the trig point and just South of where the paved road joined it, obviously to stop cars using the Coach Road where it passed part of the new development. Strangely, cars could still drive to just beyond the trig point and people could get out of them and have a panoramic view of the airfield, while the busy paved stretch of the Coach Road passed within a few yards of several of the new blast-resistant hangars.

The Wiltshire Police were, of course, consulted about the festival site, and were apparently pleased with it because the nearest resident, a farmer, lived over 1,500 yards away behind trees on the other side of Boscombe Down. Thus complaints from residents would be unlikely. To prevent traffic problems, the Coach Road past the festival site became a voluntary one-way street for the duration of the festival. We didn't get a proper order to do this, so it had no legal force, but the police didn't mind. This meant that the organisers had to put in some quick spadework filling in the two ditches so that cars could cross them, and cars could then drive the whole length of the new development.

Like the first campsite, the festival site had no running water, but this difficulty was overcome with lots of containers and two hired plastic tanks, which were filled by a milk lorry.

Performers from all over Wessex were invited, though there were no big names. Posters and A4 leaflets were produced and distributed all over Southern England. More money was needed. As a result of discussion with a CND national official, it was understood by some organisers that national CND would help pay the costs of our free festival but the only help they gave was to give us an advance announcement in *Sanity*. Extra cash had to be found in a hurry.

On Thursday, 14th June, 1984, the first campers arrived in a Volkswagen mobile home to help set up the festival. They spent the night at Low Flying Corner. They brought with them fine, warm weather and almost cloudless skies which stayed with us throughout the festival and for the first days of the peace camp, so we were glad of the water supply which proved more than adequate for the festival.

By 08.00 hours on Friday other people had begun to arrive and by 09.00 hours the marquee hired from Southampton was being erected beside the Coach Road. By mid-afternoon the information tent was up and the site was rapidly turning into a tented community. That evening's *Southern Evening Echo* carried a big headline: 'Airbase is new peace camp target', and revealed that A&AEE at Boscombe Down with 1,300 employees was South Wiltshire's biggest employer. It also gave details of the weekend's events supplied by Carolyne Lanyon of Salisbury CND. It said that the land we planned to use as a peace campsite was MoD land. In fact, this was wrong, as it was County Council land and its forthcoming sale to the MoD hadn't even been hinted at yet. Was this a mystical prophecy?

The first thing to go up in the marquee was the exhibition of autonomous buildings from Kernow Environment Research and Insolation Developments Company (KERID) of Southampton, including the model autonomous village that had won a prize at Geneva. Here were models of homes that would, so far as land was concerned, let you have your cake and eat it. Sections for these houses could be manufactured in quantity, in the blast-resistant hangars that would be made redundant when the F1-11s left Boscombe Down, when the proposals of the Boscombe Down Action Committee were put into practice. Demonstration autonomous buildings could also be built on Boscombe Down and the growing of food in them brings them into the scope of a horticultural college, which was one of the proposed alternative uses for the fifty-seven acres of land in the new development. KERID had been trying for many years to get funds and land, with little success, and the conversion of this land at Boscombe Down could have done them good. On Saturday Will Sandey and his wife arrived from Southampton and he began explaining all about autonomous buildings to anyone who would listen, of whom there were many. They returned on Sunday and Will again spent the whole day explaining his models.

Greenpeace literature from A1 Beale and Martin in London took up another trestle table in the marquee. BDAC were represented in the marquee with their petition and details of proposals, which they claimed could provide up to 2,000 more jobs in the area. In the marquee and on the outside of it was an exhibition showing the history of protest at Boscombe Down. There was more to come.

On Saturday morning my camping stove was making coffee at a horrendously early hour and we set about getting the site ready again. The Peace Pledge Union film van arrived from Yorkshire and Dennis Gould came and laid sheets on the grass where he spread an enormous display of books and pamphlets for sale. The big tepee from Andover was erected. The Green Roadshow arrived with entertainers, loads of props and a field kitchen. The kitchen, which did mainly, if not wholly, vegetarian food, was a pleasant surprise to those who had been advised in poster and leaflets to bring their own food as there was not likely to be any on site. The leaflets and posters had to be printed before we were able to complete the arrangements for the kitchen, and we were uncertain if we could get anyone to cater for an unknown number of people at a free festival. Yet more food, in the form of home-made 'goodies', was being sold on the Warminster Peace Group stall.

Back in the spring of 1979, publicity put out for the Stonehenge Free Festival that year by Greenpeace from Endsleigh Street, London, had invited festival-goers to think about and visit Boscombe Down where new hangars were being built. Greenpeace had also helped us with advance publicity for the march in June 1979. Now, at last, people came to Boscombe Down from Stonehenge Free Festival in noticeable numbers, though still not as many as we had hoped. Two of the youths who came told how they were stopped and searched for drugs by police on their way through Amesbury. Now that long hair was going out of fashion and they couldn't find enough young people with long hair to search (they seemed to think if you had long hair you had drugs), Wiltshire police were turning their attention to people wearing CND badges in the fight against illicit drugs.

Several people who were touring Britain from overseas saw our publicity in *Peace News* and *Sanity* and came to the festival.

Saturday evening began with a march from the camp to the airbase main entrance. Councillors Mary and Austin Underwood drove to the main entrance in good time to meet the march. (They would arrive in good time, wouldn't they? Austin's Army training saw to that!). They saw no sign of the march, so drove round to the campsite by A345. When they arrived, the main body of the march, which had left late, had just crossed the summit of Boscombe Down on the Coach Road. One or two others and I were tidying up at the site before running to join it. I was in the marquee, when through the doorflap Austin's crisp military parade-ground voice bellowed a message to 'Young Waugh' about time-keeping on marches!

The march was led by Colin Webb and Green Roadshow's dragon with many marchers' legs carrying its body. A superb picture of this dragon, taken by Roger Elliot, appeared on the front page of the *Salisbury Journal* on 21st June, 1984. The photo showed a policeman escorting it and one of the new blast-resistant hangars behind the security fence. It clearly showed a sign on the fence, which in the photo appeared right beside the policeman's helmet, but was too far away for the wording to be visible. Roger must have been able to read that sign when he took the photograph. The sign told us that the Official Secrets Acts forbade photography there. Did Roger have official permission to take photographs there and use it to debunk the Official Secrets Acts, which forbade the photographing of things in public view? What did he intend?

We held an hour-long silent vigil outside the main entrance where there was a Modsquad cordon. The Ex-Services CND banner was there. The three Ex-Services CND members, one of whom was a D-Day veteran, gave us hope and determination by their powerful presence and dignity. No aircraft flew. Only a couple of vehicles drove quietly past. Nobody spoke. In the silence you could have heard a pin drop.

Back at the festival Site the Green Roadshow kicked off with music, poetry, folksingers and a bit of theatre. A local rock band (probably Opera for Infantry) were playing a few numbers down below at the Southern end of the site, using the film van's battery for power. As the evening drew on a young lad who could not have been more than five years old, if that, stood up unannounced by the main bonfire and started reciting poetry. His diction was clear; his memory accurate. When a delighted audience encouraged him, he recited more. At last his act came to an end long after most children his age would have been in bed asleep and the audience gave him tumultuous applause. A group of folk-singers from the Foc's'le Folk Club in Southampton performed individually. Two police cars were drawn up along the Coach Road with their crews enjoying the show.

A policeman asked one of the folksingers if he knew 'Tambourine Man'. He started to play it and the policeman shone the Range-Rover spotlight on him. This was too much! Some years before I had been a roadie for a local band and through that experience I had been with them practising on Boscombe Down. One of their numbers was 'Tambourine Man' and my mind went back to happy times. I went off on a transport of delight, my mind zonked out of its socket. Soon the music died and gently a fog of euphoria settled over the campfires as friends talked quietly into the night and others slept.

On Sunday yet more people arrived for the festival, and the afternoon developed a family picnic atmosphere. Again the sun shone from an almost cloudless sky.

A meeting, which started at 15.00 hours on Sunday afternoon, decided to set up the peace camp as sufficient people volunteered to keep it going for the first few weeks.

In the beginning the campers included Steve and Sophie Harrington-Ellesmore and their son Caleb from Penton, John Fuller and his son Martin from Andover and a woman called Vee Wright. At the beginning of July, Vee Wright was the only person living on the site and her tent was the only one there, though a jolly young man called John came to live at the site soon after.

Near the tent was an open fire, beside which was a low canvas windbreak of a type designed for casual beach use and a shelter built out of wood and blue plastic sheeting on the South side. This gave some shelter from the wind on this very exposed site and, if one crouched under it, shelter from rain as well.

Jet aircraft make up to 150 decibels of noise on take-off. Apart from jets taking-off sometimes two at a time from Number One Runway which ended only a few yards from the camp, the only noise was from traffic on A345 and Porton Road and a very faint hiss from the three MoD floodlight trained on the camp from inside the fence. At night the roads were deserted from about midnight to 07.00 hours and at night and at weekends there was normally no flying (but not always). So the site was sometimes very noisy indeed and at other times, usually at night, really quiet.

It was a site with many beautiful wildflowers, lots of Chalk Blue butterflies, and vicious, blood-sucking ladybird beetles that would settle on shirtless campers and pierce their skins to extract blood. Campers rarely wore shirts during the camp's first three months as the weather was nearly always sunny and warm.

It was about this time that Robert Key, Tory MP for Salisbury visited Boscombe Down to see one of the biggest employers in his constituency. He was investigating the recent loss of 500 jobs at A&AEE, and the latest announcement that 125 more jobs were to be axed there. Some time before, I had written to Bob Mitchell, then MP for Southampton Itchen,

Picture courtesy of the *Salisbury Journal.*

about Boscombe Down, and asked about the loss of 500 jobs there. Bob lost his seat to Chris Chope, a young enthusiastic Tory contemporary of Robert Key. Bob passed my letter on to Chris, who contacted the minister responsible and got a reply for me. I believe Chris mentioned my letter to Robert who then asked to visit Boscombe Down. Robert then tabled five parliamentary questions about the workers at Boscombe Down and the privatisation of MoD work there.

On Sunday 1st July, a demonstration took place at the government laboratories four miles away on Porton Down. Some of the Porton demonstrators came to Boscombe Down Peace Camp, apparently on their way back to the Stonehenge Free Festival, which was still continuing.

This visit appears to have taken the police by surprise and there were not enough of them to prevent people from lining up along and shaking the security fence behind the campsite. Then a wonderful person, a hero whose name I have been unable to discover, drove a van or coach into Crash Gate Red. He knocked it down, breaking off both its gateposts just above ground level and lifting part of the fence right out of the ground. Other demonstrators pulled and pushed at it until a total of twenty-nine metres of fence, including Crash Gate Red, were either badly damaged or knocked to the ground. The Porton people left for Stonehenge.

The unknown hero and his friend Brindley Price were later arrested by Wiltshire Police who stopped their coach as it was returning to Stonehenge. They were taken to the cells and brought before the county bench of magistrates in Salisbury Guildhall the following Tuesday. Sadly, the peace camp's legal back-up system at this time was non-existent. Apparently Vee Wright did not know of the arrests and neither did anyone else concerned with the camp organisation, simply because they had not been told. According to press reports (*Amesbury Journal* 5th July 1984, and *Southern Evening Echo* 3rd July 1984) Brindley Price was fined £50 for obstructing a police officer and three men (including our hero) and a woman were remanded in custody for a week charged with criminal damage. At least one of these charges must have referred to the broken gate and the others almost certainly also referred to the gate and fence damaged at Boscombe Down. Apparently prosecutor Inspector Brian Sharpe had the court at his beck and call as no defence solicitors were there.

After this direct action, the authorities made tempo-

rary repairs. The fence looked battered and bodged, straining wires, which should have been taut were loose, the gate was wonky, the gateposts though re-erected were still moved out of position at the breaks by four centimetres and nine centimetres respectively and there were gaps under the fence which should not have been there. These gaps were to prove useful to peace campers later. I could find no press reports of the results of the court cases of the four people remanded on criminal damage charges. Presumably the MoD as in so many other similar cases had played things down to minimise publicity and unfortunately these people were either unable or unwilling to make publicity from their cases for our cause. This is where a legal back-up system would have helped.

In July 'Baby' George Smith and Colin 'Boris' Grey joined the camp with the big 'Broken Bondage Collective' tent, which could sleep six. Steve 'Scumbag' Rixon, 'Beatle' (named after his haircut of course), Debbie and another local woman followed them.

Soon after arriving some of these people applied for their social security money to be sent to them at the camp, as they were living there and four peace campers in a group visited the DHSS offices in Salisbury. There clerks told 'Boris' and another camper that the peace camp was not a proper place to which the DHSS could send their giros and they could not claim benefit if they lived there. (Yet a city council paid the rent and rates of a flat for another peace camper who was spending about as many nights at the camp as he was in his flat, which was unoccupied for days on end. Had it insisted he live solely at the camp, it would have saved itself his rent and rates.)

The four peace campers held a sit-in there and then to protest at this decision. When they saw this had no effect, they changed tactics and ended the sit-in. They then left without causing any disturbance or difficulty for the staff and split into two groups to attend to other business. 'Boris' and his friend were later stopped by police, who accused them of causing a disturbance in the DHSS office! After a discussion the police left without charging them. It is important that the police did not interview them at the DHSS office as a result of being called there to evict them. The police could not have known they were there and certainly could not give eye-witness evidence in court about any disturbance, as they did not see any. Without asking the campers to leave or warning them that the police were being called, the DHSS had telephoned the police. They had given details of the campers to the police in contravention

Daniel, 'Scumbag', Barry, 'Pinkie' and kneeling in front, Tracie. The author is standing to the right. Taken at Boscombe Down, Summer 1984. Picture courtesy of the *Salisbury Journal*.

of their own confidentiality rule. 'Boris' went to the *Salisbury Journal* office and told a reporter about this. The paper published a sympathetic report mentioning the peace camp.

Pressure was applied to the DHSS and soon afterwards they accepted the camp as a proper address.

In those days the Modsquad used to leave the Porton Road Gate open in daylight with a modplod in the little guardroom so that workers could drive in and out of Boscombe Down without stopping. As the gate was on a minor road it was almost never used by strangers and any who used it would be stopped by the modplod holding up his hand if they didn't stop at the guardroom anyway.

It had to be closed when the main runway was in use as the road from it to the A&AEE led across that runway. This practice ceased and the gate was kept closed at all times, only being opened for individuals on production of passes after 'Yandy' and 'Spooner' visited the peace camp.

Carolyne Lanyon had left a bicycle for the use of

campers. She thought we would need it, as we lived two miles from the nearest village. 'Spooner' rode this cycle in through the open Porton Road Gate one day, cycled round inside for a few minutes to the consternation of the modplod on duty and rode out of the gate. The modplod was ready when 'Yandy' rode through his gateway. He knocked 'Yandy' off the cycle. The young man picked himself up and ran outside leaving behind the cycle, which a modplod later threw over the perimeter fence into the peace camp. A brief report of this incident, originating from the camp, appeared in a local paper.

There was usually little, if any, flying on Saturdays unless a special event on the airbase required it, in which case a full day's flying programme might take place. There was no flying at all on Saturday 28th July because Doug Read was holding a kite flying and photography festival at Low Flying Corner. He had told the authorities about it in advance and also publicised it through the peace movement newspapers, including *Peace News*. Rather than risk damage to an aircraft in a collision with a kite, the RAF let the festival continue and stopped their own flying. Amesbury residents were pleased with the peace and quiet and the festival was good for our morale, even though only twenty-five people came.

At the end of July George and a friend put together a leaflet about the camp. Tony Hill of Sarsen Press in Winchester printed a thousand free copies without even charging for the paper. These were ready for Hiroshima Day. Shaun Barney (a youth who had come to the camp from West End, near Southampton) and I were going to the Hiroshima Day commemoration in Southampton. On his way from the camp to Southampton, Shaun collected some leaflets from Sarsen Press, and we distributed them at the commemoration ceremony, while the Mayor officially declared Southampton a NFZ.

By early August the camp had been joined by two Scots, who were to be of immense value to it – Colin 'DT' Cunningham and Tracie. 'DT' had been at Lossiemouth, Faslane and Upper Heyford camps before coming to Boscombe Down. Tracie was a woman in a million. They brought with them a young man called Michael, who was kind, intelligent and sociable but who had some weird ways. Tracie had met up with him at Stonehenge and adopted him. From then on she virtually mothered him until he left to live alone in Salisbury, and not having Tracie to look after him got into trouble. These all came in Colin's magic bus, a petrol-engined Leyland Redline with a wheelchair tail-lift that didn't work. The bus was a marvellous addition to the camp.

Down at a Bournemouth squat 'Pinkie' seemed to be wrecking himself on the drugs scene, so two friends bought him an explorer bus ticket and put him on the Salisbury bus with instruction how to change buses to get to Low Flying Corner. 'Pinkie' was a helpful guy and did all sort of jobs willingly, including cooking. I remember one day he needed something with which to stir the stew he was making. He found an absolutely filthy fork in the ashes beside the fire. Neither washing nor wiping the fork he plunged it, dirt and all, into the stew. I don't know exactly what was on that fork, but I do know the stew tasted fabulous!

Barry from Basingstoke was a bit older than most of us. He had been married with children and was good at looking after them, as well as bender building. He began with the shelter of blue polythene and, bit-by-bit, extended it into an enormous bender with tents and little benders on the sides and an old oil drum for a stove in the middle. In a bad storm in late autumn, the Broken Bondage Collective tent was wrecked and other damage occurred but Barry's work was sound and the main bender survived. 'Boris' and Barry then built a lined bender with sods piled around the outer edges designed to withstand storms and be warm on the coldest night – which it was. I slept one night in it and my body heat alone was enough to keep the temperature tolerable, even though it was freezing outside.

A homeless youth called Daniel came to stay. He told me he had no previous experience in the peace movement. He left for Heyford in November after several months at Low Flying Corner.

Our hardworking telephone contact and first *Peace News* contact was Heather from Amesbury. She rarely spent time at the camp as she was always either busy looking after her beautiful home and family, teaching or out cruisewatching.

Doug Read was a pillar of strength in our support network. He used his car to run campers to CND meetings in nearby towns and kept us supplied with plastic containers of water. Often Doug would go into his office in the morning, get an afternoon phone call that Cruise was out and, immediately after work, go out and spend the night cruisewatching. In the morning he would be back in his office and after a day's work he would drive out to the peace camp with some filled water containers, with an apology for not being there the evening before as he had to chase Cruise missiles. 'Baby' George wrote of Doug:

"Without the commitment he made to bring us water, there would probably never have been a peace camp at all." [*Radiator* December 1984]

Terry Wynne and his family were active in the support network but as they lived and worked thirty miles away they were not often at the camp.

THE PEACE CAMP STARTS A WAR

About half-an-hour later two armoured Transits drew up on the main road and about twenty burly policemen emerged. They went to our banner and started to take it down. Some campers ran down to the main road and were told the banner had to come down as it was erected without county council approval, and was therefore illegal under the Highways Act 1959. The police agreed it would also be illegal if erected facing onto the track by the peace camp where it had been all along and they had said nothing. We got the banner down and they let us keep it and re-erect it facing the track. We did not wish to risk prosecution and confiscation of our banner as we felt there would be little publicity gained that way. As we were the only people using the track regularly we weren't surprised that they let us put it on the track, though it could be seen from Porton Road as well. We marvelled at how it took twenty policemen and two armoured Transits to get a banner moved. One friendly bobby on a motorbike could have done just as well.

In 1979 John Hard, then the owner of the Druids Motel in Amesbury, erected road signs advertising his motel without county council approval, apparently contravening the same law as our banner. Despite complaints from other local traders about these signs the police took no action and it was left to someone else to take some extra-legal direct action and steal four of them. Then the Parish Council condemned them. There seems to be an inconsistency of law enforcement here.

It was obvious by mid-August that the Hiroshima Day leaflet was not bringing the massive support we needed. The whole camp met and decided something had to be done.

The weather on the night of Monday 13th August was ideal, with a thick fog setting in. Shortly after midnight, two peace campers cut a hole in the fence about 500 yards up the Coach Road from the camp and painted CND symbols on buildings. They returned to the camp, reported their mission accomplished and went to sleep.

A few minutes after 06.00 hours the following morning, a cyclist quietly pulled his bicycle from under one of the benders and rode away from the camp under cover of the fog. He rode into Porton village and used the public phone there, which was less likely to be tapped than public phones nearer the peace camp, and where he was less likely to be seen by passing policemen. After this he rode on to Salisbury and made about a dozen more phone calls, all like the first, to the local press.

It appears that as a result the local newspapers were telephoning Boscombe Down and their publicity officer, a civil servant called Terry Heffernan (of whom we will read more later), was flatly denying that any campers had been inside during the night. Most of the journalists accepted that as true, but John Dudley, the news editor of the *Salisbury Journal*, accepted the invitation of the peace campers on the phone and came out to the peace camp to investigate. It was Tuesday afternoon, he was right on top of his news deadline, and he needed a story badly. When he arrived there was no sign of the fog; the sun had been shining brightly for several hours. A routine check on his Mini by the modplod observing the camp from the caravan caused a panic. The news editor himself had arrived – this was serious. A Land Rover appeared inside the fence, the modplod driver observing everything. After talking to the peace campers, John walked up the Coach Road with two of them and inspected a hole in the fence and a CND sign. The sign painted on a building inside was clearly visible to even a car driver on the track outside the fence but not to the modplod in the Land Rover inside, who was behind the building. As the three began walking back to the camp, another Land Rover appeared coming southwards along the track. It followed them back to the camp and stopped when they did. The Modplod sergeant driving it asked John why he was there. John told him, without mentioning what he had just seen.

The Sergeant replied: "We shadow every move they make. There is no way they broke in last night and even if they had we would have discovered it by now. We had a man patrolling this stretch of the fence all night." (*Salisbury Journal* back page, 16th August, 1984)

John Dudley still didn't tell the policeman what he had seen. He waited until he got back to his office, then he wrote up a sympathetic report which showed the Modsquad and Terry Heffernan in very bad light for not discovering the incursion. I followed it up with a letter in the next week's *Salisbury Journal* criticising the Boscombe Down security and asking what would happen if trained terrorists stole one of the nuclear bombs from Boscombe Down. The MoD did not reply.

The *Salisbury Journal* for 23rd August carried something else as well – a report of the rapid reaction to the incursion in the North-West Planning Sub-Committee of Salisbury District Council. Councillor Terry Heffernan from Boscombe Down was a member of this committee.

Discussion of the peace camp apparently began when John Davies, the county surveyor, told the committee a little about the peace camp (not entirely accurately) and said the county council preferred a 'wait and see' attitude to it. He claimed that, after a summer that had been warmer and sunnier than average, a return of normal weather, (i.e., a cold, wet, windy autumn) would probably result in us leaving. Clearly, the county council wanted us to leave of our own accord and didn't want to have to pay to evict us from a site, which was believed to be their land. Terry Heffernan said he could not understand how anyone could believe how a return to normal weather would move us; we were camped illegally and should be moved. Councillor Mrs. Phyllis Titt agreed, adding that Porton Women's Peace Camp had survived the most appalling weather. Councillors agreed that, as the county council was believed to be responsible for the campsite, they should pay for any eviction. Obviously, that night incursion had caused embarrassment and annoyance on the other side of the fence.

Thanks to this meeting and the *Salisbury Journal* report of it headlined: 'Councillors at war over peace camp site', Boscombe Down Peace Camp became the only peace camp that could claim to have started a war!

On 14th August I strolled into Salisbury District Council's imposing offices in Bourne Hill and asked to see an up-to-date list of Civil Defence community advisers. A new list had just been published and should have been available for me to inspect there. It was not. The council officials could have phoned the public library and either had their copy sent over or sent someone post-haste to get it, or even told me that it was temporarily the nearest copy and sent me there to see it. They did none of these things. They simply gave me an excuse and said they hadn't got one, but would get one soon. I reported my visit to Austin Underwood who mentioned it in an article on Civil Defence. ('Safe in Wiltshire' published in *Radiator* October, 1984) I had a genuine reason for seeing the list of advisers as I was preparing a survey of the advisers for the Parish of Idmiston. Fortunately I later saw copies in both Amesbury Public Library and Salisbury Public Library.

On 27th August I visited Molesworth Peace Camp as a representative of Boscombe Down Peace Camp and brought back a report, which is included in 'Guided Tours of Alconbury and Farming at Molesworth'.

Also in August two occasional campers who lived in London most of the time, 'Caz' and Martin, painted CND symbols all over the village of Amesbury. They were caught, convicted and each given a conditional discharge.

At the beginning of September the nights were drawing in and the long dark evenings were coming upon us. All the other campers were asleep, but something I could not explain was keeping me alert and awake, when at about 02.40 hours on the morning of 2nd September a vehicle drew up outside and shone a spotlight and headlights on the camp. Without moving the cover of the bender, which would have revealed that someone was awake, I managed to observe it through a hole. It was a modsquad Land Rover A151-MPR. After observing us for half a minute or so and seeing no movement, A151MPR drove away. Frequently Mod-squad Land Rovers patrolled inside the perimeter fence but this visit was unusual in that the Land Rover had approached along the tarmac Porton Road outside the fence. Because of this I made a special note of the visit.

A few minutes after the Land Rover had left something very unusual happened. A continuous roar began, rather like that of a jet engine, but unlike any jet I had heard. It was smoothly increasing in intensity. I have already commented on the quietness of our location and this roar coming across the silent Salisbury Plain was positively eerie. The visit of the Land Rover might have been connected, I thought, and the RAF could be doing something odd behind the fence.

I went outside to see if I could find any clues as to what was causing the noise. I could see none. Then lights, like vehicle headlights, appeared over A345 to the North. The ever-increasing roar seemed to come from the same direction. It seemed that the roar did not have one source, but many. A number of vehicles were climbing the hill out of Amesbury.

We would all have egg on our faces if a Cruise convoy, accompanied by carloads of cruisewatchers, passed the peace camp with only one camper awake.

At 02.43 precisely the first vehicle passed along A345 towards Salisbury. It was the lead vehicle in a British Army convoy travelling at about 35mph. Some of the vehicles were track-laying, others were equipped with cross-country type tyres. The weird roar was orchestrated by a combination of their engine noises, the noises of their tracks and the noises of these tyres. The convoy disappeared over the hill at High Post taking the roar with them.

I was still the only person outside. By now the mod-plod in the caravan would have seen me and reported that I was awake.

I went into the bender to find none of the others awake. I woke them and explained with difficulty about the convoy to bleary-eyed people, asking what we should do if another convoy came past. We had no prepared drill. Had it been a Cruise convoy, we would certainly have gone out and tried to stop it, if we had been awake, but this was just another Army convoy not likely to be carrying nuclear weapons. It was decided that if another convoy came through that night I should note the details of it and only panic if it was a Cruise convoy. Then I was to kick the other campers out of bed fast. We were not equipped to take any real action. The nearest telephone was over a mile away and the fastest vehicle we had was a bicycle. Even then it was unlikely that anyone could get to the telephone without being stopped by the police and if they did get to it there was no guarantee that it would work. We had no CB radio. We had not all had non-violence training, and we had not trained together as a team. Some of us had never seen a sit-down. We were less than a dozen in number. What could we have done?

At 0.300 a Modsquad Cortina drove very slowly past on Porton Road. Clearly, they were worried about us for this was the second time that night one of their patrols had passed on that unusual route. We were all inside and quiet when he passed, and some of us were more asleep than awake.

Soon another roar brought me out to observe a second convoy of Army vehicles heading south at about 35mph. This time I observed it from beside A345. This convoy was similar to the first. As I walked back to the camp, I spotted some more vehicles approaching very fast. They had no flashing blue lights, but I suspected they were several police cars.

Everyone was asleep when I ran into the main bender at 03.20. I tried to waken them and warn of the police raid. Alas! I did not succeed, as within thirty seconds a posse of CID men, uniformed Wiltshire

Police officers and Modplods arrived at the bender entrance. Some entered one by one as quickly as they could while others stayed outside. The sleepers were wakened, and asked who they were, while police torches shone everywhere. These big, heavily-coated policemen were moving awkwardly among the prostrate and rising bodies under the low roof of the bender and its even lower extension. They got campers out of their bedrolls to see how they were dressed, and campers started to talk with them. They said nothing about the convoys apart from admitting they existed. As the search continued I heard another convoy approaching. I managed to get out of the door, and do a rough vehicle count as they passed without alerting the police to the fact I was counting them. The police told us the main reason for their search was that a caretaker had been stabbed at Stonehenge a few hours before. Police have been known to invent a fictitious crime as an excuse for a search but this stabbing was later reported in the local press and appeared genuine. However the camp was under constant Modsquad observation, and it was a clear night, so it was extremely unlikely that a fugitive from a violent crime would have slipped into a peace camp unseen and been allowed to stay in it. Wiltshire CID probably thought it would be worth a look just in case, as Modsquad vigilance had recently been shown to be erratic by our incursion and their failure to observe the results even in bright sunshine. It would also give them a chance to intimidate campers and establish what level of control, if any, was required to prevent us from hindering the progress of the convoys. The vehicles involved in the search were A151 MPR and two Ford Escorts of Wiltshire Police. One Ford had a registration plate beginning with the letter 'A'; the other was registered NMR 942X.

After the raid and the police had all left, all of us, even including 'Baby' George, 'Boris' and 'Scumbag' were wide awake. When a fourth Army convoy came we all went out to the main road to watch them pass.

Several more convoys passed and I counted the vehicles in all of them. This was the effort of an untrained, amateur observer with a single ballpoint pen and a scrap of paper working in the dark all the time. Between the first vehicle passing at 02.43 hours and the last at 05.38 there was a gap of two hours, fifty-fve minutes. There were several convoys, each containing fifteen to twenty vehicles with approximately thirty minutes on time separating the lead vehicles in each convoy. I was unable to accurately

count the total of all vehicles, but I estimated there to be between 100 and 150. There were between fifty-six and sixty-one track-laying vehicles, at least two Alvis-built six-wheel-drive vehicles and many four-wheel-drive vehicles, some with trailers.

We found out later that these convoys were going from Salisbury Plain to Southampton where they were embarking (or trying to embark) onto cross-channel ferries as part of 'Operation Lionheart'. There were many other Army convoys converging on the Channel ports that night, too.

'DT' was arrested on three charges and remanded in custody one Monday in September, after he had shown an astonished modplod and other campers how to unwind the chainlink fencing to make a hole without wire-cutters. The following day being Tuesday, the county bench of magistrates was conveniently sitting in Salisbury Guildhall. He was hauled before them, convicted and sent to Winchester Prison before the rest of the peace campers could find out what had happened to him. Even the local press was unable to get a story.

The campers discovered 'DT' had been sentenced to a fortnight in Winchester, after one of them asked a modplod on Tuesday afternoon. Our attempt to help him and get him visited in prison achieved nothing because of its lateness and a collection of errors. Fortunately he got maximum remission and was released before his fortnight was up. He came straight back to the peace camp.

It was this event which began our realisation of the need for a back-up system for peace camp residents and visitors in trouble with the law.

Later 'DT' did a second fortnight in Winchester after another conviction for criminal damage to the Boscombe Down perimeter fence. This time the campers kept track of him and managed to visit him in prison. Being anarchists, they believed that fines only financed the state while prison meant that the state had to keep you and therefore as a rule refused to pay fines. On this occasion, however, Colin was having a bad time in prison and he wanted to get back out and help at the camp where numbers were low. The campers had had the foresight to go to Winchester with sufficient money to pay off the part of his fine that was still outstanding and the prison authorities let him out as soon as they paid.

On 5th September, officers of Wiltshire Police visited the camp and told campers they would all be arrested the next day if they had not left. They returned the following day to find the campers had called their bluff and were still in residence. Instead of arresting everyone they arrested only one camper, who was unsuccessfully searched for drugs and then released.

Doug Read's letter in the *Salisbury Journal* of 6th September likened Terry Heffernan to Hitler and called on him to publicly declare his interest in evicting the peace camp.

In the evening of 17th September, the Boscombe Down Peace Camp banner was raised inside the Michael Herbert Hall in Wilton. In spite of torrential rain this, the largest hall in this country town, was packed to standing room only with people listening to Bruce Kent of CND debating nuclear weapons with Nicholas Baker, Tory MP for North Dorset and Parliamentary Private Secretary to the Secretary of State for Defence. There were a couple of questions about the peace camp, too long and involved to repeat, and a disagreement over George's enterprising method of raising money for peace camp funds, which led to Bruce Kent stepping in and preventing a fight from developing between myself and another angry man. The very next morning Bruce posted a postcard to the camp wishing it luck and I later apologised to him for my behaviour in getting overheated. It was an upsetting incident that grew out of long-standing rivalry; I think neither of us won that argument after the meeting. If winning matters, Bruce won.

During September nuclear-capable French Mirage bombers visited Boscombe Down.

As a result of the lobbying by Terry Heffernan and his committee, several councillors raised the subject of our eviction at Wiltshire County Council's September meeting. Documents circulated to councillors included copies of a letter from County Councillor Richard Griffiths (who represented the parish of Idmiston on whose boundary the peace camp lay and within whose boundary RAF Boscombe Down lay), which was clearly not in support of the camp, and copies of a letter written by George and published in the *Salisbury Journal* on 30th August, 1984, describing us, our way of life and why we were there. George and I were both pleased this letter was getting such a wide circulation. Councillor Underwood, who had inspected ancient documents beforehand as he knew there was once common land around Low Flying Corner, asked who if anyone, owned the land whereon the peace camp lay, during the debate. The county solicitor admitted he did not know for certain if the county council owned it, which most people had been assuming, and said he would find out and report back to the October meeting. Thus further discussion of our eviction was delayed for another month.

The peace camp next organised a ramble, which was sponsored to raise funds. We also wanted to get the camp better known and as many people as possible to see Bulford Garrison and its Army ranges which Cruise convoys had roamed. This was expected to be a pleasant morale-boosting walk for peace campers. The ramble was to follow a return route along the Marlborough Coach Road Northward to Silk Hill, six miles out and six back. Sympathetic newspapers gave us advance publicity. Thousands of leaflets about the ramble were distributed and posted to people all over Southern England.

The Post Office, with whom we had already had misunderstandings about deliveries, stopped delivering mail to the camp altogether from Wednesday 10th October because according to the Post Office the camp mailbox had been burnt and there was no longer a suitable place to which mail could be delivered. Campers claimed the box was stolen which seems more likely, as we used to get visits from thieves from time to time, and it would be easy for someone to walk off with the mail box if he was strong. I don't know what happened.

As soon as campers learned that the Post Office needed another lockable mailbox they provided one and informed the local sorting office. Deliveries were not resumed and important mail did not arrive. When I arrived from Southampton I was faced with an empty new mailbox. I went and tried to telephone the sorting office. After getting through twice and not being able to speak to anyone, on the third attempt I managed to speak to someone in authority, who realised I wasn't going to go away when he put the phone down. I asked if there was any mail for the camp at his office, and he said there was, and that we could collect it, but a delivery could not be arranged that day. He promised to resume deliveries the next week. Needless to say, by the time I contacted the person in authority, I was very angry with the way the Post Office was handling my complaint, and I made it clear to this man that I thought he was not doing his job, that he was not needed on the Post Office, that there were plenty of unemployed people who could do his job, and I would be writing to higher authority to try and get him dismissed.

The important mail was needed immediately so a car was found to go into Salisbury and collect it, resulting in more delay and extra expense for us.

Tony Hill of Sarsen Press had helped the ramble publicity by printing very cheaply 5,000 leaflets and 500 cards for sponsored ramblers. Some local groups also helped. Southampton CND was not so co-operative however. Their newsletter not only announced that the ramble was to be held at Upper Heyford Peace Camp, but also made it known that at the last minute the CND group had decided to hold their first (and only so far) daytime annual general meeting on Saturday 13th October – the day of the ramble!

Friday night had been a clear night and the camp was under constant Modsquad observation. This did not deter a thief from stealing my bicycle, which was parked outside on the campsite with both wheels locked. The necessary search found the cycle still locked several hundred yards down Porton Road, fortunately undamaged. This caused delay, which I could ill afford.

At last about fifteen ramblers were assembled at Low Flying Corner in cold, cloudy but dry weather. Doug Read said he would act as guide and asked if there was an alternative route. I said I didn't need one as the Army Land Warden's office had said the route was clear, and the police had said as far as they were concerned there would be no problems. I had prepared an alternative route, but this could only be used if it was possible to divert walkers before they reached the bridge over the old railway. Doug didn't appear to share my confidence, though he didn't ask for a copy of the map of the alternative route. He didn't need to, because few if any people knew more about Salisbury Plain than Doug.

For about an hour after Doug's group left Low Flying Corner, a few more ramblers left in ones and twos. Then I set off on my cycle to patrol the route.

Just before Sheepbridge the ramble route turned right off the tarmac road to follow a track across the Bulford Ranges. When I arrived there I was unable to proceed as the track was almost blocked by a Land Rover with a military policeman (MP) guarding a 'road closed' sign. I doubled back and by-passed this by another track out of the MP's sight. I got back to the first track which was the Old Coach Road and found that further up there was a gate closed with another 'road closed' sign. A red flag was flying which warned that the ranges were closed to the public and I could hear firing from a closed small-arms range near the road to Tidworth. Obviously the Army had decided to do this at the last minute to try and hinder the ramble.

I returned to the tarmac road and began to look for the ramblers who had all vanished. Even the rambling archaeologist I had left only a minute or two before finding the MP in his Land Rover had vanished. I did not speak with the MP, who being an Army man, was under no obligation to help me and was more likely to deliberately hinder me. I crossed Sheepbridge and cycled up some tracks, which eventually led to a hilltop with a good view but saw nobody I knew. Had they gone up the Coach Road out of sight? Had they given up and caught a bus to Amesbury? Had they all been arrested? The possibilities were endless.

Meanwhile 'Tid', driving his Morris Minor Pickup with a dummy Cruise missile on the back was prowling round the Bulford Ranges. These ranges occupied the valley of the Nine Mile River which was a shallow oblong bowl set right in the middle of Salisbury Plain. Around the rim of this bowl were a number of Army watchtowers, linked by radio and each with a good view of a large part of the valley. Thus when the watchtowers were staffed, the whole valley was under Army observation. 'Tid' wanted to see if the towers were staffed, so he drove onto the ranges by means of a track that was not closed, and parked in front of one of the towers. He did not have long to wait. A soldier popped his head out of the tower's first floor window, saw 'Tid' and his Cruise missile, and the soldier's eyes nearly popped out of his head. He pulled his head back into the tower and radioed for help. Having achieved his objective and engaged the enemy successfully, 'Tid' decided to withdraw before the arrival of enemy reinforcements made his position untenable. As he drove off the ranges, a Land Rover full of modplods hurtled past him heading toward the watchtower. It didn't stop and he escaped without being challenged.

I had waited near the roadblock for about an hour before four ramblers, who had been with Doug, appeared.

They said Doug, on finding the Coach Road closed, had led them over Sheepbridge and onto the ranges by a different track, to a place where a Cruise convoy had 'dug in' recently. The men with the convoy had left much litter, some of which was clearly marked with what it was and where it was made and information that it had been supplied to the US military authorities. There was a nice hat in the middle of it all. The ramblers collected this litter and took it to Heather, who was going to catalogue it. The younger ramblers were delighted with their find.

The rambling archaeologist had found the others simply by asking the MP which direction they had taken, and following a track that was not closed until he saw them.

The best thing that resulted from that ramble was the inspection of the Cruise site and the litter collection. There was no media publicity of the actual event except for a brief mention in *Peace News*, which was probably just as well as after nearly 5,000 A4 leaflets had been distributed only just over twenty people rambled. The money spent on publicity was donated by a peace camper, otherwise the ramble would have made a financial loss. As it was, it only made a very small amount of money.

Subsequently I kept my promise to the man on the other end of the telephone and complained bitterly about him and the failure of the Post Office mail deliveries to two Members of Parliament. One of them, Tony Benn, wrote to the head postmaster at Salisbury, Mr. Crowle-Groves who sent me a formal letter of apology. He had already resumed deliveries on the Wednesday after the ramble, and we had no further problems with mail.

A gang of five camp wreckers arrived at about 02.00 hours on Thursday 18th October. They demolished Debbie's bender, and she awoke screaming underneath it. The wreckers also began to smash up the main bender. The modplod started walking down from his caravan, the wreckers saw him and fled in their yellow Ford Cortina. Apparently nobody was able to get the number of the car.

Before the bad weather began in late October we had several visitors from the Continent of Europe. Many were 'Greens'. On one of these visits everybody was sitting in the smoke-filled room that formed the centre of the main bender. I couldn't stick the fumes and smoke inside so I went out and tried to get a hole put in the crown of the bender so the fumes and smoke could escape. I lost my temper and said one or two things I should not have said.

For the rest of the afternoon I was Public Enemy Number One and in the evening I was put on trial in the magic bus. All the campers then living at Low Flying Corner questioned me and sat in judgement. I was alone with neither advisor nor lawyer. I admitted guilt, apologised and promised to avoid a repetition but was not punished. We all remained friends. I can think of a parallel in the trial of Socrates, where he was condemned to death, except that I was not punished in any way. Are death sentences, imprisonment and all the punishments meted out by courts necessary? I did not repeat my offence.

At the October meeting of Wiltshire County Council Planning Committee's Southern Panel, the county solicitor announced the land we were camped on belonged to the county council. He said he knew of no county council plans to use the land, and it was surplus to highway department needs. He told the meeting that the MoD were interested in buying the land, but only with vacant possession. The councillors agreed to do nothing until the MoD made up its mind, and intimated they were willing to clear the site if a reasonable offer was made to buy it. This left the camp with another month's breathing space before an order in possession could be discussed.

Salisbury Journal reported this meeting under the headline 'Peace camp truce' on 25th October. The war, which started on 23rd August, had ended.

On 8th November the camp received more publicity when *Wessex News*, a Southampton University newspaper, published 'Peace of the action' an essay written by myself about the camp. It filled a good half page with small print. The fact that it was the unedited contribution of a peace camper showed we had friends in influential places living away from the camp.

Some Royal Observer Corps members, preparing for an exercise due to take place on 28th October, visited their bunker, which lay in a field between the Coach Road and A345 about 300 yards from the peace camp. They found the locks had been superglued. Unfortunately, this was the only protest we made against the nuclear defence exercise, as there were not enough people at the camp to mount an effective protest, and no outside groups had offered to join one.

ACCIDENTS AND ARGUMENTS

There were two routes from the camp to Amesbury, one via the Marlborough Coach Road and Earls Court Road and the other via A345. Both were about the same length. A345 was a fast main road (the stretch past the peace camp was known as Amesbury Flats, where local people would take their cars and motorcycles for speed testing) with neither footpath nor lights most of the way, while the Coach Road passed through a hollow where there was always deep mud, except when it was frozen or snow covered. Though campers often used the dangerous A345, there was only one camper injured on this road throughout the camp's eleven-month existence.

Boscombe Down Peace Camp had no rules of admission and no formalities. Campers did not need to bring money or supplies, though most did. Each person contributed what they could. Daniel and

Michael had both been homeless when brought to the camp, and stayed because they found our welcome friendly, not because of any previous commitment to nuclear disarmament. They both helped in the work of the camp and learned about the peace movement. At least three people hitching on A345 looked in to see us and stayed several days. The obvious problem here was keeping out government and MoD secret agents. We 'twigged' two obvious ones who claimed to be off duty soldiers genuinely interested in what we were doing.

Another problem could arise when people who came to the camp did not get on with some campers already there. This problem arose when the hippie tribe came from London and Carlow in Ireland shortly after the sponsored ramble. The tribe was led by two women, Daidi and Michaela, and contained several men, including Neville and Ben, along with Michaela's baby daughter, Nadine, and a delightful dog called Bert. Poor Bert, through no fault of his own was at the centre of the big argument, but before that arose, other things happened at the camp.

A camp supporter from Amesbury, who had no reason to lie in an unprompted conversation on 12th January, 1985, told me of an accident shortly after the hippie tribe arrived. He was visiting the camp when Michaela was run down and seriously injured by a motorcyclist on a 125cc machine on A345. This happened near to the camp on Amesbury Flats. I don't know who was to blame but I believe there were no prosecutions. Ben ran up to the motorcyclist and threatened him with a knife – not routine peace camp procedure! Although the campers had no means of summoning an ambulance quickly, one came, probably called by the modplod in the caravan or a passing motorist. Michaela was taken to Odstock Hospital in Salisbury where she spent several months and never returned to the camp. Michaela was sincere, almost fanatical, in her belief that nuclear weapons must be destroyed because they threatened the life of her daughter and really believed in what the camp was doing. Tragically, I first met her in hospital.

Happy things happened too. One camper, being a Quaker, used to attend Salisbury Meeting of the Religious Society of Friends from time to time. On a cold Sunday in November, he returned from the meeting with food left over from a lunch in the Friends' Meeting House. The Quakers, rather than take home food that was perfectly good and only surplus to requirements, asked him to take it to the camp. About half the food was in the form of meat rolls and the entire camp was either vegan or veg-

etarian. The camper who brought the food didn't realise that everyone there at the time would refuse the meat rolls so brought them anyway. The embarrassing problem was solved by Bert, who on being presented with the meat rolls, eagerly scoffed the lot. Thanks, Friends.

While Bert was the resident guard dog, we were neither troubled with thieves nor camp wreckers.

When Michaela went into hospital, she left her daughter Nadine behind. Daidi promised Michaela that she would see that the baby was looked after, and kept her promise. The rest of us helped her, especially Barry, who had a wife and child of his own and changed nappies with a skill born of long practice. Daidi had a problem with the police and council authorities at one time, who wanted to take Nadine and put her in a council home, but Daidi refused to part with the baby without Michaela's consent, which the authorities could not obtain. She made such a fuss that they drove her and the baby back to the camp and left them alone thereafter. Nadine became a camp mascot, representing the children for whom we adult campers wanted to make a better world.

During the dark, cold and wet November nights, with up to a dozen people staying at the camp every night and hot water needed for the baby Nadine, the campfires consumed much wood. The oil drum stove was burning most of the time people were awake and a second fire was also burning outside from time to time. Consequently, foraging parties had to roam Salisbury Plain looking for more wood. Trees overgrowing the Coach Road, except the fruiting apples, had already been cut back and local woods had been raided for all their dead timber, even to the extent of sawing dead branches off trees. Still the fires had to be fed.

A new source of logs was found. Peace Campers sawed the tops off some fence posts, which extended several inches above the top wire, giving enough to make a log without interfering with the wires and destroying all the effectiveness of the fence as a stock control device. I'm not sure if the local farmers would agree with this line of reasoning but then they weren't consulted.

This new source of logs led to an interesting NVDA, which caused problems for the RAF at Boscombe Down. In a field across Porton Road, viewed from the peace camp over decapitated fence posts, stood some of the Southern runway approach lights for the airfield. There were stout wooden fences around these lights. These fences were to keep stock off the lights but as there had been no stock in that field throughout the year – a grain crop had been growing there – a camper concluded that the fences were redundant and could be used for firewood. These lights and fences were in full view of the Modsquad caravan by day and, with the help of the floodlights directed across the camp, by night also. The modplod in the caravan had no way of seeing through fog, however. One foggy night when the runway lights were switched off one or two of these fences disappeared. The Modsquad did nothing. Then a few days later when the RAF switched on the lights they didn't work. Investigators found that the cables had apparently been cut with an axe.

Although the modplods found an axe belonging to 'Boris', they found no saws and took no firewood, and nobody was arrested and charged with the £5,000 worth of criminal damage which they alleged was done. It is believed the lights would not have been sabotaged without the help of the hippies – or were Russian spies the real culprits? Only the people who did it know.

We paid little attention to safety at the camp, and many careless acts took place. Most came to nothing, but a chain of carelessness produced a real tragedy in mid-November. This account has been pieced together second-hand from what others have told me, as I was not there at the time. I have done my best to sort out the conflicting points as both sides told different stories.

A camper purchased paraffin for some cooking or lighting device and put it in a plastic water container. This for convenience was placed near the oil drum stove in the main bender. Some time later Daidi, making a pot of tea, filled the kettle from the nearest water container and put it on the fire. Nobody told her she had used the paraffin and amazingly she did not notice it! Around the stove sat half a dozen people on highly inflammable bedrolls and a three-piece suite in a nice dry bender made of inflammable material, which had only one tiny exit. Bert, the dog, was lying in this exit. Daniel was sat facing the hole in the oil drum, which gave access to the fire. A kettle full of paraffin will stand a certain amount of heating before doing anything unusual. If the heating continues long enough, flames will start dancing on the surface of the liquid. Even at this late stage prompt action by someone familiar with elementary fire prevention procedures could prevent damage or injury. Flames started dancing on the paraffin. With the best will in the world, Daniel then did the worst possible thing – he grabbed the kettle and threw it to-

wards the exit. The burning paraffin fell on Bert, who fled through the exit in terror, his coat ablaze. Some things in the doorway also caught alight. The flames in the doorway were quickly doused, but it was some time before Bert was caught and the flames in his coat extinguished. as he was running around madly outside with the fresh air fanning the flames in his coat to greater ferocity.

Immediately after this accident there was a row. Apparently one camper's knife cut another camper's face before a third could step between them. Even though threatened himself, he managed to cool things and prevent further injury. The third camper told me nothing about this; it was only by piecing together accounts from others that I discovered the part he played. Fortunately, the other camper's facial cuts were not serious and he did not need to be hospitalised, but poor Bert was so badly burned he had to be 'put down'. Disagreements had already started between the hippie peace campers and the campers who were there before them. This accident brought things to a head.

When I arrived to stay the weekend at the camp on the following Saturday, all the old campers except 'Boris' had left. Then he also departed. I cycled as far as Amesbury with him, did some shopping and returned. He went on to Shrewton where he was to meet Daniel and Barry. All three were going then to Hay-on-Wye in Wales. 'Boris' didn't say why they were going there. Back at the camp when I commented on the smoke marks around the doorway and the absence of Bert, I was told very little and nothing about the knifing incident.

On Monday evening back in Southampton I had a phone call from 'Baby' George and 'Caz' in London. 'Caz' had just returned from Hay-on-Wye where 'Boris' and Daniel had told her an amazing story about a row at Low Flying Corner. She and George related to me a tale I found difficult to believe. Unfortunately, it was obviously one-sided, with apparent exaggerations, and, because neither had actually seen the row and the tale was second-hand, I couldn't cross-examine them properly, so I needed information.

George then issued a statement to the press without consulting many of the campers, including myself, which meant that the statement only represented the views of his own group, and not all the campers, as it implied:

> We, the Boscombe Down Peace Campers, would
> like to make a statement concerning the camp at

this time. The Peace Campers would like to make it quite clear that the people staying at the site of the Peace Camp are not peace campers and we have no connexion with them. Their actions and ideals are not those of the Peace Campers who had to leave due to the atmosphere created by these people.

With the consent of all the Peace Campers who intended to stay the winter at the Peace camp and others concerned, the Peace camp has temporarily closed. This is due to several reasons but mainly this group of people who have moved in and taken over the camp and have no intention of protesting for a peaceful world; they are not peace campers.

Another reason is that the support was minimal from local CND groups, which is an important part of any peace camp. Having said that, we would like to thank Michael Waugh for his continual support and the successful events that he has organised and Doug Read for his great support – without the commitment that he made to bring us water there would probably never have been a peace camp at all.

The Peace Campers are going to set up a new Peace Camp, which will be totally committed to the intentions of the original Peace Camp. We have formed a Boscombe Down Peace Camp Support Group which will keep all the funds and belongings of the previous camp in readiness for the continuation of the Peace Camp. [*Radiator* December 1984]

There followed a London telephone number to contact, but no address.

Although George sent me a copy of this statement, there was no letter with it inviting me to discuss it or giving a release date, so I assumed it was for immediate release. There were details with which I disagreed, and maybe I should have sent a letter to *Peace News* saying I wished to be counted out of the people who sent in the statement, and pointing out that I was a part-time resident at the camp who intended to continue through the winter, but I did not.

By 22nd November, the hippies had moved on and that night only 'Boris' and I were at the camp. The hippies did not return and when *Peace News* published a report based entirely on George's statement, without checking facts with anyone else on 30th November, only campers from the earlier band were there. George had not up-dated their information, which he could have done in time. Unfortunately, *Radiator* followed this by publishing the whole of this now obsolete statement. I was hoping the hippies would put their side of the story into print, but we heard no more from them.

A few minutes after 08.00 hours on Friday, 23rd

November, I left the peace camp on the first leg of my walk to London to present the 'RAF Boscombe Down – Nuclear Bombs or Farm fresh food' petition at the MoD Main Building. On the walk, which totalled about 100 miles, I spent the four nights in friends' houses in Hampshire and Surrey and addressed meetings in Alresford, Alton, Farnham, Guildford and Kingston. At Farnham I met a local Quaker, who claimed he had assembled a nuclear weapon at Boscombe Down about thirty years before.

On 27th November, I collected the big box of petition forms and letters from Friends' House in London to which they had been sent ahead and added the petition forms and letter I had collected on my walk. I then completed my walk, accompanied on the last quarter mile from Parliament Square by George. We entered the Main Building carrying a box holding over 5,000 signatures and twenty-nine letters of support and were courteously received in an outer lobby by the security guards. We were told to wait and a Scotsman appeared. He eventually admitted to being a senior security officer (although we were sure he was the duty head of security) but refused to give his name. He promised to deliver the petition to Michael Heseltine's office and subsequent correspondence proved he kept his promise.

Publicity for this walk and presentation was not as well organised as it might have been, owing to a lack of cash. The result was only a few small news items in local papers and a small write up in *The Friend* of 21st December, 1984.

The walk to London commemorated the late Mary Harrison's walk from Salisbury to 10 Downing Street, London, to petition the Prime Minister to get rid of Britain's nuclear weapons. This took place thirty years before in 1954.

At 17.00 hours on Tuesday, 1st December, a typical day at Low Flying Corner – four peace campers were sitting round the stove in the main bender; Paddy, 'DT', Phil and myself. Paddy, who had lived in Greenham Common Peace Camp before it had gone all female, was brimming with enthusiasm tempered with experience. We had just been visited by three people from Odstock and awaited the return of 'Boris' from Salisbury. Michael Arthur had recently left the camp to live in Salisbury. Shaun had gone to Faslane Peace Camp where he and 'Boris' were later to take a lead in some imaginative NVDA. The conversation ranged over several topics. Recently some Boscombe Down peace campers had published a letter about animal liberation. We tried to find the relevant issue of *Peace News* but as usual when we wanted a particular paper it was impossible to find it among the piles of paper and books in the main bender. We discussed the media in general, Prisoners for Peace (it was Prisoners for Peace Day and we had sent cards), mail deliveries and the kindness of a modplod who had chased off some camp wreckers.

Camp wreckers and thieves were a recurring problem. Their visits in October have already been described. On another occasion camp wreckers arrived by car in daylight and started knocking down our signs. Barry emerged from the main bender and confronted them. He then put his head across the entrance and shouted in to us, "Have you got the shotgun ready?" He turned away and resumed the argument. After a minute or so the wreckers left. Barry, the only person outside, did not get their car number because he could not see it and was far too busy concentrating on negotiating with a man "built like a brick shit-house" (Barry's description) who may have wanted to do him an injury. We had no shotgun. It is not unreasonable to assume that the shotgun bluff had a deterrent effect on the wreckers and helped Barry persuade them to leave. That does not prove it would be effective on another occasion, or that all deterrents work, however.

At about this time, I slept in the lined bender which 'Boris' had built after a storm had wrecked the Broken Bondage tent. I had taken my own tent home, as after several months constant use on the camp, it had got tatty and no longer stopped the wind from getting at its occupants. The lined bender had turfs stacked around its base and an entrance dug into the ground to keep it from blowing down and to keep the bitterly cold wind out. This bender was big enough to sleep three in spacious comfort. Inside I was alone and had no other heating but that of my own body, yet when I awoke it was pleasantly cool inside, while outside it was bitterly cold with a touch of frost. Later when numbers got low on the camp, this bender was left unoccupied and rats settled in it. Sadly it was burned to the ground in order to get rid of the rats.

Over Christmas 'DT', Barry, 'Scumbag' and 'Boris' staffed the camp in grim weather when it stayed either below or around freezing throughout the Christmas period. On the night of 26th December the camp had its first snow and about two inches fell.

I cycled to the camp on 29th December. The others left to spend New Year's Eve elsewhere and I was alone from the afternoon of 31st December until 'Boris' returned about lunchtime on New Year's Day

1985. I was not lonely for I had plenty to eat and drink and something to read.

Thus throughout Christmas and New Year we had kept the camp staffed continuously, except for a couple of periods of less than thirty minutes each, when campers were collecting firewood locally and shopping. Terry Heffernan had been right when he told the sub-committee he couldn't understand how a return to normal weather would move us.

On 5th January a load of logs was delivered, the cost being split between campers and peace camp friends. This was either the second or third load and should have lasted a month if used sparingly but actually lasted just over a fortnight.

COURT CASES, COMMUNITY ADVISERS AND PROTEST MARCHES

Since the hippie tribe left, though we had managed to keep the camp open we were having trouble getting people to stay, and for days on end there would be only one person living on the camp, which led to periods when it was completely deserted for hours at a time.

One time the camp was deserted for several hours was the evening of Saturday, 12th January, when 'Boris' and 'Scumbag' were playing at a gig in Amesbury, which we had adopted as a peace camp social. All five of the campers staying that weekend went into Amesbury. At the gig we chatted with teenage camp supporters and others about the camp. We split up and the five of us returned to the camp in ones and twos over a period of about two hours after the gig had finished. This appeared to worry the modplods as they kept seeing people trudging through the snow on the coach road beside the perimeter fence and they didn't know when the next person was coming, who it would be, or even how many people were coming. We began passing the Modsquad caravan just before midnight and it was gone 01.00 hours when I, as last man, passed it. We were using a CB radio, which probably worried them also.

At the camp, one person crawled under the fence into the base and came out again. He was not caught, but he left his scarf inside. Then I rolled under the fence and back out without getting caught. I did not know about the scarf.

Shortly afterwards, the other camper and I were walking down Porton Road as we had a perfect right to do, when a Cortina Estate pulled up in front. A Modsquad sergeant got out, stopped us and gave my friend the scarf. Things seemed scary to me. The sergeant said we would be in trouble if we went any further and suggested we return to the camp. I stopped a passing motorist in a Capri, in case we needed a witness.

Not knowing how to open a conversation in the circumstances I asked him: "What police force are you with?"

"MI5," he replied, and drove on – and has probably been laughing about it ever since.

The sergeant radioed his station. We decided not to insist upon exercising our right of passage and turned and began walking back to the camp. As we walked back, three more Modsquad vehicles and two Wiltshire Police cars arrived, giving a ratio of six police vehicles to five campers. Unfortunately, detailed lists of registration numbers and policemen's numbers were not taken, or we could have sent the list to a sympathetic MP and asked him to find out why six vehicles were needed to handle five campers, three of whom were sitting peacefully in a bender. The police must have been paranoid. They checked the camp, and the civilian police said they wouldn't be back that night as they were leaving the Modsquad in charge.

Now some weeks before this, a camper had crawled under the fence behind the peace camp and had turned over one of the three floodlights trained on the camp and was not arrested. We were not sure precisely how he did it, but going by his timing we knew there would be ample time to turn over two of them before the modplod could come down from his caravan. Shortly after 02.00 a friend and I crawled under the fence and ran to the first light. My friend took one side and I the other and we carefully turned it onto its face. We ran to the second light and repeated our act. Neither light was damaged. We then returned to the peace camp. Had we thought of it, the whole operation had gone so quickly and smoothly we could easily have turned the third light round to face the caravan and leave the camp in total darkness, with the lamp illuminating the caravan as the modplod came out and collected his dog.

We hid in the main bender, with Terry sitting quietly in his car as legal observer. After a few minutes five vehicles (once again, my count and not substantiated by registration numbers) appeared along with Sergeant Wright and his dog Blake from the caravan. In answer to requests, the four of us came out of the bender. The police wanted to know who had been inside.

Unaware of the finer points of NVDA as taught by the Committee of 100, which would have required him to say everyone had been inside, little 'Scumbag' shouted: "No-one".

Then Blake was put to work, sniffed my trail, and came to me and also took a lunge at my friend who had been inside with me. I was arrested; my friend was not. I was put in the back of the Cortina Estate. I continued to shout to the others. One Modplod mounted guard on me, then left me. They seemed to be somewhat disorganised. I got out of the car and started shouting again. I was put back into it and driven to Boscombe Down MoD Police Station, where I was detained under constant observation and interrogated with many irrelevant questions about bank accounts and other things, which had no bearing on the alleged offence. (A solicitor later suggested that the Modsquad were trying to find out how peace camps were financed.) I refused to answer them. After a sleepless night and declining a cup of tea, I was taken back to the MoD Police Station where I collected my belongings, then to Low Flying Corner and released. No-one else was arrested.

As I was pleading not guilty to the criminal damage charge, I consulted a solicitor Richard Griffiths, who gave good advice and represented me once under the green card scheme. Richard was the Tory county councillor for Idmiston Parish, which included Boscombe Down and on whose boundary lay the peace camp. He had actually circulated a letter complaining about the camp in a council meeting. When I found out about this I asked him about it, then decided to stay with him. I believe I made the right decision although, as legal aid was refused and he needed £100 to carry on, I didn't retain his services much longer but finished the case myself.

Some days after being released, I went to Low Flying Corner and, helped by 'Boris', took measurements and notes for a detailed diagram of the damaged fence under which I had entered the airfield. As the modplod in the caravan was watching our every move, I was careful to avoid being seen writing anything or using a camera. The latter would have been illegal and the police would not like me doing the former either. I couldn't hide the tape measure. We finished measuring and 'Boris' went to look for firewood. I was inside the main bender completing my notebook entry when a car drew up outside. I hid the notebook and pen and went out to see who it was. A policewoman from the Wiltshire force was there. We chatted. She said she had just called as she was passing to see how we were but it was obvious from the way her eyes were roaming that she had come in answer to a Modsquad request to try to find out what we were doing. She did not find the notebook. Had she done so she would almost certainly have confiscated it and sabotaged my evidence collection.

On 5th February, when my case came before Salisbury magistrates, it was adjourned until 26th February because I was pleading not guilty. This meant the MoD needed to brief a prosecuting solicitor in place of Detective Sergeant Gareth Williams, who interrogated me and who would have handled my case if it had been a guilty plea.

About forty people took part in a march from Low Flying Corner to the main gate shared by the Microbiological Research Establishment and the Chemical Defence Experimental Establishment on Porton Down on 23rd February. Most of the peace campers were involved in opposition to what went on at Porton and some were in animal rights groups. This march was planned as a 'Celebration of Life' without the threat of nuclear, biological or chemical war and to oppose and publicise animal torture at Porton. Though it was cold – lying snow was defying the sunshine – we had a pleasant march and saw the new fence and gates at Porton. No-one was arrested. We got publicity for the march and the peace camp in the local papers. The modplods got in a lot of well-paid overtime.

With other campers I was planning to visit all the Civil Defence community advisers in Idmiston Parish to conduct a survey and find out about the system. So as to be able to put their houses in a visiting order and to save time on the actual visits, I looked up the locations of some of them on the way back from Porton Down. I entered a shop in the main street wearing a badge of protest, asked for an address in Beech Close and was told where it was. I went and saw the bungalow and then walked up the hill towards Boscombe Down.

A car containing two men in civilian clothes stopped. One got out, said he was a policeman, and asked me my name, address and where I was going. He said suspicion had been aroused when I asked the way to Beech Close and questioned why I wanted to go there. I said I wanted to see someone I knew there.

Fortunately he asked no further questions and he didn't search me or he might have found and confiscated my notes. This could have led to police action to thwart the survey. Never before have I been stopped by police as a result of asking directions.

On 26th February, Salisbury County Bench of magistrates adjourned my case to a special sitting on 11th March.

On 27th February, the Southern Panel of the Planning Committee of Wiltshire County Council met. Boscombe Down Peace Camp was introduced. After preliminary remarks and the presentation of a report by the county secretary and solicitor on the progress he had made in trying to sell our campsite to the MoD, the panel went into secret session. We are not allowed to know the details of what they decided.

A short while before this meeting, county council men had erected a chestnut paling around the peace camp. One end was tied firmly to the RAF perimeter fence and the other was tied loosely to it. The loosely tied end could be swung aside to give access to the peace camp. The campers were delighted when the county council men started clearing away the rubbish that had accumulated around the camp, and helped them load it onto their lorry. As soon as the council men had left, campers modified the paling by putting a break in it for easier access to the camp. Nobody was prosecuted for damaging the brand new paling even though there was no question here about exactly what was damaged, as there was no existing damage and there were only a small number of campers at the camp at the time. Had the Modsquad kept the camp under constant observation as they claimed, they would have clearly seen the damage being done and the person or persons doing it. They could then have reported the matter to the Wiltshire Police who would have prosecuted for criminal damage to the paling. There was neither arrest nor prosecution. This new fence was significant. Although cut, it was still there as a warning that the machinery of eviction had been put in motion. The campers didn't need to see the minutes of the meeting when it took place on 27th February to know what had been decided, probably even in advance of the meeting.

The next fence to be damaged was much bigger, and there was much more damage. Graeme Stuart 'Spud' Reid cut down thirteen sections (well over 100 feet) of the airfield perimeter fence beside the Coach Road. He was almost certainly helped by other campers, but the Modsquad arrested him and nobody else. He was charged with causing £900 worth of criminal damage. On his first appearance on Tuesday 5th March, Salisbury County Bench sentenced him to twenty-eight days in detention and confiscated his boltcutters.

'Spud' was a typical Boscombe Down peace camper, nineteen years old and a pacifist. He came from Scotland and was trying to make a career in alternative medicine.

His mother in Cumbernauld heard of the sentence, Richard Griffiths got involved with the defence and an appeal was launched. At last some sort of legal backup system had developed.

The day before 'Spud' was convicted, Richard Griffiths had defended a group of cruisewatchers including Blue Joyce, Ann Hodgson, Lynda Moody, Dawn Russell, Sian Jones, Karen Morris (all of the Women's Peace Camp, Greenham Common) and Vicky Orba (of Southampton) on an assortment of charges at Devizes Magistrates Court. Some charges were adjourned. Pleas of not guilty had been entered by eight women on minor charges of trespass on the military land on Salisbury Plain and when these charges were brought up, prosecuting solicitor Michael Jeary asked for adjournments as he did not have his witnesses present. Apparently the charges were straightforward, and could be dealt with then and there, which was what the women who had travelled a long way to the court expected. After some discussion, Richard Griffiths persuaded Chairman of the Bench Reginald Buttery to throw out these trespass charges and reprimand Michael Jeary for not coming prepared to deal with what were after all pettifogging charges!

My case came up in Salisbury Guildhall for the third and last time on 11th March, at a special sitting of the County Bench in the Grand Jury Room. Before my case began the MoD tried to get my most important defence witness locked up and out of the way without me knowing until it was too late, but by meticulous preparation I foiled their attempt. They had waited months to bring 'Boris' to court for not paying a fine arising from a small theft at the peace camp. He was sentenced to fourteen days in prison, but I found out that the same bench that were due to handle my case were hearing his case in the Grand Jury Room, so I went in and heard the end of his case and prevented him from going to prison before he had given evidence for me. Court ushers are useful people and meticulous preparation by the defence also helps!

Once my hearing began the MoD evidence was full of errors and discrepancies. Their album of photographs of the fence (all taken after the alleged offence) did not show the wire I was supposed to have broken. As the fence had been repaired only the

week before after a seven-week wait, the magistrates could not inspect the fence and the straining wire that I was charged with breaking themselves. My diagram came in handy to show how much of the fence was already damaged and had been repaired roughly and temporarily at the time of the alleged offence. The MoD solicitor, Brock Trethowan, claimed I threw the floodlights to the ground yet they were already on the ground and when asked about damage to them he could produce no evidence and said it was not the concern of this court! I left the magistrates to work out for themselves how I could have thrown them without damaging them. The case was a cliff-hanger right up to the conclusion at about 17.30. Late in the afternoon 'Boris' said that several times a camper had gone under the fence with the permission of the duty modplod to collect a football that had got itself kicked into the airfield. Of course, Sergeant Sergey denied this had happened. Then 'Boris' told the court that campers had photographs of the damaged fence, which would prove that I went through an existing gap. This caused a five-minute adjournment while the defence decided whether it was worth getting the photographs, which were in London, brought up for an adjourned hearing later. We decided not to do this but that if I was found guilty I would appeal and produce the photographs. Nobody on the defence side mentioned my friend who had been with me, as he was not in court and no purpose could be served by mentioning him. The MoD solicitor throughout the four-and-a-half-hour case did not mention him at all. The magistrates found there was not enough evidence to convict me and I walked free.

Graeme Reid's appeal was heard by Judge Martin Tucker, QC in Winchester Crown Court on 13th March. Griffiths had engaged a barrister called Christopher Leigh to defend 'Spud'. During the course of the appeal, a modplod told the court that there had never been any nuclear weapons stored at Boscombe Down (a white lie the MoD could not prove), and that Boscombe Down bore no resemblance to Greenham Common. It probably didn't resemble it before the RAF put airfields on them both, but that was a long time ago. I wish Christopher Leigh and 'Spud' had exposed these lies, but it appears they didn't. Graeme lost his appeal.

An official came to the peace camp on 19th April, and on behalf of Wiltshire County Council, served notice that an application had been made to the High Court for an order in possession. He also gave campers copies of the affidavits in county council evidence.

Wiltshire included large areas of military land and

many nuclear war targets, as well as a disproportionately large number of retired army officers. Thus it was no surprise to find that Wiltshire County Council invented community advisers, though its decision to appoint the first ones was by no means unanimous. Socialist councillors, including Austin Underwood, were highly critical and the Tory government in London did not like the idea of community advisers. Later the Tory government changed its mind and other councils, seeing what Wiltshire was doing, started appointing their own community advisers. These people are civilian volunteers, many with experience gained in the armed services, from an assortment of different walks of life and political persuasions, who go on twelve-week spare-time courses, which train them what to do and how to advise in the event of any large-scale emergency, including a nuclear war. Most of the training seems geared to the nuclear war business. Some are appointed survey meter readers, and these people are supposed to go on a further course to teach them to read radiation meters and do more advanced work. There are about a dozen community advisers in each parish, including one or two survey meter readers.

After Austin Underwood's criticism of the community advisor set-up came to our notice, some peace campers thought it would be interesting and informative for us to conduct a survey of the local advisers. The peace camp sat on the parish boundary between Idmiston and Winterbourne. RAF Boscombe Down was itself in Idmiston. Because the villages and community advisers of Idmiston were closer to the camp than those of Winterbourne, we decided to go to Idmiston for our in-depth survey. This all developed from my interest in the new lists of community advisers. I was eager to see how up-to-date they were.

Our survey was conducted on Saturday 27th April. Gary II (there were two Garys on the camp – Gary I helped on the ramble in October and left soon after), 'Pinkie' and myself walked the three miles into Porton Village to start the survey. We had seven questions for the advisers to gather information about them, what they could do for us and what we could do for ourselves. We used the examples of a hurricane and a nuclear attack on RAF Boscombe Down. Everyone received us politely. Only one adviser politely refused to help and said he wanted nothing to do with us, when we told him who we were. The next one we saw made up for this by not only answering our questions, but also inviting us into his kitchen for cups of tea and cake, showing us some of his paperwork and telling us all about his voluntary

part-time job as a community adviser. By the time we left his bungalow the snow was not only falling but lying as well, for the morning's pleasant weather had given way to a blackthorn winter. By the time the three of us had returned to the camp, we had walked about nine miles and conducted seven interviews. This may seem slow, but it must be remembered that although Gary and I had done a little doorstep selling, Pinkie had no relevant experience at all, none of us had ever done a survey like this before, and the Railway Hotel in Porton was an excellent pub.

The survey had been planned for some weeks, but had been delayed for several reasons, the main one being inclement weather. Thanks to the delay and the need to get the results circulated before the l local elections on 2nd May, the photocopying had to be rushed and was of poor quality. We simply did not have the money to do a better job in the time available. Copies were sent to Labour councillors, but no action resulted. The results of the survey are printed at the end of this chapter.

Before Mr Justice Simon Brown, QC of the Queen's Bench division of the High Court, sitting in chambers in Room 128 of the Royal Courts of Justice, there appeared four Boscombe Down peace campers and a solicitor representing Wiltshire County Council. The council applied for and got an order in possession against defendants described as persons unknown. This open order forbade camping on the verges of Marlborough Coach Road and Porton Road, alongside the RAF Boscombe Down perimeter fence. It was effective immediately, so the council could legally send in bailiffs at any time – even before the peace campers could get the message about the impending eviction back to the people living at the camp. The camp had no telephone, but the council had one.

The wait for the bailiffs began. We decided to stay until evicted, although we didn't have the resources and numbers to fight an eviction, and all had other homes to go to when the camp ended. Also there was the offer of immediate accommodation for the entire camp, if needed, in a large house at 7 Archers Road, Southampton (since demolished). Letters protesting at the proposed eviction and sale of the campsite to the MoD were sent to the Chairman of Wiltshire County Council by at least three local organisations.

The council elections then took place on Thursday, 2nd May. Austin Underwood was not standing for re-election because of ill-health, and his long, controversial career on three councils was coming to an end with his reputation for integrity, tenacity and hard work unblemished. Both Doug and Audrey Read stood for the county council, but neither was elected. We had lost our sympathetic county councillor and no-one on the new council was sympathetic. The voting results were known on Thursday night.

On the morning of 3rd May, the Mothers for Peace set off on the third day of their walk from Christchurch on the south coast of England to Faslane in Scotland. From Salisbury their route took them past Old Sarum Castle and the famous Ordnance Survey Gun along a road that had been in continuous use for two millennia and had known the tramp of the feet of Britons in the centuries before Christ. The main road was narrow and there was no pavement beside it. Their legs were aching; their feet were tired and blistered, and they were sick of the fast traffic whizzing past very closely. I was later told A345 was one of the worst roads on their entire route of over 450 miles. They were looking forward to a hot cup of tea and a rest at the peace camp just over a hundred yards from A345 at Low Flying Corner.

Wendy Chivers told me over the phone what it was like when they arrived:

> There were council workmen putting up posts for a new fence. The peace camp had all gone. It looked all burnt. All that was left were a few bits of trees, and they looked dead.
>
> No sooner had we arrived than police turned up and started getting heavy. We were not allowed to stop there. They thought we were going to set up another peace camp. We walked on up the track and the police followed us from inside the fence.

Because of the demise of the peace camp, the women had nowhere to sleep that night so walked up the Coach Road to Amesbury to look for accommodation where there was none. Supporters had to drive them to Sixpenny Handley – twenty miles away – and back so they could get a night's sleep.

The county council officials timed the eviction well. Their bailiffs arrived at 06.00 hours on 3rd May, the first day on which the camp had no sympathetic county councillor. The campers were asleep when the bailiffs came and their numbers were down, as there were usually fewer campers on site on nights in the week than at weekends. I understand the hourly paid council workers were delighted with the extra overtime and unsocial hours payments they got for doing this job and the only resistance they met was a reluctance on the part of the campers to leave warm bedrolls.

Boscombe Down Peace Camp had become merely a training centre, tying up resources and people that could be better employed elsewhere. It had gained much publicity for what was happening on the airfield, and several young people had learned about pacifism, non-violence, nuclear disarmament and NVDA there. It had not been possible to get enough people and resources up there to maintain twenty-four-hour observation of the base from the peace camp as at Greenham Common, though SAND had maintained a limited observation from Amesbury. I made good friends there. These peace campers and their supporters were the finest crew ever assembled on an anti-nuclear protest; it was a privilege and a pleasure to have been among them.

The new fence and gates at Low Flying Corner were not completed until about February 1986. They were built to the specifications for anti-intruder chain link fencing 2.9 metres high given in MoD Circular 7/77, which was sent to all the local councils in the area and Wiltshire County Council in 1977. When this was sent out, it only proposed replacing the old fence with this higher fence on the Northern and Eastern boundaries of Boscombe Down, but the authorities decided to replace more fence on the South and West when they erected the fence around the campsite, enclosing it as part of the airfield. I only found out about this circular after 1985; had local CND members noticed this circular, and asked questions when it originally came out, we would have known earlier about the expansion for the F1-11s.

In the spring of 1986, USAF bases all over Britain were getting new by-laws. The MoD wanted to introduce them to Boscombe Down and, so that local people would know about them, published them in advance. They proposed to ban all sorts of things inside the security fence (which the authorities outside accepted) and to set up a controlled area just outside, encompassing the married quarters, NAAFI shop and barracks which housed USAF airmen on exercises and modplods drafted in for Cruise convoys. Here they wanted to ban many ordinary things, including leafleting, selling ice-cream, garden bonfires, camping and canvassing. A Salisbury district councillor called the by-laws 'draconian' and the council, which normally eats out of the MoD hand, bit the hand that fed it and objected to the by-laws, particularly the ban on political canvassing.

After discussion and a few concessions had been made, the by-laws were introduced. At short notice, the modplods, who had not been properly briefed in advance, were instructed to erect signs showing the new by-laws around the airfield. These had been up for several days, when Doug Read pointed out that the maps on them were upside-down. All the signs had to be replaced.

What follows is the full and unabridged text of the Community Advisers' Survey Report. Copies were supplied to County Councillor Austin Underwood and others immediately after 27th April.

Boscombe Down Peace Camp
Low Flying Corner,
Salisbury Road,
Near High Post,
Amesbury,
SALISBURY, Wilts

CIVIL DEFENCE COMMUNITY ADVISERS' SURVEY

Dear Friends,

On Saturday 27th April 1985, 'Pinkie', Gary II and Michael Waugh, being three residents of Boscombe Down Peace Camp, conducted a survey among the community advisers appointed for the Parish of Idmiston by Wiltshire County Council. We attempted to visit all eleven community advisers on the County Civil Defence list. As these included three husband and wife teams, we had to call on only eight houses, all in Idmiston Parish. We especially stress that we used the latest most up-to-date list and that this list was in fact already out-of-date when it was published seven months before. Only one community adviser declined to help us; we thank all the others who helped us complete this survey with neither prior notice nor payment of any sort.

It is noted that two of the community advisers were interested in addressing the peace campers at a meeting, provided proper notice is given. It is hoped something will come of this (nothing did).

Names and addresses in this document, other than those of the community advisers, which are already published, are not for publication.

We have tabulated our results below and starting with the seven basic questions. Some people did not answer all the questions; one gave us much extra information. One person we contacted was the male half of a husband and wife team and replied on behalf of his wife as well as himself. There we counted one person contacted but two replies. We have mentioned this as some women may regard this data as invalid. Unfortunately the husband made it clear that he did not wish us to speak to his wife, who was

out at the time, and it was not possible in the time at our disposal to contact her independently. Information gained through asking extra questions and in discussion, is added, where relevant, under each community adviser's name and address. Answers to the seven standard questions are introduced by the question number only "i.e., we asked Mr Thomas question 2 "What training, if any, do you get?" and he replied, "twelve weeks training." In the report this appears as: Q2 – twelve weeks' training.

Standard Questions

Q1   Are you a community adviser for the Parish of Idmiston?

Q2   What training, if any, do you get?

Q3   We understand that the costs of keeping a force of community advisers to advise and assist in emergencies come out of taxes and the County Rate. Is this correct?

Q4   We live in tents on an exposed hillside adjacent to Boscombe Down Airfield in the Parish of Idmiston, and would like know what to do if an aircraft crashes on our camp, and would like to know of any way we could cheaply protect our camp from a crashing plane.

Q5   Can we do anything to protect ourselves in the event of a nuclear war?

Q6   What should we do in the event of a hurricane destroying our camp, and have you any suggestions to minimise damage in advance on a 'prevention is better than cure' basis?

Q7   Would you be prepared to come to our camp, and talk to us, and answer questions on your subject?

Analysis of Sample

No. of community advisers listed	11
No. out of this total interviewed	6
No. of replies (includes one via husband)	7
No. of community advisers moved within one year	0
No. of community advisers moved away over one year	2
No. of homes visited	8
No. of community advisers not contactable after two visits on Saturday (excludes moved away)	2
No. of husband and wife teams listed	3
No. of community advisers who had ceased to act as community advisers	3 (at least)

No. of males listed 7

No. of females listed 4

No. of survey meter readers, both not listed and both untrained 2

Answers to the Survey from the Community Advisers.

MR & MRS COPELAND, PORTON.

Q1 I don't do it any more.

Q You and your wife are on the lists.

A My wife doesn't. I don't have any part in it any more.

(The last interviewee, Mr Pafford. gave some further information, which appears to contradict this. He told us Mr & Mrs Copeland were still on the lists and had not resigned to his knowledge and that though Mr Copeland was listed as a survey meter reader, he was pretty sure this man had not done the meter reader's course.)

MRS D M HOPPER, PORTON

Q1 Yes.

Q2 12 week course.

Q3 I have no idea. We are volunteers.

Q4 There is not really much you can do, except to keep yourselves covered and protected. Stay inside.

Q5 It depends on where the nuclear bomb is. (We understood the "is" to mean "explodes".)

Q On top of Boscombe Down?

A You haven't a chance.

Q6 There is not much you can do, being as you live in tents.

Q7 Answer not obtained and interview concluded.

MR C E THOMAS, PORTON

Q1 - Yes.

Q2 - 12 weeks training.

Q3 - No.

Q4 - Only by going into bunkers.

Q5 - No, you can't in fact.

Q6 Hurricane? In this county? Again, bunkers.

Q Where is the nearest bunker?

A Probably in Amesbury.

Q7 I might, provided you gave me enough notice. I

should probably be able to. Interview concluded.

DR I LEADBETTER, PORTON

Q1 No.

Q You are on the list.

A I was a long time ago, not now. (Remember we are using the latest list – only SEVEN months old.) Interview concluded.

MAJOR & MRS PARRY, PORTON

We called twice, but both times this husband and wife team were out and we were unable to ascertain when they would return.

MR S G & MRS P H WHITTICK, PORTON

Q1 A puzzled look on the face of the gentleman who greeted us on being asked this question, led to us discovering he was not a community adviser. Neither was he Mr Whittick: Mr Whittick had moved.

Q How long ago did they move out?

A They have moved over a year ago. They haven't moved far, only to Amesbury.

The occupant of "High Plains" was interested in the community advisers list and where copies could be inspected. We informed him that copies were kept in public libraries and council offices in Salisbury and Amesbury and concluded the interview.

LIEUTENANT COMMANDER A F SYMONS, MBE., BEM., RN., EAST GOMELDON

Q1 Yes, one of them.

Q2 Why? Who are you? (Oops! The boot is on the other foot now. He is asking questions of us instead of answering ours. One of us answered.)

Interviewer: We're from Boscombe Down Peace Camp.

Symons: Sorry! I refuse to answer your questions. No, I don't want to speak to you people.

We walked in the direction of Mr Pafford's bungalow and were sure Commander Symons saw us go in that direction. We thought he would phone a warning that we were coming, but he didn't.

MR M C PAFFORD, EAST GOMELDON

Q1 Er, hum, yes.

Q2 Ah! You want to speak to my son who has done

the course. (Father fetches son, who is the man we want.)

Q1   (To son this time) Oh! My God! Well, would you like to come into the kitchen? (Father, Mother, Son and three interviewers enter kitchen and sit at the table. Son fetches big red folder and opens it on table for us all to see.)

Q2   Basically a 10-week course. (This is different to the other answers of 12 weeks. The course could have been lengthened or shortened for a second intake or Mr Pafford may have signed on late. At any rate this discrepancy is almost certainly unimportant.)
Each week has a different aspect: the first is basic introduction, in the second we learn about radiation hazards, radiation sickness, dose rates, burns and so on. Advisers go on this course full of enthusiasm because they are pressured by parish councils. Many of them are parish councillors themselves.

Q3   Yes, I believe that is true. We don't get paid. It's entirely voluntary.

Q4   In an aircraft crash, your main danger is the fireball with aviation fuel.

Q5   Yes, I believe you can, up to a point; whether you survive later is another matter. It depends on the size of the bomb, location of the explosion etc. A 120 kiloton bomb as on the SS80 (Soviet missile) would give you pretty bad problems. You have to think about blast radius, heat radius and whether it's an air burst or ground burst. A ground burst would have lots of muck flying about in the wind.

Q6   Hurricane? Aren't you in a hollow? (We aren't, but we returned to Q5 as he did not want to go on with hurricanes and we felt it would be wise to let him release some of his immense knowledge about nuclear explosions.)

Q5   Fifty pounds per square inch over-pressure will destroy a house. The further away from an explosion you are, the less overpressure you get. One pound per square inch overpressure will crack windows. A five megaton bomb on Southampton will crack windows in Salisbury (with over-pressure).

Q   Would it crack them here?

A   Probably.

Q7   Yes, well I wouldn't mind.

We then drifted into a general discussion involving all six of us without formal questions.

Interviewer: Why did you do the job?

Mr Pafford Jnr: I did it because I was interested.

Mr Pafford Snr: When you did this course had you joined the Campaign for Nuclear Disarmament?

Mr Pafford Jnr: Yes, but I did not tell them (Wiltshire County Council). Did you know about the survey meter readers (SMR) organisation?

Interviewer: No.

Mr Pafford Jnr: Before conflict starts, SMRs of which I am one, will be issued with radiation counters so that we can go round after the war checking radiation and knocking on doors telling people when it is safe to go outside. SMRs are supposed to go on a special one day course. I was going to take the course but have not yet done so. My boss in the organisation, Mr Copeland (see first interview) told me he had not taken the SMR course.

Interviewer: Any bunkers around here?

Mr Pafford Jnr: Well, no. We've got Dean Hill. The hill is hollow. You may be interested to know that in the event of a war a certain percentage of the Army will be detailed to work in this country and not go to Germany.

Interviewer: What is the (community adviser's) job?

Mr Pafford Jnr: The job was invented by Wiltshire County Council, originally against government guidelines. Now the government have accepted it, and it's within their setup. You receive updates (of information) every year by mail. We are getting people to do the job on the old boy network. (Where is my Old Probians school tie?) It is criticised because of this but it is said they get good people this way. To get volunteers Idmiston Parish Council put up a public notice – Winterslow asked in the Parish Magazine inviting people to go on the course.

Interview concluded.

In reporting this last interview, I have tried to separate the wheat from the chaff, so as to exclude local gossip and other trivia. We were talking in the kitchen for over an hour. Mr Pafford Jnr., had a list of advisers apparently identical to the one used to organise this survey and as the other community advisers should have received lists like this with their own names on them, there was really no excuse for those who said they weren't on the list. Mr Pafford showed us, in books, dummy emergency exercises advisers do in training and much literature, including some bought out of his own pocket. He had purchased a Bruce Sibley book – Sibley being probably the best known author in this field – which had excellent charts. One question we might have asked, but didn't was: "Are there any SMRs in Wiltshire who HAVE been on the SMR course?" Dean Hill, which Mr Pafford Jnr mentioned, is a Royal Naval Armaments Depot about twelve miles away and whilst Civil Defence in that area may use it, it is extremely unlikely that anyone in Idmiston would go there in a nuclear war, unless on Naval business.

RAF BOSCOMBE DOWN

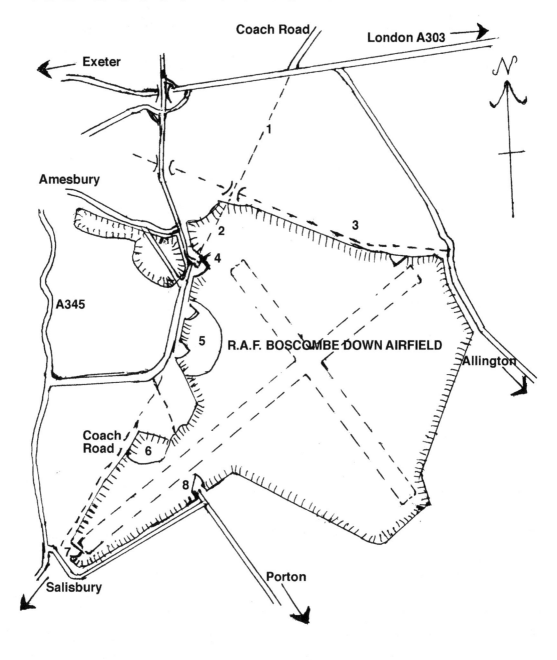

SUBWATCH
AT
BRAWDY

In 1980 journalists discovered what appeared to be the largest underwater surveillance base in Western Europe with submarine cables stretching far into the Atlantic Ocean. This was the USN submarine tracking base at Brawdy near St. David's in West Wales – the subwatch base.

Its first big demonstration was on 6th June 1981, when 1,500 people assembled there and demanded the removal of the subwatch base, after a walk from the village of Newgale organised by CND Cymru and the Welsh Anti-Nuclear Alliance.

On 27th May 1982, a women's peace march started in Cardiff and marched the 120 long miles to Brawdy. On 5th June when they arrived they blockaded the base for a time and then went off to the beach at Newgale Sands where they made enormous CND signs with stones. This was the famous Women for Life on Earth March with its beautiful banner later depicted on postcards and posters.

In was not until nearly a year later, however, that a peace camp was set up at Brawdy on 24th May 1983.

In July 1983 women campers twice invaded the base and were released without charge by the authorities. Also in July some women decorated a bus shelter and this led to three criminal damage charges.

Campers planned to commemorate Hiroshima Day with a die-in on a piece of land just inside the base

at the front, that was easily accessible from outside, and had invited journalists and broadcasters along to see it. However by the evening of 5th August the authorities had erected a new boundary fence, which made access to this plot of land apparently impossible. On 6th August the media people arrived and were told about the new fence, which they could see. While this was going on and the authorities were congratulating themselves on an amazing victory over the peace campers, women climbed into the base at the back, walked between the buildings and 'died' on the plot of land behind the new fence that they had planned to use. Delighted media people gave them good coverage.

Around the end of August this camp closed and the three cases of criminal damage to the bus shelter were heard in October. Not guilty verdicts were returned on two and the third woman was found guilty and given a conditional discharge.

Another peace camp was set up at the subwatch base in support of the Greenham women in America attempting to stop the deployment of Cruise by legal means. This camp only lasted twenty-four hours on 8th and 9th November 1983.

On April Fools Day 1984, disarmers cut the fence at Brawdy in several places.

A third camp was set up on 25th May 1984 and, on the night of Saturday 26th May, women from this camp travelled a short distance to Trecwn Royal Naval Storage Depot, where over forty caves with steel doors are set in one side of a secluded valley. Apparently there were plans to move the stored supplies to another place and refurbishment work was obviously being done on the depot, which gave rise to speculation about its future use. The women arrived at Trecwn and some entered the depot. They were inside for two hours before being caught, questioned and released without charge. This camp, which had been set up for International Women's Day was closed on Monday 28th May.

Since April Fools Day the MoD had erected several new fences at the subwatch base and replaced the security chief.

On 7th June an expedition went to the back of the base, which they found guarded. They were obviously not going to enter here, as the women had done on Hiroshima Day. Then six women went to the front, and found they could walk straight through the front gate. Here they discovered the Americans had orders not to touch protesters and, as there were no British police there, they had to wait three hours for the British police to come. When the police came, the women left of their own accord.

On 24th August a fourth peace camp was set up. One camper, an Automobile Association member, had a key for the AA telephone across the road, so campers could use this phone. Apart from Faslane, this is believed to be the only peace camp that had a telephone. I telephoned Boscombe Down Peace Camp's greeting to them from my home. Campers blockaded the main entrance once on 24th August and made several incursions. On each of two incursions on 24th and 30th August, four women got through the second security fence into the inner compound. There were ten arrests on 24th August, one woman who had entered the base was released, nine blockaders were charged with obstruction and bailed to appear in Haverfordwest Magistrates Court on 4th September. The other women on incursions were apparently released without charge. This camp closed

and the women left voluntarily after a few days.

The next camp ran from 20th to 30th September 1984, and was part of a campaign against NATO military manoeuvres that were taking place at this time. Peace Camps were set up throughout Britain and West Germany to protest at these manoeuvres. In Britain at least, they coincided with a women's strike, which meant that many striking women used their time off to attend their nearest peace camp.

The first Welsh 'snowball' action took place at Brawdy and resulted in Joe Furnell, Donna Cowley and Bruce Watkins being charged with criminal damage to total value of £46. On 18th November 1985, they were fined £40 each by Haverfordwest magistrates. These were first convictions in all three cases. Bruce did not pay his fine and was prepared to go to prison, if necessary. Bruce Watkins then made history by becoming the first person ever to be awarded an attachment of earnings order for a fine incurred on a 'snowball' action.

His case had been transferred to the magistrates' court in the extremely beautiful town of Llandeilo which made the attachment of earnings order. This order imposed a legal duty upon his employers to pay the fine out of his wages in instalments, taking each instalment out of its respective pay packet (or salary cheque) before they paid Bruce. If the employers failed to do this, they could be hauled before the court. His employers did not want to defy the magistrates.

Unlike Molesworth and Greenham Common, which are both in easily accessible places in the populous Southeast of England, Brawdy lies in a remote part of West Wales, beside A48 between Haverfordwest and St. David's. Fewer people live around the subwatch base and it is harder to muster a crowd of protesters there than it is at Molesworth and Greenham. Thus it had not been possible to build up a continuing presence here, as has been done at the two Cruise bases. However, activities have succeeded in giving much publicity to the subwatch base and to Trecwn and have also given good publicity to, and got new supporters for, the peace movement in West Wales.

BRIGHTON
BEACH
PEACE CAMP

At the Metropole Hotel on Brighton Sea Front the British Government held a great Arms Fair to promote sales of ammunition, guns, bombs, tanks, gas masks, military clothing and all sort of military impedimenta manufactured by British firms. Representatives from many countries made expenses-paid trips to the Metropole.

The Arms Fair attracted protests in May 1983 when three people were arrested and charged with obstruction.

Members of the Campaign Against the Arms Trade (CAAT) organised the biggest protests to date in 1985. First they took action through the local council, then they set up a peace camp on the beach for the duration of the fair and they organised NVDA. The action in the local council succeeded in getting a planned civic reception for the Arms Fair stopped. The peace camp was set up across the road from the Metropole on the beach. This provided a base for a continual presence of protesters throughout the three days of the Fair, 14th to 16th May, so that everybody who passed the front of the Metropole during that time knew something was going on. The camp also provided accommodation for supporters from outside Brighton.

There were many police outside the Metropole throughout the three days.

In an obscure place where the police could not see them, twelve people gathered together and entan-

gled their bodies in a chain so as to form a human barrier held together with steel. The two ends of the chain were left free and the people at the ends of the barrier each had snap-action padlocks open and ready for use. Nobody on the barrier had keys for the padlocks. Meanwhile, a large crowd of protesters sat down in the road outside the hotel and blocked it. Policemen guarding the hotel went to clear the road and arrest some of the protesters. While the police were thus distracted, the chain gang quietly walked up the front steps of the hotel. The chain's free ends were fastened to the railings on either side of the entrance with the snap-action padlocks. The entrance was effectively blockaded. The police then turned back to the front steps to try and clear them, but had to wait until boltcutters were brought before they could move the chain gang and arrest them. There were thirty-two arrests on Thursday 15th May, and there were two more on 16th May. Most were for obstruction and breach of the peace.

This NVDA was filmed, and a video has been made of it (Concorde Films Council, 201 Felixstowe Road, Ipswich, Suffolk, IP3 9BJ or Brighton Peace Centre, 28 Trafalgar Square, Brighton, should be able to locate a copy. They can be phoned respectively on 01473-715754 and 01273 692880.)

This protest received national and local publicity and got a lot of people around Brighton thinking about arms exports and won new support for CAAT.

BURGHFIELD
PEACE
CAMP

Hidden in the Berkshire lanes fourteen miles to the east of Greenham and five to the east of Aldermaston, lies Royal Ordnance Factory Burghfield Place. The M4 passes within 1200 yards of this factory, whose lights can be seen at night to the South of the motorway between junctions eleven and twelve and to the west of the railway between Mortimer and Reading West stations. ROF Burghfield is just four miles from the centre of Reading.

This factory was originally built in 1941 and has worked on nuclear weapons since around 1954.

In 1976 the MoD told the Ordnance Survey (OS) that ROF Burghfield's security classification had been changed and it has been omitted from all subsequent OS maps. Apparently the MoD thought that maps with it marked would be useful to terrorists. This was a case of closing the stable door after the horse had bolted, for thousands of the old maps were still on sale and in the hands of libraries and individuals all over the world. There was no obvious change in 1976 to warrant this alteration in classification. Aerial photographs taken with official permission and the old maps showed ROF Burghfield to cover about 280 acres surrounded by a narrow strip of land owned by the MoD.

> There are three major complexes; half a dozen explosives storage bunkers on the Northern side of the site; three 'igloos', two of them large and concrete-capped by the East Gate; more than 300

large buildings; a new office block; filter beds; four fuel storage tanks and numerous high earth banks around buildings. [ROF Burghfield Page 3]

These earth banks were blast walls designed to contain explosions.

The Mearings is a road running along the Western side of ROF Burghfield. The Factory Main Gate leads off it. On it are about twenty-five homes, a sports and social club and a farm. When I rode through on a moped there was only one gate, which was open and one guard hut, which was empty. Both were at the Northern end.

On 24th April 1982, Greenham Common peace campers, who came originally from all over the United Kingdom and who wanted to start a mixed peace camp, came to Burghfield and set up a peace camp at the Northern end of The Mearings near St Mary's Church. They maintained a continuous presence there for a month, sleeping in sleeping bags and sheets of plastic because the police banned tents. They placarded workers and leafleted houses.

The Factory Secretary claimed in a press statement issued when the camp started, that ROF Burghfield was for the 'production and assembly of atomic warheads for the services'. [*Berkshire Mercury* 28th April]

After a month the camp moved to a site about a mile north of the factory, not because of an eviction, but because the new site was a better one with water laid on, and tents could be erected without hassle there. The new site was actually on a caravan site. Apparently the police had approached a local land-owner and persuaded him to have the peace camp on his caravan site. The campers disliked the new site because it was too far away from The Mearings for them to maintain a continuous presence there with their limited numbers.

On 18th May 1982, an entry in the peace camp's diary timed at 12.15 hours reads:

> Fenella and Caroline went to look for the footpath and take photographs of the assembly building. MoD van with two officers (presumably mod-plods) stopped us and asked us what we were doing, saying that it was illegal to take photographs. We disputed that and carried on walking – they followed and once stop us to ask us to wait while their 'hierarchy' decided whether or not to arrest us. We carried on, but then decided to go back and take some more (photographs). Having used up the film in C's camera we started walking back again and eventually they made up their minds to arrest us. We sat down on the verge and they very gently picked us up and put us in the van. (They) took us through back entrance of The Mearings to [an] office just inside Main Gate. Two WPCs searched us and took names and addresses – we refused to give any more information. 'The Chief' came and said it (photography inside the factory) was against the Official Secrets Act: discussion about DC. Sgt Bygraves (local Thames Valley Police) came in and called us mischief-makers etc., took C's camera (F's was empty) took the film out, returned the camera and let us go.

On May 19 a modsquad inspector came out of the factory, and gave Caroline some prints from her film. He said the others were spoilt.

> Fenella's camera was empty when they were arrested as the film had been left in a hedge, un-til they could safely return and collect it. This was done and the film taken to a commercial developer in Reading. When someone went to collect it the following day, it was only to be told that it had gone missing

(Both quotations are from ROF Burghfield, page 5. The first four comments in brackets are my own ex-planatory notes; the other two came from the diary entry. I do not know the meaning of DC.)

Neither woman was charged as a result of these pho-tographic sessions, nor was anyone arrested on Sun-day 28th May when between twenty and forty peo-ple walked round the factory taking photos from the outside. Afterwards there were more photographic sessions, at which apparently there were no arrests and many photos were kept by the campers and the photographers.

Betty was arrested for sketching, and failing to give her name and address on the public road outside the Assembly Building on 8th June. Her sketch was sent to the Attorney General and the Director of Pub-lic Prosecutions, but Betty was released and never charged.

During June and July peace campers had noticed building work going on in the factory. After read-ing in the *Reading Evening Post* of 3rd July the state-ment of a factory spokesman that 'no building work was currently going on there' (Quoted on page 9 of ROF Burghfield.) They decided to investigate. They contacted the press and the Factory Director. The Director's letter in reply explained that building work was in fact going on to update and improve facilities, but that this work had nothing to do with the new project at Aldermaston.

The issue of radioactive and other potentially harm-ful discharges also arose. Here campers did much research and asked many questions following on from original research done mostly by Josef Rotblat, the pioneering nuclear scientist and CND sponsor. Some information came from the *Annual Survey of Radioactive Discharges in Great Britain* published by the Department of the Environment, which men-tioned Burghfield specifically in Table 40, and from figures of discharges published by the Reading Evening Post. As usual the research was hindered by Government secrecy.

> In order to garner more information the peace camp conducted a traffic survey from 5.30 am on Monday 12 July 1982 until 6.30 pm on Friday 16. The three entrances were covered almost continu-ally despite weather and terrible boredom.

> We enlarged our list of companies dealing with ROF Burghfield, got a fair amount of detail of a military convoy entering the factory and have plenty of material for assessing the number of employees and their shifts.

> On the first day we took many car numbers, but largely discontinued this after we realised that it was causing a lot of resentment and providing us with a mass of detail that we probably would never be able to usefully process.

> For the Tuesday, the camp diary records the fol-lowing:

> 'Back Gate,

> 2.50 First unusual happening. MoD opened gate, walked out to road, looked left and right gave no

response to my half-hearted greeting, walked back inside gate and stood against it clicking wire nervously.

2 MoDs (one called Donna) arrive on foot.

3.45 Gate opens. Thames Valley Police motorcyclist arrives. 3 MoDs come out. Radio on and the following extract heard:

…ROF convoy…

-convoy waiting to be picked up at Junction 11-

-motorcyclist gone past three times now-

-it's due 3.00 and I'm on overtime now-

-OK it's just gone past – you can come and get it now-

-Is the gate open? Can we get straight in?-

3.47 TVP motor cyclist leaves, turning right.

3.55 3 TVP outriders.

1 MoD white van, 2 MoD occupants.

2 green MoD vans, 8 occupants in each: 46 AC 98, 47 AC 00

3 armoured lorries, padlocked.

1 green van, 3 passengers and driver: 47 RN 20

1 green Land-Rover, 3 occupants: GAN 31 V

(number possibly transposed with previous vehicle number)

1 green fire tender.

1 motor bike: 21 KA 62

1 coach, 4 occupants: 47 RN 10

All occupants wore green berets and blue shirts.

3.56 Gate closed.

Similar convoys have been seen numerous times on the M4, both East and West of the Reading area. Locals report that such convoys frequently use the small country lanes between Junction 11 and the East Gate of the factory.

One such was seen on 7th October 1982 travelling at 40 to 50mph on the motorway. Two motorcyclists were with it, travelling ahead to clear junctions when it left the motorway.

Land Rover, blue 65RN11, 2 or 3 occupants.

Transit Custom, green 50 AC 36, 3 aerials.

Mammoth Major lorry, green 30 AJ 84.

.... ditto .... 30 AJ 85.

Fire engine, green, full sized 31 AJ 48

Transit Custom, green 50 AC 32.

Land Rover, green.

Bus, green 47 AC 92.

This convoy took a route from Junction 12 along the Bath Road through Calcot into Reading and then out again on the Burghfield Road.

This is a route also used quite frequently by a very different sort of convoy. Typically they consist of a very ordinary looking grey box truck, with small radioactivity symbols on the back and sides. In front and behind are turquoise Range Rovers, bristling with six aerials each and containing police. The whole thing is preceded by a civilian police traffic car, and followed by a minibus or Land Rover. This last vehicle has no passengers and is presumably present as a precaution against 'contingencies'.

Previous reports had suggested that 550 people may work at ROF Burghfield. In fact on Monday morning, 750 people entered between 6 AM and 9 AM. Another ninety entered before noon, but many of them were making deliveries. Most vehicles use the Reading Road entrance to The Mearings, especially deliveries and first time visitors. The James Lane entrance is used by no more than forty or so before 9AM and then hardly at all. This does include the occasional chauffeur driven car, however on 12th July, a red saloon, SRD 647S and on 14th, JJB 928N.

The East Gate is opened for employees for two hours in the morning and again in the evening. Otherwise, it is seldom used. About 270 employees use it during the week.

As well as direct employees, a number of contractors work at the factory and numerous companies provide services and materials. (This quotation from ROF Burghfield pp. 13-14 includes extracts from the peace camp diary written by an observer at the gate at the time. Times given are PM. For 2.50 read 14.50 hours.)

There have been other convoys like the one, which closed M4 for seven hours, allegedly because of a brake drum fire. I quote again:

Possibly the most worrying feature of ROF Burghfield in this respect are the convoys. The movement of nuclear warheads by road is an essential part of the operation of the factory. There used to be a rail line entering the factory but it has long since been lifted. (As railways go through towns rather than around them it is possibly just as well that warheads are not transported by train.)

But although motorways may by-pass most towns there is still enough potential for mishap. No amount of legislation prevents road accidents.

In September 1981, the M4 was closed for seven hours while firemen dealt with a fire in the brake drum of a twenty-ton lorry loaded with Sidewinder aircraft missiles. Numerous convoys use the M4.

In July, 1982, the MP for Swindon demanded a top level enquiry after a document was found in a street in South Glamorgan. It detailed vehicle registration numbers, drivers' names and times for munitions convoys from Barry Docks to USAF Welford. (*ROF Burghfield*, p. 19)

Even with the danger posed by conventionally armed Sidewinders and a serious brake drum fire with lots of smoke rising from overheated linings, it should still have been possible to extinguish the fire, cool the load with a hose, inspect and make safe the load and get the vehicle moving again in less than half the seven hours quoted. A normal lorry brake drum fire can be treated with a bucket or two of cold water. Then a fitter need only adjust the brake and the vehicle can proceed. There appears to be something more than just a brake drum fire here.

As for nuclear warheads not being moved by rail – in ROF Burghfield's case this may well be true, but RAF Chilmark, RNAD West Dean and RNAD Frater all have storage for nuclear weapons, and regularly use their railway lines and sidings for loading and unloading goods trains. So almost certainly, nuclear weapons are moved by rail as well as road. When ROF Burghfield was written, public knowledge of the movement of nuclear weapons was much less than it is now.

The traffic survey helped to produce a comprehensive list of firms dealing with ROF Burghfield. The survey was operating between April and August 1982. A copy of the list is reproduced at the end of this chapter.

It was getting difficult to keep people at the camp all the time, as well as keeping someone at the factory entrance and the camp had to be left deserted for short periods. Campers did not want this, so they decided to close the camp and as a final fling, close the factory at the same time. On 26th September, the camp was formally closed and twenty people who blockaded the factory managed to close that too for a short time. No traffic passed through their blockade and no arrests were made.

Northern entrance to ROF Burghfield.

At Christmas thirty to fifty people took part in a ninety-six-hour fast in a portacabin. Unfortunately this was not at the factory entrance, but was parked beside a dungheap on wasteland near the railway. Apparently a local farmer was squatting the land with his dungheap and was claiming ownership of the land by virtue of his use of it under the twelve-year squat law, and he didn't try to evict the campers.

On 31st March 1983, National CND gave whole-hearted support to civil disobedience for the first time in its history when it organised a massive and successful blockade of the factory all day without any arrests. On 1st April, which was Good Friday as well as April Fool's Day, this was followed by a great demonstration with a human chain between Burghfield and Greenham Common via Aldermaston. I was on the chain, and I believe figures given for the number taking part understated the numbers because of the sheer enormity of the demonstration. Nobody will ever know exactly how many came, but I believe we were around 300,000 in number. Coach parking facilities were full before half the coaches had arrived. There was chaos by 22.00 hours, when people, whose coaches should have collected them at 18.00, were still waiting in the rain. Some coaches were collecting people right up to midnight, long after their passengers should have been home. This had all been caused by the numbers of demonstrators, which had exceeded the organisers' wildest dreams.

Two people entered ROF Burghfield on the night of 10th February 1985, leaving messages and decorations behind them. As far as I can ascertain, they were not arrested.

On 19th September, nine Greenham women entered the factory to protest about the 'Brave Defender' military exercise, were arrested and charged with criminal damage. Their trials were adjourned pending a decision by the Director of Public Prosecutions on whether to charge them additionally under the Official Secret Acts. At this time some RAF airmen were being tried on serious Official Secrets Acts charges as a result of their activities at a RAF base in Cyprus. They were found not guilty and the government lost face over the trial. Probably because the government didn't want to lose face again, all charges against the nine were dropped just after the Cyprus trial ended.

On Christmas Eve 1985, fifteen members of Christian CND cut holes in the fence and entered the factory grounds from several different directions at once. They were all arrested.

The campaign against ROF Burghfield continues.

Camp site at ROF Burghfield.

The two peace camps and the ninety-six-hour vigil played important parts in it.

Below I reprint the entire Appendix from *ROF Burghfield* so readers can know the firms which supplied the factory during the time of the April – August check.

Appendix:

We believe the following companies deal with ROF Burghfield. Most of them were seen between April and August 1982.

AIR PRODUCTS (liquid nitrogen)

ALAN HADLEY LTD (bricks and cement)

D. ALDRIDGE & SONS, Southampton

ALWARDS BROS. Taynham, Kent

A.R.C. PREMIX, Theale

ASTRAMARK AIR FREIGHT, Newbury

BDH Mn SCIENTIFIC LTD, Poole

BICC PCL, Basingstoke

BOC (Liquid argon)

BARLOW HANDLING LIFT TRUCKS, White Waltham Industrial Estate, Maidenhead

AG BARTHOLEMEW (sand) Bentham Hill, Thatcham

BAYNES, Reading

BERKSHIRE FENCING COMPANY

F BEWSTOCK, Pontypool

TY BISSETT, Woolhampton

BIFFA WASTE SERVICES

BRANTS TIPPER LORRIES, Tadley, Berks.

BRITISH TELECOM

BRYNTON

BUCK & HICKMAN TOOLS DISTRIBUTION

CAMPBELL-GREY PLANT HIRE, West London

CAPLIN SCAFFOLDING

CASE & SON FISH MERCHANTS

WE CHIVERS & SONS, 108 London St. Reading – Civil Engineers and Builders

CLEANSING SERVICES GROUP, Newbury

CLIMAX PARTS

CUNNING & HOLBROOK LTD

*DB INDUSTRIAL FASTENERS LTD, Milford Rd, Reading

CDCL YEAST (UNICOL FOODS)

DELIVERY SERVICES LTD.

F DIXON TRANSIT, Croydon

DREWS IRONMONGERS, Caversham Rd., Reading

DYNOROD

EBENEZER MEARS & SON, Byfleet, Civil Engineers, Builders

HN EDWARDS & PARTNER LTD, Builders, Basingstoke

ESSO (Fuel Oil)

ESTCOURTS, Devizes & ESTCOURTS PLANT ENGINEERING (these two are part of the CHIVERS GROUP)

EVODE ROOFING

EXPRESS CATERING FOODS

FEBREY TRANSPORT

FISONS SCIENTIFIC

FLU-LINE CHIMNEY LINING SYSTEMS

GKN (Scaffolding & wood)

GRAHAM FORD (building contractors)

GROVE & PHILLIPS

WW HALL, Elgar Rd, Reading

HARE & PARTNERS

WJ HATT (water installation)

FA HAWKINS TRANSPORT,Eaton Bray

AP HENDRICKS TRANSPORT

INFAST, Thatcham

INTERCOUNTY EXPRESS

JAMES WHITE& SONS ENGINEERING LTD., Commercial Rd. Reading

JOHN STACEY LTD. Tadley, motor repairs, etc.

KASVIN LAUNDRY SERVICES, Windsor

KELSEAL

KEYPLANT

KITSONS INSULATION PRODUCTS

KODAK, Maylands Ave, Hemel Hempstead

*LEWIS ELECTRICAL MOTORS, Bell St, Maidenhead

LOVELL PLANT HIRE, Halifax Rd, Cressex Industrial Estate, High Wycombe

LYTOG LIGHTWEIGHT AGGREGATES

MBS, Thames Bank

F MAHER CIVIL ENGINEERING

MALONE ROOFING, Newbury

MAN EQUIPMENT LTD (protective clothing and equipment) Godalming

MANOR BUILDING & PLUMBING SUPPLIES, Darwin Close, Reading

NATIONAL CARRIERS LTD

NESTLES LTD

NEWEY & EYRE (ELECTRICAL DISTRIBUTORS) LTD

PALMERS SCAFFOLDING, Bracknell

PARKERS, Andover

PARKER PLYWOOD, Sandford

PEARCES FARM

PILLAR ENGINEERING SUPPLIES

PORTSMOUTH AVIATION, The Airport, Portsmouth

POST OFFICE

PRAKE BROS CATERERS (ed. note: may be a misprint for BRAKE BROS. caterers)

PRESTONS OF POTTO, DISTRIBUTORS, St Neots, Cambs

*PSIMAT (high pressure water cleaning)

RADCLIFFE, Guildford

READING SCREEDING

REIGATE WAREHOUSES

ROADLINE

ROCON PLANT HIRE, Basingstoke

ROWE GROUP

SOUTHERN ELECTRICITY BOARD

SECURE SCAFFOLDING, Henley

SECURICOR PARCELS

SECURITY EXPRESS

SELWOOD ENGINEERING, Chandlers Ford, Hants. (Construction plant & digger hire)

SHERWOODS CLEANING CONTRACTORS, Wokingham

SONNING HAULAGE, Reading

SOVEREIGN

SPRINGWOOD ENGINEERING

STERLING CABLE CO., Bath Rd., Padworth

STONEFORD

SUNBLEST

*SURREY FASTENERS LTD. Fernbank Rd, Ascot

TW FLOORING, 6 Howard St. Reading

TANKS & DRUMS LTD.

*TAYLOR & GOODMAN LTD (electrical motor repairs & sales) Craddock Rd, Reading

TYDESLEY INTERNATIONAL HAULIERS

UBM BUILDING MATERIALS

WAKEFOLD ENGINEERING, Basingstoke

WALLINGTONS, Twyford

WHITE ARROW MAIL ORDER EXPRESS DELIVERIES

DS WILCOCK, Newbury

WILKINSON TRANSPORT, Milton Trading Estate, Abingdon

WILLIAM KIRK LTD.

WITHER & STAFF

YOUNG & WILDSMITH

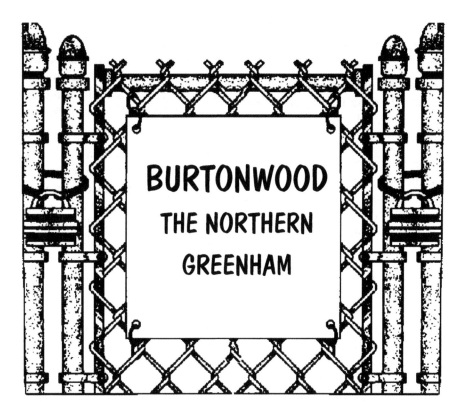

BURTONWOOD
THE NORTHERN
GREENHAM

Between the villages of Great Sankey and Burtonwood, near Liverpool, lies RAF Burtonwood. During World War II the RAF used this depot, but in the 1960s the US forces moved in, and some land on the RAF station was sold for housing and development. Prior to this, there had been several demonstrations at Burtonwood involving the Committee of 100, but after the sale of the land, the peace movement appears to have forgotten about the place, except for a few local disarmers. The few found out that RAF Burtonwood was being converted into the biggest military storage depot in Western Europe and believed that it contained underground storage on three levels, in addition to the many large warehouses at ground level. This was an integral part of the NATO nuclear war fighting machine.

Greenham and Molesworth were a long way from the densely populated North West of England. Consequently many people in the area found it difficult to get to these places to demonstrate. Some people then looked at RAF Burtonwood and decided it would be a good place for a peace camp. It was close to both Manchester and Liverpool, there was a railway station nearby and many Midlands and Northern cities were within easy reach via A57 and motorways. Burtonwood would be a good place to publicise and oppose the US military build-up in Europe.

On 17th March, 1982, opposite the US Army married quarters bungalows in Sycamore Lane, Great Sankey, women from Greater Manchester CND, along with other women from Northern England, set up a peace camp and immediately dubbed it 'The Northern Greenham'. Though set up by women, this appears to have been a mixed camp.

For some inexplicable reason the local CND group, Warrington CND, were not told about the new peace camp, which meant back-up from local disarmers was not as good as it might have been. This was especially true at the start.

For the first month or so campers faced harassment from a local farmer, who laid claim to the wasteland whereon they were camped. After a time the harassment ceased without him getting an order in possession to evict them.

The US troops were ordered not to speak to the campers. Civilian maintenance and construction workers at the base were told they would be sacked if they talked with campers. Once the peace camp had become established, the MoD put a new fence around the base and increased the number of security guards.

This peace camp was becoming well-known. Campers were travelling about Britain distributing leaflets about 'The Northern Greenham' in a quite professional manner. Important visitors included Lord Brockway. As a result, the camp grew so big that it was decided there were enough campers to set up a second camp on the other side of the base.

On 20th June, a group of campers moved to the new site. Now Burtonwood had two peace camps a mile-and-a-half apart.

Just after this, Peter Baker and Ken Cole visited

Burtonwood on their sponsored hitchhike around the seven peace camps.

On Saturday 3rd July 1982, a march from Warrington town centre to a festival at the new camp on the Warrington and Runcorn Development Corporation land attracted 5,000 marchers.

The corporation quickly obtained an order in possession and evicted the new camp only three weeks after it had begun. The campers returned to Sycamore Lane. At the time of writing the land where the Mark II camp had lain was all developed with a new road leading into a suburban estate.

In contrast to this, the farmer had apparently acquired the plot in Sycamore Lane simply by squatting it and erecting a fence. This might help to explain two things; first his aggressive attitude to and harassment of the campers and second the inability of the local council to discover who owned the land when they wanted to act against the landowner for allowing a campsite contrary to planning regulations.

In January 1983 mail was apparently being taken into the US Army base for interception and inspection before being delivered to the camp. Cheques were being returned to sender marked 'not payable', even though the camp to which they were addressed had not received them.

The campers celebrated the camp's first birthday with a festival at Sycamore Lane over the weekend of 4th to 6th March.

Some campers were going to Stonehenge for the Summer Solstice and some wanted to go to other peace camps. It was felt that not enough people would be left to keep a constant human presence at Sycamore Lane, so the camp closed on Monday 6th June 1983.

A blockade of the US army base on 8th/9th November 1983 was accompanied by Burtonwood Peace Camp Mark III, in solidarity with the Greenham Women Against Cruise who were fighting a legal battle in the USA to get Cruise missiles banned from Europe. At the blockade nine people were arrested on obstruction of the highway charges, which were altered to obstructing the police four days before the court hearings began. In court eight defendants were bound over, each in the sum of £50. The ninth was a coal miner involved in the national miners' strike that was taking place at the time, who had already been banned from the Warrington area until a court case, which was not due to be heard until one week after the blockade. Whilst the others were released on bail, he was detained in prison until this other court case came up and was dealt with separately.

Burtonwood Peace Camp Mark IV was started on April Fools Day 1984, on the Sycamore Lane site. Within an hour of the campers' arrival the farmer had returned and was getting very nasty. He was carrying a big stick as if preparing to chase the campers away like a herd of cattle. He knocked one child over, fortunately without causing injury. The atmosphere was

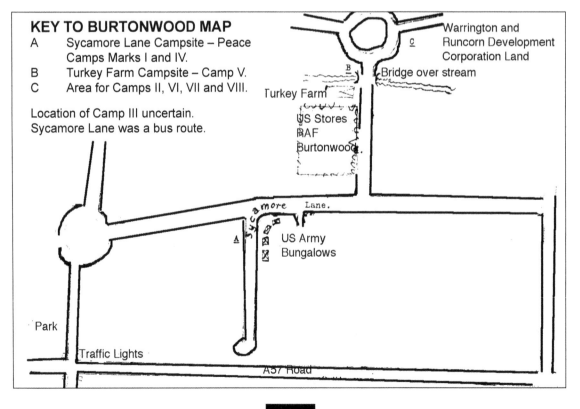

KEY TO BURTONWOOD MAP

A   Sycamore Lane Campsite – Peace Camps Marks I and IV.
B   Turkey Farm Campsite – Camp V.
C   Area for Camps II, VI, VII and VIII.

Location of Camp III uncertain.
Sycamore Lane was a bus route.

Warrington and Runcorn Development Corporation Land

Bridge over stream

Turkey Farm

US Stores
RAF
Burtonwood

amore Lane.

US Army
Bungalows

Park

Traffic Lights

A57 Road

heavy and threatening. Campers were worried in case someone got hurt, and to prevent this they packed up and left.

They went straight to a new site near the Turkey Farm owned by the MoD and set up camp unopposed.

Burtonwood Mark V became the base for a new campaign involving much NVDA including fence cutting. One interesting little direct action took place when somebody, by merely removing the ignition key from an army lorry, caused considerable inconvenience and delay on the base.

14th April saw what was probably Burtonwood's biggest ever demonstration, when Granada TV estimated that over 8,000 people demonstrated at the perimeter fence. They put balloons, flowers, photographs of loved ones and children and cut-out replicas of children on the fence. People stood holding hands all round the perimeter 'embracing' the base and singing. There was neither aggro nor arrests.

By late April this fifth peace camp had grown big, with a very large kitchen tent, and another large tent for supplies. Graham Gavin, who was there, recalled that there was also "a large home-made tarpaulin roofed structure that housed the main camp fire". Here they ate, held meetings and as Graham recalled enjoyed "evening music sessions with Skip on drums and Dave on guitar".

"We also owned (some would say most importantly of all) a tent for the chemical toilet! Apart from these, there were various other tents and a bender for use by visiting campers." (Both quotations are from a letter sent to the author in 1986. Graham Gavin inserted the brackets.) It apparently took the MoD three weeks to find out that this peace camp, which was causing so much trouble on the base, was on their own land!

When they found out, they acted quickly. A few days after the big demonstration bailiffs arrived and evicted the entire camp. They collected the tents, benders and gear in their own vehicles, and took them all to vacant land near the site of the Mark II camp of June 1982. They dumped everything there and the campers, without hesitation, set up Burtonwood Peace Camp Mark VI on that site.

Warrington and Runcorn Development Corporation once again applied for and was granted an order in possession. Another eviction was expected soon, so the campers decided to make the camp really active starting with a rock concert and picnic on 2nd June.

The miners were still on strike. Miners from Bold Colliery were regularly visiting the camp, bringing gifts of coal, coke and firewood. They brought a tarpaulin to extend the homemade structure with the fire in it. Some peace campers reciprocated by joining the miners on their picket lines and giving them little gifts.

In spite of all the activity, or perhaps because of it, some campers were tired and disappointed after the concert and only three were left living at the camp.

During the weekend of 9th/10th June, many campers and camp supporters were in London demonstrating during a visit by US President Ronald Reagan. In spite of this, on the Sunday Christian CND managed to raise about 400 people to march from Burtonwood village past the peace camp to the main gate of the US Army depot where they held a Peace Pentecost service. Afterwards the marchers returned to the village. Late on 10th June two women entered the base and held another Peace Pentecost service inside. They were arrested, strip-searched and detained for about twenty-four hours by modplods before being released with criminal damage and trespass charges. They were given bail on condition they kept at least one mile away from the base perimeter until their court cases on 6th August Their cases dragged on until 9th September when Warrington magistrates found them all guilty and fined them a total of £285.

Graham Gavin recalled an incident that weekend:

> Gina, our son and daughter (then two and five years old) and I stayed at the camp the weekend of 9th/10th July. We were awoke early Sunday morning by the sound of stones hitting the outside of our tent. The stone throwers proved to be three locals from Burtonwood. With what I considered was great restraint on our part, we convinced them to stop their violence and talk to us sensibly. This proved too much for them. They couldn't present a coherent argument against us. Their main grouse seemed to be that our presence was upsetting the status quo between them and the base personnel. Their other gripe was that our camp was an eyesore and a danger to the environment!! (From a letter sent to the author in 1986. This was the only hostile violence Graham encountered)

On Monday 11th June there were only four people left at the camp when the corporation bailiffs evicted them. These residents immediately set up Burtonwood Peace Camp Mark VII, only to be evicted again.

Once again they moved a few yards, and set up another camp. Burtonwood Peace Camp Mark VIII was, like its predecessor, evicted. After three evictions on one day, they had had enough so they left.

Around 16th July, an attempt was made to set up

another peace camp at Burtonwood but this one did not materialise.

'The Northern Greenham' still gets frequent attention from disarmers with vigils and 'snowballing'. Criminal damage charges followed eleven arrests at a 'snowball' here on 3rd September 1985. Although women were very much to the fore in all the actions at Burtonwood, the peace camps were apparently not women only. The biggest US Army store in Europe hasn't been closed down yet but it hasn't been forgotten either...

THE BUSTARD PEACE CAMP

This camp was set up on MoD land in the middle of Salisbury Plain when some women, including Greenham women, held a women's walk from Avebury to Stonehenge. They were determined to walk across the plain along the track which had once been the Salisbury-Devizes road and which ran via Redhorn Hill and the Bustard Hotel. The police arranged with the Army not to fire their guns on that part of the plain and on Thursday 2nd May, 1985, the women walked along this old road to the Bustard Hotel and set up camp on land nearby.

The pub had been named after the bird which had once flown over this part of the plain. The last wild British Great Bustard had flown here many years ago. More recently the great aviator Colonel Cody had flown his primitive aeroplane near here from a now forgotten airfield. He experimented with it and demonstrated it and did all sorts of things with it to please the Army top brass in an effort to get them interested in aeroplanes. Aeroplanes were great fun but would never be of any 'military value' was their opinion as they declined to renew his experimental contract in 1910. (In 1911 they changed their minds, however).

On 3rd May the women walked on to Stonehenge. They camped near it for two nights and on both nights they cut the razor wire coils and went inside the compound containing the stones.

On Sunday, 5th May, the women split up and left. A group of eleven went back to the Bustard campsite and tried to set up a second Bustard Peace camp, but police arrested them when they tried. On the first occasion there had been more of them and the authorities had received notice of their plans in advance, while the second camp was apparently not notified in advance to the proper office. The authorities may have been feeling a little peeved about the fence cutting at Stonehenge, too.

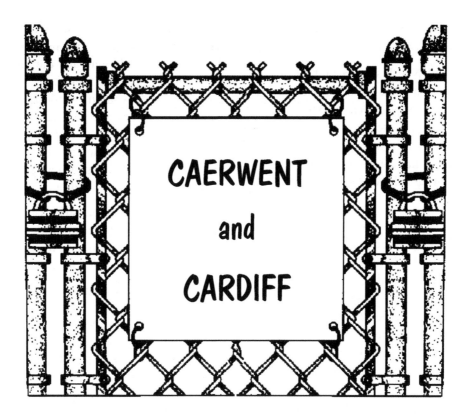

CAERWENT and CARDIFF

The Roman walls around Caerwent bear witness to the strategic importance of this hill town seventeen centuries ago. Within the walls was a haven of rest for travellers on their way between Gloucester and Newport on what must have been a difficult and hilly road in Roman times. From these walls Roman soldiers kept watch over, and repelled, the rebellious natives.

In 1982 the natives were still rebellious, although the Romans had long since left, and the main road (now known as A48) by-passed the old Roman town. Indeed, the new bypass had itself been bypassed by the M4 motorway. Caerwent was now a quiet, beautiful village set amid Roman ruins.

The new conquerors were the Americans who had moved into RAF Caerwent on the northern side of the bypass.

After the Romans left, Caerwent declined in importance until 1943 when the Royal Navy found this obscure village to be an ideal place to set up a propellant factory that had to be kept top secret. After a couple of decades, changes in naval armaments meant that the factory's products were no longer needed and the factory closed in 1967. Some of the buildings were kept in use for storage as The Deep Sea Stores. Then rumours started to circulate that the Americans would be moving in and grew until Remembrance Day 1967 when Welsh disarmers demonstrated at Caerwent against the US takeover. The protests had begun.

The protesters saw evidence that American forces had already arrived there.

Then on 22nd November the cat was let out of the bag, when the British government announced that the US Third Air Force was moving into Caerwent. On 29th November the USAF officially took over the old Royal Navy propellant factory, now renamed RAF Caerwent. It was announced that £4,000,000 was being spent on modernising, repairing and adapting the old factory for them and that this work would provide up to 800 jobs for local people.

On Saturday, 7th September 1968, the first British National CND demonstration in Wales took place at RAF Caerwent's Main Entrance. It was followed by a march to a park in front of Newport Civic Centre. I was there with a contingent from Salisbury. Many demonstrators saw USAF trucks hidden behind buildings at the factory.

Local people believed the USAF planned to store armaments there, in particular its European stocks of nerve gas.

In spring 1982 in a house a dozen or so miles away in Newport, Gwent, a group of disarmers discussed what was to be done about RAF Caerwent. Only a few months before some of these people had helped the WFLOE march on its way from Cardiff to Greenham Common and naturally they were fans, if not supporters of the Greenham Common Peace Camp. A similar camp was suggested for Caerwent. Dr John

Cox ex-Chairman of British National CND asked: "Who's for the camp?"

Nick Fisher, son of Neil Fisher, Secretary of Newport CND (in whose modest terrace house they were gathered), said he was for the camp. That was how it all started. Nick was elected Peace Camp Co-ordinator. At this time victory was in sight at Bridgend Bunker just forty miles away, and it was thought great things could be achieved at Caerwent with a peace camp.

On Easter Eve, Saturday, 10th April, 1982, Joan Ruddock, National Chairperson of CND, at the victory rally at Bridgend Bunker announced that a new camp was being started at Caerwent. The Mid-Glamorgan CND peace caravan was towed down there. Many people from the Bridgend rally went to Caerwent to help start the new camp. When they arrived to start the camp, Sue Sullivan and Nick Fisher handed a letter to Squadron Leader Stuart Holland, the RAF Commanding Officer of Caerwent, explaining why they had come. Although he accepted the letter, he refused to shake hands with them.

Before long, there were two caravans and six tents on the verge of A48 Caerwent Bypass where Dinham Road led off through military quarters in the grounds of the old factory. This was the main entrance.

Nick in front of the house where Caerwent began.

Gwent Police came and told the campers that if they did not move the police would move them because they were on MoD land and the police had powers to remove trespassers therefrom. The campers told them their bluff wouldn't work because the campers already knew they were on land owned by Gwent County Council from which any eviction would need a court decision and an order in possession. An eviction was unlikely as the camp was supported by at least two county councillors.

However, Monmouth District Council began plotting to get the camp declared illegal because it had no planning permission, and by Tuesday, 14th April, the campers were waiting to see what they would do.

The following weekend Mid-Glamorgan County Councillor Ray Davies was living at the camp when at about 23.30 hours on the evening of Saturday 18th April, "…an unidentified group of thugs, about a dozen men…" (*Sanity* No. 3, 1982, p. 34 col. 1) arrived. One camper said there were about fifteen men.

Andy Thomas of Caldecott CND takes up the story:

> They threw chairs over, tore our tents down and smashed our signs. One tore up a pointed metal tent pole and rammed it through a tent. They said we had to go. They didn't want us in the village. One or two of them were drunk. We did not resist them. Ray tried to talk to them and told them he would keep his arms by his sides. They kicked a fire brazier at him and then one of them punched him. (Quoted from a document possessed by the Fisher family)

County Councillor Davies was knocked unconscious. The visitors, apparently satisfied, then ran off. Soon after, the police arrived, having been called by local people – presumably from the village houses across A48. The ambulance was next to arrive. It took Ray to hospital, where he was kept for a couple of days. Fortunately, he was not seriously hurt, and suffered no lasting ill effects.

In view of this violence, the cramped nature of the site and police advice on road safety (the site was at a dangerous cross-roads on a fast curve), the campers moved to a larger site one and a half miles to the West on 19th April. Caerwent Peace Camp Mark II, though still in Gwent County, was in Llanvaches Parish in Newport Borough. This got Monmouth District Council off the campers' backs. (At the time of writing boundary changes since 1982 had placed the site of Caerwent Peace Camp Mark II into Monmouth District) It was on a big lay-by on A48 in front of the historic Tabernacle United Reformed Church. Between the old road, which now formed the lay-by, and the new road there was enough land for peace campers to set up an exhibition and to dig for peace. They dug a garden as soon as they arrived.

Newport Council soon got to hear of the camp and sent their public health inspector to inspect it daily to ensure that it posed no health risk to the good burghers of Newport. He was a friendly chap who seemed to see sense in the idea that nerve gas and nuclear weapons were bigger risks to public health than a peace camp. He also gave good advice on keeping the camp healthy.

At about this time, campers had been planning to force the wooden door of a Royal Observer Corps bunker near the camp and occupy the bunker. Suddenly the authorities replaced the wooden door with a stout, firmly fastened steel door. Were they gifted with telepathy, or did they have a spy in the camp?

This leads us to Bert McCann. This rather odd abrasive Scot who seemed obsessed with drugs appeared on the scene almost as if from nowhere just after the camp started. Nobody knew exactly whence he came though he had been seen at Bridgend Peace Camp. Neil Fisher was suspicious of him and warned son Nick that he appeared to be up to no good. Bert was seen speaking to the police and military on a number of occasions, always, it would appear, where campers could not overhear his conversation. Then came the raid on 18th April. After it, Bert was confronted by two CND members with the information that he had got into a car with military men and had a military friend. He left the camp without giving a satisfactory answer and was never seen again. Campers believed it probable that he was involved in the planning of the raid and some regretted they had not got rid of him as soon as Neil had warned Nick. They were sure Bert McCann was not the name with which he was born. It is possible the authorities had spies at other peace camps but none were as clumsy as Bert and there is no record of him elsewhere except at Bridgend.

There were threats of more violence against the peace camp but none materialised.

Police arrested three of the raiders on Sunday 19th April, and campers made statements. The three who were prosecuted seemed on the face of it to be nice respectable local people. One was an off-duty modplod and scoutmaster. Although other accounts said there were about twelve to fifteen raiders, the prosecuting solicitor, Mr Boland, told the local magistrates that there were only seven. He admitted some of the men were carrying mallets and one an iron bar.

I find it odd that nobody was prosecuted for carrying an offensive weapon.

Stephen Jacob Grumbach, a twenty-two-year-old family man who lived in Caerwent, pleaded guilty to assaulting Ray Davies and was fined £50. With Walford Ronald Brandon, a family man of thirty-two, and Arthur Paul Richards, twenty-eight, he admitted damaging signs at the camp. For the criminal damage offences all three were bound over in the sum of £50 each. Apparently a whip-round among Grumbach's modplod colleagues helped pay his fine. We could compare these cases with those of 'snowballers' with blunt hacksaw blades!

On 27th April, Nick Fisher sent letters to both of Caerwent's commanding officers, Squadron Leader Stuart Holland (RAF) and Colonel Stringer (USAF), inviting them to a public debate on unilateralism. They did not accept.

In early May, Mr J B Williams, Newport Borough Council's environmental health officer, reported to a council committee that he was able to give the peace camp a clean bill of health. The camp could not, therefore, be evicted on health grounds. Though the daily checks ended then, the inspector did call from time to time afterwards. Each time he found nothing worth reporting.

During the summer campers reported extensive building work going on in the old factory. They also reported a big increase in traffic entering and leaving it during the Falklands War.

Local Tory MP John Stradling Thomas was agitating for the eviction of the camp at the lay-by and Llanvaches Parish Council were also trying to get it moved and lobbying the Labour-controlled Gwent County Council with this end in mind. They, in turn, asked the Welsh Office about moving it. The Welsh Office was not prepared to take any action until the autumn, after the crops in the peace camp garden had been harvested. So, as owners of the land involved,

Caerwent Mark II

the county council took a vote on it at the beginning of June. They voted to start eviction proceedings.

Then began a few days of intensive lobbying by peace campers and supporters, helped by County Councillors Ray Davies and Paul Flynn, of the members of Gwent County Council. The council voted again and reversed their earlier decision.

Ray Davies was not only a camp supporter, but also lived at the camp from time to time, which made him probably the only county councillor who was also a peace camper at the same time and who gave his address as a peace camp. Gwent County Councillor Paul Flynn, who later became an MP, never lived at the peace camp but visited several times.

On 22nd June, Peter Baker and Ken Cole visited Caerwent on their sponsored hitch round seven peace camps. They found the site tidy and liked the 'Dig for Peace' vegetable garden. No doubt they saw the exhibition, which was not only visible from the road but also admired by many people who stopped their vehicles in the lay-by.

In June, Juliet drew up plans for a peace centre on the campsite. It was to have two permanent wooden cabins. These plans were submitted to Newport Borough Council for planning approval, which would be needed before negotiations over the land with Gwent County Council could be concluded. Newport Council deferred its decision when it first discussed the plans to its meeting at the end of July. The proposed permanent peace centre, which would have needed a lot of money to build and set up, came to nothing in the end.

On 4th July, the campers demonstrated at RAF Caerwent. A declaration of independence was read out in Welsh and English and a cherry tree was planted in memory of the victims of the Hiroshima and Nagasaki A-bombs.

The camp hosted another demonstration on 1st August. Demonstrators released 100 balloons with labels that stated that if there was a nerve gas accident leading to a release of gas at Caerwent, a deadly cloud could drift just as the balloon had drifted, and the finder of the balloon could be dying because of that accident. It is believed that one of the balloons was found in Southern Ireland. This demonstration took place some time before the disaster with gas at Bhopal in India.

On the same day, there was a meeting and Caerwent Peace Camp Mark II closed. Although the campers left taking tents and caravans with them, some later returned to tend the garden and harvest the crops.

The campers then set up Tathan Peace Studies Centre at Paul Flynn's house in Newport. This was planned to be the first permanent peace studies centre in South Wales, but it, too, met with council opposition. When the people involved applied to Newport Council for planning permission for the change of use, their application was turned down on the grounds of insufficient car parking space, so Tathan Peace Studies Centre in turn also closed.

The two Caerwent Peace camps had uninterrupted mail and milk deliveries. Newport Borough Council took the rubbish from the Mark II site. Newport CND had organised the camp with the help of Gwent CND, and Mid-Glamorgan CND's caravan had been at the camps throughout their 112 days of existence. When the caravan left, it had a rest and a cleanup and was then taken to Llanishen in Cardiff.

There were placards in the roadside exhibition asking motorists passing the lay-by site to hoot for peace and some did. Farmer Keen, whose farmhouse was about 300 yards across a field behind the lay-by, did not find the hooting peaceful, however, and complained about the noise the hooters were making.

Caerwent Peace camp Mark III was held on 9th-10th November 1983, by Welsh women supporters of Greenham Women Against Cruise in the United States. There were two reasons for setting up this third camp:

First back in 1981, the march from Cardiff to Greenham Common had come by Caerwent; second, the USAF was here.

There are no reports of Caerwent campers being arrested for any offence in connexion with RAF Caerwent. I am sure that some campers must have gone into the MoD establishment for a stroll round the factory grounds occasionally.

Various actions have taken place at RAF Caerwent since. The campaign against the USAF nerve gas store there has by no means ended.

About twenty miles south west of Caerwent, ROF Llanishen was involved in the manufacture of nuclear weapons, handling and machining radioactive materials. This factory is in the suburbs of Cardiff with its front gate on Caerphilly Road, Llanishen, and its back gate at the end of Malvern Way, on Ty Glas Industrial Estate near Ty Glas Halt on the suburban railway.

A peace camp was started on Christmas Eve in

front of the Cardiff Royal Ordnance Factory. It started as a round the clock camp until the council removed the Portakabin they were using early in the New Year. They're now vigilling outside the factory from early morning until late evening every day. They intend to establish a new permanent base at a different site by the factory's perimeter. (*Peace News* 3rd February, 1984)

The Portakabin would have been in Caerphilly Road.

Early in 1984, Mid-Glamorgan CND's caravan (ex-Bridgend, ex-Caerwent) was brought to a patch of wasteland off Malvern Way by the factory's back gate. Here it apparently served for many months as a centre for vigils, incursions and other activities.

However, the only peace camps at Llanishen appear to have been temporary ones secondary to vigils taking place there because no house that could be used as a centre was handy. Nobody appears to have lived at Llanishen as they did at primary peace camps like Caerwent. When I went to Cardiff to investigate Llanishen, I expected information about a camp at the front gate and one at the back, but nobody knew of any! However, I persevered and later received a letter from Sheila Rees of Cardiff Peace Shop part of which I quote:

> We have never had an actual camp at ROF Llanishen, now renamed the Atomic Weapons Establishment, incidentally. There have been regular vigils there, however, since 1984, and these continue on Monday and Friday mornings. We did once have a week-long vigil in which all the city groups participated, but not overnight. Very occasionally, we might have an overnight vigil as during the recent "Snowball" activity earlier this month, when some people did hold a vigil the night before. (From a letter to the author, 12th October, 1987)

The Welsh people's perseverance in their pursuit of peace at Cardiff and Caerwent is an example to us all.

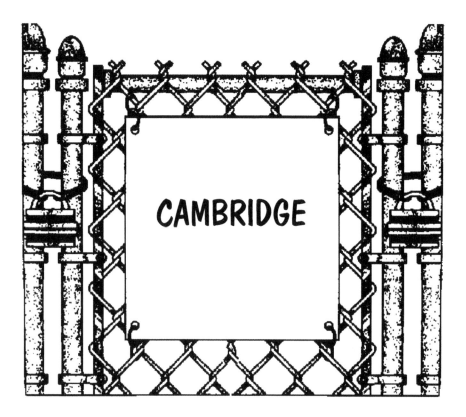

CAMBRIDGE

Alconbury, Colchester, Cottesmore, Lakenheath, Molesworth, Wethersfield peace campsite, and several nuclear bases are all within fifty miles of Cambridge as the crow flies. The Rainbow Village, after its eviction from Molesworth in 1985, travelled in this area. Consequently there were many pacifists moving around and visiting Cambridge who needed accommodation there, usually temporary accommodation.

Groups of people, including convoy people, some of whom had been on peace camps at bases, helped to set up several short-lived squats and at least one camp around Cambridge. They were usually run on anarchist lines. One of the groups was the Legion of Dynamic Discord. The camps and squats did not go much for publicity for peace campaigning themselves but concentrated on playing a supporting role and pioneering the idea of urban peace camps in a practical way. Generally, they tried to avoid NVDA and confrontation at eviction time as these could be a drain on their limited resources.

There was a big camp on Grantchester Meadows and several squats included one in a Salvation Army building. Perhaps the most famous was the squat set up in the centre of Cambridge in a disused parsonage owned by the Diocese of Ely at 45 Jesus Lane. On 12th August, 1982, after contacting the diocesan authorities, the Cambridge Peace Collective moved into the old parsonage. They set up a library, provid-

ed a 'crash pad' for visitors, and set aside rooms in which peace groups held meetings. They also made it a home for themselves with art, music and other trappings of a civilised small community. This squat lasted several months before ending in a massive party immediately before bailiffs were due to evict it, and the squatters left of their own accord.

Anybody looking for 45 Jesus Lane today would be stumped by finding a high stone wall fronting Jesus Lane here. On turning the corner into Manor Street, however, one finds on the right-hand side Parsonage House, a hostel for married students. This was built on the site of the old parsonage, which was demolished when the squatters left.

Parsonage House in Manor Street.

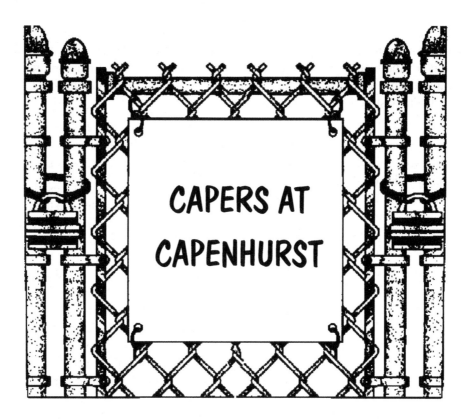

CAPERS AT CAPENHURST

The reprocessing plant of British Nuclear Fuels Limited (BNFL) at Capenhurst is located on the densely populated Wirral Peninsula not far from the ancient city of Chester.

Normally, nuclear plants are situated in areas of low population density well away from cities. They don't require very large labour forces being highly mechanised with labour saving electronics and because they do not handle large quantities of goods as does a food warehouse or car factory. Thus they don't have to be near cities. They do need large areas of land, which is expensive in densely populated districts. Any accident could have serious consequences for people living nearby and the greater the population density the worse the effects of any given accident. Also the greater the population density the greater the problem of protests, as was illustrated at BNFL Capenhurst.

The BNFL plant has a railway station nearby and buses running past the front gate. Many anti-nuclear activists live in the area. All this made it easy for activists to come out and survey the place and organise actions there. The reader is invited to compare the continuing campaign at Capenhurst with the campaign at Torness in an area of low population density.

After Capenhurst had been publicised in the peace movement nationally and there had been some locally organised protests, a peace camp was set up beside the front entrance where a luxuriant shrubbery now grows on 13th November 1982.

On 21st or 22nd February,1983, (reports disagree) thirteen women and a boy went into the BNFL plant and paddled on the duckpond using rubber dinghies and BNFL's own boat. They then rampaged around the grounds, blockaded the main gate so traffic had to be diverted through a side gate and wreaked havoc. As a result six women were arrested and charged with obstructing the police. Subsequently four were conditionally discharged with £15 costs for each to pay and magistrates conditionally discharged the other two with £20 costs each.

A human chain was made between the Marconi torpedo factory at Neston and BNFL Capenhurst on 6th March 1983.

Although this peace camp closed on 8th March, the campaign was by no means ended. Some of the campers returned on 20th September and were involved in a successful blockade. Without any advance warning to the authorities, one women's coach and one mixed coach arrived at the gates. Coach passengers quickly disembarked and locked all the gates using 'Kryptonite' cycle locks. This was done immediately before the morning shift change and took the authorities by surprise. Workers inside could not get out to go home, workers outside could not get in to start work and deliveries could not be made. The Cheshire Police were called and were delayed in the traffic jams around the plant! The

'Kryptonite' lock shanks required special cutting gear and by the time this had arrived and had been used to open the gates the blockade had lasted one and a half hours and seven women had been arrested. They were charged with obstruction and subsequently fined £25 each by local magistrates.

Campers were again involved when on 25th March 1984, a group of sixty women made an incursion into the grounds. In spite of their not being able to surprise the authorities this time, they managed to cut the fence in several places. Some women climbed onto the roof of the building where work was being done on the Trident project and this building was painted and decorated. There were nineteen arrests, all of which led to criminal damage charges. An estimate gave £1,500 as the cost of repairing the fence and there was also the damage to the building to consider.

An attempt to set up a women's peace camp in May 1984 was foiled by a large number of police, who were ready for the women and just rolled up their tents and gear and put it all back in their van.

On 7th June about a hundred yards of fence was taken down and cut up so it could not just be re-erected.

BNFL were claiming that they had increased security at Capenhurst. To test this increased security on the night of 4th September several women broke into the plant and easily entered a building. Over 100 building plans were stolen, machines were damaged and slogans were written on the floor in bitumen. The women then left of their own accord and were apparently never caught.

Much of the uranium used at Capenhurst and its sister plant at Springfield, Lancashire, originated in Namibia. Now Namibia was administered by South Africa in a way which caused great annoyance to many people who wanted all British trade with Namibia stopped. Some of these people got

Capenhurst peace camp site.

involved with the Capenhurst campaign. There was another blockade on 2nd November, this time protesting against the Namibian contract. There were two arrests for obstruction at this NVDA.

On 7th November 'Kryptonite' locks were again fixed to all three gates. Police arrested two people at 05.00 hours, alleging that they had locked the gates but could not find the keys to the locks.

Later on the same day at Chester Magistrates Court seven of the nineteen demonstrators arrested on 25th March were fined a total of £1,090 and ordered to pay £400 compensation to BNFL. At an earlier hearing one of the nineteen had been found not guilty of obstructing the police and two more people had been each fined £20 with £50 costs and compensation. This left nine women. On 3rd December Chester magistrates found them all guilty of criminal damage and fined them sums ranging from £90 to £180 each. The nine women were ordered to pay £2,785 in compensation between them. Subsequently, they caused a stir by paying £550 of their fines to a Namibian group, the South West African People's Organisation, instead of to the magistrates' clerk. Needless to say the clerk did not accept this as valid payment.

Pat Pulham and Tony Crawford were each sentenced to twenty-eight days imprisonment for locking the Capenhurst gates on 7th November. They were sentenced on 3rd January and released from prison on 30th January so they do not appear to have been awarded any remission.

On 4th January magistrates fined one Capenhurst woman £120 for two offences, one of obstructing the police and one of obstructing the highway, both having occurred at the blockade on 2nd November. The fate of the other arrested person is not known.

On Hiroshima Day 1985, several Merseysiders cut the fence, entered the plant and inspected the new gas centrifuge due to start work in October. Police with a dog stopped them and the four were arrested, held briefly and released without charge. Obviously the authorities did not want the embarrassment of court cases publicising the fact that these people had got inside the plant as far as the centrifuge.

On Saturday, 31st August, shortly after Bruce Kent had been arrested in a blaze of publicity cutting an MoD fence, a United Kingdom Atomic Energy Authority policeman spotted people picnicking inside the grounds and asked what they were doing.

'Oh, we're just the diversion. Bruce Kent's coming

across the railway lines with his boltcutters now.'

'He's coming tonight is he? I'd really like to meet him.' [Conversation reported in *Peace News*, 6th September 1985]

Exit policeman.

The picnickers then strolled around the factory grounds with cameras and left without being arrested.

Hilda Murrell was murdered near Capenhurst in mysterious circumstances. Karen Silkwood, a worker in the US nuclear industry, was also murdered in mysterious circumstances. In neither case has the murderer been apprehended. On the second anniversary of Hilda's murder seven people climbed over the fence and quietly held a memorial vigil in the factory grounds. Local people would have known Hilda for she had lived nearby before her death on 21st March 1984. A simple white wooden cross, a Peace Rose, some bulbs and some leek seeds (to represent nuclear leaks) in memory of Hilda, Karen and all the other people killed by the nuclear industry were planted. Then the seven set up a peace camp in some woods in the factory grounds and slept until wakened by Atomic Energy Authority Police at 05.00 hours. The police removed them and dumped them two miles outside the Main Gate. They walked back and set up camp at the Main Gate for two hours until morning broke when they left of their own accord.

It was at BNFL Capenhurst that 'Kryptonite' cycle locks were first used and showed how, with about £60 worth of locks, a factory can be closed for 90 minutes costing untold thousands of pounds in lost production. Most important of all no violence was used and nobody was hurt.

There have been many more minor events here and a peace camp at BNFL Springfield reported elsewhere in this book under 'Springfield and Styal'. The peace camps at Capenhurst have been an integral part of a campaign that has ensured this evil factory will never be forgotten.

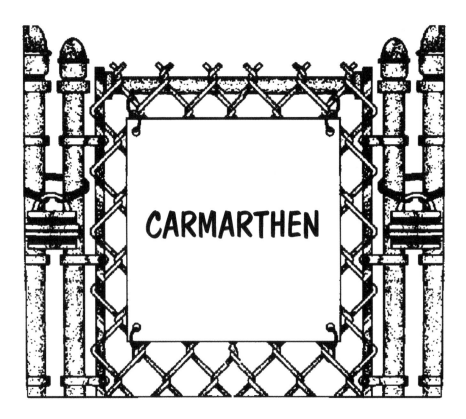

CARMARTHEN

About thirty miles North West of Swansea lies the peaceful, proudly Welsh town of Carmarthen. Well, it was peaceful, until Carmarthen District Council started to build a new parlour for its chairman in the car park beside its HQ in 1985.

The story began in Bridgend, fifty miles away, where in 1982 Mid-Glamorgan County Council had to cancel the building of a huge extension to the Waterton Complex of civil defence bunkers. In the end they were forced to demolish the partly built extension, which had cost thousands of pounds. [See 'The Fifty-seven Days of Mid-Glamorgan Peace Camp' elsewhere in this book] Although the Home Office sent out literature and offered bribes to encourage local councils to build and extend bunkers, no other council in Wales seemed interested. As a result of all this the Home Office became very concerned, so they sent Eric Alie (a civil defence expert on contract to Department F6 of the Home Office) over to Wales to talk to some Welsh councils to encourage them to build bunkers, thinking that an expert on the doorstep as it were would have more success.

Carmarthen District Council was the only council that would build a bunker after Eric had visited them in Spring 1985, just after their planning committee had approved plans for a new parlour for their chairman. After listening to Eric Alie the full district council, which did not have a clear NFZ policy, decided by a vote of thirty-one to two to incorpo-

rate into the new building a special basement with the equipment needed for a bunker. They worked out a deal which they reckoned would save their ratepayers money and the Home Office agreed to pay £45,000 of the £60,000 combined total cost of the bunker and the new office. The new office alone would have cost well over £15,000.

In June construction started.

In August a member of CND Cymru found in Hansard a reference to the government grant for the Carmarthen bunker and by early September 2,350 people had signed a petition against it whilst Plaid Cymru (the Welsh National Party well represented in local government in the area) came out solidly against it.

The district council found Friday 13th September, to be unlucky. On that date at 06.30 hours protestors occupied their building site just before the workers arrived and a campaign of direct action against the bunker began.

Work on the building was halted by about eight protestors, who set up that morning a peace camp, which was to occupy the site for five weeks. Some, but not all, of the workers were angry but at least one was friendly. By the time a lorry had arrived with some blocks there were about thirty protestors on the site. They immediately swarmed onto the lorry, which left without delivering its blocks. A policeman made things easy for the lorry driver and gave him a reason to leave which he could report to the consignor of his load by telling him he had 'no right delivering' [*Peace News* p. 7, 7th February]. This issue carried a news item (p. 5) and an excellent feature about the entire campaign against this bunker (pp. 7-8) during a peaceful protest.

On 25th September the district council held a public meeting to discuss the bunker where guest speakers opposed to it included Gwynfor Evans of Plaid Cymru, Tony Simson of END and Carmarthen MP Roger Thomas. The councillors then voted on whether to evict the peace camp and, as only four voted against eviction, they went and asked Lord Justice Saville for a possession order so they could legally evict the camp. When he heard their application Lord Justice Saville was told by the peace campers representative that the council did not own all the land involved. They had not obtained the consent of their landlord to seek the possession order. The order was not granted and the council was told an order could not be granted on all the land involved without the landlord's co-operation.

Peace campers were already in their sleeping bags on the evening of 30th September when they were surprised by a visitor, Mayoress Lorraine Maynard. She told them she, her husband and the entire town council were behind them and she would like to be evicted with them

This needs explaining. There were three councils involved: Dyfed County Council which had declared a NFZ and was opposed to the bunker, Carmarthen District Council which provided local government for Carmarthen and the surrounding district and which had responsibility for the bunker, and Carmarthen Town Council which had limited powers over the town only and no jurisdiction over the bunker. The district council planning committee dealt with building regulations and planning applications.

Thanks once more to the efforts of Mike Reed, the camp solicitor who was doing a grand job in the court conflicts with the district council, the council failed in their second attempt to get an eviction order on 5th October, but it was third time lucky for them on 8th October and the camp was told to be prepared for an eviction.

On the morning of 10th October the Sheriff arrived to carry out the eviction and told the campers to leave. They stayed. The Sheriff left. The campers knew that building materials already on the site would make it difficult for the council to evict them if they did not leave when asked.

The next day contractors arrived and dug holes for fence posts, the object being to fence off the site with posts set in concrete. As soon as the postholes were dug campers got into them. This prevented the contractors from installing the posts and pouring their soft concrete round them, as any attempt to remove the campers would lead to a charge of assault and court. The police were not willing to remove them. The concrete, which should have gone in straight away, stayed in the contractors' van and went hard. The contractors abandoned work there.

On Monday, 14th October , an interfaith religious service was held on the site and in the evening of that day Carmarthen Town Council held a public meeting to discuss the bunker.

The contractors restarted work on 16th October after twelve peace campers had been physically evicted by the Sheriff and his men who had arrived at 04.45 hours that morning.

On 25th October the High Court granted an injunction against the district council to stop them building the bunker because their planning permission only covered the original plan for a chairman's office. In their haste to start work the council had not even bothered to give a copy of their revised plans to the planning committee, which could have passed them 'on the nod'. They had also by-passed the usual procedure of advertising the contract and putting it out to tender. Instead they gave it to a local firm whose owner was related to a member of the council staff.

The council decided not to appeal against the injunction. Instead it did the simple job it should have done in the beginning and got its planning committee to grant permission.

The town council met the Local Government Ombudsman to call for an investigation of the flouting of proper procedures by the district council. Both Roger Thomas MP and Gwynfor Evans backed the town council's request at the meeting. As a result, far from reprimanding the district council for bungling things, the Home Office offered to be flexible over construction costs and to pay extra costs arising out of protests. The planning committee awarded planning permission for the bunker on 6th December although it was shown at the planning meeting that the number of anti-bunker district councillors had grown from four to nine. Now the district council not only had permission to do what it wanted but also had been given what amounted to a blank cheque to pay for it by the Home Office.

A petition against the bunker attracted 9,000 signatures. A pro-bunker petition displayed by protestors beside the other in order to be scrupulously fair and to gauge public opinion attracted only 190 signatures. Over ninety-five per cent of signatories, therefore, voted against the bunker.

Security guards were violent when 150 people, including Sue Pitman of Lampeter, treasurer of CND Cymru, demonstrated at the bunker on 11th January.

> The demonstration had been called because of a previous assault by a security guard on one of the vigillers there. Many people got onto the bunker site and Sue Pitman was given a 'leg up' to look over the fence. She was pulled down by a security guard so viciously that both hands were injured: The little finger on her left hand was ripped off. Henrietta and Annette Miller were also admitted to hospital after being injured by guards. [*Peace News*, 4th April 1986]

Yet the district council's policy and resources committee rejected a motion requiring Pritchard's men to "only use reasonable force" [*Peace News*, 4th April 1986] on the protestors and instead agreed a motion expressing confidence in the company. They did however agree eleven to ten to meet local protestors. The same committee recommended that the district council abandon plans to build the chairman's parlour and that tarmac be put over the roof of the bunker. So the chairman may not get a new office after all! Even with all the Home Office money the council seemed to be hard pressed to pay for building the bunker and also for keeping out protestors.

Dyfrig Nicholas of Pontardawe, allegedly the security guard who tore Sue Pitman from the fence, was charged with assault causing grievous bodily harm to which he pleaded not guilty. The case eventually was sent to Swansea Crown Court where it was waiting to be heard at the time of writing.

Since the peace camp had been evicted there had been several vigils at the bunker like the candle light vigil with twenty-five people held on 17th January.

Several local bodies expressed opposition to the bunker including Dyfed County Council. Many local Christian ministers and congregations were also opposed. During the bunker occupation several local traders expressed support for the occupiers in tangible ways with goods and services.

The district council then obtained legal writs to stop seventeen local activists from trespassing at or obstructing access to the bunker site. Any action these seventeen took there from now on rendered them each liable to imprisonment for disobeying a writ.

There were several attempts to occupy the site again and whilst some people got into it no new occupation was started. Of course, the site was by now guarded by high fences and Pritchard's men, who weren't exactly angels.

> Apart from the continuous stream of verbal abuse directed towards protestors it had been graphically shown that they do not flinch from using actual physical violence. Lately headless nails have been found driven into the trunk of a tree near the bunkers outer fence obviously intended to injure anyone who brushed against it. [*Peace News* 4th April 1986]

In atrocious weather at Easter 1986, in what was probably the biggest anti-nuclear demonstration ever held in Wales, 4,000 people marched through Carmarthen to the bunker being built to protect the chosen few in the event of a nuclear war. The banned seventeen, each wearing a numbered tabard, paraded across the road from the bunker where they could not be arrested for disobeying writs. Other demonstrators 'embraced' the bunker site with a 'chain of peace' and then held a 'die-in'. Welsh daffodils were everywhere. David Morris MEP, Paul Johns, chairman of CND, and two of the banned seventeen spoke at the rally afterwards in the grounds of Dyfed County Hall.

This bunker site had been for some time prominent in the media including Harlech TV. In London it had been raised in Parliament several times by both Plaid Cymru and Labour MPs. Several county councils were denouncing the bunker project as a breach of the NFZ policy of every county in Wales. David Morris MEP had called for the whole district council to resign. At Easter 1986 the campaign against the bunker project was growing stronger. There was still a chance of getting the construction of the bunker stopped and the site converted to wholly peaceful uses or the bunker filled in and forgotten. The peace camp in occupation, proudly flying its Welsh dragon flag, had been an extremely valuable part of the campaign.

PEACE CAMPS IN THE CHILTERN HILLS: CHRISTMAS COMMON, DAWS HILL AND NAPHILL

The Chilterns are listed as an 'area of outstanding natural beauty' and are part of the 'Green Belt' around London. If you live there you will have a job getting planning permission to erect anything more than a small back garden shed. You will encounter objections from local people, local government and national government as well as various conservation groups. Nobody wants these beautiful hills to become one great industrial slum dotted with jerry-built housing estates!

The British Government, however, builds what it likes and where it likes in the Chilterns. A mile or two south of High Wycombe they drove the London to Oxford Motorway M40 through these hills in spite of much local opposition. They also built two large ugly radio towers on hilltops beside it and also beside it the USAF Daws Hill command bunker. At Naphill RAF Strike Command have their old HQ alongside their brand new bunker built on National Trust land and there are radio towers here too. Right on top of the Chilterns at Christmas Common and Stokenchurch are two more large ugly radio towers.

To get to Daws Hill Peace Campsite one takes A404 towards High Wycombe from its flyover junction with M40 to a steep hill down into Wycombe. Immediately after the hill begins a right turn across the dual carriageway takes one into Daws Hill Lane. The entrance to Daws Hill USAF Bunker is on the left-hand side just before the lane crosses M40 on a

bridge. The peace camps were here, one on land now fenced in to the left of the entrance and one on the road verge on the other side of Daws Hill Lane. A little to the East on top of a hill beside M40 stands a British microwave radio tower and further East is a second ugly radio tower also beside M40.

During World War II Daws Hill contained the HQ for the USAF in Britain. From 1952 to 1965 it held the control centre for the USAF aircraft in Britain. It has quarters for USAF personnel, its own school and its own medical facilities.

In 1980 the USAF's Theater Mission Planning Squadron arrived here to control British-based Cruise missiles. Improvements were made in the Daws Hill Bunker, which became a vast affair of 23,000 square feet on five levels all dug into the hill. The improvements were said to have cost £50,000,000. Soon after, 7555 Squadron was joined by the rear field command centre for EUCOM, the USAF's European HQ. Should the main EUCOM HQ in Stuttgart become inoperative for any reason, Daws Hill would take over as the USAF HQ for all Europe. It is linked by radio with Hillingdon Communications Centre in West London, RAF Croughton next to Upper Heyford, Stuttgart and the USA. Daws Hill had no proper airfield but did have a sports ground suitable for helicopters. EUCOM was not committed to NATO. Whilst USAF planes can operate as part of NATO, EUCOM can also operate them separately, which it did when USAF planes raided Libya without NATO approval as this book was being written.

About four miles north of High Wycombe lie the adjoining villages of Naphill and Walter's Ash, both on a hilltop in this 'area of outstanding natural beauty'. In these villages are many RAF married quarters and houses for MoD employees who work at RAF Naphill, which lies between Walter's Ash and Park Wood. Here lay our second peace camp at the entrance to the new bunker construction site. Bradenham Estate to the South West of these two villages was given to the National Trust in 1956 on condition it would be 'inalienable'. This meant the trust could not sell the estate or any part of it and they could lease the whole or any part of it only with the approval of the Charity Commissioners in London. The 1,111 acres of Bradenham Estate includes Hollybush Farm and Park Wood. Through Park Wood runs a prehistoric man-made ditch believed to have been built for defence purposes! Rare orchids grow in the wood which the national government has designated a 'site of special scientific interest'. All this makes Park Wood into a sort of 'holy of holies' where doing anything other than breathing or looking could be illegal. RAF Naphill was HQ for RAF Bomber Command until this was incorporated into RAF Strike Command when it became the HQ for the latter. It controlled all the British nuclear bombers as CND Easter marchers who walked from Naphill into Trafalgar Square in 1965 will remember. Hollybush Farm adjoins RAF Naphill and Park Wood.

In 1978 the National Trust were approached by the MoD and negotiations were started with a view to the MoD leasing about forty acres of Hollybush Farm for the construction of a bunker to extend facilities at RAF Naphill. The terms of the lease were not agreed until July 1981 as the negotiations were unprecedented and needed great care. The approval of the Charity Commissioners was sought but ordinary members of the National Trust were not told and didn't find out about this deal until February 1982. They did not have time to mount a successful campaign against the leasing of Hollybush Farm before, in April 1982, the lease was signed with the Charity Commissioners' approval. The cat, however, was out of the bag. Members of the Trust were being persuaded by their colleagues who were opposed to the bunker to join the campaign against it. There was much publicity. Members of the public also started learning about the MoD plans for Hollybush Farm and as a result were also joining the campaign. Professor George Hutchinson, who was

for a time Chairperson of Southern Region CND, was a member of the National Trust and a leader in the campaign, which obtained over 3,000 signatures of National Trust members calling for an extraordinary general meeting of the trust to be held to discuss this deal. At this meeting, if there were sufficient votes in favour, members could void the lease of Hollybush Farm to the MoD, which would have to stop building the bunker and restore the land to its original state. The date for the extraordinary meeting was set for September. The MoD and its contractors seemed confident that the meeting would find in their favour and work, which had started as soon as the lease had been signed, continued. They knew that if the National Trust voided the lease they would have to pay for the land to be restored and would probably end up paying the MoD compensation as well. The MoD would not find another site easily and knew that the cost involved would be a factor in deciding whether to void the lease or not. The greater the cost to the Trust, the less likely they were to void the lease, obviously, and so the more work the MoD contractors did before the extraordinary meeting the better it would be for the MoD. Then the officers of the Trust postponed the meeting until 6th November, thus making conditions even better for the MoD.

At Easter 1982 Wycombe Peace Council organised 'the biggest demonstration the town has ever seen' [*Radiator*, February 1985] as part of the campaign to stop the building of the Naphill Bunker. At the entrance to the construction site and on the grass in front of RAF Naphill, 3,000 people gathered. They then marched down into High Wycombe, across the town and up to Daws Hill. The march was news and it got the bunker into the news as well. There could hardly have been a resident of Buckinghamshire who had not heard of the Naphill Bunker and the USAF bunker on Daws Hill within a week.

The Naphill Bunker was to be known as the United Kingdom Air Primary Static War HQ. It was to contain two establishments, National HQ, RAF Strike Command and HQ, NATO United Kingdom Air Forces. Thus it would control all air defence and attack forces in the United Kingdom except those controlled from Daws Hill. One estimate of its costs was £300,000,000, six times the cost of the Daws Hill Bunker improvements. It was to cover an area of no less than eight acres and would be under a mound thirty-three feet high set in a compound of twelve acres! At sixteen houses to the acre, a common density, that land would accommodate 192 three-bedroom houses. The bunker was to be surrounded by two fences, one of which was to be a security fence illuminated at night. Inside the fences a road would link the four main entrances. An emergency exit was to be installed along with two ventilators (each twenty-two feet by twenty-four feet), two diesel exhausts for engines inside the bunker and a sunken compound housing evaporative coolers. Peace campers invaded the bunker and discovered four underground levels, giving a floor area of nearly thirty-two acres in all! The spoil being dug out was spread partly on the roof of the bunker and partly on the ground around, so as to make an artificial mound.

All the National Trust appears to have persuaded the MoD to do, as a concession to the natural beauty of the site, was to grass over the mound completely and to supply trees to replace those they had cut down.

By a happy coincidence the local water board were building a reservoir a few hundred yards further up the hill. This was to be underground so would not be immediately affected by blast or fallout in a nuclear war, as an open reservoir would be. It was a simple matter to plumb in an extra pipe and lead it to the bunker, which could be given priority over civilian users of water when necessary. Spoil from the reservoir was being spread on land which drained away from Park Wood, so as not to affect the wood.

Meanwhile, on 2nd October, a caravan was parked on district council land at the entrance to the bunker construction site. A new dimension in the campaign to get the National Trust to void the MoD lease had begun: Naphill Peace Camp. At first it consisted of a series of vigils in daylight hours only and the caravan was not continuously staffed, which was a disadvantage because vandals took to wrecking it when it was unoccupied.

The National Trust sent out notices to its members, announcing the extraordinary meeting now to be held on the same day and in the same place as the annual general meeting. The campaigners were allowed to explain in a 200-word statement enclosed with the notice why they had called the meeting and why they wanted to void the lease. The Chairman Lord Gibson allowed himself a 250-word statement of the case for the other side and added an 'Expanded Statement' [*Radiator*, November-December 1982]. Copies of all three statements went with the notices. Although the executive had apparently misused its privelege of office by sending out fuller statements than the objectors, the meeting was not nullified. Lord Gibson was biased against the campaign obviously.

Many Trust members and supporting organisations would not be at the meeting and he knew it. Their votes would be proxy ones sent by post and would be based largely on the information sent out with the notices. They would not participate in the debate at the meeting and would not hear any of the information and arguments produced by the campaigners there.

In the meeting the campaigners based their case on the inalienability of the forty acres of land used for the bunker and ancillary works, in that the Trust was trying to lease it for a purpose not in keeping with its aims, and on the actual and possible damage to Park Wood. A new road from RAF Naphill to the bunker was to be driven through Park Wood. The other side did not mention the RAF nuclear weapons, which would be controlled from the bunker, but instead came out with irrelevancies, one of which consisted of an MoD official, in evidence under oath, saying that the bunker 'would have nothing to do with Polaris, Trident or Cruise missiles' [*Radiator*, November-December 1982].

The people in the 6th November meeting voted 972 for the motion to void the lease and 793 against. Thanks to Lord Gibson's persuasive statements the postal votes were 169,000 against the motion and 26,000 for it. The motion fell.

Over two Christmases, 1980 and 1981, students from High Wycombe had held vigils at the entrance to Daws Hill Bunker. Each time they had set up a peace camp to do it. In a torchlight procession just before Christmas 1982, 400 people marched out from High Wycombe to set up a third camp on this site. This one became permanent and was visited by some very important people, including Lord Brockway.

On 29th January almost 1,000 people marched through Wycombe to a peace festival at Hollywell Mead held to publicise the new Daws Hill Peace Camp. Many of them visited the camp.

Meanwhile, Naphill Parish Council was making legal attempts to move the Wycombe Peace Council's caravan from the entrance to Naphill Bunker. Other people were making illegal attempts by persistently damaging the caravan. Several times campers arrived for their daily vigils to find damage and broken windows. NATO stickers and National Front symbols were also found. On Saturday, 26th February, 1983, 'peace campers at the daytime camp at the World War III bunker at Naphill arrived to find that their caravan had been taken to pieces during the night and daubed with swastikas' [*Peace*

News, 4th March 1983]. In spite of these problems the picket continued here until Wycombe Peace Council decided it had served its purpose of publicising the bunker and withdrew the caravan.

At Daws Hill American airmen, apparently drunk, attacked the camp, destroyed a bender, stole some signs and the camp flag and ran back into the base. They were not stopped — no, not even for a security check – by US guards on the gate.

Daws Hill peace campers visited Naphill on 6th March and four students among them climbed two tower cranes on the bunker construction site. The cranes were 150 feet or more high. Jane Anderson was quoted:

> Security is not very tight. The students just climbed up to the cabins' (*Radiator*, February 1985). In addition on March 8 a group of women blockaded roads to the site. This resulted in work, which already had stopped over most of the site, being stopped all over the site completely except for talking and telephoning in the site office. It ceased until the last man was brought down from the cranes. Sean Hawkey, Robert Crampton, Neil Bailey and Jason Topping occupied the cranes. Bruce Kent saw them when he visited the site. Jason was brought down from his crane on the Wednesday after injuring himself and fainting. He was taken to hospital but was not detained and when the others came down after four days aloft, he welcomed them on the ground.

This crane occupation had received 'widespread national and international media coverage' [*Radiator* February 1985]. Although police removed banners from the cranes and the modplods 'gave the cranemen a severe grilling when they finally came down' [*Radiator* February 1985], nobody was arrested and charged on either the crane occupation or the blockade.

Immediately Wycombe District Council got to hear about the International Days of Action Festival planned for 9th-10th March they banned it. One thing planned was a human chain between Daws Hill and Naphill, which would have required at least 10,000 people. Not enough people came to make the chain but over 1,000 people did come to the other events. Once again there was much publicity. BBC TV showed film of both Daws Hill and Naphill on the 18.00 and 21.00 hours news bulletins and subsequently it was discovered that TV news broadcast in Australia had covered the festival! Greenham Women and Lords Jenkins and Brockway were among the speakers, whilst personal messages of

support came from the Bishop of Salisbury, Michael Foot and Tony Benn. One person was arrested during the days of action for painting CND and anarchy symbols on the inside of a fence at Daws Hill. When he was caught a US Sergeant tried to hit him. He pleaded not guilty so that the MoD lawyer would have to bring US witnesses to court, which the MoD did not want done. This would enable the defence to ask questions they would not otherwise have been able to ask and this would give more publicity to Daws Hill and why it was there. After three adjournments he was found guilty in July 1983 and fined £50 with £30 compensation and £46 costs to pay. He was not given time to pay, even though he was living on only £16 per week. Friends paid there and then to keep him out of jail.

After the district council ban, the festival organisers' strategy for circumventing it and this fence painting, hostility towards Daws Hill Peace Camp grew. Even some of the 300 or so members of Wycombe Peace Council were critical, especially of the painting though they had not criticised decorating at Naphill.

Soon after this five campers tied themselves to a large wooden cross and obstructed the Daws Hill entrance. They were arrested, charged with obstruction and fined £50 apiece.

In spite of the loss of the peace council support and its caravan, which ended the Naphill Peace Camp, a camp was started again there, this time on National Trust land. From it campers and 'Walk for Life' activists entered the bunker, removed some plans and occupied the trench being dug for the pipeline from the new reservoir to the bunker. This severely niggled Audrey Urrey, Wycombe Peace Council Press Officer who called the removal of the plans 'theft' [*Radiator*, February 1985].

On 25th July, three Daws Hill peace campers were arrested at the Wycombe Army Recruiting Office. They were in court on 15th August on obstruction charges.

The National Trust obtained an order in possession against the new camp at Naphill. It seems ironic that the huge bunker and its ancillary works were acceptable to the Trust while a small peace camp was not! On 26th July they sent in bailiffs who evicted the camp.

All the campers were at Naphill preparing to resist the eviction and there was nobody at Daws Hill when without warning, Department of Transport staff, civilian police and US guards cleared the entire Daws

Hill Peace Camp. As a result £300 worth of campers' personal property was never seen again, despite the loss being reported to the police. The campsite was covered with heaps of chalk and chippings on the orders of Wycombe District Council to make it difficult for another camp to be set up there. Apparently a 'mole' leaked information to the unsympathetic *Bucks Free Press*, so that the resulting publicity over the evictions would be favourable to the authorities.

The campers were back at Daws Hill within hours and Richard Weiss anchored his evicted caravan to neutral ground at the edge of a wood to restart Naphill Peace Camp. He displayed great courage in doing this and living in the caravan alone.

For a time Daws Hill was continually harassed by police and guards. On 28th July some campers managed to enter the grounds of the bunker there, were caught and released without charge, probably because the MoD did not want the publicity of court cases.

On Hiroshima Day, Helen Trask started a fast at Naphill in the 'Fast for Life' campaign.

In September the 'Walk for Life' people came and started a peace camp actually inside the bunker at Naphill. Needless to say this Naphill Peace Camp Mark IV did not last long before being evicted.

On 6th November, as part of a series of protests in support of Greenham women in America taking legal action to try to get the US Government's deployment of ground-launched Cruise missiles in Britain declared illegal, Wycombe Peace Council ran a motorcade around the local bases. A convoy of more than forty cars visited Naphill, Daws Hill and Christmas Common Radio Tower. During the motorcade one peace camper was arrested inside the grounds of Daws Hill Bunker and spat at a US guard, who drew a gun on him. Another was arrested for alledgedly attempting to set fire to Daws Hill's solid wooden perimeter fence. At about this time the Peace Council organised a weekly picket to support the peace campers at Daws Hill who were reducing in numbers.

Molesworth peace campers visited Naphill in November and organised another occupation of the bunker. They got the same treatment as did the peace campers who camped in it in September and were arrested, questioned and released without charge.

Also in November 1983 the last four cases from the Naphill eviction of 26th July were heard in High Wycombe Magistrates Court: two campers had their charges dropped and two were given conditional discharges.

Late in November Wycombe District Council Planning Committee received an application from the British Government Property Services Agency to extend the perimeter fence at Daws Hill further out towards the road and enclose the land on which the peace camp lay. The campsite was on redundant MoD land, left outside the fence to act as a visibility splay to improve safety at the turning into Daws Hill Bunker. The USAF who apparently rented the land from the MoD wanted to spend £5,000 on enclosing the campsite. In spite of there being no known advance public notification of the planning application (which the law requires) and the possibility of a road accident being caused by the loss of the visibility splay (hardly obstructed at all by the low tents of the peace camp), the planning committee approved the application and its approval was endorsed by the full district council meeting. Peace campers, informed of this decision as soon as it was made, appealed for help to resist the inevitable eviction.

On Human Rights Day 10th December Wycombe Peace Council held a torchlight procession to Daws Hill.

Days of action which included a planned blockade of Daws Hill had been announced for 18th and 19th December 1983.

In order to disrupt as much as possible the preparations for the days of action and the peace camp organisation as a whole, the authorities evicted Daws Hill Peace Camp just before 18th December. Campers resisted with NVDA – one was arrested after climbing onto a JCB digger – but the camp was evicted and the construction of the new fence began.

Like an army unit evacuating one strongpoint and retreating a few yards to another, the campers moved across Daws Hill Lane to the grass verge opposite and set up a new camp with military precision. This was not surprising as at least one camper had been trained how to do this during twelve years in the British Army!

The first day of action took place as planned with Christian CND organising events in and around Wycombe on Sunday, 18th December.

The second day's actions were centred on the peace camps and began with a blockade of Daws Hill Bunker. At 06.00 hours on 19th December, groups arriving from all over England started registering for the blockade at the peace camp. By 08.00 the police had begun arresting people. They maintained access to the bunker – though traffic was delayed – by a policy of instant arrest. As soon as each police van was full of blockaders, it was driven to High Wycombe Police Station. Around 300 people took part in the blockade of whom 152 were arrested. The blockade ended at 11.00 hours.

Then about 400 protestors found their way down the hill to Rye Park and formed up there into a silent procession which marched into Wycombe. When they passed the police station the marchers waved to blockaders they could see inside. They finished by silently leafleting Christmas shoppers in the town centre.

In the afternoon some people drove and about 200 others walked out to Naphill. There they planted young trees to replace trees felled by construction crews. Civilian police and modplods on duty for the event helped them. This was apparently done with the knowledge and approval of the MoD and the National Trust, who were planning to do this, as the planting of trees was a condition of the lease the MoD agreed with the Trust.

Altogether, counting everyone, including those providing backup services such as vehicles and telephones, about 1,000 people participated in the days of action.

Operations at Daws Hill were not diminished by the moving of the camp. There were several sorties from the new camp into the grounds of the bunker. A visit was paid to Number 3, Officers Married Quarters, which was the commanding officer's bungalow. Only a vigilant off duty guard prevented peace campers from stealing the USAF's flag.

Not all the news was good news, however. Americans were harassing the campers but stopped when the commanding officer made some of his men apologise for stoning the camp. Campers were banned from several pubs in Wycombe and one was arrested after an incident in The Three Tuns, a pub then frequented by civilian police.

On 15th January, Martin Luther King's birthday, a regular picket of Daws Hill began. For a time during 1984, it was held on Thursdays from 10.00 to 16.00 hours.

By 2nd March 1984 all the 152 cases from the 19th December blockade had been heard. Some, involving not guilty pleas, had been adjourned. Those that had pleaded guilty before High Wycombe magistrates

were mostly fined £20 each for obstruction with £25 costs. Some refused to pay and were sentenced to seven days in prison. The 113 who had pleaded not guilty were sent home on bail and their cases were adjourned until late March.

Showing solidarity with the arrested campers, eleven people from Brighton NVDA Network entered the bunker site at Naphill on Friday, 2nd March at 04.00 hours. They occupied parts of the site, including cranes at least 150 feet high; three people went into the bunker itself; five onto the two smaller tower cranes and three onto the taller cranes. At 07.00 the workers began arriving but they did not start work. Some climbed the two smaller cranes and tried to intimidate the activists in their cabs. Then police and workers found the people in the bunker and started to physically abuse them. Still no work was being done on the bunker and the workers were playing a waiting game, aiming to starve out the activists on the cranes.

Christmas Common can be reached from High Wycombe by taking A40 through Stokenchurch to just before descending Aston Rowant Hill where a side turning leads to the American radio tower at Christmas Common. This is not to be confused with Stokenchurch BBC Radio Tower two miles away. The tower at Christmas Common is linked into the EUCOM network and is an important relay station for the USAF in Europe, carrying radio messages to and from the USA. It is about seven miles from High Wycombe and within easy reach of many bases including Greenham Common, Brize Norton and Daws Hill.

While everybody's attention was attracted to the Brighton activists in the cranes at Naphill, at 03.00 hours on 3rd March two Daws Hill peace campers, Steve Pritchard and Dominic Clancy, occupied the 120 feet high radio tower while other activists occupied the radio station and took down about 400 feet of fence. There was nobody on duty in the radio station at the time but it was not long before US and MoD officials found out what was happening and came and told them that they were at risk from dangerous microwave radiations on the tower, which was still switched on. Of course they would not switch it off. Steve and Dominic decided to face the risk of the microwave radiations until Monday, 5th March, when they came down and went to the gate. By this time the authorities had re-erected the fence, which had only been pushed over. In doing so they had not noticed that the lock on the gate was sealed with superglue! Getting the two activists out of the radio station compound then took some time. Steve and Dominic were arrested but later released without charge, though criminal damage charges were laid against the peace campers who pushed down and damaged the fence and painted the buildings.

The occupation of the Christmas Common Radio Tower was really a peace camp in an unusual place. The campers had food and clothes with them and had erected a plastic tent and chemical toilet on the catwalk of the tower.

Meanwhile at Naphill campers had started to come down from the cranes where they were having an unpleasant time. The cranes were swaying like ships in storms. In high winds tower cranes like these can sway and fall and their loads can also sway danger-ously and be impossible to lower onto anything. I am reliably informed that had the cranes been free, the contractors would almost certainly not have used them at this time anyhow because of the winds. In addition, workers had climbed up to the cabs of the two smaller ones and 'started to physically and verbally intimidate the five people who were occu-pying them' [*Peace News*, 16th March 1984]. Tony Hemingway and Jan Clarke were among the crane occupiers and the last to descend was Sean Hawkey, who was on one of the taller cranes.

> At 9.30 on Sunday Jan Clarke, who had been occupying one of the taller cranes in extremely high winds, came down nauseous and exhausted. She was arrested, questioned for five hours and body-searched by police looking for a 'hacksaw'. During the afternoon two site workers climbed up to the cab of one of the taller cranes which was being occupied by Sean Hawkey. One of them kicked open the door, grabbed him and threw him out onto the ladder. They started punching him in the head and kicking his hands. Another protestor, Tony Hemingway, saw what was happening. He shouted to the Ministry of Defence police at the bottom to tell them what was happening but he said: "They have consistently refused to intervene when violence was being done to protestors" [*Peace News*, 16th March 1984].

Tony Hemingway and Sean Hawkey were charged with criminal damage and were due to appear before Wycombe Magistrates on 26th March. They were seeking legal advice in connexion with the alleged assault on Sean. Other protestors were charged with breach of the peace and a third crane occupier was charged with obstructing a police officer on duty.

During this event the three bunker occupiers tried out a novel idea. Even though they were made to leave early they managed to raise £100 by getting their sit-in sponsored.

In solidarity with the activists appearing in court on that day on 26th March, eight Brighton activists returned to Naphill, cut the wire and occupied the bunker again. They were arrested and charged. Subse-quently they were each fined £50 with £40 court costs and each was ordered to pay £22.50 compensation to Taylor Woodrow, the contractors building the bunker.

Details are not known of all the cases that arose out of the NVDA in the Chiltern Hills but some information is known. It is believed Sean was sentenced to youth custody in East Anglia by the magistrates who dealt with his case on 26th-28th March. In June the activists arrested for demolishing the fence and painting on the radio station at Christmas Common were each fined £50 and £20 costs. Probably the highest individual to-tals of fines, costs and compensation were amassed by two peace campers, who had to pay £167 each. By the summer of 1984 the total of fines, costs and compen-sation awarded against activists in the Chilterns had risen to well over £1,000. The indefatigable Dot Clan-cy organised a bust fund to help activists pay fines. She and her two sons, Steve and Dominic, were in the thick of it themselves and lived locally at this time.

Of course not everybody was fined or had to pay costs or compensation. Some people were sentenced to youth custody or jail, others were awarded condi-tional discharges, a few were found not guilty and some who were fined did not pay so were sent to jail.

Many of the activists involved especially at Naphill were in the Brighton NVDA Network. Although not all of these came from Brighton – some of them came from as far North as Nottingham – most came from the Brighton area as did Sean Hawkey.

After the end of March things became quieter at Naphill Peace Camp. Once again Richard was alone for long spells in his caravan in New Road, Walter's Ash, he being the only permanent resident of this peace camp.

On 3rd July, Naphill campers, two of whom were not permanent residents, entered the compound at Christmas Common Radio Station and painted it with graffiti. This was done in response to a message 'Cruise is out', on the Cruisewatch telephone tree. It would look nice in daylight when the sun rose over it on US Independence Day, or so they thought.

The campers were not caught and apparently the police were not aware of their identity until they called on Richard Weiss in his caravan in New Road and interrogated him. Richard was not used to police interrogation procedures and he admitted to being involved along with Steve Jones and Steve Pritchard. On 25th July all three were charged with criminal damage for cutting the perimeter fence and painting on the buildings. At least one newspaper reported that they had damaged the fence and buildings at Stokenchurch BBC Radio Tower. This may have been engineered by MoD publicity officers to draw attention away from the US tower and transfer it to the BBC tower.

Also in July 1984 activists entered the Naphill Bunker yet again. This time they spread thirty pounds of very lightly radioactive mud from Sellafield on its floors. They announced what they had done publicly and work on the bunker halted. A decontamination team had to be brought in (probably from Harwell in Berkshire). After examining the mud they declared the bunker safe for work to continue. The MoD announced the radioactivity was a hoax. The site workers were not amused but they did resume work.

Later, thirty-six workers walked out and struck because of the bad working conditions. This was an amazing strike! Strikes almost never occur in the British construction industry, where workers are renowned for their tolerance of bad and sometimes unsafe working conditions with mud, dust, fumes, rain, frost or heat from the midday sun to contend with on jobs where any delay could cost a great deal of money in contract penalty clauses. With all the demonstrations and publicity that the Naphill Bunker had already attracted, this was the last thing the MoD wanted. The MoD would probably be very embarrassed too as they are very keen on providing good and safe working conditions for their own employees and expect their contractors to provide them too. The press came along. *Bucks Free Press* quoted one of the workers talking about working inside the bunker. "The place is like something out of Dante's Inferno." The media seemed to be on the side of the workers for a change. The MoD was embarrassed. Taylor Woodrow acted quickly to improve conditions and work was resumed.

Richard Weiss and the two Steves went to Thame Magistrates Court on charges arising from the action on 3rd July. Peace groups from Chinnor, Thames and Wycombe all mounted a vigil outside the court on the day that they were appearing to give them support. The magistrates adjourned these cases to October and released the three campers on bail.

As Richard Weiss walked out of court that morning he was arrested by a plainclothes modplod who took him to Thame Police Station and interrogated him.

The vigil outside the court disbanded and reformed outside the police station where it stayed until he was released, apparently without charge, in the early afternoon.

It being Hiroshima Day, the two Clancy brothers along with Steve Pritchard, Gail, Simon and Richard then set up a peace camp for Hiroshima Week at Christmas Common. All stayed the whole week there except Richard who only stayed two nights. There were no arrests for NVDA at this camp and the campers left of their own free will on 12th August.

The numbers at Daws Hill Peace Camp were dwindling. People either working in the USAF bunker or connected with it were making their lives unpleasant by showing continuing hostility to the few campers that were left. Mainly because of these factors Daws Hill Peace Camp closed at the end of August after twenty months of existence. Campers either went to their other homes or went to strengthen the camp at Naphill.

This was not the end of activity at Daws Hill. During autumn 1984, six women broke into the establishment when a Cruise convoy was out and painted buildings numbers 807, 808 and 809 with slogans. They were in a top security area for one and a half hours before giving themselves up. They were charged with £820.98 worth of criminal damage but were 'fined only £75 as compensation; one who admitted possessing boltcutters was fined an extra £25. The magistrates were obviously out to impress' [*Radiator*, February 1985]. There was more protest activity at Daws Hill later.

On 10th October Richard Weiss, Steve Pritchard and Steve Jones were all fined by Thame magistrates. As they did not want to go to prison, they all paid their fines. They paid slowly and reluctantly.

In autumn 1984 Naphill Peace Camp published the first two issues of its magazine *Angry Pacifist*. Issue number one was financed by a sponsored walk, which was obviously more financially rewarding than the one we had at Boscombe Down Peace camp in October 1984! The proceeds from the sales of the first paid for the second issue, which was 'a mixture of poetry, humour and serious comment' [*Radiator*, February 1985]. *Angry Pacifist* cost thirty pence per copy.

On 14th December there was a torchlight procession from High Wycombe to Daws Hill to commemorate the fifth anniversary of the NATO decision to base Cruise missiles in Europe.

Between April 1983 and December 1984 about 190 people had been arrested at actions at the three establishments in the Chilterns. Many had been imprisoned or detained in other institutions. Well over £1,000 had been paid in fines.

On New Year's Eve 1984 about another fifty arrests were made at a great party held by Naphill Peace Camp. The high point of the evening was the practice of an old Scottish Hogmanay custom, first footing. (In this, people visit neighbours bringing presents during the night of 31st December – 1st January.) Activists took gifts of coal, whisky and bread through and over the perimeter fence of the bunker construction site and were first footing all over the place. Some were in the RAF HQ, others were inside the bunker itself. It was hoped to get a large Trojan loaf, a theatrical costume resembling a huge loaf of bread draped over a number of activists into the bunker site, but there were so many police around that it would have been useless to attempt it. The loaf was therefore diverted to Daws Hill where a hole was cut in the fence and the loaf entered the grounds of the USAF bunker and walked to a high security area where it was stopped by guards. The women inside the loaf then sat down and the guards had to cut into it to get them out. Soon after arresting these women, the authorities released them without charge.

In February 1985 Naphill Peace Camp was closed and *Angry Pacifist* ceased publication. There were now no peace camps left in the Chilterns.

Daws Hill Peace Camp was born again for a brief period on American Independence Day, 4th July, 1985. Several women camped on the site across the road from the entrance to the USAF bunker. They did a lot of singing and held a ceremony calling for British independence from the USA. There were insufficient volunteers to make this camp permanent so it closed after the ceremony finished.

Throughout 1985 the courts were dealing with cases arising from NVDA at Naphill, Daws Hill and Christmas Common even though the last arrest for NVDA was made in January or February at the latest. Steve Pritchard who had already paid a fine imposed on 10th October 1984, was jailed for thirty days for not paying other fines and two Southampton Cruisewatch women were each sent to prison for fourteen days for not paying fines.

The peace camps in the Chilterns proved of great help in the campaigns against these bunkers and Christmas Common Radio Station. They got great publicity for the nuclear war preparations going on there and caused much delay in the construction of the bunker at Naphill. Many local people joined the campaigners because of the publicity. It would be unfair not to mention the family who were the leading lights in the campaigns, Dot Clancy and her sons Dominic and Steve, without whom they would never have been so big or effective.

Having neither a nuclear weapons store nor an actual nuclear base nor any nuclear weapons convoys proved no handicap to the energetic and enthusiastic disarmers in the Chilterns!

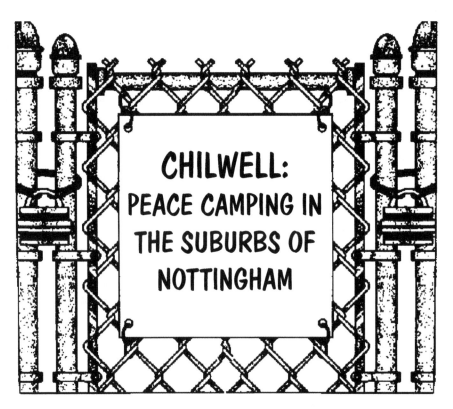

CHILWELL: PEACE CAMPING IN THE SUBURBS OF NOTTINGHAM

In November 1983 rumours were circulating of a forthcoming USAF takeover at the big British Army stores and maintenance depot at Chilwell beside A6005 road in the suburbs of Nottingham. They were not denied by the government.

The area was leafleted and then a small demonstration was held on 3rd December.

Next the first Chilwell Peace Camp was set up and stayed two weeks until Christmas. This camp organised no large actions against the depot but concentrated on simply being there and on telling people what the MoD were doing.

What is believed to be the first peace squat in military premises in the world was set up in an empty British Army married quarter at the depot on 1st January 1984, by women from Nottingham and Birmingham Women for Peace. Police soon removed and arrested all twenty-five of them. The women refused to be interviewed separately and were all later released without charge.

On 14th February the rumours were confirmed: the government announced that this depot was to be the first of sixty-four additional bases offered to the US forces and that it was being leased to the USAF. Local disarmers reacted quickly. On the following Saturday 18th February, there were no fewer than five linked protest demonstrations in the City of Nottingham and Nottingham Women for Peace held their first 'Breakfast Picnic'. Out of these actions grew the Reclaim Chilwell Group.

On 13th April, ten people entered the base to paint graffiti all over it. The two arrested were released without charge.

A thousand people took part in the 'Airstrip One' demonstration on 15th April. This included a cycle ride and an incursion by twenty-nine people who entered the depot and occupied Army tanks. Of these twenty left when asked and nine were taken into the country in a police van. When the police dumped them there they proceeded to blockade the van and the police could not get it out of the blockade until they gave the blockaders lifts back to Chilwell! Nobody was arrested and charged.

The depot was entered by fourteen people to paint graffiti on 2nd May and by six people for a midnight party on 17th May. On these incursions there were seven arrests of which three were for criminal damage to the fence (priced at £106 per person) and four were for being there with intent to cause criminal damage. The cases were to be heard at Shire Hall Magistrates Court on 25th September.

In June 1984, 800 redundancies were announced by the MoD at Chilwell Army Engineers Depot adjacent to the stores depot that had been leased to the USAF. We had heard a similar tale at Boscombe Down. Exactly what the USAF were going to do with the depot was at this time uncertain but Nottingham CND believed it was to be used to garage a rapid deployment force of 1,500 vehicles to back up other USAF activities in Britain.

Unfortunately for the authorities, *Peace News* had recently moved its offices from London to Nottingham. This newspaper began putting out advance publicity for a 'Reclaim Chilwell' action involving a mass incursion on 1st July to readers all over Britain and abroad. The authorities prepared, erecting a high chain-link fence topped with barbed wire and with barbed wire coils at its base. The disused Main Gate on A6005 road was surrounded with coil upon coil. The depot looked ready to withstand anything the peace movement could do.

What might have been a lively local affair turned into a very big demonstration. County and city councillors came and one was arrested inside the depot. The new fences were brought down, pulled up and crossed with ladders by many of the 4,000 protesters who were there. Some local residents were among them. The MoD claimed that 300 entered the depot while Reclaim Chilwell Group said that between 1,200 and 1,500 got in and 150 went through the inner security fence, too. As all this was going on, soldiers filmed it on video. The civil police when removing demonstrators were 'friendly and reasonably gentle' [*Peace News*, 13th July 1984], but the troops and modsquad were 'pretty hostile, protesters were pulled along the ground and thrown into barbed wire fences'. [*Peace News*, 13th July 1984] Although about 200 people were caught and held for a time only eleven were eventually charged with any offences. These were for criminal damage. This demonstration had taken an immense amount of planning and preparation beforehand. The Quaker who had been working full time for many weeks for no wages and the people who helped him to organise this demonstration must have been very pleased with the results.

At about this time Reclaim Chilwell Group found that the old stores depot was being used by police on picket duty for the miners' strike.

On 8th July at Nottingham Peace Festival, Reclaim Chilwell Group held the first in a series of follow-up meetings.

The next peace camp began on 29th September 1984. Some women involved in the nationwide actions that were taking place at that time started planning the camp only four days before. On the Saturday evening they pitched their tents on a grass verge next to the depot fence near New Main Gate in Swinet Way. Their camp was quickly planned and quickly evicted. Within an hour modplods had arrived and offered them the choice of moving or being arrested. They moved. They had another site they could use across the road and they were soon settling on land owned by the local Co-op. In no time at all a Co-op security guard appeared. He threatened to set his Alsatian dog on them and grabbed one woman who tried to photograph him, but the women would not leave so he did.

Throughout Saturday evening and Sunday the camp had many friendly visitors and one camper was interviewed on local radio. The camp finished at 17.00 hours on Sunday as planned.

On 19th February 1985, Jeremy Deacon was found guilty of criminal damage for crawling under the perimeter fence – yet Salisbury magistrates, in March 1985, found me not guilty of criminal damage for doing the same thing on Boscombe Down! I can only surmise that it was proved that he had actually done some criminal damage whilst crawling under the fence, which was not proved in my case. Jeremy was also found guilty of obstructing a policeman when on top of a MoD building in the stores depot. His fines and costs totalled £170. When confirming a transfer of fine order, Nottingham Magistrates in error sent him a letter intended for Leicester Magistrates. In this letter the section titled 'Relevant Information' said 'Defendant is a member of CND and does his utmost to attract publicity. He will force the court into a situation of committing him for non-payment if he gets the chance'. On being shown this NCCL expressed concern. [From Janey Hulme's 'Roll Call' in *New Statesman* 5th April 1985]

One feature of all the actions here has been the reluctance of the authorities to arrest and charge protesters. This has been evident, particularly on incursions at other bases but nowhere has the reluctance been so strong as at Chilwell. This may be due largely to three factors, the 'respectable' support for the campaign, which involved city and county councillors, the constant contacts with *Peace News* and the media maintained by demonstrators and a desire on the part of the MoD for minimum publicity for the American takeover. The more protesters that get arrested and charged the more go to court and the more publicity is got for the takeover and for the campaign against it. Publicity is valuable nonviolent ammunition for protesters.

A colour VHS video account of the preparation, organisation and actions on the 1st July 1984, Reclaim Chilwell mass trespass has recently been released. It lasts forty-two minutes and should prove a useful discussion starter for NVDA training. It can be either hired or bought from: Jerky Video Collective, 42 Foxhall Road, Forest Fields, Nottingham telephone 01602 784963.

As I write the campaign to get the US forces out of Chilwell continues.

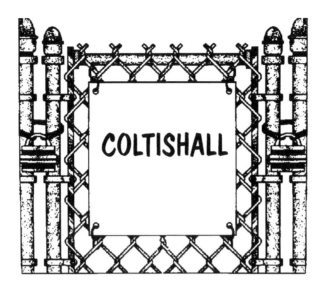

At the RAF airfield of Coltishall in Norfolk a peace camp was set up and was well reported in the local press. The camp is believed to have taken place sometime between June 1983 and October 1984. At the time of writing the author is trying to get more information about it and would be grateful for any information readers may have, especially the name and date of the newspaper that reported this camp.

RAF Tornado nuclear bombers were based at an airfield on very good agricultural land beside the village of Cottesmore in Rutland.

Because of this on 26th June 1983, a peace camp was set up here. Peace campers leafleted and talked with local people. Apparently there were no arrests. The camp was planned to stay for only one week and ended on 2nd July without being evicted. This was apparently the first protest here. Though it got little publicity the campers did manage to alert the local peace movement to RAF Cottesmore's existence and start a lively campaign against the base.

Subsequent NVDAs here produced much more publicity. West Midlands CND organised a demonstration on Friday, 16th December, 1983. This included a two and a half hour blockade, which turned back all traffic except for a health visitor. The blockade was followed by a carnival. Only one arrest was reported – that of a man charged with breach of the peace and obstructing the police. He was remanded in Welford Road Prison, Leicester, for six days. His eventual fate is not known.

Activists visited the airfield on 6th January 1984 and were stopped by police but were allowed to proceed when they said they were birdwatchers looking for dotterels. They were actually doing a reconnaissance for an NVDA planned for 2nd February. The six of them could not have done a perfect job because they failed to see a lake, which seriously delayed activists from Nottingham and Leicester, who in the early hours of 2nd February went in, climbed two navigation towers and brought all work on the airfield to a standstill. They believed that police had discovered their plan to enter the base and so at the briefing meeting on the eve of the NVDA it was decided to bring the action forward several hours in order to enter the airfield before the police expected them. In spite of delay caused by the lake, this tactic worked. When police eventually found the activists on the towers there were nasty threats, at least seven arrests, four charges of wilful obstruction of police officers and evidence taken for possible breach of the peace and criminal damage charges, which were later dropped. Two activists who refused to give their names were remanded in Welford Road Prison for three days. Two, who were arrested for stealing their own car, were later conditionally discharged and ordered to pay court costs of £20, while one was conditionally discharged with £40 costs.

Simultaneous to this action, 2,000 leaflets were given out in Leicester and Nottingham and the Army Recruiting Office in Leicester was occupied. National TV, national radio, four national and five international newspapers as well as the local media covered the tower occupation whilst the actions in the cities got slightly less publicity [*Peace News*, 17th February 1984 carried a detailed report].

Apparently Cottesmore was 'snowballed' for three arrests for fence cutting on 3rd September 1985 were reported.

Although Cottesmore remained a nuclear base it was subsequently forced out of the limelight by developments at Molesworth, the proposed East Anglian Cruise base less than forty miles away.

There is an interesting postscript. Leicester is the nearest city to Cottesmore and was on Thursday, 17th May, 1984, a NFZ. On that afternoon in broad daylight a convoy with Mammoth Major nuclear warhead carriers drove right across the city, getting held up alongside the commuters in the rush hour traffic. This convoy was travelling from North to South on A46 and did not visit RAF Cottesmore. Although Polaris-watchers trailed the convoy they were unable to stop it.

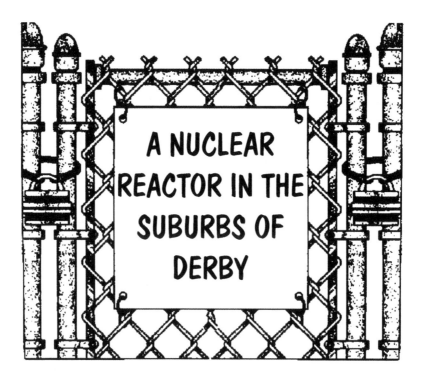

A NUCLEAR REACTOR IN THE SUBURBS OF DERBY

Until 1984 it was not widely known that a nuclear reactor existed in premises in Raynesway, a section of Derby Ring Road running through an industrial area. The offices and factory containing it belonged to Rolls Royce and Associates, part of the Rolls Royce Group. Companies in this group were contracted to make parts for the Trident nuclear submarines.

On Saturday, 21st July 1984, at 07.15 hours these offices were quietly entered by people from Derby NVDA Group, apparently by just walking through the door which was open for cleaners. Banners reading, 'BOMB FACTORY' and 'TRIDENT OR 500 HOSPITALS' were displayed on the roof about a hundred feet up by six people for four hours while others outside chained the entrances, and told folk what was happening. This also told about this firm's involvement with Trident and about the nuclear reactor. After attracting much attention from passers-by on the busy ring road and folk working in the other factories in the area, the six came down off the roof voluntarily. They had been photographed for at least one newspaper [*Peace News*, 10th August 1984, published the photograph and a report].

The local police arrested the activists and apparently charged them with blemish of the peace, under the Justices of the Peace Act 1361. A charge under the section dealing with blemish of the peace requires that the person charged be detained until the next sitting of magistrates and cannot be released on bail, as is usually done in breach of the peace cases. Thus the six were imprisoned for the weekend until the mag-

istrates released them on bail the following Monday. Apparently, people arrested under this section could only be bailed by a court.

The magistrates later bound over the six in sums of £50 and £75. David Davenport was the only person who refused to be bound over. He felt the law was being used to silence peaceful protest. On 9th January 1985, Derby Magistrates sent him to Leicester Gaol for three months. Apparently the offences these people committed were not classed as criminal, yet six people were quite legally detained to await release by a court and David, not being a criminal, was not allowed any remission for good conduct on his prison sentence.

As part of the campaign to draw attention to the work of Rolls Royce and Associates and the plight of the six activists on 17th December, five members of Derbyshire Women for Peace set up a peace camp on the grass verge outside the Raynesway offices. Several hours later after the press had photographed it, they were all arrested and charged with obstruction of the highway. Here police treated the verge as part of the highway as they did when closing Alconbury Peace Camp Mark II. [See 'Guided Tours of Alconbury and Farming at Molesworth' elsewhere in this book] Apparently the women were later all convicted.

The main reason for the authorities' paranoia over any activity at this factory must be the fact that the Rolls Royce Group are one of the two biggest employers in Derby and employ many other firms on sub-contract work. Money talks.

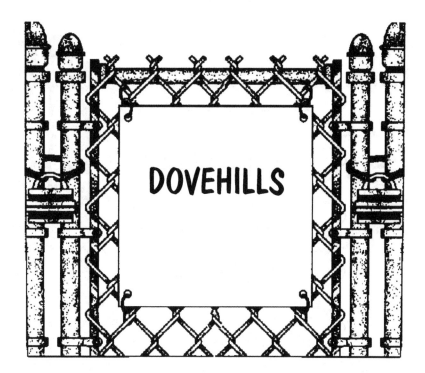

The Hawkhills is a large country house with a gate lodge and a long drive, one mile South of Easingwold on A19 to York on the Eastern side of the road. It is used by the government as the Home Defence College where Civil Defence or Civil Emergency officers are trained at residential and day courses. It appears that officers on courses at The Hawkhills are indoctrinated with right-wing MoD propaganda.

A peace camp was set up, operating at weekends only, on 23rd October 1983, at the front gate on the wide grass verge beside A19. This camp was named Dovehills Peace Camp, as a play on words. At the time belligerent politicians were being called 'hawks' and those advocating peace were being termed 'doves'. The countryside was flat and the 'hills' obviously came from the name of the college.

Special activities were planned at Dovehills in support of the big action at Greenham Common in December of that year. Many local women went to Greenham but the men and children stayed behind to organise supporting actions.

The first took place on Thursday, 8th December, when seventy people walked into The Hawkhills. They met and talked with College Principal George Harrison and several tutors before leaving without being arrested.

On 9th December, a three-mile long line of white crosses was set up to link Dovehills with the local council's Civil Defence bunker at New Parks, Shipton.

Dovehills peace campers took part in a 'Burn the Bomb' march and bonfire in York on Saturday 1st December.

On 11th December, three peace campers were arrested when they entered the grounds of the college and refused to leave.

After that the peace camp ceased its existence as The Hawkhills had become much better known publicly, which was a main reason for setting up the camp in the first place. Also it was not as important as the campaign on Cruise at Molesworth and Greenham to which the Dovehills peace campers were also committed.

Entrance to the Hawkhills looking North along A19: Peace camp site in right foreground.

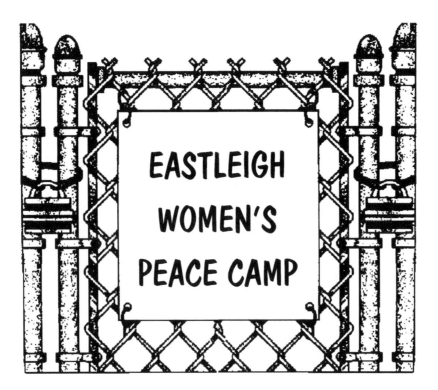

The main claim to fame of Eastleigh, Hampshire, is its large railway works but the fast trains between Southampton and London don't think it an important enough place to call in and pass through without stopping. One can drive right across Eastleigh on the dual carriageway without realising one is passing through a town. Greenham Common, Boscombe Down and Brambles Farm are all within thirty-five miles. In 1976, the author was involved when Eastleigh achieved a historic national 'first' and the first CND flagday was held here.

To commemorate International Women's Day for Disarmament on Tuesday, 24th May 1983, women from the recently formed Eastleigh Campaign Against Nuclear Weapons, some of whom had been involved with Greenham and Brambles Farm Peace Camps, held a peace camp on The Common in Leigh Road with a tent or two, straw bales and a table. This site was a good one, being slap in the town centre between the old Town Hall (now the Town Hall Centre) and Upper Market Street. The Borough Council gave permission for the camp to be there.

The campers gathered signatures from visitors and passersby for a petition to the Soviet Women's Peace Committee, which said that they wanted their children to grow up to be wise people free from fear of destruction by nuclear weapons and that they believed that Soviet women had similar desires. They took a strong stand against nuclear weapons.

The camp, which only lasted one day, issued a statement which, after saying the campers were women, said:

> We are half the World's population. If we make our stand for ordinary human values and sanity we really can change things. The arguments politicians use to increase their spending on arms have a logic but where does it lead? It is terminal logic. It doesn't change our common sense knowledge that the arms race is madness.

The women returned to the town centre on Wednesday, 25th May, to join local disarmers for a silent vigil of protest at the Old Town Hall when it was visited by Her Majesty's Secretary of State for Defence, Michael Heseltine.

The peace camp received local publicity. Throughout both actions there was no NVDA and there were no arrests. The actions were good for morale and got many local people to think about disarmament.

In June 1950 the USAF moved into the RAF airfield about a mile south of the village of Fairford in the South East corner of Gloucestershire. Its main runway was about 4,000 yards long and this was adequate for their B47 and B52 bombers. After thirteen years inter-continental missiles were replacing some of their long range bombers and they didn't need so many airfields in the UK, so they left and the RAF returned.

On 23rd March 1975, Her Majesty's Under-Secretary of State for Defence, Brynmor John, assured every-one that though RAF Fairford would continue as a relief landing ground, there were no plans to make it into an active airfield or expand it. Three and a half years later Her Majesty's Secretary of State for Defence, Fred Mulley, reversed this by announcing that the USAF KC135 Stratotankers that had been rejected from Greenham would be stationed at Fair-ford. On 5th February 1979, the details were spelled out: 1,100 USAF personnel and about 1,700 depend-ents coming to live in the area, a £20,000,000 cash injection to pay for construction work on the airfield which would employ about 300 local people and many airfield buildings which lay derelict and de-serted would be put back into use.

On hearing this local people were not slow in bring-ing up environmental issues, starting with possible effects on the Cotswold Water Park. On 1st June the Commanding Officer of Fairford Rex Sullivan said the USAF would monitor Cotswold Water Park for effects. On 4th June the villagers of South Cerney and Down Ampney under the Airfield's western flight

path were told that if they received over 110 decibels of noise they should qualify for noise insulation.

On 19th June further details of the development were released. The USAF would require 108 new married quarters and bachelor quarters for 300 men as well as other new housing for ancillary staff in Oxford-shire and Gloucestershire. Many local builders were delighted.

The Secretary of State for Defence realised he would have to handle local opposition carefully. He set up a local RAF liaison committee under Lady Agnes Humphrey, the widow of a former Chief of the Defence Staff on 4th July. Lady Humphrey was to appoint the other members. Straight away the min-ister found himself in dispute with local Councillors Martin Harwood and Philip Beckerlegge. His idea of a local resident was not theirs. Lady Humphrey lived only twenty-five miles (forty kilometers) from Fairford, England, and people who lived there did not consider her as local. The organisers were not active in the Fairford area. Also they felt there was no guarantee of any truly local people getting onto her committee.

The first Stratotanker arrived on 12th September 1979, and ten days later the USAF officially took over the airfield. The MoD was still acting as land-lords, of course.

In November there was a rumour of surface to air missiles being based at Fairford. A farmer who leased some land including an old bomb dump from the MoD suddenly found his lease cut short. Was this to make a missile testing range?

On 7th February 1980, one of the USAF's biggest aircraft, a C5A, delivered one of their biggest wheeled trucks. It was a fire engine. Airfield fire engines have to be fast, powerful and capable of delivering quickly vast quantities of whatever is needed to fight a fire. As a rule, it is vital that any aircraft fire be got under control within two minutes otherwise the aircraft could be lost. A fire with a Stratotanker on Fairford would be a far worse nightmare than a fire on a civil jet on a commercial airport. As at Greenham one of the fears of local people was of a KC135 crashing and setting fire to a wood or village. Then they were reminded of another fire risk on 5th March, when a petrol tanker crashed into a field and the road running outside the airfield fence was closed for eight hours, while the fire brigade and a breakdown crew recovered the petrol tanker.

Whelford villagers were complaining about noise and smells from the airfield and Parish Councillor Clem Wakefield acted as their spokesman when they presented a petition of 100 signatures on 25th February. This petition appeared to have some effect as on 5th March the USAF announced they would install blast deflectors to curb the noise of the Stratotankers on the ground and said that from 1982 they would be fitting new quieter engines in them. This did not stop the noise problem from growing. Alan Hughes, Environmental Health Officer, reported to Cotswold District Council that 248 houses in Whelford, Marston Meysey, Down Ampney and on the edge of Fairford Village were subject to excessive noise. At the council meeting Chairman Joe Clark spoke out against the noise and the council agreed to tell the MoD it expected them to keep their promise to pay for sound insulation for houses that received over 110 decibels of noise.

On 25th March the USAF took over fifty-three more houses in the area for its personnel.

On 1st June, three B52 bombers arrived on a six-day visit. These aircraft could carry thermonuclear bombs and air launched Cruise missiles. On the very next day, South Cerney Parish Councillor John George asked the USAF if Cruise missiles were coming to Fairford. They said no. A small picket against the B52s took place at the Main Gate on Horcott Hill on Monday, 16th June.

Then on 25th June ambulances raced through villages near the airfield with sirens wailing. Ellen Wakefield, a worried Whelford villager, phoned the USAF at the airfield for information about this. On asking to speak to an officer she was told, "You cannot speak to an officer. There is an emergency." Actually all that was happening was a mock accident exercise.

A girl was raped outside the Officers Mess on 2nd September. Investigations were handed over to the

R.A.F. FAIRFORD

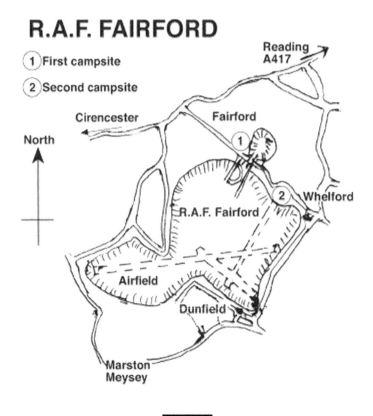

① First campsite
② Second campsite

Americans by Cirencester Police who were well aware that American servicemen on duty who raped girls in this country were only subject to English law if the US authorities handed them over to our government, which they need not do.

The USAF Commanding Officer of Fairford, Colonel William Brown, addressed a dinner of Gloucestershire builders on 4th December. He told them there were eighty construction projects at Fairford just waiting for official approval to spend the money. He admitted that the airfield was a potential target for any enemy, adding that all runways of 10,000 feet and over like Fairford's would be a target. Obviously our American guest had not been long in Britain and had been wrongly informed, because he then said there were only six of that length in Britain. He was wrong. There were over a dozen that long and longer marked on Ordnance Survey maps available to the public.

On 8th December the USAF took over 300 married quarters at RAF Little Rissington for the use of Fairford personnel.

On 31st January, 1981, complaints from Whelford villagers about the large USAF trucks driving through the village on their way to and from M4 prompted the reply,

> We cannot guarantee anything but we will look into the possibility of keeping the big ones off the road by using the smaller trucks.

On 19th February one of Colonel Brown's construction projects got in the news when the USAF and the MoD announced they were going to build a leisure centre on the airfield for the personnel and their dependents. Local people took notice when it was said planning permission was not required.

An appeal for rate reductions because of annoyance generated by RAF Fairford was launched by thirty-four residents of Kempsford, Bunfield and Whelford on 6th January and the valuation court heard it on 26th March. The villagers were represented by Councillor Philip Beckerlegge. Some lost their fight but others got a ten per cent reduction. They had asked for reductions ranging from seventeen to twenty per cent.

On 27th March the MoD after all its promises announced it would give no money for noise insulation in the village homes because the laws on sound-proofing under which it would have been paid only related to new public works and had no provision for existing private houses. The USAF aggravated this wound when just six weeks later on 6th April their Stratotankers flew no less than eighteen missions in

one day as part of an exercise called 'Cloudy Chorus'.

About 75,000 people attended the 1981 Fairford Air Show on 16th August.

On 20th October three more B52s arrived, unarmed, for a three-week stay.

Cotswold District Council officials made noise checks around the outside of the airfield perimeter on 29th October and reported back to the subsequent council meeting. On 5th December the USAF admitted it was behind schedule in replacing noisy generators in the aircraft parking bays with quieter ones and Alan Hughes asked for more pressure to be put on them to get the work done quickly. He again asked for more pressure a few days later, this time though it was to be applied to the MoD to get them to reverse their decision not to provide sound insulation for the villagers' houses. They didn't reverse it.

Meanwhile some Bristol CND members on their way home from the CND National Conference stopped at Greenham Common Peace Camp and stayed there awhile. They thought about setting up a peace camp in their own area and RAF Fairford a few miles North of M4 between Greenham Common and Bristol seemed the obvious choice. Bristol CND members then surveyed Fairford and found at least two possible campsites. It was decided to go ahead and secret planning began. Every detail was meticulously worked out even down to who would go in which vehicle to Fairford. They planned to meet up on A429 at RAF Kemble and from there travel in two separate unmarked convoys to Fairford. The layby where the campers met up may well have put the idea of Kemble Peace Camp in someone's mind, because it was later the site of Kemble Peace Camp which was set up after the local police were informed. They planned to run Fairford on a rota basis so there would be plenty of people to keep it alive and all the hard work would not fall upon the usual overworked few.

D-Day Saturday, 6th February 1982, arrived and the invasion went like clockwork. The non-violent invaders established a bridgehead just across Whelford Road from the main entrance to RAF Fairford. They were on MoD land, which they almost certainly would not have been allowed to occupy if they had announced their intentions in advance. About twenty people from Stroud and Bristol took part in this successful operation.

The weekend at the camp was enlivened by the European Theatre of War from Groundwell Farm near Swindon performing street theatre in which some parts involved wearing military uniforms. They had everyone including USAF personnel and police in stitches of laughter. This company gave tremendous support to Fairford Peace Camp throughout the camp's existence.

The camp got publicity from the start. On Monday, 8th February, a Cotswold District Council official told the *Swindon Evening Advertiser* that the council would only get involved with the camp if it became a public health risk. 'If there is no proper sanitation our director of environmental health would start to take an interest.'

By the end of the week the MoD had evicted the camp and campers had moved about half a mile down the road towards Whelford to a piece of county council land. The council had been given rights over this land in 1956 so that a dangerous bend in the road could be straightened. After twenty-six years the council had not yet got round to straightening the road so the land was still vacant. This plot had been the second choice of the campsite hunting survey. Their first site had been ideal from a publicity point of view and had been helpful in getting good publicity when the camp started, but as a site for a permanent peace camp it may have had drawbacks. At any rate campers did not seem to mind the move.

On 14th February the new campsite hosted a meeting of the camp's support group who reviewed the first week of operation and the rota and decided to continue.

In a local hall they hired on 16th February, peace campers gave a public filmshow with a film called *The Bomb*.

Peace campers claimed nuclear weapons were kept at Fairford. Russell Johnson, Liberal Party Parliamentary Defence Spokesman, took up the issue and asked the MoD if they were. The MoD answer was apparently noncommittal because the whole subject was covered by the official secrets acts.

At about this time camper Peter Ford made Mr Red Tape, a nicely sculptured scarecrow. People calling at the camp and asking who was in charge were told he was. Titles such as 'Our Leader' and 'Chairman' were bestowed upon him. His 'Vice-Chairman' was Trev's eighteen-month-old son Dan.

Campers also set up the Alternative War Research Establishment, which was a real means of researching and teaching alternative methods of resolving conflicts – alternatives to violence that is. The initials AWRE were chosen deliberately as a sort of skit upon the other AWRE in Berkshire, which did much the same job with atomic weapons. AWRE Fairford even had its own headed notepaper using the peace campsite as an address!

At 20.00 hours on Friday, 19th March, the AWRE held a weekend school for campers and supporters at the camp. It included such subjects as 'How did we get here?', responses to problems, public speaking, strategy, effectively working in groups, yoga, alternative defence, resistance to persuasion and responses to aggression. The school finished at 18.00 hours on Sunday.

The weekend school used the secondhand marquee, which camp supporters had bought with £200 from camp funds. This marquee later was erected on the Thirty Acre Site at Upper Heyford. In addition to the marquee there were several smaller tents, two caravans, a loo and a vegetable garden at Fairford. The loo was a primitive unisex affair.

From the outset the camp had been getting frequent shouts of abuse especially around pub chucking-out time in the evenings and placards placed by campers along the perimeter fence were being smashed. Around May this campaign was accelerated when a letter threatening the camp was published in a local paper and threats were shouted by someone using a loudhailer from a passing car. Then the British National Party announced they were going to hold a rally beside the peace camp.

On 7th June Fairford Peace Campers went to the CND rally in London touring the embassies of the nuclear powers and the Defence Sales Office. They erected their own peace camp banner in Hyde Park and put up their own poster exhibition there. They issued a press release about their visit to London, which cunningly used pictures of posters to get the message across.

Campers were thinking of leaving but a leaflet published by the British National Party entitled 13th June D-Day, which called on people to protest by supporting the demonstration against 'the CND traitors', made them decide to stay until after the rally. The peace camp produced its own leaflet, telling people how to remain calm and non violent and decided to play it low key and stay on their own site during the rally, which was to be held on another part of the vacant county council land beside the peace camp.

The first thing that happened on Saturday, 13th June, was the arrival of a coach load of Quakers from all over Gloucestershire, several of whom had been involved in the peace camp. They took over the marquee and held a meeting for worship in it. More vehicles arrived. Then an Anglican vicar walked into the marquee and held an Anglican service. The next turn was that of a Roman Catholic priest. By now about 100 supporters had assembled. Campers were surprised. They had expected a few visitors but not all these and certainly not a coach! The Nationalists and Young Conservatives marched past and went onto the grass just beyond the peace camp. They assembled around a man on a soapbox. There were only about twenty of them listening to his speech. The police surrounded the peace camp and kept their beady eyes on the Nationalists and Young Conservatives in case of trouble but after the rally they left quietly. To the relief of some very worried people at the camp the whole day had passed off peacefully.

On Tuesday 22nd June Peter Baker and Ken Cole passed through Fairford on their sponsored hitch round the peace camps. They particularly noticed that Fairford Peace Camp was very tidy with neat gardens.

The camp closed on 27th June. The main reason was given in a leaflet published by the camp and distributed throughout six local villages:

ANOTHER ACRE OF LAND FOR THE US AIR FORCE?

On July 20th Gloucestershire County Council will apply to magistrates to extinguish their rights over a piece of land on the Whelford Road outside RAF Fairford. As a consequence the land will be entirely controlled by the Ministry of Defence and will be fenced in as part of the US Air Force Base.

PEACE CAMP SITE

The land in question is the site of the Fairford Peace Camp. While the Peace Campers have never denied access to anyone, including the British National Party, Ministry of Defence now intends to fence it in.

COUNTY COUNCIL WASHES ITS HANDS

In making this move the council is both washing its hands of the responsibility for dealing with the Peace Camp and its responsibility for road safety. It was originally given rights over the land in 1956 to straighten out the dangerous bend in the road. Twenty-six years later the bend remains and the council is handing over another acre of Cotswold countryside to the US Air Force.

YOU COULD STOP THE COUNCIL MOVE

You could write now to object to this move and prevent the further encroachment of the US Air Force into this area. Write to: Mr Witherspoon, Chief Clerk, Gloucestershire County Council, Shire Hall, Gloucester or to your County Councillor.

WE CAME IN PEACE AND WE WILL GO IN PEACE

In coming here in the first place we wanted to show our opposition to militarism and our belief in nonviolence. We feel it would be a sad result of our actions if this land was to become part of the base and part of the American military presence in this country. The move to enclose the land has obviously been prompted by the presence of the Peace Camp so we intend to leave on June 27 so that this excuse no longer exists.

FIVE MONTHS AT FAIRFORD

For five months the peace campers have maintained a presence outsite RAF Fairford. During this time there have been vigils, demonstrations, theatre events, meetings and celebrations on the camp. They have created a flourishing garden and planted trees on the site, which will remain for everyone's enjoyment.

Fairford Peace Camp probably had the best relations with its civilian neighbours of any of the British Peace camps, with the exception of the anti-nuclear power camp at Luxulyan. [See my account of Luxulyan's camp 'Victory at Luxulyan' elsewhere in this book] Unlike most, they asked to pay rates but Cotswold District Council turned down their offer. This council agreed to collect the camp rubbish and in return for this service was persuaded to accept a donation of £40 to cover costs. There appears to have been neither fence cutting nor incursions nor blockades nor arrests during the period of this camp.

Fairford Peace Camp's last act before closing was a tea party. The leaflets that were distributed in the villages in the area contained an invitation to tea at the camp on the afternoon of 27th June that was open to all.

The campers didn't stop campaigning when their camp closed. Already they had been active in London and at RAF Welford in Berkshire [See my account 'Artists and Greenham Women at RAF Welford']. On 25th July some returned to picket RAF Fairford's open day. People Against Militarism (PAM) grew out of the Fairford camp and was active for about two years after it closed. Probably their most famous action took place when four of the PAM chained themselves to railings at the Czech Embassy in London.

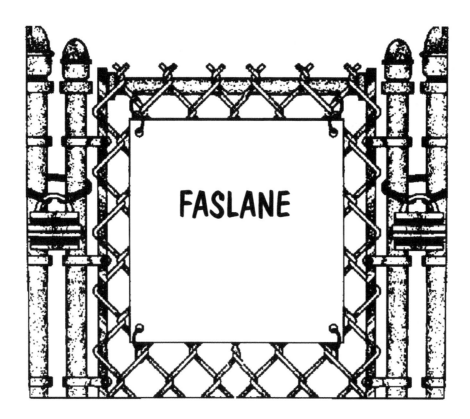

MONSTERS IN THE GARELOCH (1960 - May 1982)

In 1960 with the consent of the British Government, the United States Government set up a nuclear submarine base in Holy Loch. Shortly after this, the British Government set up a store for nuclear weapons and supplies at Coulport, a few miles away on Loch Long and upgraded its own World War II submarine base in Faslane Bay, on the Gareloch, by building new, and improving old facilities, so that Faslane could handle nuclear-powered submarines. All these facilities were constructed in lochs on the North side of the Clyde, North West of Glasgow. They were all within thirty miles by boat from the centre of Scotland's biggest city. Outside the US and the USSR they constituted the biggest complex of nuclear submarine bases in the world.

The nuclear warheads for the British Polaris submarine-launched ballistic missiles were to be built and serviced at the Royal Ordnance Factory, Burghfield, Berkshire. The missiles themselves were American. The monsters that were to carry the Polaris missiles and be based in the Gareloch were to be built at Camel Laird's shipyard in Birkenhead and Vickers at Barrow-in-Furness. Albert Booth, Labour MP for Barrow, to his eternal credit, joined demonstrators outside rather than go inside to the official launching of one of these submarines, which were being built to the order of a Labour Secretary of State for Defence. Albert was one of the CND's original sponsors.

Although the first sub – *HMS Resolution* – was said to have cost £42,242,000 [Sanity', May 1968: 'In His Concrete Box'] the later ones cost more. At one stage the average figure for the cost of each sub was said to be around £70,000,000 – more than three and a half times the cost of the magnificent *Queen Elizabeth II* liner then being built twenty miles from Faslane at Clydebank. Vickers themselves could build a 100,000 ton tanker for around £5,000,000, which represented £50 per ton. With a Polaris Submarine weighing in at 7,000 tons it represented a cost per ton not far off £10,000! [*Sanity*, November 1967: figures from 'Polaris – the threat to jobs' by Albert Booth MP] Originally the submarines carried sixteen missiles each and each missile had one 800 kiloton warhead but these were soon replaced by Polaris A3 missiles each with three warheads of 200 kilotons and later these were in turn replaced by Chevaline missiles.

The Admiralty claimed the construction of *Resolution, Renown, Revenge* and *Repulse* was "the largest single undertaking this country has ever attempted within a given time scale" and "one submarine's firepower will be greater than all the bombs dropped by both sides during the Second World War, including Hiroshima and Nagasaki" [*Sanity*, November 1967 p. 2].

Originally it had been planned to build five subs but one was cancelled as a result of Labour taking the reins of government from the Conservatives at a British general election, so only four were actually built. Maintenance and repair facilities were built on farmland beside the existing submarine base at Faslane Bay and assistance with maintenance and repairs was provided by Royal Naval Dockyard, Rosyth, on the Firth of Forth. The crews were trained mainly at *HMS Dolphin*, Gosport, which meant good business for British Railways (as they were then) moving sailors between Gosport and Helensburgh/Faslane on rail warrants.

The first monster fresh from her fitting-out berth crept stealthily through the Rhu Narrows in 1967 as Lieutenant Commander Kenneth Frewer sailed *HMS Resolution* up to Faslane. She left for her first patrol in the chamois-leather-gloved hands of Lieutenant Commander Frewer with her full complement of 130 ratings and thirteen officers in May 1968.

CND continued to campaign against the Polaris subs and by 1972 feelings were running high in Scotland about them. Many Scots wanted rid of not just the British Polaris fleet but the US nuclear subs in Holy Loch as well, so a big event was planned for Easter 1973. This was to take the form of a series of linked demonstrations at seven nuclear bases in Scotland. The main feature was to be a vigil at each base with vigillers and visitors signing a register. CND organised a train up from London so that visitors from the South could get to Faslane.

The seven vigils ran concurrently at Coulport, Edzell, Faslane, Glen Douglas, Holy Loch, Machrichanish and Rosyth.

Coulport on Loch Long is about fifty miles from Glasgow by road or nearer if you go by boat down the Clyde. It had its own dock with warehouses for weapons and supplies in 1973 but has since been extended to accommodate Trident missiles and the much larger subs needed to carry them. In 1973 the Polaris subs used to call there to arm themselves before going on patrol and to disarm on return.

Edzell is in Eastern Scotland near the North Esk River and the town of Brechin. It was a very low frequency radio transmitter station. Its aerial occupied the runway of what was once a RAF airfield. Through the aerial Edzell communicated with submarines submerged at sea.

There were US Navy personnel on the base.

At Faslane Bay on the eastern side of the Gareloch about six miles North of Helensburgh lies the home base of the British nuclear submarine fleet. Owing to the narrow entrance to the loch at Rhu Narrows, it is virtually inaccessible to enemy vessels and easy

to guard at this point. The surrounding mountains shelter it from very high winds and make if difficult for enemy bombers, missiles and radar to get at Faslane (and make the Gareloch an extremely beautiful setting for an establishment that looks really ugly). The base is thus a natural marine fortress, hence its choice many years before as a submarine base.

The fourth base was Glen Douglas, which lies in the mountains between Loch Long and Loch Lomond, accessible by public single-track road from either loch or by a military road from Glenmallon Jetty on Loch Long where the ammunition ships berthed. Trains use rail sidings within the base. There are probably nuclear weapons stored here as the base was built as a rear store for NATO for all sorts of arms and ammunition with deep bunkers inside the mountains.

Holy Loch, the next loch down the Clyde from Loch Long, contained the USN submarine base, which consisted of a depot ship, a floating drydock (both anchored offshore), a jetty and offices onshore at Sandbank.

Machrichanish was a World War II airfield used by civil and military aircraft in 1973. It was also used as a weapons store, troops reinforcement airfield and standby airfield for nuclear bombers.

Rosyth Royal Naval Dockyard across the Firth of Forth from Edinburgh was the last base for a vigil. This dockyard was equipped for fitting out and refitting nuclear submarines. There was some grumbling among the workers there when special rates of pay were given to people working on the nuclear subs. Many of these were Transport and General Workers Union members. Rosyth has all sort of engineering facilities installed regardless of cost. I found this out when later in 1973 I helped to move an engine testing brake capable of testing engines up to 20,000 horsepower from Rosyth to Portsmouth for Mr Pound, the Portsmouth war surplus dealer (who, incidentally, does a nice line in used submarines). The heaviest section of this machine weighed seventy-five tons.

I read of these demonstrations being planned and decided to ride up to them and visit as many vigils as possible on my AJS motorcycle, which was then being rebuilt. I have always been keen to see CND out demonstrating at the bases and looked forward to joining these demos in Scotland.

On Maundy Thursday I hurried to my parents' house in Leicestershire after work and set about completing the rebuild and preparation of my AJS for the tour of the bases. At times like this one finds many more things have to be done than one expects and after Friday's exertions I did not get to bed until 04.00 hours on Saturday which meant I did not get up until late. Loading began. Onto the carrier of the bike went my tent and my toolbox, which contained just about every tool I was likely to need to fix the bike including a big hammer. This toolbox, a war surplus grenade box, weighed about half a hundredweight full and if left unattended could easily start a bomb scare. With this lot on the carrier the bike was somewhat top heavy. It was almost impossible to lift it onto the centre stand and the sidestand was useless with this load. Unwisely, I packed the light items in a rucksack which went on my back and put a strain on it. Bang had gone my dreams of an early start; it was 12.15 when I headed North.

Up over Carter Bar on A68 I was dodging between snow showers and it was bitterly cold. I saw a petrol station with an 'open' sign. I pulled up by one of the pumps and I was so numb with the cold that I was unable to prevent the AJS from falling over. After a struggle to pick up the heavily laden 650cc twin and put it on its stand, I found the pumps locked and nobody on the premises. I concluded that this petrol station, contrary to the information given on its sign, was in fact closed. I made a mental note never to call there again even when it really was open and rode on to Jedburgh where I fuelled up and found some food.

I arrived in Edinburgh at 22.15 hours and decided to celebrate my arrival in Scotland's capital with a quick pint of ale in a nice warm pub. I waited for a group of men to come out of a friendly looking alehouse before entering and one spoke to me, "It's closed." "What time do they close here?" "Ten o'clock."

If there is anything more annoying than dropping one's newly painted motorcycle because a brainless idiot puts up a sign saying a petrol station is open when is is not, it is finding a city where all the pubs have just closed.

The first bit of luck that day was finding solo motorcycles crossed the Forth Toll Bridge free (this was still true in 1986). I was beginning to cheer up, thinking of tents, a campfire, folk singing and maybe even a mouthful of someone's beer at Rosyth vigil.

On the far side of an enormous car park loomed the gates of the Royal Naval Dockyard like US turnpike gates. As it was nearing midnight they were closed and there was no traffic, nor was a vigil to be seen anywhere. After searching the area in vain I unrolled my sleeping bag in a bus shelter and slept like a log.

In the morning it was raining. I again went to the dockyard gates and again saw no sign of a vigil. It was no good asking the modplods on guard for if they gave me any information it would almost certainly be misleading. Faslane seemed the most likely place to find a vigil so I rode the seventy miles to Faslane.

There I found a vigil and asked, "What happened to the 'Rosyth vigil last night?" "Oh we were all at a party in Clydebank."

I had suffered a dropped bike, a closed petrol station, closed pubs and now I had just missed a party! Despair and disgruntlement grew to immense proportions.

I erected my tent on the beach just above the high water mark near the others. There seemed to be a very small rise and fall in the tide here, another factor in favour of Faslane Bay as a submarine base. Sunshine had replaced the rain and the tree-edged beach was beautiful and peaceful that Easter Sunday morning.

Soon an old Ford arrived carrying a gang of lads who had come up from Leicester. Some but not all of them were acquainted with Leicester CND. Some were in favour of nuclear disarmament; some were against it but they all wanted to know more about it and debate it. They joined the group on the beach and a tremendous debate ensued.

I left my tent on the beach and once again headed the AJS Northwards. I rode through the pretty village of Garelochhead and onto the pass with its spectacular view down the Gareloch. I descended back to near sea level alongside Loch Long and then turned right up the public road, which steeply climbed the moun-

Faslane 1973 Peace Camp behind the white post in the distance

tain to Glen Douglas. I signed the vigil clipboard at the entrance to the base and then rode back to Gare-lochead and over the Peaton Hill to Coulport. After signing that clipboard near where operations were going on to extend the facilities at the base, I returned to Faslane. We had a marvellous evening around the campfire there, after which the group from the old Ford split because all were not yet convinced of the importance of nuclear disarmament. Some camped with us, while the pro-bomb lads slept in the car. We were all full of friendship and tolerance.

On Easter Saturday morning over 300 English people had arrived in Glasgow Central Station aboard the special train CND had chartered from London. At lunchtime they and Scottish disarmers met for a rally in Glasgow with Jimmy Reid and David Boulton (prominent Scottish union leaders), Bruce Kent and Dr John Cox (of CND), Councillor Olive Gibbs (of Oxford) and Councillor Geoff Shaw (of Glasgow) among the speakers. They then marched to Clyde-bank, where they stopped the night and enjoyed the party I had missed! There were about five councillors from Glasgow alone on the march that day. On Sunday the march continued to Faslane and at about 17.00 hours arrived at the South Gate where speeches were made, a letter was handed in and Bruce Kent exorcised the evil from the base. The exorcism got excellent publicity in the Scottish media.

Later on Sunday evening the London people returned home and on Monday morning I broke camp, while the old Ford, after a push start, headed North on a search for the Loch Ness Monster. Not long after I left the vigil ended at Faslane. Thus the first Faslane Peace Camp, which started up on the morning of Good Friday, 20th April 1973, finished on Easter Monday, 1973.

The campaign against the Polaris subs continued with a big march and rally with crowds of English people in Glasgow in 1974. This was followed by an arms conversion conference in March 1975. One of the socially useful alternatives which was discussed and on which considerable research was done, was converting Faslane into a dockyard for building and repairing submersible marine oil drilling platforms. In May 1975 another big march and rally in Glasgow was followed by a visit to Faslane.

On 21st July 1978, in pursuit of a pay claim, MoD workers blocked all work on nuclear subs. At Coulport missiles could not be loaded onto *Revenge* for her patrol; *Repulse,* which had just finished a twenty-month refit at Rosyth could not go on sea trials and

Renown's refit at Rosyth was delayed. Then on 25th July Labour Defence Minister Fred Mulley ordered the Navy to load *Revenge* themselves and she went on patrol. This led to a twenty-four-hour strike in support of the pay claim and during this *Resolution* returned from patrol on 2nd August. Work on *Resolution* was blacked two days later. Eventually 200 workers were suspended and the industrial action came to an end.

The march from Aldermaston to Faslane in 1979 included survivors from the atom bombing of Hiroshima and two Buddhist monks from Japan Buddha Sanga when it arrived at the South Gate of Faslane. This march took seven weeks from 16th April until its arrival on 2nd June with 1,000 marchers. Marchers and hibakusha (victims of the atom bombing) laid a wreath for those who had died as a result of the atom bombing of Hiroshima and Nagasaki at the gate. Keith Bovey, Bruce Kent and the Leader of the Labour Group on Strathclyde Council made speeches to the base workers and disarmers. The day of action and the disarmament conference in Glasgow, both on 4th June 1981, led up to the 'March for the Future' when Bruce Kent handed in a letter and a leaflet to the authorities at the base on the morning of Saturday, 6th June. About 6,000 people then marched from Faslane to Clydebank where as usual there was great hospitality. On Sunday the march ended at a rally in Kelvingrove Park, Glasgow with many important speakers and about 20,000 ordinary folk.

On 8th July 1981, Strathclyde Regional Council passed the motion 'That this council opposes the atomic missile base at Coulport and demands the removal of all atomic weapons and bases in Strath-clyde and Scotland'. [Quoted from *Faslane, Diary of a Peace Camp* written by the campers and published by Polygon Books.] Because the MoD were making sneaky approaches to local farmers to try to buy land piecemeal and were not revealing the extent of the area they required for expansion to accommodate Trident missile stores at Coulport, Strathclyde Council passed yet another nice motion in September 1981 opposing the MoD's acquisition of extra land at Coulport. At the time of writing Strathclyde is not only a NFZ but also the council has affilliated to CND.

The Scottish Campaign Against Trident was formed in September 1981 to fight the British Government's plan to replace the existing Polaris subs with much bigger Trident nuclear armed and powered submarines. This was an organisation to which other groups and organisations could join and which would help collate facts and coordinate campaigning. It later changed its name to the Anti-Trident Campaign.

The planned new nuclear powered and armed submarines displaced 16,000 tons each, more than twice that of the Polaris subs. Trident missiles were to be fitted with a battery of twenty-four to each submarine. The Trident missiles were bigger than the Polaris, had more warheads and a greater range, about 6,000 miles. At this time the British Government was wondering how it could raise the money to build these new subs and to construct the new onshore facilities for handling them and their weapons. The Polaris weapons stores would be inadequate and a whole new range of ship-repair facilities and berths would be required at Faslane, among other things.

PERMANENT PEACE CAMPS BEGIN AT FASLANE
(June 1982 - May 1984)

On the morning of 12th June 1982, Les and Louise Robertson, Bobby and Margaret Harrison and ten other people erected two tents on a site beside the Faslane Base. These four campaigners in particular devoted their lives to making this peace camp work.

At midday, modplods appeared and told them they would have to remove the camp as it was on MoD land. They told the campers that Strathclyde District Council would not evict them immediately if they camped on a piece of land in front of St Andrews School beside A814 where the road leading to the South gate turned off the main road. This land was apparently earmarked for possible dualling of the main road some time in the future and was at this time wasteland.

Faslane Peace Camp Mark II was taken down. Soon after it was again erected, this time as Faslane Peace Camp Mark III on the land in front of St Andrews School owned by Strathclyde Regional Council. The campers had moved about 500 yards. About six people completed the first week on the new campsite.

The campers had twenty-eight days' grace in which to apply for planning permission for the camp. As soon as they had settled in they sent their application to Dumbarton District Council, their planning authority, so that there would be no evictions, fines or prison sentences for breach of planning laws. The landowners, Strathclyde Council, had given them permission to stay there but could not give planning permission.

Right from the start campers worked on establishing friendly relations with everyone in the base. They would go down to the gates and vigil as workers arrived in the morning and wave to them and greet them as the day shift went in and the night shift came out. There would always be friendly greetings for sailors or workers passing the camp and in the evenings campers would often walk back to the base with sailors returning from the pub. This policy was to pay big dividends in the future.

By end of June numbers at the camp had risen. The campers were getting more confident and were arranging their first big event, which was to be the Peace Camp Open Day on Hiroshima Day, 6th August. Jimmy Reid, the leading Scottish trade unionist, was among the guests who spoke at the meeting that day along with a survivor of the Nagasaki A-bomb who planted a cherry tree, which sadly was uprooted a few days later by the MoD. Some campers held a twenty-four hour fast to commemorate Hiroshima Day. A dividend from the policy of maintaining good relations with everyone on the base came in the form of a donation given to the camp on the open day.

On 8th August the peace camp celebrated International Peace Day.

In a surprise action immediately after the Greenham eviction of 29th September, twelve campers sat down in front of the main South Gate of Faslane and blockaded it. Nobody got through and the traffic jam stretched for four miles down A814. After half an hour the campers got up and left. There were no arrests.

Chevaline had now replaced the Polaris A3 missile as the standard armament on the nuclear armed submarines. This was

Part of Faslane Mark III Below St Andrews School

a new type of missile, with greater range and firepower. It took a decade to develop, mostly in secret, and its development cost the British taxpayer a cool £1,100,000,000. Chevaline was expected to stay in service until replaced by Trident after about ten years.

Dumbarton District Council granted the peace camp a caravan site licence, originally for two years. The licence was granted on condition that the camp was brought up to commercial caravan site standard by June 1983 with a fence at the front, fire safety equipment, refuse disposal facilities, running water, toilets, etc.

A new Commanding Officer was posted to the base in November 1982. Campers baked him a cake and went to the main gate to give it to him and welcome him to Faslane. Their request to meet the commander was refused so they sat in the road. Police asked them to move. They moved and said they would return next day. When they returned their request was again refused. Then six campers sat down in the road and were once again asked to move. This time they stayed. Still the commander did not appear. The campers were arrested, charged with breach of the peace and released on bail. They were finally sentenced in May 1983.

On 12th December the base was again blockaded in sympathy with the big blockade at Greenham Common that day. All three gates were blockaded and fourteen or fifteen people were arrested, charged with breach of the peace and released on bail late at night. All pleaded not guilty so the Sheriff's Court at Dumbarton did not deal with their cases until June 1983.

On Martin Luther King's birthday, 15th January, the fence was crossed for the first time in inclement, squally weather when campers climbed over the fence and spent six hours in a gun turret. This was planned as a surprise action. Campers managed to get TV people and press photographers along to see the action without alarming the authorities unduly or disclosing the details of their plan. There was a last minute hitch at the peace camp when the ladder they were to use was found to be too long to fit inside the van, so when they set off for the fence in a convoy of assorted vehicles the ladder was poking out of the van window for all to see. Upon arrival at the fence, seventeen people quickly climbed over. By then sufficient police had arrived to prevent their supplies from being passed over to them. A number of ruses were tried to divert the police and one involving another attempt to climb the fence 200 yards away succeeded enough for warm clothing to be passed over

the fence, although it appears that police and Royal Navy personnel still managed to prevent tea flasks and food from getting over to the people inside the fence. The MoD announced that they would wait for the campers to give up in the gun turret which they had occupied but after six hours they gave up waiting and started removing sandbags to get at the people inside the turret. Campers watching outside cheered. The seventeen 'peace gunners' were arrested, charged under the Faslane bylaws and subsequently convicted. The three of them who refused to pay fines were sent to prison for fourteen days.

On Sunday, 6th March 1983, well over 1,000 – probably over 2,000 – women took part in the Scottish Women's Day of action at Faslane. All the workers who normally would have worked that day were given the day off, so that they would not have to risk running a blockade. The peace camp men helped the women's protest in various supporting roles, including cooking, running a creche and cleaning the toilets.

People started arriving on Saturday, 19th March, for the festival on 20th March and tents were once again pitched on the beach where the first Faslane Peace Camp had lain. Although the festival had taken several weeks to plan, details of the plans had been kept out of the hands of the authorities so that a site near to the South Gate could be used. Inevitably the authorities got wind of the festival plans but they did not find out all the details. First thing on Sunday morning police came and asked campers to fill in forms requesting permission to hold a festival. As the campers know that permission would either be refused or delayed until it was no longer wanted, they did not sign the forms.

Military precision and split second timing were therefore required to place the stage, a forty-foot-long trailer, on a site fifty yards from the South Gate. It was necessary to park the vehicle, wind down the trailer legs, disconnect the trailer from its towing unit and get the unit away before the authorities realised what was going on. Failure would mean the authorities would be able to compel the driver to tow the trailer away and there would be no stage for the festival. At 10.20 the articulated lorry pulled up at the peace camp. The driver was briefed, while the loading of the peace camp van with the generator and other equipment was completed and the two vehicles then headed for the festival site. So far so good: The authorities had not spotted them. Within two minutes of arrival, the trailer was dropped and the unit had left. All that remained was to wire the trailer for sound and set up their equipment.

By 18.00 hours the festival was over, the sun was setting, the bands (including the well known Fallout Marching Band) were off home and the litter was being cleared by campers. About 2,000 people had spent an enjoyable afternoon in good weather. When the lorry driver collected his trailer there were no problems.

Many people stayed overnight for the blockade on the Monday when twenty people were arrested at the North Gate. One of the people arrested, Chris, was deliberately doing nothing illegal because he was a legal observer; another, Brett, was taking a cine film of the action when arrested and also doing nothing illegal. The trials were spread over six months. Nearly all resulted in guilty verdicts but not guilty verdicts were given by the Sheriff in two cases when he chose to believe defence evidence, which was consistent, rather than widely conflicting police evidence. The first person found not guilty was Brett, who proved he was legally filming and not laying in the road as the police claimed when he was arrested. The second, Jeremy, had a solicitor called Brian Gilfedder. As Jeremy's defence was different from the others his application for legal aid had been granted. He was the only person granted legal aid. His solicitor produced photographs which proved that some of the police were lying and two policemen who claimed to be the arresting officers of Jeremy were not in any of the photographs of him being dragged from the blockade. This case was not finished until 21st September.

Most Faslane campers preferred to represent themselves rather than have a lawyer do the job, especially where minor offences were involved. Lawyers, particularly those on legal aid, tended to concentrate on the legal aspect of the case and ignore the reason the defendant was at Faslane in the first place. When representing themselves, defendants had more opportunity to air the nuclear disarmament issue in court and thus get it more publicity. Certainly in minor cases the use of solicitors did not seem to make much difference to whether the defendant was found guilty or not, nor to the fines and sentences of convicted persons. People also found this true at Greenham Common.

A march, rally and carnival in Glasgow on Saturday, 2nd April, was followed by a demonstration on Easter Sunday, 3rd April, at Faslane. About 3,000 demonstrators formed a human chain along the perimeter fence between the North Gate and the South Gate and the fence was decorated. The base was entered by five demonstrators, who were arrested. The human chain from Burghfield to Greenham Common meant that there were few English demonstrators at Faslane but to make up for that loss Northern Ireland sent over a large contingent.

On 5th May the court hearings for the November blockaders were held. Sheriff Kelbie found the campers all guilty of one of the thinnest breaches of the peace he had ever handled and admonished them. An admonition is similar to an English unconditional discharge but with an official reprimand added. It is not used outside Scotland.

Vegetables were by now being planted in gardens at the camp, a sure sign that campers were expecting to live there for some time.

One hot day in May, Pauline and Lyn were sat on the grass beside A814 when some motorcycles followed by military vehicles and then a line of green trucks sped past. Pauline shouted to the others to come out of the shelter, where they were in a meeting and they ran out in a vain attempt to stop the trucks. Except for one vehicle this convoy did not slow down and campers were unable to stop it.

The exception was a Land Rover, which broke down just past the peace camp. Campers ran up and surrounded it. The troops inside were hostile and did not speak to them. Soon a Transit van came up and towed the Land Rover away, leaving campers upset with the hostility shown by the troops.

Also in May, 5 campers went to court following a climb into the base. Their cases were adjourned until October.

Glasgow City Council supplied and fitted flush loos at the peace camp to help it comply with the caravan site licence conditions imposed by Dumbarton District Council. Thanks to the efforts of Councillor Ian Leitch the date for the camp to comply with the licence had been deferred to the middle of August.

The camp celebrated its first birthday on 12th June and the 200 people at the party enjoyed the running water from the mains and the new loos all of which had been recently installed. Sadly there was also running water from the heavens above and no tap with which to turn off the rain!

By late June campers had found out much about the convoys with the green lorries.

Nuclear missile warheads deteriorated when subs took them out on patrol primed for use as was the normal practice. They had to be returned frequently from Coulport to Burghfield for overhaul and fresh warheads had to be taken to Coulport to replace them. The Royal Navy formerly moved these warheads by sea, using a port in Southern England (believed to have been Gosport) near to landlocked Burghfield.

Decorated caravan.

Enquiries revealed that now the warheads were being moved all the way by road, in convoys, approximately once a month. The unmarked green lorries Lyn and Pauline had seen were AEC Mammoth Majors each carrying four warheads under a special roof, with a front section which telescoped back under the rear section. Both then lifted on hinges at the tail to reveal a flatbed lorry. This ingenious cover of armoured steel not only protected the warheads but also gave an airtight seal. Under new laws every vehicle carrying radioactive substances must have placards describing its load attached to the sides and rear. Were these warheads being moved by private carrier this would apply but the MoD is exempted from the Radioactive Substances Regulations! [There are several laws dealing with road transport of radioactive loads, the main ones at the time of writing being the Radioactive Substances (Carriage by Road) (Great Britain) Regulations 1974 (Statutory Instrument 1974 No. 1735) made under section 5 subsections 2 and 3 of the Radioactive Substances Act 1948 and the Radioactive Substances (Road Transport Workers) (Great Britain) Reg., 1970 (SI 1970 No. 1827).] There were usually from two to five warhead carriers in a convoy, which would suggest loads of up to twenty warheads per convoy. Also on each convoy were usually four police motorcycle outriders. A Strathclyde policeman told campers that these were RAF Regiment soldiers disguised to look like police. Each convoy was completed with four plain green Ford Transits, a fire engine carrying foam and a command and control vehicle. This last contained a motor-cycle for carrying messages in an emergency, tools, an armoury of weapons including machine guns, all sorts of communications equipment, scientists and a special safety team trained to handle accidents with nuclear warheads. The command and control vehicle that came past the camp at any rate on the early convoys was apparently always the same one bearing the registration 31 AG 63, but all the other vehicles were not the same ones each visit and there were many green Mammoth Majors and Transits. This meant it was possible that there were several other convoy routes, each covered by control vehicles unique to that route. The RAF organised the convoys and staffed them with people trained by Special Air Services at Hereford along with people from Commachio Company, Royal Marines. Trunk roads and motorways were used and towns and cities were avoided as much as possible on the two-day journey from Burghfield to Coulport and on the return journey. However the RAF liked to use the shortest practical route to cut down running time. This meant the convoys usually went past the peace camp and through Helensburgh, the alternative routes being much longer. Similar convoys were seen subsequently in Peterborough, Leicester, Luton and Northumberland far to the East of the direct Burghfield–Coulport route, in Wales visiting ROF Llanishen and in many other places.

On 27th June, A814 and the railway nearby were closed because of a suspected gas main leak at Dumbarton or so the authorities claimed, about twelve miles South East of the camp. Just after the road had been closed a convoy appeared at the peace camp. It was coming from Dumbarton and must have used that stretch of road. One Naval recovery vehicle drove onto the closed road from the north, after the road had been closed, but campers suspecting an accident or breakdown involving a convoy vehicle were unable to see where it went or what it did. The Navy said the convoy was out of the danger area before the road was closed. One report said that a gas main had been fractured by a mechanical digger. A mishap might have befallen a convoy vehicle and the government closed A814 not only as a safety precaution but also to keep peace campers away. Frequently government secrecy hides unpleasant facts. After an overnight stay at Coulport during which the fresh warheads would be unloaded and used warheads loaded onto the Mammoth Majors, a convoy would normally leave the next morning, which in the case of this convoy would be 28th June. It did leave then but returned to Burghfield via the Garelochead Pass and the Loch Lomond Road, which avoided the peace camp and Dumbarton but involved about two hours extra driving.

It did not dodge the peace campers, most of whom went to Coulport to vigil all night and wait for it to leave so they could attempt to blockade it. Here the MoD must be given full marks for the timing of this convoy, for on that same morning fifteen campers were due to appear in Dumbarton Sheriff Court all with not guilty pleas as a result of the 12th December blockade. The convoy was still inside Coulport when ten campers left to reach the court on time. When they appeared in court they were found guilty and fined £25 each. Donald and Ardo cut it too fine when they left Coulport on the twenty-mile journey to Dumbarton. The convoy had not emerged when they left. On their way to court they were arrested for being late and were remanded in custody for eight days until the next available court sitting. Shortly after the convoy left Coulport and some time after the court had begun to sit, Kenny, Spud and Les were arrested. They had sent a message to the court apologising for their absence, explaining it was due to the imminent emergence of the convoy, which could not be adjourned! Kenny was remanded in custody along with Donald and Ardo for eight days. Spud and Les Robertson were dealt with straight away however. Spud was found guilty, fined, fined again for breaking his bail and also fined for an earlier contempt of court charge when he along with the other sixteen defendants arrested at the gun turret occupation of 15th January had refused to stand when the sheriff had entered the court. Les apparently refused to pay the fines and was sent to prison. While he was there a peace camp was set up outside and he received daily visits and lots of mail. The remanded defendants were later found guilty and fined. Kenny refused to pay and was sent to prison for seven days. All fifteen defendants were thus found guilty of breach of the peace.

In June Strathclyde Regional Council held a public enquiry into the presence of the nuclear arms dump at Coulport asking if it was really needed there. Of course the MoD carried on as before because, whatever the findings, Strathclyde Council had no direct power to call a halt to their activities.

On the evening of 4th August, while the public relations officer from Faslane was visiting the camp and discussing the arrangements for events over Hiroshima Day and Nagasaki Day, a taxi pulled up. Two sailors got out and walked into the camp. They were warned in whispers who the other visitor was and decided nevertheless to stay a while.

After the public relations man left the sailors had a long discussion with campers before returning to their quarters. Later Frank, one of the sailors, came out of the base with some personal belongings and spent the rest of the night at the camp. He wanted to leave the Navy and become a peace camper.

At 10.00 hours the next morning the public relations officer arrived along with Naval Provost and civilian police with what they called a search warrant. Campers inspected the warrant, saw it was not a search warrant but a warrant for Frank's arrest and refused permission to search the camp. Frank was told they had come for him and said he did not want to be arrested. The police and public relations man left but soon they were back and this time they did have a search warrant. Frank was in a bender with Kathy and Pauline holding onto him and Lee lying in the entrance. The police went straight into the bender, pulled Frank out along with Kathy, Pauline and Lee and dragged them right across the road to their Leyland Sherpa van. The three campers were held five hours and bailed on charges of obstructing the police whilst Frank was detained in a Naval Provost cell.

On 6th August campers and camp visitors joined the International Fast for Life to draw attention to the plight of the world's starving and the waste of resources on arms. Fasters were only allowed liquids for the ninety-six hours of the fast until it finished on Nagasaki Day. They spoke to many people, police, workers from the base and members of the public at the site at South Gate where they vigilled and fasted.

Lee, Kathy, Pauline and Frank were all in court on the same day. Frank was convicted of resisting arrest and assaulting the police although he appears to have remained nonviolent throughout. He was fined £100 and later discharged from the Navy (and just after his discharge he joined CND). The three campers were given fantastic charge sheets alleging that they hindered, molested and resisted the police and struggled violently! Lee pointed out to the sheriff that the charge sheets were fantastic and to underline his statement tore his sheet in half in front of the sheriff. After discussion the prosecution dropped the completely fictional parts of the charge sheets. The campers were then found guilty on the remaining minor charges and fined £25 each.

Due largely to lack of cash the camp had been unable to meet four of the caravan site licence conditions by August. There were no standpipes and the fence at the front was not of the post and rail type favoured by Dumbarton Council. One reason campers were reluctant to spend money on the fence was the damage it was suffering. Not only was it damaged at the arrest of Frank but there was also a local resident of Shandon who smashed it at least once as well as breaking caravan windows and assaulting at least one camper. The council decided to refer the matter to the Procurator Fiscal with a view to prosecuting the campers for breach of the licence conditions. Notwithstanding, campers plodded on trying to get the camp up to standard and in September they moved some caravans so they would be twenty feet apart to comply with the licence conditions. The general management committee of the local Labour Party criticised the council for referring the matter to the Procurator Fiscal and stated that the camp was much more attractive than Faslane Base in a letter published in the Lennox Herald of 16th September.

The 'Bandit Alarm' was set off, a shift change was delayed and a seven-mile long traffic jam built up along A814 as workers waited to come in through the locked gates in the morning of 3rd November, 1983. A few minutes before the shift change a peace camper just happened to mention to someone on the base that a large section of fence appeared to have fallen. When the fence was checked in the area mentioned forty yards of it were found to have fallen on the ground. The alarm was set off, the base gates were closed and the whole base was searched for intruders. The establishment was sealed for about an hour and during this time movement was restricted inside. Nobody could get in or out and the traffic jam reached its maximum length of seven miles in only half an hour, stretching away down through Rhu. There appeared to be chaos inside. The beautiful thing was that even if there had been intruders in the base they had left before the hue and cry started, so the searchers had to search all the more because there was nobody in there to find. They had to search everywhere and not just until they found an intruder or two. No arrests were made.

A rumour did circulate to the effect that the stretch of fence that fell might have been demolished by peace campers about two-and-half hours before the panic began but rumours are not very reliable!

Blue, Jamie and Les went over the fence and climbed a 150 feet high radio mast in the early morning of 15th November. Marines who followed them up threatened to throw them down. The campers stayed. Eventually at daybreak police came up and replaced the marines. A 'No Cruise' banner was flying from the tower reminding people of the official announcement the day before of the arrival of the first Cruise missiles on British soil. The banner was eventually confiscated and thrown down by police. After six hours up the mast the campers were arrested and charged. Campers on the ground outside the fence but within earshot continued to shout support to their friends throughout the entire occupation of the tower.

At 12.30 hours on Sunday, 11th December, 1983, a Cruise missile replica left the car park on Helensburgh sea front carried by two people and followed by 2,000 more, commemorating the fourth anniversary of NATO's decision to base Cruise missiles in Europe. They walked past the peace camp to the South Gate of Faslane and held a rally. Speakers included local councillors Ian Leitch and Iain Mac-Donald, Billy Wolfe of the Scottish National Party, a Fire Brigades Union member, Nicolette Carlow of the Medical Campaign Against Nuclear Weapons and peace camper Louise.

A number of people stayed overnight so as to participate in the actions on the Monday when all the gates were blockaded. Traffic was delayed but not completely stopped and there was no repeat of the seven-mile jam. Blockaders exchanged friendly greetings with people walking and cycling to work. Arrests at North Gate totalled twenty-seven. There do not appear to have been any at South Gate and the Tunnel (under A814).

The blockade over, several demonstrators left the peace camp in two groups and were seen by a group of pressmen who joined them as they walked northwards past the base. When the pressmen asked where the demonstrators were going they were invited to 'come and see'. Soon an unguarded gun turret was spotted. Over the fence and into it went five campers. The press cameras worked hard recording the incursion. Soon police came and dragged the five intruders off into a police van. Campers were charged under the Faslane, Coulport and Rhu Narrows Bylaws 1971, with three offences – entering the base, being in the base and refusing to leave when asked. With regard to the last charge, if the police did ask them to leave they did not make their request audible and they did not wait for the campers to acknowledge it and leave if they wanted to. Later that day the fence was cut and there were more arrests. Altogether about 300 people took part in Sunday's actions and fifty-six were arrested.

On 20th December most of the campers were at a local TV studio in the audience at a debate on defence. There was little participation by the campers and the debate on the platform was pretty one-sided and mainly biased towards the British Government view.

As a result of the radio tower occupation of 15th November, Blue, Les and Jamie were in court all pleading not guilty on 21st December. Jamie ended up pleading guilty on two charges and was fined £50. The other two stuck with their not guilty pleas and had their cases adjourned six months to 21st June 1984.

Towards the end of 1983 the camp received some welcome gifts, including the single-decker bus used on the March For Life. This was followed by a council grant of £200 for peace education, which helped equip the bus as a mobile peace centre. Glasgow Friends of the Earth donated a solar panel, which Owen fitted up to a practical hot water system very cheaply. This came in handy, especially for washing clothes, though it had ceased operating by 1986.

'First Footing' is a Scottish custom where people call on neighbours with gifts on Hogmanay, 31st December. Lyn and Louise 'First Footed' into the base causing a big security alert in 1983. They were arrested on New Year's Day 1984 and each subsequently spent seven days in Cornton Vale Women's Prison.

A peace camp was set up outside the prison on the Thursday evening prior to their release and campers were there greeting Lyn and Louise when they were released on Friday at 07.30. Antonia (who was in the gun turret on 12th December) and Dawn were also in Cornton Vale for Faslane actions at this time.

Throughout the first four months of 1984 there were several minor actions and people were getting into the base frequently. Much effort was being expended on supporting campers in court and in prison. Around Easter, Helen Steven was arrested for unlawful entry.

Closed circuit TV cameras installed by the MoD on the tops of many fence posts to increase security just did not seem to see where people were cutting the fence and getting into the base, probably because the people operated outside the cameras' restricted fields of vision. These cameras had been installed at great expense during 1983. Almost every time the fence was breached, the 'Bandit Alarm' went off, and the base had to be closed, with all traffic through the gates stopped and movements within the base restricted for up to two-and-a-half hours while the base was searched for intruders.

People were facing problems with unsympathetic sheriffs in the courts; any honeymoon of leniency

there was in the early days of Faslane Peace Camp Mark III had now ended.

At about this time Tony, a clerical officer on the base, told peace campers he had resigned from his job on the base. Yet another person from behind the fence had come over to our side!

In March a Dumbarton District Councillor complained about the length of time it was taking to prosecute the peace camp for not complying with the caravan site licence.

Just after this, Les Robertson, an active founder member of the camp, stood for Bonhill Ward of Dunbarton District Council in the local government elections. Bonhill includes the Nobleston housing estate, built to house workers at Faslane and other MoD installations. Now discussions with Faslane workers showed peace campers that many people only worked there for the money and because there was a lack of suitable employment elsewhere in the area. Some preferred not to work on nuclear subs. The peace camp and the Labour Party, whose red flag Les was flying, had been involved in research into an alternative project (done mainly by the trade unions) to make submersible oil drilling platforms at Faslane instead of looking after nuclear subs. This idea had got nowhere with the authorities. Those workers who favoured this idea of alternative employment would probably vote for Les, along with local people who supported the Labour Party and the peace camp, but would this give him enough votes to get in? This would mean upsetting the status quo and canny Scots don't like making radical moves that might upset the status quo without thoroughly thinking them out and ensuring they would be good for them. There was much publicity against Les. Local papers made no secret of his record as a peace camper and his court appearances. It was his first time standing for Bonhill. On 3rd May when he was elected Les just about doubled Labour's majority in the ward.

Dumbarton Council now had eleven Labour councillors most of whom supported the peace camp, three independents, one Tory and one Social Democrat.

The Procurator Fiscal now decided to prosecute the peace camp for not complying with the caravan site regulations made by Dumbarton Council. There was to be a further delay before the case could be heard. It was not a question of simply taking the matter to the next sheriff's court sitting, getting the campers all convicted, locking them up and clearing the campsite. The case was vitally important to Scottish disarmers because Faslane was now the only peace camp left in Scotland. Les's election had shown the amount of respect with which it was regarded locally.

Whilst preparation went ahead for this prosecution, much else was happening and peace campers were by no means idle.

On Tuesday, 15th May, Dumbarton District Council declared Dumbarton a NFZ. The whole district was in Strathclyde NFZ already so all the district council needed to do to carry out its new policy was to wholeheartedly support Strathclyde's anti-nuclear policy. Ironically we now had a complex of nuclear submarine bases and a nuclear arms depot in a double NFZ!

TRIDENT: BIGGER MONSTERS TO COME (May 1984)

USS Ohio, the first American Trident sub was nuclear powered, 168 metres long and thirteen metres wide, displaced 19,000 tons and carried twenty-four nuclear armed Trident missiles.

Francis Pym, Her Majesty's Secretary of State for defence (later replaced by Michael 'Tarzan' Heseltine) announced in July 1980 that the British Government had decided to buy the Trident missile system from the USA and to start building four new Trident subs in 1986. These would be slightly smaller than *USS Ohio* but would still carry twenty-four missiles. They were to be built by Vickers at Barrow-in-Furness. The missiles came in several versions: the 1-C4 which the British Government intended buying, had a range of 4,000 miles (compared with 2,750 on the latest Polaris) from eight to twelve warheads, each of about 100 kilotons and each with its own independently target-table rocket (IRV) to take it to its own target; whilst the later 2-D5 had a range of 6,000 miles, sixteen to twenty-four IRV warheads on each missile and about 600 kilotons of 'bang' in each warhead. Alterations and new equipment were needed at Chapelcross, Aldermaston and Burghfield to manufacture the fuel for and maintain up to 800 new Trident warheads. As the new subs were to be at least twice the size of their Polaris predecessors many alterations were needed to accommodate them at the British bases. As the early stages of the project progressed, the MoD saw it would be more economical for some Trident servicing to be done in the USA. The whole project was so costly and enormous that even the British Government could not cost it accurately. Although they usually gave a cost of around £5,000,000,000 they did once reveal in March 1981 a figure of at least £6,000,000,000 for the cheapest variant of Trident. The government were also considering building a fifth Trident sub which could cost an additional £500,000,000 [Figures from *Sanity*, June/July 1981]. Independent experts reckoned these estimates understated the actual costs by large margins.

The MoD planned to expand Faslane and Coulport to accommodate Trident subs. A new shiplift and berth would extend about 300 metres into Faslane Bay with a shed on it 185 metres long by fifty wide and forty high, a new finger jetty would extend about 175 metres into the Bay with two cranes and a sixty metres long access platform, there were to be torpedo handling facilities and in order to include all this the Faslane Base was to be extended to include the former Garelochead Shipbreakers Yard. At Coulport there was to be a 3,000 acre extension to accommodate new nuclear warhead stores, a floating jetty with cranes and a shed similar in size to the big new one at Faslane, new magazines and processing works, a new access road and extensive landscaping with trees. Coulport was to be continuously floodlit at night and was to have two new security fences, one of which was to be over three miles long. At both bases a total of over 1,000 steel and concrete piles, each weighing an average of fifteen tons would be driven into the ground by noisy pile-drivers. Two new reservoirs were to be constructed for the Navy. The Garelochead Bypass was to be built, enabling traffic between Faslane and Coulport and through traffic on A814 to avoid the village with its steep narrow hill. All these and other minor additions were to cost an estimated £350,000,000 and would take about seven years to construct. During this period up to 1,600 people would be working on the project at any one time and while Polaris was being phased out and Trident phased in, a further 1,300 would be needed for staff jobs. None of these jobs would be permanent and there was no guarantee that the people employed would be local as far as possible (it was later found that many were not). There would probably be fewer jobs in the bases for local civilians when the project was complete but some jobs would be created elsewhere in the MoD network and there would be about 500 more jobs for people serving with the Royal Navy.

These plans were revealed to an audience of invited regional district and community councillors and journalists at a meeting in the Denny Civic Theatre in Dumbarton on Wednesday, May 16. Dumbarton Council who owned the theatre explained that they were honouring a commitment made by the council before local government elections, which gave Dumbarton an anti-nuclear majority and had the present council received the MoD's application to book the hall, they would almost certainly have refused it. It must not be forgotten that only the day before they had declared Dumbarton a NFZ.

Though they weren't invited, some peace campers got to the theatre early, along with Dumbarton CND members. About eight of the campers climbed onto the roof with banners bearing messages like: 'They lie, we die' and 'Nobody wants it, nobody needs it'. Sailors went up onto the roof to remove the protestors. One protestor was held out over the edge of the roof. CND people and others below, worried that someone could get hurt and about people being denied the right to protest peacefully, complained. Cameras were produced and shutters began to click. "Councillor Ian Leitch went in and told the Navy if they didn't stop our people from being arrested then they were being thrown out of the building." Jane wrote in a letter to me afterwards. She was on the roof along with Phill, Huw, William and other peace campers at the time.

The sailors were recalled. Police arrived, went onto the roof, removed the protestors, arrested them and announced that they would be reported to the Procurator Fiscal for breach of the peace offences.

Dumbarton CND members then picketed the front entrance to the theatre and a partial blockade developed. Protestors from the roof action joined in just as soon as the police released them. They sat and lay in the entrance as the invited audience went into the theatre. Vice Admiral Anthony Tippett the senior officer of the MoD crew, paused briefly as he got to the door and Jane took advantage of the pause to lie down in front of him. The blockaders were removed and released by police. They were not, at this stage, arrested and charged. Several returned again and again. They also chalked messages and signs at the entrance. Police eventually arrested two of the most persistent blockaders, Phill and Fiver. One of the founders of the second and third Faslane Peace Camps (in June 1982) Louise Robertson was sat on the picket with her baby. She was left alone by police. When her husband Les came to enter the meeting to which he had been invited as a Dunbarton District councillor he spoke with her. After a few minutes he announced he would refuse to enter the meeting. Strathclyde Regional Councillor Ian MacDonald also refused to cross the picket line into the theatre. All eleven Labour Dunbarton councillors arrived and spoke with pickets. Apart from Les they all went into the meeting. The other councillors entered, mostly ignoring attempts by pickets to talk with them. Vice Admiral Tippett's MoD crew in-

cluded Rear Admiral John Grove, Commodore David Morse (the Commanding Officer of Clyde Submarine Base) and Michael Ellison from the Property Services Agency of the MoD. They all went through the picket line, though one or two did speak with pickets on the way through.

One of the first things to be mentioned in the meeting was the case of the two environmental impact assessments. Michael Ellison had led the MoD team which prepared one without inviting anyone to their enquiry to help establish the facts. Not surprisingly, this assessment concluded that we needed Trident and Strathclyde would be a good place to put it. The Regional Council's assessment, with evidence from many experts (including for instance the Caldecotts from the USA) but without MoD evidence because the MoD had declined to assist, concluded that Trident was not needed! Apparently the MoD now regarded both assessments as incomplete because neither included evidence from the opposing side! The MoD crew were not answering all the questions, they would not explain how they calculated their 'yellow' and 'purple' safety lines around Coulport nuclear arms store. They thus rescinded a promise made by Minster of State for Defence Viscount Trenchard in 1981 that he would answer this question. (In this connexion I recall the safety line calculated around Bikini Atoll for a H-bomb test. The Japanese fishing boat *Lucky Dragon IV* was fishing well outside this line when fallout from the test dusted her, resulting in at least two deaths and problems with her catch which had been sold on the markets in Japan before anyone realised it had been dusted with dangerous radioactive fallout). Soon after, the Dumbarton Labour councillors all walked out of the meeting explaining that there wasn't much point in them staying because they had not been given a proper chance to study the documents in advance of the meeting. As the debate continued various questions arose but apparently nobody mentioned the large asbestos dump on the site of the old Garelochead Shipbreakers Yard where the MoD planned much construction and excavating. The environmental impact assessments appeared not to mention this dump, the importance of which was not to be realised until much later. The big meeting ended peacefully and everyone went home with the MoD plans substantially unchanged and the opposition ideas also substantially unchanged.

A phone call on Friday, 18th May, warned the peace camp that a nuclear warhead convoy had been seen near Preston in Lancashire and had parked up for the night in the Central Armaments Depot, Longtown, a few miles South of the Scottish Border in Cumbria. Nuclear warhead convoys regularly stopped overnight here. It appears that the crew left the convoy here and went off for a long weekend for the convoy did not come past Faslane (just under a day's journey from Longtown) until Tuesday, 22nd May.

After spending the night at Coulport a convoy would normally leave at 10.00 hours. The campers decided to go to the gates of Coulport and blockade this convoy as it left on its return to Burghfield. As campers were getting up and preparing to go to Coulport the convoy sped past the peace camp at about 07.00 hours. Some people going to the blockade in a taxi arrived at the camp immediately afterwards and in no time at all ten protestors were aboard the camp van in hot pursuit of the convoy. Despite being stopped at least twice by police and being deliberately delayed by them the van arrived at Longtown not far behind and without any speeding tickets. Campers could see the lorries that carried the warheads inside the gates but modplods asked about the convoy denied its existence.

LONGTOWN PEACE CAMP AND ACTION IN LONDON (May 1984 - September 1985)

CAD Longtown Peace Camp was set up. A member of Cumbrians for Peace contacted the campers on the Wednesday evening, bringing blankets and promising to return with more supporters early the next morning. At 07.30 on Thursday 24th May, ten Cumbrians arrived to reinforce the ten campers from Faslane along with several journalists. At about 08.30 the convoy guards and drivers returned from their lodgings and went to their vehicles which then started to move about inside the base. Campers at the main gate lost sight of them. At the time only the main gate had a presence and it wasn't until 09.30 that campers' fears were confirmed: the convoy had left by another gate and driven through Longtown itself, which it had not been known to do before.

There was general mayhem at the main gate with campers frustrated by not being able to blockade the convoy. The modplods retired to the guardroom as campers spent two hours cutting the fence, painting buildings around the main gate and paintbombing the base. Signs reading 'CAD Longtown' were amended to 'CND Longtown'. One woman was arrested, cautioned and released ten minutes later by the modsquad. The painting and fencecutting continued with renewed vigour. Eventually Cumbrian police came to the rescue of the beseiged

modsquad and arrested two or three people for spraying paint on a sentry box. They were charged with criminal damage. Having thus ensured media coverage for their peace camp and having ensured that a second act of the same drama would take place in the local magistrates court, the campers broke camp and returned to Faslane that Thursday.

As a result of the convoy driving through Longtown the local council sided with the campers against nuclear convoys.

Of the peace campers charged with criminal damage at CAD (or should it be CND!) Longtown, one was found not guilty and another, Jean, was fined lightly. They had an excellent local lawyer who wore a CND badge in court. When he received a complaint about his wearing the badge, he pointed out that one of the magistrates was wearing a Rotarian badge and an argument with this magistrate ensued. In the end both agreed to remove their badges while the court was in session. (It is recalled that the late Donald Dickenson, a Quaker and a magistrate, was reputed to wear his CND badge when sitting in Salisbury Magistrates Court and apparently never had to remove it.)

On 11th June another raiding party went much further into England to an objective over 400 miles from Faslane. While Ian De La Mare waited outside with press releases ready, his six colleagues entered the lobby of the MoD Main Building in Whitehall, London with some tins of red paint. They put superglue into doorlocks as they went. They then threw the contents of the tins of paint, symbolising blood, all over the lobby before security guards could stop them. The five Faslane peace campers in the lobby were arrested and later charged with criminal damage to the tune of £8,000.

Having seen the action and the arrests, Ian quietly slipped away and contacted the press, radio, TV and a lawyer. He gave his name and a contact address and telephone number to the media of course.

Now, unfortunately it appears that Ian's shoes were accidentally spashed with red paint before the cans were taken into the building and as a result of his giving his name and address to the media the police knew where to find him. When they went to see him later that day they said that they had found spashes of red paint on his shoes. Ian had deliberately kept out of the action so as not to get arrested. He was detained, interviewed and subsequently charged with aiding and abetting the others in committing criminal damage.

After formal appearances in the Magistrates Court and committal proceedings, the full trial at Southwark Crown Court did not take place until February 1985. A report of the trial is included in chronological order.

Faslane peace campers celebrated the second birthday of their camp with a festival on one of the beautiful banks of Loch Lomond on 12th June 1984.

From 3rd to 6th July, peace campers fasted for three days to draw attention to the links between the uranium used in the Trident project, the poor conditions in the Namibian uranium mines and apartheid. During the fast they commemorated US Independence Day by calling for independence for Britain with an 'Alternative American Independence Day' event.

In August campers commemorated Hiroshima Day as was their custom and there was a fire in a drydock at Faslane. Just a few yards away lay a visiting sub, the USS Nathaniel Green with it full complement of Poseidon nuclear missiles. Had that fire got out of control...

The site where the new MoD offices were being built in Argyll Street, Glasgow, was occupied by some women who got both support and abuse from workmen on 21st August. Apparently Faslane peace campers were involved, there were five arrests and the two women in their support group were arrested and held for thirty-two hours without charge.

A fortnight later on Monday, 3rd September, the two tower cranes on the site were climbed by four Faslane peace campers with banners reading: 'Glasgow's miles better – without Trident' and 'Turn the tide of war'. Work was stopped for over six hours. Then five workmen with hammers and crowbars climbed one crane while another group of workmen sang Give Peace a Chance. The campers, including Jamie Donoghue and William Peden, descended, were arrested and were later charged. Their two legal observers were arrested at 04.00 hours on the Tuesday morning even though they had not participated in the action. Everybody pleaded not guilty to everything.

Immediately to the north of Clyde Submarine base on the site of the old Garelochead Shipbreakers Yard lay a vast tip, believed to contain something like 10,000 cubic metres of asbestos, the dust of which can cause a very serious disease, asbestosis. The MoD had already announced their plans for a sixty-two acre extension of Clyde Submarine Base to accommodate Trident subs but had taken care not to mention the asbestos buried on the site which they

owned and had surveyed. Since the public meeting in the Denny Theatre and even before, many objections to this expansion had been sent to the MoD but apparently none mentioned the asbestos. Moving this asbestos to another site and dumping it there could cause people to develop asbestosis. Even merely disturbing it in the course of excavating could cause the workmen to develop asbestosis, unless the most stringent precautions were taken to see that no part of any one of them came into contact with the very fine dust given off by the asbestos.

In about October 1984, the closing date for objections to the Faslane expansion arrived. On the very next day the MoD announced it was starting work on the Garelochead Shipbreakers Yard and that it had awarded a contract for the removal of 3,000 tons of asbestos, which had been tipped there years before. This announcement hit Strathclyde like a bombshell. Protests began immediately. At an enquiry Dumbarton and Inverclyde District Councils called for the loads to be declared abnormal. This would mean that every time a loaded lorry left Garelochead Shipbreakers Yard, Strathclyde Regional Council (who had already declared an NFZ and whose majority were opposed to the Clyde Submarine base and Trident project) as highways and bridges authority, would have to be informed in advance along with the police. They would probably have been able to put special conditions on the movements of these lorries. Before long several different estimates of the weight of asbestos to be moved before the work would be finished were circulating and they varied from 16,000 tonnes to 100,000 tonnes. Regional and district councillors from all over Strathclyde were opposing the movements. Glenboig where the asbestos was being dumped came within the bounds of Monkland District. Monkland District Council was trying to stop the dumping by every legal, democratic method known to man, including an eighteenth-century law. This opposition had no effect whatever and the lorries started to roll. Glenboig villagers protested as the lorries drove past them to the tip. Then sixty villagers went to the tip and blockaded it, physically preventing some of the lorries from entering and unloading their hazardous cargoes. Surprisingly the police did not remove and arrest the protestors and at least one policeman showed signs of sympathy with them. Eventually the contractors, Shanks and McEwen, voluntarily suspended operations. The villagers then took their campaign to the British and European parliaments. Before this stage of the campaign had run its course, however, the MoD made the suspension of operations permanent. They were stuck with the asbestos. They announced that they would keep it inside the new expanded base even though it would make their excavations and construction more difficult, especially the dredging of new berths and the piledriving.

This important victory was won by the Glenboig villagers, not over the MoD, but over a firm of civilian contractors, who were doing the MoD's dirty work for them. Their lorries, unlike the Mammoth Majors carrying nuclear warheads, had no police escorts. The tip they used, whilst being licenced for the dumping of asbestos, was not on a military base where a blockade could be easily defeated but in a distrct where the local people, the local council and the regional council were all opposed to the tipping. By acting in place of the MoD, Shanks and McEwen provided a buffer between the MoD and the protesting public, so the MoD were able to alter their plans to accommodate the asbestos in the enlarged base without losing face. The contractors were in rather an awkward position because the MoD wasn't their only customer. Anybody who hires out tipper lorries knows that local councils use them from time to time and when this happened at Glenboig the councils in Strathclyde could quite legally have boycotted Shanks and McEwen and hired lorries from other possibly more expensive firms instead.

In November the peace camp held a month of small actions and deliberately got visiting groups to participate as much as possible. They kicked off on 1st November with a day of protest against the Namibian uranium contract, which included street theatre from a visiting group.

Then just after 09.30 on 9th November a nuclear warhead convoy was halted for a few minutes by blockaders who sat in front of it as it travelled south through Garelochead. The police were ready but were not able to prevent a brief sitdown.

This was the first time protestors had managed to stop a Polaris convoy. There were to be many more stoppages.

A few days after this *Faslane: Diary of a Peace Camp* was published by Polygon Books. Back in the summer when the book was being compiled, William Peden had inserted in it a promise that a Polaris convoy would be stopped by the peace campers before the book was published. The campers had cut their timing a bit fine but they had kept the promise!

On 25th November, 200 Women for Mines not Missiles marched to the main gate of Faslane and held a two-hour blockade. Also during this month of small

actions there were many incursions into the base including one where Scott was arrested on 30th November. Lyn, a visitor from Greenham Yellow Gate, was also arrested on the base at this time.

Another little mishap struck Clyde Submarine base when a crane collapsed onto a sub in dry dock during a high autumnal wind.

The court cases for the Argyll Street crane occupation were held on 4th December. Jamie Donoghue was sentenced to sixty days in prison, Tim Roberts and William were each fined £120 and the fourth case was adjourned for social enquiry reports. On 20th December the fourth crane occupant was sentenced to do community service.

Nuclear weapons convoys made at least two journeys in this month. On Saturday, 8th December, five campers lay in the road at Garelochead and once again stopped a southbound convoy. Police removed them while legal observers looked on. One camper held onto the front bumper of a vehicle with his arms, as if it were his child and it took five policemen to remove him. These blockaders were arrested and charged with breach of the peace. A convoy was obstructed outside Faslane Peace Camp eleven days later and four campers were arrested by Strathclyde Police. The cases of these four blockaders were finally heard in May 1985.

Faslane peace campers were also going out to meet other people and tell them about the camp and its campaign at this time. They were performing street theatre in Glasgow. They joined a miners' support march where they gave out leaflets linking coal mining with the nuclear industry and the closure of pits with the increasing use of nuclear power. Many coal miners were on strike at this time over the threatened closure of certain pits.

On New Year's Day fifteen campers were on a vigil at the South Gate of Faslane and here four or five arrests were made, resulting in breach of the peace charges. Initially all these people pleaded not guilty in Dumbarton Sheriff Court on 10th January but two then changed their pleas to guilty and were each fined £25 which they refused to pay. They were then sentenced to seven days in jail each. Two others maintained their not guilty pleas and their cases were adjourned.

Throughout the winter there were incursions and cut fences at Coulport, Faslane and the nearby Glen Fruin torpedo testing centre. On 2nd January at Glen Fruin six sections of fence were cut and 18 sections were cut at Coulport on 16th January.

On 24th January, 1985, another convoy was stopped. This time three peace campers were arrested. One was caught on top of a Mammoth Major warhead carrier. Apparently this was the first time a warhead carrier had been boarded in this manner and as it was done without special equipment or proper training it showed that these vehicles were difficult to protect from non-violent demonstrators.

Jamie Donoghue was released from Low Moss Prison on 28th January and on 5th February, Helen Steven, a Quaker, was sentenced to seven days in Cornton Vale Women's Prison after refusing to pay a £30 fine imposed for entering Clyde Submarine base in April 1984.

The trial of the seven Faslane peace campers involved in the raid on the MoD Main Building the previous June began on Monday 4th February 1985, in Southwark Crown Court. Malcolm Boatman, Lizzie Strata and Antonia Lindsay-McDougall conducted their own defences on the serious criminal damage charges. Jayne Fox and Sean Hawkey also facing serious criminal damage charges apparently had lawyers. David Kelbie also charged with criminal damage did not appear and a warrant was issued for his arrest. Ian De La Mare, charged with aiding and abetting the other six, appeared to have a lawyer.

All the Faslane peace campers had either been to court, where many had been fined or imprisoned, or had a friend who had been fined or imprisoned. Nevertheless, they found this trial a harrowing experience because of the strange environment of Southwark Crown Court, because £8,000 worth of criminal damage was a great deal more damage than had ever been alleged at any other trial in their experience and because this was the first time ever that they could recall anyone being prosecuted for damaging the MoD's hallowed head office.

Judge Butler started off by threatening some campers and friends (some of whom were in the public gallery and around the courthouse giving moral support to the six accused) with contempt of court if they continued to leaflet near the court. The judge was concerned that their leaflets might influence the jury.

One MoD security guard gave evidence that when the campers went limp and were dragged from the Main Building they had used 'passive violence!' [*Peace News* 22nd February 1985]

Lizzie Strata cross-examining a policeman who denied assaulting her during her arrest, tried to

show the disparity between the non-violence of the campers and the violence around them which they opposed. Judge Butler stopped her, disagreeing with her that the issue of the case was about violence.

Campers voiced their fears about the arms race from the dock and told how back in May and early June they had noticed an increase in activity in the submarine base. They had interpreted this as a sign that the Royal Navy was preparing to get involved in fighting in the Iran-Iraq War, almost certainly with nuclear-armed ships. They claimed that this preparation was against International Law and the Genocide Act and, in view of the urgency of the situation, felt this action was appropriate. They said that by doing the criminal damage, which they all admitted, they were acting to prevent a greater crime and therefore acting with lawful excuse. The judge instructed the jury that this defence was inadmissible.

The jury consisting of six men and six women found all five guilty of criminal damage. Judge Butler then sentenced them to three months each.

Ian's case for aiding and abetting was different. He had deliberately kept out of the action because he wanted to stay law-abiding. However police claimed they saw splashes of red paint on his shoes even though they did not see him at the scene of the crime. They eventually arrested him, apparently as a result of seeing the name and address he distributed widely to the media with his press release. When arresting him they found a list of publications and press agencies he had contacted along with the name of a solicitor he had contacted on behalf of the five activists in the Main Building. The Judge held these documents to be evidence of aiding and abetting and after the jury had found Ian guilty sentenced him to three months in prison. This latter case has serious implications for secretaries and press officers of groups which include people who might get convicted of a crime on a NVDA, for although they themselves may have no intention of breaking or even challenging the law, phoning the press or contacting a lawyer on behalf of their friends could get them three months in jail with the precedent of Ian's case.

These trials were over in one week.

On Friday, 8th February, campers from Boscombe Down and Faslane who had come to support their friends on trial, blockaded US Secretary of State Caspar Weinbergers car as it left the Channel 4 TV Studios. Police soon cleared them and Caspar Weinberger went on his way. This action was partly to gain publicity for the trial at Southwark crown Court and partly to protest about the Molesworth takeover which Huw had been warned about by a journalist on 5th February.

Like all the others, David Kelbie, the seventh defendant in the trial at Southwark Crown Court, had been out on bail but unlike the others he did not appear at the appointed time. A warrant was issued for his arrest but he gave himself up about a week after the trial ended so the warrant was not used to get him. David was then tried and convicted of criminal damage and sent to prison for three months. No extra punishment appears to have been levied on him for failing to surrender to his bail on time.

On Tuesday, 28th February, Faslane peace campers again blockaded a weapons convoy. This one arrived on the Wednesday evening with new warheads and left on Thursday morning with warheads for reconditioning at Burghfield. Police and campers were ready and waiting when it passed through Helensburgh on its way South. Here it was halted for a few minutes by seven campers who were all forcibly arrested. Public sympathy was on the side of the peace campers for this action, which took place in a town street in front of lots of people, many of whom disapproved of the way in which the police arrested the campers. They were later released on bail and ordered to appear in court on obstruction charges on 7th March.

During this action all the public telephones in Helensburgh were mysteriously cut off a few minutes before the convoy arrived and stayed out of action for at least fifteen minutes. Cruisewatchers also have noticed this phenomenon in the South of England when Cruise convoys have come out of Greenham Airfield.

On Good Friday, 5th April, William and some other campers cut the fence and chopped padlocks at Coulport. Some entered, including Phill, who went onto a roof inside the base. The action was in solidarity with the Easter demonstration at Molesworth. About ten campers were found, arrested, charged with vandalism, malicious mischief and breach of the peace and released on bail. Their court cases eventually came up in August 1985.

On East Saturday about 200 CND walkers went onto the hills of the Rosneath Peninsula, which the MoD were taking over to expand Coulport Base. They were not arrested. It is believed they had hassles with the authorities because of the NVDA on Good Friday and consequently they were annoyed with the activists.

Mail deliveries including recorded deliveries to the peace camp were unreliable. In April a postman told Huw that mail was being delivered to Clyde Submarine base before being redirected to the peace camp so that it could be intercepted by the authorities and undesirable items removed. Huw wrote to the Head Postmaster at Helensburgh inviting an explanation.

The Head Postmaster replied indignantly that the Post Office did not do this to people's mail and that he had interviewed the postmen, none of whom had admitted telling Huw that it had been done. Peace campers then went to the Post Office and complained. The Post Office staff then started working to rule insisting that the peace camp provide a proper mailbox. The postmen rarely used it when it was provided. Instead they used to pull up on the main road by the camp and hoot. If nobody came out immediately to get the mail it would wait until next delivery. This work to rule made deliveries virtually non-existent for two weeks as the postmen never waited. They would just drive off and leave anybody slow to come out to get the mail standing empty-handed. After two weeks, however, things got back to normal with postmen stopping and waiting for campers to come and sometimes even getting out of their vans to put mail in the mailbox.

When Huw and I were discussing mail interception and telephone tapping some time later he told me: "We have heard from three different sources that our phone is tapped." Up to the time of writing no complaint has been made about this.

Chaos was caused when Clyde Submarine Base was closed for half an hour just as the shifts were changing on 30th April and nobody was able to enter or leave the base.

Shortly before a shift change seven peace campers went into the base and split into two groups. Guards were slow to spot them entering but when the guards did see them the bandit alarm was set off and the Tannoy loudspeakers blared out their recorded message all over the base: Bandit! Bandit! Bandit! Lock all your windows and doors. Put on your hard hats. All doors to be guarded."

One group caused a diversion and the authorities followed them but lost the second, who went and sat in the cab of a truck. Searchers in another vehicle arrived and parked near to the intruders in their truck but did not spot them.

The seven intruders gave themselves up to the mod-plods, who rounded them up, took their details and released them pending charges. The incursion was part of the Anarchist 'Stop business as usual' campaign and it had done just that for half an hour at Faslane.

On 14th June, 1985, the front cover of *Peace News* consisted of a superb photograph taken by William Peden showing Legge and a policeman apparently dancing on top of a Mammoth Major with the caption: 'NUCLEAR CONVOYS – WE'RE GETTING ON TOP'.

This came about in the following manner. A convoy including five Mammoth Major warhead carriers passed Faslane Peace Camp heading North towards Coulport on 13th May. No doubt they would have been warned in advance by radio that there was only one hazard left, a peace camper, all alone at the North gate of Clyde Submarine Base and that after that they should have a clear run into Coulport in good weather. They would be parked up in Coulport well within the hour. It would seem that the police escort had been lulled into a sense of security by a trouble-free journey with no trouble at the peace camp. The lone camper vigilling at the North gate was unlikely to cause any problems. The faster police vehicles had speeded up leaving the Mammoth Majors at the back, their diesels working hard to move the trucks, each weighing over twenty tons, as fast as they could be moved. Around the bends in A814 by the North Gate, the Mammoth Majors slowed to a safe speed. Phil, the lone camper there, walked out in front of the last Mammoth Major and it stopped. The other vehicles in the convoy were out of sight and had to be radioed. It was some time before some of them could turn round and come to the rescue of the halted lorry. Phil was arrested and detained overnight. (N.B. I believe there were two guys called Philip. One spelt his name Phil, and the other Phill to be different but I can't be sure.)

Without further incident this convoy spent the night at Coulport and set off on its return journey, passing the peace camp at about 10.00. Campers stood on top of caravans to photograph the convoy. Suddenly three campers emerged from bushes on the other side of the road and sprinted to the fronts of vehicles shouting "Stop!" They stopped with Lynn laying in front of one Mammoth Major and Legge climbing on top of another. He started to dance on its roof. A policeman climbed up and joined him and for a moment they seemed to be dancing together. Legge was then arrested as were the two others who had stopped the convoy. This second action would not have happened as it did had the campers not had the confidence born of the knowledge that Phil had stopped a Mammoth Major single-handed the previous day.

The camp celebrated its third birthday on 12th June in a fit, active state.

No peace campers were near when at 14.15 hours on Thursday, 20th June 1985, in Sinclair Street, which, being in the centre of Helensburgh, was crowded with shoppers at the time a Mammoth Major in a convoy travelling towards the traffic lights at the Western end of the street collided with a Mammoth Major stopping in front of it. The police escort immediately cleared one side of the street and the convoy's fire engine came alongside the two Mammoth Majors. Local police joined in as soon as they could reach the site. Police then closed some shop doors on the side of the street near the accident – though they deny doing this, people in shops reported it – for up to twenty minutes. Less than five minutes walk away was the office of the *Helensburgh Advertiser* and reporters with cameras were on the scene very quickly, with the result that this newspaper had excellent photographs and a scoop along with comments from one or two experts who were highly critical of the movement of nuclear weapons through town centres. A nose to tail shunt had produced one broken windscreen and a few dents and scratches that could hardly be seen – or so it seemed. The vehicle with the broken windscreen was registered 81 AE 13. Unlucky No thirteen had run into the back of his colleague!

Apparently there were no injuries and nobody was charged with any offence, neither from the shunt nor from an earlier incident on the same journey when the convoy was reported to have forced an oncoming vehicle off a 'B' road near Helensburgh.

Dumbarton District Council demanded a full explanation of the shunt from the MoD who at first would not reveal the cause because they were holding their own enquiry. Two previous incidents were recalled by Councillor Ian Leitch, one when a gas main had exploded at Cardross minutes after a convoy had passed over it, and another when two warhead carriers had slid off the road in February 1984 on Peaton Hill.

On Sunday, 23rd June, the damaged warhead carrier, 81 AE 13, which the MoD claimed had only a broken windscreen went past the peace camp on a suspended tow. At least one driver appeared to be getting paid double time for an expensive tow job. The truck was chased by seven peace campers in their own vehicle. They were stopped at a police roadblock, which police claimed was just a traffic check at Rhu and asked for their names. William Peden was arrested as soon as he gave his! Had the police wanted to arrest William they could have done it easily at the peace camp without setting up a special roadblock. Then another camper said that he suspected this was a fake traffic check and he too was arrested. Both campers were charged with breach of the peace! Not only were they pleading not guilty but were also complaining to the SCCL and the authorities about their arrests.

Maybe the campers had been stopped from chasing No 13, the police roadblock had worked this time to stop them, unlike their attempts to stop the chase to Longtown on 23rd May 1984, but it had not got clean away. Cruisewatch spotted it near Oxford, photographed it and followed it back to Burghfield.

This damaged vehicle could quickly and cheaply have been professionally inspected at Coulport. I'm sure it was. Likewise the windscreen could have been replaced at Coulport, also quickly and cheaply. The lorry could then have gone straight back into service running to Burghfield with its back load without further problems. This is almost certainly what any transport manager worth his salt would have arranged. So why if a broken windscreen was the only serious damage, was this vehicle taken out of service and given a suspended tow, at least part of which took place on a Sunday when wage rates are at double time, for over 400 miles? Did it have defective brakes that could not be repaired at Coulport? Was it not possible to unload at Coulport because of damage to the load? The MoD would not answer.

Apart from *Peace News*, the national media ignored this accident when it happened, though later it featured in a Yorkshire TV film and a few articles in radical magazines. Thank God for the *Helensburgh Advertiser*.

An evening of typical British summer holidays weather in August gave peace campers the chance to enter Clyde Submarine Base without being seen by the modplods who were all sheltering from the terrific storm. Once inside the base, the campers took shelter from the rain in a Navy van for an hour where they remained unseen until they gave themselves up. They were charged with trespass under the Rhu, Coulport and Faslane Bylaws.

Hiroshima Day was commemorated with a vigil, which presented the Faslane Modsquad with a pot of home-made jam and a book *Hibakusha*. Campers spoke with sailors, some of whom didn't know it was Hiroshima Day.

At this time several people were in prison and there was also activity in the courts.

Scott MacDonald's trial was held on Hiroshima Day. It was alleged he had spray painted 'Victory to SWAPO' on a naval building inside the base during the 'Turning the Tide on Trident' action on 30th November 1984, and he was charged with trespass and malicious mischief. Scott was questioning Gill Durber of the Campaign Against Namibian Uranium Contracts when Sheriff Murphy ruled her evidence was not relevant to the case and ordered her to leave the witness box. She refused to go. A policeman lunged at her, picked her up and carried her down to the cells. Two women in the public gallery rose to protest at this ruling and were also taken down to the cells. Sheriff Murphy then continued with Scott's case, found him guilty on all charges and fined him a total of £210. After half an hour the three women were brought back into court and asked if they wanted to apologise or face contempt of court charges. One apologised and was released. Gill and Judith Lambe refused and were remanded overnight in Cornton Vale Women's Prison. The next day Gill was fined £20 for contempt of court and Judith was admonished. It is believed Lyn was fined for her part of the action at Dumbarton Sheriff Court in February.

Records are sketchy of trials arising from the Easter Saturday incursions, which dragged on into August 1985. About ten campers were in court including William Peden, Jane and Linda. William's fine of £210 was apparently the heaviest, probably because he actually cut the fence and he very nearly got a police inspector convicted for aiding and abetting him! He asked the friendly inspector to hold his rucksack, William then rummaged in it for his boltcutters, which he eventually found. He withdrew them and cut the fence. The Inspector just stood holding the sack speechless. Jane, probably helped by Linda, then began unravelling the fence. They were all arrested. In August Jane was found guilty and admonished. Only one of the two police witnesses identified Linda and as this meant there was not enough evidence to convict her, she was found not guilty.

Over the weekend of 17th-18th August the Army held an exercise on the ranges above Garelochead Army Training Camp and fourteen peace campers got involved. They told the Army to go away and leave the countryside in peace. The Army was flummoxed. They called the Modsquad who then told the peace campers to go away and leave the Army in peace. Some campers left. The two modplods who had come in a jeep then arrested Steve and Mary-Anne after warning them they would be charged with breach of the peace (for interrupting an Army exercise!), took them to a carpark in the jeep, transferred them to their Transit and took them to Faslane Modsquad Station, then to Helensburgh Police Station, which would not accept them. They were then turned away from Dumbarton Police Station too before being taken to Vale of Leven where the police held them until the modplods could collect the other three and charge all five of them. When the modplods arrested Pauline they were violent and when arresting Shawn one punched him in the mouth, though they were not so rough with Tommy. They were probably a bit flummoxed, too, there being only two of them to arrest five peace campers out of an original group of fourteen and with the civilian police telling them to go from station to station. The campers were eventually released from Vale of Leven at 06.30 in the morning after their midnight walk on the ranges.

Also in August, Exercise Short Sermon involved a simulated nuclear accident at Faslane with enough Navy top brass to mould a Big Tom and vans from British Nuclear Fuels Limited all over the place. The visitors to Rhu Radiation Centre all got out of their radiation suits and went off to the pub for a two-hour lunch break. One wonders if this would be done in the event of a real nuclear accident occurring. Faslane peace campers joined in the spirit of the thing. They gave Clyde Submarine Base a twelve-foot long artificial leek vegetable, representing both radiation and information leaks. They also put warning placards on the fence in case members of the public hadn't noticed there was supposed to have been a simulated nuclear accident there.

At about this time Huw became the third convoy blockader to be jailed. On 17th May he had been fined £50 for convoy blockading and intended to pay the fine. Part of his defence concerned the safety of the convoys as a 'road liable to subsidence' sign had been erected 300 yards along the convoy's route from where it was blockaded. In his view this subsidence added to the hazards of moving nuclear warheads. (Huw was a prophet! Road subsidence contributed to the causes of a much-publicised, serious accident when a Mammoth Major left a minor road in Wiltshire and overturned on 9th January 1987.) After the collision in Sinclair Street, Helensburgh, Huw changed his mind and decided a more effective protest was needed about these hazards. He stopped payment so that the authorities would have to call him back to court where he could voice his fears and reasons for not paying and there was another chance of the media reporting them. The authorities did this and as no payment was forthcoming jailed him for about a week.

Ruth, Rufus and Scott MacDonald invaded the South African Consulate in Glasgow to protest about the import of Namibian Uranium. Ruth, a South African, demanded her right to telex President Botha. They would not let her do it. The protestors were removed from the building, Rufus and Scott being charged with displaying banners illegally and behaviour likely to cause a breach of the peace. Ruth was not charged.

Soon after Short Sermon a document called the Clyde Area Public Safety Scheme was distributed to selected interested parties by the MoD. Peace campers had to study someone else's copy. This document gave details of the telephone tree to be activated if there was a nuclear accident at Faslane. The first two tiers to telephone were military and naval people. Then came civil nuclear authorities like the United Kingdom Atomic Energy Authority. Last to be told would be the local councillors and health authority officials.

By the beginning of September Faslane Peace Camp and CND had published copies of a *Polariswatch Information Pack*.

THE MOON CAMP AND THE RAINBOW (September 1985 – April 1986)

In early September Moon Camp was set up almost dead opposite the North Gate of Clyde Submarine Base. This camp, set up in addition to the existing camp, was also known as North Camp. It stood on land reserved for the Garelochead Bypass. This would relieve the village of Garelochead with its tight bends and steep hill of heavy vehicles. Most of the heavy vehicles going through Garelochead in the nineteen eighties were on MoD business. No doubt the shunt with the Mammoth Majors in Helensburgh in June influenced the authorities in the decision to build the bypass. They didn't want an embarrassing shunt like that with its attendant publicity in the middle of Garelochead. Because of the gentle curves and easy slope of the bypass, vehicles using it would have quicker journey times and improved fuel consumption, thus making their journeys quicker and cheaper, as well as safer. Had it not been for the heavy lorries on MoD business, particularly in connexion with Trident, the bypass would never have been built. The main reason for building it was to improve the route for MoD vehicles, thus making it more difficult for peace campers to stop them, and helping the MoD at the expense of the civilian road construction programme. How many traffic-jammed villages have been campaigning for bypasses for years? So, in order to highlight all this and to maintain a presence near North Gate, peace campers moved onto the muddy, puddle-covered site for the new road.

The Rainbow Actions were an organised plan of escalating actions, involving some NVDA organised primarily by the peace camp, designed to stop nuclear subs from using the Clyde.

The first Rainbow Action was the Red Action – 'red for danger and red for stop' was the slogan, which took place on 16th September 1985.

Good preparation, advance planning and thorough briefing led to the activists being inspired with confidence. They formed into affinity groups and spent the night at the two peace camps. They moved into action early. By 06.00 hours there were around 200 activists at South Gate and more elsewhere. The rumour got around that all the civilian MoD workers at Faslane had been given the day off and that only essential naval personnel and modplods were working this Monday morning. The blockaders' morale was high. Work had been severely disrupted already! However the arrival of workers in vehicles soon proved the rumours to be false. Both entrances were blockaded. What was known as the Tunnel Entrance in fact led to a car park outside the South Gate, so a blockade of the South Gate was all that was needed to stop the people from the married quarters across the main road from getting into the base. The North Gate was the other entrance to the base. A massive traffic jam grew at the South Gate as blockaders completely closed the road. Then police started to get rough, arresting people and bringing in police horses. After much delay the morning shift entered the base, with blockaders either arrested or cleared to the roadsides. Meanwhile at North Gate over seventy people with candles and rainbow banners shining in the half-light blockaded and sang. These included the MAFIA, one of three affinity groups formed at Moon Camp. Over half of this affinity group was arrested during the day and they seemed to have borne the brunt of the arrests. Perhaps the police confused the Molesworth and Faslane Into Action Affinity Group with a Sicilian organisation also called the Mafia!

All this blockading did not affect the sailing in eerie silence of a nuclear submarine. Protestors saw a timely reminder of the reason they were there.

Shortly afterwards ten peace campers piled into a van with two ladders and a carpet. For a while they drove up and down the fence along A814 followed by a friendly journalist. Rain restricted visibility and stopped sound carrying any distance so when they arrived at what appeared to be a good place to enter the base they did not notice a rugby match in progress on the other side of the fence. Their diversion was late. Then as campers rushed up their wooden ladder to cross the fence it broke. When they eventually got over it twenty-two burly submariners welcomed them as an amusing interruption to their rugger. Legge and Josie evaded capture for a while, with a chase involving Josie jumping into a burn three times and dancing on the roof of a cycle shed.

It had been hoped to show the journalists how easy it was to make an unauthorised entry to the base. I think campers felt that this particular NVDA, which was only done virtually on the spur of the moment, could have done with more advance planning. It would have helped if people had known the maximum load for the ladder, so as to avoid overloading it, the diversion could have been better synchronised and some way of circumnavigating an obstacle like the rugger match should have been planned in advance.

Around 22.00 hours that night the local police were inundated with phone calls as a minor earthquake rocked that part of Scotland. People did not know what was happening. Was the Earth moving in sympathy with the Red Action?

Faslane was not on a fault line. The nearest one was situated North of Glen Douglas. Slight tremors from this line had occasionally been felt in the area. Apparently they usually came just after demos at Faslane though nobody knew why. This was the first proper earthquake here since before 1973.

On the morning of Tuesday, 17th September, the public gallery of Dumbarton Sheriff Court was filled to overflowing with peace campers and their supporters. In the dock were seventy or so people arrested at the Red Action, not all at once of course. Most were charged with obstructing the highway. Some who pleaded guilty were fined straight away and the others were bailed to return later. It is not possible to deal with all the cases individually here. Subsequently the SCCL took up the cases of several women arrested at the Red Action who complained of being strip-searched at Maryhill and Clydebank Police Stations. They were also investigating allegations that the police handled people extremely roughly, especially at South Gate and outside Maxine's house, and reports that an inspector and a police sergeant had lost their self-control at South Gate during the demo. This entailed preparing a report for the Strathclyde police committee, and the SCCL were appealing for witnesses to come forward.

On 18th September campers noticed a convoy with five warhead carriers passing the peace camp on its way to Coulport. They did not stop it then but by 07.00 hours on Thursday 19th September a 'Citadel' cycle lock had been put on the gate of RNAD Coulport, while a small group of protestors and a visiting fire-eater had entertained the modplods on guard. Nobody inside noticed they were locked in until they went to release the convoy. Boltcutters only cut the plastic cover on the lock's shank. Oxy-acetylene cutting gear had to be brought up to cut the shank itself. It was 09.45 before they could release the convoy, hours late. As usual peace campers noted details of convoy vehicles.

On 21st September there were five arrests at another 'snowball' action to cut the fence at Faslane.

At 16.10 on 3rd October another convoy was spotted by peace campers. Faslane Peace Camp's alert of their phone tree crossed with another alert on the Cardiff Polariswatch phone tree because another convoy had been spotted in South Wales near ROF Llanishen. On 4th October police and campers assembled at Garelochead. The three campers took photographs and noted details of the vehicles as they passed on their return to Burghfield. Police, who said they were only there to stop people from jumping into the road and obstructing the convoy, arrested nobody. In the past campers had been arrested for photographing convoys, while visiting American Nukewatch people photographing a convoy in England with nothing to show their Nukewatch identity were merely asked to stop.

Faslane Peace campers arrested at the 'Stop Business as Usual' protest in Summer 1985 were tried in court on 31st October and 4th November.

Yorkshire Television's documentary *Britain's Bomb* was not shown as planned on 5th November because of problems with the MoD. The peace campers had helped to make this film, which contained many shots of the convoys. The film was shown later.

The MoD had by this time announced their plan to extend the Rhu, Coulport and Faslane By-laws to cover an extra 3,000 acres extending across the isthmus of the Rosneath Peninsula, leaving only one public road down the Eastern side for access to the town and villages on the peninsula. They also planned to modernise the by-laws to bring them into line with new ones introduced for other bases under the Military Lands Act 1892. Although it would be possible to enter this area legally at certain times (provided one complied with certain conditions in the by-laws), 600 acres of it – nearly a square mile – was completely closed to the public, right on top of the hills where the best views were to be had. Previous to this the land had been used for sheep and forestry and one could walk freely across nearly all of it (provided one acted responsibly as a hill walker should anywhere). The MoD had used compulsory purchase powers to acquire some of this land from farmers who did not want to sell. The MoD did not have it all their own way however. They were inundated with complaints about the 3,000 acre extension to RNAD Coulport and the new by-laws from walkers, ramblers and local people as well as the peace campers whose spokesperson Phill said the camp was pleased with this "encouraging indication of local feeling" [*Peace News*, 15th November 1985]. Panda, a peace camper, wrote objecting to the new by-laws and subsequently received a letter from the MoD saying Panda could walk on the hills, around Mam Mor between Coulport and Garelochead without being arrested. Later this was proved a lie, when Panda was arrested walking there.

There were problems at Faslane where the construction project was said to be delayed for six months because the asbestos could not be removed and dumped elsewhere.

To add insult to injury, on 5th November four peace campers strolled across this asbestos dump and sat on a jetty until modplods found and arrested them. They walked over the dump because they wanted to show how easily children could enter and play on the site. They were released without charge probably because the MoD wanted to avoid publicity and children finding out how easy it was to enter this super playground!

About now people were getting to know about MoD plans to blast Rhu Narrows so that Trident subs could sail through them up to Faslane. Apparently while this entrance to the loch suited all the other subs perfectly, Tridents being wider could not navigate it.

Strathclyde Police's enquiry into the allegations of strip-searches and violent arrest at the Red Action was now taking place.

By 20th November Polariswatch had spread to the rest of the United Kingdom. Meetings as far south as Oxford and London had organised people into a network for observing convoy movements. Janet Convery at the CND head office became national co-ordinator. People were asked to look out for convoys and when one was spotted they were asked to supply Janet or Faslane Peace Camp with at least the following information: the number of warhead carriers in the convoy, their registration numbers, where sighted, the direction of travel and the time and date of the sighting. In much of Southern England the existing Cruisewatch network helped.

On 3rd December Yorkshire Television's documentary *Britain's Bomb* received its first showing. The campers seemed to think it was well worth the wait and was a very good film.

On 5th December fines of £20 each were levied by Dumbarton Sheriff Court on three campers found guilty of breach of the peace as a result of their being on an Army training ground during an exercise. These campers were almost certainly three of the five arrested on the ranges above Garelochead Army Training Camp on 18th August.

The high security section of Clyde Submarine Base was entered just after Christmas by three campers who had crossed the Faslane North construction site (formerly Garelochead Shipbreakers Yard). Nobody seemed to notice them even though they were wearing bright red Santa Claus outfits. They strolled into the high security area and boarded a diesel-powered sub. Then they left it and climbed onto the nuclear powered hunter killer sub *HMS Conqueror*. Neither carried nuclear missiles but they might just have had nuclear depth charges on board, though it was unlikely. Before leaving *HMS Conqueror* they hung a stocking from the conning tower cable. Only when the campers were leaving were they found and arrested. This protest made the national press and the BBC reported it in the Radio 4 news broadcast all over Great Britain. Nobody was charged with any offence at this action.

In January 1986 the pile-drivers began their noisy work piling for the new Trident jetties at Faslane.

Also in January the peace camp published a list of over 100 contractors involved in the expansion at Faslane and Coulport. The list included a firm said to be involved in the road building which had rendered yeoman service to the MoD at both Molesworth and Greenham Common – Tarmac. Shortly afterwards *Peace News* reported that Tarmac had been awarded a £4,000,000 contract to 'clear 80,000 tons of asbestos buried beneath the site of the base expansion. At Coulport scores of Portakabins have been erected in connexion with Trident expansion work there' [*Peace News*, 7th February 1986]. In view of the recent failed attempt to clear the asbestos off the construction site by Shanks and McEwen and their subcontractors Yull and Dodds, I believe the contract

had been amended so that Tarmac now had only to move the asbestos out of the way of the construction work and bury it elsewhere on MoD land.

On 23rd January a convoy left Burghfield accompanied by calls on the peace camps telephone tree reporting convoys all over the place, one with three warhead carriers and another with only one. As a result the campers were expecting a convoy probably on Monday, 27th January. The peace camp was crowded with visitors that Sunday afternoon when suddenly 'what should come thundering past our camp but a convoy with five carriers with a CND member and a Strathclyde Regional Councillor in hot pursuit'. [*Faslane Focus* February 1986: 'Polaris Convoy Capers'] This convoy had taken three days on the journey north, one day longer than usual and had spent the extra night out somewhere near Stoke-on-Trent. Out of the many convoys that had visited Coulport this was only the second to arrive on a Sunday. Polaris-watchers made sure its arrival at Coulport was reported on Radio Scotland. Callum, Jane, Phil and Sam, waiting for it to reappear on Monday, saw a Polaris sub sailing up the loch (do they sail, steam or what?) and submerging before entering Coulport, but no convoy! It left a day later than usual on Tuesday, 28th January, again spent a night somewhere near Stoke-on-Trent (or maybe even in the town) and was tracked most of the way back to Burghfield where it arrived on 30th January. During this tracking a tracker's car was forced off the road by police. Road conditions on 27th January had been icy and the Strathclyde Regional Councillor was going to ask questions of the Strathclyde Police Committee about the speed of the convoy as it went through thirty miles per hour areas. A complaint about this was made at the time to a police chief inspector at Coulport. (Another factor contributing to the cause of the Mammoth Major accident on 9th January 1987, was ice on the road.)

In Autumn 1985 Moon Camp had spent £75 on applying for planning permission to Dumbarton District Council, the planning authority in whose area the camp lay. Earlier in 1985 a petition from some local residents had not prevented Dumbarton Council from renewing the older Faslane Peace Camp's caravan site licence originally granted in 1982. Dumbarton Council granted planning permission for Moon Camp. The application was treated as a personal one from camper Pat Freeborn, and the proposal that the permission be granted was moved by a friend of the camp, Councillor Ian Leitch. There were several conditions, none of them impossible to comply with, including one which limited the duration of the planning permission to five years.

At their January meeting Strathclyde Regional Council had a petition from 969 residents of Garelochead asking the council to close Moon Camp. Strathclyde also had at hand a subcommittee recommendation that they should not grant permission for Moon Camp to be on their land, which of course it already was. This land was earmarked for the Garelochead Bypass of course. Permission to camp there was not granted but no action was taken at this meeting to obtain an order in possession so as to evict the camp. The camp was not then in the way of contractors building the new road and would not be in their way for some time to come.

In no way did this grant Moon Camp permission to be on Strathclyde's land and would not prevent Strathclyde from evicting it, but if the camp complied with the conditions they could not be prosecuted by Dumbarton for breach of the planning laws. The Secretary of State for Scotland could still purchase the site and evict them, or use a complex legal procedure to revoke their planning permission and then prosecute them for breach of the planning laws. Moon Camp was not yet as safe as houses.

One Saturday in January nine women and nine men went to the perimeter fence at Clyde Submarine base and began to cut it. One person then 'concentrated on unravelling the fence to make a big hole' [*Faslane Focus*, February 1986]. At Faslane they took their 'snowballing' seriously, scratching the wire with a blunt hacksaw blade was not good enough here! Chief Inspector Carson of Helensburgh and his men were reinforced for the day by women police constables from Glasgow. They were chatty and relaxed as they had been told in advance what to expect and the 'snowballers' were friendly and non-violent. All eighteen were arrested and charged with criminal damage.

Friday, 14th February, saw a great increase in activity at the two peace camps when people started arriving for the Orange Action and spent the night there. At least 200 people came for the action and they were all active. On three occasions people entered Faslane North and walked on the asbestos dump. Only one of them was held by the police and that person was later released without charge. However, the three people on the roof of Rhu Radiation Centre were not treated so kindly by police. All three were arrested and one later complained about racist abuse. They were compensated by getting at least one photograph published in a newspaper. Throughout the action a telephone blockade of the base was attempted and many supporters unable to attend the action joined in by phoning the base to apologise for not being there. On the

Saturday buskers and leafleters covered the whole of Dumbarton, followed by an evening ceilidh in the Rhu Halls. On Sunday there were workshops on several subjects including information on construction work for the Trident Project and planning for future Rainbow Actions. These were a series of seven actions each taking as its theme a particular colour of the rainbow, starting with red and taking the other colours in their order across the visible spectrum. The co-counselling workshop was probably the best attended. On Monday leafleters leafleted the workers actually inside the South Gate and at North Gate leaflets were handed to a chaplain who said he would give them to the workers in the Tarmac Portakabin. Also on the Monday nine people went for a ramble on the hills around Coulport where Panda was assured by the MoD that one would not be arrested, and were arrested. Altogether fourteen people were arrested over the three days. All the men were held in Maryhill Prison and the women in Clydebank. It was 04.00 hours on Tuesday before the last one was released after being charged.

Thanks to the list of contractors published by the Faslane Peace camp, supporters identified five sites occupied by firms involved with the Trident Project in South Hampshire and on the Saturday morning they held vigils at two of them in support of the Orange Action. The first was at Plessey's factory in Titchfield and the second was at Vickers' office block, Wessex House, in the centre of Eastleigh. Though normally open with people working in it on Saturday mornings this building was closed. A friendly police sergeant told the demonstrators that Vickers had closed the building when someone told them there was going to be a demonstration. These small vigils involving a total of less than twelve people received good local press coverage. A crafty security policeman contacted by a TV cameraman, who said he was coming, conned the demonstrators into leaving Plessey early, so that the TV cameraman missed them by a few minutes. However, he came to Wessex House and filmed the demo there. His film was shown on TV that night. The present author is rather proud of the publicity these two vigils got as he wrote the press releases!

From time to time similar small actions inspired by the Rainbow Actions took place all over Britain.

Shortly after John's van had brought the arrested campers back to Faslane early on Tuesday, 18th February, and everyone was asleep, Kitty was awakened by a fire in the caravan next door. She woke other campers but they could not put out the fire, not even

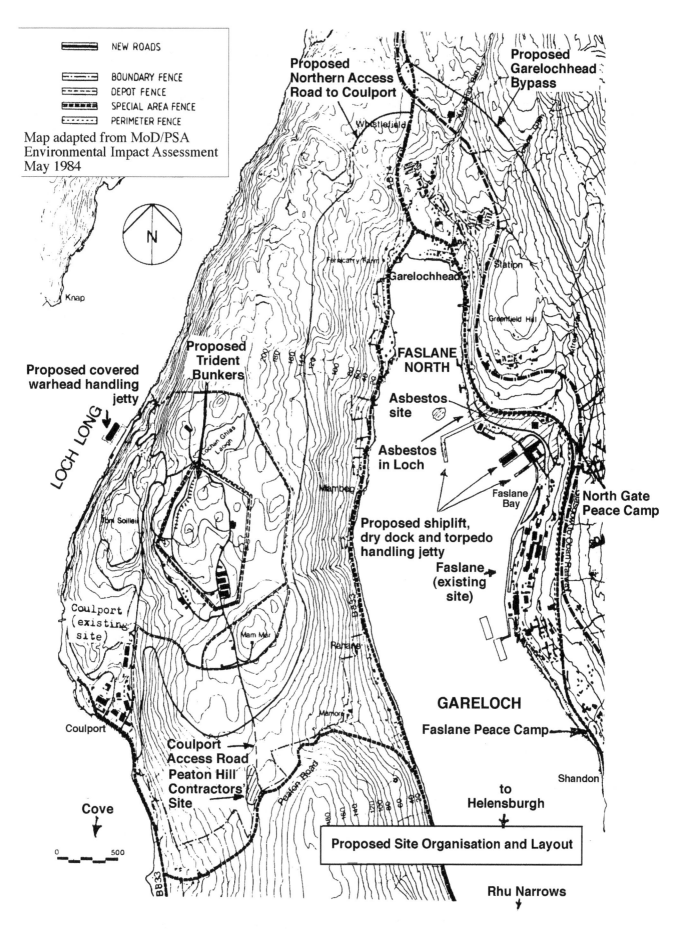

FASLANE MAP

with the extinguishers offered by passing taxi drivers. A passing policeman phoned the fire brigade. A taxi driver took some photos with her camera, which she was going to submit to a local paper. By the time the firemen had put out the fire the caravan was a gutted ruin. They were treating the fire as arson, the police were treating it as suspicious and two peace campers saw and followed a suspicious person to the Clyde Submarine Base…

While the cruise convoy was out during the period 19th-24th February beacon fires were lit all over Britain. The following poem from *Faslane Focus* for March describes what happened at one fire. It was inspired by a trip up the Peaton Hill to light a beacon there.

THE PEATON BEACON

Jim and Phil went up the hill,
With Jenny, Chris and Mark.
Tommy, John and Peter too,
Went to light the dark.

Despite the chill on Peaton Hill,
We made a little spark,
And huddled round our beacon,
We soon light up the dark.

Up on the hill we used our skill,
For we wanted no mistakes.
We found some wood we thought was good,
Thank Tarmac for their stakes.

Then up the hill as modplods will,
They came to see this sight:
The Cruisewatch flaming beacon
Was lighting up the night.

Then modplod Bill came up the hill.
He fetched, with him some water.
He used the same to douse the flame,
Though we said he shouldn't ought'r.

With peace we fill the Peaton Hill,
Our dreams, our hopes they will not weaken,
For we can stop the building work,
With you around that beacon …
… THE YELLOW ACTION … HELP US STOP THE WORK
     Reprinted with the kind permission of *Faslane Focus*.

Reference to the Yellow Action is a call for people to get active in organising the next event in the series of Rainbow Actions, which was due to take place on 2nd June 1986. The March issue of *Faslane Focus* carried information about the plans for it.

At the end of February yet another window was broken in the communal caravan when three children from the local school threw bricks at it.

On 7th March two people arrested at the Red Action appeared in the Sheriff Court. Anne F was fined £60 and Alison was fined £50. In the other cases resulting from the Red Action, already heard, there were three not guilty verdicts, one not proven and three people who refused to pay fines were imprisoned. The number of people fined is not known but the total of all the fines levied to 7th March was £805. Some cases were still to be heard, notably those of Anne P, Chris B, Jan S, Paul McG, Jeanne M, Andy D, Martin, Keith and Mark.

At about this time the report on the alleged police violence at the Red Action was published. The procurator Fiscal in Paisley saw it and it was believed that the Lord Advocate for Scotland was consulted. As was to be expected Chief Constable Andrew Sloan defended his men, saying that he thought their violence was justified by the behaviour of the blockaders. He was at the blockade in person. His presence was believed to be the reason for the alleged uncontrolled behaviour of some officers. Prosecutions on assault charges were considered for two policemen and subsequently one of them who had dragged a woman out of a bus by her hair was found guilty of assaulting her and fined £40. Nothing happened about the strip searches.

In March the two caravans and all the equipment of North Camp were moved by hand a few yards South to a new site. A vehicle with a towing hitch could not be found in time. The reasons for this move appear to have been rather complex. Notice was given in a local paper on 28th February that Secretary of State for Scotland George Younger had drafted a compulsory purchase order – the Garelochead Bypass (Side Roads) Compulsory Purchase Order 1986 – in order to buy land for the construction of a bypass to ease the passage of heavy vehicles between Faslane and Coulport. Many objections to the order were submitted to the Scottish Development Department before the deadline of 19th March but they did not stop George Younger's plan to take over this land, which included the old North Camp site. Before the camp was moved, trees were being felled behind it and work on the actual campsite was expected to begin any day, which could lead to eviction hassles. The campers were planning actions that required them to be camping off but near to the bypass construction site.

The new site was to be known as Life Camp. The move to Life Camp resulted in Mike being charged with trespass and as his case was not to be heard until August the camp was safe until then, for until the court had made a decision nobody could legally act to move Life Camp. Campers started to raise the £75 needed for planning permission for the new camp to give it yet more security.

Campers arrested at the Orange Action were originally charged under the old by-laws but the new by-laws made under the Military Lands Act 1892 had come into force on 5th February so the authorities had to change the charges. Faslane was not the only base where the authorities were apparently taken by surprise by the introduction of these by-laws.

For four years the residents of Helensburgh had been campaigning for a bypass to relieve the town of heavy vehicles and nuclear warhead convoys and the authorities had said it was impossible to build one. In March the MoD announced plans to build a military road for the exclusive use of vehicles on MoD business and with MoD permits which would take the contractors, lorries and convoys away from Helensburgh. This road was to be dug up when the construction work for the Trident Project was complete. Of course the construction of this road and more importantly its destruction when the Trident Project was finished would in themselves generate much traffic of heavy lorries with tippers and contractors' plant going to and from the roadbuilding site.

It was reported that the Vice-President of the Scottish Conservative and Unionist Association regarded the plan for this road as the last straw in a collection of blunders in the treatment of Scotland by the Tory Government. He resigned. The MoD would have to buy land from Sir Ivor Colquehoun to build this road. It was reported that he, too, didn't want the road built.

In this account publicity has only been mentioned rarely and usually only when national publicity has been involved. In fact much national publicity has been missed out and practically every event at Faslane has had some sort of local or Scottish publicity, usually lots of it. I have not mentioned the numerous meetings and rallies Faslane peace campers attended, sometimes with an exhibition, nor the links and friendships they have forged with disarmers all over Britain, nor their contacts with visitors from all over Europe and North America.

Some of the keenest campers came from outside Scotland, among them Phill, Jane and Shawn from Hampshire and Colin 'Boris' Gray and 'Scumbag' from Wiltshire, all with previous peace camping experience. Faslane Peace Camp had become a Mecca for disarmers.

The postal address for the camps was: Faslane Peace Camp, below St. Andrews School, Shandon, Helensburgh, Dumbartonshire.

PEACE CAMPS IN THE FENS: FELTWELL, LAKENHEATH, MILDENHALL AND SCULTHORPE

General Tooey Spaatz, leader of the United States Army Air Force, and Marshal of the Royal Air Force Lord Tedder signed the Spaatz-Tedder Agreement in secret on 6th July 1946 (before the USAAF dropped its first 'A' for 'Army' in September 1947 and before Britain exploded her first atomic bomb in 1952). This agreement laid down the terms and conditions under which the USAAF was to base B29 Superfortresses in Britain.

The B29 was quite simply the aircraft which won World War II. It could fly higher and further than any other fixed-wing aircraft of its day. B29s had proved their reliability in delivering two atom bombs and a huge tonnage of incendiaries to Japan in 1945 though they were not then used in Europe. The Americans wanted bases for them in England because a B29 could fly from here to European Russia, deliver its bombs and return for a second load. Under the agreement they were to be based on five airfields that had been used by the USAAF and the RAF in World War II: Bassingbourne, Lakenheath, Marham, Mildenhall and Scampton. The first ones arrived in 1948 but their presence got little publicity.

About twenty miles East of Cambridge, RAF Mildenhall was by 1982 no longer a nuclear bomber base though it could still handle them. It was a command and distribution centre. The USAF Tactical Airlift Wing was based there with troop-carrying C130 aircraft. The Electronic Security Wing based

there had the use of two U2 spy planes and had just acquired one of the latest SR71 'Blackbird' spy planes. Mildenhall also had fifteen KC135 tanker aircraft equipped for in-flight refueling, though these may have been moved soon after to another base. Mildenhall was on the list to receive the huge C5A 'Galaxy' transport planes. 'Operation Silk Purse' is the name given to the organization, which put up airborne command posts for US generals in the event of another big war in Europe and its four Boeing 707s converted to flying war rooms were based at Mildenhall. In a false alarm on 6th June 1980, alerts went round the world to the first five US bases before the information was checked and the alert signal cancelled. One of these five bases was Mildenhall which shows how important it was, probably because of the 'Silk Purse' aircraft.

RAF Feltwell, beside A1065 about twelve miles North of Mildenhall and ten miles North of Lakenheath, was a storage depot for the USAF. Short take off and landing aircraft could use its airfield but it is believed no aircraft were based there. Feltwell had a school for 850 USAF children and housing for service personnel. There was in the early 1980s a plan to build an underground hospital for American servicemen in a war here but this plan seems to have been abandoned because of the difficulties of excavating in the low lying fenlands.

At the Northern end of A1065 a left turn onto A148

leads to RAF Sculthorpe, an airfield normally used exclusively by the RAF about thirty miles North of Feltwell and near Norwich. It is on slightly higher ground on the edge of the Fens. Between Feltwell and Sculthorpe lie RAF Marham and RAF Swaffham both of which hosted big nuclear disarmament demonstrations in the past.

It was not until 1979 that news of a crash in about 1955 was officially released to the public. This crash involved a B29 carrying a quantity of high explosives, which apparently did not explode when it crashed into a store at Lakenheath, although three members of the crew were killed. There were three atomic bombs in the store at the time. Had the B29 exploded would it have set them off as well?

Lakenheath Airfield is twenty-two miles East of Cambridge and lies immediately to the East of Lakenheath Village and Maids Cross Hill. It was laid out during the Depression in the 1930s by mostly local labourers paid 7/6d. (37 1/2p) per day, with food tickets thrown in. Since then it has grown until at the time of writing it had 1,600 married quarters, a ninety-bed hospital, schools for over 2,300 pupils and about 18,000 USAF personnel and some British, of course. The secure part of the base was surrounded by a seven-and-a-half mile fence, outside of which lay much of the housing and some shops and social facilities. Local civilians, including some peace camp supporters and campers, were thus able to mix with Americans and did so. There was a rumour that some peace campers smoked 'dope' with American servicemen. It is fact that the daughter of Hazel, one of the Lakenheath peace campers, married an American security officer without severing connexions with her mother who got on with the American quite well.

An excellent view could be had of this airfield from the Ordnance Survey Trig Point on top of Maids Cross Hill. Although only thirty-one metres above sea level, this trig point is higher than any other land between it and the Ural Mountains thousands of miles away in the USSR. That's good news to a bomber pilot limping back to base with a badly wounded bomber after being shot up over Moscow.

Progress marches on. The B29 that out-performed its contemporaries was in its turn out-performed by jets. By 1982 RAF Lakenheath was home to the F1-11 fighter bombers of the USAF's 48th Tactical Fighter Wing and blast-resistant hangars were being built for them and for USAF 'Thunderbolts'.

Members of Nottingham CND and Nottingham FAB got together following a visit to Greenham Common and decided to set up another peace camp in Eastern England in addition to Molesworth. They looked at several bases and finally settled on having a camp in the area around Lakenheath and Mildenhall. Contact was made with disarmers living there and they were very helpful. They inspected several possible sites and found out about who owned what land in the area. A site was chosen. The location was kept secret so that the authorities would not block it off and prevent access. An appeal for all sorts of things was made in the *Nottingham CND Bulletin* of April 1982. On Saturday 29th May a lorry left Nottingham carrying six people, tents and camping gear. It headed south. On Sunday, 30th May, a mini, a van and a minibus also left Nottingham loaded with people (17 this time) and camping gear and also went south. On that afternoon all four vehicles gathered at a house in Suffolk where they joined up with some local supporters and nine Molesworth peace campers.

Meanwhile RAF Lakenheath was holding its annual air show nearby. Traffic on the roads around the airfield was heavy and the guards at the entrances were kept busy.

Nobody paid any particular attention when at about 17.00 hours several unmarked vehicles, including the four from Nottingham, pulled up on A1065 Brandon Road almost opposite Gate Two of the airfield. The people on the vehicles started unloading camping gear and erecting tents. Still nobody appeared to notice. By 19.00, ten tents and a tepee had been erected, a fire had been lit, water had been collected, the campers were already eating their first meal cooked by Louise, and Richard had already started contacting the media to tell them about the camp.

Almost certainly it was the phone calls to the media that alerted the police and USAF for it was not until 20.30 hours that they put in an appearance. Two police cars arrived with two policemen and an American whose big hat, boots, belt and check shirt earned him the nickname 'JR' after a TV character. The police told the campers they were on private land. As they had been unable to trace any registration of the land to an owner, the campers said they would stay until legal action was taken to remove them. Presumably they thought that their only problem would be over planning permission for the camp and that sort of a legal wrangle can be dragged out for quite a long time, even if planning permission is not obtained in the end. It was a pleasant evening, the discussions were friendly and the official visitors left happier than when they arrived. Some of the people who had helped to set up the camp left, as they had to go to work in other places and about nine or a dozen campers stayed. Right from the start the campers had some wonderful local supporters, especially Bernie and Mandy Fry from Icklingham and later the Brown family from Lakenheath. The camp could not have survived without these local people in its first year, for the main body of campers came from Nottingham, ninety miles away and had family connexions, work and other commitments there.

Richard continued to phone the media while the campers settled themselves into their new camp. As a result of his persistent phoning at least three local radio stations reported the camp, as did three national dailies whilst the *East Anglian News* carried 'a very sympathetic article with a large picture!' [*Bulletin* June 1982] *Peace News* and the *Bulletin*, both published in Nottingham, carried reports.

Among the people who set up the camp were Louise and Ted Gabb and their three children, Sue and her two children and Ann Wood. These all came from Nottingham. During the first month or so about nine people lived at the camp permanently with their pets. Animals seem to have been present at all the camps at Lakenheath as pets.

Soon the campers had leafleted many houses in Lakenheath and Mildenhall. They also asked for an interview with the commanding officer of RAF Lakenheath but it appears that their request was not granted on this occasion.

The first campsite was on what was thought to be common land or wasteland, but on 28th June a notice was nailed to a tree beside the camp by two men. This notice stated that on 9th July if the campers had not left the landowner would be applying for an order in possession, so he could evict the campers. The notice was checked with three solicitors including the camp's own solicitor. They said the landowner had a good case even though the eviction notice did not name any actual campers but named a local camp supporter as the responsible person. The notice was issued by Elvedon Estate, controlled by Lord Iveagh, a member of the Guinness brewing family. *Peace News* reported:

> A member of the Guinness family owns the land on which three villages and the peace camp stand. He also rents the base to the US Air Force for $1.00 a year. [*Peace News*, 9th July 1982]

However, 4th July, American Independence Day, came before the eviction. To celebrate it the USAF at Lakenheath were holding an open day when the public would be allowed onto the airfield to see their aircraft and displays. The peace campers were determined to take full advantage of this event to publicise the nuclear war preparations going on there and persuade people that these preparations had to stop. They bought much extra food and made many visiting supporters welcome at the camp. About ninety activists all told were present. At 10.30 hours on the day some of them began to leaflet the long queue of vehicles waiting to go into the base, while other leafleted inside. At about 13.30 the activists conferred and made their plans for the afternoon. It was only now that the sit-down was properly planned. After the conference some activists went to hold a vigil at the gates while others went inside the base. Then at 15.00 about twenty adults and eight children who had gone into the base ducked under a cordon holding back spectators when a klaxon was sounded, walked briskly about 150 feet to a runway and sat down on it in a circle. They sang and shouted peace slogans. USAF police immediately surrounded them and after about three minutes some vehicles came and were parked so as to hide the demonstration from the spectators. The activists moved back into view. All flying stopped but was resumed after about ten minutes as the demonstration was not on the main runway but on an emergency runway at the side. After fifteen minutes British police arrived followed by the senior RAF officer, a Wing Commander. He said the children were in a dangerous place and asked the activists very politely to take them away. Activists said that the nuclear bomber airfield endangered the lives of the children anyhow and stayed. After about forty minutes and three more refusals to leave the demonstrators, pleased with the effect of their action and not wishing to be arrested this time, got up to leave of their own accord. They were stopped and told to wait for an escort to take them off the airfield. A bus came. They got on the bus and were driven off the airfield, with placards showing in the windows. Once outside the bus stopped and police asked for names and addresses. Everyone gave their surname as FAB and their address as that of the peace camp. Eventually the police gave up and released them all. They then joined the vigil at the gates, which stayed until 19.00 hours when the visitors to the open day had left. The entrances to the airfield had been open all the time, though in the afternoon police were drafted in from many miles away to handle the vigils at the gates. The authorities probably feared blockades and more action on the base. Dozens of activists had been into the base, some having been removed as many as eight times, and thousands of leaflets had been dis-

Lakenheath peace camp site Mark III – now a rubbish compound.

tributed without anyone being detained or charged. At least one newspaper gave the actions a big report. In the July *Bulletin* an activist summed up:

> We were all very elated and felt that the day had been a huge success.

When Elvedon Estate's application for an order in possession came before the High Court in London on 9th July, three families from the peace camp attended and assured the court that the camp would leave immediately. This meant that no order was needed and no costs were awarded against the peace campers and supporters, some of whom were people of substance who would suffer if an order for court costs was enforced.

Meanwhile other campers had begun preparing to move and the move was completed soon after the court had risen. Reliable, knowledgeable people told the campers that the new site was owned by the local council but on their first day on it they were visited by Mr Henry Black who told them Elvedon Estate owned the new site as well and wanted them off it. They were now camped on an interesting area of ditches and banks called The Warren, which had been used for breeding rabbits in years gone by, when their skins and fur were in great demand for hat-making.

On a hot summer day campers sweated as they moved all their gear to the site of Lakenheath FAB Peace Camp Mark III. All this moving was upsetting for the children, interrupting their schooling and also creating difficulties for campers who were planning things. By Hiroshima Day they were settled on the third site beside a back gate to the airfield on common land at the bottom of Maids Cross Way, which was administered by the Parish Council. Later part of this site became a council rubbish compound. At the time of writing this gate was not in normal use and blocked off

a road, which had once led through to Brandon Road.

Out of a £300 donation given to the camp when it first started by Nottingham CND campers bought some second-hand white clothes in a local shop, forty feet of chains and thirty-nine padlocks. They also obtained some theatrical make-up. The clothes were partially burned in the campfire to make them look right for the job.

By 05.00 hours on Nagasaki Day the campers were up and dressing themselves in these fire-damaged clothes. Then they applied the make-up to make themselves look like victims of a fire bomb. At 07.30 they set off for the main gate, Gate Two on the other side of the airfield, in several cars. There they chained themselves to the fence beside the entrance along with a sequence of six placards, which announced:

HIROSHIMA, NAGASAKI AUGUST 6-9 1945.
21,000 PEOPLE KILLED 37 YEARS AGO.
PEOPLE ARE STILL SUFFERING TODAY.

They stood in the bitterly cold wind for an hour, watched by press and TV reporters. The demonstrators then released themselves and wandered around to try and get warm. In doing so they found that they were more effective at attracting the attention of passers-by. Police arrived and when told what was being done left the campers to continue. Traffic was entering and leaving through Gate Two all the time. Soon the day grew hot and some demonstrators lay down in the gutter at the side of the road where there was a little shade, which seemed to startle passers-by who saw them. When the commanding officer had visited the demonstrators and talked with them, somebody asked him if he was planning to commemorate the Hiroshima and Nagasaki bombings. He walked away without answering so a letter was sent to him via the police on the gate repeating the question. He did not reply to it. The demonstrators decided that if he wouldn't tell them of any arrangements to commemorate the day on the airfield, they would ensure that as many of the base workers as possible would be forced to join them in a commemoration, by means of a blockade mounted to coincide with knocking-off time which was 17.00 hours for most of them. They would be able to reflect upon the reason for the blockade as they waited for the police to clear the road. Apparently there were no police at the entrance at the time but people inside the airfield who saw the demonstrators forming up into a blockade contacted the police. At 16.45 hours about twenty police led by a Chief Inspector, who talked to the demonstrators and on finding out what was planned agreed to stop the traffic going through all the gates to RAF Lakenheath for two minutes at 17.00 hours and arrange two minutes of silence. He kept his word and the demonstrators who didn't mount the blockade, as their side of the bargain, were delighted with this climax to their day-long vigil. They left just after the two minutes was over and the traffic queue had cleared Gate Two.

It is possible that the police chief ordered the two minutes silence simply to avoid the blockade, which would have delayed the traffic longer and made hard work for his men but even if this was so he and his men must surely have left Gate Two with a better understanding of the meaning of Nagasaki Day and why the peace camp was at Lakenheath.

Over the weekend of 3rd-5th September the campers mounted an exhibition about the camp at Rougham Tree Fair, which was organised by Green Deserts. There they made some useful contacts, gave out literature, collected for the camp and sold badges.

Then the peace camp banner went on the march to Sizewell and the campers had a stall at the fayre, which ended the march on 17th September, where once again they made new contacts.

On 6th September, Lakenheath Parish Council voted, by six votes to two, to give the camp twenty-eight days to move. If it had not moved from the site by the back gate to the airfield by 4th October the council would get an order in possession and evict it if necessary. All the time the campers were trying to persuade the councillors not to evict them or if that was unavoidable to find them an alternative site. Their lobbying probably delayed the council in its actions and earned themselves breathing space, but it did not prevent the eventual eviction, for had the parish not evicted them the district council could have prosecuted the parish council for permitting a camp on the common without planning permission.

Meanwhile campers were not idle. They were busy preparing for a public meeting and leafleting every house in the village with leaflets about it. On 28th September their hard work paid off and about 100 people were in the hall to see the Dimbleby film *The Bomb* and to hear a lecture on disarmament given by Chris from Cambridge. At that time there were only nine people living at the camp. After the talk all nine got on stage to answer criticisms of the camp and other questions and a lively discussion was enjoyed by all present.

Lakenheath Broom Road site.

On 4th October the camp was still on the same site, its third, and the part-time parish council clerk set the wheels in motion for an eviction. They moved slowly. On 17th November the High Court heard the application and granted an order in possession giving the campers one week to leave before it took effect.

Alas! I can find no report of the exact location of Lakenheath FAB Peace Camp Mark IV to which the campers moved in November but it is known that the site was owned by the Elvedon Estate. The winter there was one of struggling to survive. There was no activity like there had been in August and September at Mark III.

According to the diary of Ann Wood who, as Nottingham CND's press officer was frequently at the camp and was kept informed of what was happening there, the one happy event of the winter occurred on 10th November. Other records disagree. A report in the newspaper *Nottingham Trader* put the date at between 11th November and just before Christmas, Simon Brown who had lived at the camp gave the date as 12th December and his father, a keen camp supporter agreed; *Sanity* in March 1983 gave the date as 8th December. This is one of several cases where contradictory reports had to be sorted before writing this book but in this case alas! I was unable in the time available to contact the family at the heart of the matter to check the date. Poppy arrived into a caravan without even a water standpipe. Her father 'did the honours' because the midwife he had called did not arrive until after she did. As father rummaged around for something in which to wrap her, he disturbed a poppy left over from Remembrance Day which floated down from a shelf to land beside the baby. Hence her first name Poppy after the flower which symbolises the end of war. Her second name was Tau – Chinese for 'safe and peaceful'. Her surname Gabb she inherited from her parents, Louise and Ted Gabb who had been living on the camp since it started in May, moving with it from site to site. They returned with Poppy and their other children to their home town of Nottingham for Christmas. Photographs published some time after her birth showed Poppy to be a fine healthy child.

On Saturday, 12th February, over 200 people marched round the village and the airfield to Gates One and Two and briefly blockaded both gates. Although the weather was bad, morale was good and there were no arrests on this first event of 1983.

On 15th March the High Court granted Elvedon Estate an order in possession for the fourth campsite and gave the campers two weeks to leave. This order banned peace camps from all Elvedon Estate lands in the area for twenty-five years. The campers had to pay £75 court costs.

The campers wanted to stay in the area and, aided by local supporters searching through documents in libraries and council offices, they at last found some land that nobody had claimed among the pine trees at the top of Broom Road. This unadopted road, no more than a rough track, led from the village main street, past houses and bungalows up to Maids Cross Hill. The lower end was used by buses on their rare visits to the village and in spite of its poor surface, Broom Road was treated as a public highway by everyone.

By Easter Monday, 4th April, the camp had moved to this new site. It seems moving camp had prevented the campers from organising any activity over Easter.

The campers were not idle though. They were preparing for their biggest demonstration to date. Just three weeks later on Sunday, 24th April, more than a thousand people took part in a 'Fly for peace, not war' event there, a sort of alternative air show. The fun started early when one of the Nottingham coaches attempted to take its load of demonstrators onto the airfield by Gate Two by mistake instead of taking them to the dropping off point further along Brandon Road. The guards on the gate seemed put out by this mistake. The coaches were dropping demonstrators on the opposite side of the road from the airfield and a policeman earned their gratitude by being a 'lollipop man' and shepherding them across the road. The demonstrators then walked round the base using a public road which separated some married quarters and the 'Anglo' housing from the airbase itself, so the Americans saw them and they saw the Americans at close range. Their walk ended upon Maids Cross

Hill where the entertainments, including the flying of balloons and kites to hamper the operations on the airfield below, took place. The demonstration ended happily with neither arrests nor accidents.

It was followed by a blockade which started at 06.00 hours on the Monday morning in pouring rain. This was planned as a twelve-hour blockade of all the gates, but as only about eighty people took part, a full blockade was not possible. At first all three gates in use were blockaded and vehicles were delayed for up to five minutes for a time, but police kept moving people out of the way and the activists were being worn down. At around noon Gill and Helen from the 'Peace Chariot' of Sheffield were warned that if they sat in the road again they would be arrested and charged. Gill sat down again, was arrested and charged. Helen then sat down in solidarity with her and was also arrested and charged with obstruction of the highway. They were bailed to appear before Mildenhall magistrates on 16th May and released. Possibly the rain had kept people away. Whatever the reasons there were just not enough people to keep the blockade going now the arrests had started. Fortunately Lakenheath campers seemed always equipped with a trick or two up their sleeves and were good at changing tactics to resume direct actions that looked lost.

Next, some activists parked a hired van beside the fence and put a carpet over the barbed wire. In no time at all some of them had climbed onto the van and over the perimeter fence. They were roughly ejected by police without charge.

In the afternoon one group continuously attempted to blockade Gate One to keep the police busy. Simultaneously a second group went to a place out of sight of all the gates where a hole had been dug the night before and crawled into the base and a third group simply ran in through an entrance that was not well guarded. A total of fifty-five persons, including two babies and a young boy, had entered the airfield. They danced, sang and picnicked until British police arrived. They ignored orders to leave. The police did not charge anybody with any offence but after forty minutes just escorted the activists off the airfield.

The day ended with a vigil at Gate Two as people left work in the base. Activists were dancing, singing, smiling and waving at workers going home, many of whom waved back. These included Americans, who had all been instructed not to smile at or have any communication whatsoever with any activists or demonstrators.

On 12th May a group of visiting activists from Burtonwood and Upper Heyford Peace Camps showed the Lakenheath campers a new trick when they climbed a water tower on the airfield. Heyford campers were renowned for their skill at climbing water towers!

For three days in May a NATO exercise excited the Lakenheath campers so much that they decided to join in. On 24th May, seven women walked onto the airfield and made a large CND symbol at the end of the runway. Then more women went in by another entrance and put flowers in some camouflage netting. This was followed by a thirty-minute blockade of Gate Two during which a sentry box was garlanded with flowers. The resulting queue of traffic took two hours to clear apparently. On 26th May, ten campers climbed over the perimeter fence and onto the top of a hangar where they displayed the camp's huge FAB banner. They were arrested, questioned and detained for five hours before being released. Their banner was confiscated. Do I detect a school-teacher touch in the police handling of this action? This series of actions was brought to a close when on Friday, 27th May, a group of activists climbed a water tower but came down after only a short time. Throughout the series, which must have caused considerable inconvenience on the airfield, nobody was charged with any offence.

At the weekend, however, a heavy police presence made it clear to campers and supporters that the peelers would arrest and probably charge anyone trying to disrupt the USAF air show at Mildenhall Airfield. The visiting Lakenheath peace campers and their friends restricted their activity to leafleting people entering and leaving the airfield and did not leaflet inside the gate. The peelers did not trouble them.

Not only was Monday, 30th May Lakenheath FAB Peace Camp's first birthday but also it was Spring Bank Holiday, so it was an ideal day for a celebration. The campers had earned it by organising many demonstrations of up to a thousand people and quite a few very good direct actions in spite of being moved on four times from site to site. Of course their local supporters, without whom they would never have survived the first year, deserved a party too. It was a happy, friendly, relaxed sort of party and the high point of it appeared to be a picnic in the countryside involving about thirty people sitting on top of a mound of earth with about sixty US servicemen watching them from behind riot shields. The picnic lasted for over an hour before the British police arrived and escorted the picnickers off the top of the

blast-resistant fuel store on which they were sitting. The police took them off the airfield and released them without charge.

There were plans to improve the airfield facilities and resurface the runway at Lakenheath at a cost to the USAF said to be in the region of $3,000,000,000. While this was being done the F1-11s and several lorry loads of equipment would go to RAF Sculthorpe for four months. The big move began on 1st June.

FAB decided to set up another peace camp at Sculthorpe to continue the protest against these nuclear bombers there. They decided to march to Sculthorpe so as to get the maximum publicity and after a march of four days up A1065 arrived on 11th June, 1983. The march passed RAF Feltwell (soon to have its own peace camp) and two RAF stations that had been the scene of nuclear disarmament demonstrations in the past; Marham and Swaffham.

All the time the peace camp was at Sculthorpe it worked closely with Lakenheath Peace Camp, where a couple of campers on Broom Road Campsite kept a presence at Lakenheath. After about a month it was felt that keeping both camps going stretched resources too far, or so it would seem, and after about six weeks Sculthorpe Peace Camp was closed. This camp does not appear to have done anything important, had any arrests or an eviction. When the Sculthorpe campers closed their camp they left the campaign in the hands of the local peace movement, which in the light of later events proved a wise decision.

Sculthorpe Peace Camp was not connected with Angie Zelter who lived on a farm in Norfolk. It may have inspired her though when she got the idea (apparently in her bath – Eureka!) to cut the perimeter fence at RAF Sculthorpe in 1984 and start the 'snowball' campaign. The first time just three people cut it; then three people cut it and issued their famous statement, then nine people cut it and in January 1985, twenty-seven cut this famous fence. From there the campaign grew just like a snowball being rolled through fresh snow and spread to many bases, involving people at many peace camps in it.

While some campers were still at RAF Sculthorpe, in spite of reduced numbers at Lakenheath, the Lakenheath campers still managed to organise a vigil at Gate Two on 4th July, 1983, to commemorate US Independence Day. It is believed that a similar vigil took place at Sculthorpe at the same time. Also at the same time a camper mounted a one-man blockade and refused to move from Gate Two until the

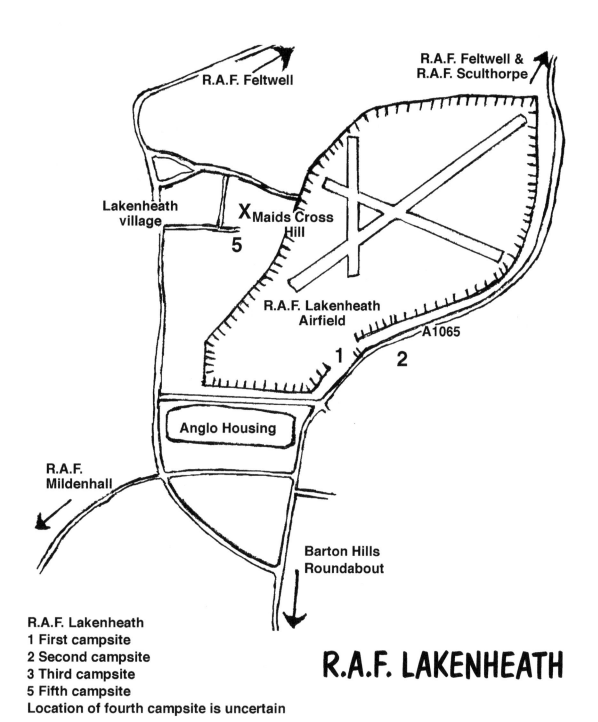

Lakenheath village

XMaids Cross Hill

5

R.A.F. Lakenheath Airfield

A1065

1

2

Anglo Housing

R.A.F. Mildenhall

Barton Hills Roundabout

R.A.F. Feltwell

R.A.F. Feltwell & R.A.F. Sculthorpe

R.A.F. LAKENHEATH

R.A.F. Lakenheath
1 First campsite
2 Second campsite
3 Third campsite
5 Fifth campsite
Location of fourth campsite is uncertain

camp banner, confiscated on 26th May, was returned. He was arrested and imprisoned. The modplods returned the FAB banner undamaged.

On the night of 30th-31st July the camp in Broom Road was attacked by a gang of about twenty skinheads. Nobody appears to have been seriously hurt but much damage was done. Apparently an empty caravan was overturned and a tent was collapsed on top of two children aged ten and twelve. More caravans may have been damaged. Fortunately some local bikers were around who were friendly to the camp and they chased the skinheads away.

This seems to have led to people leaving the camp or it could have been that none of the Sculthorpe campers returned to Lakenheath, for in August the camp was appealing for more people to come and join it. There was obviously a severe staff shortage that autumn because no activity was reported there during August, September and October and there was at least one more appeal for new campers.

RAF Lakenheath was believed to be involved in the 'Polaris Convoy of the Air'. Aircraft flew to and from the USA at intervals of about six weeks. It was believed that they carried nuclear weapons to the USA for reconditioning or scrapping and brought back reconditioned or new weapons.

Late one November evening in 1983 a Lakenheath resident observed some cruise missiles of a type designed for air launching arriving on a USAF freighter aircraft. They were apparently to be fitted to a new version of the F1-11. The unloading area was well lit and the observer had a clear unobstructed view from Maids Cross Hill, which was in darkness.

There was a twenty-four-hour vigil on 9th November in support of Greenham Women Against Cruise in the USA who were trying to get Cruise deployment in Europe declared illegal in the US courts. The few remaining campers worked hard at persuading camp founders and local supporters to join them for this event. It was obvious they could not keep the camp going due to lack of volunteers. Apparently they decided to close it but return from time to time for single events.

At the same time at RAF Feltwell ten miles to the North there was a women's twenty-four-hour peace camp also in support of Greenham Women Against Cruise. Here the campers tried to deliver a letter to the commanding officer but were turned back. Servicemen and police who spoke with campers were quite friendly, though most could not understand why this storage depot had been chosen for a peace camp until much explaining had been done. It appears no order had been given to them to avoid contact with and speaking with peace campers.

'LIGHT FOR LIFE' BROOM ROAD AND MILDENHALL IN 1984

At Winter Solstice a beacon was lit on Maids Cross Hill to signify the start of the 'Light for Life' fast which took place at Lakenheath Peace camp from 22nd to 31st December. On 1st January, 1984, the fasters having eaten set off on the 'Light for Life' walk to Sizewell via Snape Maltings. [See my account 'The Camp For A Safe Future' elsewhere in this book.]

The four families, several single people, five dogs and five cats living on the camp on Friday, 6th January, 1984, were joined by supporters for a barbecue.

This was followed by an all-night vigil at Lakenheath protesting against the US domination of Britain and the presence of CND 'reds', organised by the National Front. Peace campers didn't take part in this!

On 7th January campers and supporters held a march from Bury St. Edmunds Railway Station to Lakenheath.

During January when Cruise missiles were arriving on Greenham Common peace campers spotted extra activity on Lakenheath and Mildenhall Airfields.

All the campers went to Gate One in Brandon Road on 12th February along with visitors from Swaffham and Fakenham Peace Groups and Molesworth Peace Camp. They decorated the perimeter fence and handed in a letter addressed to the commanding officer asking about the presence of Cruise missiles at Lakenheath. They promised to return if they got no reply.

Apparently at this event Richard Kennet was arrested and charged with criminal damage. He was later convicted and the other campers had a whip-round to pay his fine and keep him from prison. When he was fined for not having a current road fund licence on his car two weeks later, the Brown family paid the money to tax his car.

As they had received no reply to their letter, the campers returned on Tuesday, 14th February, and blockaded a gate. The authorities still wouldn't answer their questions but asked them where they got the idea that Cruise missiles were in RAF Lakenheath. While the authorities' own camera crew filmed the blockade from inside the base so as to have pictures of who was there for future reference, a BBC TV crew filmed them from outside.

Suddenly three blockaders got up and bolted through the entrance into the base. They ran to a bunker. One went to one side of it, one ran onto the top and one ran 'underneath' according to the report in *In-Sanity* the Lakenheath Peace Camp's irregular newspaper. Presumably it meant that the camper ran into the bunker underneath the 'shell' of it. The police quickly removed them and ejected them from the airfield without charge. The man who had been on top of the bunker spoke to the BBC TV *Look East* reporter and the action got three minutes of airtime on the *Look East* TV programme.

That blockade broke up and a second blockade was started at 16.00 hours, which stopped virtually all traffic on both Gate One and Gate Two for a whole hour. As the blockaders left at 17.00 hours or thereabouts, police reinforcements were arriving to help the small number of police on duty to pull the blockaders off the roads.

The diversion caused by the actions at the gates on Brandon Road had enabled two peace campers to nip into the base unseen and scout around for ninety minutes among some high security bunkers. They then gave themselves up and were removed from base apparently without charge.

TVAM that morning had denied that any form of Cruise missiles were at Lakenheath but the campers and their supporters had done their homework and knew Cruise missiles were handled there from time to time.

On 15th February some campers from Lakenheath visited Faslane Peace Camp and in March a Lakenheath camper visited Daws Hill, Naphill and Christmas Common and saw the peace campers up Christmas Common Radio Tower [See my account: 'Peace Camps in the Chiltern Hills' elsewhere in this book] which they had occupied. Following this visit some campers went up a water tower at Lakenheath and stayed on it for two days.

Peace News on 17th February reported another baby due at Lakenheath Peace Camp. The second baby to be born there, Jenny arrived on 21st February 1984.

Two miles South of Gate Two A1065 met All Road at Barton Mills Roundabout. All was one of the government's secret Emergency Service Routes (ESRs) for use in the event of a nuclear war or national emergency. On 29th February Lakenheath peace campers and supporters demonstrated with their banners at Barton Mills Roundabout to show the motorists they were on an ESR. Beside public toilets nearby demonstrators erected a banner, which used humour to impress its message on passing motorists and people using the toilets:

THREE MINUTES TO WET YOURSELF

A police motorcycle patrolman came and threatened the eight demonstrators. When he saw they weren't packing up and leaving he radioed for reinforcements. The demonstrators left, taking their banners with them before the reinforcements arrived, as they did not want any arrests and charges and they had not planned a permanent display in any case. The fact that the police patrolman had radioed in about the demonstration would be logged, so the police could not claim later that there had been no demonstration as they probably would have done if the demonstrators had left in answer to a simple verbal request.

At this time there were five vehicles on the Broom Road Campsite that could be described as runners and five families had been living there during the 1983-4 winter. This gave hope for much activity in spring and summer.

The Anglian Water Authority received an application for a water supply made on the official form from Richard Kennet of Lakenheath Peace Camp on 23rd March.

Some cyclists arrived at the camp from Islington, London on Saturday 31st March and joined some peace campers who rode bicycles on a 'cycle vigil' all round the airfield.

The six Islington CND cyclists also joined in the events on All Fool's Day, 1st April, when the star turn seems to have been Richard wearing a flying helmet, riding up a ramp outside Gate Two and trying or pretending to leap the fence. The humour seems to have been appreciated on both sides of the fence as there were no arrests reported that weekend.

During 1984 there were frequent vigils outside the gates to the airfield one of which began at 10.30 hours on 14th April. Like most of them, this did not lead to any direct action or arrests and the few that did lead to other things are mentioned elsewhere in this account.

On 15th April a silent group of CND people marched from Gate One to Gate Two. When the march reached Gate Two, the main gate, a marcher sounded an air-raid warning on a portable Klaxon. Some marchers then dropped to the road in a die-in, pretending to be dying in a nuclear attack while others ran around in a simulated panic. No arrests were reported.

About thirty activists took down several sections of perimeter fence at Lakenheath on 16th April. Only two were arrested, one of whom was released without charge. The other, Jonathan Frank Jackson, was taken to court, convicted of criminal damage, conditionally discharged and ordered to pay £54.50 compensation towards £109 worth of criminal damage to ninety feet of fence.

On the same date police stopped John Riding and several other visitors with him and tried to prevent them from leaving the camp by Broom Road. John Riding and his colleagues were neither campers nor wanted criminals. It is true that John himself was a camp supporter but he was also a reputable villager and prominent in the local Labour Party.

On Saturday 21st April some Christian CND Easter marchers arrived at RAF Mildenhall where to accommodate them over the Easter weekend a temporary peace camp was set up. Mildenhall Christian Peace Camp stayed only until Easter Monday, 23rd April.

From Mildenhall on the Monday the Easter March came to Maids Cross Hill for a final rally. All along the march route police were horrible to the marchers, warning people to lock all shed, car, house and caravan doors securely before the march came past.

They also spread all sorts of rumours about the peace campers, most if not all of which were untrue. The parish council's new household refuse tip beside the old Lakenheath Peace Camp Mark III Site would normally have been open during the day over Easter for the villagers to dump rubbish and large items in skips provided, but not this Easter!

> Police informed the tip manager that the tip would have to be closed for the whole of the Easter holiday as it was likely that 3,000 members of Christian CND would rush the gates and grab iron bars with which to attack the police [Quoted from *InSanity* the camp's own newspaper].

There were threats of a National Front attack on the peace camp at Lakenheath over Easter. Though some earlier FAB campers had been pacifist, the present campers were not known for pacifism and Glenn certainly wasn't. So a punch-up couldn't be ruled out. Then Superintendent Burrows and his policemen raised the level of tension by warning the campers that two coachloads of National Front troublemakers were coming. They said they had stopped the coaches but were unable to prevent them continuing their journey. In the end only about twenty National Front people came and held a separate demonstration before departing peacefully.

There was no direct connexion between Lakenheath Peace Camp and the rally which had been organised by Christian CND, though some campers went to it. The shortest route between the main road from Mildenhall and the rally was up Broom Road past the camp. Between the camp and the main road police set up a road block and stopped all except Broom Road ratepayers, their families and their visitors, from passing through it. This meant many people going to and from the camp and the rally had to detour by Mill Lane and Wings Road further North. As the road block was set up by the police apparently on their own initiative, on a private road, it was of dubious legality. Among some people stopped trying to go up Broom Road to the peace camp was John Riding, stopped for a second time. He was arrested, forcibly photographed and fingerprinted but was not charged with any offence at the time. He was later released.

The march when it arrived was well received by the Lakenheath villagers, many of whom watched and clapped as it passed through the village to the rally. Thousands of people attended the rally including some villagers. Afterwards the Christian disarmers went home.

Forest Heath District Council decided on 16th April to serve an enforcement notice under section 284 of the Town and Country Planning Act 1977 on Lakenheath Peace camp. It was addressed to Richard Kennet and Hazel Wright and served on them on 30th April. It said that if they were there after a certain date without planning permission they would be breaking the law and would be in trouble unless they appealed against the notice. Of course the district council, which was the planning authority, would not grant them planning permission. They had until 5th June to lodge an appeal with the Department of the Environment.

Also in April more sections of perimeter fence came down.

At 04.00 hours on Friday 4th May, 1984 a robbery at Rob Hunter's small supermarket in Lakenheath was reported to the police. By 04.30 the local police, operating quickly and efficiently, had a list of the stolen goods: nine bottles of spirits, twenty-nine tins of baked beans and three million cigarettes.

At 07.30 a lone policeman was parked in Broom Road between the camp and the main road. He was searching campers' vehicles and by 10.00 he had stopped and searched a Land Rover driven by Deb no less than three times. He was joined by 10.30 by a small convoy of police vehicles and as the day wore on more came until there were nine. This force was commanded by Chief Superintendant Burrows in person. He had with him a chief inspector, an inspector, four plainclothes police, two women police constables and a dozen or so uniformed men. They had search warrants authorising them to search for and remove stolen goods.

> The first call was to a caravan parked near the peace camp proper. A skin-head youth was dragged out, handcuffed and taken away. Some items were taken from where he spent the night. No one seemed to know him or from whence he came although his arrival the previous night had caused some concern.
>
> Having recovered some goods and detained a person the police thought to be connected with them, all officers and 'other ranks' began to search each and every caravan, vehicle and latrine.
>
> One of our number insisted that if his home was to be searched the search was to be absolutely legal. After some time more detailed warrants were obtained.
>
> Since by that time the police could not have had reasonable suspicion that either stolen goods detailed on the warrant or any fugitives were in that caravan, one wonders at the searching questions

asked by their tame JP before signing the warrant.

Due to the good humour of the p.c., which was shared by the local police, the search reached its hilarious conclusion without incident. Needless to add the police found nothing of the stolen goods at the p.c.... but then of course they didn't expect to. [Quoted from *In-Sanity*. In this item read Justice of the Peace or magistrate for JP and read peace camp for pc.]

This search was probably instigated by outside pressure using the supermarket robbery as an excuse. Was the skinhead just a thief who used the peace camp as a base? Or had he been bribed to rob the supermarket and plant himself with some loot on the peace camp to provide the authorities with an excuse for the raid? The search of the camp was unnecessarily time consuming and thorough; police even searched through the very file I examined at Lakenheath while researching this account. What could they have found in a file – twenty out of three million cigarettes? The police seem to have made only one small mistake when the warrants they had prepared for one caravan gave its location wrongly and mis-spelt the name of the occupant. This caused a delay as he would not allow them to search his caravan until they had got correct warrants. Although the police and campers seemed to have parted in good humour after the searches were complete, relations between the police and the campers may have been hindered in the long term. As a result of the raid campers got increased support in the village, which seemed odd in a constituency that sent Eldon Griffiths to Parliament.

At this time Cyril Brown, a staunch supporter of the peace camp (as were his whole family including his son Simon who lived there for a time), was standing for election to the local council as a Labour candidate. In spite of the help of several campers including Hazel, Jean-Paul and Richard with his campaign he was not elected.

Later in May the campers started touring East Anglia leafleting and telling people about RAF Lakenheath, RAF Mildenhall and their peace camp. As part of this touring, which they apparently did intermittently throughout that summer, they held a very good exhibition at a Green Deserts event, Thorpe Tree Fair.

On 27th May campers were on a protest march from Lakenheath to Mildenhall.

During May there had been a meeting of some kind of nuclear security inspectorate at RAF Lakenheath. The peace campers got wind of it and were nipping in and out of the base, showing the inspectors many different breaches of security. After they had got into the base and painted a radar scanner, spotlights were put round it to prevent a repeat, so they painted the spotlights. About seventy yards of fence came down beside Brandon Road during a twenty-four-hour alert when security was supposed to be extra vigilant. Campers cut bits of wire from the perimeter fence, mounted them on cards and sold them for £1.50 each to raise funds for the camp. Another letter to the commanding officer about Cruise missiles at Lakenheath went unanswered so campers occupied a bunker. They were removed and ejected from the airfield by police. Apparently nobody was charged with an offence during all this activity, probably because the authorities didn't want RAF Lakenheath's breaches of security getting any more publicity than they actually got.

Forest Heath District Council were threatening to prosecute Richard and Hazel for having no planning permission under section 284 of the Town and Country Planning Act 1977. The NCCL were contacted and were able to put the campers in touch with a lawyer who had much experience in dealing with campsite problems. Mr Lidgey of Mayne and Lidgey, a London firm, was a legal adviser to the Gipsy Federation. From the summer of 1984 until the camp ended Mr Lidgey worked for the camp.

On 31st May Mr Lidgey wrote informing the district council that Richard Kennet and Hazel Wright were appealing to the Department of the Environment against the enforcement notice and said the appeal would be based on the following points:

a) That permission ought to be granted.

b) That copies of the enforcement notice were not served as required under section 85, subsection (5) of the Town and Country Planning Act. 1971.

c) That the period allowed for Richard and Hazel to comply was unnecessarily short.

Though the enforcement notice had been served, it had not been done in the precise manner laid down, so the solicitor was making the most of this point. He also pointed out to the council that if the campers' appeal failed they would appear to become gipsies from a legal point of view. He asked the council if they then adapted the campsite to comply with regulations for official gipsy camps would they be allowed to stay?

A Department of the Environment report issued on 12th July 1983, listed no less than twenty-one unauthorised gipsy camps in that area and not one single official campsite built to comply with the law that required county councils to provide them.

On Friday, 1st June, the peace camp held a party to celebrate its second birthday. A special birthday edition of *In-Sanity*, the peace camp's own newspaper, was published. I was pleased to read in it a 'plug' for the forthcoming Festival of Peace at Boscombe Down.

Mr Lidgey managed to get the appeal date for the planning appeal extended from 5th June to 14th June. On 8th June the council replied to his letter querying the legal definition of a gipsy. Also they had had some correspondence with the Department of the Environment and were claiming Richard had no *locus standii* to appeal. On 12th June Mr Lidgey wrote to the district council again arguing about the definition of a gipsy and on the same date wrote to Richard and Hazel enclosing another form from the Anglian Water Authority along with a letter saying he was lodging their appeal with the Department of the Environment. The costs so far, including the £47 fee for lodging the appeal, had been paid by legal aid. Richard and Hazel did not receive Mr Lidgey's letter so he sent a duplicate on 11th July, which was delivered. The peace camp was having problems with its mail. On 18th July he sent them another form for the water supply, which the campers completed and posted on 28th July.

John Riding was charged with obstructing a police officer on duty at the road block in Broom Road seven weeks after he had been stopped there the second time. He pleaded not guilty.

The lawyer who had been the camp solicitor in the beginning was no longer acting for the camp. No local solicitor would act in John's defence as they thought he had no hope of an acquittal. Lakenheath was in the heart of Conservative law and order country and Eldon Griffiths, who was sponsored in Parliament by the Police Federation, was their MP. This Labour Party member was being charged with obstructing one of their guardians of law and order! Of course the composition of the local bench reflected this attitude. There was only one local magistrate involved with the peace movement and she used to stand down whenever a peace camper was before the bench because she felt she might give a biassed judgement.

The NCCL was contacted and introduced the campers to a solicitor who took on the case, unsuccessfully. There was an appeal, which failed so John received a criminal conviction.

On 20th June most of the campers were arrested, imprisoned and threatened with criminal damage charges over an alleged £8,000 worth of criminal damage to buildings, equipment and fences at RAF Lakenheath. They all appear to have been released later without charge.

On 21st August Mr Lidgey sent the campers counsel's advice about their appeal along with his own comments and confirmed that the Department of the Environment had received the appeal application and would be organising an appeal. In his letter he referred to the departure from the camp of a mysterious Mrs Morrison and some others who had been living there in a bus. Apparently everyone was pleased they had gone because they had been a nuisance to other campers. Mr Lidgey asked for detailed measurements of the campsite and photographs of it with a simple fence to pass on to Anglian Water who were asking all sorts of questions about the camp.

West Midlands CND and the 'Peace Chariot' organised the 'Conspiracy Blockade' in protest at the USAF's alleged part in the international conspiracy to commit genocide with nuclear weapons and at the charging of Alconbury peace campers with conspiracy charges. [See 'Guided Tours of Alconbury and Farming at Molesworth' elsewhere in this book.] As the blockade took place at Lakenheath, a protest about the arrests of 20th June was included. There appear to have been no arrests at this event, which took place on 31st August.

On 4th September Anglian Water wrote asking for confirmation that Richard Kennet owned the campsite and Mr Lidgey replied explaining who owned what.

On 20th September Mr Lidgey wrote to the campers explaining that though he could get paid for his work so far on legal aid and he could get paid by legal aid for the application for water, he could not get legal aid to pay for the representation at the enquiry, for which a barrister would cost the camp about £800 assuming a two-day enquiry. If he represented the camp himself he would charge £460 plus hotel expenses. The question for the campers was, could they raise this kind of money? A few days later he wrote advising the campers to delay the application for water until after the planning enquiry as a victory in the enquiry would make things easier with the application.

On Thursday 27th September, four protestors spent three hours up a water tower with a banner, which read:

PEACING IT TOGETHER

As a result floodlights were moved to the main gate to try and prevent further incursions during the hours of darkness, which were now lengthening.

Hallowe'en came on Wednesday, which was awkward for a demonstration or action of any size, so the campers held their 'Spook the Base' action on the nearest Saturday, 3rd November. About 250 people took part.

Early in 1985 about five, though it may have been as many as eight, caravans were burnt and damaged, one beyond repair, by four drunken local lads. They were all subsequently arrested, charged, taken to court, fined and ordered to pay compensation. The campers, who felt the lads had been punished too severely and wanted to do something nice for them, met to sort it all out. There is no record of what if anything was done for the local lads. The compensation money had to be spent on repairing and replacing the caravans as all of them were on loan to the camp apparently.

On 23rd January 1985, the Department of the Environment informed Mr Lidgey that they were ready to hold the planning enquiry and on 1st February he wrote to Cyril Brown at his house in Lakenheath and to Richard at the camp telling them the news about the enquiry. At the time the campers were having problems with surviving the winter and with burnt caravans and it appears they were unable to raise the money for their representation at the enquiry. To make things worse relations between the campers and local supporters were growing strained over some niggling matters.

Only days short of its third birthday 8th May, 1985, Lakenheath Peace Camp was laid down. It being Easter Monday all the Cambridgeshire and Suffolk police were either on leave or busy with an event at Molesworth. This enabled the campers to move off unobserved as some of their vehicles were of dubious legality and they did not want to be stopped on the road.

The camp at Lakenheath was only laid down not closed. At the time of writing the nuclear bombers were still there and camp supporters still lived in the village. They knew of suitable sites and had a sum of money frozen in a bank awaiting a new peace camp.

So this camp could be reactivated at any time. It did an immense amount of good campaigning while it was active and it is hoped that it will be active again.

None of the peace camps in the Fens had permanent sites and none had electricity, water or telephones laid on. Mail was sometimes not delivered. Until the Lakenheath campers arrived at Lakenheath Peace Camp Mark V in Broom Road they had recurring problems with evictions. Here they might have got their camp made as permanent as Faslane and could have established an East Anglian regional peace centre had they won the planning enquiry. There may yet be developments here.

During demonstrations and actions at Lakenheath, though not at Feltwell, US servicemen were under orders not to communicate with demonstrators and activists in any way. So every time people had to be removed from the airfield British police had to do the job. Sometimes there was delay while sufficient British police were brought to the scene and activists used this delay to their advantage.

Since the camp was laid down there have been several actions at RAF Lakenheath one being on 12th October 1985, when three peace women were arrested with a roll of film which included shots of the airfield. They were threatened with official secrets and criminal damage charges but were apparently later released without charge.

In December 1985 soldiers caught four Cambridge women in a hangar at RAF Mildenhall. The soldiers allegedly beat them up and then handed them over to the Modsquad who arrested and questioned them. They told the Modsquad about being beaten and were asked to write statements and give them to the police, which they did. The authorities took no action.

After their release the women were interviewed on *Look East* television programme and complained to a Member of Parliament about the alleged beatings. The Modsquad took more statements and as RAF Molesworth came into the same Modsquad area, modplods from there were called in to help investigate the women's allegations. The final result appears to have been a letter of apology and a request to the troops to be less enthusiastic when apprehending trespassers.

Another action took place on 23rd February, 1986, in the full glare of searchlights when four women cut the perimeter fence. They were arrested, stripsearched and released without charge. They later complained about the strip-search.

The campaign continues.

A FOUL PLACE ON FOULNESS

Hidden in the middle of the MoD's Proof and Experimental Establishment which tests weapons on 8,000 acres of land and 20,000 acres of mudflats around Foulness Village is a branch of Atomic Weapons Research Establishment (AWRE).

Foulness Village lies on Foulness Island off the Essex coast. One can't just drive up the road from Southend and expect to drive straight onto the island. The only road onto Foulness has been gated by the MoD and in order to visit the island one needs an MoD permit. This even applies to civilians visiting civilian villagers.

On 30th January 1983, Southend CND set up a peace camp at the gate on the road to Foulness. Peace campers went leafleting all over the area and got the existence of the AWRE branch on the island publicised. Many local people were completely unaware of its existence. This was believed to have been only the second demonstration here; the first had taken place over ten years before.

On 6th February the campers with the caravan that had been the centre of the peace camp moved to the new peace camp at Wethersfield. [See 'A Staffing Rota that Worked and Violent Opposition at Wethersfield' elsewhere in this book for further details of this camp]

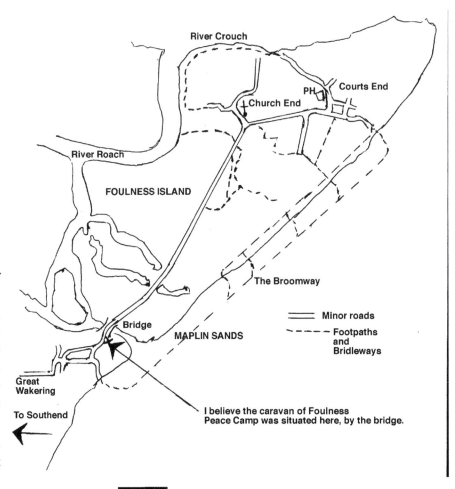

I believe the caravan of Foulness Peace Camp was situated here, by the bridge.

GREENHAM
COMMON

SUB TABLE OF CONTENTS FOR GREENHAM

IN THE BEGINNING THERE WAS A COMMON

Bolivian television has shown film of them; so has television in Fort Hood, New Jersey, USA; the Soviet press has reported them; a national Japanese conference has discussed them. There can be few people in the world who have not heard of the Greenham Common Peace Camps. Much of the publicity has, sadly, been propaganda, which has avoided facts which did not fit in with its own message; most of the writing has been done by journalists in a hurry, who may not even have visited Greenham Common. In this brief history I have tried to record all the facts, and have written slowly and with care, about a place I have visited many times. I apologise for omissions and for treating many events with brevity in order not to bore the reader with excessive detail. Cruisewatch has been mentioned in passing, but it really needs a book all to itself.

In 1938 Newbury Council purchased an area of common land on the Commons of Greenham and Crookham in Southern Berkshire, so that this area could be kept for the enjoyment and recreation of local people in perpetuity. Then, in May 1941, the Air Ministry (as it was then) requisitioned 900 acres of this land on top of the hill. An assurance was given that the land would be returned to the local people after World War II had ended. Had he won the war, would the late Adolf Hitler have kept this promise?

During the rest of World War II, the United States Army Air Force (as it was up to September, 1947) used Greenham Common, although the Air Ministry still was responsible for the airfield. Aircraft from here played a vital role in the back-up for the troops invading France on 6th June 1944 – D-Day. The USAF was, of course, in the war on the British side. American troops and airmen were bivouacked around Greenham Common, and billeted locally, in large numbers.

There was one ugly wartime incident, which many folk would prefer forgotten, but without a mention of it, this history would be incomplete. A few miles down the road to Basingstoke (A339) lies the peaceful village of Kingsclere, which is still even now peaceful, because it is far enough away from the airfield and its flightpaths for the big jets not to disturb it and road traffic noise has been taken away by a new bypass. In 1944, an American Negro airman, stationed at Greenham, visited this village. There was a quarrel of racial origin, and he went into the churchyard opposite the Crown Pub. People came out of the Crown. A gun started firing from the churchyard, and nine white, British people fell, dead and dying. There is still local ill-feeling about the Kingsclere Massacre forty-two years after it happened.

The war ended, the USAAF went home, and in 1946 even the RAF left Greenham Common. At around this time RAF stations at Quedgeley, High Post and

R.A.F. GREENHAM COMMON

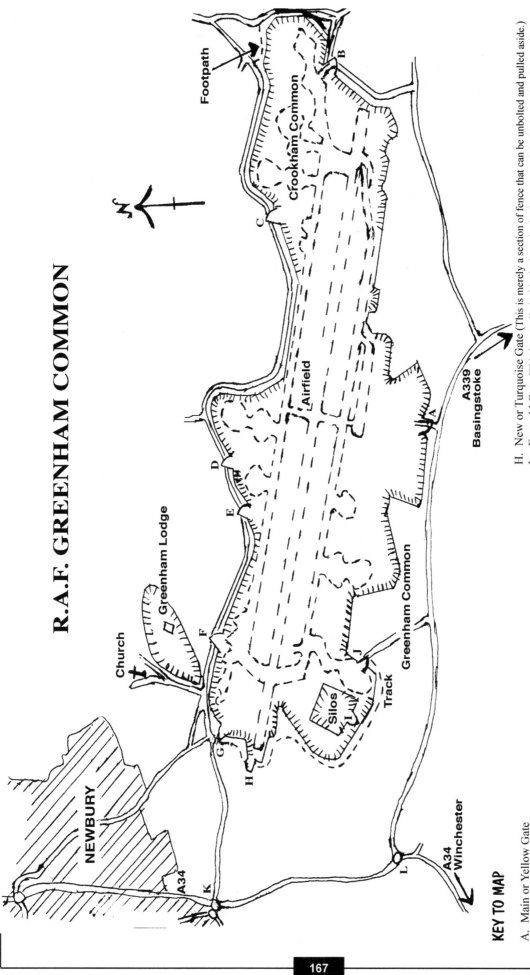

NEWBURY

Church

Greenham Lodge

Footpath

Crookham Common

Airfield

Greenham Common

Silos

Track

A339
Basingstoke

A34
Winchester

A34

KEY TO MAP

A. Main or Yellow Gate
B. Music or Orange Gate
C. Artist's Gate or Red Gate
D. Religious or Violet Gate
E. Forgotten or Indigo Gate (This was closed and replaced by Woad Gate beside it, set in the fence at an angle supposedly for greater safety, but more likely to enable lorries to leave and enter more quickly when on exercise.)
F. Pedestrian Gate
G. New Age Gate or Blue Gate
H. New or Turquoise Gate (This is merely a section of fence that can be unbolted and pulled aside.)
I.   Emerald Gate (This is actually inside the base, in the fence around the high security silo area.)
J.   Green Gate
K. The Double Doughnut Roundabout
L. The Swan Roundabout

In the interests of clarity, the various campsites have not been marked. Their locations are described in the text, in relation to the gates, which are marked.

⊥⊥⊥ Boundary of MoD Land

other airfields were demilitarised and converted to civilian uses, but not this one. The buildings and runway were left for vandals to attack and weeds to engulf. Newbury Council sent two registered letters asking the Labour Government about returning the land to the people; they were ignored. Newbury Chamber of Commerce produced a poster calling for the airfield to be handed back to the local people. All this came from a safe Tory parliamentary constituency, and Labour ruled in Parliament with a large majority, so they could afford to ignore it all. Then, at the 1951 general election, Labour's majority was so reduced as to make government almost impossible.

However, in 1952 they authorised the supply of certain airfields and facilities to what was now the United States Air Force, in addition to those already supplied under the Spaatz-Tedder Agreement [See my account, 'Peace Camps in the Fens', elsewhere in this book]. Greenham Common was one of these airfields handed to the Americans in 1952. Shortly after this, another general election was forced upon the government by the difficulties of governing with a very small majority, and Labour lost to the Tories. I wonder if their apparent willingness to lend British airfields to the USAF, publicised in the media at the time, had anything to do with Labour's losses at the two general elections?

In 1952 nobody outside air force circles thought of nuclear weapons on Greenham Common. On Good Friday of that year, in "Operation Gandhi", fifty people demonstrated at AWRE Aldermaston. They boarded the workers' buses, and leafleted the workers about the terrible new weapons being developed there. While this went on, the USAF men and aircraft were preparing to come to RAF Greenham Common, just seven miles to the west. American long-range piston and turboprop-engined bombers arrived. After a few years, they were replaced by jet bombers. Quietly, without fuss or fanfare, nuclear weapons came to Greenham Common.

For ten years the heavily armed airfield was left in peace, until a group of activists in the Oxford Committee of 100 discovered it. They organised a twenty-four-hour blockade, but after 315 people had been arrested, on 13th June, 1962, the remaining activists had to call it off, with about twenty hours still to go. The arrested activists were forcibly fingerprinted, detained for a while, then apparently released without charge.

Soon things reverted to normal, with the only protests consisting of occasional letters, complaining about aircraft noise, being sent to the authorities and the *Newbury Weekly News*. Neither local nor national organisations appeared to be opposing the nuclear bomber base. Even when, shortly after the blockade, RAF Greenham Common featured on a list of nuclear bases in *Sanity*, the CND magazine, nobody took much notice.

Then, at the beginning of 1978, the Tory Government planned to 're-activate' Greenham Common. The US Government had asked for a base for aircraft moving troops between Europe and the USA, and for KC135 tanker aircraft. These jet-powered planes carry large quantities of jet fuel for the use of other aircraft, and can refuel them in flight. In 1963, whilst refuelling in flight, a USAF nuclear bomber went out of control and crashed, losing two nuclear bombs, in a blaze of international publicity. This led to an outcry, which caused General Franco to ban all nuclear weapons from Spain. This was clearly remembered by many of the people living around Greenham.

Newbury Weekly News held an opinion poll, which showed that, out of 1,100 votes cast, 875 were against having the KC135s, and 152 were for having them. [Quoted in *At Least Cruise Is Clean*, by Lynchcombe.] This newspaper also published maps showing the flight-paths and noise corridors for the big jets using the airfield.

A campaign against the 're-activation' began, with the support of many prominent local people, including the world-famous Andrew Lloyd Webber. The local Tory MP, Michael McNair-Wilson, opposed his own government on the issue. Deputations went to London and Washington; the American Ambassador in London not only received a deputation, but also came to Greenham to see the problem for himself.

Into the middle of this came a group of about twenty folk, mostly Quakers from Newbury and nuclear disarmers from Southampton CND. They held a vigil at the Main Gate (now Yellow Gate) against the nuclear bombers that used Greenham Common, and were happy to add the KC135s and transport aircraft to their ticket. In addition to the vigil, they held a meeting and several other events, around Newbury over Easter, 1978.

The anti-reactivation brigade were not keen to add nuclear weapons to their ticket, though, and were not represented at any of the Southampton CND events. When one of their deputations visited Her Majesty's Secretary of State for Defence, there was confusion until they made it clear to him they were nothing to do with CND. He had been briefed that they were part of a CND protest.

The 're-activation' for KC135s and troop transports was prevented (RAF Fairford was used instead) but Greenham Common was kept as a nuclear bomber base. [See my account 'AWRE Fairford', elsewhere in this book].

The Americans were keeping a low profile, behind a rusty, old perimeter fence, which had many holes. At least one hole, where Green Gate was later installed, was large enough for a big man to enter the base easily.

On 12th December 1979, a meeting of NATO Ministers decided to site 464 ground launched Cruise missiles (GLCMs) and 108 Pershing missiles, in five European countries, and agreed for them to be under sole US control. Greenham people paid no special attention to this decision, for there was no mention of the missiles being based on their common.

Things changed radically when, in June, 1980, Her Majesty's Secretary of State for Defence, Francis Pym, P.C., MP, (known to some as Frankie Pimple) dropped a bombshell on Greenham Common: He announced it was to be a base for USAF GLCMs that NATO ministers wanted to deploy in Europe.

There are several different types of Cruise missiles: ALCMs can be air launched, as are the ALCMs fitted to B52 bombers; some can be launched from USN ships (SLCMs). GLCMs of the Tomahawk type can carry a battery of nuclear warheads on each missile. Most Cruise types have conventional high explosive warheads. Tomahawk GLCMs are fitted in batteries of four to each transporter-erector-launcher semi-trailer (TEL), which is coupled to a German MAN

unit to tow it. The whole vehicle, loaded, is said to have a gross train weight of fifty-eight tons.

The campaign against Cruise took off like a rocket (the way the Americans would have liked all their Cruise missiles to have taken off when being tested!). Joan Ruddock, who worked at the local Citizens' Advice Bureau, was at this time Chairperson of Newbury Constituency Labour Party, and had stood for Newbury in the General Election of May 1979, against Michael McNair-Wilson, the Tory who was elected. Within a week of Francis Pym's announcement, Joan and her friends had sent letters to hundreds of organisations in Southern England. Newbury had beaten the KC135s and troop transports; there was hope they could beat Cruise, too. Newbury Campaign Against Cruise Missiles had been launched.

About this time, Liberal County Councillor Trevor Brown's survey in East Newbury showed seventy per cent of the people interviewed did not want Cruise. On 26th June 1980, *Newbury Weekly News* held another opinion poll: Out of the 127 who voted, seventy-four opposed Cruise and forty-five were "not opposed" to Cruise. Yet just one year later, on 25th June 1981, the same newspaper quoted Michael McNair-Wilson, MP: "The great mass of my constituents did not oppose the suggestion that ground launched Cruise missiles should be stationed at Greenham Common." In 1980, however, the Whitehall Government were not so sure. They decided that something had to be done to curb the restless local folk. Glossy brochures full of pro-Cruise propaganda were liberally distributed around Greenham. The front page photograph was so good that it was immediately pinched by anti-Cruise campaigners for their posters and leaflets. On 24th July, Francis Pym came trouble-shooting to speak at

Greenham Main Gate.

a meeting at Newbury Racecourse, where he planned to promote Cruise, answer questions and allay fears.

Newbury District Council, now in favour of Cruise, distributed tickets for the 400 seats, doing their best to exclude campaigners against Cruise. The front rows of seats were reserved for local councillors, many of whom did not appear. Some Labour councillors were outside, picketing the meeting, with campaigners who could not get tickets. Many people were outside. The Chairman of Newbury Council chaired the meeting and questions had to be submitted to him in writing prior to the start. Francis Pym began by making a speech, which was much heckled. Obviously, some campaigners had managed to get into the gathering. Then the Chairman called upon the Mayor of Newbury to ask the first question (surprise!). There were many questions, quite a few of which were critical of defence policy and developments on Greenham Common. Not many of the audience appeared to like Cruise. When Michael McNair-Wilson closed the meeting with a short speech, there was a chorus of jeers and boos. In spite of all this, government publicity officers still managed to get the national media to publish the nonsense that the meeting had been a government success! They referred to protesters as 'loony left' and 'rent-a-crowd' minorities.

In July, 1980, the Newbury Campaign Against Cruise Missiles organised the first of several protest marches against Cruise. It was well supported, in spite of being held on the same day as Newbury Agricultural Show. *Newbury Weekly News* gave the show full coverage, but this clash meant only one of its reporters was able to cover the march, and then only in a few rushed minutes snatched from his work at the show. Surprisingly, the national press gave the march good publicity.

On Sunday 21st September, a new group, Southern Region Campaign Against the Missiles, organised an anti-Cruise rally, and 3,000 people marched up the hill from Newbury to a field near Greenham Parish Church, in beautiful weather. Several anti-nuclear groups had stalls there. On stage there was live pop music interspersed with speeches. Joan Ruddock and Bruce Kent both spoke. Sadly, none of the speakers mentioned that Greenham Common was already a first strike target because of USAF nuclear bombers already there; nothing was said about Greenham's sister base, RAF Welford, [See my account 'Artists and Greenham Women at RAF Welford', elsewhere in this book], which we could see from the rally field, and which was reputed to be the biggest arms dump in Europe; and thirdly, even though *Peace News* had

recently published a detailed description of a Cruise missile, no speaker appeared able to tell us anything about the missiles themselves. Although the march to the rally field passed along Bury's Bank Road, alongside the northern perimeter of the airfield, the gates here were then unimportant and the march did not stop at any of them. The Main Gate (now Yellow Gate) faced onto A339 trunk road on the Southern side of the airfield. The organisers failed to ensure even a token presence here. They failed to collect rent from stall-holders, some of whom borrowed trestle tables, which meant they were missing out on a source of income that would help them cover their costs. They did not properly organise litter clearance, with the result that the farmer sent them a litter clearance bill for £400, which came as a nasty shock. Afterwards, they appealed for cash to pay it from other groups in the area. I felt at this rally that the organisers had a lot to learn and there was a need for some form of training to prevent repetition of past mistakes.

Then on 22nd September the Whitehall Government, attempting to play cricket, got hold of a political football and scored two own goals with it! When campaigning to get people to accept Cruise missiles, they had claimed that nuclear weapons bases would not increase the danger to the inhabitants of nearby towns, above that which would have existed if the bases had only conventional weapons. With the help of local authorities all over the country the government launched "Operation Square Leg" (square leg being a position in the game of cricket) in which a number of missiles were launched at Britain by an enemy. It was an odd sort of cricket match. The political football scored two own goals, when missiles aimed at RAF Greenham Common and AWRE Aldermaston hit Newbury and Thatcham instead. Although this was only an exercise, the fact that the organisers allowed these missiles to go off course and hit two local towns made nonsense of their claim of no increased danger, as this did not appear to happen in places like Winchester, which had large, conventionally-armed army depots nearby.

When choosing a site for their nuclear war bunker a few months later, Newbury Council did not use their offices or depot, both near Greenham, but instead chose a site as far from the airfield as possible.

Southern Region Campaign Against the Missiles soldiered on, with letters to the press, leaflet distribution, another march in Newbury and even their own newspaper, which was distributed free around Greenham.

In April, 1981, Tarmac Limited started installing facilities for Cruise on the common. About £61,000,000 worth of work was involved.

Anne Pettit lived on a smallholding in Wales. From there she took an interest in what was going on at Greenham. She didn't like it, so she organised a protest march and in August 1981, forty women and four men left Cardiff to march the 110 miles to Greenham Common. They spent the night of Friday, 4th September, in a church hall in Newbury. The following day, when they set off up the hill, their ranks had been swelled by local disarmers to about 300. They planned to finish at a minor gate on the Northern perimeter, believed to have been Blue Gate, but on the march they asked the police if they could change their destination to Yellow Gate and the police agreed to shepherding the march for the extra three miles. Everyone was polite and friendly.

When the march arrived at Yellow Gate, some women, dressed in black, sat down in a circle and started wailing and crying as if in mourning. A thoroughly unpleasant American, dressed in casual clothes, took pictures of the demonstrators without telling them he was doing it. Some demonstrators were interviewed by a journalist and a cameraman. Later, an interview with Johanna New of Southampton saying in German why she was there and what she was doing, was broadcast on East German television. Johanna was delighted when relatives in Germany informed her that she had helped to publicise the campaign against Cruise in East Germany and that her German had come in handy. Although one British newspaper published a photo of the arrival at Greenham Common, most of the British media virtually ignored the march of the Women For Life On Earth (WFLOE) and their demand for a televised debate with the government, which was denied them because the government claimed they had held sufficient discussions to satisfy their democratic obligations. Although WFLOE members went frequently to Greenham Common during the following week, it is believed they were staying in Newbury at the time and did not actually live on the common until the first peace camp was formally established on 12th September, under a blazing, hot sun.

Meanwhile, the Property Services Agency of the Department of the Environment contracted with H. L. Goodman and Son (Bristol) Limited, Fencing Division, Berkeley Avenue, Reading, for the repair, and replacement where necessary, of the rusty, old chainlink perimeter fence. The price agreed was £121,512.

THE FIRST GREENHAM COMMON PEACE CAMP AND THE COSMIC COUNTER-CRUISE CARNIVAL

In pursuit of their demand for a televised debate, on Saturday 12th September, early in the morning, four women chained themselves to the fence near Yellow Gate in a suffragette-style protest. After a short while, at a predetermined time, another four replaced them and they kept up their presence by means of a rota. Meanwhile, some mainly local campaigners set off to march from the centre of Newbury to Yellow Gate. When the march arrived, it met a group of women, four of whom were chained to the fence, and a letter was delivered to the Commandant of RAF Greenham Common. The media had been told and were there in force. Local residents, off-duty airmen, and others debated vigorously with campaigners at Yellow Gate. The women chained to the fence were released. It all seemed friendly, if somewhat chaotic. WFLOE wanted to continue the debate at the gate, as they weren't being granted a television debate, so they set up the first Greenham Common Peace Camp beside Yellow Gate. This was just a camp, and there were people of both sexes and a large age range at it. Several complete families stayed there. This had been a historic day.

In those days, CND National Conference did not hold collections for money. At the 1981 conference, however, the Greenham Common campers were allowed to make a collection and raised £402 from the 800-plus people there. This was almost certainly the first formal collection to have been made at a CND National Conference in nearly twenty-five years.

In addition to collecting this respectable sum, the campers helped this conference pass a motion, which was a fundamental policy change for CND:

> CND supports regional and local groups, in undertaking considered NVDA in pursuit of the British campaign, and would be willing to organise and lead national direct action if considered necessary. This is particularly urgent in view of the government's continued rejection of popular demand for a stop to the Trident programme and the basing of Cruise missiles in this country. In particular, conference supports the peace camps at Greenham Common and elsewhere and actions against Operation Hard Rock next autumn. [From *Green CND Newsletter* issue no. 4].

By November the peace camp at Yellow Gate had grown to ten caravans and two tipis, and campers of both sexes were getting used to what they thought were difficult conditions, with the cold rains and fogs of autumn. Had they known of the frost, snow and evictions in store for them, they would have thought differently!

At about this time, seven of the WFLOE went to Porth, in South Wales, where two of them lived and set up a peace camp in solidarity with the one at Yellow Gate. At first they chained themselves to railings by the General Post Office in Porth Square, but they were later lent a portable hut, in which they lived for about a week. This camp is believed to have been unique in two respects: It was the first British exclusive women's peace camp, and campers had the use of the police station lavatories!

Campers and their supporters marched from Yellow Gate into Newbury on 13th December 1981 to commemorate the second anniversary of the Nato decision to deploy Cruise in Europe. This was the first of many annual commemorations of this decision.

On 21st December peace campers used NVDA to stop sewers being laid into the base.

Also in December, Leonnie Caldicott took news of Greenham Common to Japan, and addressed a huge Japanese women's peace rally. She visited the women at Shibokusa, and brought news of that peace camp, older than Greenham Common and very different, back to the Western world. [For details, see *Women at the Wire*, by Leonnie Caldicott and Lynne Jones, published in London by the Women's Press].

In January 1982, a second attempt to lay sewer pipes into the base was delayed, and eventually stopped by women lying in the trenches, again using NVDA. These two sewer actions inspired actions at several other locations, including Brambles Farm. [See my account 'Torpedo Town' elsewhere in this book].

National Conference of CND elects a National Council, which meets regularly throughout the year, between conferences, to interpret policy and conference decisions. Council agreed, at its January meeting, to organise a national demonstration against Cruise on 6th June.

Then, on 19th January, the Recreation and Amenities Committee of Newbury District Council, meeting in camera, decided to evict the peace camp. As eviction from commons can be complicated, the committee naturally obtained the best available legal advice. On 20th January, Helen John and the other campers received a letter from Newbury Council, serving notice that they intended to ask for an order in possession for the campsite. Then began long and involved discussions among the campers, which considered all the angles and aspects of this new problem. It was

decided to resist any attempted eviction. It was felt the camp would have a better chance of survival and there would be less risk of violence, if men were not living at the camp, and only women were there to resist evictions. These appear to be the main reasons the men left, and on 1st February 1982 the Yellow Gate camp became exclusively a women's peace camp.

This started a great controversy in the peace movement. Many people, some obviously not peace campers, complained about men being excluded from Greenham Common, and others tried to explain and defend the decision of the peace camp. Not only did many debaters ignore the existence of mixed peace camps, but they even ignored Fran De'Ath's mixed peace camp at Green Gate.

At about this time, Fran De'Ath from Bristol began her picket of the Works Entrance (Green Gate). She had a primus for cooking, and a tipi for sleeping, and invited campers of both sexes to bring their tents along and join her. Slowly her camp grew, while day after day Fran sat with her placard, talking to the workers, either as they came in and out, or through the fence, about nuclear disarmament.

The Green Gate peace camp played an important part in the next big event on Greenham Common, when, on 21st and 22nd March, the Spring Equinox and Mothering Sunday were celebrated by about a thousand people with a festival, in a large clearing in the woods, near the perimeter fence, immediately to the West of Green Gate. The many acts included the Fallout Marching Band and people of both sexes were there.

On Monday, 22nd March, between 200 and 300 women successfully blockaded all the gates at once. The authorities appeared to admit defeat and stopped trying to keep any of the gates free. They then sneakily opened a section of fence at the end of the main runway, to let traffic in and out of the base. Soon women found that it was being used, and rushed up the track through the woods to blockade it, so that traffic was stopped here, too. This time police moved in and dragged the women off, arresting thirty-four and charging each one with obstructing the Queen's Highway. The traffic began moving again.

On Good Friday, 9th April, a crowd of young people gathered by Southampton YCND left that city to walk the forty miles or so to Greenham Common. They were joined by other young people along the way and, after spending two nights up the road, arrived on Easter Sunday. About thirty had marched the whole way. When they reached Yellow Gate with their banners, the peace campers, who were having a quiet Easter, were surprised to see them. This appears to have been caused by inadequate advance liaison and publicity. The young people returned home that night in supporters' cars.

On 14th April, twenty-two of the women arrested on 22nd March appeared in court, all with not guilty pleas prepared. The first case was taken as a test case, so the same judgement would apply to the others and there would be no need for twenty-two long and involved trials. Defence Counsel Helena Kennedy argued, in Newbury Magistrates Court, that a deliberately made gap in a fence was neither a highway nor a normal access, and to be guilty of wilful obstruction of the highway, the defendant would have had to intend to obstruct a properly defined highway. This defence failed, and the first woman was found guilty as charged. After several speeches pleading innocence, some of which were applauded from the public gallery, the other twenty-one women were convicted for obstructing the highway. A week later Newbury magistrates found all the remaining twelve women guilty. Fines of £15 with £10 costs were levied on each of thirty-two women and £1 nominal fines were imposed on each of two Buddhist nuns with no personal income. The first woman to be fined announced that she would not pay, as she considered herself not guilty as charged.

On the night of 22nd April, the Washington State to Moscow Peace Walk visited Greenham Common.

At Green Gate, on 12th May, Trades Union CND got union officials, including one from the Union of Construction and Allied Trades, to talk to construction workers on the base. English law obliges employers to let union officials talk to workers. A discussion took place, with union officials, workers and peace campers.

The Sanctuary was a small, privately owned plot of land, without any fences or buildings, in the middle of the woods on Greenham Common. At one time the rill flowing down one side had filtered through the remains of an old, dumped Ford car, in an amusing manner, reminiscent of custard-pie comedy films. Indeed, even the name on the car seemed right – a ford is a shallow place where one can cross a rill or a stream, so one would expect to find a Ford there. However, this rill was crossed by a bridge. There were tents and tipis on The Sanctuary, but no caravans as the path and bridge were not wide enough for them. Campers used The Sanctuary as a rest camp,

and as a place to leave valuables, where they would be safe from bailiffs in evictions.

At the Royal Courts of Justice in London, on 14th May, a high court judge in chambers heard Newbury Council's application for an order in possession for all the common land on Greenham Common and Crookham Common. The order excluded the airfield, of course; the road verges, which belonged to the Department of Transport and Berkshire County Council; The Sanctuary and other private properties. After refusing to take the hearing in open court, the judge granted the council their request.

Outside the Royal Courts of Justice, as this was going on, there was a peaceful picket, which included Buddhist monks praying and banging on small drums. Suddenly the police arrested the two Buddhists and tried to drag them to a Sherpa van. Protesters immediately sat down around them. When the police eventually got the monks into the van, about fifty people sat down and blockaded it so it could not leave. Police reinforcements arrived and twenty-six more people had to be arrested before the Sherpa could move. All twenty-eight appeared before a stipendiary magistrate at Bow Street, who adjourned their cases until 28th May and 2nd, 3rd, 4th 8th and 9th June.

The next stage in the fight against eviction came when a group of peace camp supporters, including local residents who also happened to be Newbury Council ratepayers, exercised their right to call upon the council to debate the eviction before it took place, in order to gain time, publicity, and a slim chance for the council to change its mind and allow the camp to stay. The council found they could legally delegate the discussion to a committee, which they did, in order to save time. Alas! The committee decided to evict.

As soon as the debate was over, the first eviction began. It took nine hours. During it, five women were arrested: Ioma Axe, Amanda, Beatrice Schmidt, Tina and Sara. Both the camp at Yellow Gate and the camp at Green Gate known as the Other Peace Camp were evicted. The Sanctuary, and caravans and tents on road verges near Yellow Gate were left alone. Some people left and the Women's Peace Camp reformed entirely on the road verges.

In court all five arrested women were convicted of committing breaches of the peace, for which four refused to be bound over and were imprisoned for seven days each. Beatrice, who was roughly treated on arrest, and received mild concussion, accepted the binding-over order and was not sent to prison. It is believed she did this because she had a small child on Greenham Common. These women, like many in court after them, took advantage of opportunities afforded by the court for defendants to explain their actions and the reasons for them, They contrasted their idea of a breach of the peace – a Cruise missile base – with the police idea of a breach – a peace camp.

Meanwhile, Fran from Green Gate was also in court. Shortly before the first evictions she sat down in front of a mechanical digger, which was digging a trench in Brockenhurst Road, the lane leading from the A339 to Green Gate. Work was delayed for an hour, after which she was arrested and charged with obstruction of the highway. A charge of behaviour likely to lead to a breach of the peace was later added. Fran conducted her own defence on both charges. She refused to plead, so the court assumed not guilty pleas. She called police and site workers to give evidence that her behaviour was "at all times peaceful" [*Radiator*, August 1982] and told the court that if anyone had been likely to become upset, she would have got up and made tea. As Brockenhurst Road had already been closed by the authorities, with proper road signs so that the trench could be dug, the obstruction charge could have been bounced back at the prosecution and made them look silly, if it was argued out in detail in court. For this reason they offered no evidence and agreed to the magistrate's request to drop the charge, hoping that dropping it would improve their chances of a conviction on the second charge. After hearing the evidence, however, the magistrate found Fran not guilty of behaviour likely to cause a breach of the peace and she left the court a free woman.

The CND national demonstration on 6th June did not take place on Greenham Common as at first planned, because after planning for it began, the government announced that US President Ronald Reagan would be visiting London then. About 250,000 demonstrators attended the rally in Hyde Park, and Greenham women spoke from the platform.

Following this, about eighty Greenham women, in London for the rally, held a "die-in" on the streets around the Stock Exchange. About six were arrested.

Keening is an American Indian custom involving a sort of humming. In the House of Commons, on 8th June, Ronald Reagan became the first US president ever to address the British Parliament. Outside, as he spoke, Greenham women held a keening, and another "die-in", at which there appear to have been no arrests.

On Tuesday 22nd June, at about 08.30 hours, John Eddie, the new Labour mayor of Basingstoke (a town about twelve miles down A339 from Yellow Gate) called at the Women's Peace Camp. With him in the mayoral car he had Peter Baker and Ken Cole. They had hitched an official, civic lift with him, in a blaze of television, radio, and press publicity, at the start of a sponsored, 600-mile hitch-hike around seven peace camps. After Greenham Common, they hitched to Upper Heyford, Fairford, Caerwent, Burtonwood, and Waddington, where Ken had to finish. Peter continued, via Molesworth and 10 Downing Street, returning to Basingstoke in the remarkably fast time of thirty-two hours. As a result of the sponsored hitch, money was raised for the peace movement and letters were delivered to the Prime Minister from organisations involved with the hitch-hike. This is believed to be the first occasion, and at the time of writing, the only occasion, in world history, that a mayoral car has picked up a hitch-hiker as part of its civic duties!

Every year, on Midsummer night in June, a festival takes place at Stonehenge, on Salisbury Plain, about thirty miles west of Greenham. In recent years, crowds of young folk have come, and added their own music festival to the traditional one. In 1982, some of these folk had been to the Spring Equinox Festival by Green Gate and wanted to hold another anti-Cruise festival there.

They made plans, and a small notice was inserted in the *Peace News* diary page for 25th June: "1-8 July Greenham Common. Peace and Alternative Lifestyles Festival". That appears to have been the only advance publicity, outside of handbills and newsletters these folk may have produced themselves. There were no posters all over the area, and no mention in the media in Southampton, less than forty miles away. Thus many local anti-Cruise campaigners knew nothing about the Cosmic Counter-Cruise Carnival until after it was over.

"On Wednesday June 30th about 130 vehicles, carrying 500 people," [from the *Radiator* August 1982] arrived at about the bottom of Brockenhurst Road. Some had "THE PEACE CONVOY" painted on their sides. The authorities, who were expecting the convoy, had dug trenches to stop vehicular access to the common from Brockenhurst Road. It appears that the police had not expected such a big convoy, because when the festival folk arrived, they found few police and a group of them were able to lift, with their own hands, a Ford Transit with only the driver sat in it, that was parked blocking Brockenhurst Road, filled part of the trenches, and drove onto the site, which was on the common a short distance to the West of Green Gate.

Tents, tipis, and traders' stalls were erected around the parked vehicles. Among the newcomers were campers experienced in setting up camps in the face of official opposition, and these people proved to be of immense value in getting the camp set up quickly. The women from Yellow Gate were not much help at all – indeed, they seemed not to want the carnival there. Soon the camp became a bustling hive of activity, even to the extent that it produced a daily newspaper, *The Greenham Free Press*.

Newbury District Council took no action at the carnival site. The *Peace News* announcement had mentioned 8th July as a date for the end of the carnival, and the council hoped the convoy would leave then. The police kept a low profile.

Representatives from the carnival addressed the CND National Executive on 3rd July, appealing for funds and help to set up the stage and generator. National CND was only able, at that stage, to give moral support, but Green CND donated £50, and set up a site office at the carnival. CND Chairperson Joan Ruddock agreed to visit the carnival on Tuesday, 13th July. This meant that it would continue beyond 8th July.

On 4th July the flag of the 501st Tactical Missile Wing of the USAF was raised over Greenham Common, at an Independence Day ceremony behind the fence. Ironically, 4th July commemorated the US gaining its freedom from the United Kingdom; now the boot was on the other foot, for the US was taking over the UK. Lakenheath and Upper Heyford were flying US military flags.

Outside the wire, the Cosmic Counter-Cruise Carnival held its own ceremony, and issued its own Declaration of Independence, as the People's Free State of Greenham. They issued a statement, part of which read:

> The most serious threat to life on this planet is that of nuclear war. The most serious escalation in the nuclear arms race will be the installation of 96 American Cruise missiles at Greenham Common in the Autumn of 1983. Britain is the one European country that is keen to be the first with Cruise. If it is stopped here, it will be stopped for the rest of Europe. [From the *Radiator*, August 1982.]

Two carnival campers were arrested for cutting down saplings for firewood. They must have been inexperienced, for green, living wood does not burn well and had they looked, they would have found plenty of dead wood, which burns better. Many campers thought living trees very important, and wanted to preserve them, so these arrests did not lead to

protests, and would not have been worth a mention, but for their importance in the light of a later event.

By 8th July, the day the carnival was originally going to finish, about a thousand people were enjoying themselves there. At least one meeting had been held to plan NVDA and it was clear from subsequent events that neither police nor military spies had infiltrated that meeting, for the authorities were not prepared and nobody was arrested, when late on Thursday night a hole was made in the fence and two people entered the airfield, where they sabotaged and painted equipment used for constructing bunkers. At this time, bunkers and silos were being constructed just inside Green Gate. The two people came back out after their incursion, and were stopped by neither police nor US guards. As they were working inside the fence, a section of chain-link fencing fell away from its posts, probably assisted by other campers. As soon as the Modplods saw what had happened, they produced a searchlight, and shone it along inside the fence. This prevented NVDA for a time.

When, in the early morning, carnival campers watched the MoD contractor bulldoze flat a large area of saplings just inside the fence, they were saddened and angered. Not only were trees important to them, but they also remembered the arrests of the two campers caught cutting down saplings outside the fence. They retaliated by systematically and deliberately demolishing the perimeter fence, which, though two new double gates had been built into it at Green Gate, was still the rusty old chain-link fence repaired by H. L. Goodman and Son. The campers knew what to do; they had prepared themselves for just such an action. The fence posts were broken with sledge-hammers a foot above the ground, and vehicles were hitched to the fence to pull it down and at the same time bend any reinforcing rods left undamaged inside the fence posts. People pushed and pulled, too. About 250 metres of fence were completely flattened. It was done quickly, and took the few police and troops inside by surprise. The whole 250 metres was wrecked beyond repair, and there was nothing between the carnival campers and the airfield.

What would have been the outcome if a mass incursion had taken place at this point, and campers had occupied buildings on the airfield? We don't know.

It was alleged that stones had been thrown at bulldozers working inside the fence. As the carnival site was stony, people who wanted to make trouble for the campers, or had some other crazy idea, could easily have picked up stones and thrown them. However, the police arrested no stone throwers, who could have been charged with behaviour likely to cause a breach of the peace, or a more serious offence. In fact, the police arrested nobody. They just stood around taking photos.

A group at Green Gate were picketing and blockading as people drove into work. By pushing, shoving and dragging people out of the way, police were getting traffic through, when suddenly, a van leaving the airfield knocked down a man, who reacted violently. In the ensuing disturbance three people, including a press photographer, were arrested. Their release was demanded. Then police chained the gates closed, next to the flattened fence, and the traffic stopped. If there was to be a mass incursion, it would have to take place now, for police reinforcements were beginning to arrive. No incursion occurred. Everybody just waited. Some folk started winding things up; some tried cooling down the crowd that had gathered. Two women from Yellow Gate played a part in calming the crowd. More and more police were now arriving, though they were making no arrests. It was suggested that if they went onto the site, everybody should sit in front of the stage. Then a long row of police formed up and, walking slowly forward, side-by-side, they came onto the site. Groups of police in riot gear were walking behind the ordinary police.

"Get that one. I saw him," shouted a senior police officer.

A man was arrested.

The senior officer shouted again, and the process was repeated four more times, until, having apparently satisfied their craving for arrests, the police retreated and stood around for a while, before leaving the scene.

Meanwhile, a male motorcyclist on his way to the carnival was stopped in Newbury and arrested. Along with six of the people arrested at the carnival, he was detained. They were detained for periods of from six to ten days. An eighth person was allowed out on bail 'because there were only seven cells' [From *Radiator*, August 1982]. There are no reports of what happened to three of these people, but on 28th February 1983, five appeared in Reading Crown Court on serious criminal damage charges. The cases against four were dismissed for lack of evidence, after they had pleaded not guilty. Perhaps that senior police officer, who had only just appeared on the scene when he started shouting for arrests, had not really seen the accused at all when the fence came

down. Indeed, he may not have been on the common when it happened. One of the four, Jerry Barford, was found guilty on a lesser charge of breach of the peace. The fifth defendant, Kevin Hutton, from West Wales, and aged nineteen, pleaded guilty, saying he was not ashamed of doing something which he regarded to be a justified protest against the coming of Cruise and the bulldozing of the saplings. He was sentenced to three months in a prison in Southern England, which meant his family had a round trip of about 400 miles every time they visited him.

Things would have been easier for those in court, and records would have been better kept, had a legal back-up system been arranged for the carnival, but if one was, it was ineffective. A legal back-up system for a crowd of people as large as that at the carnival can have disadvantages. Had one been properly arranged, leaflets about it would have had to be produced and distributed, and more meetings would have been necessary. These things almost certainly would have alerted the authorities to the planned actions, resulting in there being too many police and troops around on the night of 8th July for the incursion and the fence demolition to take place.

Although at least one press photographer was at Green Gate on 9th July, the media seems to have largely ignored this NVDA, and, indeed, the whole carnival. Several pressmen were in court on 28th February, but again the media seems to have ignored this event. Even peace movement and radical journals gave the carnival and the court cases poor coverage. Certainly, the authorities did not want the carnival and the not guilty verdicts publicised. While the authorities employed professional publicity people and gave them offices and telephones, the carnival relied on ill-equipped amateurs.

Immediately after the 9th July arrests, the US Embassy in London contacted national CND, claiming carnival campers had attacked RAF Greenham Common with petrol bombs and bows and arrows. Petrol bombs and bows and arrows, are fairly easily made, and can be used by amateurs, so one can't rule out the possibility of this allegation being true. However, the facts suggest that the allegation was untrue, for nobody was arrested doing these illegal acts, nobody appears to have been hurt by a petrol bomb or an arrow, and no publicly available account of the carnival mentions any such attack. Folk who were there, and with whom I spoke, didn't remember one, either. CND's next act was unpardonable. Without consulting any of the carnival campers, CND accepted the American allegation as true, issued their own statement dissociating themselves from the carnival and cancelled Joan Ruddock's forthcoming visit. In spite of their 1981 National Conference decision to support NVDA, apparently no National CND officer ever visited the carnival.

Understandably, *Greenham Free Press* criticised CND. Out of all this fog of uncertainty and allegations, one fact emerges clearly: on the night of 8th July and in the morning of 9th July history had been made, with the first non-violent demolition of an MoD fence by nuclear disarmers. Of course, it led to much discussion on the common, about violence, non-violence and direct action. Alas! The victory was short-lived, for the MoD soon had a new fence built.

When the carnival ended, most of the folks involved left on 18th July – ten days after the big night. Only about 150 people remained in a peace camp by Green Gate, to continue campaigning against Cruise.

Around 5th July, the Department of Transport were planning to evict the Women's Peace Camp from road verges near Yellow Gate.

Also at about this time, Sue Cowgill announced she was holding a sponsored prison sentence, after being told she would be imprisoned for not paying a fine. Then Helen Blackwell and Helen Murphy (who were also active at Upper Heyford) refused binding-over orders for offences on Greenham Common. Imprisoned in Drake Hall, they, too, held sponsored prison sentences.

Then, on 23rd July, *Peace News* reported receiving a telephone call from a man claiming to have been told by an American worker on Greenham Common, that Cruise missiles and lorries to carry them had been flown into Greenham Common by KC135 aircraft on 1st March 1982. If this had been a made-up story, it is unlikely that KC135 tanker aircraft would have been specified; a type of freighter aircraft would. An inexperienced observer could have mistaken freighter aircraft for KC135s, or may have described them as looking like KC135s. It is not easy to mistake Cruise missiles and TEL trailers for anything else.

In the morning of Hiroshima Day, 1982, campers from Yellow Gate filed past the War Memorial in the corner of Newbury Parish Churchyard, each laying a small stone at its foot as she went. They planned to lay 100,000, to represent 100,000 Hiroshima victims. It is believed they actually collected that many stones on the common, and took them to the War Memorial in cars and vans. Although some passers-by joined the women in laying stones, many were rude, and jeered. One Greenham woman was slapped, the National Front arrived, and the atmosphere got heavy. Our old police friend, Ken Scott-Picton, newly promoted to Chief Superintendent, offered to arrest the women and lock them up for their own safety. To prevent violence, the women ended their demonstration after laying about 10,000 stones and returned to Greenham Common.

On the next day, Greenham women marched through Edinburgh, Britain's first NFZ, in solidarity with other women imprisoned for not paying fines earned blockading the airfield.

On Nagasaki Day, a group of women, who had never been on the airfield before, walked through Blue Gate and sat down inside. The lone modplod on duty tried to stop the women but could not. He radioed for help.

Japanese people believe that folding 1000 paper cranes will bring the folder good fortune. A girl called Sadako Sasaki, dying as a result of the A-bombing of Nagasaki, believed that if she could fold a thousand paper cranes, she would get well. The folding of the cranes kept her mind occupied, as she lay, in pain, in hospital. She managed to fold 645 cranes before she died.

The women sat on the airfield had the paper to make 366 paper cranes, to finish her thousand in her memory. They sat folding cranes as police reinforcements arrived. After about thirty minutes, the women were politely asked to leave. They refused and asked to see the commanding officer. He came. They presented him with a paper crane and a letter of explanation. They still wouldn't leave, so were carefully loaded into a van, driven off and released outside Yellow Gate, all under the personal supervision of the commanding officer, who worried in case they got hurt. A film crew outside Blue Gate filmed the entire event, apparently without Modsquad interference.

A lone modplod was in the guardroom at Yellow Gate when about twenty women strolled casually up the approach road. He ran out towards one in front, Helen John, saying that the women weren't allowed in. Helen kept walking. The modplod made a grab for her. Suddenly, the others made a dash for the guardroom, and occupied it.

After about twenty minutes, the Modsquad had the building surrounded, and one modplod managed to get in, using a small window that had been left open. The doors were unbolted. The Modsquad arrested nineteen women, and charged them with breach of the peace. They finally appeared in Newbury Magistrates Court on 15th and 16th November.

The planning and execution of the Yellow Gate takeover and the paper crane action had been superb.

On 29th September the Women's Peace Camp was at last evicted from road verges near Yellow Gate by the Department of Transport. It was raining steadily throughout the eviction. The women's caravans, with their belongings inside, were hitched to lorries and towed off to a pound in Newbury, where the women were later allowed to collect their belongings. Tents were wrecked and removed. The women moved onto Newbury Council common land, where police not only stopped them from fixing umbrellas fixed in the ground to keep children dry, but also tried to put out their bonfires. The women slept that night on the council land with plastic sheets over them. Unlike the umbrellas, these were not structures and did not contravene the by-laws.

At the same time, the Other Peace Camp was evicted by Newbury Council bailiffs from common land near Green Gate. This camp reformed outside Orange Gate, where Green CND planned to hold a Hallowe'en festival, involving people who had been at the Cosmic Counter-Cruise Carnival.

On the day after these evictions, which were well covered by the media, Helen John addressed a special meeting on Greenham at the Labour Party Annual Conference, where a collection was taken for the Women's Peace Camp.

Peace campers blockaded the main entrance to Faslane submarine base in Scotland, in a surprise action in solidarity with the evicted Greenham campers. The blockade caused traffic chaos, with a four-mile jam on A814. Then, before the police could arrest them, the blockaders got up and left (For further information, see 'Permanent Peace Camps Begin at Faslane' elsewhere in this book).

A few miles away in Edinburgh, about twenty people occupied the US Consulate for twenty minutes on 1st October, after which all but two left. These two were allowed to stay and dictate letters to Margaret Thatcher, NATO and Ronald Reagan, protesting about Cruise missiles and the Greenham evictions.

Back on Greenham Common on 1st October, amid the disorder and discomfort, women from the peace movement all over the world came together with Greenham Women and some British visitors, to plan their peace campaigning and share experiences and information. The Women's Peace Camp received lots of donations. The evictions hadn't prevented their gathering, obviously!

On 4th October, workers arrived to make another attempt to lay sewers into the base. The women went onto the construction site, sat and laid themselves down in the way of the pipe layers and wove webs of wool over themselves. The webs created an odd legal situation, and the police for a time were uncertain what to do. They explained politely that if the women didn't move out of the way of the pipe layers, they might cause a breach of the peace, because the men were anxious to get on with the job and might throw them out of the way violently.

Other women were frantically alerting the media and the telephone tree, probably from a private house belonging to a supporter in Ecchinswell. Reinforcements were desperately needed.

Nobody moved. Then the policemen roughly pulled the women off the site, and nothing happened for some minutes. Some workers went onto the site and began hammering survey posts into the ground. A group of women ran back onto the site and removed the posts. Police were at first amused, but when a woman threw a hammer into the bushes, they acted and arrested Rebecca. They eventually arrested twelve more women before the action came to an end. After being charged with behaviour likely to lead to a breach of the peace, the women were released in the late afternoon. They were finally tried by Newbury magistrates on 17th November.

DHSS officials visited the Women's Peace Camp at Yellow Gate on 8th October, and discussed raising the social security money, for claimants living there, from £7·70 to £18.

On 1st November, at 07.00 hours, six people began to picket the works entrance (Green Gate). The authorities would not open it, so traffic, including all the lorries, had to divert through another gate, and was delayed.

As much of the traffic was people going to work, many started work late, and construction was delayed. When the six women saw the success of their picket, they called it off. They hadn't planned a blockade, but their picket had the same effect as a blockade, without their getting arrested.

At Newbury Magistrates Court, on 15th, 16th and 17th November, the trials were held, first of the women in the Yellow Gate Guardroom take-over, and then of the women in the sewer pipe action of 4th October. The accused were represented by three lawyers who rendered great services to Greenham women in the courts: Jane Hickman, Isobell Forshall and Elizabeth Woodcraft.

Simone Wilkinson, one of the defendants, said in a statement to the court: "I am on trial for my life, not just for a breach of the peace, but if we lose this case, we stand to lose our children." (Several quotations from women on trial are in *Women's Peace Camp*, published in February 1983, by the camp.)

All the women were bound over to be of good behaviour, but twenty-three refused to be bound over, and were each imprisoned for fourteen days. Of these, eleven were sent to East Sutton Park Borstal in Kent and twelve went to Drake Hall Open Prison. The Drake Hall women refused to work and all ended up in Allen House, which was the punishment block. Apparently this filled Allen House. The Committee of 100 ideal, to have so many people committing civil disobedience that the jails would be filled with them, had been realised here. About ninety-five women took part in a peace camp with a vigil outside, which ensured the outside world knew who were inside, and that the prisoners got many visitors. This upset the authorities, so the Drake Hall women were moved: three went to Styal Prison, three to Crookham Hall, three to Holloway, and three to another prison. When the three were released from Holloway Prison in London, they were welcomed by a huge crowd outside and excellent publicity. Ironically, they were released on 30th November, the day before the War Resisters International Annual Prisoners for Peace Day, so didn't qualify for Christmas cards. (For a fuller account of the prison sentences and the camp, see "The Inside Story", by Sue Lamb and Lynne Fort, *Radiator*, February, 1983; also 'Springfield and Styal', elsewhere in this book.)

At the 1982 CND National Conference, a number of Greenham women were elected to the National Council.

There were many demonstrations to commemorate the third anniversary of the NATO decision to site Cruise missiles in Europe. One was at Smithfield US Army Depot in South Australia; another was in London, England, on 10th December, when a mock Cruise missile was delivered to Tarmac's head office. Once inside, the Greenham women and friends, who had brought the missile, were greeted by a Tarmac employee, who said it all, when he told them: "We don't want this missile here." (Quoted in *Peace News*, 7th January, 1983.)

To commemorate the NATO decision, the women wanted to surround the airfield on 12th December, with a human chain of 16,000 people, nine miles long. In fact, about 30,000 people came, and the chain was a huge success. All the gates were closed all day, CB radios and vehicles were used effectively. Men were allowed to participate at one mixed gate, and men arriving at the other gates were sent there. The other gates were, of course, all women-only. The perimeter fence was decorated all round with a vast variety of objects – pictures of children, locks of their hair, banners, flowers, etc.

On Monday 13th December, from dawn to dusk, between one and two thousand women were sitting in all the gates continuing the blockade. Police, dressed in overcoats obscuring their identity numbers, tried to move them. At most of the gates, their method seemed to involve a large group of police approaching the blockade from outside, and another large group coming at the gates from inside. While the insiders pushed the gates open outwards into the crowd of blockaders, forcing them apart so their linked arms could not hold, the outsiders dragged blockaders away roughly, and opened a passage for traffic. There were no arrests.

> Many women received bruises and grazes; at least one woman was kicked in the head, another run over by a police motorbike, another by a coach (and received a broken foot), another was picked upon because she was known to live at the camp and kicked in the back, pressure pointed behind the ears while having her arm twisted, and trodden on. Police trampled on stomachs and legs, pulled hair, and twisted breasts. Two women in a car from inside the base deliberately ran down a woman walking along the road." (Reported by S.G. in *Radiator*, February, 1983)

The road was near Blue Gate; the woman was a Dutch woman, Mirjam Harmsen. Dreike Hall and Mirjam came with a group of Dutch women (NATO had sited Cruise missiles in Holland, too, and the Dutch people were protesting even more than the British) to Greenham to take part in the actions on 12th and 13th November . In a letter published in the *Radiator*, in April 1983, they revealed how this car ran down Mirjam who was walking along the roadside.

> … On Monday, however, it seemed as though the evil contained within the base's perimeter fence reached outside it: A Dutch woman was deliberately run down by a car (reg. no. ABL 743T – red Datsun) along the northern perimeter road. The woman driver neither used her horn nor tried to

swerve to the free side of the road: She pertinently ignored the consequences of the hatred to which she had thus given expression. These were several: Firstly the woman involved had to undergo a knee operation, and after a period in hospital and six weeks in plaster, is now learning to walk again. Secondly a feeling of wretchedness remained with us: Such incidents should not be possible. Dehumanising other people as 'opponents' and thus justifying the need for their destruction is precisely what we had come to demonstrate against. On a larger scale, this is what is happening with nuclear weapons.

In May 1986, Mirjam wrote, to me, that her knee, which had been operated on, had recovered, but that it would always be a weak part of her body. No doubt this will restrict her participation in sports and walks.

There is no record of the Datsun driver or the motorcyclist being prosecuted, and I do not recall a prosecution of the coach driver, either.

A policeman was once fined £400 for driving "… at dangerously high speed through a group of peace demonstrators" (The only record of this fine, that I found, was in *At Least Cruise is Clean* by Lynchcombe). Newbury Citizens Relief Fund was started by five local people to help pay his fine, but the authorities later stopped them paying it, as for the fund to pay it would not have been legal. This appears to be the only time that a driver or rider connected with RAF Greenham Common, the Cruise Convoys, or the policing of them, was prosecuted for a driving offence at a Greenham Common demonstration. Even when police have been given registration numbers and witnesses' names, and their own officers have seen that offence they have been unwilling to prosecute, but when a driver from CND or Cruisewatch was involved, the police were eager to prosecute, arrest and detain. The tiniest error on the part of the driver would become dangerous driving. One man was arrested, and detained, for sleeping in his legally parked car! He was later released without charge.

During the blockade, women were able to roll back the perimeter fence at one place. They went onto the airfield, where they planted seeds and bulbs and lit candles.

Throughout all the actions of 12th and 13th December, there were only three arrests for minor offences. Police kept the numbers of arrests down for several reasons: Firstly, they avoided the hassles of charging and detaining large numbers of people; secondly, fewer folk appeared in court making speeches

against Cruise; and thirdly, they wanted the media to commend them for their restraint, which, of course, the media did. There may have been other reasons, known only to the authorities, but these were the obvious ones.

The actions were reported widely in the British media and abroad. A CND member in Bolivia sent "… several news cuttings from La Paz, Bolivia, which when translated turned out to be very accurate accounts of events at Greenham over the weekend of 12th and 13th December." ('Good News, Bad News' by Celia Whiteside, *Radiator*, February, 1983)

All the publicity helped to make for a hectic Christmas, with lots of visitors bringing the camp many presents. Nearly all the presents were sensible, practical and useful.

1983 BEGAN BEFORE DAWN ON 1ˢᵗ JANUARY

The campers were not idle, just because it was miserable weather, and they had to get over a hectic Christmas. They were planning their next action. They held meetings, sometimes three in a single day, to get the details right.

A crowd of women walked into a shop in Reading, bought ten ladders and walked out with them. Fortunately the shop staff, though left guessing about the use of the ladders, didn't report their purchase to the police. The crowd of women were not in working overalls. Had the shop staff thought it suspicious that they should buy so many ladders and contacted the police, the police would have immediately searched for the ladders on the common and increased security.

Carpets were acquired. This time more carefully.

By the evening of 31ˢᵗ December, the carpets and ladders were stowed out of sight on the common. An objective had been identified and inspected as best it could be. A route to the objective had been surveyed. A banner was ready and safely stowed. The campers' security appeared to have held, and the police seemed to suspect nothing. The New Year's Eve blockade at Heyford drew police away from Greenham Common.

The campers were left with the tricky problem of alerting the media about their forthcoming NVDA, without alerting the authorities. It was decided that a press conference at the Women's Peace Camp, to be held at the eccentric time of 06.00 hours on New Year's Day would get the media along without unduly alarming the police. It would also serve as a useful diversion to draw police from the area around the objective, which was over a mile from the Women's Peace Camp. The campers told the media they were going to reveal big plans for 1983, and made no mention of any action planned for that morning. Would the media folk get out of bed that early on New Year's Day? That was the $64,000 question.

A few media people came to see if there was a New Year's Eve party, and to try and get advance information of what was to be given out at the press conference. They were told to return in the morning. The small party ended early, so that the women could get a good night's sleep.

Before dawn on 1st January, 1983, the ladders were pulled out of hiding and put against the perimeter fence near Turquoise Gate. The carpets were put on top of the fence. As the first light was spreading through the clouds, the women were over the fence, and running up the muddy slope onto the top of a newly-built silo. For an hour, forty-four women danced on top of it, with a huge banner: "PEACE '83". By this time sufficient police had arrived to arrest them, and charge them all with breach of the peace. They were remanded on bail, and their charges were later tried by Newbury magistrates on 15th and 16th February.

The media people went to Yellow Gate in time for the press conference, and were sent post-haste to the scene of the action, where they took some excellent pictures through the fence, without being stopped by the police.

In January, 1983, another peace camp was set up at Green Gate to replace the mixed camp that had closed in autumn, 1982.

Also in January, *Makepeace Daly's London Roadshow* went on stage at Friends' House, London. This musical review, performed by a Quaker theatrical group called the Leaveners, included a sketch with a peace camp set up on the stage, in which the song 'Women of Greenham' was sung for the first time.

The House of Commons went into session on 17th January. MPs were lobbied about Cruise by women from all over Britain. This date was chosen for the lobbying because it was the first day the MPs were working, in the year when the first Cruise missiles were due to arrive.

Some women had found a law of 1666, which stated that anyone found causing a disturbance in Parliament could either be imprisoned there or tried by Mr. Speaker in the House of Commons. The normal breach of the peace law did not apply in Parliament. This offered possibilities for publicity.

At 15.30 hours, some women formed a circle in the lobby of the House of Commons, diverting police attention from about forty others, who then rushed the door to the Commons Chamber. Moving quickly, however, police managed to bar the door, and the women were prevented from entering. All the women then sat down and started singing 'You can't kill the spirit'. They continued singing as police dragged them into a corner of Westminster Hall. The singing appeared to have a calming effect on everybody, especially the police, and things stayed good-humoured. The women were held for three hours, and then released without charge, after being told they had been mentioned in the House of Commons, and therefore would be reported in *Hansard*. Although they were not able to enter the Commons Chamber, and read out their statement, at least MPs knew they were in the lobby and why.

On 22nd January, the Modsquad noticed some women erecting tents on Newbury Council common land at Blue Gate, contrary to the council by-laws. They arrested three women. Later, in the magistrates court, two had all charges dropped and one case was adjourned to 21st March.

On 24th or 25th January (accounts disagree) thirteen or fifteen women were arrested blockading Green Gate.

The Conservative government planned a propaganda operation to counter the publicity the Greenham women were getting. The first big event of this campaign was on 7th February, when Michael Heseltine, Her Majesty's newly appointed Secretary of State for Defence (known to the Greenham women as Tarzan, or Goldilocks) came to address a meeting at Newbury Council Offices that evening.

Greenham women blockaded the offices. An account of this blockade was first published by the campers on page 13 of *Women's Peace Camp* in February 1983. Lynne Jones is a responsible person, who, in the course of her work, is trained to make accurate observations and to write clearly. She was on the blockade. She wrote this account, as part of a longer essay in *Women's Peace Camp*, and very kindly has allowed me to reproduce it:

> It started well. I am someone who is nervous of total lack of structure, and I came down to the camp anxious and worried, but Greenham is teaching me to be more spontaneous and in fact everything was going well. Women had been invited from all

over to come down and do what they wanted. All morning they arrived, got into groups, talked, and worked out what they wanted to do. What evolved was a temporary blockade. Groups going off to blockade different gates as and when they were ready – disrupting work rather than preventing it. Four other groups had already gone into the base, dancing and singing in snake costumes. Taking into their own positive forms of life to counteract the preparations for death. They were all arrested at the construction workers' gate. Then we decided to go into town.

It was here that for me the problems began. My affinity group had that morning discussed what action we wanted to take. We were going to stand blindfolded and silent outside the council chamber with a note saying 'don't be blinded by propaganda', and another saying 'why not come and talk to us'. We hadn't thought there would be any point in stopping Heseltine speaking. Nor did we think it would be achievable. Rather we wanted to make our own statement to the public and media who might be listening to him. We wanted it to be as strong and dignified a statement as we could make it. There was no opportunity however to really discuss this with other groups.

It was cold. There was a lot of traffic. Some women had gone to the police station, some for cups of coffee. No one seemed to know when Heseltine might arrive. About fifty of us did get into a circle and tried to discuss what we would do. We agreed we didn't want to yell, and one woman taught us to keen: a low, mourning two-syllable sound, rocking on our knees. There were many women who wanted to blockade the entrances to make Heseltine confront us. Many didn't. The result was a hurried discussion (with hindsight I think too hurried), and a decision to split into two groups with the keeners supporting a small number of women who would lie down when Heseltine arrived so that he would have to step over their 'dead bodies'. We had another hour to wait. Women danced and sang to keep warm. By 4:30 pm it was growing dark, and the police had started to arrive in large numbers. (Many more women had arrived; those released from jail after the morning's action, and those who had supported them. But there was no opportunity for discussion.) The police technique was to form a cohort of about fifty, three abreast and to quick-march into the thickest part of the crowd (in front of the main entrance), spreading women by sheer impact. A whole crowd of women spontaneously lay down in front of the main door, and what originally had been a small symbolic lie-in suddenly became a very heavy blockade confronting about 100 police. As blockades go it was quite impressive. The police were very aggressive. They didn't lift any women out of the way, they simply pushed and cleared, rolling women one on top of the other. Then Heseltine arrived. The atmosphere was already tense and angry with all the pushing and shoving from the police, who seemed to lose patience altogether and simply rammed Heseltine through, pushing him to the ground in their eagerness, then lifting him and carrying him indoors. It was over. Some women looked exhilarated and jubilant. Others were in small huddles crying. "Why are you looking so unhappy?" a friend asked me. "It didn't feel non-violent, and I don't know what we were doing" I replied. "Well some women have to express their anger," she replied.

Who was right, of course. I do not believe that non-violence is the suppression of anger, but it is the ability to turn anger into a positive force, rather than let it become confused with bitterness and hate. Differing perceptions as to what constitutes a positive force seems to be one of the problems.

The media were primed by the authorities, and seven or more national dailies gave out wildly inaccurate accounts of the meeting, saying that Heseltine was attacked and thrown to the ground by 'peacewomen'. The offending editors were the target of many phone calls and letters telling them what actually happened, and one newspaper even corrected its later editions on 8th February, as a result of the phone calls. Although the television film footage did not show Heseltine being jeered, jostled or pushed, the television news commentaries implied that he was. Later West Midlands CND published a leaflet, with the help of pressmen and a radio reporter who were there, listing the media 'mistakes'.

At the same time, there was much action on Greenham Common itself.

One of the many visiting groups was a women's group from Shaftesbury, who arrived at Yellow Gate in a minibus at 11.45 hours. They were asked to go straight to Green Gate, about a mile away, to help a blockade that was having trouble with contractors' lorries. Once there, most of them joined the blockade. Though this blockade did not prevent any vehicles from going through the gates, it made getting the vehicles through a difficult, costly and time-consuming job for the authorities. About twenty-five to thirty people were arrested, including eight from the Shaftesbury group, who were taken to Newbury Police Station, and split up among a large number of arrested women, some of whom came from other actions on the common.

This left the driver and legal adviser, along with two other members of the Shaftesbury group, free. They drove into Newbury. While the driver and legal adviser went into the police station to await the release of their friends, the others joined the blockade of Newbury Council Offices awaiting Michael Heseltine's arrival (which occurrence was the reason the Shaftesbury women came in the first place) and took an active part in the blockade when 'Tarzan' arrived.

Meanwhile, the arrested women were charged that they did without lawful authority or excuse obstruct the highway. Shortly after 18.30 hours they were all released, and those who lived on the common returned there, whilst the others, including the Shaftesbury women, went home.

On 6th February some Greenham women had made three snake costumes, rather like oriental carnival dragons.

Back on 22nd March, 1982, the authorities had opened a gap in the fence to let traffic through during a blockade. When they had finished with this gap, they had just fastened the fence with nuts and bolts, so that the gap could be re-opened quickly should it ever be needed again. This became known first as New Gate, and later as Turquoise Gate.

At about 10.00 hours on the morning of 7th February around forty women with the snake costumes bundled into two cars and two vans. They drove through the woods to Turquoise, where they got out of the vehicles, and into the snake costumes, leaving only the four drivers to take the vehicles away. Then three bolts were removed and the chain link fence turned back. Sybil, Rosie and Cecily (for these were the snakes' names) entered onto the airfield unseen by the guards, even though it was broad daylight. They had crossed the grass and travelled some distance along the main runway, before an American police car appeared. Sybil temporarily shed her skin so she could clear the car bonnet, put her skin back on and continued wriggling along the runway. By now, several men had arrived, and they got hold of Rosie and Cecily, and ripped them asunder. The women inside these two snakes got out, and walked away, holding hands. Police parked vans across the runway to try and stop them. They just split up, ran round the vans, joined hands again, and continued walking, singing and dancing towards some piles of earth where workmen were digging. At first, the workmen did not know what to make of this, but the women waved and shouted greetings, which made the workmen soon realise they were friendly. The women sat on piles of earth and stopped a mechanical digger from working. They talked to workmen. The hole they were digging was believed to be for fuel tanks.

Then modplods and RAF men were seen approaching, so the women got into the hole, linked arms and began to move in a circle.

The modplods and RAF men divided them, pulled them out of the hole, and dragged them to vans, which took them to Newbury Police Station.

Meanwhile, Sybil headed slowly for Yellow Gate. She had to find a way between some offices. This was a tricky part of her journey, but she speeded up for a minute or two, and nipped through a gate, thus accomplishing it without problems. Once between the buildings, she resumed her slow speed. She passed one office, which seemed to be a schoolroom, because it was full of children who cheered and laughed when they saw Sybil slithering by their windows. Unhappily, just before Yellow Gate, Sybil the Snake was captured by police, dissected, put in a van and taken to Newbury Police Station.

The thirty-seven women inside the snakes had been on the airfield about one hour, and had been held by the police a further two-and-one-half hours. They were not charged with any offence. However, it appears the three snakeskins were lost, except for Sybil's head, which the Sybil crew had kept with them. On the other side of the balance sheet are the disruption and delays they caused behind the wire and in Newbury Police Station; the loss of a number of man-hours digging and lost time for the mechanical digger; the loss of police time and the loss of the use of the vehicles needed to arrest the women; inconvenience to the RAF and USAF; and the influence the women might have had on the workmen and children. The action stayed non-violent, and nobody got hurt. It was a classic NVDA.

Also on 7th February, one person was arrested and charged with obstruction of the highway at another small blockade on Greenham Common.

US Vice-President Bush visited Britain on 9th February and called on Margaret Thatcher at 10 Downing Street. Some women, mostly from Greenham Common, lay down by the barriers at the Whitehall end of Downing Street. Some were arrested, and charged with obstructing the highway. In court later, it was argued that there were no cases to answer, because the barricade already obstructed Downing Street at that point. On 15th April, all these women were given conditional discharges by a London magistrate.

After these women had been arrested and it was obvious to everyone that the police thought the law had been broken, some more women silently lay down on the footpath beside Whitehall, surrounded by others standing and holding candles. They stayed for forty minutes, watched by police, before leaving of their own accord. This disparity of treatment is typical of what happened at many civil disobedience actions like this one. Here were a group of women, who claimed they had done nothing illegal, arrested for breaking the law; while another group committed an action, which both they and the watching police knew to be illegal and were not arrested even though the same police were there, the distance in time between the two actions was measured in minutes, and they took place just a few yards apart.

On Monday, 14th February, the Shaftesbury group returned to Greenham Common and joined the blockade in progress at Blue Gate. The gate was kept shut for some time against contractors' vehicles, although the women allowed a school bus with children aboard to leave the airfield. The ordinary police were quite well-behaved, though they did a few annoying little things (probably in an attempt to wear down and demoralise blockaders). A bus-load of civilian police, wearing blue anoraks without numbers, arrived after the blockade had started. They were very rough.

The Shaftesbury group were typical of groups then coming from places all over Britain, in cars and coaches, to support the Greenham women and become Greenham women. None of the Shaftesbury women were arrested on that day.

Another group of women came to Greenham Common on 14th February, and they were from Bristol. They went onto the airfield, and occupied a concrete mixing and batching plant. Police found them, fingerprinted them, and released them without charge. This NVDA, involving only eight people, who were neither charged with any offence, nor fined nor imprisoned, appears to have caused considerable disruption and delay behind the wire, especially when the women climbed over the tower-like batching plant.

This may have been the action referred to on page 6 of the *Radiator* for April 1983:

> I was told that women had set up a camp in the base overnight and upon discovery had been escorted to the perimeter and hustled out. This time no arrests were made, even though they had committed a similar offence to the group in court that morning.

Once again we have a case of disparity of treatment by the police, of two similar civil disobedience actions.

"That morning" referred to in the *Radiator* report was, of course, 15th February. The court hearings in Newbury on that day, acted as a magnet, and drew several other actions to the area. There was a vigil outside the court, with singing, dancing, and street theatre, while a group set up a field kitchen, and cooked pancakes on the courthouse steps! Late that afternoon an attempt was made to blockade the whole airfield. When dragging women away from the gates, police were "… extremely brutal. Women were dragged off the road by their hair, breasts, and in other most undignified ways. Arms were twisted and quite a few were badly bruised" (Page 6, *Radiator*, April, 1983).

There is also a report of sixty-four women being arrested, after entering the airfield on 15th February. They were apparently released without charge.

Blockade attempts continued throughout 16th February resulting in about thirty-four arrests. These cases were eventually heard in court on 15th April.

Meanwhile, the New Year's Day activists were being convicted. A total of thirty-six were imprisoned for refusing to be bound over, and apparently eight agreed to be bound over. Some, if not all, of the thirty-six were sent to Holloway Prison. Later, seven were transferred from there to Maidstone.

On 17th February, two Greenham women were arrested for drawing hopscotch – yes, drawing hopscotch – on the pavement outside Holloway Prison. One was charged with obstructing the highway. When her friend challenged the policeman and asked why she was being arrested, she, too, was arrested, and charged with verbal abuse likely to cause a beach of the peace!

On 19th February, a die-in, held in solidarity with the arrested Greenham women, blocked Prospect Street, Hull, stopping traffic for half-an-hour. The sixteen people arrested included three juveniles and one NCCL observer. When they went to court, there were 300 pickets outside the courthouse during the trials. Each defendant was convicted, and bound over to keep the peace in the sum of £200.

In 1981, Newbury Council's Commons and Countryside Subcommittee banned the Army Cadet Force from holding exercises on the Commons of Crookham and Greenham, outside the airfield perimeter fence. Later the whole council introduced by-laws banning camping and caravans, and making it technically illegal to walk a dog on the Common without a council licence. Licences were not issued, so far as I could ascertain, and people walking dogs were never prosecuted for that alone. One interesting new by-law said that anyone discharging a missile on the common could be fined £20! Newbury Council had also revoked the public 'common ground' rights over Greenham and Crookham Commons. This enabled the council to take out injunctions to deter fifty-nine women, and persons unknown, from camping on these commons. The injunction hearing was fixed for 22nd February at the High Court, in the Royal Courts of Justice in the Strand, London.

Hundreds of women, loads of police and one judge were all up at the High Court for the hearing. There were not enough women there to enable the court to proceed. Some of the women named in the evidence were in prison and could not be got to court on time. The cases had to be adjourned to 9th March.

On 25th February, several women were arrested inside RAF Greenham Common and released without charge.

On the same day, warders found a new peace camp being set up on the roof of Holloway Prison. The campers came from outside and were protesting at the victimisation of Greenham women inside. The six women campers were brought down from the roof, charged, and bailed to appear in court on 28th March.

Some women arrested for blockading Green Gate, on 24th or 25th January, were each fined £25 for obstructing the highway by the local magistrates on 28th February.

After serving their sentences of a fortnight each, the women imprisoned after the New Year's Day action were released in a blaze of publicity.

Just after being released, Jill was feeling sick and exhausted, so she sat down on the pavement to eat an apple. She was promptly arrested and charged with obstructing the highway!

On 3rd March, seventeen of the women arrested on 7th February appeared before Newbury magistrates.

Newbury Council used rear-loading dustcarts equipped with compaction mechanisms, which crush the contents in order to increase the load capacities of the vehicles. These were used on evictions. Greenham women nicknamed them 'munchers', after the way they swallowed and munched garbage, sleeping bags, tents, cameras – in fact, anything that was thrown to them.

During an eviction on 6th March, Karen Bone had all her belongings, including an expensive sleeping bag, thrown to a 'muncher'. She attacked the dustcart in desperation, was arrested and charged with criminal damage to it! She got no compensation for the loss of her own property. Nobody did.

By 9th March about 400 campers had signed affidavits (legally valid, witnessed statements) giving Greenham Common Women's Peace Camp as their home. The injunctions sought by Newbury Council were against fifty-nine named women and persons unknown living there. The 400 had a legal right to have all their claims individually examined by the judge. Over 100 Greenham women and supporters were at the Royal Courts of Justice to see how this adaptation of the old Committee of 100 tactic to jam up the courts would work here.

The judge was ready for them, and dealt justice – or maybe it was injustice – hard and swiftly. In spite of protests, he held the hearing in chambers excluding the public. He claimed that defence arguments were 'political' rather than 'legal' and because of this, granted final injunctions to the council, rather than the interim injunctions that legal experts were expecting, with another hearing later for final injunctions if needed. As a result, any person found camping on the commons administered by Newbury Council risked up to two years in jail. The judge also named twenty-one women whom he not only barred for life from Greenham and Crookham Commons, but also ordered that they should be imprisoned if (even when many miles away) they were caught conspiring with anyone else to trespass thereon!

About this time the camp by Yellow Gate returned to Department of Transport verges beside A339 road.

In March and April Greenham Common became the game board for an enormous game of snakes and ladders. The rules were simple: you either went over the fence with a ladder, or slid either through or under like a snake, Rosie, Cecily, and Sybil were still fresh in people's minds.

A group of important NATO generals visited Greenham Common on 24th March. Campers mounted a blockade in their honour.

The Highbury, London Magistrate was in a good mood on 28th March, for he not only discharged the six women arrested on the roof of Holloway Prison on 25th February, but also gave an absolute discharge to Jill, the woman who was arrested for obstruction while eating an apple.

EASTER 1983: THE BIGGEST DEMONSTRATION YET

On Maundy Thursday 31st March 1983 the mixed blockade of Burghfield nuclear warhead factory (See 'Burghfield Peace Camp' elsewhere in this book) was the first NVDA with civil disobedience ever organised by National CND. It was almost a complete success. All but twenty of the workers were given the day off. Only these twenty went in, presumably to do essential maintenance work, and they had to walk in through the blockade.

At the same time, a women's blockade of Greenham Common was mounted. This was not so successful, as police managed to clear the road and seventeen coaches went in and out.

Burghfield Blockade started up again on Good Friday, when it formed one end of a fourteen-mile human chain organised by CND. People linked arms all the way from Burghfield to Yellow Gate on Friday afternoon.

Other supporting events took place around AWRE Aldermaston, midway along the chain. I shall forever remember Bruce Kent's 'woolly hat' speech in a field near Aldermaston.

Many more thousands of people turned up for the demonstration on the Friday than either CND or the police expected. Not all of them were there at once. Some came late, some left early, some only came for the morning and some only for the afternoon. It was estimated that 1,500 coaches came. There were so many that some could not park in the allocated spaces near the chain and some collected passengers up to six hours late on that wet evening. Some demonstrators came in their own or friends' cars, others hitched, some walked to the event and others used motorcycles and bicycles. Estimates of 75,000 to 80,000 people participating, made after the event, were clearly too low. The true figure must have been easily twice that number, though, obviously, without any means of counting or seeing the crowd at any one time, any count can only be a guess.

Good Friday, being 1st April, was also April Fools' Day, and to celebrate the latter, 200 women dressed as furry animals scaled the perimeter fence and entered RAF Greenham Common, and held a teddy bears' picnic. They were arrested and later released without charge.

On 15th April, a magistrate conditionally discharged the women arrested at Downing Street on 9th February.

The Shaftesbury women were in court on 18th April, before three lay magistrates at Newbury. Each one had to pay £10 costs, and was given a one-year's conditional discharge. On the same day, that bench dealt with a number of other women arrested on Greenham Common, including some Welsh women and two of the campers. One camper objected to the magistrates on the grounds that she knew them to be hostile, and the campers' cases were adjourned. The Shaftesbury women were dealt with more leniently than they were when last before Newbury magistrates.

At lunch time on International Mothers for Peace Day, 20th April, mothers from three continents visited Greenham.

On 22nd April, *New Statesman* published diagrams of Cruise missile bunkers, and much information about them.

The first Cruise convoy crew finished training at Davis-Monthan Air Force Base, near Tucson, Arizona, USA, on 26th April. The forty-seven crewmen were to have a month's leave before coming to Britain. Their place at Davis-Monthan was taken by a second Cruise crew in training.

On 27th April, Greenham women picketed the Italian Embassy in London, in solidarity with their comrades campaigning against Cruise at Comiso Peace Camp in Sicily.

The 'Ideal Peace Camp' (See 'Peace Camps and Squats in London' elsewhere in this book) was set up by Greenham women, opposite the Royal Navy stand at the Ideal Homes Exhibition, in April.

Also in April, nine Greenham women got a great deal of publicity when they entered the Chamber of the House of Commons and shouted out a message: 'The wishes of the islanders are paramount.' They had borrowed some words of Margaret Thatcher's, taken them from their Falkland Islands context and applied them to the British Isles and Cruise missiles. These islanders didn't want Cruise.

The report of the arrival of Cruise launchers with missiles on 1st March 1982, rumoured in *Peace News* on 23rd July, may have been a false alarm. What actually arrived may have been mock-ups for trials and training. The first planeload of supplies to start the build-up for the coming of Cruise did not arrive until late April, 1983. By then bunkers and other facilities were nearing completion, having been under construction for two years. The main contract was nearly over, but *The Guardian* revealed that a new contract, worth £1,500,000, to provide servicing facilities for vehicles, was just starting and that the US Government and NATO were footing the bill.

Again in late April, on 27th April to be exact, all the gates to the airfield were padlocked closed with 'Citadel' cycle locks, which had to be released with cutting torches burning through the shanks. This type of lock was also used at Capenhurst with excellent results. (See 'Capers at Capenhurst' elsewhere in this book.)

Taxi rides from Yellow Gate to Greenham Primary School were successfully claimed for their children, by two Greenham women in spring 1983. Greenham Court was further from the peace camp than the minimum legal distance for free travel to school and there were no convenient buses. A British schoolteacher, Teresa Smith, and a German, Beatrice Schmidt, had paid a lot of money in fares already in sending their children to school. Although some Berkshire county councillors protested vehemently at this use of ratepayers' money to benefit the children of peace campers, when the matter was discussed at a council meeting, they could not stop the council paying, because the law requires them to pay.

They had to reimburse Teresa and Beatrice for fares already paid and arrange future taxi rides for their children.

During a thousand-strong Mayday rally, about a hundred women entered the airfield, and danced and sang their way to the main runway on which they burned a model Cruise missile. The police arrested them, took them outside the main fence, and released them without charge.

On 12th May, bailiffs and police, using considerable force, evicted women camped on council land by Yellow Gate, arresting four of them on breach of the peace charges.

Then eight cars were towed away, and confiscated in lieu of costs. Soon five were returned as being of no value. The other three were returned later because their owners were not named in the High Court orders to the bailiffs. Afterwards, the council estimated that the confiscation and return of the vehicles had cost Newbury ratepayers £1,500.

There were still camps on the Department of Transport road verges by Yellow Gate, and at Green Gate.

In May the Women's Peace Camp, now, of course, on the road verges, became a mixed camp for a time, when a baby boy was born there.

In early June, twenty women wearing black veils walked into the airfield and scattered black ashes. They were thrown out by police, and then lay symbolically dead in a 'die-in' outside the gate for two-and-a-half hours. When the media people had gone, police picked up the women and threw them, with considerable force, away from the gate.

For a time during 1983, the Women's Peace Camp had a London office, with a telephone, at 5 Leonard Street, EC2.

On 25th June, a midsummer celebration was held, and during it women sewed together pieces of cloth, sent from all over the world, to make a rainbow dragon, reputed to have been over a mile long when finished.

Ann Pettit, Karman Cutler, and Russian-speaking Jean McCollister went to Russia on an ordinary tourist trip to Moscow and Leningrad. Through Jean's contacts, they managed to meet and speak to the unofficial Trust Group and ordinary Russians, as well as the official Soviet Peace Committee. During June and July the travellers reported back to various people and made plans for a bigger party to visit Russia in September. (Full report in *Peace News*, 8th July, 1983.)

American Independence Day, 4th July, was celebrated inside the base by the newly arrived Cruise crew and their colleagues. Outside the fence, it was celebrated by the start of the biggest and longest series of blockades yet held on Greenham Common, which used tactics developed on the recent long blockade of Upper Heyford. The Greenham blockades ran from the morning of Monday, July 4, until the following Friday evening. Though the blockades didn't stop all road traffic in and out of the airfield, what traffic that did move in and out usually had to move in convoys, and this entailed considerable delay. The convoys, once they were made up, were then delayed themselves for up to two hours at a time. To reduce this traffic, and to keep manpower up inside the base, troops inside were confined to barracks – in other words, not allowed off the base – for the whole five days. Police used whatever means they could to keep roads open, including on Thursday and Friday, constables mounted on big horses, which terrified the women blockading, two of whom were injured on the Friday. Over the five days, 139 arrests were made, and police used Newbury racecourse to detain some of their prisoners until the magistrates were able to see them, as all the local police cells were full. At the court, Thursday's arrests spilled over onto Friday's. The magistrates added to the chaos by refusing to work late and insisting on finishing at 16.00 hours. Solicitors were showered with lists of names to represent at a few minutes' notice, and requests for assistance with claims about police violence. During this week, fifty feet of perimeter fence fell down, and some campers helped to perform an exorcism on the common, in addition to all the blockading.

While all this was happening in Berkshire, international links were strengthened when twenty women from Britain, Western Europe and America were ordered to leave Hungary on 6th July, two days after arriving in the Greenham Common Women's Peace Camp Rainbow Bus. They had planned to spend a few days camped with people in the Hungarian peace movement. However, even though the campsite had been booked in advance, there were problems, and the bus had to move on to another site, and then to a third. After two days of moving about, the police arrived. They detained the people on the bus for two hours, then gave the tourists a choice: either

leave voluntarily on the bus immediately, or leave under escort, or be evicted from Hungary by force. The tourists had five minutes to decide. They went voluntarily. At least one woman was left behind, but she was helped by Hungarian peace people and eventually found her own way home.

By 22nd July, women were camped at Green Gate, Blue Gate and Orange Gate, in addition to Yellow Gate. People going to the air tattoo called 'Star '83 – Strike, Attack and Reconnaissance 83', held on 22nd and 23rd July, could not avoid seeing them when passing through the gates. At air shows, leaflets are important, so the women gave out leaflets opposing Cruise. Air shows are also about entertainment, so some women walked onto the airfield with the crowds and entertained people with street theatre. On this occasion they bought tickets to go into the show, but on the Monday, when some very important people came to see the arms exhibition that accompanied the air tattoo, they didn't buy – or

were unable to buy – tickets to enter to decorate a top secret Blackbird spy plane. The seven women who decorated it didn't want it to appear dull; they wanted both the plane and their message to be seen. The seven were arrested and charged with criminal damage and thus became the only peace campers arrested during 'STAR '83'.

On 5th August, the 'Women for Life on Earth Star Marches' began arriving at Greenham Common. I wonder who chose the title 'Star' first? One group of marchers came 1000 miles from Machrichanish in Western Scotland, along a zig-zag route, accompanied for the last 850 miles by a contingent from Faslane. Marches came from places all round the United Kingdom, and converged on Greenham Common like the rays of a star (one with wobbly, zig-zag rays, that is). They came from Bath, Brambles Farm, Brighton, Bridgwater, Bristol, Cambridge, Cardiff, Carmarthen, Chester, Chichester, Dorchester, East Anglia, the Isle of Wight, Lancaster, Leicester, Merseyside, Surrey, South London and Wrexham. They visited many towns and cities where they addressed meetings, received welcomes and free accommodation and helped to start new disarmament groups. At the end of their marches, the marchers joined Greenham women for a Hiroshima Day vigil and fast at Newbury War Memorial. Some of them later joined Greenham women for a 'die-in' at Yellow Gate on Nagasaki Day.

During August, several Greenham peace campers joined in the 'Fast for Life' with pacifists and disarmers all over Britain.

At the trial of the women charged with painting the Blackbird, which took place on 18th August, the MoD withdrew all the criminal damage charges. Only one woman was convicted, and that was for contempt of court. Obviously the charges were withdrawn because the MoD didn't want any more publicity for the Blackbird's presence on Greenham Common.

In September, Greenham women attended the alternative peace talks in Geneva, Switzerland.

CRUISE ARRIVES October - December 1983

A messenger dropped some mail into an in tray at the London office of The Guardian newspaper at around 20.00 hours on Friday, 21st October. It included photocopies of two documents, which had no covering letter, and which had no indication as to who had sent them. They could have been routine government bumph, but the professional journalists on *The Guardian* knew better.

After some frantic telephone calls to verify the authenticity of the documents, the editor had the front page changed for the later two editions on 22nd October. Under a headline 'Whitehall Sets November 1 Cruise Arrival', was set out information about the plans for the arrival of Cruise missiles, extracted from the two photocopied documents.

The story of what happened next and the fate of Sarah Tisdall, the young civil servant who copied the documents and delivered copies to *The Guardian*, were extensively reported in the national press. (*The Guardian*, 31st October, 1983; and 24th March , 1984, and other papers)

By now planes were landing frequently with supplies for the 501st Tactical Missile Wing, who were to operate the Cruise missiles. Planes loaded with supplies came throughout October and November.

Construction work was being done not only on the airfield itself, but also on buildings in Greenham Village, including a mansion with a lake in its extensive grounds off Bury's Bank Road. This place, Greenham Lodge, was to be the HQ of the 501st and its first commander on Greenham Common, Colonel Robert Thompson.

Taking full advantage of the publicity in many newspapers about plans for the imminent arrival of the missiles, the peace campers announced they would be holding a reception for them, on the weekend of 29th-30th October. The date was chosen, not by the authorities, but by the campers. It was the ancient feast of Hallowe'en. As dusk fell after their Hallowe'en party, about 1,500 women moved along the perimeter fence and stood outside it in groups, waiting for signal flares. It was a very cold Saturday night. Suddenly one group started cutting the fence with bolt-cutters. Others followed immediately. Police and soldiers outside were too thin on the ground to prevent the fence from being cut to ribbons in many places; coils of wire, recently placed just inside, with the intention of hampering women who got over or through the perimeter fence actually hampered police and troops when they tried to reach the fence from the inside to stop the women from cutting it, and making incursions. The authorities were taken by surprise, and that night about four miles of fence fell from its posts. When police reinforcements arrived, however, nearly 200 women were arrested. Annabel Cole was charged with criminal damage to the fence. Jill Morony and Gloria Delmonte were each charged with criminal damage to one section of the fence to the value of £25.

Annabel's case was typical; that of Jill and Gloria was famous. We will read more of them later.

On Monday, 31st October, *The Guardian* published the full text of 'Deliveries of Cruise Missiles to RAF Greenham Common – Parliamentary and Public Statements', in time for that day's House of Commons debate on Cruise.

There was little time for protesters to organise or MPs to prepare, as news of the Cruise debate came out only when that week's parliamentary timetable was published on the previous Thursday. Thousands of people had gathered outside the House of Commons, trying to enter to lobby MPs during the debate. Most were not allowed in. For a time during the evening, police went so far as to keep people right away from the Houses of Parliament.

Meanwhile, as the debate started, over 2,000 people gathered for a torchlit vigil in Trafalgar Square. Police had been informed only that there was to be a vigil. Even then the vigil may have technically infringed the law governing demonstrations in Central London, because it was not agreed with sufficient notice given in the correct manner beforehand to the police. No notice was given about other events. However, police made no arrests, and, at 20.00 hours, the torches were extinguished, and the vigil ended. Next, a great crowd of vigillers surged down Whitehall like a tidal wave, from the square. The police walked with the crowd. The leaders of the crowd had planned to sit down as near as 10 Downing Street as possible, but about a thousand police had managed to form themselves up into a barrier and kept them away from the entrance to the street. After milling around for about forty minutes, the demonstrators went and sat down around the entrances to the MoD Main Building. News of this sit-down soon reached Parliament Square and people began sitting down there, too. Several Greenham women sat among the demonstrators. Although traffic was in chaos, there appear to have been no arrests for obstruction of the highway, and nobody seems to have been injured. The demonstrators packed up and left, peacefully, at around 22.00 hours.

Cruise missiles and warheads did not arrive on 1st November as expected, but aircraft continued flying in supplies to Greenham Common. The women watched them landing and unloading.

On 1st November, Michael Heseltine caused a storm in the House of Commons by announcing that trespassers on military bases risked being shot. Also at this time, security was increased on Greenham Com-mon, but was still ineffective. Proof came when a former Berkshire County councillor from nearby Baughurst drove through an open gate, behind another vehicle, onto the airfield, on 4th November. He had driven nearly a mile across the airfield, and was heading for an aircraft unloading supplies when a USAF jeep rammed his car. Nobody was hurt, and apparently neither driver was charged with any offence.

Newbury magistrates jailed eight Greenham women for fourteen days each, for contempt of court, on 2nd November.

On Sunday, 6th November, a coach full of men and women day-trippers arrived from West Wales to spend four hours supporting the peace campers. The trip was organised by Greenham supporters, but it was plain that some of the Welsh visitors had not been briefed properly about the militant feminism of some of the Greenham women. There was a clash of minds and some unhappiness. The old debate was revived: Should Greenham Common Peace Camp exclude men or not?

'Greenham Women Against Cruise' (twelve women supported by two US congressmen) had filed, in the US Federal Court in New York, a writ that claimed Cruise to be in breach of US constitutional and international laws. Supporting actions took place all over Britain. Many people and groups sent telegrams to the women in New York.

> At every one of the 102 US military installations in Britain, a peace movement presence was made on November 8 and 9 in support of the Greenham women's court case. The actions mostly took the form of twenty-four-hour peace camps or vigils. (*Peace News*, 25th November, 1983)

There were peace camps as far apart as Forss, in Caithness, Scotland; Hythe, on the south coast of Hampshire; and St. Mawgan, Cornwall. (See my account: 'The Forgotten, Unfenced Airfield') At RAF Brize Norton, Oxfordshire, two dozen people camped the night and about seventy-five people visited and joined them for short periods. RAF Feltwell (See my account 'The Fenlands Peace Camps') in Norfolk, was a USAF storage depot, mainly for furniture, with only a few married quarters, about twelve miles north of Mildenhall, one of the main USAF supply airfields in Europe. There was a women's peace camp here. Some campers tried to take a message to the depot commander, but were turned back. Many of the American and British personnel were friendly with the campers, and discussed with them why they were there. There were temporary camps at other places, some of which are mentioned elsewhere in this book.

On 9th November, Home Secretary Douglas Hurd announced that policing Greenham Common over the past twelve months had cost £1,520,000 of which £951,000 was supposed to have been extra money needed for policing demonstrations. The current cost of policing Greenham, in 1983, was later estimated at around £50,000 per day. These figures cover civil police costs only and exclude the Modsquad's costs.

Newbury magistrates jailed three women for not paying fines on Thursday 10th November – one for a week, one for a fortnight, and one for a month. At about this time, a former magistrate was dragged from this court after being remanded on a charge of criminal damage on Greenham Common.

The ninth anniversary of the death of Karen Silkwood was commemorated at the peace camp on 13th November.

On 14th November, *The Guardian* announced that ground launched Cruise missiles and warheads would come to Greenham the next day, but on that very afternoon Michael Heseltine told the House of Commons that the missiles and warheads had already arrived. The newspaper report may have been inspired by information deliberately 'leaked' from the MoD in order to mislead the peace movement.

A torch-lit vigil was hastily organised for the night of Tuesday 14th November on Greenham Common. On Wednesday a blockade of the gates and demolition of large lengths of fence resulted in over 140 arrests. According to one eyewitness, the entire fence, from Orange Gate to Yellow Gate, on the eastern perimeter of the airfield, was pulled down. The police appear to have been taken unawares by the number of prisoners they took and they had to use lock-up garages behind Newbury Police Station to accommodate the overflow from their cells.

Demonstrations took place all over Britain. On Tuesday and Wednesday evenings the House of Commons was blockaded, with over 300 arrests on the second evening. Also in London, about thirty members of the Religious Society of Friends (Quakers) sat down outside the Guildhall and held a meeting for worship, while Margaret Thatcher addressed a gathering inside. The Quakers were arrested, charged with highway obstruction and bailed to appear in court on 22nd February.

At Manchester University Students' Union on Wednesday Michael Heseltine was met by angry, frightened people, and sprayed with red paint on his way to address a meeting there. He couldn't start speaking for nearly an hour such was the uproar. Even then, he was interrupted many times. He left by a back door, to a tirade of abuse; rubbish was thrown at his car as it departed.

On Wednesday, over a hundred people took part in a 'die-in' in Norwich City Centre, most of them lying on the ground for about five minutes. There were five arrests. Shantum, the only coloured demonstrator, who had sat for only thirty seconds before rising of his own account and was not a ringleader, was subsequently detained by a policeman who asked him a racist question. He was held for five hours, and was not charged with any offence at the time.

At about this time, the National Greenham Conference was held in Manchester, and involved Greenham women in fruitful discussion with other peace movement people.

In November, the US Pentagon admitted that many Cruise test flights failed to produce the desired results and all six types of Cruise missile were behind in their development.

One autumnal evening, some Greenham women organised a mixed action, along the perimeter fence between Green Gate and Blue Gate. They held a silent vigil from 17.00 hours to 18.00, then sang until 22.00.

A meeting of Covenant for Peace, an American peace group, was held in a suburban church in Detroit on 2nd December 1983, not far from the Williams International factory, which made Cruise missile engines. The meeting was to publicise and raise funds for the court case to stop Cruise coming to Europe. A film was shown and Greenham woman Jean Hutchinson exhibited a piece of wire cut from the Greenham Common perimeter fence. There were four or more plainclothes police at the meeting and so the organisers were not surprised when, shortly after the meeting had ended, the police searched the church for the film and other items of interest to them. They did not find the film, but arrested Jean and charged her. She was ordered to stay in the US, and appear in court on 13th March. All this was apparently caused by a court injunction to stop, among other things, campaigners from urging people to demonstrate outside Williams International.

On 11th December, the nearest Sunday to the anniversary of the NATO decision to bring Cruise to Europe, about 30,000 people attended an all-women action – 'Sounds around Greenham' – on the common. About the same number had attended 'Embrace the Base' the previous 12ᵗʰ December. Women brought songbooks, mirrors (to reflect the base back in upon itself), photos, plants, candles and other small items to make their protest with symbolism. Some talked with policemen, and made good contacts. At around 15.00 hours, the first sound began. It was an odd sound, for the women used an assortment of drums, whistles, pans, spoons and keys, as well as their own voices singing. Then some sections became silent for a period, until another wave of sound was sent onto the airfield. After a while, some women grabbed the fence and started pushing and pulling. Their weight and strength eventually pushed sections of the fence over, and women ran onto them and over them. Armed reinforcements came hurrying to the aid of the police behind the fallen fence, and helped them push it back up. Unlike July 1982, when the fence posts had been broken with sledgehammers, on this occasion the damage was easier to repair. Nobody wanted to tempt the armed men to use their guns, and the women retreated.

Suddenly there was a scuffle. A fence post had fallen on Inspector Michael Page of Thames Valley Police, and people were clearing the crowd so it could be lifted off him, and help could be got to him. His colleagues carried him to an ambulance.

He was kept in hospital. A month later, he was still in hospital, wearing a surgical collar, and recovering from several serious injuries. He got many letters and 'get well' cards from people who had been on the demonstration. His letter thanking them was published in two newspapers. (*The Guardian*, 24ᵗʰ January, 1984; *Radiator*, April 1984 – 'Inspector Page's Thanks')

The air traffic control tower of any airfield is a vital nerve centre. Surprisingly, Greenham Common Control Tower was not well guarded at this time. At 17.00 hours on 27ᵗʰ December 1983, apparently by means of an external staircase, three women climbed onto its roof. They stood there and moved about, for two-and-a-half hours, without base personnel seeing them, even though they were silhouetted by artificial lighting, which made it possible for a journalist and some peace campers to see them from outside the fence. They then descended a staircase and broke into the control room itself, where they spent a further half hour in the control tower reading documents. Some dealt with procedures for landing aircraft contaminated by radioactivity, and handling damaged warheads, under the heading 'Hot Guns'.

Another document outlined the procedure for dealing with terrorists who had taken over a room in a building on the airfield! The area was to be evacuated, sealed off, and stormed by guards of K9 Division, who would be armed and ready to kill if necessary. K9 Division were believed to provide the armed guards on the Cruise convoys, and the guards with helmets, clothes, boots and long truncheons, all coloured black, at Seneca in New York State (See my account of 'Peace Camps Abroad' elsewhere in this book). Although only one such guard had so far been seen at Greenham fully equipped, several US soldiers had been seen there with long black truncheons. After reading the documents, the women started flashing the tower lights on and off, to the delight of watchers outside the fence. An American soldier, whom the women had earlier seen go onto the control tower roof to observe the peace camps with binoculars, came down into the control room by the same route the women had used. Upon discovering them, he was terrified. He panicked, rounded them up, and roughly pushed them down the internal stairs to the ground floor. Only modplods and soldiers without armed K9 guards, arrived in answer to his request. After being held about nine hours and questioned by police, the women were released. Even though they had apparently contravened the official secrets act and a case could be made against them for breaking and entering the control tower, they were only charged with the most minor offence for which they were liable – criminal damage to the perimeter fence. Serious charges would have publicised the useless MoD security too much.

By the time the three women were released, *The Guardian* reporter had left. She returned a few days later and showed campers a report that had been cut by her editor and which had not yet been published. It never was.

Recently, Michael Heseltine, Secretary of State for Defence, had publicised the arrival of paratroops for guard duty and other security improvements on Greenham Common. He said it had been made impossible for the women to enter 'sensitive areas' on the airfield. The main object of these women, who saw no evidence of improved security on their way to the control tower, was to prove Heseltine wrong by entering a 'sensitive area'. To do this, they needed publicity, which is precisely what the MoD did not want! Was pressure put on the editor of *The Guardian* and other editors? In order to keep up the 'whitewash', they even denied that the papers the women had read were in the tower at all! Now that was daft, for, obviously, in an emergency and in training, the air traffic controllers would find those papers useful. This raised two questions: firstly was the failure to make Greenham Common secure part of a plan to mislead people into believing that Cruise missiles were kept there, whilst in reality only vehicles, equipment and men were there? And were the real missiles hidden in a better-guarded base without a peace camp, ready to be flown to airfields near the launch sites, or driven there directly at a moment's notice? (For further details see *Peace News*, 3rd February, 1984: "A Stroll into the Monster's Lair".)

CAMPS AT EVERY GATE

On New Year's Eve, 1983, Indigo Gate was occupied. Now every gate in the perimeter fence that was being used had a women's camp at it.

Greenham Common Women's Peace Camp had survived into another year. The authorities had as yet been unable to deploy Cruise missiles on launchers outside their base, and the campers claimed some of the credit for this. On New Year's Day, 1984, the campers had much to celebrate and did so by flying a giant wool web, suspended from helium filled balloons, over Greenham Common, hoping that it would interfere with air force flying. On the same day, the MoD announced the attainment of 'initial operating capability' by Cruise. None of the campers noticed Cruise attaining anything! They countered this with a press conference, telling the media they believed there were no Cruise missiles on Greenham Common; that the camp would stay, at least until Cruise missiles left Britain; that the women would continue to expose MoD lies; and they would connect with women's movements around the world. The

Greenham Common

Who stole the Goose off the Common?
    Who stole the Common off the Goose?
Who stole the land for airfields?
    Who turned the scientists loose?
Pigs and Sheep, Goats and Cattle
    Horses and Asses roaming at will
Crisscrossing paths with sightless vision.
Farewell to Lords and Ladies
    Welcome the Lord of Misrule
Farewell to Kings and Queens
    Welcome the Goddess and Fool
Welcome the Lord of the Dance
    Welcome the Goddess of Chance and Mystery
Some place their faith in religion
    Some place their faith in dope
Some place their faith in military bases
    Some place their faith in hope.
Men and women wear sea-green ribbons
    Like The Levellers of old
Carrying armfuls of daffodils
    As our Spring Rites unfold.
Marching to a different drummer
    Marching to a different song
Marching out of step and out of time
Feminists, Quakers, Anarchists, Pacifists
Non-violent Revolutionaries out of line.
From Watership Down to Stanley Spencer's
Cookham Chapel
From Grimsbury Castle   to Aldermaston
From Cold Ash to Portway Roman Road
    From Cottington's Hill to
Noah's Ark Cottage on long lost
    Greenham Common
Civil Disobedience & Fertility Celebration
    Chanting Buddhists & Rhyming Priests
Acoustic Musicians and Dervish Dancers
    Silent Ecologists and Bawdy Feasts.
From Cottington's Hill to Noah's Ark Cottage
    On longlost Greenham Common.

media then began a 'black-out' on news of Greenham Common, publishing only occasional mentions from MoD handouts.

In the USA, in early 1984, Greenham Women Against Cruise had their case heard in the New York Federal Court.

On 21st January, a Royal Marine was given a suspended six-month prison sentence for assaulting two Greenham women.

Olga Medvekova and other Moscow Trust Builders, on the way to attend the trial of Oleg Radzinski in Moscow, were arrested and detained a whole day by plain-clothes police. Oleg was charged with 'forcible opposition to the militia', and it was alleged she had assaulted a policeman. The others with her all made statements that this did not happen and that nobody had offered any resistance to the militia. They were told that since their accounts contradicted militia reports, they would be charged with giving false evidence. The Greenham women learned all this through their direct contacts with the Trust Builders. Maintaining these links was not easy and involved much expense.

'Greenham women everywhere' was a slogan often used by the campers, and it was just as often true. At this time, some were already in the USA, and others were planning a trip to the Soviet Union to protest at the treatment of the trust builders. Their first move was a visit to the Soviet Embassy in London on the morning of 25th January, when four Greenham women met the first secretary there. After five-and-a-half hours, their talks seems to be going round in circles, so the women shut up and stayed completely silent for the next ninety minutes. At last the first secretary picked up and read the copy of the *Trust Builders' Appeal*, which the women had brought for him. Dialogue was resumed. Soon after, the meeting ended inconclusively, but amicably.

Subsequently, David Barnesdale (see 'Boscombe Down: How it all began', elsewhere in this book for an account of his arrest there, in 1983) organised a vigil outside the Soviet Embassy, with sixty-five people, on Sunday 5th February, in support of Olga Medvedkova. An attempt to see the ambassador failed; a petition was presented, but not accepted; and the embassy insisted: "Mrs. Medvedkova … has had no charges brought against her." (*Peace News*, 17th February, 1984)

At the beginning of 1984, Newbury District Council took on two new, full-time bailiffs, so that they could increase the evictions of campers.

Around the end of 1983, in answer to a request from Newbury magistrates for help with their increased workload, the Lord Chancellor had appointed a stipendiary magistrate, David Miller, to Newbury court. A stipendiary can sit alone, unlike lay magistrates who must normally sit in a bench of three. It is easier to raise one stipendiary for a special sitting than it is to raise three part-timers, who have other commitments.

One of the first things our stipendiary did was to refuse to accept Greenham Common Women's Peace Camp as a legal address (yet government departments, Newbury Council and the Post Office accepted it as a legal address) and then imprisoned a woman who gave it as her address and needed time to pay a fine. This ruling was overturned on appeal to a judge in Reading Crown Court on 13th January. Nevertheless, in February, on another case, David Miller again refused to accept the camp as a legal address.

In January, David Miller fined one of the Hallowe'en fence cutters, Annabel Cole, £50 for causing £200 worth of criminal damage, and confiscated her bolt cutters. This was the normal way fence cutters were treated, but Jill and Gloria, who were also Hallowe'en fence cutters, were treated very differently, as we shall read later.

On the weekend of 11th-12th February, contingents from Wales came to swell the numbers of campers on the common. On the Saturday, the campers held a fence cutting exercise and on the Sunday a Cruise TEL was seen outside a silo on the airfield.

Peace News announced, on 17th February, that the Greenham women had been nominated for the Nobel Peace Prize by the Swedish Peace and Arbitration Association. Some Labour members of the European Parliament supported this proposal. After due deliberation, it was decided not to award the prize to the Greenham women.

Some interesting government lies were told when the Department of Transport evicted peace campers from its land so that road widening could start on 2nd April near Yellow Gate. What was publicly announced as road widening only was also an attempt to get rid of the peace camp, as a confidential document 'leaked' to peace campers revealed. When the campers were evicted from the DoT road verges, they just moved to another part of the common near Yellow Gate. Imagine their surprise when they read in the newspapers that they had finally been evicted and were no longer on the Common! Obviously, the authorities had issued a press statement that had misled the press.

About this time there was an attempt to stop people camping around Yellow Gate by dumping lorry-loads of hard-core and lumps of concrete on the common. Though this 'landscaping', as the authorities called it, spoilt some little flower beds the women had planted, it did not stop them from moving and setting up camp again beside the rubble. The authorities were stumped, for they could not cover the whole common with a layer of rubble.

Early March saw the snow on the ground melting (but not for long – more fell in late April) in the spring sunshine. This seemed to be the cue for an increase in incidents of harassment, assault and battery. A dossier was being compiled.

An example of the sort of things that were happening was an incident at Orange Gate early one morning, when a woman was awakened by someone grinding a foot into the ground near her tent. Afraid, she shouted for help. A man ran away. Nobody was able to get a close look at him, so there was no description that could be used to identify him. Later, when women searched the area, they found a tennis ball cut open which had been full of petrol, a wick, a bottle half-full of petrol, and some pornographic magazines. Obviously an arson attempt had been stopped in the nick of time. The police were told.

Later that day, some men with American accents, entering the airfield by car through Orange Gate, shouted to the women nearby that they wouldn't fail next time. The modplods on the gate did not stop and question them and, so far as I know, they were never questioned about the attempted arson. (Case reported by Ann Fairnington in a letter published in *Peace News*, 3rd May, 1985)

Evictions, which eased up in mid-winter, were now being enthusiastically executed daily with the help of the two new bailiffs. On 25th February, Berkshire County Council had decided to evict the women from land mainly along Pinchington Lane and Bury's Bank Road, and appointed Newbury Council as its agents to do the 'dirty' work. Newbury Council, who were already evicting from other land on the Common of course, began evicting women from the Berkshire land on 5th March.

The DoT was also evicting at this time, from its verges by Yellow Gate, for its road widening scheme. The MoD seemed to be the only authority not evicting.

Jill Morony and Gloria Delmonte, in spring, found the criminal damage charges of 29th October, 1983, replaced by new charges, which alleged that they had taken down and damaged a total of eighty-one fence sections, which cost £5,397.65 to repair. The Ordnance Survey grid reference, and therefore the location, of the alleged crime had been altered – yet police claimed to have arrested Jill and Gloria at the scene red-handed! The increase in the value of the alleged damage entitled the women to elect for a full crown court trial in Reading, instead of a hearing before the local magistrates, which was all they could get with the smaller amount of alleged damage. The crown court trial would mean more publicity for the campaign against Cruise. An appeal was launched to raise funds for Jill and Gloria.

The first Cruise convoy, a TEL and two support vehicles, left Blue Gate just after midnight on 9th March,1984, and headed along Pinchington Lane towards A34, M4 and RAF Lyneham. It returned the same night.

Between the time of the first convoy and the emergence of the second, Rene Gill from nearby Maidenhead stayed on Greenham Common on 13th and 14th March. Rene wrote a delightful account of her stay in a pamphlet brilliantly illustrated by Richard Kennedy, which describes the atmosphere on the Common at that time far better than anything I could write. Rene very kindly permitted me to reprint the pamphlet in full, for which I am extremely grateful. The pamphlet copyright still rests with Rene, so I regret I can't supply separate photocopies. The pamphlet is out of print, but Housman's Bookshop or CND national office may be able to supply a copy (addresses in Bibliography). This pamphlet was published by Maidenhead CND around September, 1984.

Photo of cover of *Twenty-four Hours at Greenham*

by Rene Gill • Illustrated by Richard Kennedy

Everyone knows where Greenham is, and why it's there. But what is it? Its character changes like clouds. To the numerous women who are, or have been there, and who call themselves 'Greenham Women', it is an entity: a new focus.

This time we drove first to the camps along the North side, distributing goods as requested: fruit, lettuces and a bike pump at Blue Gate; a plant for Violet, (several of the camps – there are ten in all at present, have started gardening: little flower and vegetable beds, like hummocky graves, edged with stones); toilet paper and an umbrella for Red, potscourers, dustbin bags, candles and matches for Yellow, (which used to be called Main Gate, but that sounded too hierarchical). Red needs a water container refilling. There's only one source of water for all the camps, a standpipe opposite the main gate to the base. The police took away the original standpipe, now the women, or wimmin, or womyn (they are not sub-species of men) have bought their own, and keep it hidden. It's quite a palaver, setting it all up, filling the container, dismantling and hiding it again. But as with all the many other forms of harassment, the womyn respond with patience and resourcefulness. ("It doesn't take long to re-light the fire after the police have extinguished it. But it is irritating when they come along and put it out again straight away.") Gone are the big, humped, comfortable shapes of the benders. The womyn live on the bare ground; rain-proof gortex sleeping-bags have been invented in the nick of time. The main gate to the base has been sealed off by two wire fences, between which men with earthmoving equipment are at work widening the road, ostensibly to facilitate the emergence of the Cruise convoy, in reality yet another attempt to dislodge the womyn. A few maintain a small camp behind; the rest have decamped onto the common on the other side of the road.

We decided to do our night watch at Red Gate, as only three womyn are in permanent residence there at present: J., a recent Cambridge graduate; L., from Sweden and R., from California. Day and night they are watched by leering soldiers with binoculars on the other side of the fence. J., L., and R. keep all their belonging neatly stacked on three old prams, for ease of removal during 'evictions'. Behind the camp is a small copse with a colourful banner slung between two trees: it provides privacy when they wash, visit the latrine, or 'shit-pit', dug deep into the stony earth among the trees. To one side of the camp is an area of burnt gorse, with new bracken snaking up out of the blackened earth, among the grotesquely twisted black skel-etons of the gorse. J. describes her pleasure at dis-covering that she can live like this, with none of the amenities with which she has grown up, apart from a few books. A pan, a pot, a kettle, firewood, a plastic plate (to fan the flames) her extra long sleeve for a pot holder, these for her meals of veg-etables and pulses; and for entertainment, talking with visitors, or visiting other camps, getting to-gether from time to time for a party, singing and dancing to the music of an accordion. For sleeping, a sheet of plastic draped across three cords strung between two trees and a sleeping bag. Sh.e has no wish to live any other way. All the womyn we met, radiated this same sense of well-being and con-tentment, although each camp has its own peculiar atmosphere, partly dictated by its physical posi-tion. Violet is on an embankment right up against the fence; the womyn there indulge in a great deal

of back-chat with the uniformed men inside, and also make frequent daring incursions into the base when the gate is opened for a military vehicle. At Orange Gate, the atmosphere is poisitively refined. The camp is in amongst the trees, and the womyn sit comfortably on chairs in various stages of col-lapse in a ring around the fire, with two cats gam-bolling about. When we visited them they were ac-tually sipping wine and passing round a large box of chocolates.

When you walk along the perimeter fence, you are escorted by a soldier on the other side who reports your every movement over his field radio: "Krrr! Romeo to Tango. Am with two women moving in a westerly direction. Over. Krrr!"

They are eager to talk to you, and have evidently been instructed to elicit information. This they do very subtly:

"What are you planning to do?"

"Oh," we reply, "a million women are going to storm the base tonight." He gulps audibly and re-lays this message to Tango. If you stop for a while and rest your hand on the fence, you can hear the man on the nearest watch-tower nervously spring to life:

"Krrr! Krrr! Juliet to Bravo! One woman testing fence in your sector. Over. Krrr!"

You can cause consternation by disappearing from sight in a ditch or behind a bush. Soldiers come running and shouting, the radios splutter, the tall searchlights swing round, a Jeep drives up – until you arise and stroll on.

The central issues are often discussed, and the soldiers trot out the familiar arguments about the need to deter, defend and retaliate against the evils of communism. Presumably the Army is afraid the soldiers might be convinced by the womyn, as the guards are changed every week. They are quite clearly indoctrinated with wholly unrealistic information about nuclear war:

"Have you considered what will happen when they launch Cruise?" "I'll be all right; I've got protective clothing."

While we were eating our filling supper, two hired mini buses drove up, and out jumped some two dozen womyn, members of the Manchester Greenham Common Women Support Group, who were given the same warm welcome as we had been. After they had put up their banners, swarmed about talking for a while, and eaten, they dispersed to undertake night watches at other camps.

While J. and L. slept, R. rode off on her bike to visit friends. Three very young girls from Manchester and I sat around the fire and talked.

One of them said sleepily: "Let's stay here forever."

"Why?" I asked. "Why do you like being here?"

"Because, just by being here, you're doing something."

They dozed off. I watched the base, bathed in the bluish glare from the search lights; the fences, look-out towers, buildings in stark silhouette. Vehicles moved about in there all night; a generator throbbed and gurgled ceaselessly; behind me in the trees a nightingale sang, trying out an infinite variety of trills, runs and melodies. A fawn mouse with circular black eyes dodged out of a gorse

bush; the moon rose above the base, blurred and golden. The message of the soft warm night was clear. I thought of the womyn's camps encircling the metal and concrete of the base, and wondered whether a symbol could possibly be strong enough to defeat so much misbegotten hardware.

During breakfast next morning, J. and L. looked up and groaned. The red chomper had arrived; we were to be 'evicted'. "Not on Sunday!" I asked what we should do. "It varies. Don't do anything for now." They strolled over to the bailiff and talked to him companionably. They asked about his working hours – he was on flexitime. They discussed their mutual problem: the council. "Basically, they don't want you to camp on the common." The upshot was that a few ropes were unknotted in a desultory way, while he sat in his van, watched and read his Daily Express. Then he drove off and the knots were tied again. "That," said J., "was a very gentle eviction. It isn't always like that. Sometimes they snatch our belongings out of our hands and throw them in the chomper. But generally we tell them what they can take and pile the rest on the prams and push them into the woods. Which is how we get rid of our rubbish. We're meant to be getting a car today from some womyn in Brighton. That'll make evictions much easier."

This day happened to be Pensioners for Peace day at Orange Gate, and, confusingly, Grannies against Cruise at Green.

Busloads of grey-heads started arriving. I joined my mother at Orange. There were a few speeches, a good deal of singing and a very relaxed and musical blockade. Then a military vehicle tried to force its way through the milling groups, and one elderly

woman tried repeatedly to sit in its path, but was forcibly removed by the police, who suddenly materialized in hundreds from their concealed busses when their leader signalled with one hand. The last we saw of them, the pensioners were linking hands and were weaving in and out of the police and the vehicles in an ever-lengthening, singing snake.

Published by Maidenhead CND. © Rene Gill 1984

The road widening mentioned here needs further explanation. Only the approach road to Yellow Gate and its junction with the A338 were actually widened. The reasons given by the authorities were not the whole truth: there were others. The approach road and its junction could accommodate an RAF Queen Mary, longer than any vehicle yet seen on a Cruise convoy, without difficulty. This road had been adequate for traffic up to now. Any road widening here was likely to meet opposition as the sewer pipe laying had done. This would add considerably to its cost. The authorities considered it vital to widen the road and the junction, however, so that Cruise convoys could leave and return via Yellow Gate as fast as possible and not give way at the main road as normal traffic was supposed to do. The high fences erected to keep the women from obstructing the road works also served to keep them off the approach road, making it easier for the police to prevent sit-downs on it. They helped to hide the peace camp from the view of the public driving along the A338, too. Narrow roads had made the progress of the convoy in leaving Blue Gate difficult, because they were easier for the women to obstruct, and, with the convoy moving slowly, people were much more likely to run in front of vehicles, or drive in front of them, to make them stop. Also, the USAF wanted to cut the response time for convoys to the minimum, so that they could fire missiles from the launching sites as soon as possible after being ordered to go there.

The second Cruise convoy, which emerged twenty days after the first, used the same route to go to Lyneham and back. This convoy had no fewer than twenty-six vehicles. When it was returning, some vehicles went in through Blue Gate, and there was a short pause before the rest of the vehicles came up the road. As the remainder of the convoy appeared, Di McDonald reversed her white Volkswagen Kombi into the road, partially obstructing it. The road was not blocked, and there was room for the rest of the convoy to get round, but they would have to slow down to do so, The leading vehicle swerved around the Volkswagen, clipping a fence and a signpost to Greenham Church as it did so. Next, six burly

policemen forced themselves into Di's car, and pulled her from the driving seat. In the confusion they tried to move the car, but could not. Di was then released and moved it herself. A BBC reporter was standing a few yards away, and gave listeners to the early editions of the Radio Four news bulletins an accurate account of what happened, recorded as he watched it happening. In later editions, this was replaced by a police statement prepared by someone who did not seem to have been there and who seemed more interested in slandering the activists, than in reporting accurately. Press coverage included at least one front-page report.

On 30th March, Janey Hulme, writing in *New Statesman*, estimated that there had been 1,775 arrests of demonstrators and activists at Greenham since September 1981. Many had been imprisoned.

In early April, the Reading Crown Court trial of twelve Greenham women was halted by the judge after a daily newspaper named one of the women in a report of the case. The judge accepted the defence submission that this report might have prejudiced the court against the defendants.

6th and 7th April saw the worst spate of evictions yet. There were thirty arrests of people allegedly obstructing evictions on 7th April alone. They were all charged. Perhaps the arrival of more Cruise missiles by air on 6th April had something to do with all this.

On Good Friday, six people went onto the airfield and held a Christian religious service. As they were being arrested, they continued worshipping. All were strip-searched, and later released without charge, except for one person, who was charged with criminal damage.

Charges of criminal damage were brought against four women arrested on the common on Easter Monday, 23rd April.

The roads around Greenham, and the perimeter fence, were extensively painted and decorated on 7th May. Arrests totalled thirty. Of these people, sixteen were charged with various offences and released on bail. The remaining fourteen were released without charge.

At the perimeter fence on 12th May, twenty-six women were arrested and charged with cutting it – criminal damage in other words. On what I believe was their second appearance in Newbury Magistrates Court, they were remanded to trial dates of 19th and 20th June. A condition set for bail was that each keep at least five miles from Greenham Com-

mon, and twenty-one of the women refused to accept this condition, so were remanded in prison until their trials. The others were released on bail.

On the weekend of 18th-20th May, nearly a thousand pensioners demonstrated their concern about 'nuclear weapons and the survival of the younger generation', (*Peace News*, 15th June, 1984, p. 7) in a 'Grannies Weekend' on the Common. One of their banners proclaimed:

GRANNIES AGAINST NUCLEAR WINTER

(*Peace News*, 15th June, 1984, p. 7 has a photograph.) This demonstration may have originated the term 'Greenham Granny'; though grannies had demonstrated there before this, not only at the 'Pensioners' Weekend' on 13th-14th March, but also at least as early as 5th September, 1981. Those who came for the 'Grannies' Weekend' sang with the regular campers around the campfires and held a silent vigil.

Monika Timm was sentenced to fifty-eight days in prison in May, as a result of four separate criminal damage charges. An appeal was planned, as everyone was horrified at the length of the sentence. Monika had been arrested in December 1983, as a result of two incidents. She was German and her English was poor. After ten hours of questioning in custody and being awake for nearly forty-eight hours without a break, she had made admissions, which led to the police charging her with four offences of criminal damage.

Some Greenham women were arrested inside the Atomic Weapons Research Establishment at Aldermaston, on 12th June. Charges of £150 worth of criminal damage were laid against five of them, and they were told to attend Bradfield and Sonning Magistrates Court on 4th July. One woman was released without charge.

On 21st June, Barbara Weston was charged with criminal damage to a USAF vehicle.

One command vehicle, four Cruise launchers (TELs) and eleven support vehicles left Orange Gate at 01.00 hours on 26th June. They drove to the A339 and then headed East along it. This convoy was tracked to and from army ranges near Longmoor in Hampshire by Alton CND and Basingstoke CND. About a hundred yards short of Yellow Gate on the return journey, one vehicle broke down. It was quickly towed in through Yellow Gate 'without incident' (MoD press release) and to the accompaniment of cheers from the peace campers and cruisewatchers. Convoy 3 returned on 29th June.

By now women were getting onto the airfield much more frequently than Cruise convoys were getting out! Not all those on incursions were caught, and not all those caught were being charged.

One interesting incursion took place just after Convoy 3 had returned. Yellow Gate was open, and guarded by three policemen and a soldier when Di McDonald, with Blue Joyce and two other women as passengers, drove her white Volkswagen between these guards and through the gate. She had driven across the airfield and onto the runaway before she was stopped. These women and their car were escorted off the airfield, and released without charge.

On 5th July, a Greenham woman chained herself to a helicopter exhibition in London. She was arrested and charged. When she attended court on 24th July, she was given a conditional discharge.

At Bradfield and Sonning Magistrates Court on 11th July, the five women arrested at Aldermaston and charged with criminal damage elected to go for jury trial at Reading. The committal hearing was set for 22nd August.

On Monday, 23rd July, after serving four months of a six-month sentence, reduced by remission for good conduct, Sarah Tisdall (the woman who gave the photocopied secret documents to *The Guardian*) was released from East Sutton Park Open Prison.

On 24th July, two launchers, one control vehicle, and twelve support vehicles left Yellow Gate at 01.00

hours. They headed west by A339, then south along A334. Then the Andover group of Cruisewatchers spotted them turning off A303 at Parkhouse, onto the Northbound A338. Now Parkhouse is a flyover, but in 1984 it was a roundabout. This, the fourth convoy, turned onto Bulford Ranges and deployed there.

The convoy left Bulford Ranges by 'C' crossing, and turned North along A345, to arrive back at Greenham Common at 02.00 on 26th July. This convoy was a quarter of a mile long when spread out and moving at speed (50-55 mph) on the open road. On the ranges, during this deployment, eight Southampton women were chased by paratroops, tanks and a helicopter, before being arrested, detained six hours and charged with, or cautioned about, offences under the Salisbury Plain and Bulford Ranges By-Laws.

At about this time, in Reading Crown Court, ten people were imprisoned for actions at Greenham Common and three were acquitted. Anne Francis, a Welsh cleric's wife, and Margaret Johnson, a Quaker grandmother, were both involved in this trial apparently, and during it they refused to submit to intimate body searches. For this they were imprisoned on remand for the two weeks the trial lasted. Anne subsequently complained about this treatment to her MP, John Stradling Thomas.

Southampton City Council declared itself a NFZ on 28th July and in September donated two tents to Greenham Common Women's Peace Camp. The council also offered its staff the chance to go there on unpaid leave during the Women's Strike, without affecting their holiday entitlement.

At the beginning of August, four campers entered a high security zone and got to within a hundred yards of some missile silos. They left cards saying: "Greenham Women are everywhere", and "Prepare for peace, not war", all over the place. After an hour, they were arrested, then released without charge.

A military event held there prompted some Greenham women to climb onto the canopy on the front of London's Whitehall Theatre on Hiroshima Day. After four hours, during which their protest was seen by many passers-by, the women came down of their own accord. They were arrested and taken to Rochester Row Police Station, where it appears that the eight were additionally charged with criminal damage. Some women had sat down on the steps outside the police station and the police apparently arrested six of these, whom they later released without charge. The trial of the theatre-goers was set for November.

On 7th August, two people were arrested on Greenham Common and charged with criminal damage to a wooden fence erected by Newbury Council.

Nagasaki Day was commemorated with a blockade and a 'die-in' at Yellow Gate. The women taking part had covered their bodies with oil, ash and tomato paste, to make themselves look like atom bomb victims.

Newbury magistrates, on 16th August, jailed Greenham woman Leslie Westbury for not paying £101 in fines.

At about this time Reading magistrates fined another Greenham woman, Caroline James, £100. She refused to pay and was sentenced to fourteen days in jail.

On Tuesday, 21st August, a great, white bird landed on Greenham Common. It was probably a C5A Galaxy of the USAF. A Cruise TEL and a Cruise control vehicle were driven out of the for'ard door, while four long, white crates and a smaller item were unloaded from the rear door. More Cruise convoy vehicles arrived in a Galaxy, which landed at about 10.00 hours on Bank Holiday Monday, 27th August. Both of these deliveries were observed by Greenham women, who were developing their technique in plane-spotting and observation. Some of the early deliveries do not appear to have been observed, or if they were, no reports were made.

Also in August, the Federal Court judge in New York who had been hearing the Greenham women's case against Cruise in Europe in international law, ruled he was not competent to hear the case. Therefore he granted no injunction to stop the US Government from deploying Cruise in Europe. Greenham Women Against Cruise planned to appeal.

On 3rd September, Newbury magistrates were busy. They dealt with two women charged, on 12th and 13th May, with criminal damage to the perimeter fence on Greenham Common (sentence unknown); and with two more similarly charged on 7th May, who were fined £40 with £15 costs, and £50 with £15 costs, respectively. They sentenced Barbara Weston, charged with criminal damage to a USAF vehicle on 21st June, to fourteen days in jail, when she refused to pay her fine. They fined Bat Dimyon £40 with £10 costs on a criminal damage charge dating from 26th July, and sentenced her to seven days in jail when she refused to pay. Also at about this time Newbury magistrates dealt with Megan Williams on a charge of criminal damage to an MoD padlock (sentence unknown) and in court in Reading Greenham woman Margaret Norman was bound over to be of good behaviour for three years in the sum of £100.

There were plenty more people for the courts to convict where these came from. On 19th September, four women were arrested on the Common and charged with criminal damage to the perimeter fence. Likewise, Jean Hutchinson (who had earlier been arrested in Detroit, USA) was arrested for damaging the same fence, on 25th September, charged with criminal damage, and bailed to appear before Newbury magistrates on 4th October.

The fifth Cruise convoy, consisting of one articulated tractor unit (suitable for use on TEL or Cruise control vehicles) and nineteen support vehicles, left Yellow Gate early on the afternoon of Sunday 16th September. Two more tractor units left Indigo Gate at the same time. All headed for Salisbury Plain.

THE WOMEN'S STRIKE (September-December 1984)

Between 20th and 30th September the Women's Strike was organised, partly in protest at the large number of British personnel taking part in NATO manoeuvres in West Germany. Greenham women were active in it.

These NATO manoeuvres caused at least thirteen new peace camps to be set up. As part of the anti-NATO action, Greenham women started one outside the Atomic Weapons Research Establishment, Aldermaston (see my account 'Aldermaston: the first peace camp', elsewhere in this book), which brought Aldermaston's evil work back into the news. A group of Nottingham women started a camp at Chilwell (see: "Chilwell: peace camping in the suburbs of Nottingham", elsewhere in this book) and were evicted from the grass verge by the base entrance within hours. The depot at Chilwell was an appropriate place for this camp, as it had recently been leased to the USAF. A women's peace camp was set up near the United Kingdom Warning and Monitoring Organisation nuclear bunker in Alexandra Park, London (see my account 'Peace Camps and Squats in London', elsewhere in this book). Peace camps were established on Brandon Hill, Bristol; at Brawdy; (see my account, 'Subwatch at Brawdy', elsewhere in this book) and at Petersfield, Hampshire, during the ten days. From Thursday 27th September until 30th September there was a peace camp at Colchester, Essex, with women mainly from Essex CND. An international peace camp was set up for the duration of the NATO exercise at Grebenheim, West Germany and peace camps were set up

outside four other West German bases: Fulda, Hanau, Alsfield and Wildflecken.

During the Women's Strike, there was an appeal for ten million women to demonstrate between 20th and 30th September. People were asked to do so for ten minutes or ten days; there was no need to participate for any special period of time, so long as the participation took place during the ten days of the strike. The women were allowed to demonstrate at bases near their homes, as many did, and there was no need for everybody to travel to Greenham Common. No list recorded the names of all the participants. To make such a list would have been impossible with the resources available. What is known is that an immense number of women did take part, and some actions may well have gone unrecorded.

On Greenham Common, there were many incursions onto the airfield. On one incursion, some women entered a briefing room and took away documents giving instructions on how to deal with a nuclear attack or nuclear accident, and which told how to wash down Cruise convoys with detergent to remove fallout. The documents revealed that this could not be done, as the equipment with which to do it had not been bought. Perhaps they were waiting for the Betterware salesperson to call.

Large sections of the perimeter fence on the common were brought down during the ten days in several separate actions.

In September, with support and funds almost healthy in their defence campaign, Jill Morony and Gloria Delmonte were preparing to defend themselves in Reading Crown Court on their criminal damage charges, when the charges were suddenly reduced to committing £65.76 worth of criminal damage. This put everything back into the magistrates court, as crown court trials could not be had for alleged offences of under £200 worth of damage.

Evictions had cost Newbury District Council £9,000 up to the end of September. (According to Janey Hulme, *New Statesman*, 23rd November, 1984.)

During September, campers began noticing mysterious symptoms and ailments, of which more later.

Cruise convoys emerged three times in October 1984. Convoy 6 went to Salisbury Plain on 10th October and returned on Sunday, 14th October. Convoy 7, consisting of two launchers, plus seven support vehicles, left Indigo Gate at 11.00 hours and drove to Kidlington, Oxfordshire, returning 13.30 on the same day, 17th October. This was the first time any Cruise convoy vehicle had left the airfield in daylight and is also believed to be the only time a convoy left by Indigo Gate. At 11.10 on 30th October, again in daylight, a full convoy of twenty-six vehicles left for Salisbury Plain, and returned at 06.38 on Saturday, 3rd November. Just before it left Blue Gate, an eviction had started at Yellow Gate, and nearly all the campers had gone round there to resist it, so Convoy 8 slipped out almost unnoticed. This was the first convoy to rehearse a 'broken arrow', which was a training exercise assuming a major accident with a nuclear weapon. A convoy of the type used to carry Polaris missile warheads was seen in the area at the same time. There probably was a connexion between the 'broken arrow' rehearsal and the proximity of the Polaris convoy.

The campers paid a £65 deposit, along with water rates, to the Thames Water Board, for a standpipe on a hydrant near Yellow Gate. Apart from two little rills in woods near the A339, this was the only source of water on the common available to campers and was used for drinking water. Bailiffs from Newbury Council took the standpipe during an eviction. When asked for its return, they denied taking it. However, on 5th November, Thames Water Board said the council had admitted taking it.

Apparently, when the council took the standpipe, they handed it to the water board, as it wasn't theirs to keep and they didn't need it. The water board refused to issue a new standpipe to the camp, claiming, firstly, that the camp had changed hands since the eviction and the new occupiers were not the people who had rented the standpipe; and secondly, that the standpipe constituted a prohibited structure under the Greenham Common By-Laws and needed planning permission, which it didn't have. The camp had not changed hands. The standpipe was not left in position when not being used, and was much smaller than a fire brigade connecting pipe. If the fire brigade had to apply for planning permission every time they had to use a connecting pipe to fight a fire in any of the houses dotted on and around the Common, it would be a case of 'burn, baby, burn' for the house would be a burnt-out shell before planning permission could be granted. The Water Board also refused to sue the council for the return of the standpipe.

The campers could have prosecuted Newbury Council for theft, and a guilty verdict against the council would have enabled the court to order the return of the standpipe. There was no guarantee that the campers would win and, even if they did, a prosecution could involve long delays, (which could

be years) and much expense, so they didn't prosecute. Had they obtained and fitted their own standpipe, they would have risked yet another confiscation and maybe prosecution for fitting an unauthorised water standpipe.

What they did was to issue a successful appeal for plastic containers full of water, which served their short-term needs. The campers also got more people to support their campaign to get their standpipe back, and argued their case in the relevant offices. After much haggling, and a brief occupation of Newbury Council Offices, the standpipe was returned in November.

Following the actions of 20th-30th September, camp morale and numbers were at a low ebb. The authorities took advantage of this to launch a series of very bad evictions in October. Not only was the standpipe taken, but also, on several occasions, personal belongings, blankets and sleeping bags were deliberately grabbed and thrown into the dustcart before the women could get them out of reach of the bailiffs.

The women covered in oil, ash, and tomato paste, who were arrested at the Nagasaki Day 'Die-In', came before Newbury magistrates on 16th October. Caroline Griffiths was fined £35 with £20 costs for obstructing the highway. She paid. Similar fines were meted out to five other, who all refused to pay and were each imprisoned for seven days. A warrant was issued for the arrest of one woman who did not come to court. Dee West was the only woman found not guilty.

On the same day, six other women were arrested for obstructing A339 past the approach road to Yellow Gate. They refused to pay fines, so the magistrates sentenced each of them to seven days in prison. Also Caroline Powell was fined £50 with £10 costs and Claire Roberts £25 with £20 costs. Further details of these two cases are not known.

An unusual case, which came up with these, was that of Carolyne Jarvis, fined £50 with £10 costs for abusive and threatening behaviour. She had thrown two eggs onto the airfield from outside the fence, narrowly missing a USAF officer.

Stella Mann-Cairns had been arrested at a water tower occupation on the common in December 1983. This was one of the many incursions onto the airfield around that time and obviously was a minor action, for I have been unable to trace any report of it. When arrested, she was strip-searched. A week later, she made a formal complaint about the way in which the arrest and search were conducted. She was interviewed by a Modsquad chief inspector in March, and then heard nothing until October. The case became important at this point, because Stella had been actively pursuing her complaint along several avenues and had now been awarded legal aid to conduct it. This is believed to be the first time ever that legal aid has been awarded to conduct a complaint against the Modsquad.

At Hallowe'en forty women got onto the airfield, in several separate groups. Some of them reached silos, others got to the runway and two women occupied the Air Traffic Control Tower. This was the second time (the first being 11th December, 1983) that women had occupied this vital objective. On this second occupation, tomato sauce was poured over computers and other electronic equipment. The sauce symbolised blood. The women hope it would do a lot of damage to the sensitive electronic internals.

Shortly after this a water tower was occupied.

On Sunday, 4th November some women borrowed a USAF bus inside the airfield and drove round by the fence collecting passengers who had come through or over it. Eventually the coach stopped at a silo, and the women got out and started cutting the fence around it. They were well inside the main perimeter fence. Soon American troops arrived, and arrested them. They were handed over to the Modsquad, who charged each of the twenty-one or twenty-two women with taking the motorcoach without consent and allowing herself to be carried in it and three additionally with criminal damage to the silo fence. The women were ordered to appear in Newbury Magistrates Court on 22nd November. The coach tour had taken place during a 'broken arrow' exercise, when a nuclear accident was being simulated. The passengers saw some of the exercise, including soldiers wearing gas-masks dashing hither and thither.

Cyril Parkinson, MP, a member of the Tory government, went to St. Albans in his car, and two Greenham women, who were also there at the time, caused the car to stop by sitting down in front of it. As a result, they attended St. Albans Magistrates Court on 13th November, charged with obstruction of the highway. Defence solicitor Mary O'Dwyer successfully proved that their actions didn't amount to obstruction. Then she applied for costs to be awarded to the women, and the magistrates awarded them £50 each, on top of their not guilty verdicts. Campaigners should keep this case in mind, so that if they are in a similar position one day, they can refer to it in their defence, and not forget to ask for their costs. (Not guilty verdicts, followed by cash awards for costs, to the defence, have occurred in some subsequent cases involving cruisewatchers.)

When Convoy 3 left Greenham Common in June, it went to Longmoor Ranges in Hampshire. Cruisewatch didn't publicise it as they usually did, because this route and these ranges offered possibilities for actions against Cruise, and they did not want to discourage the convoys from coming this way again. The convoys liked to keep to dual carriageways and flyover junctions, but most of this route was on narrow, two-lane roads, some of which were only fourteen feet wide, which is not wide enough for two lorries the size of Cruise TELs to pass. Cruise TELs are about the same size as civilian articulated, thirty-eight-tonne lorries, though they are somewhat heavier. When the road is not wide enough for two heavy lorries to pass on the straight, the situation is much worse when there are bends, as there are in the narrow main street of Selborne. Cruisewatchers were talking of carelessly parked vehicles and non-violent ambushes. The Longmoor area is much more densely populated than Salisbury Plain, and the military is not the biggest local employer, as it is on the plain. Without the same pressure of military employment, there were greater percentages of active disarmers and potential protesters in the population around Longmoor, which is also much nearer London, with its big easily-mobilised concentration of disarmers. If a Cruise convoy was on Longmoor Ranges over a weekend, there was no telling what Cruisewatch would do with it!

Luck was in for Cruisewatch, when on Thursday, 15th November, Convoy 9 left Greenham Common by the same route that Convoy 3 had used in June, along A339, by-passing Basingstoke and Alton, but driving down the narrow, winding main street of Selborne. It was tracked all the way to Longmoor, where it was virtually surrounded by disarmers when it stopped on the ranges. The disarmers were either chased off or arrested by the police.

Experienced Cruisewatchers expected the convoy to return on the Friday night, to avoid weekend protesters, but it stayed. More activists kept appearing, and swelled the numbers in the crowds on the ranges. Although the police were managing to keep most activists away from the convoy itself, some Southampton women got close enough to paint and decorate many convoy vehicles, so that when they moved the media could see that Cruisewatch had spotted the convoy, and any newspaper photos and television crews would show up their artwork. This was done in the expectancy of the convoy moving on Saturday night, but it stayed. The crowds waited, watched and grew.

At 02.00 hours on the Monday morning, roadblocks were set up, and police diverted what little traffic there was from the public roads around Longmoor. A few cruisewatchers saw what was happening, and quickly went into 'phone boxes to alert the telephone trees. It seems most of the phones were working properly, so British Telecom hadn't disconnected them, as they often did when a convoy was moving nearby. The telephone trees brought out more activists, some of whom had already arrived when the roadblocks were suddenly lifted at 02.45, and police and military activity returned to the level it had been earlier in the night. Apparently they had decided to delay departure until there were fewer cruisewatchers around Longmoor.

Many weekend activists had to leave early on the Monday morning, after helping to stop the convoy moving, but the police showed no signs of going home.

When roadblocks were set up again on Monday night, many extra police appeared. Police cars tailed cruisewatchers' cars and prevented them from stopping to 'phone the telephone trees. Cars were stopped and searched by police. In spite of all this, two people did manage to alert the telephone trees when the convoy started to move. As on the previous night, the trees brought out more activists. Police got even more 'heavy' as the convoy left the ranges, and headed for Alton, which it by-passed before following the old A32 onto A33, then M4. It came off M4 onto A34 and returned by Newbury Ring Road and Blue Gate, in the early hours of 20th November.

Cruisewatchers managed to follow it all the way, but the big police escort prevented them from overtaking it. The new route appears to have taken Cruisewatch and the campers by surprise, for crowds were awaiting the return of the convoy at Yellow Gate. It was much longer than the outward route.

The MoD wouldn't admit that activists had delayed the convoy by twenty-four hours; nor did they say much about the withdrawal of civil liberties that took place around Longmoor while the convoy was there. Public footpaths were closed, and public highways were blocked without prior notice and without either accident or other emergency to justify the closure. People were being stopped, searched and interrogated at random. Property, including maps and telephone number lists, was being taken from them. People were being warned they risked prosecution if they used perfectly legal CB radio sets. The inhabitants of the Longmoor area had to endure much extra noise and loss of privacy. In one of several incidents, a thirteen-year-old girl and her mother, who lived in the village of Greatham, were out walking their dog, when they were arrested and detained in a pit, along with some cruisewatchers. A total of forty-five people were arrested, but all were apparently released without charge. People were complaining about the way police and troops treated them and some were taking court action, claiming among other things, wrongful arrest. The resultant legal battles are continuing at the time of writing.

Local disarmers found that a Cruise convoy in their own area over a weekend could work wonders in reactivating old CND members, and recruiting new ones. It beats a Bruce Kent debate any day.

On Thursday, 22nd November, the women who had toured RAF Greenham Common by motorcoach appeared before Newbury magistrates, pleading not guilty to taking a coach without consent, and there were adjournments. The crown court trial, with judge and jury, did not start until 2nd December 1985 – a year later.

On the same day Sarah Hipperson was jailed for six weeks for criminal damage, and two other women were each jailed two weeks for not paying £50 fines.

In the two months from 21st September to 22nd November, no fewer than 110 people were in court on various charges. The total of arrests to 22nd November, for the whole period of just over three years since WFLOE had arrived from Cardiff, was estimated at 2,013. (According to estimates of Janey Hulme, *New Statesman*, 23rd November, 1984.)

The prosecution claimed a total of £1,700 worth of damage was done to the Whitehall Theatre in the Hiroshima Day demonstration. At court in November, apparently five women were given conditional discharges, and some women were ordered to pay compensation of £280 at £3 per week each, on the criminal damage charges.

At the beginning of December, there were nightly incursions onto the airfield. As time went on, and their experience was growing, women were finding it easier and easier to reach fences surrounding high security areas on the airfield. Many incursions were completely undetected by the guards and police.

9th December was the nearest Sunday to the

anniversary of the Cruise deployment decision, and Greenham women were planning to commemorate it. Because of this, evictions were increased, taking place at times twice daily and sometimes even after dark. The incursions, which were obviously another reason for the increased evictions, did not seem to be hindered much by them.

One eviction which took place after dark at Blue Gate on Friday, 7th December, conducted in the same way as previous evictions, which had preceded the emergence of Cruise convoys, sparked off an alert on the Cruisewatch telephone trees. When no convoy left, news of the false alarm had to be phoned through, resulting in twice the number of phone calls of a normal Cruise alert and one or two wasted journeys.

Several coachloads of women came to Greenham Common on 9th December and there were many small actions, with the biggest single action being a blockade of Yellow Gate with about 200 women. The authorities were well prepared and had lines of police at important locations behind the perimeter fence. Behind the police were lines of British troops and behind them Americans. Up until recently the Americans had not been formally involved in guard duties. When they had encountered unauthorised persons in the airfield, they had merely detained them and called out the modplods to actually arrest and process them, or release them, as sometimes happened. Now the Americans were helping the modplods to guard the airfield, and were actually arresting people, and handing them over to the modplods to be interviewed, and charged, or released as required.

At about this time, some Greenham women visited Faslane, and, living up to their motto of 'Greenham Women Everywhere', entered the submarine base. They were arrested painting graffiti inside the base.

MORE CRUISE CONVOYS OUTSIDE; COMPETITION TO BREAK NEW BY-LAWS INSIDE THE FENCE; AND TILSHEAD PEACE CAMP (December 1984-April 1985)

At 01.00 hours on 11th December, a convoy of twenty-six vehicles, including a full flight of two command vehicles and four launchers, left Blue Gate. They went to Salisbury Plain, where other military vehicles set up roadblocks on public highways. The roadblocks, thick fog and a British Army full brigade exercise near Tilshead, made this convoy difficult to track. As usual, the Greenham

women kept their airfield under close observation, and had spotted signs of a convoy forming up to leave in time to spread a warning on the Cruisewatch telephone trees. As was their usual practice, they made a second telephone call as soon as the convoy started to leave, and gave the gate it left by and the direction it took to the telephone trees. They also helped track it to Salisbury Plain and across the Plain. Half this convoy had returned to Greenham Common by 02.40 on Friday 14TH December, but it is not clear what happened to the rest of it. Some vehicles may have gone into other military bases nearby. Salisbury Plain is pockmarked with military bases.

Recently, many people had been picking up litter, some of which bore informative American labels, left by Cruise convoys on Salisbury Plain. The British Government sent in the Gloucestershire Regiment to clear up after this convoy. This was the first time that a British regiment has cleared litter left by servicemen of another nation, and many Cruisewatchers thought it humorous.

On 11th December, a Greenham woman was arrested and taken to Newbury Police Station. She had no criminal record and had never been convicted of anything. According to one account, once in the police station she was put in a cell. Then plainclothes CID officers dragged her from her cell and pinned her arms to her sides. One officer held her head. She was then photographed against her will. She made a complaint.

Duncan Campbell, in *New Statesman*, (14th December 1984) published the rules governing the circumstances in which British service people were permitted to shoot civilians at bases in England and Wales.

These rules were printed on pink cards given to troops and police guarding the bases. US troops and airmen came under their own set of rules and were covered by the Visiting Forces Act, which meant they had wider powers to shoot British civilians than our own troops and police had. As a result of Duncan's article, sympathetic MPs asked questions about troops shooting civilians. When the questions were asked in the House of Commons, there was uproar.

On Sunday, 16th December, at 14.30 hours, the Southern Area Peace Committee of the Religious Society of Friends (Quakers) held the first of many monthly meetings for worship at Blue Gate. At the same time, I was with some West Country Quakers and other Christians, holding a Christmas carol service at Yellow Gate. Richard had brought Gary and myself over from Boscombe Down Peace Camp in his car.

At the time, Richard was a supporter of both camps, though I don't believe he ever lived on either camp.

Greenham Common had a quiet but jolly Christmas.

The first event of 1985 connected with the peace camp took place not on the Common, but at North Peckham Civic Centre in London at the beginning of January. Here Tabitha Salmon held an exhibition of drawings and water-colours, which she drew during her stay at the women's peace camp during the 1984 winter.

One of the signs that a convoy was due to emerge was an eviction. A particularly nasty eviction on 14th January alerted the campers, so they were able to warn Cruisewatch in advance, of the departure of part of a Cruise convoy, at 01.00 hours on 15th January. This was followed by an incursion, on the night of 15th-16th January, when women found more Cruise convoy vehicles in hangars, and painted graffiti on them. Then, at 01.20 on 17th January, the rest of the convoy left for Salisbury Plain. Later, twenty-eight women, arrested on the airfield during the incursion, were released from the Interrogation Square.

Cruisewatchers tracked this convoy to a copse between Greenland Camp and Tilshead, where five of them were arrested when they tried to approach it. They were detained for some hours, given cups of tea, and released. The police refused to charge them with any offence, even when challenged to do so.

At nearby Orcheston, on 20th January, four more cruisewatchers were arrested. This time Blue Joyce, Hazel Bingham, Ann Hodgson and Victoria Lee Orba were all charged with entering onto MoD land on Salisbury Plain when public entry was not permitted. When these cases were presented to Salisbury magistrates, they were adjourned to 22nd April.

Snow fell and lay thickly everywhere and the temperature rarely rose above freezing during all the time Convoy 11 was out.

Cruisewatchers in cars were chasing across the plain, often on tracks normally used, even in dry summer weather, only by farm and military vehicles. Needless to say, some were pushed as far as they were actually driven on the tracks. Di McDonald was there, with her famous white Volkswagen Kombi. On at least one occasion the snow and ice got into the steering gear and jammed it solid, so she had to get underneath to clear the snow and ice to free it. Having one's steering jam as one is driving with passengers on board is not a pleasant experience. Out on the exposed plain, she and her passengers virtually lived in the Volkswagen for nearly a week.

Then, on the night of 21st-22nd January, Di, with four women passengers, parked on a tank track leading onto Salisbury Plain at Foxley Corner, near Urchfont. A Cruise launcher was coming from manoeuvres on the plain along that very track, on its way back to Greenham Common. The police could have politely asked Di to move her car out of the way and pointed out the offences she and her passengers could be charged with if they didn't move immediately, but they chose a different approach. About fifteen police, at least one wielding a crowbar, proceeded to attack the vehicle. The body was damaged, windows were broken, and women were dragged from the vehicle, which was then manhandled out of the way, causing more damage. Blue Joyce, one of the passengers, was taken to hospital in Devizes with her injuries, which is probably why she was not in the photo published in the *Southern Evening Echo* showing the women and their battered Volkswagen. When Doug Read came in response to the women's cries for help on the CB radio, he tried to read the number on a policeman's shoulder and was threatened with arrest for assault. The women in the Volkswagen were all charged with a catalogue of offences. This was the infamous 'Redhorn Rape'. (For further information see *Redhorn Rape* published by Campaign Atom, 34a Cowley Road, Oxford.)

Within a few hours, the convoy was back inside RAF Greenham Common.

Meanwhile, on 21st January, Greenham Women Against Cruise, in the USA, had begun their appeal in the Second Circuit Court of Appeals, against the judgement of the New York judge. On 8th February, the appeal judge ruled: "US courts have no power to decide the legality of Cruise missile deployment." (*Radiator*, April 1985.) This meant that these women and their US friends had lost the campaign to get US courts to make Cruise deployment in Europe illegal.

Cruise convoy 12 left Blue Gate at 01.00 on Friday 15th February. The twenty-five vehicles went to Salisbury Plain, whence they returned on the night of Tuesday, 19th February. Once again, cruisewatchers and Greenham women were out in the snow and frost tracking the convoy.

On 19th February, Carol Westall entered Greenham Common Airfield and was arrested with other women at Hangar 301. The authorities threw them all out without charge. Just four hours later, Carol sneaked in the emergency door of a bus without passengers, which had stopped at a gate to be checked before entering the airfield. (Unlike British buses, some US buses have handles which can be opened from the outside on their emergency doors.) She hid in the bus and was not detected, until it reached an area where troops in gas masks were on 'black alert' practice. She had her camera with her when arrested. She was detained by the Modsquad and questioned by their detectives, who wanted to charge her with a serious offence under the Official Secrets Acts, but later decided not to. It appears she was not charged with any offence in the end.

The proposed new by-laws for Greenham Common and Molesworth were published on 25th February, with twenty-one days allowed for objections. There was no copy at RAF Greenham Common! Someone had to be sent to RAF Upper Heyford (not yet affected by new by-laws) to fetch a copy. At this time only the two Cruise bases were named in the by-laws, but there was a provision for other named military establishments to be added. Section 2 (i) of the new by-laws threatened a fine of £100 for anyone attaching "any handbill, leaflet, sign, advertisement, circular, poster, bill, notice or object" to a perimeter fence. Also, there was a provision for a similar fine for trespass. The Secretary of State for Defence made the by-laws under Section 5(iii) of The Military Lands Act, 1982.

In February, the peace camp's London office, which had existed in several temporary locations for about two years, had to close. An appeal for office space in London or Newbury produced none straight away.

Chris Drake from Blue Gate, jailed for fourteen days, after refusing to pay a fine for highway obstruction, told the court, on 4th March "I am not paying £60 for doing a conga down the side of a road and obstructing nothing." (Quoted by Janey Hulme, *New Statesman*, 3rd May, 1985.)

On 5th March, seventeen Cruise support vehicles left in daylight, and were tracked to Tidworth Cemetery on Salisbury Plain, where they entered the Eastern part of the training area. On the same day, four other support vehicles entered this area from Beeches Barn, between Everleigh and Netheravon. They all gathered in Ablington Furze:

The convoy remained in the Furze for three nights, continuing what seems to have been a mainly infantry-type field exercise, with men of the Light Infantry posing as the enemy. Some of this training took place in The Wig, where one of two cruisewatchers, apprehended in the early hours, discovered the American rules of engagement – an M16 thrust into his throat. The two were eventually handed over to the Brits, one of whom, when told of the incident, commented dryly: 'No training'.

The convoy returned to Greenham on Friday 8th March, again travelling split-up and in daylight; but not unobserved by Cruisewatch. (Part of Doug Read's report, *Radiator*, April 1985. The M16 is a type of rifle.)

This convoy apparently arrived back to a lively reception as a 'blanket the base' action was taking place.

On 9th March, with the help of the NCCL, seven Greenham women won a legal battle with Ratepayers Against Greenham Encampments (RAGE). This was a local organisation, which wanted to deny the right to vote to people giving Greenham Common Peace Camp as their address. Victory meant that the women could sign on the electoral roll and vote – or should have done. Although RAGE were faced with a huge bill for legal expenses already, they decided to go ahead and spend yet more money on an appeal. The women were not allowed to sign the register until after the appeal was heard, which would not be until May. Convoy 14 left Greenham Common at around 03.00 hours on 18th March and went to Salisbury Plain. Greenham women had advance warning when three American supply vehicles left separately during the previous week and were tracked to Salisbury Plain, which they approached by devious routes. Cruisewatch was kept informed, so cruisewatchers were ready for it. On the way out, it was delayed about a quarter of an hour by a roadblock of cars set up by Cruisewatch on a single carriageway stretch of A34 about a mile south of Greenham Common.

Soon after this convoy stationed itself on Salisbury Plain, there was a mass trespass of about a hundred people onto the land around it. A cruisewatcher got into the cab of a launcher and left a message, before being caught trying to get through the Modsquad cordon around the convoy on his way out. This convoy returned to Greenham Common on the night of Thursday, 21st March.

On 27th March, Di McDonald was sent to Holloway Prison for twenty-six days for not paying fines of £172 collected protesting against Cruise. She got remission for good conduct, and was released on 13th April.

Chailing and Titewhai, two women from the Campaign for a Nuclear Free Pacific, who had just spent a month touring Britain and telling people about the campaign, visited Green Gate on 30th March, where a farewell party was held, before they returned to their homes on the other side of the world.

There were four events in March worth mentioning.

When fifteen women cut the perimeter fence, four of them were arrested, one being rugby tackled by a soldier. As she fell her head hit a concrete fence post. She was taken to hospital, examined and X-rayed. Afterwards she was released, as she was not seriously injured.

Another group of fifteen women had more luck, when they got inside the same fence and then cut their way out through an inner security fence. They found a third fence inside that and some had started to cut this third fence when guards appeared and all fifteen were arrested. Even though the authorities found two pairs of boltcutters, which they confiscated as they usually did, they charged only one woman with criminal damage. The other fourteen were released without charge.

When they entered the base and did their washing in a wash-house on it, three women from Yellow Gate were arrested and charged with the theft of electricity.

For an hour six Blue Gate women borrowed a military vehicle and drove it around the airfield, before giving themselves up to the Modsquad. They were each charged with taking the vehicle without the owner's consent, which meant that all six could elect for crown court trials. The crown court offered more chance to publicise the campaign against Cruise than did trials which only involved local magistrates.

At midnight on 31st March, when the new by-laws (substantially unaltered from the proposals of 25th February) came into force, many people were on the airfield, all wanting to be the first to be arrested for trespass under the new by-laws. Most, if not all, had climbed over the fence, as they wanted to avoid being seen cutting or damaging it on their way in, so as to avoid criminal damage charges. As soon as midnight struck and April Fools' Day began, the Modsquad moved swiftly into action, and arrested fifty-five people. Somebody must have been the first person arrested, but such was the speed with which the modplods worked and their reluctance to reveal times of arrests, that we don't know who it was, not that it really mattered. During the next six days, seventy-eight more trespassers were arrested. All of those arrested were charged with breaches of the new by-laws.

A crown court judge, in early April, imprisoned Ann Francis for one year, for doing £150 worth of damage to a fence on Greenham Common. This was the longest sentence given to any peace activist in Brit-ain, since seven were convicted on conspiracy and incitement at the Wethersfield Trial in 1961. (See my account, 'A Staffing Rota that Worked, and Arson at Wethersfield', elsewhere in this book.) There must have been a special reason for the crown court trial here, for at the time, criminal damage of up to £200 was normally dealt with by magistrates, and the defendant could only elect for crown court, with judge and jury, if the damage was over £200. Magistrates could only give a person up to six months in jail. Ann had pleaded guilty, saying her act had been a righteous one, and not an act of damage. After conviction, she was sent to Holloway Prison and was in there planning her appeal when the authorities told her she was to be moved to Styal Prison, near Liverpool. At Styal she would have been too far from London for her barrister to visit her, which would have made organising her appeal much more difficult, so she insisted on staying at Holloway, even though it meant losing some remission and being held in the punishment block. Then, in support of Ann, a fifty-strong march went from the Home Office to the House of Commons; letters were written; politicians were lobbied. Holloway was used for short-stay women prisoners, and for longer stays the Home Office transferred women elsewhere. Ann had to be moved. Later she agreed to go to Cookham Wood Prison, Kent, only a few miles outside London.

After months of preparation, a Quaker theatrical group called the Leaveners appeared at the Royal Festival Hall, London, on Easter Monday, 1985, with a new musical by Tony Biggin, financed by the Quaker Trust. This had grown out of the song 'Women of Greenham' in the January, 1983 'Roadshow'. *The Gates of Greenham*, a history of Greenham Common Peace Camp set to music, was well received by the audiences, and subsequently a recording was made (copies of which can be bought through the bookshop at Friends' House, Euston Road, London, NW1 2BJ).

"April 11 saw reports in many papers" (Ann Fairnington in a letter published in *Peace News*, 3rd May 1985.) of an unpleasant incident on the common. Hazel Rennie (a woman in her forties) and Jane Powell were sitting beside a campfire at Jade Gate on Wednesday 10th April, when they were attacked by two men with staves. Hazel was taken to hospital with two broken ribs, severe cuts, and bruising. Jane was cut and bruised. There was evidence that the attackers were two US airmen. Later, two airmen were investigated and cleared by police, who took no further action.

On 15th April, Paula Williams was sentenced to

seven days in jail for not paying a fine outstanding from an event in 1983.

At a special sitting on 22nd April, Salisbury magistrates dealt with the Orcheston Four: Hazel Bingham, Blue Joyce, Anne Hodgson and Vicki Orba. They were each fined £30. Some paid and some went to prison instead.

At 03.05 hours on 23rd April, Cruise Convoy 15 emerged in two sections, both bound for Salisbury Plain, but by different routes. Cruisewatch had predicted the routes correctly and had a press photographer out in time to photograph one section of the convoy on its way to the Plain. Soon after the convoy had stationed itself at West Down, near T ilshead, television crews were on the spot filming it, and activists were harassing it. It then moved to East Down, followed by activists, sixty of whom were arrested there on the Sunday.

During this convoy outing Tilshead Peace Camp was set up, when cruisewatchers parked in a lay-by beside A360 just south of Tilshead, on the night of 24th April 1985. Police arrested them and destroyed their camp. The women involved – Di McDonald, Missie, Amanda, Lynne Barlow, and Hazel Bingham – were all charged with trespassing on Salisbury Plain contrary to the military by-laws. There were no red flags flying at the time in the area. The place of their offence was a lay-by onto which any motorist could have driven, without any notice warning of prosecution for trespass. Adjacent to the lay-by were the huts of a small, infrequently used Army training camp, and this lay-by served as a vehicle park for it, though there were no signs saying it was Army property. There were no troops on the camp at the time. On the afternoon of 25th April, cruisewatchers passing the lay-by noticed that fencing of metal posts and wire had been hastily erected to stop other motorists from using it without permission. Di's charges were later dropped. The authorities knew she was going to contest them in court. The police proceeded with the others and all the other women were found guilty at a special sitting of Devizes magistrates. They did not appeal, which seemed a pity, as the charges seemed so ridiculous.

The weather was dry, and, although it was dark, light from camera flashes, vehicle headlights and flares enabled cruisewatchers to take photos and video film when this convoy returned on 30th April. The convoy was paint-bombed, and one of the vehicles was forced to stop on the approach to a roundabout because Ian Lee had parked his car in the way. This vehicle was unable to move for about a quarter-of-an-hour. Taking advantage of this vehicle being stopped, Ian Lee and Ian James quickly climbed onto the roof of its cab and painted, with brushes, CND symbols on the cab windows and windscreen. This appeared to annoy the driver, who turned on his windscreen washer and wipers, thereby turning a beautiful symbol into an opaque mass, which completely obscured his forward vision. At this point, it is important to note that this vehicle's crew appeared sober, and not under the influence of drugs. Certainly the two Ians were not under the influence of drink or drugs. There were no prosecutions for being drunk or drugged either. Some of the national press reports, with their liberal use of the word 'intoxicated' implied otherwise. None of the nationals, apparently, mentioned that the vehicle was stopped when the windscreen was painted, some giving their readers an impression of a lorry travelling along a road at speed, with two drunken maniacs clinging to the cab roof, while they painted the windscreen dangerously. The police arrested the artists and tried to caution them. They refused to accept the cautions, reiterated their guilt, and reminded the police that other cruisewatchers had photos and video film to prove their guilt. Still they were not prosecuted. Ian Lee believed this was for political and not legal reasons. The police were not so much frightened by the prepared Genocide Act defence arguments of the artists, as they were by the possibility of yet more unwanted publicity for the convoy which was supposed, according to the MoD, to 'melt into the countryside', which would be inevitable with any more court cases involving cruisewatchers. Also, they didn't want to publicise the fact that cruisewatchers had stopped the vehicle that was painted for a good quarter-hour.

Bob Naylor got a superb photo of the Cruise launcher with its smeared windscreen, just before the driver smashed the glass with a spanner, and resumed his journey to Greenham Common. Several newspapers used Bob's photo and, at the time of writing, bookshops are selling packs of Cruisewatch postcards including copies of it.

Just to add insult to injury, when this convoy returned to Greenham Common two women jumped onto a launcher and rode onto the airfield on it.

On 24th April, the appeal by RAGE against the earlier court decision to allow the seven residents of Greenham Common Peace Camp the vote was heard in the High Court. The judge, after listening to both sides, applied a touch of the Alfred Hitchcock and delayed giving judgment until 1st May. The vital county council elections were to take place on 2nd May.

In April, Rebecca Johnson, Sue Horngold, and Elizabeth Galst were tried in Reading Crown Court for their incursion into the Air Traffic Control Tower, and were found guilty. Sue agreed to be bound over in the sum of £50 for three years, but the others refused, and were kept in prison overnight. They again refused when brought before the court the next morning. Rebecca was sentenced to a month in jail, and Elizabeth to fourteen days.

Also in April, a group of women, including ten from Greenham Common, entered a BBC television studio in London while the news was being transmitted. They didn't manage to get onto the news broadcast, but did photograph themselves inside the building, which proved they had been there when the BBC denied it.

ZAPPING YET MORE CONVOYS AND CAMPERS GET THE VOTE (Spring 1985- August 1985)

For some time women on the Common had been feeling uneasy and some had fallen ill for no apparent reason. Microwave radiation was one of the possible causes.

In spring, 1985, Dr. Rosalie Bertell visited the Greenham Common Peace Camps. She was a world-renowned authority of the effects of microwave radiation. She confirmed that the symptoms were consistent with low-level microwave radiation. Since her visit, tests have been conducted and scientists have plotted radiation of great strength from certain areas of the airfield. So far, the authorities have refused to explain these radiations.

Greenham Common Peace Camp residents, who had noticed the funny effects as early as September, 1984, called the mysterious business 'zapping'. They were convinced the authorities were zapping them frequently.

Naturally, it was impossible to tell whether these radiations were merely a by-product of some process or equipment on the airfield, or whether the radiations were deliberately made, and directed at the campers. If they were aimed at the campers, the authorities could not only use the radiations as a weapon against them, but could also note the results, and keep the data to enable them to improve the radiations and make them more effective and train more operators.

Low-level microwave radiations might have been the cause of the extraordinary lethargy among the peace campers on Boscombe Down on the night of the big convoy. The radiations might have been directed at us from equipment in the modplods' caravan.

At the end of April, the Ascot CND meals-on-wheels service stopped for the summer. Many women had been very grateful for it throughout the winter, because there were immense, sometimes insuperable, problems attached to cooking on campfires on the common. Policemen, bailiffs, and the weather were all trying to extinguish fires and camping stoves.

On 1st May, the High Court judge gave his verdict on the appeal by RAGE; the seven residents of the peace camps were allowed to use the Greenham Common Women's Peace Camp as an address from which to vote, and they could vote in the county council elections on 2nd May. Alas, their votes made no difference to the composition of Berkshire County Council on this occasion. However, as the judgment established a legal precedent, it meant that any bona fide Greenham Common peace camper could register and vote. A large number of women could come and live on the common in time for the next election. They would have to surrender their votes elsewhere in order to register to vote at the Greenham polling stations, but if they did so in sufficient numbers, they would have a decisive effect on the next election.

Convoy 16 went out on Salisbury Plain ten days after Convoy 15 had returned. Cruisewatchers joined it there, and three Cruisewatch vehicles drove onto the plain on 12th May, to get nearer to the convoy. Ian Lee was driving one, with at least two passengers, when Army vehicles surrounded him, and he started to slow down. His car was then rammed by an Army Land-Rover, which wrecked his fuel tank and exhaust pipe. No doubt the Army were pleased with this damage done to the car, which had stopped the vehicle whose windows were painted by the two Ians on a previous Cruise outing. Nobody was charged with any offence, and apparently Ian got no compensation for the damage. Then about 100 people went on a mass foot trespass onto the plain near the Bustard Hotel, in an attempt to reach the convoy, which apparently did not succeed. Convoy 16 was paint-bombed on its return journey and entered RAF Greenham Common in the early hours of 15th May. No doubt it carried the note left by a trespasser, who had managed to enter the cab of a launcher unseen. Unlike the last person to leave a note in a launcher cab, this person was not caught on his way out from the launcher.

Much of the paint-bombing was done with a mixture called Greenham porridge. This was, as its name implies, originally made from porridge left over from breakfast and powder paint. It could also be made from flour, powder paint and water and no doubt some women found other ways of making a gooey, sticky, brightly coloured mess for throwing. Before the invention of Greenham porridge, open tins containing liquid paint were thrown, but this proved expensive.

On 24TH May, International Women's Day, five women of Stroud Greenham Support Group set off from Stroud on a fifty-mile walk to Blue Gate. On the afternoon of 26th May, four of them finished the walk. The fate of the fifth is unknown. Their walk was sponsored and was expected to raise about £400 for Greenham Women's Peace Camp.

London Greenham Support Group got themselves an office address, believed to be only a contact address for mail and messages, in Featherstone Street, London EC1, in May. The appeal had produced something at last.

About 370 women were detained during mass trespasses onto the airfield, in support of imprisoned Ann Francis, on the nights of Saturday 25th May and Sunday 26th May. Some of these women were released without charge. Those of the remainder who gave their names and addresses were released on bail, with several court dates throughout June. About eighty gave no information, not even their names, and police were unable to get information from other sources in the time available. These were held overnight, and appeared at a special sitting of Newbury magistrates on Bank Holiday Monday on criminal damage and trespass charges. I believe they appeared before the stipendiary magistrate, but can't confirm this. Without identification the women could not be released on bail, so they had to be fed and securely housed until the court sat. As their cells were full to capacity, and they were worried in case another crowd of anonymous trespassers descended upon them, Thames Valley Police wanted rid of these women quickly, so they moved hell and high water to get the magistrates court to sit on a bank holiday. The big advantage to the eighty anonymous activists, apart from jamming up the cells and making it necessary for a special court to sit, was that if they served their sentences without revealing their identities, they would have no criminal records in their own names from these criminal damage offences.

Those on criminal damage charges were pleading not guilty; they were claiming they had entered by existing holes, and had neither damaged nor cut any fences. They may have read in a local paper (*South-*

ern Evening Echo, 12th March 1985; see also 'Court Cases, Community Advisers, and Protest Marches' elsewhere in this book) of how I was cleared of criminal damage on Boscombe Down in a court case two months before, because I had gone under the fence without breaking it or cutting it. Some, if not all of these women, were sentenced to prison. Many of the prisoners were held in solitary confinement. Some were not given travel warrants to their home towns on release (though how one can claim a travel warrant to one's home town without giving one's home address is problematical) and at lease ten sent statements to the NCCL complaining of brutal treatment in prison.

The first Phoenix Gathering took place on the weekend of 1st - 2nd June, 1985. The aim of these gatherings was to get as many women as possible to the peace camp on the first weekend of every month, to give the camp a morale boost.

At about this time, twelve Greenham women nipped onto the airfield and painted an ugly 150mm self-propelled gun with pretty flowers and symbols. The authorities didn't seem to think the result was pretty, for they arrested the twelve women and ordered them to appear before Newbury magistrates on various charges on 21st June . Apparently they all gave correct addresses, but each chose to call herself 'Katrina' after Katrina Howse, who was sent to court charged with committing criminal damage on Greenham Common. Katrina claimed the authorities knew she had not done the damage with which she was charged and that she was being victimised. When all these 'Katrinas' came to court, their cases were adjourned.

Also around this time, the people charged with trespass during the first week of the new by-laws were appearing before the Newbury magistrates. One, Margaret Robinson, was jailed for seven days when she told the magistrates she would not pay a fine. Guilty pleas were heard from seven others, who were each fined £10 with £15 costs. The many who pleaded not guilty had their cases adjourned to dates in July and August. As a result, Newbury magistrates court was booked solid for six weeks starting on 16th July.

Ann Francis had her appeal heard at the High Court, in London, on 12th June. Her sentence was reduced from twelve months to six months in prison, plus a six-month suspended sentence. Of course, she had already served part of her sentence, so, assuming maximum remission for good conduct, she could expect release in July.

Greenham women Steph, Maggie, Dee, Karen and Jane were caught inside AWRE Aldermaston on 12th June. When arresting them, a policeman told them they were radioactive, as they had been caught in a contaminated area. They were subsequently checked and found free of unnatural radioactivity, with ordinary Geiger counters at Aldermaston. Later, they were put through more detailed tests at Harwell and again cleared. The women were charged with criminal damage.

At Reading Crown Court the five women objected to all the men in the jury and managed to get themselves a wholly female jury. They also cross-examined several Aldermaston workers in open court. The policeman who had told them they were radioactive admitted he had lied: "Yes, I told porky-pies." (Quotation from *Peace News*, 12th July 1985.) On 24th June, the women were all found guilty. Each was given a two-year conditional discharge, ordered to pay £30 compensation to the MoD and pay court costs, which varied from £50 to £100 per defendant.

Kathleen Cripps, a health worker and housewife, had been a magistrate at Bakewell, Derbyshire, since 1981. After consultations, local people had put forward her name as that of a person suitable for consideration as a magistrate and the Lord Chancellor had, after due consideration, appointed her to the area commission.

When a friend appeared in Bakewell Magistrates Court, on a charge resulting from activities at Greenham Common, Kathleen was not on the bench. She was outside, demonstrating with other supporters of her friend. This demonstration received much publicity, for it is not every day that a magistrate demonstrates outside her own court!

The Lord Chancellor got to hear of it and dropped her from the commission. He was criticised for doing so. Kathleen and the NCCL appealed against his decision.

I am reminded of Ivy Strachan, a magistrate in Loughborough, only about forty miles from Bakewell, who told me herself she had been to Greenham Women's Peace Camps as a supporter. I have not heard of her being discharged from the commission.

At Newbury Magistrates' Court, on 19th June, forty-five defendants attended for cases arising out of the mass trespass of 25th-26th May, and seventeen more defendants did not appear. Not guilty pleas led to adjournments for at least nine people; a dozen guilty pleas led to four women paying fines, seven being

each sentenced to five days in prison and one being given fourteen days. The Modsquad erred when making up the charge sheets, booking seven more defendants to appear before the magistrates on a Sunday, when they would not be sitting. These charges were withdrawn, freeing the seven defendants.

In several court cases this summer, women challenged successfully the actions of bailiffs on Greenham Common.

On the weekend of 6th-7th July, the second Phoenix Gathering took place. The bailiffs, who, throughout 1985, had been calling twice a day, towed off Fast Food, Blue Gate's mobile kitchen. However, this weekend Kingston Peace Group donated Crazy Daisy, a legally roadworthy camper van with cooking facilities in it. This presentation made a welcome high point to this gathering of about 200 women.

The hot days of June set the campers to thinking about lounging on the beach after a cool swim in the sea. They didn't have a beach. They didn't even have a swimming pool, but they found somewhere to swim. Outside the airfield security fence, across Bury's Bank Road, lay Greenham Lodge, which was being renovated to become the HQ of the USAF 501st Tactical Missile Wing. In the grounds of Greenham Lodge was a small lake, hidden from prying eyes by bushes and trees.

The court cases for the charges of trespass in the first week of April began before Newbury magistrates on 16th July and dragged on through August. The first defendants, Shelley Makepeace and Listy Acons, charged with entering the airfield contrary to the new by-laws on 1st April, proved that they had actually entered on 31st March (when it was not illegal to do so) although they were not arrested on MoD land until the early hours of 1s April. They were found not guilty as charged and then released. The prosecution solicitors then rapidly changed all the other charges, so that defendants were merely charged with remaining on MoD land – just being there, in fact. The rest of the trespassers were found guilty of the new charges. On 19th July, five of them were sentenced to seven days in prison. It would appear that the women's prisons were all stretched to capacity, for these women spent their entire sentences in Newbury Police Station's cells, with only twenty minutes of exercise daily and no slops buckets in the cells. Normally people are only held in police cells for a night or two, on bail before trial. Short sentences are usually served in Holloway or another convenient prison. Apparently most of the others were each fined about £25, with £10 costs, probably because of the shortage of prison accommodation. One was a highly respected Methodist deaconess, Sister Judith Watkins, and another was Katrina Howse. Apparently other charges of Katrina's were brought up at the same time, for she was sentenced to three months in prison for a total of six or seven offences. She continued to protest her innocence of some of the charges, and again complained that the authorities were picking on and victimising her, as she had been doing for some weeks.

Just half-an-hour into the dark early hours of the morning of Wednesday, 17th July , a Cruise convoy left Greenham for Wadman's Coppice, in the Imber Ranges, on Salisbury Plain, near to Deptford Down airstrip, which was used when Convoy 5 went out (Convoy 5 is covered in my account of the second 'Boscombe Down Peace Camp', elsewhere in this book).

On 21st July, Cruisewatch organised a mass trespass onto the Imber Ranges, when about 800 people approached this latest convoy. Around 100 were arrested and many of these were roughly handled by police. One Greenham woman was subsequently charged with assaulting a police officer. Others were charged with trespass and other offences, under the Salisbury Plain Military By-Laws. Protesters inside a fabulous Chinese dragon costume evaded arrest on MoD land, when police gave up trying to catch them, after the dragon had done some skillful manoeuvring.

On 31st July, the women's walk across Salisbury Plain from Silbury Hill to Greenham Common began. It is believed the walkers arrived at the Yellow Gate camp in time for the third Phoenix Gathering, held on 3rd-4th August, which was "jolly despite the wet" (Peace News, 6th September 1985).

Another walk, this time with twenty-seven women, set off, from a disarmament rally on Southsea Common, Portsmouth, for Greenham Common, by way of Friends' Meeting House, Winchester, where they spent the night. These walkers arrived in time to commemorate Hiroshima Day with the peace campers.

On Hiroshima Day, eighteen women went onto the airfield, and ten of these entered a silo area and inspected a silo, which they found to be empty. All eighteen were arrested and spent twenty-four hours in police cells. It is believed that no-one was convicted of any offence in connexion with this incursion, and there were no public court appearances, The MoD announced that no breach of security had

occurred and no silo had been entered.

Nagasaki Day was commemorated by three Greenham women getting into AWRE Aldermaston. After wandering around inside for some time without being challenged, they telephoned the Press Association from a telephone box in the grounds. When the Press Association phoned AWRE offices to check the story, AWRE police were alerted, but they did not find the women until a full twenty minutes after the women made their phone call. This was the second incursion within two months, and still: "The security was non-existent. The main thing that stopped us going in a lot of the base was our fear of radiation." (Lorna, one of the AWRE visitors, quoted in Peace News, 6TH September 1985.)

The women were released, but were tailed on their way back to Greenham Common, where each was arrested again. Initially, they were going to be charged with criminal damage, but then the police found a document was missing. This document detailed the duties of the AWRE police and listed the arms they possessed, including machine guns. On the second arrest the women were searched and interviewed, but the police could find no trace of the document. A day or two later, however, Peace News received a copy of the missing document, apparently from a source within the peace movement! The MoD announced that the document was not confidential. Subsequently, the three women were charged with the theft of the document and elected for crown court trials.

Also commemorating Nagasaki Day were twenty-seven women arrested inside RAF Greenham Common. They were painting and decorating everything they could, including some vehicles in a lorry park. According to the MoD, several vehicles were 'semi-permanently immobilised' (Ah! Jargon). When these women appeared in court, some paid fines and others had their cases adjourned to late August and September.

This is a good place to quote Churchill: "If you had just one more brain cell you would be a plant." (Quoted by Janey Hulme, in New Statesman, 30TH August 1985.)

In court on a charge in connexion with campaigning against Cruise, Greenham woman, Nicola Churchill made this comment to the judge when he refused to hear her reasons for going onto Greenham Common airfield.

Greenham women and local women, accompanied by young children, were arrested in Hackney shadow-painting, on Hiroshima Day. They were released when the borough council refused to press charges.

The MoD attempt to convict two scapegoats for the National Day of Action, as a deterrent to further fence-cutters, proved to be a damp squib when Jill Morony and Gloria Delmonte, on 14TH August pleaded guilty to charges of criminal damage totalling £65.76. The Reading Crown Court judge awarded each of them two years conditional discharge and ordered them to pay compensation to the MoD.

A convoy leaving Greenham on 27TH August ran through a blockade. The trailer of one vehicle ran over Ann Harrower's leg, and she was taken to Basingstoke Hospital with a multiple fracture. Thames Valley Police held an enquiry into the accident. They wanted to know why the driver did not stop, as he was required by law to do (unless claiming exemption under the Visiting Forces Act, 1942). Subsequently, further information became available to Ann, of which we will read later. This accident apparently delayed the convoy much longer that it would have been delayed otherwise. After the enquiry, police took no action.

Paula Yates and four others were sentenced to nine hours in police cells, on 30TH August. Paula claims she was held down forcibly by policewomen and given an intimate body search, while two policemen watched. The Police Complaints Authority investigated her claim.

PEACE CAMPERS AND CRUISE-WATCHERS RESTRICT CONVOY MOVEMENTS - OFFICIAL! (August - December 1985)

General Charles Donnelly Junior, commander of the USAF in Europe, told *Aviation Week* magazine in 1985, that USAF officers remained surprised at the persistence of Cruisewatch and Greenham Common Peace Camp. Convoys were "only able to move out into designated areas of Salisbury Plain about seventy-five per cent of the time". (*Aviation Week* quotation via *Peace News*, 6TH September 1985.)

The enormous cost of policing the convoys was the reason he gave: about 300 police were needed to shepherd each convoy along its route, with about 100 more keeping the women back on Greenham Common. Considerably more police would be needed if a

convoy were to leave on the day of a big demonstration there, so they did not leave during demos. The cost of policing each convoy was around £60,000. Also, the civilian police had a big say as to where the convoy went, what route it took, how the vehicles were divided into sections of the convoy and even whether it went out at all!

In spite of all this policing, cruisewatchers were still managing to stop convoys. So far the USAF and the civilian police had not fallen out, but if this had happened, it might well be ordered from above that a convoy leave Greenham without its civilian police escort. The modplods were already fully occupied with guarding the base and helping the civilian police on Greenham Common. Bussing in extra modplods would take time, and their officers would not be skilled in shepherding the Cruise convoys, which was different from escorting the Polaris convoys. Armed troops billeted at the base could be used to shepherd the convoy, but this would almost certainly raise big problems on the public highways in peacetime, with soldiers stopping traffic, and not a police officer in sight.

General Donnelly's revelations no doubt embarrassed the MoD, because they had always claimed that the convoys were not affected by the peace camp and Cruisewatch. Here we have evidence that they are not always free to go where and when they like. There is no mention of the additional cost of cleaning up the mess when the convoys are painted and of the Gloucestershire Regiment clearing up the litter after the Americans left the Cruise parking places on the plain.

Nevertheless, Cruise convoys, as they were sent out, seemed always to have hundreds of police to shepherd them around, but Camden Women's Centre had to move from its offices into Camden Town Hall because attacks on its offices were becoming frequent, even though the police claimed they were giving the centre policing twenty-four hours a day, every day.

September saw the camp celebrating its fourth birthday and holding its fourth Phoenix Gathering. Hundreds of people were at the camp for the four-day celebration, which combined these two events.

At the beginning of the party, on 5th September, a welcoming committee, including the Japanese woman Juki, dressed in an elegant orange overall, was formed to greet two women who had done something special. The two emerged from the woods, carrying sleeping bags and camping gear and walked towards the welcoming group. One of them was a

Briton and the other a New Zealander. There was nobody else there. The two women turned and walked along the track parallel to the fence towards Yellow Gate. The welcoming group followed them, through the woods outside the fence. An American car appeared on the track. The driver stopped and asked the women for their IDs. (IDs are identity cards, which must be carried whenever they are inside the base, by people living or working there.) The women just kept on walking. The American car drove off. When the women had almost reached Yellow Gate, two police vans and two American cars pulled up. The women outside sang 'Happy Birthday' as the two inside were arrested, after spending four days and nights camped in the woods inside without being detected until this happened. Had the women cut a quick hole so the women inside could have got out when they first reached the fence, it is almost certain the authorities would not have caught them. They wanted publicity for what they had done, however, and being caught at this stage would give them a better chance to get publicity, which would enable them to expose the poor security on Greenham Common and to further spread the campaign against Cruise.

Another version of this story involved three women camped inside the fence, in woods, for three days, and it was rumoured that, about six months before this, two women had camped inside the base for a week in the winter of 1984-85.

Jacoba Seman and Maria Pengelinan, from the Northern Marianas Citizens Committee Against Nuclear Waste Dumping visited Greenham on the Saturday. Once again, campers were delighted to welcome guests from the islands in the Pacific Ocean, on the other side of the world.

During the fourth anniversary celebrations, the bailiffs once again tried and failed to evict peace campers. This time one of the bailiffs got covered in red paint, and two women were charged with criminal damage to his clothes. It had obviously not occurred to the authorities that the bailiff might be a red spy!

On the Sunday, there was a picket protesting at the intimate body searches being carried out by the police. One woman lodged an official complaint, at Newbury Police Station, about her own body search.

There were many incursions, especially on the Sunday, and these led to some arrests.

Greenham women on an incursion at about this time found a Modsquad memo, with guidelines on photographing peace campers, which said photos "should not be taken against their will and no physical contact or inducement should be made to secure a photograph". On the same visit a small album holding photos of campers was found, which included formal shots of women in custody; also some random shots of women in custody, at the camps and standing at the perimeter fence, who seemed unaware they were being photographed.

On 28th April, nine women entered the base, and were all caught, and taken to Portakabin One (where arrested people were held). One by one they were then taken to Two and questioned there. These women were prepared, with a strategy ready for the photographer, to prevent their photos being taken. Part of this strategy was for each woman to say, and get it written down, when she was arrested: "I do not give my permission to be photographed." (*Peace News*, 18th October 1985, p. 18)

Thus the modplods knew if they wanted photos, they would have to use devious methods. They did. The first four women to enter Portakabin Two were surprised by a man who jumped up from behind a screen and snapped them with his camera. After questioning, they were taken to another portakabin, where they were held until they were taken, again one by one, to be charged in a fourth portakabin.

The next woman entered Portakabin Two with her face covered and asked the sergeant in charge why photos were being taken when the women had expressly withheld consent.

She got the reply: "You had the right to refuse when being questioned, but now you are being charged we have the right to photograph you." (*Peace News*, 18th October 1985, p. 18)

After some discussion and a hint that if she did not allow herself to be photographed, she would not be let out on bail, this fifth woman surrendered and allowed herself to be snatch photographed.

It appears that by now news of the jumping photographer was spreading, and the next women had been warned about him in advance, for all four of them flatly refused to be photographed, and kept scarves over their faces. These women were charged and released after three hours without being photographed. Had they been forced to pose, the modplods may have laid themselves open to prosecution for assault. Threats to frighten the women into posing for photographs for police files might also have been illegal. Otherwise the law was vague about photographing suspects. Already, there had been complaints from women who had been held by policewomen, and forced to pose for photos, a short while before.

The women on the 28th April incursion then contacted MPs and the NCCL, and one result was that Renee Short, MP, asked a parliamentary question beginning: "In what circumstances are military police entitled to photograph demonstrators after arrest?" (*Peace News*, 18th October 1985, p. 18)

Although the Military Police and the Modsquad are two different forces, with different powers in respect of civilians, they both ultimately come under the control of the MoD, as do the RAF Police, etc. Here Renee appears to be using the term 'military police' in a broader context, to cover all MoD police forces.

The reply was:

> It is usual practice of MoD and Home Department police forces to photograph persons taken into custody and suspected of having committed a criminal offence. These photos may be needed as evidence if a prosecution takes place, but if no proceedings take place, the photograph is destroyed. It would be administratively impractical either to return unused photos automatically or to invite witnesses to their destruction. (*Peace News*, 18th October 1985, p. 18)

The women who had been photographed on 28th April also made formal written complaints, as soon as they were released, after complaining verbally to the Modsquad Superintendent at Yellow Gate.

When the nine women were in court, they all conducted their own defence and cross-examined the arresting officer. He confirmed what had happened in the portakabins, and how the photos were obtained. The stipendiary magistrate, Mr. T. Maher, listened closely and confirmed that snatch photography was improper. Subsequently, after they had finished in court, the women approached one of the clerks to the court, and discussed what might be done about the photography. The clerk had a word with Mr. Maher, and then sent an official letter, signed by the clerk to the justices, saying that Mr. Maher considered it highly improper for threats to withhold bail to be used to obtain photographs, and that any confession obtained under similar circumstances would be of no value as evidence. This letter was sent to Detective Superintendent T. G. Hughes, head of the Western Division Modsquad Criminal Investigation Department, on 13th August.

Since Superintendent Hughes received that letter and the parliamentary question was asked, the Modsquad photographers had been less enthusiastic.

The nine women were all found guilty and fined £15, with £10 costs, which seemed to be normal for a straightforward incursion at this time. They were given the alternative of one day in prison if they did not pay.

Kathleen Cripps' appeal to the high court against the Lord Chancellor's decision to drop her from the Royal Commission on Justices of the Peace was rejected. She and the NCCL were now faced with a legal bill of thousands of pounds. They considered appealing to the European Court of Human Rights, but decided not to. Of course, Kathleen could still carry on in her job as a health worker.

On 18th September, in Reading Crown Court, Judge Blomefield sentenced Katrina Howse to two months in prison for criminal damage and activated four months of a previous suspended sentence, to run consecutively. This equalled Ann Francis' sentence of six months. On this latest charge Katrina was convicted on the evidence of two US soldiers. The other women who were with her at the time claimed she had no boltcutters and had not cut the fence, which was what she was charged with doing. She had lived on Greenham Common for three years and was consequently well known there. She was claiming she had been framed, and the authorities were picking on her. In her defence, she had read out a letter received at the CND office in London, purporting to be from an SAS guard stationed on Greenham Common, saying that Greenham women would be framed to get them into prison, if they couldn't be got in there any other way. Apparently, leave to appeal was not given. Katrina served her sentence at Ballwood Hall Prison in Essex.

It was at about this time that police detectives made what they said was an unofficial call at Yellow Gate to ask for the return of certain items taken from the airfield on a recent incursion. The detectives said they wanted the items returned directly to them, and they did not want the uniformed branch involved. The campers could not give the goods to them, as the documents that had been removed had been distributed to the press already, and the other items had been placed in a black plastic sack, labelled 'property of CID', and left outside Newbury Police Station. Some women went to look for the bag, and found it where it had been left. One of them then telephoned the police from a nearby phone box, and was put through to a CID detective, whom she told where the sack rested. Within seconds, a uniformed police-man came out of the police station and took the bag, observed from a distance by Greenham women. So much for the detectives' wish to keep the uniformed branch out of the affair! Subsequently, detectives arrested one of the women and were threatening to charge her under the Theft Act.

In late September, ten women were alleged to have stopped a lorry carrying a tank, and painted it. They were all in court on 30th September on charges of criminal damage, and the cases were adjourned to 16th October.

Also in September, the British Army had been having fun with Exercise Brave Defender. Their guards didn't succeed in defending Greenham from incursions: there were several during the exercise.

By the end of September, some women, brought to court on minor charges, were being sentenced to one day's imprisonment, detained at Newbury Magis-trates' Court or Police Station and released as soon as the court rose, because the prisons were full. One woman, sentenced to one day in prison, was locked up for precisely four minutes before the court rose and she was released. Is this the shortest prison sentence ever – or is it not counted because it was not actually served in one of Her Majesty's Prisons?

Throughout the autumn, evictions were continuing daily, and at times more frequently.

Phoenix Gatherings were held on the first weekend in October and on 2nd-3rd November.

On Thursday 7th November, a convoy of Cruise support vehicles went to Bramshott Common, near Longmoor in Hampshire. Before returning, on 10th November, this convoy split into four sections which travelled separately, to try and evade Cruisewatch. This convoy, incidentally, was the first to come out of Greenham Common for three-and-a-half months.

Section One, on its return, approached Yellow Gate along A339. Women moved into the road to blockade it. No civilian police appeared to be on the spot to stop them, so RAF policemen and modplods dashed down from the gate and dragged them aside. Just afterwards there was confusion at the gate, and in the confusion an American civilian car rammed Yellow Gate, putting it out of action.

> As the second section arrived the most dangerous incident occurred. A US Dodge Ram lorry saw a lone woman camper vigilling on the side of the road – opposite the camp — and for some reason careered away from her across the middle of the

road. A second Dodge Ram lorry drove straight at the woman who was standing on the verge, bounced off the kerb and flew across the road, and in swerving back out of the way of the oncoming traffic, overturned its trailer. After dragging ... along on its side for a distance, the trailer righted itself. (*Peace News*, 15th November 1985)

Further on in the same *Peace News* report, we read:

> Eyewitnesses say that the US drivers were speed-ing recklessly and that it's amazing no-one was seriously hurt. Women later took photos of the skid marks that the vehicles made.

Owing to the damage to Yellow Gate, the latter sections of this convoy used Indigo Gate to enter the airfield.

By mid-November, the accommodation problem in the prisons seems to have eased, and women from Greenham were again being sent to proper prisons. Anne Ingold, from Orange Gate Peace Camp, was sentenced to seven days in Holloway Prison for not paying a £15 fine.

CND National Conference at Sheffield expressed support for Cruisewatch, Polaris-watch and the peace camps. Chairperson Joan 'of Newbury' Rud-dock retired and was replaced by Paul Johns, who impressed Conference, before his election, by brandishing a piece of razor wire he cut in a 'Snow-ball' action.

Ronald Reagan of the USA and Mikhail Gorbachov of the USSR met in Geneva, for a summit confer-ence with nuclear disarmament and Cruise missiles on the agenda. This was on 20th November.

Some Greenham women believed that a fourth flight of sixteen Cruise missiles was delivered to Green-ham Common on the eve of the Geneva Summit Conference, but a phone call to Colonel Kennet, Publicity Officer of the 501st Tactical Missile Wing, failed to confirm their sighting. Not all the six flights of Cruise missiles planned for Greenham had been delivered yet. There was a theory going the rounds at this time that there were no real Cruise missiles at Greenham, and there never had been any there. No member of the public or reliable media had been shown a real one, and seen it stripped to prove it was real, on the airfield. It was believed that the missiles that had been seen there were all dummies and the real ones, if there were any, were kept in safe places well away from peace campers and would normally be used only in the event of a real war. It was thought that the convoy which went to Bramshott Common, and which had no launchers with it, may have met up with a launcher equipped with real missiles when it was there.

By odd coincidence, the American Colonel Kennet was working on an airfield overlooking the British Kennet River which flows through Newbury.

On 20th November, a Cruise convoy, including one control vehicle and two launchers, left for Salisbury Plain. This convoy moved about a bit. Vehicles were sent back to Greenham Common, and more vehicles were sent out. It finally returned in the wee small hours of the morning of 26th November.

This convoy was widely criticised in the media for its bad timing. Many commentators thought it should not have come out on the day of the summit, though, sadly, most of them would not have minded it coming out on a day when a summit was not taking place.

While this convoy was out, Cruisewatchers leafleted Devizes; about 200 people trespassed on the plain; and Tony Jillings twice got his car into the convoy and drove along with it until stopped by police, who then beat him up, allegedly, and charged him with various motoring offences. When the convoy returned to Greenham Common, there were 600 police shepherding it along the road – twice as many as normal. They were guarding every bridge and junction. They even had police at every private driveway between Newbury and Greenham common. Searchlights scanned verges. Because of this extra security, the convoy had to travel very slowly. As the returning convoy went in the gate, women threw paint at it. Some police got their uniforms splashed with paint, but continued working until the convoy had got safely home. Afterwards they were sent to hospital for a check, probably to make sure no paint remained in their eyes. None were detained for treatment, but Chief Inspector Bracken told the press they needed treatment because of "paint in their eyes". (*Peace News*, 13th December 1985) Women were thrown into bushes; one woman was repeatedly kicked before being arrested; and another was hospitalised with back injuries after being slammed into a bus shelter by police. Di McDonald told *Peace News*:

> The fact that no police were actually hurt showed the great restraint shown by Greenham women in the face of police brutality. (*Peace News*, 13th December 1985)

Of the thirty-nine women arrested, thirty-three were later released without charge, and six were charged with various offences, including criminal damage to police uniforms with paint.

The dull days of late autumn in the dole queue at Newbury Unemployment Benefit Office were enlivened for some unemployed Greenham women when they saw an old friend in the dole queue – 'Baldy-the-Barbarous-Bailiff'. At least he wasn't doing evictions again!

After an incursion on 30th November, there were eleven arrests. The detained women were remanded in custody for the weekend, and appeared in Newbury Magistrates Court on the Monday, when five were charged with stealing the USAF uniforms they were wearing when arrested, and the other six were charged with boarding a USAF pickup. One or more of the women charged with wearing a uniform may also have been charged with boarding the pickup, as three pleaded guilty and four not guilty to the pickup charge. The three women pleading guilty were each fined £15, and the other cases adjourned. The MoD wanted the women accused with stealing uniforms kept in custody, but they were released on bail on condition that they each sign-on at Newbury Police Station daily until 3rd January, when they were next due in court.

The twenty-one women who had driven across the airfield in a USAF bus on 4th November, 1984, went to trial over a year later, on 2nd December. The three charges of cutting the fence were dealt with earlier by Newbury magistrates and the verdicts were all guilty. However, the theft of a bus being a serious offence, the women were entitled to a crown court trial, which they requested and got. When the big trial began, the women successfully challenged all the male jurors, and obtained an all-women jury. The prosecution could not prove to the satisfaction of the judge and jury that the twenty-one women on trial were the same ones who had taken the bus. Because of this element of doubt, they were acquitted.

The sixth anniversary of the NATO decision to deploy Cruise in Europe was commemorated by the 501st Tactical Missile Wing, who sent a Cruise Convoy to Salisbury Plain. This provided an appropriate centrepiece for the peace campers' commemoration planned for the weekend of 14th-16th December, as it went out on 11th December and gave Cruisewatch plenty of time to organise big protests around it. On the Saturday night, lots of Greenham women joined a mass trespass onto Salisbury Plain near the convoy. It is believed that about 100 people were arrested for trespass on the plain and five of them were charged with criminal damage.

Meanwhile, on the common, campers organised a

demonstration with the theme of 'Widening the Web'. The original web was one of wool stretched over women activists, lying and sitting in the way of men and machines trying to dig trenches for sewer pipes on 21st December 1981. The web succeeded then. The widening bit involved the peace camp support network. During this demonstration, the base was embraced. This meant a row of people held hands all around the nine-mile perimeter of the airfield.

The weekend's events were well covered by the media. *The Morning Star* reported there were 25,000 at the 'Widening of the Web'; the police said 3,500. Janey Hulme reported sixty-six arrests at this demonstration, including three people charged with criminal damage and sixty-three with trespass. According to her, this brought December's arrests on and around the common to ninety-one, whilst the total for the month of November was thirty-seven. (Janey Hulme's 'Roll Call', in *New Statesman*, 17th January 1986.)

The media were out in force again on the night of Monday, 16th December, when the convoy returned. Cruisewatch got television cameras to the route, and the next day film was shown on television of Brixton-style riot tactics being used by police against non-violent demonstrators in a picturesque country village.

The MoD, to commemorate the anniversary, issued the first official photo of a Cruise TEL, with a World War II phrase to describe its location. It had no registration plate, and was off the paved road, "somewhere in England".

Bat-Dimyon was apparently assaulted by two policemen not displaying numbers, near Violet Gate, at around 01.00 hours on 15th December. After putting out her fire, which would probably have meant the area was in total darkness, the policemen hit her, she claimed. She said loudly: "You have assaulted me and I want your number." (Quoted in *Resister*, April 1986)

As a result she was charged with a breach of the peace. She was also taking legal action against the policemen for assault. There can't be many people who witnessed this incident, in darkness, in the middle of the night, near a minor gate. Nevertheless, Bat-Dimyon wanted anyone who saw the incident, or had information, to write to her, care of Friends' Meeting House, Highfield Lane, Newbury.

One of the women arrested during the 'Widening the Web' demonstration telephoned home, asking for reverse charges. She made a comment about being arrested, and the operator asked if she had been arrested at Greenham. When she said, "Yes", he said that it was a free call, and told her to take her time!

ZAPPING, POLICE VIOLENCE AND OTHER PROBLEMS (Late 1985-April 1986)

Bat-Dimyon was not the only woman reported as being roughly treated by police in late 1985. Lynette Edwell reported that Sarah Hipperson was beaten by police, and thrown into a ditch, and that police stated Sarah had been "attempting to escape up a tree", "creating a diversion" and "stage-managing an incident." (Quoted by Lynette Edwell in her report, *Resister*, February 1986)

The mysterious symptoms and ailments first noticed in September 1984 were slowly identified. Doctors were consulted (at least one Greenham woman helped here as she was a qualified doctor) and they found the following when they examined the women: headaches, nosebleeds, disorientation, diarrhoea, vomiting, lethargy, pain behind the eyes, pain in the ears, chest pain and skin burn. Many people said they found decision-making difficult and experienced extreme mood swings. Some appeared to be getting sensitised to whatever was causing the symptoms. Later, changes in menstrual patterns and menstrual disorders were reported. All these things were felt by both residents and visitors.

I recall a medical doctor talking about the effects of low level radiation on people, ten years before it was first detected on Greenham Common. The word 'zapping' was not used to describe it then.

Low level radiation was identified as a probable cause of the symptoms and ailments by Dr. Rosalie Bertell, an eminent electronics scientist, in the spring of 1985.

On the night of 20th December, in an effort to identify and locate the source of the zapping, twenty-one women forayed onto the airfield and entered the HQ of the SAS. They found no evidence of zapping equipment before they were spotted and arrested. Later they were released without charge, probably because the MoD didn't want the SAS humiliated in open court. If the regiment supposed to be guarding Greenham Common couldn't keep the women out of their own HQ, it was no wonder the women were getting onto the airfield most nights, and sometimes during daytime as well. Often they were not caught.

Katrina Howse was released from prison on 28th December. In a letter from prison, she had claimed that false evidence had been laid against her, and several other Greenham women. She also claimed: "The Cruise missile programme is not working at Greenham" (*Peace News*, 13th December 1985).

In an internal memo circulated in the base, the USAF commander summed up 1985 and said it had been a successful year for them. Accidentally included in the list of achievements was "… and we hit one peacewoman with a vehicle".

This was believed to refer to Anne Harrower, who was still receiving treatment to the leg broken on 27th August. It seemed an odd achievement. A copy or two of this memo managed to escape from captivity, in spite of the large number of guards and high wire fences designed to prevent just such an escape. At least two peace movement newspapers quoted it. In the end, poor Col. Doug Kennet had to admit that the author of the memo had been reprimanded.

Another Cruise convoy left Yellow Gate in mid-January. It was paint-bombed yellow by women who wanted the world to know it had emerged from Yellow Gate.

Campers were attempting to colour-code the convoys. The police guard was tight and nobody got near this one on Salisbury Plain. When it returned in the early morning of 21st January, some women got close to it and two were charged with criminal damage. One was also charged with assaulting a policeman.

Frosty winds moaned about Green Gate and through the trees on the night of Saturday, 18th January, as two women from Leamington Spa settled down in their tent for the night. The police from that gate had gone back to their warm beds, and only a handful of soldiers remained behind the wire there. Shortly after midnight, one of the women thought she heard a movement. She opened her tent flap, looked out, and was met by a hail of kicks to her face from a stout boot. The other woman was kicked through the side of the tent several times. Two men, with crew-cuts and dark clothing, ran away silently. They had obviously come prepared, with their dark clothing and silence, so they could run away and people would neither see nor hear them disappear into the woods, and of course, there were no voices that could be identified. They appeared to know the lie of the land, and that there were no police on duty at Green Gate that night. The soldiers refused to call an ambulance for the injured women, so someone went to Yellow Gate, and after some delay, the mod-plods there called an ambulance. The two women

were quite badly knocked about, and in hospital they were treated for eye, head and back injuries, along with shock. Civilian police did not arrive until three-quarters-of-an-hour afterwards and even then were reluctant to properly investigate the assault. The women had to show them what to do! As a result of this, a formal complaint was made at Newbury about police handling of attacks on campers.

On 23rd January, Newbury District Council held a meeting, to which senior police and air force officers, along with selected local residents, were invited. The press, public and Greenham women were excluded. 21st On January, a group of Quakers had met Brian Thetford, who was organising the meeting and he agreed to let a paid Quaker worker attend. Subsequently this invitation was withdrawn and the Quaker refused admission. Anthony Meyer, of Ratepayers Against Greenham Encampments (RAGE) was also refused admission, because he represented a particular pressure group. This notwithstanding, he gatecrashed the meeting, and was allowed to stay and harangue it. He wanted the council to take out specific injunctions against women living regularly at the peace camps.

This led to letters in the following week's *Newbury Weekly News* warning ratepayers of the cost and ineffectiveness of injunctions, one of which came from the Tory chairperson of the meeting, Councillor Gareth Gimblett. *Newbury Weekly News* also published a letter from Newbury Campaign Against Cruise Missiles, saying that if injunctions were used and rates increased to cover the cost, members of the campaign would withhold their rates.

Women picketed the Nottingham office of the National Association of Local Government Officers. They had found out that the Greenham bailiffs were NALGO members. This picket took place on 27th January 1986.

On the same day, in Oxford Crown Court, a group of women were fined £75 each. They had entered the base, found a Land-Rover unlocked with keys in the ignition, and took it for a drive across the airfield. This time the Modsquad took more care with their identification than they did with the women charged with taking the USAF bus.

Evictions were occurring daily, and sometimes even hourly. On an eviction on 27th January, which was probably taking advantage of the fact that one or two Greenham women were in Oxford at court and others were picketing the NALGO office in Nottingham, bailiffs stole the Green Gate mailbox, with mail in it, and put it all in the muncher. Thames Valley Police were informed, and, with Mr. Reeves, head bailiff, searched the muncher. They found an empty mailbox and a few items of mail scattered around. A complaint was made to an MP, who took the matter up with the Home Secretary.

In London, on 28th January, Cruisewatchers and Greenham women met MPs and discussed the increasing police violence on convoy duties, and on Greenham Common.

Copies of a request for an enquiry into the policing of Greenham Common and the Cruise convoys had been delivered to Thames Valley Police, the Home Office, Mr. McNair-Wilson, MP for Newbury, Mr. David Mitchell, MP (Labour, Basingstoke) and Berkshire County Councillor Trevor Brown. This request formed the basis for most of the London discussion on 28th January. One thing that particularly worried the people in the discussion was the paramilitary riot control tactics of the police in white vans, who accompanied the convoys. Another thing which came up was that Greenham women were frequently being turned away from Newbury Police Station when they went to make official complaints, while for some mysterious reason, Campaign Against Cruise members were better treated and received instant co-operation.

At about this time Cruisewatch postcards, including Bob Naylor's famous photo of a painted and stopped

Cruise launcher, became available all over Southern England for sixty pence per set of four.

Also at around this time the Nature Conservancy Council designated the non-military parts of Greenham Common a site of special scientific interest (SSSI). I am uncertain why this was done. Near Brockenhurst Road, I know of a cotoneaster that is probably the only one of its type growing in the wild in Britain. It is a garden escape from a distant garden and on its own wouldn't warrant such attention. There may be an esoteric reason for this move that could show itself later.

Contractors working on the airfield pumped water out of excavations into the Bury's Bank Road drainage system, which could not cope with the extra water. This water overflowed the road, just outside the Greenham Common perimeter fence. It being January, the water froze and the road became an ice rink. Fortunately, there were no serious accidents before County Councillor Trevor Brown wrote to Wing Commander Michael Marsh, the RAF Commander of Greenham Common, who got the flow of water from the pump diverted. The road was treated by the council and the ice thawed.

It is interesting to note that now the RAF had a wing commander in charge of Greenham Common, whereas in 1978 a squadron leader commanded both Greenham and Welford. A wing commander is one rank higher than a squadron leader and is approxi-

Van stopped at blockade

Photo of van courtesy of Upper Heyford Peace Camp Library.

mately one rank below a colonel in the USAF. This suggests that Col. Bacs was still the real boss on the airfield.

In January Greenham Parish Councillor Chris Ridler complained to the police about illegally parked vehicles on double yellow lines in Pyle Hill, near to a peace camp. The police told him they were not prosecuting the women because it took six months to get them to court. At the parish council meeting councillors instructed Parish Clerk Brian Smith to write to Chief Superintendent Colin Gillot, of Thames Valley Police, that this answer was just not good enough and that they wanted the drivers prosecuted. It was interesting to note that it was automatically assumed to be peace campers' vehicles at fault and not the cars of journalists, lazy local house-owners, door-to-door salesmen, doctors, tourists and visitors. These people never park on double yellow lines – or do they? There is, of course, the tale of one enthusiastic Greenham Granny, of about eighty, who had been driving for decades before double yellow lines were invented and displays a Greenham Common sticker on her car window. She often parks on 'double yellows' – and has never been prosecuted!

During January, thirteen women were arrested on the airfield. All were charged under the new by-laws, and prosecuted by the police.

The largest Cruise convoy for ten months, with four launchers, two control vehicles, two spare tractors, and support vehicles left Greenham Common on the night of 18th-19th February. The first section of Convoy 20 left at midnight and went by A34, A303, A345 and Netheravon, to West Down on Salisbury Plain. This secret route was accurately predicted by Cruisewatch. As usual, as soon as the first vehicles began to emerge from the base, supporters were alerted by the telephone tree. This alert was unique, for instead of covering just the area around Newbury where Cruise could roam, this alert covered the whole United Kingdom. Arrangements had been made beforehand for beacons and bonfires to be lit all over the country, and this night they were lit at Land's End, Stockport, Stoke-on-Trent, Ware, Manchester, Birmingham, Luton, Witney, Alderley Edge, Petersfield, Devizes, Southampton, Brighton, Portsmouth, on the West Pennines, and Peaton Hill (For further details of Peaton Hill, see the poem 'The Peaton Beacon' in 'The Moon Camp and the Rainbow' elsewhere in this book). There were also beacons, bonfires and torches lit, to light the way for Cruise all along the route.

There were several incidents. A police van in the convoy stopped, and police started beating one woman against the side of the van. She was then put in the van and promptly escaped out of the side door. So police grabbed someone else – Katrina – and the van drove off with her aboard. Katrina then had a tour of part of the convoy route, seeing beacon, bonfires and flares as well as a large crowd of cruisewatchers at Bullington Cross, before being taken into Andover Police Station. On the fast dual carriageway A303, the sides of Cruise launchers were paint-bombed as they sped past Longparish. Helen and Anna, who did it, were arrested and taken to Andover Police Station. Soon a crowd of Greenham women had assembled outside, shouting for their friends' release.

Meanwhile, the second section of this convoy left Orange Gate, at 01.00 hours on 19th February, and headed Southeast on A339 towards Basingstoke, where they turned West on the A30 towards Salisbury Plain. At one point on the route: "They arrived just as cruisewatchers were doing inept, twenty-three-point turns in the road, stalling engines, etc. … So protesters were able to walk along … about thirty stationery US vehicles," (*Resister*, March 1986) and talk to the drivers.

A third batch of vehicles left Greenham Common by A34 and A4 and approached the West Down traffic jam from the North. The rest of the convoy and the cruisewatchers' vehicles had already arrived at the turning off A345, where the convoy had to go up the track to West Down. Turning off a paved main road onto a narrow track, meant the convoy had to slow right down, and cruisewatchers running about slowed it even further. Hence the jam. All the military vehicles eventually got into the new security compound in West Down Plantation followed by at least two cruisewatchers – Blue Joyce and Simon from Southampton. The convoy was under the command of the new boss of the 501st Tactical Missile Wing, Col. Bacs. The massive police escort included twenty-five vans and innumerable cars and motorcycles. In some vans there were ladders, so the police could climb trees to remove cruisewatchers, and see over hedges and walls. This was believed to be a new development. In spite of all these precautions, and not forgetting splitting the convoy, the second section was stopped by cruisewatchers for ten minutes. Incidentally, this was the deployment on which Col. Bacs, whose wife had a passion for blowing the housekeeping money on antiques, fell and hurt his back. I, as a sufferer from back pain, sent him a get-well-soon card.

As this convoy was preparing to return on the evening of 24th January, what appeared to be local idiots, including someone calling himself 'God Squad', on citizens band radios, were disrupting Cruisewatch communications. This used to happen frequently and, as usual, in this case they were asked to get off the Cruisewatch channel. A cruisewatcher phoned HQ from Durrington Roundabout, by Stonehenge Pub, and said: "Er, you know who 'God Squad' is? Bruce Kent." (*Resister*, April 1986)

On 20th February, Katrina Howse was in court again. She had been found guilty several times previously on charges arising from NVDA against Cruise. She had been arrested on 6th February, after an action in which she was alleged to have done criminal damage. Women who were at the action came as defence witnesses and claimed she was not there. Katrina claimed that the charge on this occasion, like at least one previous charge on which she had been convicted, was a frame-up, but the magistrates appeared to take no notice.

Although evictions in late February were not as frequent as they were in January, they were still happening. People bringing firewood and supplies were threatened with arrest for aiding and abetting an illegal occupation. Council bailiffs gave police the registration number of one vehicle bringing firewood, and police supplied them with the name and address of the owner. This is certainly not normal practice with Hampshire police, although Thames Valley may have different rules.

Lucy Mallard was arrested on 25th February and she formally complained about rudeness and rough handling during her arrest and detention. It is probable that she was arrested during a particularly nasty eviction, which took place early that morning. Cruise had returned the night before. While the women were sleeping off the exertions of the Cruise return, bailiffs arrived, and started taking everything. When the women awoke, the bailiffs were rude to them. Bailiff Ducket then "banged a woman's head against a lamp post, and further assaulted her." (*Resister*, April 1986) She subsequently needed medical attention and at the time of writing was suing Newbury Council, Mr. Duckett's employers, for compensation. The police present did nothing and they said they saw nothing. The impending legal action seems to have improved the behaviour of the bailiffs, though how long this improvement was to last only time would tell.

Two women from the Campaign for Nuclear Free Pacific visited the peace camps on 1st March. One came from Rongelap, and the other from Belau, a tiny country with less than 300,000 inhabitants. At the time of writing, Belau was the only country in the world with a constitution declaring it to be a NFZ, although pressure was being applied to change this, so that an American base there could handle nuclear weapons.

Convoy 21 left Greenham Common on Tuesday 11th March. Cruisewatch had again anticipated this exercise, so there were plenty of cruisewatchers tracking it to Salisbury Plain. During this exercise, nine people were arrested and complaints were made about police behaviour. On the night of Monday 18th March, the real excitement began. Even the local papers admitted that 1,000 people watched the convoy return. The people had been gathered by the organisers of at least thirty-eight local groups from all over the area within Cruise patrolling range.

The police were nonplussed. This convoy was stopped for ten minutes on Thruxton Hill, on A303, by cruisewatchers. Bicycles were being ridden all over the place at Bullington Cross, each requiring its own motorcycle escort, to prevent it getting in the path of the convoy. Japanese monks and Paul Johns, Chairperson of CND, were among a crowd of 200 or so at Swan roundabout, where A339 joins A34, and the convoy had to slow while police dragged women out of the road here. At this time a bonfire was burning merrily right across the drive up to Yellow Gate, which was known to be the entrance that the authorities wanted the convoy to use. The women lit the bonfire about an hour before the convoy was expected. An air force fire engine came up to the other side of the fence, stopped and waited. A Newbury fire engine appeared, was told by the women it wasn't needed, and went home. Then, suddenly, more police arrived, put the fire out, and moved the women from the road. In sped the convoy.

The star of this exercise was the driver of a support vehicle, who overturned his vehicle on the A339 near Kingsclere. According to a BBC Radio Four report, nobody was hurt. Notwithstanding this, the road was blocked all of four hours, while the driver and crew kept people away from the vehicle and refused assistance from tow trucks, apart from the USAF wrecker, which righted the vehicle and towed it into Greenham.

Experienced cruisewatchers were developing interesting tactics, with some success in restricting movements of convoys. Masses of people were joining them, and their numbers kept increasing. Police were going to have to use lots more vehicles, and men, along with citizens band radio jamming, telephone tapping and air support, to keep convoys moving in future. For air support, the Optica, built on Salisbury Plain, had already been tried by Hampshire police, who helped with policing Greenham and the convoys, though it had yet to be used here; helicopters had already been used on Salisbury Plain. Splitting the convoys over several routes had in the past stretched Cruisewatch resources,and at times succeeded in evading the disarmers, but the increasing numbers of cruisewatchers were making this tactic useless.

Even when Cruise was out, life still continued on Greenham Common. On Sunday 16th March 1986 upwards of a thousand troops, airmen and police were going about their business on the common, and there were women living at the camps outside, keeping an eye on the place until the convoy returned. Outside Blue Gate, at 14.30 hours, members of the Religious Society of Friends, or Quakers, as they are commonly known, met for their sixteenth monthly meeting for worship, which lasted an hour. These meetings were supported by Quakers, and occasionally other Christians, from Berkshire and surrounding counties. They took place regularly on the third Sunday in each month, in the open air in all weathers and were continuing at the time of writing.

On 17th March, Blue Joyce was on a charge of criminal damage to a Cruise control vehicle at a special sitting of the county magistrates in Salisbury Guildhall. The case took all day. Blue defended herself, with Rebecca Johnson as her 'McKenzie friend'. Police produced a statement signed by Blue, purporting to say she agreed she had thrown the paint on the vehicle and why she did it. This was their only substantial evidence. Their witnesses disagreed, and there was some courtroom argument. In spite of this, Blue was found guilty. The prosecution was expected to ask for compensation of $792.92. Could they not have converted this into pounds and pence, or did they really want it in greenbacks, dimes and nickels? I wonder. However, probably because of this odd request, and the apparent sloppy presentation of the prosecution case, the magistrates refused the prosecutor's request for costs and compensation.

Before Devizes magistrates, also on 17th March, Mick Ambrose successfully pleaded not guilty to a charge of remaining on military land after being warned off. Originally he had been charged with the less serious offence of trespass, to which he was willing to plead

guilty, but then the MoD amended it to remaining on military land. He argued his case, and was acquitted. Often in court a serious charge is reduced to a less serious one to ensure a conviction in a case where the evidence may be insufficient to give the more serious charge a good chance of sticking. Here the prosecution were not able to get a conviction on the more serious charge, and one would have thought that they would have seen this possible outcome and asked to reduce the charge to simple trespass, but they had already acted contrary to normal practice in increasing the charge.

Other court cases in March included one for trespassing on Imber Ranges, after a convoy visit, where the signs said the maximum fine was £20. In spite of pointing this out, Sylvie Atkins was not given leave to appeal when the magistrates fined her £50, because the maximum fine had been £100 at the time of her offence. Apparently the maximum fine had been changed since the signs were erected. Bob Naylor was charged with returning to military land after being warned off it. What he apparently did was to stand on a public road, and photograph some military and modsquad vehicles, and a van containing children. The military tried to confiscate his film, and failed so they charged him. He was acquitted, but the magistrates refused his application for costs against the prosecution. Bob was lucky: the newspaper for which he was working paid the costs and probably because he was a press photographer, local papers criticised the quality of local justice after this case. Both amateur and press photographers are advised to take great care in taking cameras into situations where police or military are about, because nasty things can happen. All the following things have happened in England since 1977: An elbow has 'accidentally-on-purpose' smashed an expensive lens; photographers have been detained and had film confiscated; and when someone went to collect a film which showed scenes of Burghfield Royal Ordnance Factory, the film got 'lost' in the chemist's shop (see my account 'Burghfield Peace Camps' elsewhere in this book).

On the weekend of 22nd-23rd March, around 100 London women initiated a 'Heavy Metal weekend', with the campers, on Greenham Common. The main feature was the use of lots of tinsel, cymbals, and baking foil, to deflect the authorities' zapping radiation. There were workshops around Green Gate, where women campers and visitors learned about zapping, and how to combat it. Up to now the women had collected some evidence, but not enough to present a watertight case to prove zapping was used here. Experts from Electronics for Peace and a MP had helped them. The media had carried a few stories, not all of which were the truth, and nothing but the truth. Nobody outside the military authorities could print the whole truth. The search was hampered by a lack of equipment. When the authorities found out the women were searching (with what gear they could beg, borrow or buy) the readings on the dials of the searchers' equipment would suddenly drop, or go to zero, suggesting military zapping equipment being disconnected. To search for the source of, and identify, the zapping needed an electronics wizard. He would need a large van equipped with a generator and about £250,000 worth of electronic gear, parked on or near the common for some hours at least, without the authorities knowing it was there, to do conclusive tests. Also, there were problems getting enough doctors to systematically examine and interview all the people who were affected.

In North America there was considerable knowledge of zapping done with anti-personnel electronics. Its potential for crowd control was well known there. There is documentary evidence that the US military authorities have been sponsoring experiments with electronic weapons. Alas, in Britain the paranoia over government and commercial secrecy has prevented information about zapping in this country from leaving the places where it is known, and there was still no solid evidence of zapping on Greenham Common – only uncorroborated test results and the mysterious effects.

On Good Friday, 28th March, a Christian vigil, consisting mainly of visitors, was held at Blue Gate. Over Easter, many visitors came to all the gates that had camps. Several gates on the northern side had been abandoned because there were insufficient women to maintain a presence at all of them. However, the camp at Violet Gate had recently been set up again, and there were plans to start the others again, too.

Sylvie Atkins was due in court again, this time at Newbury, on 14th April, for touching the Greenham Common perimeter fence; Di McDonald, Simon Parker, and Blue Joyce were due to appear at Devizes, on 21st April, charged with trespass on Salisbury Plain; on 25th April, Dawn Russell and Vicki Orba were due in Pewsey Magistrates' Court, charged with painting a message on the road for an approaching Cruise convoy; and on 12th May, Mary Millington II and Rebecca Johnson were due in Devizes, charged with trespass on Salisbury Plain. There almost certainly were others, but this is all the information available at the time of writing.

Since getting her leg broken on 27th August, Ann Harrower had been in hospital having several operations and was still suffering pain and restriction. After pressure from local people, Thames Valley Police instigated an enquiry to discover exactly what had happened, and why the driver did not stop after hitting her. Obviously, the driver reported the accident to the police within twenty-four hours (a policeman probably went to him and asked for a report) and thereby kept within the law on that score. The police would not necessarily have shown this report to members of the public, and as the driver was not prosecuted, it was not used in evidence in court. As Ann was injured, the police were obliged by law to give to her the details of the driver and vehicle that several policemen had seen at the time and place where she was hit. This revealed that the driver of the US vehicle was, in fact, British and therefore was not immune from prosecution under the Visiting Forces Act. However, the police stated it "would not be in the public interest" (*Resister*, April 1986) to prosecute him. After the "We hit a Peacewoman" memo, Michael McNair-Wilson, MP, wrote to the commander of Greenham Common, asking about this accident. He was surprised to receive a reply from Lord Trefgarne, who wrote that it was normal for him to reply to letters sent to the commander of Greenham Common. This was news to everyone! If the driver of the vehicle had committed no offence, I would have thought a prosecution to clear his name of the accusations levelled at him would have been in his interest, but other issues, such as national security, were obviously considered along with the reputation of the driver, in reaching a decision, by the police. With the police on the spot not willing to act as witnesses, a private prosecution would have stood no chance, so now Ann was involved in a complicated legal battle, claiming damages against a driver, who has apparently caused her injuries, but was not prosecuted for any offence. Fortunately, she had several Greenham women who were prepared to give evidence about what they saw, even if the police were unwilling to give evidence in a civil court case. How different it would have been if a cruisewatcher's car had broken a policeman's leg!

Evelyn Parker was a well-known and respected, middle-class, middle-aged local villager. She lived in a nice cottage in a very nice village about twelve minutes' drive from Green Gate and was the sort of sensible, down-to-earth woman the daily press would tell you is typical of the local people opposed to the Greenham Common Women's Peace Camps.

During one of the many evictions in the winter of 1985-86, Evelyn was at Yellow Gate, when bailiffs went to move two vehicles. They called out for drivers. One appeared and drove off one of the vehicles. No driver appeared to claim the second, so Evelyn made a run for it, so she could drive it to safety and thus prevent the bailiffs from taking it. She was manhandled, and physically prevented from driving it, while the bailiffs towed it off to be scrapped.

Evelyn just happened to be a Newbury Quaker, with a record of demonstrating against nuclear weapons on Greenham Common that went back at least to Easter 1978. So much for the daily press!

At the end of March, there were about 1800 US service personnel stationed on Greenham Common, in addition to MoD, RAF and Army personnel. Under construction at this time were new housing and leisure facilities for these personnel; shops, including a vast supermarket; and an aircraft refuelling and servicing facility. This was costing US taxpayers around $250,000,000 – well over £100,000,000. There was much building going on inside the base near Orange Gate.

Outside the fence, building any structures on the common was forbidden. There was also a ban on new residential building in the areas under the airfield flightpaths.

I have made many visits to Greenham Common since 1977. On one visit a note was put under a windscreen wiper on my van, which was parked on the drive up to Yellow Gate. There were no double yellow lines then. The note said to contact a Newbury box number if I was prosecuted for parking on the common. I wasn't, so I didn't. On another visit, I was told that the Newbury District Council Medical Officer of Health had recently visited all the camps in an attempt to get them declared a health risk. The idea backfired on the council, for he gave all the camps a clean bill of health. On yet another call I was told that the women at Yellow Gate were lamenting the lack of mains electricity. One of them acquired a plug, a socket and a length of wire. The socket was screwed to a table, and the plug inserted. The wire had one end attached to the plug; the other buried in the ground beside their bonfire. A policeman wandered over for a casual visit and noticed the plug and socket. He asked what they were doing there. He was told that this installation was the opposite of an electric imitation wood fire, of which there were many in the front rooms of houses all over England, and that it was an imitation electric fire burning wood without the help of nuclear power. He withdrew, apparently satisfied with his inspection of this wonderful new invention. The next day, two policemen and an electrician with a big bag of tools turned up to investigate it and find out how the electricity was getting into it.

The women's peace camps on Greenham Common have no leaders. This has proved awkward to the media, who like a 'chairman' (a very rude word in the camps) or a 'spokesperson', or 'spokeswoman' to misquote. All the camps are of equal importance; one may be greater in size than another, but not in importance.

Now that the camps have been women's peace camps for some years, an understanding has grown up between the women and regular visitors. To help in the smooth running of the campaign against Cruise missiles – and all nuclear weapons – on the common – it is important that men:

a)   never approach the camps or gates

b)   never Cruisewatch by parking opposite a camp

c)   do not take action likely to invite arrest on or near the common

d)   keep off A339 between Yellow Gate and the Swan roundabout

Of course there are exceptions. Sometimes a man may be asked to deliver firewood or supplies and will usually be given permission to drive his vehicle up to the camp. Men are allowed to attend the monthly Quaker Meeting for Worship outside Blue Gate Women's Peace Camp. Women, on special occasions, invite men to join them, making details clear when they do so. Men are asked not to invite themselves. Men do not need to visit Greenham Common to see a peace camp or to campaign against Cruise. At the time of writing there are several mixed-sex peace camps in the United Kingdom and Cruisewatch needs men elsewhere.

The campaign at Women's Peace Camp, outside Main Gate, RAF Greenham Common, Newbury, Berkshire (the postal address) and at the other camps around the perimeter fence continues, and is growing as I write.

HEXHAM:

THE BUNKER, THE ABBEY AND WEST END METHODIST CHURCH

This peace camp had a tremendous impact on the people of Hexham, Northumbria. It occupied a prime site, on a main street only a few hundred yards from the town centre, with toilets and kitchen provided. Campers held regular vigils in the town centre and also at the bunker entrance, which was right beside the busiest road junction in town.

Local people had noticed construction work going on at an old World War II cold store beside the main Newcastle-Carlisle Railway. This store was conveniently sited for access to Hexham Railway Station and trunk road A69. Enquiries were made, and it was discovered that the old cold store was being converted to a sub-regional HQ for the government in Northern England and a deep bunker was being dug under it. This work was discussed at a NVDA weekend in Newcastle in early 1982 and again at the Peace Action Newcastle (PAN) meeting on 28th February 1982. The military connexion was checked, possible actions suggested, and it was decided to pursue the path leading to a peace camp. Planning and preparation began.

On 1st March, a meeting to discuss the bunker and the proposed peace camp was attended by, among others, John Fielder and some Quakers from PAN; Liz Harris; Rev. Sam Yeo, a retired United Reformed Church Minister; and County Councillor Rev. Eric Wright. Eric was the minister responsible for West End Methodist Church, and was the member of Northumbria County Council who had cast the deciding vote for the council to make Northumbria a NFZ. Another meeting was held in Hexham on 9th March. Sam Yeo, Eric Wright and sympathetic farmers were asked about possible peace camp sites. No site was found.

Meanwhile, activists were carrying out a survey around the houses in Hexham, asking questions about disarmament and the bunker.

Eric Wright was approached about a campsite again, and the disused tennis court beside his church, was discussed. The Methodists owned it. The tarmac surface posed problems for the erection of tents, but there were church hall loos and a kitchen available to offset this and the site was on a busy street near the town centre. Eric Wright agreed to it being used, and on Good Friday, 9th April 1982, the peace campers moved onto the site.

The Boys' Brigade was already using the kitchen, so a demarcation line had to be drawn there, but sharing the loos posed no problems. The campers had friendly relations with the Boys' Brigade; there were discussions about all sorts of peace issues with the adults in charge and some of the boys.

Campers were worried on Easter Saturday night lest drunks came onto the site and caused trouble. This didn't happen on the Saturday, though drunks gave trouble late on Sunday night, after the campers had returned from the Easter Sunday service in Hexham Abbey Church.

On 12th April, peace campers took banners to Hexham Peace Fair, where they sold beads, and gave out leaflets.

The campers soon got into a routine of protest. At lunchtime they held regular vigils at the Abbey in the town centre, and in the afternoons, when in the rush hour the road junction at the bunker entrance was busiest, they held regular vigils at the bunker entrance.

The police were friendly, which was a relief for the campers, because whilst the Methodist Church adjoined one side of the campsite, Hexham Police Station was on the other side.

Hexham Peace Camp sits beside West End Methodist Church. This 1986 photo shows it is a building site.

Of course, the big issue all over Britain at this time was the Falklands War. A local group called Northumbrians for Peace (NP) took the place of a CND group in Hexham. NP was not, as a body, opposed to this war, but PAN apparently was and Hexham Peace Camp certainly was, for it included members of pacifist organisations wholly opposed to violence. Helped by Pat Wilmott of the local Labour Party, campers gave out leaflets against the war in the Market Place.

News of the camp was spreading and visitors from other towns in North-Eastern England were calling. The local punks, who had been banned from almost everywhere else in town, visited, were welcomed, and declared their support for the camp. John Fielder was using the PAN duplicator to great effect in getting out information about the camp, and the campers included two very experienced activists, Jean Hutchings from Molesworth and Jean Charlton from the Committee of 100.

West End Methodist Church appeared to be split down the middle, with some of the congregation supporting Eric Wright in allowing the camp to be there and others opposing it, because they didn't like the untidiness, banners and things on the tennis court fence, wood smoke, and the inconvenience it was causing people using church facilities ,which the campers had to share.

The campers announced, via the press, that they were going to stay on the tennis court until after Operation Hard Rock, a military and Civil Defence exercise, had ended in the autumn. This surprised NP and the Methodists, who had not realised they planned to stay so long. The Methodists reacted against the campers and Eric had to ask them to leave. They left towards the end of April.

Margaret Wright, a peace camper who was not related to Eric, returned with two other people, to Hexham Railway Station on 1st May. Caroline Westgate, Secretary of NP met them there, and took them to Haugh Lane, where there was a plot of land not being used by its owners, the local council. It was near the bunker.

It was a real Blackthorn Winter, bitterly cold and snowing, when the campers erected their tents. Caroline apparently left. Then a policeman arrived.

The policeman asked: "Have you permission? What are you doing here?"

Margaret Wright replied: "No. When the peace camp was being planned, we tried to get permission."

Policeman: "This is council land. You know what the council's like."

Margaret: "What would they do to us?"

Policeman: "Send workmen to remove tents, etc.… We've had a complaint."

Margaret: "What would you say, in theory, if I said we weren't going to move?"

Policeman: "Council would remove your tents, etc.…"

Margaret: "Are tents the problem?"

"Yes," said the policeman. (I thank Margaret for writing down this report of the conversation as it happened, and for allowing me to reproduce her report.)

After considering the possibilities of slow removal, such as spending two weeks taking down a tent, the campers dismantled their tent. The policeman then told them he was not actually throwing them off the land, which meant they could remain, so long as they didn't erect a tent. The campers attempted to stay without shelter, but inclement weather and a lack of plastic sheeting made this impossible. Phone calls were made from a nearby callbox, and a local resident rescued the freezing peace campers.

The Second Hexham Peace Camp was all over in just ninety minutes.

Meanwhile, the Young Quakers (YQs) were holding their Junior Yearly Meeting in Newcastle. They knew about the bunker at Hexham and were in contact with Hexham peace campers – indeed, some Hexham campers were probably at the meeting.

Suddenly, about eighty YQs descended upon Hexham, which was only twenty miles away, and set up a vigil outside the Abbey. The Abbey didn't usually host services on Sunday afternoons, but this Sunday was 2nd May and a Boy Scouts' Founders Day Service was being held. The Rector, Rev. Timothy Withers-Green, came round a corner of the building to be faced with about eighty banner-waving Quakers. He went berserk and apparently had to be restrained, before threatening to call the police if the demonstrators didn't leave right away.

Not wanting to be prosecuted on breach of the peace charges, and seeing that they had made an impression at the Abbey, the demonstrators left and went to the front of the bunker. Some of them climbed the fence and entered the bunker, which was still being constructed and was not sealed off against intruders. Later they came out of the bunker voluntarily, without being arrested. The demonstrators then returned to Newcastle.

An inquest on the two peace camps was held at an NP meeting in Hexham, on 10th May, 1982. It seemed to Margaret Wright that the atmosphere there was very heavy, and there was much anxiety. A query arose about the Abbey vigils: Were they a bit too aggressive and impairing the good relations that NP had been establishing with the Abbey authorities? The secretary wasn't very enthusiastic about the extra work the camps had entailed (especially as it was she who was out in the snow with the second camp) and seemed to think the effort was counter-productive. NP had originally, as a group, supported the first camp, which got much local publicity, mainly in the *Hexham Courant*. In spite of an editorial criticising the campers, the *Hexham Courant* gave them much accurate reporting and several big headlines. This led to publicity for the bunker, which was what the campers wanted. Over four years afterwards, everybody in Hexham I asked about the camp, except for one new resident, remembered it and nobody was solidly opposed to it.

The story doesn't end there, however. One camper was a national member of the Natural Childbirth Trust. In October 1982, she attended her first meeting of a branch in Newcastle of which she was not a local member. The speaker, a county council scientist involved with Civil Defence, was the husband of the trust member whose home it was.

He told the audience he was angry at the cancellation of the Civil Defence side of Exercise Hard Rock, which had just occurred. He then revealed plans for a Civil Defence exercise based on Hexham. It involved troops, probably the Territorial Army,

Hexham Bunker (1986). Note the English Heritage sign at the entrance.

being threatened by peace protesters. The troops would have to contain them at Hexham, and stop them making a nuisance. When he told everybody the bunker was just an old meat store, our peace camper brought him up to date, told him what the bunker was, and revealed she didn't share his views. She left soon afterwards, because it doesn't pay to go into a man's home and call him a liar in front of his friends.

Clearly the government took Hexham Peace Camp seriously, even to the extent of using the campers in their military exercises!

In 1986, the square, red-brick, Sub-Regional Seat of Government, with its steel radio tower, dominated the lower part of Hexham. Inside there were reserved places for one cabinet minister, one police chief and one Army chief to rule the North of England in the event of an emergency, or nuclear attack. There was only one sign on the wall at the entrance: a small brass plaque saying 'English Heritage'. This referred to a separate, fenced-off yard behind the bunker, which had some wooden huts in it and was used as a local depot by English Heritage. The depot shared the same front drive as the unmarked bunker.

Despite local opposition, the district council bowed to pressure from the Whitehall government and voted to build a bunker for selected – not elected – officials under its offices in Hexham. Unlike the first tier of sub-regional HQ, this would be a small third-tier bunker for local government only. The vote to construct this was taken on April Fools' Day, 1st April, 1986.

THE UPPER
HEYFORD
PEACE CAMPS

Why and Where

The Heyford biplane bomber aircraft used by the RAF in the nineteen-thirties, before and during World War II ,was named after one of their airfields – RAF Upper Heyford, in Oxfordshire.

The USAF arrived there in 1951. The British government remained the landlord. In 1970 the USAF 20th Tactical Fighter Wing arrived. This wing eventually brought the F1-11 nuclear-capable fighter bombers and their brothers the EF1-11s. The latter flew with complex electronic countermeasures equipment designed to jam enemy radar, so that they and the aircraft they were escorting could get through enemy airspace.

In 1978 plans were announced to build blast resistant hangars at many airfields in Europe to a new NATO standard. This was in order to make them impregnable to virtually everything, except a direct hit with a nuclear weapon. To do this, the MoD wanted to extend RAF Upper Heyford, so that the USAF could have fifty of these hangars built, spread out around the airfield sufficiently thinly to satisfy the NATO specification. The MoD needed to buy a large area of farmland and told Oxfordshire County Council what they planned. Many members of the council wanted their plans passed in full and to sell them more land than the minimum they required, but Olive Gibbs (at the time a CND national councillor, as well as a

county councillor) led objectors into action. County councillors went by coach to inspect the land in question. After this and some discussion, the council approved the MoD plans and agreed to sell them part of the land, but not all of it. Olive and the other objectors had been only able to check but not stop, the Tories' enthusiasm to help the MoD. This land later became the Thirty-Acre Site.

In 1982, the airfield covered about 1,221 acres. It had a 9,600 foot runway, and a population of roughly 6,000 military personnel with around 4,000 dependents and 700 to 1,000 civilians. Then there were about seventy-one F1-11s and some support aircraft based there. (The F1-11 came in several marks; each time a new, more up-to-date version was developed, it replaced its predecessor; with the exception of the EF1-11, which was a special purpose mark.) The latest F1-11F had a nuclear firepower roughly fourteen times that of 'Enola Gay', the B29 aircraft that dropped the A-bomb on Hiroshima. Like the B29, the F1-11F could also be used to deliver conventional incendiary or high-explosive bombs. The additional 18 EF1-11s were due to arrive when the hangars on the Thirty-Acre Site were built.

It is believed that each F1-11 take-off cost about the same as a small semi-detached house in the area. Americans, incidentally, had bought several houses or rented them, and lived in the local villages. There were frequent take-offs and landings, and one end of

USAF Upper Heyford is about 15 miles north of Oxford, between the A43 Oxford-Northampton road and the A423 Oxford-Banbury road.

SOMERTON

A423

ARDLEY

TO BANBURY

RAILWAY TO BICESTER

A43

BRACKLEY →

← OXFORD

TO BICESTER

MIDDLETON STONEY

PARKING FOR COACHES ONLY

LOWER HEYFORD

UPPER HEYFORD PEACE BLOCKADE. MAY 31-JUNE 3 1983

Ⓣ = TELEPHONE KIOSKS
⋮⋮ = TRAFFIC LIGHTS
1 km = 50 mm (APPROX)
W.C. = TOILETS

UPPER HEYFORD

PARKING FOR CARS ONLY

COACH PICK UP/DROP OFF POINT

ASSEMBLY POINT

← A423

BFPO

CAMP ROAD

MIDDLETON STONEY RD.

KIRTLING

← BICESTER RD.

PEACE CAMP

W.C.

RIVER CHERWELL + OXFORD CANAL

OAK GATES

VILLAGE FARM

CRÈCHE

W.C.

30-ACRE EXTENSION SITE FOR EF111s

ELDER

RESIDENTIAL QTRS. ETC.

ROWAN (C's GATE)

LIME

W
S — — N
E

BEECH (MAIN GATE)

SPRUCE
CHESTNUT
WILLOW
HAWTHORNE

OPERATIONAL SIDE

ASH GATES

HAZEL

W.C.

W.C.

R.A.F. UPPER HEYFORD

the runway pointed between the villages of Somerton and Middle Aston on one side and Upper Heyford and Steeple Aston on the other, whilst the opposite end of the runway pointed directly over Ardley. Local people were thus in two minds over the base: they liked the money their friends and neighbours, the Americans, spent in the village shops and pubs, but they didn't like the noise their aircraft made and the risk of crashes. Some local people, including at least two farmers, were nuclear disarmers. The village of Upper Heyford and its airfield, lie in the centre of a triangle drawn between Banbury, Bicester and Oxford. The airfield has connexions with Croughton, Daws Hill, Christmas Common (See my account: 'Peace Camps in the Chiltern Hills' elsewhere in this book) and Barford St. John communications sites. Upper Heyford, Oxfordshire, is not to be confused with Upper Heyford, Northamptonshire, which is near the M1 motorway and has no airfield.

Following phone calls from Margaret Lowry, a student from Coventry, and Steve Barwick, a Sheffield student, to Steve Chasey, an initial tour of the area was made to survey possible sites for a peace camp, by Steve and Rip Bulkeley (of Oxford and Campaign Atom). Thames Valley police had blocked off all the suitable sites with wire. Maybe they had been tapping phones, and were afraid of another Greenham Common starting here. Then, in a phone conversation, Cherwell District Councillor Ru Reiss drew attention to the Portway, a disused and overgrown bridleway that came to a dead end, alongside the western perimeter of the airfield, and another possible site in Ardley Road.

On Easter Sunday, 11th April, 1982, a small demonstration against the nuclear bomber base was held with blockades at the gates during the day

That evening the Portway was occupied by campers, including Margaret Lowry, Steve Barwick and Annie Waterhouse, with tents and at least one caravan. Thames Valley Police soon moved in. Once again, they seemed to have found out about the camp in advance by phone tapping. The police harassed the campers, claiming that they had consulted the definitive map of the area held at County Hall and the County Council Chief Executive Floyd, and that they had provided proof that the Portway was no longer a public bridleway. After being there less than four hours, the campers had to move just before 23.00 hours. They adjourned, with their caravan, to the yard of Village Farm, which belonged to Ru Reiss.

Councillor Roland Pomfrey was a member of the Ramblers Association and this little dispute was right up his street. He proved that the police could have neither inspected the definitive map nor consulted Floyd, as County Hall was closed throughout the Easter holidays. He further proved, using his skill at dealing with blocked-off footpaths, developed through his being a rambler, that someone had tampered with the definitive map at County Hall. Therefore it was no longer a clear statement of the position of the Portway in law. There was also evidence that a fence was where it should not have been.

Once this had been sorted out, campers were told of the position and agreed to establish a second camp in the Portway.

At 13.00 hours, on Saturday, 17th April, 1982, local gypsies, at the request of Steve Chasey, dropped the peace camp caravan at the end of the bridleway. At the same time thirty people arrived on cycles and in under thirty seconds the caravan had been dragged down the Portway. Steve Barwick, Sian Charnley, Steve Chasey and Margaret Lowry were among that gallant band.

Within minutes a policeman arrived. He ordered the campers to move, as they were obstructing the bridleway, which was illegal under the Highways Act. Steve Chasey then told him of the fence around the MoD's fuel compound which was blocking off the last fifty-five yards of the public bridleway. This certainly constituted an illegal obstruction, as it was immovable. At least a caravan could be moved to clear a path for animals or people. The policeman's reply to this was forthright and honest. Faced with having to do some extra overtime, he replied: "You rotten sod – I finish my shift in five minutes." (Quoted from *Chronology of Upper Heyford Peace Camp* by P. N. Rogers.)

A police sergeant arrived and threatened to arrest everyone. Steve Chasey told him he would be sued for false arrest if he did so on the evidence of the map (believed to have been the altered definitive map.)

Soon after, lawyers Michael Payne and Andy Shaw arrived, and explained in detail the legal position of the camp to the sergeant, who then realised that he was going to need assistance if he wanted to arrest all these people. He contacted his police station on his radio.

By 16.00 hours the local press had turned up, as a result of a peace camper phoning them. They found three tents, a caravan and a crowd of campers and police. Annie Tunnicliffe told them that the campers would stay there until the air base closed.

Police officers kept arriving. Each one seemed higher ranking than the last. This process came to a head just before 19.00 with the arrival of Chief Superintendent Brian Romaine and Chief Inspector Andrew Wallis from Banbury. Still the campers would not go and the police would neither throw them off the site nor arrest them. The police left. By 20.00 many visitors, including USAF personnel, had begun arriving. A rota was finalised, to ensure at least three people would be at the camp every night. On some nights up to twelve people were able to stay. The youngest of these pioneer campers appears to have been Sian Charnley's three-year-old daughter, who helped promote a happy family atmosphere.

On 20th April the police called, and tried to move the campers again, saying the camp was an obstruction. The camp stayed where it was.

Also on 20th April, Councillor Roland Pomfrey went to the Radio Oxford studio, where he was interviewed. He asked, in his statement to Radio Oxford, for Cherwell District Council to be impartial, pointing out that in order to legitimise their case for the removal of the peace camp, they would have to move the MoD's fuel compound perimeter fence (which was blocking off fifty-five yards of the Portway beyond the camp) and many other obstructions on local paths and bridleways, caused mainly by farmers.

It is interesting to note here that when the airfield at RAF Wethersfield was fenced, several footpaths were blocked without diversions. At Burghfield and Molesworth, later, footpaths were closed with all the due process of law and were diverted, although at Molesworth the MoD did have to move a wrongly erected fence at Peace Corner. My accounts of the peace camps at these places give details.

Roland Pomfrey's interview was broadcast, and Radio Oxford quoted his statement on the other blocked footpaths, but edited out his reference to the fuel compound fence, which the government would not want mentioned. Nevertheless, as a result of this broadcast, the council relented and the peace camp was allowed to stay on the Portway.

On 24th April, Steve Chasey received a letter from Brigadier-General Dale W. Thompson Jnr, USAF Commanding Officer of Upper Heyford, confirming the Oxfordshire County Council had been wrong to remove the whole of the Portway from the definitive map at County Hall without the public consultation required by law. In effect this meant that the fifty-five yards of the Portway inside the fuel compound was still a public bridleway and the fence was an illegal obstruction, and he was admitting he understood this. This letter also showed that, although the signs outside read 'RAF Upper Heyford', the USAF was in command there.

The Oxfordshire Times for 7th May reported that Cherwell District Council were discussing the sale of the Thirty-Acre Site to the MoD. This adjoined Ru Reiss's land.

28th May was Women's World Day of Peace. To celebrate it, thirty women leafleted at the entrances to the airfield. They also sent letters to the Prime Minister and Tony Baldry, Conservative MP for Banbury Parliamentary Constituency, which included Upper Heyford.

At around this time, Upper Heyford Parish Council met and declared its opposition to planning permission for the peace camp. The Conservative Chairman, Paddy Quinn, owner of the 'Three Horseshoes' pub, vigorously denounced the camp as dirty and an imposition on the village community. It was suggested that his attitude may have been due to the USAF Commanding Officer telling publicans and shopkeepers that he would declare their establishment off-limits to his free-spending personnel if they served peace campers. Apparently no establishments were actually declared off-limits for this reason, even though village traders continued to deal with the campers.

Winston Churchill, MP (a right-wing Conservative, and a grandson of the late Sir Winston, whose country house was near Heyford) had suggested that CND should demonstrate outside the Embassy of the USSR in London. So while peace campers from Greenham Common and Molesworth were dying-in around the Stock Exchange and US Embassy respectively on Whit Monday Bank Holiday, five peace campers from Heyford, with a friend, 'died-in' outside the USSR Embassy. Although 7th June was a bank holiday in Britain, in New York and Geneva (where the UN had their main offices) it was a normal working day and it was the first day of the UN's Second Special Session on Disarmament. The 'die-ins' were to mark the first day of this great conference and to remind governments, particularly our own, that people wanted them to disarm. The six who demonstrated at the USSR Embassy were all arrested and charged with obstructing the highway. When they appeared in court the next day, 8th June, their cases were adjourned to late August.

In June, President Ronald Reagan of the USA, Commander-in-Chief of all US Armed Forces,

Original Upper Heyford Peace Camp.

visited Britain and addressed the combined Houses of Parliament. In mid-June one of his subordinates, the USAF Commanding Officer at Heyford, forbade his base personnel from having any further contact with the peace campers. The local presses made an issue out of this: one minute Reagan was saying the American forces were in Britain to defend freedom, but the next his Commanding Officer at Heyford was restricting the freedom of base personnel to speak with and socialise with their neighbours!

On Tuesday, 22nd June, Peter Baker and Ken Cole arrived at the peace camp from Greenham Common, on their sponsored hitch-hike around the peace camps. After a brief stop, they continued to Fairford the same day.

Mail was delivered directly to the camp. Its postal address was Upper Heyford Peace Camp, Portway, Camp Road, Upper Heyford, Oxfordshire. Camp Road took its name not from the peace camp, but from the RAF camp. As the peace camp had no phone, however, a local supporter had to act as telephone contact. Steve Chasey replaced Ru Reiss as telephone contact in the *Peace News* of 25th June, and was still telephone contact at the time of writing.

A Christian open-air church service was held in June, with the support of the peace camp.

4th July, US Independence Day, was marked by the campers and some visitors reading their own 'Declaration of Independence' for Europe at the Main Gate and erecting placards declaring: "British Independence from American Nuclear Weapons".

On 23rd July, the *Oxford Times* reported on a meeting of Cherwell District Planning Committee, chaired by Conservative Vice-Chairman Douglas Spencer. They discussed the peace camp. Letters supporting it, including one from Councillor Roland Pomfrey (not on this committee), were rejected by Spencer as ideological. This brought protests of political bias from Labour councillors. When a vote was taken, it came out five to five, so Spencer, remarking that two Conservative committee members were not there, used his casting vote, and the committee decided to evict the peace camp because it had no planning permission. It was clear they would not give the camp permission, no matter how well its case was presented. The same planning committee meeting cleared the plans for the proposed development of the Thirty-Acre Site by the MoD. Although planning permission was not normally required for MoD work, the MoD was, as a matter of courtesy, in the habit of showing their plans to local planning committees. Knowing they had no power to stop the MoD, the committees normally approved the plans without question. Occasionally they would suggest planting a tree screen, or some other minor addition, and the MoD usually obliged.

Campers Mark Harris and Richard Shappiro were quoted in the *Oxford Journal* as saying the people at the camp were all committed to fighting any eviction attempt. They also said campers were getting verbal abuse from passing US personnel. It would seem that the Commanding Officer's recent order to them not to speak with the campers excluded shouts of abuse.

During June and July 1982, campers observed three mysterious convoys of heavy lorries, escorted by police, visiting the airfield. They believed these visits had something to do with the construction of the Chemical Warfare Bunker, designed to store nerve gas and similar shells, in the Special Weapons Compound, though they appeared unable to get any official information about these convoys.

On 2nd August, a meeting was held by the peace camp and Oxfordshire peace groups, in the Upper Heyford Village Hall, which they had hired to organise the Oxfordshire Peace Alliance and to plan a big 'Farm Land Not Base Land' rally in September, The planned protest was against the MoD taking over the farm land on the Thirty-Acre Site, which had already been agreed, and developing it as part of the USAF nuclear bomber airfield. The MoD had not yet fenced the site nor had their contractors started work there.

On 20th August, Annie Hacksley, with thirty letters of support, protested against the legal refusal of the peace camp's request for an appeal against the order telling them to leave, which had been issued by Cherwell District Council. The camp still had several months before the final date, after which legal action could be taken against anyone living on the campsite.

In court in London on 24/25th August, the six protesters from the USSR Embassy demonstration were each given a conditional discharge for a period of six months. They apparently received a message of congratulations for demonstrating peacefully outside the Soviet Embassy from Winston Churchill, MP. After the court appearances had finished, "… supporters marched in colourful style to the offices of several national newspaper to complain of the lies told about peace groups. Their placard was a parody of the *Daily Mail* advertisement:

> 'WARS EVERY YEAR: STARVATION EVERY WEEK; LIES EVERY DAY.'"

[*Peace News*, 3rd September 1982]

At 06.00 hours on Wednesday 25th August, USAF Upper Heyford Main Gate was blockaded for a quarter-of-an-hour by twelve peace campers. Traffic had to be diverted to other gates. Nobody was arrested.

Later on the same morning, Steve Barwick chained himself to the USAF's flagpole. Police removed him and dumped him outside the base violently. He had, nevertheless, succeeded in delaying the raising of the Stars and Stripes for two hours. Steve was arrested and charged with obstruction.

On 26th August, brief, small blockades at two gates necessitated the authorities diverting traffic again. No arrests were recorded.

'Take the toys away from the boys' was the theme of the demonstration on 27th August. About twenty people (mostly adults) came to the Main Gate with balloons, yo-yos and skipping ropes. They played 'peace games'. This demonstration and the three actions preceding it, were part of a series of small actions planned to disrupt a week-long NATO 'war-games' exercise involving animated nuclear attacks, in which Air Force personnel at Upper Heyford were taking part.

THE THIRTY-ACRE SITE

The 'Farm Land not Base Land' demonstration planned at the village hall took place on Saturday 25th September. Some 200 people marched about nine miles from Bicester to Somerton Field, near the north-western edge of the airfield and joined more demonstrators already there to make a crowd of about 1,000. Peace groups from Woodstock and Kidlington brought a Channel Four TV crew to the demonstration, using a narrow boat along the canal as far as Somerton Wharf. Many demonstrators walked onto the Thirty-Acre Site from Somerton Field. The demonstrators left the site of their own accord, and no arrests were reported. This was the first demonstration on the site, which was still farm land. The sale, to the MoD, had not yet been completed. The main speaker at the Oxfordshire Peace Alliance rally was Dorothy Thompson. A symbolic wheatsheaf was presented to the USAF Commanding Officer. At the end of this rally, the peace campers went back to the Portway and everybody else went home.

Appeals went out for more people to join the Upper Heyford Peace Camp, particularly for an occupation of the Thirty-Acre Site on the weekend of 16th/17th October. On 15th October, *Peace News* announced the planned occupation and appealed for people to go along and help, without mentioning plans for a permanent peace camp there. The camp on the Portway faced legal action for a breach of the planning laws if it did not move soon. The obvious destination for a move was the Thirty-Acre Site! Here, not only was there plenty of room for another camp, with sport and open-air entertainment, but people hoped to use the new camp to block the MoD's planned development and return the land to farming.

On Saturday 16th October, Nigel Anstee-Algar, Nick Chambers, John Egan, Stan Kennedy, Fred McLennan, Helen Murphy, 'Musical' Martin O'Brien, Helen 'Tin-Tin' O'Reilly, Mike O'Reilly, Jean Pike, Richard Sampson, another Richard, David Sharpe, Adrian Stanley, law student Mark Taylor, Annie Tunnicliffe, Nigel Webb, William 'Bill' Wright and about ten others went up the track alongside the Thirty-Acre Site and through the gate onto it. (No roll of honour was kept. These names were remembered by people at the Portway camp years later and listed by Paul N. Rogers in the *Chronology of Upper Heyford Peace Camp*.)

By Sunday night a large marquee, which came from Fairford Peace Camp, and one or two smaller tents were up. The campers were comfortably settled, ready to deal with any visits from county council or MoD officials and police on the Monday. It was not long before they were joined by caravans and some vehicles.

Across the track was the yard and house of Village Farm, owned by Ru Reiss, where they could obtain water. At the time nobody was living at the farm. Behind the barn, to the north of the Thirty-Acre Site, was the land that the MoD would have bought at the same time as they bought the site had not Olive Gibbs and her friends on the county council stopped the Conservative plan to sell the MoD that land as well. On 18th October, the county council had not completed the sale of the site to the MoD and now the sale was obviously going to be delayed by the new peace camp.

On 5th November, Steve Barwick drew the attention of the *Oxford Times* to a document he obtained from the US Centre for Defense Information, which gave details of the planned development of the Thirty-Acre Site, and the deployment of EF1-11 aircraft at Heyford. This document was dated 7th April 1980 and showed all the plans as a *fait accompli*, proving that despite Cherwell District Council's noises of granting planning permission and how they claimed to be the power in the land insofar as new devel-

opment at RAF Upper Heyford was concerned, the MoD would have gone ahead with the development just the same if they had refused permission. As had already been made clear at Boscombe Down and Bentwaters-cum-Woodbridge, the law was on the side of the MoD.

Peace News reported on 12th November that the camp on the Thirty-Acre Site "… could soon be under threat since the county council will need to ensure vacant possession before the sale to the MoD goes through."

Throughout all this time, the camp on the Portway remained occupied and was not evicted. However, although some people from the Portway continued to stay for periods on the Thirty-Acre Site, the new peace camp became increasingly occupied by what one might loosely term 'hippies', who used to get out of bed very late in the day and even when awake had vague ideas of time. Steve Chasey, used to the early rising of farmers, summed up the difference: "One lot could read a watch – the others couldn't." (Quoted in *Chronology of Upper Heyford Peace Camp*.)

On 26th November, the *Oxford Times* reported that Steve Barwick, Adrian Goering, Rabhya Devishi and one other camper were arrested and charged with obstructing the Queen's highway whilst vigilling at the Main Gate. In fact, they were all on or beside an MoD road, which did not meet up with the legal definition of the Queen's highway when arrested – not on the Queen's highway outside the gate. The campers told the Modsquad that if they proceeded with the prosecutions for obstruction, they (the campers) would sue them for wrongful arrest. (As yet trespass on RAF Upper Heyford was not an offence.) *Peace News* reported that these arrests had taken place during a week-long vigil against a NATO exercise in November and that the charges were subsequently dropped.

USAF aircraft were flying to and from RAF Upper Heyford throughout Christmas Day.

After an organised 'alternative Christmas' (Description from *Chronology of Upper Heyford Peace Camp*) and many meetings and much careful planning, campers helped with a twelve-hour blockade with about 1,000 people, which succeeded in stopping road traffic from moving in and out of the airfield on New Year's Eve, 1982. Flying also stopped, and non-essential personnel had an extra holiday, although a skeleton staff remained on station in case it was necessary to fly the F1-11s, some of which were kept ready to fly at any time. A legal observer was stationed at each gate, equipped with two-way radio, but there were no hassles.

Beside at least one gate, civilian police and some Americans on the base, joined in singing Give Peace a Chance, with everybody being very pleasant. There were people on the blockade from Burghfield, Faslane, Greenham Common, Molesworth and London's Jubilee Gardens Peace Camps. Campers made an 8mm film of the blockade. Different representative groups were at different gates and the base was 'embraced'. With only 1,000 people it must have been necessary to use many scarves and other linking devices in places where arms could not reach. The chief speaker at this event was no less a person than E. P. Thompson.

Once again Parish Council Chairman Paddy Quinn showed his opposition to the protesters. He put a padlock and chain on the gates of the village playground in order to keep protesters (and village children!) out and ordered Leslie Archer, the publican of the 'Three Horseshoes', not to serve demonstrators. Paddy was believed to own that pub.

At the end of the action, everybody returned to their respective homes and peace camps. In spite of 400 police from all over the Thames Valley and several other military bases being there, nobody was arrested. The cost of the policing angered many local people, who blamed the protesters for causing it.

It is interesting to note that before dawn, in the early hours of New Year's Day, 1983, Greenham Common's most successful and famous incursion would begin. It had been carefully planned; its planners will have noticed that the number of police around Greenham Common would have been reduced to a minimum early on New Year's Day by two factors: first, it being a bank holiday as many as possible would be at home; second, Greenham women on the Heyford blockade will have reported to them about the Thames Valley Police officers and modplods from the Greenham area who were on duty at Heyford throughout New Year's Eve, and who would therefore be sleeping at their homes at dawn on New Year's Day. So the action at Heyford complemented the action at Greenham very nicely, and the government's tactic of moving both modplods and civilian police about the country in large quantities was outwitted.

The New Year was seen in by jubilant peace campers at both the Heyford camps, after their successful action. In contrast, the Greenham women took it quietly, in preparation for the morrow.

On Thursday 6th January 1983, a group of people including a baby, believed to have been campers from the Thirty-Acre Site, occupied part of Oxfordshire County Hall. They were demanding an answer to a letter they had sent some time before to the council's Chief Executive, Alan Brown, asking for a public inquiry into pollution, noise and loss of productive farm land that would be caused if the MoD development took place on the site. While they were inside, others leafleted outside. After about ninety minutes, the campers inside were escorted and dragged out, apparently without the answer they wanted.

On 7th January, campers blockaded the Main Gate. After twenty minutes police arrived and asked the fifteen blockaders to leave. The blockaders promised more 'peace games' if the USAF at Upper Heyford got involved in any more 'war games' and left, to the surprise of the police!

At 04.25 hours on Wednesday 12th January, Nick Chambers, Adrian Stanley and Martin O'Brien climbed the ladder to the walkway around a water tower on the south side of Camp Road. When daylight came, they were there for all to see with their banner 'No EF1-11s' (*see photo below). As they were over 100 feet up in the air, the Modsquad couldn't at first stop people from photographing them, and the press photographers clicked their camera shutters like mad.

Eventually the Modsquad threw a cordon around the tower and stopped the photography. They also prevented food from being sent up to the three activists and they were left exposed to the elements, with only the food, blankets and survival bags they had when the cordon began. Cold and hunger forced their descent at 08.30 on Monday, 17th January.

Water tower occupation with No EF1-11s sign.

The activists had climbed the tower to draw attention to the request, made by campers and other local people, for a public enquiry into the MoD development of the Thirty-Acre Site. In a public opinion poll fifty-eight per cent of the local people interviewed had opposed it. However, Oxfordshire County Council (probably mindful of the time and money spent by Suffolk County Council on a public enquiry over the extension of RAF Woodbridge and RAF Bentwaters and the way that enquiry had found in favour of the MoD) refused to call an enquiry.

When Steve Barwick had obstructed the raising of the Stars and Stripes in August, police found they could not charge him with any offence. So they unchained him, pulled him off the flagpole and dumped him on the pavement at the side of Camp Road. They then picked him up again and charged him with obstructing the highway. Steve strenuously pleaded not guilty. On 21st January, Bicester magistrates "… found police had used excess force in arresting him after freeing him from the flagpole". (Quoted from *Chronology of Upper Heyford Peace Camp*) They found Steve not guilty of obstruction and told the Modsquad to pay the court costs of £40.

When nine peace campers applied to join the electoral roll, giving the site on the Portway as their address, a retired county council groundsman, Eric Millar, applied to the Minister of the Environment, Tom King, against the acceptance of campers onto the electoral roll. The grounds of his appeal appeared to be that they paid no rates, and that their accommodation was temporary. On 26th January, Cherwell District Council held a special sitting to decide the matter. They found no legal grounds for refusing the campers admission to the electoral roll and granted them the right to vote. A precedent had been established: provided a person who was not registered to vote elsewhere could prove residence at the camp, an age of eighteen years or over, and sanity, that person could go on the electoral roll. There was no limit to the number of campers who could apply.

Persons applying to join the electoral roll did not have to appear in person before the council. They were not asked to do so. Had they been compelled to appear, Eric Millar's appeal would have succeeded in the case of at least one of the names – that of Richard Lakin's goat, Romana – and one of the campers might have been charged with a criminal offence for putting the goat's name on an application. The goat had been put on the list as a joke.

On 4th February, the *Oxford Times* reported Stan

Kennedy as testifying that four youths, in a group, had stoned the camp. Apparently this happened at the Portway and the youths made a quick getaway down the paved road from the site before police could be called.

On 7th February, nine campers from the Thirty-Acre Site were arrested after blockading the Main Gate.

Bicester magistrates found the nine guilty on 16th February. Upon refusing to be bound over to keep the peace, each was sentenced to a week in Oxford Prison. The blockaders were put in a van, which was then itself blockaded outside the court. This led to one woman's leg "… coming into contact with the wheel of the van". (Police statement) She went to John Radcliffe Hospital for treatment. Her foot, run over by the van, was not seriously injured. The police took the nine to Oxford Prison, but sixteen campers had followed them and now set up vigil outside the prison. Peter Ruddock, Vernon Truman and Donald Janice, who had recently come from the Holy Loch Aquarian Peace Camp, then camped outside the prison, using the survival bags that had been used on the water tower in January. Peter, Vernon and Donald were soon arrested and charged with obstructing the highway. There was one more time when vigillers were arrested, but in spite of the arrests, the vigillers managed to vigil until 23rd February, when their nine colleagues were released to hugs, cheers and great happiness.

On the day of the great release, county council workers were busy taking down big anti-nuclear flags, which had been hung atop County Hall the night before under cover of darkness.

The sale of the Thirty-Acre Site was closed on 24th February. The next day, a Friday, workmen sent by Stepnall, Ltd., tried to go onto the site to start erecting a perimeter fence, but were unable to gain access properly. About forty activists formed a human chain and refused to let them through the gateway in the old farm hedge. What few fence posts Stepnall's men did manage to erect during the day, in spite of activists hampering them at every turn, were later demolished with sledgehammers in the same way as the fence had been demolished on Greenham Common in July, 1982. Everybody then gathered for a musical evening at Gate 8 in the existing airfield perimeter fence, adjacent to the Thirty-Acre Site. During the night, carpets went over the fence. Two campers then climbed over the fence by means of the carpets and occupied a police observation platform sixty feet high and hung a "MAKE LOVE, NOT WAR" banner on it. They left the platform voluntarily when asked by a Thames Valley Police inspector, at 04.00 hours, and were not charged.

On Monday Stepnall's men returned to try and start work again. Campers immediately started hampering them, and were soon assisted by visitors who had come as a result of calls on the phone tree. Jean Pike, then aged sixty, stood up to the workmen alone, and when this seemed to be insufficient to stop them, rolled herself up in their chainlink fencing. For them to use it would necessitate them assaulting her. Altogether ten people were arrested for obstructing the contractors, and taken to Banbury. They were charged and got a solicitor, Roger Rose to defend them. He had then only a quarter-of-an-hour to prepare the defences for all ten. He asked for more time, but the magistrates would not allow it, so he quit the job, saying: "Justice is not being seen to be done". (Quoted from *Chronology of Upper Heyford Peace Camp*) No adjournment to engage other counsel was allowed, so the defendants, including a law student (Mark Taylor) stayed silent in court. They were each found guilty and bound over in the sum of £50 for a year. Obviously here the rule that no plea, or a silence, is automatically taken as a not guilty plea made no difference to the outcome.

On Monday, 3ʳᵈ March, Banbury magistrates tried nine people who had been arrested on the Thirty-Acre Site, sitting in post holes and standing by fenceposts. John Birbeck, Stepnall's foreman, said they were "... making work impossible" (Quoted from *Chronology of Upper Heyford Peace Camp*). They refused to be bound over, and so were imprisoned for a week. Dr. Gillian Duncan chaired the magistrates on this occasion.

The next day Adrian Stanley, thankfully not seriously injured, was taken to hospital after sustaining a bang on the head from a tractor he was blockading. Once again nine activists were arrested.

On the following Monday, as Stepnall's vehicles were arriving, activists lay down in front of them, got underneath them and hung on to their chassis. The magic figure of nine came up once again, when yet once more nine activists were arrested. Although some activists were arrested at least twice, the nine were not the same gang each time.

On Tuesday, 8ᵗʰ March, supporters were expelled from Banbury Magistrates Court for singing, "You can't shut my mouth when I sing". They did this when Magistrate Whiteley stopped Steve Barwick from making a statement from the dock. Steve, Colin Hodt and Paul Dolman agreed to be bound over in

the sum of £100 for a year. Tim Rawlings and Chris Henderson went to prison for a week.

On 9ᵗʰ March, five activists were arrested for obstructing workmen on the Thirty-Acre Site. The nine was in the date this time.

The next day, twenty-four people were arrested when they occupied a contractor's trailer and bound themselves to it with wool. Martin O'Brien and Fred McLennan climbed the police observation tower and hung a banner: 'NO F1-11s'. During the descent Fred fell thirty feet. He had to be hospitalised.

On the same day, Banbury magistrates were dealing with the people arrested on 7ᵗʰ March. Stepnall's foreman again gave evidence, testifying that: "At times it was impossible for his men to work, and one journey across a forty-metre stretch of field took an hour-and-a-half" (Quoted from *Chronology of Upper Heyford Peace Camp*). As before, most if not all the charges were for breach of the peace. For the second time in a fortnight, the same four people (Sarah Chard, Sian Charnley, Mark Dennison and Stan Kennedy) were convicted of breach of the peace. Again they each refused to be bound over and they were each sentenced to a week in prison. The other six activists (Colin Baker, Barbara Harrison, Richard Miller, Thomas Minney, Martin Robinson and Adrian Sinclair) each agreed to be bound over in the sum of £50 for one year. During the sentencing of the four, supporters in the public gallery sang. Here *Chronology of Upper Heyford Peace Camp* contradicts itself. It says all these ten were involved in actions on 7ᵗʰ March, but records only nine arrests that day. Either at least one, unrecorded arrest, took place or the extra case may have come from another day's arrests.

Overnight on Friday 11ᵗʰ March, Stepnall's men quietly finished the fence while the campers were sleeping. When they awoke they found a fence nine feet high, patrolled by modplods with dogs, cutting them off from the rest of civilisation. Food and drink were not allowed through and the only visitors allowed in on the first day of the siege, 12ᵗʰ March, were a BBC TV crew. The press people who came had to stay outside the wire and Nigel Anstee-Algar conducted a press conference through the chainlink fence! Vernon Truman was arrested and charged with criminal damage when he, along with other demonstrators, climbed over the new fence into the Thirty-Acre Site in the morning of the first day of the siege

There were now about thirty people living on the Thirty-Acre Site, all inside the new fence, where

Nic on the caravan roof.

there had only been six living at the beginning of January

While the siege was continuing, campers were also in Banbury appearing before the magistrates. Some will no doubt have left the Thirty-Acre Site to attend court, only to return and find it impossible to get back in.

Richard Sampson, Annie Tunnicliffe and Bill Wright agreed to be bound over when they appeared before Banbury magistrates on 15th March, but Catherine Robinson and Peter McFail were jailed for a week on charges arising from the same direct action, which involved occupying a tractor and interfering with fence posts. Catherine and Peter were put in a van to go to prison and it was blockaded by a crowd of protesters. Fred McLennan and one other person wriggled under it and were arrested.

Meanwhile in the court next door, five people (Dominic Fletcher, Wendy Graham, Eric Morrison, David Sharpe and Mike Sparks) were convicted of breach of the peace on 9th March. They all agreed to be bound over.

Although visitors and newcomers were stopped from entering the site completely, campers were allowed in and out of the gates towards the end of the siege of the Thirty-Acre Site. However, each person going through the gate was thoroughly searched; searches took up to ninety minutes each. This prevented food, drink and other supplies from getting onto the site.

Thursday, 17th March, was a cloudy but dry day with a cold wind. At about 09.30 hours the telephone tree alerted the Thirty-Acre Site occupiers that their eviction was im-

minent. As they had no telephone on the site, the message must have either been relayed to them from the tree by CB radio or by someone coming up to the fence and speaking a warning through the fence. At 10.00 about 100 modplods and RAF personnel arrived with tow-trucks and gave the campers half-an-hour in which to leave under their own steam. They got their belongings together and into the caravans, but did not leave, as they had no tow-trucks of their own on site. Adrian sang peace songs, with his guitar, on the roof of his caravan, while Nick, David Sharpe, Jackie and Zen also got onto caravan roofs and others, including Hazel Webb and Nigel, barricaded themselves inside caravans, shouting: "Where are your eviction orders?" It took until noon for the modplods and RAF personnel to get all the caravans hitched to their vehicles. Although the campers did not appear to be actually obstructing them, they weren't helping either! Then, with retreat inevitable and imminent, Zenophone climbed the camp flagpole and struck their flag . Down came the pole, too. A few minutes later the odd convoy retreated through the gate onto the track and headed north. There were apparently no arrests during the eviction.

Immediately the convoy pulled into a lay-by on A43 trunk road at Ardley, the camp flag went up again. The halt had been necessitated by a caravan axle breaking. The campers settled there for awhile. They threatened to return to the Thirty-Acre Site. Their eviction was illegal on at least two counts: the

Xenophone on the flagpole

authorities had not taken out an order in possession, which might have taken much more time than the procedure adopted; and towing a caravan with a passenger aboard on a public highway had only recently been made illegal, following one or two horrific accidents involving caravan passengers. Passengers had not only been in the caravans, but had also been on the roofs as they were being towed. Proving all this in court and getting convictions and compensation, would have involved heavy legal expenses for the campers, so they were unable to pursue these matters through the courts, much to their disappointment and that of their lawyers.

After a spell at Ardley, the caravans came to a stop at the Portway and swelled that camp. Sid Rawle, famous since his days with the Slough Anarchists in the late sixties, was one of the occupiers who came with the caravans to the Portway.

A sentry box was erected on the Thirty-Acre Site to enable the Modsquad to add a permanent presence to their patrols if needed.

There were several other court cases, all before Banbury magistrates. The court dates appear to have been 16th, 21st, 29th and 30th March, though there may have been other dates as well. Anne Quicke and Lucienne Jenkins refused to be bound over and were imprisoned for a week; Anthony Davis, Wendy Graham, Chris Henderson, Colin Hodt, Dr. Levene (of Campaign Atom), Anne Olesson, and Adrian Stanley all agreed to be bound over to keep the peace. In a five-hour hearing, Nigel Anstee-Algar, Helen Blackwell, Jennifer Hammond, Colin Patrick, Tim Quentin, David Sharpe and Nouala Young each agreed to be bound over to keep the peace in a sum of £50. Fred McLennan was fined £30 for obstructing a van taking two prisoners from Banbury Court to prison. There may have been other convictions, but records are incomplete. It is known that seventy-three people were arrested on the Thirty-Acre Site up to Monday morning, 14th March, and there may have been one more arrest known only to the *Peace News* reporter, for that renowned newspaper reported seventy-four.

On Sunday, 20th March, 150 people gathered on the track by the new fence for a Christian service, led by Sidney Hinks. Franciscan friars planted white crosses and other people put wreaths on the new fence.

Stan Kennedy began a week-long vigil outside Oxford Prison for the activists jailed within its walls on 21st March. As people given a week in prison on a Monday are usually released on a Friday, to encourage good behaviour and to keep the weekend prison population down, Stan was able to end his vigil on 25th March.

On the same day Cherwell District Council revealed in discussions that there were plans for 2,000 new married quarters on the airfield, but the Commanding Officer said he only wanted to erect 900. It would appear that Upper Heyford Parish Council also met on that day as it is reported that they were discussing the regulation of flight paths for the USAF aircraft and ways to reduce their engine noise. Probably this was at a meeting held to sort out the final details of the annual parish meeting, which was to be held on April Fools' Day, 1st April.

At the annual parish meeting, Parish Council Chairman Paddy Quinn predictably attacked the peace camp for litter and disruption, especially for litter and disruption caused by the New Year's Eve blockade. Certainly the peace campers and their activities had caused some disruption, but it was not so certain who had caused the litter. (Whilst peace campers were willing to co-operate with villagers to minimise disruption, villagers like Paddy Quinn were unwilling to co-operate with them. No peace campers ever appear to have been prosecuted for dumping litter at Upper Heyford, and this also applied to visiting demonstrators. Complaints were vague and apparently didn't name individual campers or specific incidents. USAF personnel, visitors from cities and even careless villagers appeared to drop litter, but there were no complaints about them.) Margaret Lowry and two other peace campers were ejected from the Village Hall during this meeting and banned from it for all time, apparently after trying to raise support for their opposition to the MoD development of the Thirty-Acre Site. Councillor Blythe (Cherwell District Council) said it could take months to move the peace camp, even though it should not have been there in the Portway. It had no planning permission. He argued that the other site had been cleared because it was on MoD land, and the MoD were able to use their own personnel to move that peace camp. His district council didn't have as many spare men and vehicles as the MoD had, and, unlike the MoD, they had to use expensive and time-consuming legal eviction procedures.

With the county council wanting the Thirty-Acre Site cleared for the MoD; the MoD actually clearing it themselves; the parish council wanting both camps evicted, but not being willing to pay for it; and the district council (unable to move the Portway Camp by getting police to read the riot act and the obstruction law) denying the Portway Camp planning permission and then claiming it was illegal because it had no planning permission, the eviction situation was somewhat chaotic! However *Radiator* for April 1983, briefly explained the situation of the Portway Camp: "The Peace Camp had been served with what amounted to a notice to quit in November. They had until Feb. 1 to comply with planning regulations. An appeal against this decision was granted, and then dismissed. They are now appealing against this decision to a High Court."

When the Portway Camp and the Thirty-Acre Site were both in operation, they had two different ways of working. Remember what was said about one lot being able to read a watch and the other lot not being able to read one. The Portway campers generally did the paperwork and produced and distributed advance information to get people to come to events. Much of the information I have used in this account, along with several photographs, came from the Portway Peace Camp. Most of the Portway campers avoided NVDA, and thus spent less time in court and in jail than did the others, some of whom, on returning from Banbury Magistrates Court or prison, immediately took action against the new fence for a second or third time, thus inviting another arrest. They took part in NVDA at County Hall, too, with a sit-in and later a flag on the roof.

Now that the two camps were together, friction developed between campers, though at this stage it was not serious.

The camp in the Portway grew to six caravans and a bicycle shed, along with temporary tents, benders and a communal geodesic dome. I'm sure Richard Buckminster Fuller would have been amazed to see his revolutionary building method in use here!

THE BIG PEACE PENTECOST AND THE LONG BLOCKADE OF 1983

Campers in the Portway awoke to terrifyingly loud bangs at about 03.30 hours on 8th or 10th April (*Chronology of Upper Heyford Peace Camp* gives 8th April. *Radiator* for May 1983 clearly identifies it as 10th April, both in a news report and in a feature.). At first they thought guns were being fired at them, but the bangs were apparently fireworks. American accents were heard as people ran away. In addition to exploding fireworks, the visitors left a crude incendiary bomb made out of a pack of matches and a petrol-soaked rag packed into a baked bean tin underneath a caravan. It exploded but only did minor damage. Police were called and inspected the firebomb. No prosecutions resulted from their somewhat unenthusiastic enquiries.

This was not the only incident of its kind. Already verbal abuse and stones had been directed at the caravans on several occasions, and windows had been broken.

On Sunday, 10th April, Kidlington Peace Group and the campers organised a sponsored 'pedal and plod', with people walking, running and cycling around the airfield as near to the perimeter fence as possible and outside it. This event was a remarkable success, given the existing circumstances, and it raised about £200.

CND National Council (the governing body of CND throughout the United Kingdom) had met on the weekend of 15th-16th January, and had decided to support a proposal for a week-long blockade of RAF Upper Heyford. National advance publicity had been organised and the first of it had gone out by April. On 10th April campers met and divided Britain into eight regions. Each region was allocated to a team of one man and one woman. Their mission was to visit the peace groups in their regions and to address public meetings, to tell people about the blockade, invite them to join it and most important, to give lessons in elementary NVDA to people expected to come. Out of these visits and meetings local affinity groups were to be formed. The skeleton of a sound organisation had been constructed; now it needed people, equipment and expertise to put meat on the bones.

The blockade was to run from Tuesday, 31st May, to Friday, 3rd June. Monday being a bank holiday left only four full working days in that week. This would make the blockaders' tasks slightly easier, as they would only have four days to cover instead of five, in order to prevent the people on the airfield from having a normal full working day throughout a period of nine days, including two weekends. Contingency plans were prepared in case it was decided to work over a weekend, but were not needed.

The blockaders were attempting to do something that had never been done in Britain before – to non-violently lay siege to a military base and seal it off for four consecutive days and nights, in order to effectively close it for at least a week.

On 18th April, campers started to get blockading practice in for the big event. In the morning six campers blockaded the Main Gate for an hour, and in the afternoon eleven blockaded it. No blockaders were arrested in the morning, but five were arrested in the afternoon. Of these five, one was charged with obstructing the highway and four with breach of the peace. A second gate may also have been briefly blockaded.

Vernon Truman, after being charged with a minor breach of the peace in the direct action against the new fence on 10th March, had jumped bail and left Oxfordshire. A warrant was issued for his arrest. The police managed to locate him and he was arrested. He and his police escort were then flown back to appear before Banbury magistrates. Both Sir Neil Martin, the Conservative MP, and Banbury Trades Union Council complained about the money wasted on flying this petty criminal to his trial, when there were cheaper ways of moving him. It is believed he landed at Oxford Airport, not Upper Heyford!

On 27th April, Alan Human from the peace camp

(originally a Thirty-Acre Site occupier) was in a local magistrates court where he was bound over for a year in the sum of £100 "… for being a 'thorough nuisance'. He had apparently tried to visit Field Cottage, Fewcott, believing it to be the home of an author, G. Thomas. When he discovered Mr. Harry Waitland – the actual resident – there, he put him in a headlock and was arrested" (Quoted from *Chronology of Upper Heyford Peace Camp*). I regret I can shed no more light on this fascinating story.

On a fine Saturday afternoon (30th April, to be precise) an Upper Heyford blockade non-violence training team visited Southampton. Regrettably few Southampton people attended the training session, held at Friends' Meeting House, and even fewer Southampton people went on the blockade.

On 5th May, *Bicester Advertiser* reported that Brindley Price was challenging the legality of the arrest on the Thirty-Acre Site and around it. Ru Reiss had demonstrated that part of the fence was outside the site boundary and technically obstructing the Portway. This was on another section of the same road that the Portway Peace Camp occupied. The two sections were separated by the main runway and fuel compound, which bisected the Portway, so it was no longer a continuous road. Thus, ironically, the growth of air transport had made it necessary for a road which had been used since Roman times, and possibly before, to be blocked. The fence around the fuel compound, which has already been mentioned, was a different matter. When the fuel compound was constructed, the outer fence was erected fifty-five yards further up the Portway than it should have been, thereby denying access to fifty-five yards of dead-end road and illegally obstructing the Portway. When

Scene taken during the four-day blockade. (All Upper Heyford Peace Camp photos are courtesy of Upper Heyford Peace Camp Library.

Brindley Price brought the matter of the Thirty-Acre fence up in court where he was on trial for an offence alleged to have been committed on the Thirty-Acre Site, the magistrates referred the matter to Oxfordshire County Council for comment and adjourned the case until they received a reply from them. This Brindley Price is believed to be the same person prosecuted for his part in direct action at Boscombe Down on 1st July, 1984. (For more information see my account of 'Boscombe Down Peace Camp' elsewhere in this book and Page 23 of *Southern Evening Echo*, 3rd July, 1984. The *Chronology* spells Price's name in two different ways; I am using the spelling employed by *Southern Evening Echo* in the report of his court case.)

Campers originating from the Thirty-Acre Site had initiated a call for direct action against the airfield on the sixth day of each and every month. In line with this on 6th May a group of them occupied the police observation tower and sentry box on the Thirty-Acre Site. The five of this group who were arrested were charged with assaulting the USAF duty guard.

On 11th May, the *Bicester Advertiser* reported that Squadron Leader David Jenkins, the RAF officer responsible for RAF Upper Heyford, had written to Barbara Eggleston of Christian CND, that he would not accept a gift of a cherry tree, as this was against MoD policy, and nor could he allow Christian CND members to meet and talk with Captain Thomas Gallenbach, the USAF chaplain, and present him with a wooden cross. Access to the church on the airfield was also refused. So it appeared that the forthcoming Peace Pentecost demonstration would be entirely an 'outside' job (except for activists on incursions, of course).

On Saturday, 21st May, between 1,500 and 2,000 Christian CND members and supporters marched from Manorsfield Road Car Park in Bicester, to the Main Gate of Heyford with Anglican Canon Paul Oestreicher marched.

It was obvious that the authorities rated this an important demonstration, because Peter Baker, MP, agreed to come to the Main Gate and receive the cherry tree and cross on behalf of the MoD. He accepted the gifts graciously and then made a speech about appeasement. Canon Oestreicher replied, giving reasons why a Christian nation should not possess nuclear weapons. The USAF Commanding Officer was not there. He had refused to have anything to do with the Peace Pentecost.

The march continued along Camp Road, across the Portway, to Somerton Field, up by Village Farm. There marchers held an ecumentical service, at which Father George Zebelka, who had been chaplain to the crew of the atom bomber 'Enola Gay' delivered the Eve of Pentecost sermon. A festival began and some 600 people camped there overnight. They planted 10,000 white wooden crosses, bearing names on them (some had more than twenty names). Counting the people on Somerton Field and on the Portway, there must have been nearly 1,000 people staying overnight – by far the biggest number of peace campers yet to stay the night at Heyford.

At 21.00 hours, a candle-lit vigil began at the Main Gate and continued through the night until 0.600 on Sunday.

Later, at Gate 6, 200 people attended a Whitsunday service of worship, conducted by Roger Ruston, an Oxford Dominican monk. Children at the service released six white peace doves.

The rest of Sunday was spent in workshops (with Rev. Merfyn Temple, Fr. Owen Hardwicke and others) and NVDA training, mainly on Somerton Field.

Another Christian service was held at noon on Monday. Then ten Christians went to the Main Gate, and asked to speak to the USAF chaplain and Christians. As expected, the request was refused but they waited for a time at the Main Gate, just in case anything should happen, or someone change their mind, and contact was allowed, after all.

A group of Christians went to the USAF supermarket, just off Camp Road on the married quarters side. They were threatened with removal, but after discussion they were allowed to hold a service and give out leaflets for an hour in the car park in front of the supermarket. When they left, the women in this action kissed the hands of a police officer. Although a hedge separated this part of the airforce station from Camp Road, modplods were not guarding every entrance and the only high security fence was around the back, facing the fields.

A group of some thirty-five people, who had done NVDA training the previous day, then climbed over the fence at one end of the runway, with F1-11s flying overhead. They held another service at the end of the runway and put posters, balloons, candles and white crosses everywhere. They weren't there long before modplods escorted them off.

Then a group including Rev. Merfyn Temple tried to enter the airfield, in order to go and see the chaplain, Captain Thomas Gallenbach, but police stopped them.

Throughout the Peace Pentecost there were apparently no arrests and the police were friendly and helpful. Christian CND's first national demonstration had gone off quite well.

Over Pentecost, Bruce Kent preached at St. Mary the Virgin Church in Oxford. Some peace campers went to hear him. Apparently Lady Olga Maitland, of the pro-bomb organisation Women and Families for Defence was also around giving out umbrellas and offering a multilateralist prayer.

The next event was the biggest ever single NVDA ever attempted in Britain up to that date. The four-day blockade produced more arrests and charges than any previous NVDA.

People came from all over Britain. One group came from Bristol on bicycles and camped on the way at Fairford Peace Camp on the night of 30th-31st May. Throughout the weekend people had been gathering at the Portway Peace Camp. Probably the first arrivals on the morning of Tuesday, 31st May, were on Campaign Atom's bus from Oxford, which pulled up at the crossroads where the Portway crossed Camp Road, before dawn.

At 06.00 hours, 600 people marched off from the peace camp along Camp Road. As they passed the first gates, groups peeled off and sat down in front of them, until the march ended at the eleventh gate. Exactly who went to which gate and when, had already been arranged. It was done by allocating different gates to different affinity groups for specified periods on a shift system and issuing clear and detailed instructions to each group. Arranging this had taken a lot of hard work.

To begin with, it appeared all the gates were successfully blockaded and by closing all the gates in Camp Road, the blockaders had effectively cut the USAF base in two. The airfield, all the aircraft facilities and some offices and sundry buildings were on the North side, along with some senior officers married quarters; but most of the married quarters, the USAF supermarket, the modsquad HQ and several offices were on the South side of Camp Road. Right from the start the marchers were outnumbered by 1,000 Thames Valley police and many modplods.

Police waited until traffic arrived, then started dragging blockaders to the sides of the roads at the various gates. Like grains of sand rolling back down the sides of a pit being dug, blockaders just returned and sat down on the roads again. Relations were good between both sides: at Ash Gate a police-

woman who fainted was given a drink of water by blockaders, who then lifted the blockade when an ambulance arrived to fetch her. Nevertheless, after a while police started getting tired of this game, and reports went out on the CB radios of the first arrests at Main Gate. Soon after, arrests began at Spruce Gate, followed by Ash Gate, Hazel Gate and the others. The numbers of blockaders were maintained by fresh shifts arriving at pre-arranged times during the day. By evening there had been seventy-one arrests and one demonstrator's foot had been run over by a car with an American driver, without serious injury.

Lady Olga Maitland and her pro-nuclear organisation Women and Families for Defence, were also active. During the first day of the long blockade they collected 400 signatures from local people, supporting the American presence. They continued to collect signatures throughout the blockade. Although most Upper Heyford villagers, appeared to agree with the aims of the blockade, most people living in the area seemed opposed to it. The 'Three Horseshoes' pub remained closed during the blockade, so as to deprive blockaders of drink. This was done on the orders of Councillor Paddy Quinn, who apparently owned it. The other pub in Upper Heyford, the 'Barley Mow', got extra business from villagers (and at least six blockaders, in spite of its ban on serving people from outside the village) because of this. One local caravan site owner claimed to have lost £1,000 because of the blockade. Other residents were kept awake by blockaders singing and music, delayed by them on the local roads and subjected to questioning by visiting police who might have thought them to be blockaders. Villager Eric Rhodes pointed out: "We can live with nuclear weapons. Lots of people around here make a good living out of that base" (Quoted from *Chronology of Upper Heyford Peace Camp*).

On the second day, police tried arresting large numbers of blockaders and carting them off. They still had difficulty getting vehicles and people through. More activists replaced those arrested and the blockade continued. The people who came had nearly all received training in NVDA, many from the training teams that had been sent out around Britain from Heyford. They came, knowing they might be arrested, strip-searched and charged as soon as they sat down in the road, and also knew something about how to react when provoked towards violence. Affinity groups were working well as groups and in co-operation with each other, until a new tactic was tried – the moving blockade. This caused the affinity group structure to start to break down, but it had a great advantage in that a crowd of slowly moving people cannot really be held to be causing an obstruction, because an obstruction must be stationary; there is no legal minimum legal speed for walking.

Jet planes occasionally roaring into the sky reminded blockaders that the F1-11s were still at Heyford. A typical arrest was that of Ross Bradshaw:

> My own arrest was at the 'Hazel' gate, near the extension site for the EF1-11s. It followed a few hours of sitting down, being dragged off and returning. The police started penning us in away from the road. They forcibly photographed all who were arrested – and later asked us to read a list of our rights, which included the right not to be forcibly photographed – mass protests will follow. Generally, however, the police were reasonable, though the group I was in had to threaten complaints and non-cooperation before we were given access to toilets.

> After initial processing we were detained in a gymnasium where we kept our spirits up by applauding all new arrivals and people being released. We were allowed to keep our belongings, and were given free access to CND lawyers. It was here that the police were most friendly – going out for chocolates and (unfortunately for non-smokers) cigarettes, and sometimes sharing their police ration tomato soup with those of us who refused the prisoner ration of meat soups. Sadly, though many detainees accepted the South African apples we were also given! (*Peace News*, 10th June, 1983).

The *Radiator* reported:

> Many people were forced to be photographed after their arrest, and also asked many questions, which could only be useful for political files (*Radiator*, July 1983).

After negotiations with the police, the activists arranged for a moving blockade to march on the Main Gate and conclude the action on the Friday. The march set off and all went well until it reached the Main Gate, when suddenly the police support unit "… inspector panicked" (*Radiator*, July 1983). The police started a concerted push against the crowd, forcing it in upon itself. For a few frightening minutes, it looked as if old people, children and at least one person in a wheelchair were going to be crushed, knocked down and trampled. Fortunately, the activists stayed calm (the non-violence training was helpful here) and dialogue was possible with the police, who eventually released their push. The action ended and people left, peacefully and in a happy mood.

About 412 affinity groups had taken part; around 4,000 blockaders had participated; no less that 752 were arrested and charged mainly with breach of the peace and obstruction. Although the airfield had not been closed (flying had gone on throughout the blockade), road access had been difficult – and for short periods impossible – throughout the four days. As the four days came between a three-day weekend and a normal weekend, and as the authorities kept overtime behind the fence to a minimum, the disruption of their working routines really lasted nine days. The activists in Camp Road had divided the USAF station in two as effectively as a river without bridges divides a town. The action got much national and local publicity, although as usual, the national press got a lot wrong.

On Monday, 6th June, Heyford was returning to normal, with people moving around unimpeded by blockaders, and peace camper Stan Kennedy starting a fast for "… all children all over the world born to live, not die in a nuclear war" (Quoted from *Chronology of Upper Heyford Peace Camp*). His fast, planned to last a week, finished after five days on medical advice.

The first blockaders were before Banbury magistrates on the same day. To list the details from every one of the 752 cases would use up a lot of paper to little avail, so I will confine my record to general information.

The activists had been told that the peace camp hoped that they would all plead not guilty, on the grounds that the Genocide Act, which made genocide and preparation for it illegal, gave them a lawful excuse to obstruct, etc. … This excuse was that they were breaking the law in order to attempt to prevent a much greater violation of the law – preparation to commit genocide with nuclear weapons. However, some blockaders who lived far away (activists from Faslane in Scotland had made a 700-mile return trip, for instance) pleaded guilty because they could not afford one or more extra journeys to Oxfordshire for not guilty hearings. The first people were tried by Colonel Henry Morrell and his bench. Colonel Morrell caused uproar when he criticised Mark Bianco from Brighton – obviously the officer was not a pacifist! On the first day, fourteen activists pleaded guilty, whilst seven pleaded not guilty. On the second day most pleaded not guilty. It appears that, overall, the proportion of not guilty to guilty pleas was about fifty-fifty. At the beginning, it was expected that the 752 cases would take two months to clear at the rate of twenty per day. After that, more time would be required to deal with the adjourned not guilty pleas. Early ones were adjourned to dates in August. On the first day, when the press was in court, no costs were awarded against guilty persons, but on the second day, when the press were not there, costs of £25 a head were awarded against them. Most people seemed to be getting conditional discharges. On the second day, a lady magistrate who had been dealing with blockaders drove away in a car with a 'Vote Conservative' sticker on it. Had defence lawyers seen this sticker before she started work, they might have objected to her on the grounds of bias, and delay would have ensued, with the possibility of a fresh magistrate. Each day peace campers were in court, providing moral support for defendants, checking on cases being tried and ensuring the legal back-up system worked, but they weren't able to check every car and its occupants in and out of the car park.

On 8th June, *Oxford Times* reported that the development of the Thirty Acre Site, and logistical support, for the EF1-11s, would cost £45,000,000. That was many millions more than the costs of policing the blockade and the peace camp, about which some locals were vociferously protesting!

Using their powers under the Representation of the People Act, Upper Heyford Parish Council called a parish meeting on 16th June, 1983. Apparently, Tony Baldry, MP, had recently promised that the peace camp in the Portway would be evicted, or words to that effect. The meeting was chaired by Paddy Quinn, who advised everyone to write to Tony Baldry and remind him of his promise. There were threats of violence if the camp was not moved. Indeed, camper Mike Sparkes noted that the camp was already subject to insults and stone-throwing, and that an incendiary bomb of a type used in military exercises had been used against the camp (in addition to the firebomb discovered in early April) and swastikas had been daubed on his caravan. The meeting asked the parish council to send official letters to the Chief Executive of Oxfordshire County Council and to the Chief Constable (Peter Imbert, soon to be promoted to Metropolitan Chief of Police). The council was asked to strengthen existing links and make new ones, with pro-nuclear groups, including RAGE at Greenham and Lady Maitland's group. Parishioners were concerned that they would have to pay the costs of policing blockades. The only person consistently voting against these resolutions was Mr. Parry, the local schoolmaster.

DIRECT ACTIONS GALORE

On 24th June, *Peace News* reported that a new peace camp had been started at Hazel Gate (Gate 10). The people involved included people whose caravans had been damaged in the eviction from the Thirty-Acre Site. Recent storms had added to this damage. Consequently, they were appealing for money to help repair their caravans. They also published a leaflet from Hazel Gate Peace Camp, calling on all the remaining blockaders, who had not yet been sentenced, to get together and stand firmly behind not guilty pleas based on The Genocide Act and international law on genocide. If all their not guilty pleas had succeeded, appeals could have been mounted on behalf of the activists already in prison.

On Monday, 4th July, American Oxford University teacher Claudia Beamish, a Campaign Atom supporter, rode Billy, a horse belonging to Ru Reiss, up to the Main Gate. There she handed a scroll announcing the 'British Declaration of Independence' to Flight Lieutenant Bill Perrins. He was deputising for the RAF officer in charge of Heyford. Behind the gate the Americans were busy celebrating the anniversary of the United States getting its independence from the United Kingdom.

On 6th July, *Oxford Times* reported that Tony Baldry, MP, had discussed the policing at Heyford with the Home Secretary and the Chief Constable, Peter Imbert.

On 8th July, Steve Barwick, Margaret Lowry and five other Portway peace campers left for Small Heath, Birmingham. They were setting up an office there to co-ordinate the defences of the people charged at the Long Blockade. This left seven campers on the Portway, including Bill Wright and Brindley Price. Bill told the media that spontaneous actions would be taken against the airfield.

At the beginning of July, the Hazel Gate Peace Camp was evicted, apparently by a local farmer towing their caravans away to a lay-by. Later they returned to the Portway. This may have had some bearing on the decision of the seven campers to go to Birmingham.

It is sad to record that a petty squabble now started over money which Stan Kennedy and John Egan – who had appointed himself camp treasurer – were alleged to have collected at a CND demonstration in London. It was to grow into a long and bitter wrangle. It is not for me to judge who was right and who was wrong.

Cherwell Peace Group had recently been formed by Ru Reiss and some friends and was now campaigning against the USAF nuclear bombers locally, co-operating fully with Portway campers.

Two campers, in a spontaneous action on 10th July, scaled the fence and painted the word 'Peace' in block capitals on a wing-tank inside it. Their artwork was clearly visible to the public outside the fence.

After a public meeting chaired by Tony Baldry, MP, the petition supporting the American presence at Heyford was presented to Michael Heseltine, PC, MP, on 11th July. It was presented by no less a personage than ex-prime minister Lord Home.

A meeting of Long Blockade defendants was held on 12th July, in Room 180, County Hall, London, to co-ordinate their defences. All the cases were being heard at Banbury Magistrates Court, but the defendants came from all over the United Kingdom and County Hall was centrally situated for defendants in the South, using road, rail or river transport.

On 1st August, magistrates began hearing adjourned not guilty pleas. A backlog had developed in the primary hearings, and the Lord Chancellor had given permission for a full-time, stipendiary magistrate to come and help clear the backlog. The same stipendiary, Terry Mather, was called to Newbury to handle cases from Greenham Common. Conditional discharges were awarded to twelve defendants. The court was cleared when supporters clapped the convicts. Meanwhile, outside, Campaign Atom was doing street theatre (a skit on Civil Defence, with a Chinese dragon and people dressed in fallout suits) and leafleting. During the cases so far, Campaign Atom had been leafleting outside the court and almost everyone in the peace movement in Oxfordshire had been helping and supporting the defendants. There was always somebody in the court, helping, supporting or just observing. Apparently, people charged with highway obstruction were being awarded conditional discharges, with costs varying from nil (on the first day) to £25, whilst those charged with breach of the peace were being bound over and being awarded similar costs against them. Danny Hodgson, a former Labour Party prospective parliamentary candidate for Banbury, paid his costs on a copy of *The Church and the Bomb*. Only one person appears to have gone to prison, in the cases heard up to 1st August. That person refused to be bound over and was sentenced to one week in prison.

On 4th August, Dr. Donald Mason of Oxford University was imprisoned for one week for refusing to pay £30 costs. He still paid his £30 – to Oxfam! Fines

which had not been in evidence before were apparently awarded against five defendants on that same day.

Karen Robinson and a juvenile were each detained for a week, on 6th August, apparently for refusing to pay fines. The court was cleared when thirty or forty supporters tried to get a minute's silence on Hiroshima Day. Normally it is the magistrates who are trying to get silence in court and they clear the court because supporters of defendants are making a noise in the public gallery, but these times were not normal times at Banbury Magistrates Court! The long blockade cases seem to have caused a muddle on the Commission of Justices for Banbury, for on 10th August *Bicester Advertiser* carried a complaint from a Mr. Eldon Squires that, because of the appointment of the stipendiary from London, he was not allowed to be a JP. Banbury justices were sitting almost every weekday in August and running three courts instead of the normal two. It appeared they just did not have room for any more JPs to sit, without going to the expense of converting schoolrooms.

RAF Upper Heyford held an open day on 13th August. Peace campers went leafleting and had their leaflets confiscated, whilst three Brighton activists were each detained fifteen minutes without charge, before they threatened to complain of false imprisonment and were released.

Most defendants pleading not guilty at the Long Blockade trials claimed their actions had lawful excuses, because they were acting to try and stop breaches of The Geneva Conventions Act, 1957 and The Genocide Act, 1969, which appeared to make the possession of nuclear weapons illegal. The stipendiary, Terry Mather, rejected this defence, but accepted a few pleas of not guilty on technical grounds, such as poor police evidence. On 16th September, *Peace News* added up the score: of those pleading not guilty, 301 were convicted, and ten were found innocent. My own arithmetic tells me that 441 more must have pleaded guilty and been convicted. There were several appeals pending.

In early September, an incendiary device was thrown at a caravan in the peace camp, without damaging it, but setting the grass and hedge alight.

In Oxford Crown Court, on 3rd November, eleven appeals against convictions of blockaders were heard. Previously magistrates had refused to listen to defence arguments involving international law, The Geneva Conventions Act and the Genocide Act. However, in these appeals, the judge agreed to hear all the evidence. As the cases were similar, they were heard as one. Two barristers argued the cases before the judge, and three expert witnesses who had not been heard by the magistrates were called. After hearing it all, the judge ruled that the question of illegality of nuclear weapons was outside the court's jurisdiction and that the court had no powers to deal with it. The barristers had not proved that there was a crime for the blockaders to prevent. Therefore the judge allowed the magistrates' verdicts to stand unaltered. Appeals to the High Court were considered, but no action was taken on them.

An alternative Remembrance Sunday Service at the Main Gate on 13th November involved Nigel Anstee-Algar and other peace campers, along with people from Oxfordshire Christians Against the Bomb and Holy Family Church, Blackbird Leys. *Peace News* reported that some families from the base were there too, and the *Chronology* confirmed that people from the base attended the service. The demonstrators, about fifty in all, including the people from the base, held a vigil from 13.00 hours to 14.00, planted flowers, sang hymns accompanied by a mouth-organ, made short statements on peace and the futility of war and placed chrysanthemums on a symbolic memorial composed of a charred tree branch surrounded by barbed wire in a tub bearing the legend 'No Next Time'.

Later that night, twenty yards of the perimeter fence was dismantled and a group walked through the gap onto the airfield. They do not appear to have been charged with any offences.

In November a twenty-four-hour vigil was held in support of Greenham Women Against Cruise in the USA, along with vigils and peace camps at 101 other bases. During the vigil, held at the Main Gate, campers danced and sang there.

During a yellow alert nuclear defence exercise on 16th November, two cyclists got onto the runway and cycled along it. One was knocked off his bike by a Modsquad vehicle, but the other managed to ride up to an F1-11 and was arrested touching it. The cyclists were arrested, charged with breach of the peace and went to Banbury Magistrates Court where their cases were dismissed for lack of evidence and the MoD had to pay £50 costs.

On the same date, a group of nine people were imprisoned for a week for not paying costs and fines arising from the Long Blockade. They included a vicar's wife and a middle-aged Quaker sculptress. One woman had her sentence sponsored by the hour to raise money for Greenham Common Women's

Peace Camp. Although cases arising from actions at Heyford went to Banbury magistrates, and Oxford Crown Court when necessary, cases of unpaid fines and costs usually came up in the Magistrates court nearest the home of the defendant. So a blockader who failed, or refused to pay a fine to the Clerk of the Court in Banbury, would normally have the debt transferred to a court near his or her home, which would ask for the money, or a satisfactory explanation as to why it remained unpaid. If the defendant could not satisfy the magistrates, they then could send him to prison, usually for a week in respect of every £50 unpaid. Cases of unpaid fines and costs were now beginning to appear in magistrates courts all over England and Wales. There were at least seven in Nottingham alone.

The Home Office gave residents of the Upper Heyford and Greenham areas what they called a 'Christmas present' on 20th December, when they announced that Thames Valley Police had agreed to pay its own costs out of funds paid for policing, partly by taxpayers nationally, and partly by ratepayers all over the Thames Valley counties. Police costs so far had been estimated at £3,000,000 excluding modsquad costs, which were paid by the MoD from taxes, and were not revealed.

Around Christmas some campers entered the fuel compound and painted slogans, including: 'Your Laws Make Wars'. For the next seven weeks the fuel compound served as the peace camp's art gallery. Every visitor simply had to go to the bottom of the Portway, to look through the fence at the slogans! For the whole of the seven weeks, it appeared that nobody on the inside of the fence had noticed them. Possibly the winter weather had kept the patrols indoors and when they did come outside, they didn't stay outside long enough to properly inspect this compound.

On Holy Innocents Day, 28th December, Paul Johns led a religious service with 150 members of Christian CND outside the base. Dolls, with countries' names on them, were hung on the perimeter fence with crosses to represent the innocent children of the world threatened with nuclear war. Two women, along with three friars from Blackfriars Priory in Oxford, got through the fence. At the end of the runway they chained themselves to crosses, or a single huge wooden cross (reports conflict here) and prayed until they were arrested, half-an-hour later. Another group, with an Anglican minister in it, crawled under the fence and got onto the airfield, where they sat praying, singing and planting little white crosses.

The five campers arrested at the sentry box occupation on 6th May were in court in December. Their cases took five days. Much of the evidence presented by the American sentry and the British police was contradictory. The jury did not seem convinced by it, preferring to believe the defendants' assertions of non-violent behaviour. They were found not guilty of assault.

A local newspaper, the *Banbury Cake*, interviewed the campers and reported on 19th January, 1984, that twenty of them were living in 'mud and squalor' on the Portway as a result of flooding caused by a burst water main on the airfield.

On 3rd February, Lieutenant-Colonel David Wesley arrived from New Hampshire, flying the first EF1-11 to be stationed at Heyford. He was met by US Ambassador Charles Price, Her Majesty's Under Secretary of State for Air Colin Humphreys and Tony Baldry, MP. About thirty campers and supporters from Campaign Atom demonstrated outside the perimeter fence, displaying banners and making brief blockades.

On 6th February, three people from the Long Blockade were jailed by unsympathetic Ipswich magistrates, for not paying court costs of £25 each to Banbury Court. They included Jennifer Hartley, the well-known Molesworth peace camper. They had been arrested on warrants before Christmas but had been bailed until February. Presumably the authorities hoped that they would change their minds and pay while waiting to go to court, thus saving the authorities the trouble of jailing them. This delay in fact gave their support group time to print and distribute leaflets and brief the press. Over 100 people assembled, with banners, outside the courthouse when the day of the trial arrived. Not only were the media in court, but also they gave the trial good publicity.

By now the original Thirty-Acre Site occupiers, including Sid Rawle, had all left the Portway, except for Mark Taylor and Rod Steine. There were reports of a fight between US personnel and a camper and a fight between two male campers over a girlfriend. As a consequence, all the women left the camp, and it became a camp for men only.

No action was taken in February over the alleged breach of planning law by the Portway Peace Camp.

To commemorate the first anniversary of the Thirty-Acre Site eviction, the 'Reclaim the Earth' action was held by about 400 campers and supporters. At 14.00 hours on Saturday 17th March 1984 it began with a decoy demonstration at the Portway Peace Camp while 300 people unobtrusively drove in cars,

walked and cycled to Village Farm. Some demonstrators quickly and quietly crossed Somerton Field. They arrived at the fence around the Thirty-Acre Site, where work was almost complete on the new buildings and facilities. Many had "... faces painted to look like Red Indians" (Reported in the *Chronology of Upper Heyford Peace Camp*). At the fence some Christians began to pray.

While the Christians prayed, people on Somerton Field and little groups of activists all along the road between Heyford and Ardley used their force of numbers to cut the fence in dozens of places. Apparently the police were nearly all on the other side of the base at the small decoy demo at the peace camp and on this side they were outnumbered ten to one by the activists at the start of the action. Gradually, however, they managed to seize all the activists' cutters, but by then sections of the fence were being pulled down, mainly where it had been cut at the posts. The police tried to stop this, but failed. A dangerous situation arose when two gates were lifted off their hinges. They almost fell on a demonstrator and a policeman.

Next, activists went onto the site and took over the two main viewpoints, three climbing the police observation tower and another group occupying the cement batching plant. A newly-arrived modsquad dog-handler chased an activist across Somerton Field until, surrounded by about forty chanting activists, he was forced to give up the chase.

The singer Nina had recently topped the charts with a song about balloons causing a nuclear war by accident. The idea for it probably came from a demonstration in Yorkshire some years before, where peace demonstrators flew balloons carrying tinsel to jam the radar in the Distant Early Warning Line Station at Fylingdales. Inspired by this song, demonstrators brought balloons to Heyford. Taking advantage of a change in police shifts, members of Chipping Norton CND and a group from Witney and Banbury got on to the runway. There they launched ninety-nine balloons. More balloons were tied to the perimeter fence and some police seemed to be enjoying themselves bursting these.

As the sun descended towards the horizon and the shadows lengthened, people began to go home and the authorities reclaimed the Thirty-Acre Site. The last activists to leave appeared to be the three on the police observation tower who were arrested and removed late at night. The occupation had nearly begun anew.

This action had clearly been very carefully planned well in advance and there was excellent co-ordination

Reclaim the Earth Day.

between groups all round the airfield. Sadly the team that planned it exists as a team no more. Two young women received minor injuries in the action. That bit was not planned but had the planners and activists not borne safety in mind, injuries could have been greater in number and severity. Arrests totalled forty-one, of which sixteen led to releases without charge and twenty-five led to charges of criminal damage. Dr. Levene from Campaign Atom announced to the media that the activists had been trained in NVDA, and had acted non-violently throughout.

On 17th April the twenty-five defendants from 'Reclaim the Earth' were in Banbury Magistrates Court. What happened is not clear, but it is known that some cases were adjourned because defendants were pleading not guilty. Their defence appeared to be based on the location of part of the perimeter fence, which had been erected, in error, outside the MoD boundary, obstructing the bridleway called the Portway running alongside. Their cases were not finally heard until 29th January, 1985.

A fund was set up to pay any fines and costs these defendants might incur, as had been done for the Long Blockade defendants. The earlier fund had caused bitter wrangling and the people running the new fund were trying to avoid this.

Another event in April was a festival organised by Campaign Atom, in which members of Kidlington Peace Group walked right round the perimeter fence, beating the bounds of the base.

On Monday, 30th April, USAF personnel walked round the villages adjacent to the airfield and talked to local people, visiting them and answering them as best they could, in a public relations operation. Some folk questioned them about USAF B52 aircraft armed with an air-launched version of the Cruise missile using Heyford.

Members of Brighton NVDA Network got involved with Portway Peace Camp and with campaigning at Heyford. With the help of the camp, this group planned and executed three actions at Heyford. Press releases from Brighton were particularly good, probably because Dominy, their publicity officer, used to work in the media.

The Brighton group's first action became known as 'The Mayday Action'. Advance notice was neither given to the media nor to the authorities, but letters were sent to all Network members and supporters, along with a few others involved with campaigning at Heyford. The letters told people to meet at a certain lay-by on A43, on the night of 1st-2nd May, 1984 and invited them to come prepared for NVDA, but did not reveal what form it was to take. In fact, it was planned that they hold a picnic on the runway. A few phone calls were made in the course of planning the action, but the information passed on by phone was limited and the rendezvous location not given. When the activists arrived at the lay-by, police were waiting. Obviously they had read their mail or put a spy on the Network's mailing list.

Notwithstanding this setback, they set off in two minibuses to try and reach the perimeter fence of the airfield. There followed a Keystone-Cops-style chase through the lanes of Oxfordshire in the early morning darkness with Thames Valley Police constantly harassing the minibuses and stopping them, alleging all sorts of minor offences were being committed by their drivers. It was clear before long that they were not going to get to and climb over the fence as there was a massive police presence everywhere. As dawn broke at 05.30 hours, the activists stopped near Hazel Gate and held an impromptu meeting. They decided to use one of the contingency plans they had prepared in advance and set off once more.

The activists then went and blockaded the Main Gate, just as USAF and MoD folk started going to work, causing considerable delay. Police kept moving the activists out of the way of the traffic, so a running blockade was started by the blockaders. Some went on to two other gates in Camp Road, where people were also going in to work. At both these gates police were unprepared and further delay was caused as blockades were mounted. Messages were sent to the Main Gate for the remaining activists to come and join the new blockades, which they did, resulting in continuing solid blockades and traffic jams, before police could transfer from the Main Gate to come and remove them. It must be remembered that the boot was now on the other foot. To start with, the police had rumbled their plan to picnic on the runway, and were ready for the activists, but they did not know what contingency plan they were using, so now they could only react to whatever moves the activists made, and therefore the blockaders were sitting down on the roads

Five-day occupation

before the police could get to them in sufficient force to start moving them. By the time they had been finally moved off, the morning rush hour had more or less ended, so the action was terminated. There were no charges.

During the running blockade, it is believed that a few people entered the base briefly, but they either left of their own accord, or were removed, and released with no charges.

There were "... eighty-odd protesters" (*Peace News*, 11th May and 25th May, 1984) involved in actions on Camp Road. Whether the two minibuses were used to ferry people from the A43, or more vehicles with local activists in them, joined the minibuses is not reported, but it seems likely that local activists joined the action. It is clear that good advance planning, mobility and communication between vehicles saved this action from becoming a damp squib when the police stopped the original plan from being executed.

The activists' dismay at missing their picnic was outweighed by delight at the success of their running blockade and by the numbers of police that had to turn out to protect the USAF.

At Banbury Magistrates Court on 2nd May, fines and costs of £25 each were levied on two people convicted of obstructing a road at Upper Heyford.

Recently, B52 bombers, capable of carrying air launched Cruise missiles, had been seen frequently at Heyford. A protest against these planes in particular took place in the early hours of 1st June, when eight visitors took a look round the airfield. Mod-plods caught five of them occupying the runway. The five were removed and released without charge.

It was obvious that covert methods of surveillance (mail interception, phone-tapping, etc.) had been used by the authorities to spy on the Brighton NVDA Network at the time of the 'Mayday Action' and had cost the activists the element of surprise in the early part of the action. We have described how they turned the tables on the authorities. To avoid a repeat on the 'Midsummer Action', they sent no letters mentioning it via the Post Office and revealed nothing in phone conversation. In spite of this self-imposed discipline, which hampered communications, the Network managed to assemble twenty-nine people from Brighton, London and South Hampshire (including 'Bill Goodwin', a fictitious character named after one William Godwin, author of *Political Justice*, who made a remark, quoted on the Net-

Ash Wednesday 1984. This Christian CND group is taking part in an Act of Repentance while a F1-11 taxis at RAF Upper Heyford. Photo: Rebecca West.

tactic almost certainly prevented some less experienced people from being charged. In the end, only one person was threatened with a criminal damage charge, mainly because he had paint on his trousers, but even this charge was dropped when all the activists were released after twelve hours.

On 29th June *Peace News* reported that two of the peace campers had been arrested after climbing a water tower and painting it with peace slogans.

work's press release in order to brighten it up and make it more attractive) in the early hours of 21st June, somewhere in Oxfordshire.

Now, in 1984 there were only coils of wire and fence about four feet high at the ends of the runway, though later a full height security fence was erected – for obvious reasons.

At 05.00 hours the activists' minibuses were approaching this fence, along a road which crossed the Banbury to Bicester Railway line by a bridge at Ardley. The driver of a vehicle, apparently on a routine patrol on the airfield, spotted them and radioed a warning, but was unable to stop them climbing over the fence on carpets. All twenty-nine reached the runway. By the time the last one was on the runway, peace symbols had been painted on it. They then formed a circle and moved along the runway with everyone singing and had gone about 100 yards before US soldiers arrived and arrested them. They went limp on arrest. There are no photographs of this action, because an American opened their only camera, removed the film and splattered paint inside.

Arrested males were put in one squash court, females in another. They sang, played games and shouted messages between the courts. When the Modsquad started interviewing them, some experienced prisoners insisted on acting as referees or advisors when the others were interviewed. This

Colin 'D.T.' Cunningham, Tracy and their Scottish friends were at Heyford during this summer. In their Magic Peace Bus, they had stayed at Lossiemouth, then visited Faslane before coming here. After the Stonehenge Midsummer Festival they left Heyford and took their expertise to Boscombe Down Peace Camp.

FIGHTS, FINES AND FIRES

About the beginning of July, there were two nocturnal arson attacks on the Portway Peace Camp, according to a *Peace News* report on 27th July. One led to a caravan being razed to the ground. It is not known exactly what happened and such is the nature of things that the true story may never be told. Two possible explanations have been suggested, however, by people who, though they were not there at the time, knew the camp and the campers well. Some campers had been misbehaving in local pubs, and all the campers had been banned from most of them because of this misbehaviour, which could have aroused animosity to the point that some local hotheads attempted to burn down the camp. A second possible explanation is that drunk or drugged campers (some campers, though not all, had been using drugs) had accidentally knocked over candles, or been careless with lit cigarette-ends.

According to Janey Hulme ("Roll Call", *New Statesman*, 7th September, 1984) two persons were arrested on Saturday, 11th August, after climbing a 150-foot tower. Stuart Morris and William Anderson, two march organisers, were arrested as a march entered Oxford and charged with obstruction. This tower incident and march may have been commemorative events in a Hiroshima/Nagasaki week at Heyford, about which I have no further information. This report apparently refers to two people climbing a tower and then being arrested on a march from Heyford to Oxford, on 11th August and charged with obstruction for climbing the tower. I do not know if they were charged with obstruction of the police (likely on a tower occupation) or obstruction of the highway (more likely on a march). At this time, climbing towers was not, in itself, illegal, so charges such as obstruction of the police or criminal damage, were likely to be used against tower climbers. On the other hand, it may be that the reference to the two people on the tower actually refers to the two arrests for climbing a water tower in June, a date got missed out, and these two arrests of tower climbers got confused with two later arrests. Communication from the peace camp to journalists and others was erratic at this time.

Another example of this communication was the only known published report of the peace festival:

> Local activists who made a sponsored walk to Upper Heyford US nuclear base, for the advertised 'Peace Festival' on September 8, were disappointed to find they were expected to organise it themselves when they arrived. The rest of the week of actions called by the camp was low-key *[Peace News*, 21st September 1984] .

The 'Train Action' was apparently inspired by the action of some Faslane campers, who had pulled the communication chain on a train running on the line above their peace camp and then run down to it. Some activists felt that trains could be used in this way to successfully enter bases with adjacent railways.

This action was planned in secrecy, without putting information in letters sent by the Post Office, and without mentioning it in phone calls. Word of mouth and notes delivered by hand were used. Planning included watching and timing all trains through the cutting at the eastern end of the airfield every day and studying the routines and

behaviour of security staff (mainly the Modsquad). This meant one activist had to live at the peace camp for a time, and travel round the airfield to the railway cutting in the early mornings and back at night.

Soon the planning was complete and everybody was told to turn up at Bicester Railway Station on the morning of 17th September. They could dress in waterproof clothing and look like ramblers off to the moors for a ramble, but on no account were they to look like demonstrators.

Some of the activists came on the train from Paddington and the rest boarded it at Bicester. Contrary to instructions issued beforehand, many of them looked like demonstrators, wearing badges and carrying uncovered rolls of carpet for all to see under their arms. As the train was leaving for Banbury at around 07.00 hours (it was the first train for Banbury that morning) the sight of all these demonstrators caused one man to panic. Carrying a suitcase, he fled from the train in a great hurry.

As the train was leaving, a woman delivered a letter to the person on the ticket barrier. This was addressed to the stationmaster and explained what was happening. It asked for the stationmaster to ensure that no other train collided with the Banbury train on the single track line past RAF Upper Heyford. The woman then rode off towards Heyford on a Lambretta.

A few minutes later, as the train passed under a road

Through the fence cutting off fifty-five yards of the Portway. Names of man climbing through the fence and his companion are not known.

bridge, three people appeared on the embankment above the line and halfway along the line towards the next bridge to the west. They waved a red scarf. An activist on the train, seeing this signal, pulled the communication chain, which caused the train to stop slowly – much more slowly than expected and hundreds of yards further down the line than planned. Instead of scrambling up a bank and reaching a road giving them an easy brisk walk to the perimeter fence, the activists had to climb the bank, and then struggle across a muddy field before climbing over the fence onto the airfield near the eastern end of the runway. The irate engine driver was shouting things like: 'You stay there! You don't leave my train! Get back on the train!' The activists were supposed to have closed the doors as they disembarked, but some forgot to do so. One man, who had just handed a note explaining the action to the engine driver, noticed these open doors and closed them before climbing the embankment to join the others.

The activists were on the airfield a good ten minutes before the Modsquad arrived, who wouldn't have been so soon had they not been alerted by the man who fled the train. The arrested folk were taken to a gym, where women were put in one partitioned section and men held in the rest of the building. The Modsquad then took them for interviews. It was during these interviews that the man who had fled the train revealed himself. He was a Modsquad inspector, who had been off duty and setting off on his holidays when he found himself in the thick of the action! It was he who had jumped off the train and ran to phone the police station on the airfield to alert them that a crowd of demonstrators were on the train passing the eastern end of the runway. He was fair when questioning people who might have been on the train. Most activists said no, or were non-committal. The person who actually pulled the communication chain is alleged to have told the inspector he drove his own vehicle to the action and to have given a fictitious registration number for the vehicle. None of these people were charged. However, out of about thirty activists, all but three of whom were on the train, about eight were recognised as having ridden on it. Even though activists had been instructed to discard their train tickets before going onto the airfield, two people were still carrying their tickets when arrested. These proved damning evidence when their owners were detained.

The activists came from Nottingham, Brighton, Southampton and Bristol, and had been brought together by the Brighton NVDA Network who had organised the whole thing. They expected to be charged with minor offences under railway regulations with a maximum fine of about £25 per offence but the authorities had other ideas. They dusted off a rarely used law, the Malicious Damages Act, 1861. Under this act the unlawful throwing of an object could lead to a death sentence, which had apparently not been abolished when the death sentences for other capital crimes were. Also under this act, trespass on railway land could lead to a five-year prison sentence. This is what the activists were faced with then they went to court charged with trespass.

This incursion took place during a NATO exercise, when security was supposed to have been tight and the activists had planned to disrupt the exercise by occupying the runway and stopping planes from using it for a time. This plan would have got much publicity for the cause. Because they were arrested so quickly, they didn't stop the planes, but their press and media handling was well organised and, even though the disruption was much less than planned, papers all over Southern England carried reports of the action. Dominy, who had issued a good press release properly timed, sat by a phone throughout the action and for some time afterwards. Here she both received reports phoned from Heyford and briefed the media.

The Network had planned a fourth action which involved cycling on the runway at Heyford but this did not take place. During 1984 the Network were at other bases, including Naphill and Christmas Common – always getting good publicity.

On Tuesday, 29th January, 1985, there were altogether forty-one outstanding cases involving damage to, or action at, the new perimeter fence in the Portway that had been constructed around the Thirty-Acre Site. Most originated from 'Reclaim the Earth'. These cases led to a test case being heard by Banbury magistrates on this Tuesday. Nigel Anstee-Algar appeared on charges of criminal damage to the fence and obstruction of the Portway. (This account is pieced together from three different reports, which appeared in *Chronicle of Upper Heyford Peace Camp*, *Peace News*, 25th January 1985 and 8th February 1985. Unfortunately none of them were complete.) Apparently Nigel had cut his way through the new fence and sat down just inside it on the part of Portway between this fence and the old boundary, which was still the legal boundary of the land the MoD had bought. Nigel, helped by Councillor Roland Pomfrey and his maps, argued that the fence was in an illegal position and blocking off access to the part of the Portway where he had sat. Therefore he was justified in cutting it and could not be guilty of obstructing a part of a bridleway to which access was blocked by a fence. The court accepted that it had been illegally erected and therefore was causing a technical obstruction of the Portway. They found Nigel guilty of criminal damage, however, as he had no 'immediate need' (The words of a magistrate, quoted in *Peace News*, 8th February, 1985) to cut the fence to get through it. He was also guilty on the obstruction charge. His fines and costs added up to £120. It is believed that this led to the other forty cases being treated likewise.

Bicester magistrates fined two women from the 'Train Action' £75 each on 1st March 1985. They were the first of the eight defendants to be tried and were convicted of trespassing on railway land and causing a train to be obstructed. They had pleaded not guilty to this charge made under the Malicious Damage Act, 1861, and had offered to plead guilty to trespass, on a lesser charge not involving that law, but this had not been accepted by the prosecution. The other cases, which the court did not have time to hear, were adjourned until 29th March.

Apparently only six of the eight defendants appeared. It was thought that two could not be traced by police because they had given wrong names and addresses and therefore would not have received their summonses, which were sent out after the Modsquad had released them on bail in September.

On 29th March, Bicester magistrates found another five of the defendants from the 'Train Action' guilty and relieved these people also of £75 each. My arithmetic says two wrong names, plus two convicted plus five convicted adds up to nine. As there were only eight defendants in all, it appears that the police had traced one of the defendants alleged to have given false names, but had not charged the person with any extra offence. Probably a letter had gone astray in the post or there had been some muddle.

These fines were a long way short of the maximum possible penalties. One reason may have been that the magistrates did not want to make martyrs of the defendants; another that this was the first time any of them had committed an offence of this nature; another – probably the main reason – was the fact that it was obvious in court that safety was, at all times, paramount to the activists. Nobody was meant to get hurt, and nobody got hurt

Also in March. some Greenham women got into an F1-11 in its hangar at Heyford and sat in the cockpit until asked to leave by the pilot.

In May, Cherwell District Council voted to prosecute the Portway Peace Camp for not complying with planning law.

On 1st June, it was reported that threats of arson were received by the campers and stones were thrown at the camp. It is believed that subsequently there were more threats and attacks of this nature, but police caught nobody.

Then, in the early hours of 18th September, John Egan's caravan was razed to the ground, in spite of the efforts of the airfield fire brigade

The following Wednesday, two men came to the camp and spoke to Mick, a resident. They then smashed him across the shoulders with a stick and drove off at speed.

On the weekend of 29th-30th September, three more caravans were destroyed by fire. Shortly afterwards, a three-ton lorry arrived, with two men, who loaded all the wrecked caravans onto it. They apparently had something to do with the district council and promised a visit from a council official. Campers had not bothered to note the lorry's registration number. No council official came. The council was contacted. They said they knew nothing of the men, the lorry or the promised visit. There is a possible explanation here, though it cannot be proved. Each council has its own procedure for disposing of scrap vehicles dumped in its district. Usually the council office sends an order to a local scrap merchant, who then removes the vehicle, strips it and sells the parts and scrap. Caravans are usually built of expensive aluminium and a scrap dealer would be delighted to have four burnt ones. Perhaps somebody on the council thought the caravans, now burnt out, were an eyesore and a health risk. An unofficial tip-off from the council office, rather than an official order probably brought the lorry out. This would have given the lorry driver the idea for him saying he had something to do with the council. However, it is just as possible that a peace camper tipped off the scrap merchant and received a back-hander for doing so. It was known that the campers were having a struggle to survive financially.

On the weekend of 12th-13th October, YCND held a national rally at Heyford. Apparently there were no arrests.

The Portway Peace Camp was issued with an enforcement notice, alleging breach of planning law, on 31st October. Previous notices only referred to particular places where particular caravans lay and could be circumvented by simply moving the caravans. This notice, however, forbade caravan parking along the entire length of the stretch of Portway where the peace camp was situated. The notice gave campers until the beginning of December to lodge notice of appeal and three months to move if they did not. On behalf of the camp, Stan Egan lodged an appeal. This meant they could legally stay without fear of prosecution penalties until the appeal was heard and, if they won the appeal, they would have the law on their side – at any rate until the council thought up some other scheme.

In November, camper Stan Nelmes claimed to have been awakened by US servicemen attacking his caravan. When I met Stan on a visit to the camp some time later, he was living in a bender. The caravan was not his own property; it was just one of the camp caravans where he slept at the time of the attack. Stan himself is a fascinating person. He had recently completed a fast for peace in London, at which he gave his age as fifty-eight, which was probably true. He walked to Faslane pushing a pram and got considerable publicity for doing so. The newspapers omitted to mention the time he took for the journey, which peace campers calculated as phenomenal. According to their calculations, he was walking nearly as quickly as the inter-city express trains travelled!

By 10th January, 1986, only John Egan and Stan were braving the midwinter weather at the camp. A report in *Chronology of Upper Heyford Peace Camp* alleged Egan had "… used violence to force Nigel Anstee-Algar and Mark Taylor (twice) and possibly other campers to leave the site".

The two of them now learned that in spite of the appeal, or perhaps because the council feared it might succeed, the council was plotting to prosecute them for obstructing the Portway. They would then be fined and would either move to avoid further fines, or be put in prison for not paying, in which case the council would tow away the caravans and benders. Things were indeed grim for our two peace campers.

This tactic had been tried before, with a different group of campers on the Portway, in April 1982. It had not worked then. The campaigners defending the peace camp used a new method in 1986. Labour councillors went rambling round the district and found many footpaths and bridleways obstructed. Some had been obstructed by local farmers who were

politically opposed to the peace camp and supported the councillors calling for its prosecution. The council debated the matter and decided not to prosecute the camp because if they did so, they would have to prosecute many other people for obstructing rights of way, some of which were disused, and the whole affair could cost them dearly in time and money.

Apparently, new by-laws under the Military Lands Act, 1892, now applied to Heyford. In January 1986, there was a report of a man fighting a case against the by-laws. This is thought to have been Mark Taylor, with the assistance of ex-policeman, John Bugg and Martin Robinson of Campaign Atom.

It was believed that the defence argument querying the legality of the by-laws was dropped on the insistence of Mark when his case reached Oxford Crown Court.

On the night of 14th-15th April, the fortunes of the peace camp were changed overnight when eighteen F1-11s took off from Heyford. In the cold, grey light of dawn they released their conventional, high-explosive bombs over Tripoli in Libya. There were many civilian casualties, including young children, and a hospital was hit. As soon as the news was out, demonstrators converged upon Heyford. Some made an incursion into a conventional weapons store in a high security area. Another group walked through the Married Quarters Area as far as the Bowling Alley, in traditional Libyan Arab dress, without being challenged! Immediately more people came to the camp, which had been doing next to no campaigning for over a year. Its future – so long as there was a nuclear bomber base at Heyford – was assured. This was good news, for an active peace camp had, in the long term proved to be a vital part of the campaign against this base.

At about this time pilots and air crew approaching and leaving Heyford had found a new landmark to aid their navigation. Even when flying on their instruments, pilots like to see landmarks that tell them their instruments are OK and they are on course. I expect they laughed when they saw this landmark. A local farmer, David Barbour, enraged some Cherwell District councillors by painting an enormous CND symbol on his barn roof!

At the time of writing, the camp address was: The Peace Camp, Portway, Camp Road, Upper Heyford, Oxfordshire, OX6 3LP.

AMERICAN MONSTERS IN HOLY LOCH

In 1960, after negotiations with the British Government, the USN anchored *USS Proteus* in Holy Loch, in Western Scotland, along with a floating dry dock. They were to act as a depot for nuclear submarines, including submarines with Polaris missiles. The USN called the depot Site One.

A few miles to the East, Faslane Bay was to become the home for Britain's nuclear submarines seven years later.

USS Proteus was reached from land by means of boats from Ardnadam Pier and a private pier inside a small naval shore base, at Sandbank, about two miles North of Dunoon. Road connexions to Sandbank were awkward, as it stood on the Cowal Peninsula, whose isthmus led up into the Western Highlands. The Dunoon Ferry was the best way of getting there from the populous Scottish lowlands. There was neither airport nor railway on the peninsula.

Apart from the small shore base, there were a few USN buildings scattered about the area. 'The Reservation' consisted of flats for USN families at Sandbank and there was a commissary (department store) run by the US authorities, where they could shop. Many USN families lived in private houses and flats locally. These they either rented or bought and on the High Road into Dunoon stood the 'Renting Building', where this accommodation was arranged.

Some of the nuclear subs to be based in Holy Loch were hunter-killers, armed with torpedoes only, and others carried missiles with nuclear warheads.

The campaign against these subs began as soon as they arrived and it involved NVDA from the beginning. Terry Chandler and Mike Nolan planted a nuclear disarmament flag on a USN ship's buoy on 3rd February, 1961.

The first Holy Loch Peace Camp was established on the beach at Ardnadam (which, by 1986, had been made into a car park) on 18th February, 1961. Activists camped on the beach and made several unsuccessful attempts to board the depot ship *USS Proteus*. They left of their own accord when the time came to end their action.

After the 1961 CND Easter March, the Direct Action Committee (DAC) marched from London to Holy Loch. This took seven weeks. On the final day, many local people joined the march and it grew to 2,000 strong. The climax came when over 1,000 of these people blockaded Ardnadam Pier, while protesters in eleven canoes and other small boats tried to board USS Proteus. Some got as far as the anchor chain, before being repelled by sailors with fire hoses. Several were arrested by British police frogmen

In diabolical weather a sit-down blockade took place at Sandbank, on 16th September. Many people going to the sit-down were delayed by police when boarding the ferry to cross the Clyde at Dunoon. At the action, police arrested over 350 people (one account gives 351, another 353) including Pat Arrowsmith, who was sentenced to three months in jail. The activists were tried in three courts; most were fined £4, with £2 costs each.

At Upper Heyford Peace Camp, many years later, I was told an amusing story about this action by Eric, who had taken part in the sit-down but not in the borrowing of the van.

Overnight accommodation was needed to house people up from England for the action. A lass from the Scottish Committee of 100 had a father who was caretaker of the Territorial Army Drill Hall in Dunoon. She booked her father's hall for a party and arranged to have the use of it all night. The relevant committee accepted the booking, without asking who was coming to the party. When the local police found out who was spending the night in the hall, the activists were already inside. At first, police surrounded the hall, but folk were allowed to sleep there and were not evicted.

In a garage behind this hall, activists found a Royal Naval van with keys in it. According to Eric, they borrowed it, drove it to Sandbank and were waved onto the USN base without being stopped. Obviously the guard thought their van was on official business. They leafleted USN personnel on the dock, before returning to the gate, where the guard waved them out without stopping them. The van was returned undamaged to its garage, and the Royal Navy apparently never found out about its unofficial journey.

Two years later, on 6th September 1963, a march from Glasgow to London delivered a dummy Polaris missile, twenty-four feet long, to the Imperial War Museum, who refused to accept it.

The Scottish Committee of 100, which had grown out of the DAC, held a fast and vigil on the beach beside Ardnadam Pier (now a car park) for thirty hours. One could hardly call this a peace camp, as there was no shelter erected and no caravan. Hardy protesters stayed out on the beach the whole time, through gales and a snowstorm, at Christmas, 1963, with just warm clothes, sleeping bags and a charcoal fire to keep them alive. They took no solid food, as they were fasting to demonstrate the contrast between nuclear weapons systems and starving, homeless people at Christmas. They collected money for War on Want to make sure that some definite good came from their efforts.

In 1971, a motorcade ended in a meeting at Sandbank.

At 10.00 hours on 1st September 1977, the historic paddle steamer *Waverley* steamed away from Anderston Quay, Glasgow, carrying over 1,200 nuclear disarmers on the first nuclear disarmament cruise. She berthed at Dunoon, whence the protesters marched to Sandbank for a rally addressed by Lord McLeod of Fuinary, Dan Smith, Keith Bovey, Jimmy Milne and an American clergyman. Disarmers from all over Britain filled the steamer to the gunwales for the trip back to Glasgow.

For a time, Holy Loch was left alone, while nuclear disarmers were concentrating their efforts at Faslane, until, on 29th January 1983, peace campers from Faslane arrived with a couple of caravans and set up the Aquarian Peace Camp on the High Road into Dunoon. Adjacent to the site was the 'Renting Building' and behind the site was a factory. All around Ardnadam was a built-up area, mainly residential, though the campsite itself appears to have been zoned for industrial development, and was owned by the Highlands and Islands Development Board.

Soon the camp was fired on by air rifles, and on 6th February a camper was beaten up by folk believed to be USN sailors. Later that night, the camper went to the local hospital for a check-up, and four other campers went to the pierhead and attempted to talk to the sailors and forgive the attackers. The sailors would not talk. Police came and told the campers to leave, and three were arrested when they insisted on staying. They were locked up and charged with breach of the peace and obstruction of the footway. Later they were bailed to appear at Dunoon Sheriff Court in March.

Only after the campers were arrested did the police take a statement about the attack, and even then they apparently couldn't find the attackers.

Just after midnight on 13th February, nearly two dozen police arrived at the camp. It was a drugs raid. Mike Shankland, who was living there at the time, described it to me in a letter:

> Nine people were at the camp that night. They were held in one caravan, then taken out individually and strip-searched in a police mobile office, then locked in the back of a police van. The police announced two hours later they had found some cannabis. It was planted: 1) the police discovered it when no member of the camp was watching, in the first caravan where people were being held; 2) they had not searched a third caravan at all, and seemed content not to carry on the search once they had found something.

The nine people present were cautioned while the drugs were sent away to be tested.

The camp's lawyer, Peter Watson of Glasgow, informed the Procurator Fiscal of Dunoon that he would ensure that each of the nine people would be represented by individual lawyers, and that he would make sure that the trial lasted as long as possible. The Procurator Fiscal later decided to take no further action.

In March the three campers charged with breach of the peace and obstruction at Ardnadam Pier came before the Sheriff at Dunoon. One pleaded guilty and two pleaded not guilty. The two pleading not guilty had their cases adjourned and were remanded in custody for three days until the cases could be heard. All three were found guilty in the end and given deferred, or remitted, sentences.

On 22nd April, ten campers barricaded themselves inside an office of the 'Renting Building' adjacent to the camp. A door had to be removed to let them out, and they were then taken to Dunoon Police Station, where they spent the weekend, before appearing in front of the Sheriff on the Monday, on charges of breach of the peace and disorderly conduct. Their cases were adjourned to 14th September.

At the end of May, at least one of the Holy Loch campers was fined £50 for participating in the Martin Luther King's Birthday incursion at Faslane in January.

The Highlands and Islands Development Board warned campers that if they stayed on their present site beyond 30th June, they faced possible imprisonment for trespass, under the Trespass (Scotland) Act, 1865. This little known act is rarely used. The warmth of summer had brought dozens of tinkers and other mobile home owners into the area, and among the local folk resentment was growing against people who lived in caravans and paid neither rent, rates, nor mortgages. This included the Aquarian peace campers. Unlike Faslane, the camp had little support from the wider peace movement, and even Dunoon CND as a group did not support it, although seven or eight individual CND members in Dunoon gave some support. One actually lived at the camp for several weeks. One of the reasons for the lack of support from the wider peace movement was the camp's isolated position on the Cowal Peninsula. Dunoon CND was not a very big group, nor was it rich in funds. According to Mike Shankland, the Aquarian Peace Camp had come to be "considered as some sort of 'black sheep' among peace camps".

So, at the end of June, this camp closed, and Mike

returned to Faslane, and some of his companions went to Lossie Peace Camp. The development board surrounded the campsite with posts, to stop vehicles and caravans from going on to it. Up to the time of writing, nothing has been built there.

People charged when the 'Renting Building' was occupied came before the Sheriff of Dunoon on 14th September. Two pleaded not guilty and three pleaded guilty. One person pleaded guilty by letter. One woman was acquitted, and five people were found guilty and fined £50 each. After refusing to pay, one was sentenced to fourteen days in prison. Warrants were issued for the arrests of the rest of the ten occupiers who had not attended court.

A nuclear powered hunter-killer sub without nuclear missiles, the USS Sam Rayburn, visited Site One on 25th February. Folk who watched her arrival and saw her hull being cleaned by sailors with high pressure hoses, tried to find out why she was there and what had happened to her, because something was clearly wrong. The Americans, and everybody else, referred queries to the MoD, who gave very little information. Apparently the Sam Rayburn had been in some kind of incident where radioactivity was involved. She left under her own power, apparently all ship-shape and Bristol fashion, on 26th February.

On 21st January, 1984, with snow on the ground, 700 women demonstrated at Sandbank. When twenty-six were arrested and charged, official complaints were made about the manner of the arrests.

The fourth Holy Loch Peace Camp was set up in Dunoon to support women in court as a result of the January demonstration. The twenty-six trials had been split into two batches, each planned to take one week, at Dunoon Sheriff Court. The first batch began on Monday 21st May. The camp, which started then, stayed for one week. Campers spoke with local people and Americans, and leafleted 'The Reservation', where some of the 4,000 US troops and sailors assigned to Holy Loch lived with their families.

On the Wednesday, PC Bisland's notebook played a vital part in Patsy's trial. When giving evidence, under oath, PC Bisland alleged Patsy had said: "You fucking American puppets. I hope you bastards are the first to die." Under questioning from Patsy's defence lawyer, he admitted the words were not written down, because his memory was so good he never needed to write details like this down.

Enter PC Sweeney, who told the court that Patsy had said: "You fucking American puppets. I hope you bastards are the first to die." No, he had not written this down; he had heard her utter these words and was sure these were her exact words, because he had, in addition, seen them in PC Bisland's notebook!

The notebook was produced. There was nothing written in it. The case against Patsy was dropped. After court had finished, PC Sweeney was asked outside how it felt to lie under oath, and replied: "Same as usual." (Extracted from the report of trials supplied by Glasgow Women for Peace, *Peace News,* 29th June1984.)

There were several not guilty verdicts during the first week. Most of the cases seem to have involved breach of the peace charges.

To provide support for the rest of the twenty-six women, whose trials began on 18th June, a fifth camp was set up. For five long days the Procurator Fiscal laboured with this second batch and succeeded in getting only one conviction. Two cases in this batch were adjourned until the Autumn, because the court were unable to hear them this week. The camp closed at the end of the week.

In *New Statesman* on 10th August 1984, Janey Hulme reported seven arrests for breach of the peace at Holy Loch.

The peace camps at Holy Loch had been an invaluable part of the campaign against the subs there. They gathered information, provided visiting protestors with a local base, generated publicity through court appearances, helped with court cases, told the public about the nuclear subs and helped to keep Strathclyde Regional Council opposed to the nuclear weapons in its region.

PEACE CAMPS AT RAF KEMBLE

This airfield sits astride the Roman Fosseway in South Gloucestershire. It has blast-resistant hangars of an old type, some of which are scattered around the airfield, and some of which are in Kemble Wood, a short distance away across A429 road. Kemble Wood is a possible site for Cruise missile deployment, though it had not been so used up to the time of writing

Following an announcement that the USAF were going to use the airfield 'for maintenance purposes', Cirencester Peace Action held a demonstration with 300 people at Kemble. They presented the base with a coffin marked with the words: 'Democracy' and 'Independence'. Exactly what the USAF planned to maintain there was a secret. However, the announcement pleased local trades unions, because it said the authorities were planning to create over 100 jobs for local people at RAF Kemble.

In 1983, more news got out. RAF Kemble was to become a new central repair and storage depot for the USAF and it was to be the maintenance centre for some of the USAF's noisiest aircraft, the A10A Thunderbolts. It was also to be used as a vehicle repair unit. Presumably the vehicle repairs would include repairs to Cruise convoy vehicles, when necessary. Kemble was also in an excellent geographical position for a USAF standby airfield for B52 bombers and other big jets, hence the 10,000 feet runway planned.

In October 1983, Kemble Parish Council asked Cirencester District Council, the planning authority, to defer planning permission for the MoD to extend the runway to 10,000 feet. Normally construction work on RAF airfields doesn't need planning permission, but it appears that this extension did.

On 8th-9th November, a twenty-four-hour peace camp took place beside the lay-by on A429 opposite the RAF Kemble runway. It was one of many in support of the Greenham Women Against Cruise in New York. (See my account 'Cruise Arrives' elsewhere in this book.)

Then nothing happened for over a year. On Monday, 24th December 1984, amid rumours of an American military hospital being established there, five people and one dog set up a new peace camp beside the same lay-by. Ron and Jenny Birch were there from Stroud, along with Rose Smith, a Greenham woman who had been on another earlier peace camp at Kemble (believed to have been the November 1983 camp). Rose saw to it that Cirencester Police had a letter about this camp well before it started, in order to avoid any police paranoia that may have arisen. This was in complete contrast to the secrecy adopted two years earlier when a peace camp was set up at Fairford, also in South Gloucestershire.

As soon as the camp began, visitors started to arrive. Several cars were there when a civilian cop car arrived, on what the crew said was just a social call to say 'Happy Christmas', and wish the campers well. Then they started taking everyone's name and address, saying this was necessary so that next-of-kin could be easily told, in the event of a camper being taken ill, or involved in an accident. Some people were reluctant to give details. After collecting the names and addresses, a policeman was overheard radioing to his base the registration numbers of all the cars at the camp, so that his base could check the names and addresses of drivers and if any of the cars had been reported stolen.

While the camp was there, many strangers passing by along the busy road stopped on the lay-by and talked to the campers. Local CND members and pacifists also visited, some staying for several hours at a time. For at least half the time it was there, the camp had one or more visitors.

Campers had no contact with folk on the airfield, no presentations were made, there were no blockades, and there was no NVDA either. Relations with the police seem to have been pleasant throughout, and local people were not hostile. However, as a result of the campers meeting the public and talking with them at their excellent, main-road campsite, many people who didn't previously know what was going on at Kemble now knew. They also knew why some people opposed it. Some may even have come over to the side of the peace campers.

The camp ended, as planned, on 27th December 1984.

Legend
1 Main Gate
2 Two gates (gates to two entrances opposite on A439
3 Back Gate
4 Entrance to Fosseway
5 Layby and grass verge (Site of peace camp?)

‿ ‒ ‒ Approximate boundaries of MoD land
‿‿‿ Tracks and footpaths
‿‿ Roads
〰〰〰 Railways

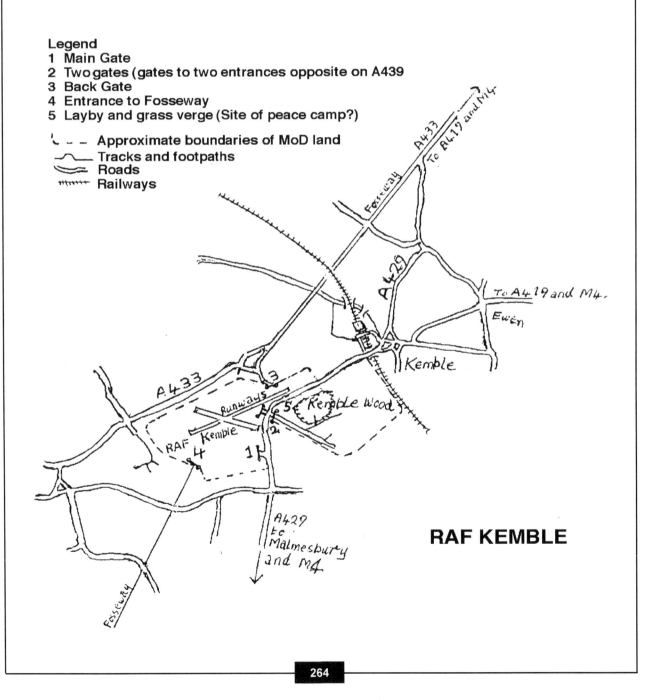

RAF KEMBLE

RAF LEUCHARS:

The Battle of Britain peace camp

Not far down A92 from the Southern end of the Tay Road Bridge in Eastern Scotland lies RAF Leuchars.

On 17th September, 1983, to commemorate the forty-third anniversary of the Battle of Britain, RAF Leuchars held an open day, with the public invited onto the base to see a small part of the air force for which they, the taxpayers, were footing the bill.

A peace camp was set up just outside the airfield for the duration of the event. It was used as a base for NVDA when thirty women from Fyfe Women for Peace went inside and leafleted folk with anti-war leaflets. In addition, a mixed group displayed banners and gave out leaflets at the entrance to the airfield. An anarchist group from Dunfermline did some theatre on the airfield runway, and chalked human figures on the tarmac, and spattered them with ketchup.

At the end of the open day the peace camp was taken down and the campers left. Nobody was harassed, nor was anybody arrested. The campers had succeeded in getting their message across in a friendly, humorous manner.

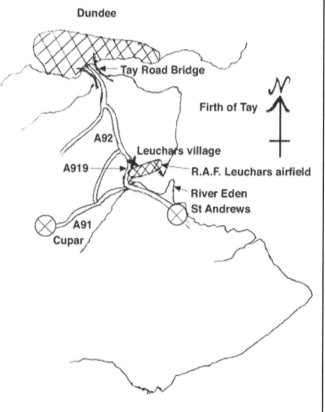

THE LIVERPOOL PEACE CAMPS

The first Fast for Life Peace Camp raised about £1300 in fifty-two hours, mainly by sponsored fasting, on its site outside Liverpool Cathedral. The money was afterwards split between the United Nations International Children's Fund and Merseyside CND's 'Peace Bus' Appeal.

The fast itself started at 14.00 hours on Christmas Eve, 24th December 1983 and by 16.00 hours the fasters were on the campsite. They erected one large tent and fourteen campers crawled into it and settled down for the night. The tent promptly blew down on top of them!

This camp was on wasteland opposite the Cathedral, because neither Roman Catholic nor Anglican Cathedral authorities would permit the camp to be on church land, so Liverpool City Council were approached and permitted campers to use the wasteland. Maybe church officials later pondered on the peace campers in the wilderness, turned away at Christmas. Maybe not.

With millions of people starving over Christmas – a time of giving for Christians, and of feasting; with the arms race and wars continuing over Christmas – a time of peace for Christians; and with the recent arrival of the first Cruise missiles at Greenham, some people around Merseyside felt it was just not possible to have a normal Christmas. Fasting seemed a logical way of getting their message across. With sponsorship they could raise money to feed the starving and to combat the waste of resources on Cruise and other weapons. Outside a Christian cathedral was an excellent and appropriate site

The camp visitors' book was signed by 208 people, some of whom stayed for long periods. Leaflets: '100,000 die in Christmas tragedy', were distributed, explaining why the fasters were camped there. At 16.00 hours on Boxing Day the camp closed and the fast ended, with neither an eviction nor any arrests.

According to Linda Lever, a camper, they "all enjoyed it immensely", and it was a "great way to spend Christmas" (In a letter to the author).

The next Fast for Life Peace Camp began on Wednesday 2nd May 1984. A chain of people was organised, each of whom would fast for a period. The chain was kept unbroken for the entire period while the International Garden Festival was being held in Liverpool.

People did not always fast at the campsite, and therefore a series of camps was set up intermittently, usually only at weekends. The longest period when a camp was on this site was when one camper fasted for 100 hours from 30th June to 4th July.

On Sunday, 5th August, the campers organised a big sit-in on the Japanese Garden in the Garden Festival, to draw attention to the anniversaries of the atom bombing of Hiroshima and Nagasaki. This NVDA resulted in no arrests. Then they went to the campsite, and set up camp there for the period of 6th August to 9th August to commemorate the atom bombing.

All the camps of this summer were held on one site, by the roundabout where Jericho Lane joins Otterspool Promenade. This was an excellent site, for people passed it on their way to and from the International Garden Festival, as well as in the course of business and pleasure in the City centre. Campers gave out many thousands of leaflets, including some printed to explain why they were fasting. They were never big camps, with only about eight people staying the night at the maximum. Foreign visitors to the Garden Festival stopped at the camps overnight from time to time. Though the Garden Festival organisers looked unfavourably on the peace campers, Liverpool City Council permitted them to camp on that site, and there appear to have been no arrests of campers. These camps succeeded in getting their message across to the crowds visiting the Garden Festival and to many Liverpudlians.

Another bigger Fast For Life Peace Camp was set up in Saint John's Gardens, behind Saint George's Hall in Liverpool City Centre with two large tents and several smaller tents and display stalls on Tuesday 6th August, 1985. The camp commemorated the anniversaries of the bombing of Hiroshima and Nagasaki. Once again the council granted permission, there was no eviction and nobody was arrested. Over the three nights of this camp from eight to thirteen people slept there and four people fasted for the whole period. Others fasted for shorter periods. A Hibakusha (survivor of the atom bombing) was well received by the crowds who saw the camp and campers felt they were really reaching the public with their message, particularly when ex-prisoners of war who came and started berating the campers later left all calm and thoughtful. Campers stressed the point

that both the ex-prisoners and the Hibakusha had suffered in a war not of their own choice. This camp, which ended on Nagasaki Day, 9th August, appears to have received good coverage in many local papers.

There have been a number of fasts in town and city centres. Most have been in daytime only. One or two ran overnight, but not in tents. The Fast for Life group were different, in that they added tents and all the paraphernalia of a peace camp to each of their fasts.

In 1985, some Greenham women wanted a peace camp put together on Merseyside to commemorate the sixth anniversary of the NATO decision to base Cruise in Europe on 12th December 1979. Merseyside activists looked for a suitable site that had not been used before and chose one hard by the gate into Brocklebank Dock, Liverpool. Some of the supplies, which passed through this dock used by the USAF on their way to the depot at Burtonwood, would certainly have been subsequently forwarded to the Cruise bases at Greenham Common, Molesworth and Alconbury. Name a better site for the camp!

Male and female members of Merseyside CND just arrived in a boxvan one evening in December 1985, without telling the authorities and set up camp. Police came, and after a discussion, agreed to the campers staying for twenty-four hours, which they did, before going as quickly as they came. There were no arrests, and the only policeman near the camp for most of that time was the one on the Dock Gate. Much city centre and docks traffic passed the camp, and many Liverpudlians got to know what was going on at Brocklebank Dock.

These camps were comparatively easy to organise. They greatly boosted morale and provided money for the local peace movement and fed some starving people.

PEACE CAMPS AND SQUATS IN LONDON

Squatting – the occupation of empty buildings by people needing homes – has been going on in the big cities in Britain for many years. With the severe shortage of housing during and immediately after World War II, squatting became popular for a time, then waned in the 1950s. Another wave of squatting arrived in the late '60s and the '70s. The techniques, procedures, and experiences of these squats influenced many peace camps. They faced similar evictions, problems with local residents and problems getting support from outside. Some were set up by folk in the peace movement, not only as homes, but also as places that furthered the cause of peace in various ways. In the early days, peace squats were just ordinary squats with peace movement involvement, so it is impossible for me to go into a detailed account of peace squats. I have personal experience of only two in London.

I recall staying at a squat in a semi-detached house with a flooded cellar in North London, where accommodation was provided for people attending a conference at Pax Christi HQ. It was cold outside and the window was broken in my bedroom.

Another squat I visited was in the most opulent house I had ever entered – 19 Cornwall Terrace, facing Regent's Park. I was attending a nationally organised meeting, held in the enormous lounge. Unfortunately, like many squats, 19 Cornwall Terrace was short-lived. The squatters had thrown the lounge open to the peace movement for meetings and could also provide accommodation, which was great while it lasted.

Tent City, set up on Old Oak Common, in East Acton on 7th July, 1982, claimed to be a peace camp where pacifists could stay cheaply in London and meet other pacifists. It had showers, lavatories, a bag store and a cafeteria, for which luxuries it charged £2/10/- (£2.50) per night. There were no reports of NVDA there. This apparently commercial camp ended on 31st August 1982.

Jubilee Gardens Peace Camp was a completely different kettle of fish. This mixed peace camp lasted over Christmas, starting about 13th December, 1982 and ending a fortnight later on 29th December. It was on a site beside County Hall, London SE1, where the Greater London Council had given permission for the camp.

To commemorate the anniversary of the NATO decision to site Cruise missiles in Europe, which fell on Sunday 12th December, campers went to St. Margaret's Churchyard the following Monday and began a vigil. St. Margaret's Church, as well as being the church for the Houses of Parliament, is just across the road from the Palace of Westminster where Parliament meets, so this was thought to be an excellent time and place for this protest. Hundreds of MPs, peers, civil servants and media personnel saw this vigil as they went into the Palace to start their week's work.

Soon the police came and arrested the seven vigillers. They were charged with obstruction, and bailed to appear in court on 13th January.

On the night of 18th December, at 23.30 hours, a group of people suddenly split up and ran at the camp in the Jubilee Gardens, smashing things and knocking down tents. Missiles were thrown. A Calor gas cylinder was upset beside a camp fire. A flame began to spout from its nozzle. Juliet Yelverton kicked and rolled it away from the fire. Fortunately the flame on the cylinder went out when it was rolled, because otherwise it might have exploded, and injured and killed folk. The youths who had attacked the camp ran way as quickly as they came. Then police arrived. Dutch camper Eddie Rose had been badly beaten. In addition to a swollen and bloody face, he had a neck wound and had lost several teeth. An ambulance was called and Simon and Juliet went with him to hospital.

The police later caught the youths who made the attack. Apparently, they had come from a National Front Christmas party in a nearby pub just before attacking the camp. Police wanted campers to give evidence, so they could press charges on the youths. The campers could not bring themselves to do this and, as an act of non-violence and forgiveness, refused. Neither did any camper hit back, nor attempt to take revenge. Instead, they took newspapers and food to the police station the next day and first asked to see the prisoners (not allowed) and then if they had a solicitor or wanted anything. They were told the youths were all right.

Of approximately twenty youths involved in the attack, six were eventually charged and convicted of threatening behaviour likely to cause a breach of the peace. The Horseferry Road magistrate sentenced them to 120 hours of community service each and said he did not share the peace campers' forgiving attitude, which had prevented the police from bringing more serious charges. The youths were sentenced in early March 1983.

After brief court appearances, on 13th January, the vigillers from St. Margaret's Churchyard came before the Bow Street magistrate in Court No. 3 on 7th and 8th April, when six were given conditional discharges for obstruction. The fate of the seventh is unknown.

London Jubilee Gardens Peace Camp had an official visit from Councillor Ken Livingstone, Labour Leader of the Greater London Council.

Greenham Women set up a peace camp on the roof of Holloway Prison in North London, in March 1983 (see '1983 Began Before Dawn on January 1').

In April, 1983, fifteen Greenham women and a baby set up a peace camp at the Ideal Homes Exhibition on its last day, and were allowed to stay, as exhibition organisers asked the police to take no action. 'The Ideal Peace Camp' was set up to oppose the Royal Navy recruiting stand at the exhibition, to publicise the campaign against Cruise, and to show that even if one can afford an ideal home, one can't defend it against nuclear attack. The women sang and talked with the crowd attending the exhibition for five hours before leaving voluntarily. Lynn Taylor said that were pleased with the public response to their efforts

Camps were set up to celebrate International Women's Day of Disarmament over the weekend from 21st to 24th May 1983. There were three in London: Turnham Green, W4; Parson's Green, SW6 and one in south London. The Greater London Council were sympathetic and so were the borough councils involved. At Turnham Green the borough council even loaned its equipment to the campers. There were no reports of NVDA or evictions. These camps were all well sited to get their message across to the general public shopping in the high streets.

In July of the same year, beside a United Kingdom Warning and Monitoring Organisation bunker in the grounds of Alexandra Palace, twenty people set up the Alley Palley Bivouac. This peace camp was publicising a government plan to use London's parks, including the Alley Palley grounds, as mass burial grounds in the event of a nuclear war. The campers had an enormous placard, showing how bodies would be distributed and what the park would look like. This short-lived camp was not evicted, and no NVDA was reported here. The campers left voluntarily.

Another peace camp was set up in the Alley Palley grounds during the Women's Strike of 20th-30th September, 1984. These campers also left of their own accord.

As I have shown, the great variety of peace camps and squats in London had no standard format or pattern. It wouldn't surprise me to find one outside one of London's important military establishments in the near future.

LOSSIE PEACE CAMP

Just forty miles north-east of the historic Scottish battlefield of Culloden, at the point where the River Lossie meets the Moray Firth, lies the fishing port of Lossiemouth. Beside it lies an airfield famous for its air-sea rescue and patrols over the North Sea and Atlantic Ocean. Not so well-known, however, is the fact that RAF Lossiemouth was home for a squadron of Buccaneer nuclear bombers. RAF Tornado nuclear bombers were also stationed there from late 1982.

Peter MacDonald, Secretary of Moray CND, lived only five miles from this airfield and knew about the Buccaneers and Tornadoes, when he went on Peace March Scotland and to Faslane Peace Camp in 1982. There he met other people interested in his nuclear bomber base. Between them they made plans for protesting there.

Jane Tallents (who had experience of several other camps, including Brambles Farm and Faslane), and five others erected a few tents on a site belonging to Pitgaveny Estates on or about Saturday 9th October, 1982. They were just 400 yards from the end of the runway used by the nuclear bombers.

The camp started on an optimistic note, with visits from lots of local people on the first day. They brought food and large quantities of cooking apples grown locally. These apples served the camp as a staple diet for weeks afterwards, with campers eating enormous quantities of apple crumble – the author's favourite sweet. Sadly, he was unaware of it so he wasn't there!

The RAF immediately ordered all personnel and civilian workers on the base not to have anything to do with the campers. Some discreetly talked to the campers, in spite of this order. This may have been where the campers learned the Tornadoes were coming early. They were not due to be stationed at RAF Lossiemouth until 1983, but campers were warned they would come early and the first ones came in the closing weeks of 1982, shortly after the campers were warned.

At first the peace camp was not recognised as an address where unemployed persons could live and claim dole money, with giros sent to the camp. They were having to hitch-hike or walk to Elgin, six miles away, and back five times a week, to sign on daily like tramps. However, some local peace groups and political organisations were supporting the camp and with their help, the camp was made a recognised address and people were able to sign on fortnightly and have giros sent to them. Caravans were acquired, and the camp grew.

Although Pitgaveny Estates appeared neither interested in prosecuting the campers for trespass nor in evicting them, the local council had other ideas. The camp had no planning permission.

On Hogmanay, 31st December, the council served an enforcement order on the campers, who were told to comply with a great collection of regulations, or get off the site by a certain date (believed to have been

27th January). Failure to do so rendered campers liable to an immediate fine of £400 and a fine of £100 for each day beyond the 'stop' date while the camp remained in defiance of the order.

Lossie Peace Camp moved across Muirtown Road to a new site owned by George Packman and Sons, builders of Buckie. Packman asked the police to investigate and they did so on Wednesday 12th January, the day after the camp moved in. They took the names and details of everybody at the camp. This was to happen frequently in the months to come.

Campers were planning to bring disarmers from all over Scotland for a march and blockade of the airfield. On 15th January, the campers held a rehearsal, with just a few people at the Main Gate. After this short blockade, which apparently stopped the traffic, the blockaders left voluntarily and there were no arrests. Security at the airfield was increased, and shortly before the day of the march the local papers announced that most, if not all, the local pubs would be banning residents of the peace camp and members of CND from their premises. Several publicans were interviewed by a local paper and gave their reasons. Peter MacDonald was surprised by the ban, because he knew of no problems caused to pubs by peace campers or CND members.

The march from the airfield into Lossiemouth town attracted about 200 supporters on 29th January. Then everybody returned to the airfield's Main Gate for a blockade, but there was no need! The authorities had sealed up the gate with barbed wire so no traffic could get through. As a result, some protesters had time to drive around the airfield inspecting it from outside. They noticed the construction work on the new blast-resistant hangars for the Tornadoes. Again no arrests were reported. The demonstration appears to have been a success, for not only was road traffic stopped, but there was no flying that day, which was unusual on a Saturday on a busy airfield like Lossiemouth.

By February, the camp had grown to five caravans, and there were problems starting with the Trespass (Scotland) Act, 1865.

In early May, seven people charged with trespass appeared in the Sheriff Court, dressed as clowns to get the maximum publicity. Their cases were adjourned to September.

After two or three more moves, by May the camp was back on, or near, its original site on wasteland at the junction of Muirtown Road and Hopeman Road, previously used as a car park by golfers on the Moray Golf Course. This was the final campsite. Campers formally applied for planning permission for the camp. This would delay proceedings against them until the planning committee had dealt with their application, and further time might be gained by submitting a second, modified application.

On the weekend of 13th-15th May, campers hosted a weekend of fun and games, while a dozen people marched the fifty or so miles from Inverness with banners, in fancy dress and with their faces painted. The march was enjoyed by those on it; they had good weather; and the people in the towns and villages on the way enjoyed meeting them.

There were more trespass charges, and whilst some appear to have been for trespass on the airfield, most seem to have arisen because the campsites were all squatted.

At the beginning of June only Dawn and Simon were living at the camp, while the others had gone to Stonehenge. Numbers did not improve much when they held a Midsummer festival and vigil. Only about ten people came to this remote camp, but balloons and streamers were everywhere. They even managed to tie streamers to the rifles of some servicemen in the back of a Land-Rover! At the festival, police were not only taking details of campers, as they frequently did, but also the registration numbers of visitors' cars, and a member of the local trades council who noticed this said that the trades council would make an official complaint.

During summer, campers were getting into ever more secure parts of the base, including, at least once, the Control Tower, where they were arrested and removed, but not charged.

Problems with numbers were eased in August when campers from the closed Holy Loch Aquarian Peace Camp arrived to live at Lossiemouth

On the weekend of 8th-9th October the camp held a first birthday celebration, but turnout was again poor because of the remote location. Even visitors from Faslane had a return journey of 400 miles across country, without any motorways or fast rail links.

There were frequent court cases. A few were for obstruction and breach of the peace charges. Most were for trespass, for which the guilty party was usually admonished (a Scottish punishment similar to an English unconditional discharge with an official reprimand added) although one camper was apparently fined £10 for his fifth trespass conviction.

The strain of the court cases, the camp's remoteness, and the beginning of a cold, wet winter must have contributed to the camp's decline until, after two caravans were mysteriously gutted in what appeared to be an arson attack in early November, the camp closed.

When the author visited Lossiemouth in 1986, French Kier, the main contractor, had almost finished constructing the blast-resistant hangars and other facilities on the airfield. Tipper lorries, removing topsoil and taking it to the golf course, were driving over the last peace camp site.

This camp started some people around Inverness thinking about the evils of nuclear weapons, and showed them that these weapons were in their own backyard at RAF Lossiemouth.

VICTORY AT LUXULYAN

The Old Packhorse Bridge, in the Parish of Luxulyan, near St. Austell, Cornwall, was demolished in January 1980, in spite of a vigorous campaign to save it by Luxulyan Research Group (LRG). This sad event was recorded for posterity in the *Courier* newspaper by a photograph of LRG members standing on the ruins and a story by Paul Humphries, their reporter.

Sometime in February, Paul stepped into the history books himself and set in motion a chain of events which altered history, when he telephoned an LRG member and asked about plans to drill holes in farmland to survey for a proposed Central Electricity Generating Board (CEGB) nuclear power station. That LRG member knew nothing. They agreed to call a meeting.

About eleven local farmers had received letters saying the CEGB were going to test drill on their land. Under English law the board had a right to do this.

All these farmers came to a meeting, with anti-nuclear speakers, called by LRG in Bridges Chapel on 28th February. Some of the farmers were very busy people who wanted to leave early, but one of the LRG members stayed by the door and persuaded them to remain until the end of the meeting and help to decide something. The meeting decided to oppose the drilling, that they did not want drilling for a nuclear power station on their land and to deny access to the drilling crews.

A full public meeting on 15th March, 1980, involving 100 local people led to a further meeting on the following Tuesday, which formed a steering committee for a campaign against the nuclear power station. This committee was at first formed of volunteers with expertise in law, sociology, biology, etc., and others with experience in campaigning. Seeing that some other people with neither expertise nor experience were showing enthusiasm, the chairman invited them to join too. Now the steering committee had all three 'E's – expertise, experience and enthusiasm

Throughout Spring and Summer this committee, now named Luxulyan Against Nuclear Developments (LAND) were busy writing letters, raising money, and generally making people aware of their campaign.

The CEGB visited Luxulyan Village Hall on 22nd-23rd April and held their 'Radiation Roadshow' there. This exhibition was meant to show the public some of the workings and benefits of nuclear power. LAND mounted a silent protest. The media came and saw it and gave the event publicity. Rumour has it that the CEGB staff were glad when the time came to move on, as their show had not gone down very well! They went to St. Austell and set up the 'Radiation Roadshow' again, only to find that Cornwall Anti-Nuclear Alliance (CANA) and several members of LAND were there with another vigil.

The 'Friends of LAND' organisation was now formed and the first member paid her subscription on 20th June 1980.

LAND affiliated to CANA. Members of LAND attended many CANA events, including the big anti-nuclear demonstration in Truro on 26th July.

In August, LAND held a 'Balloon Day' at Treddinick Farm. Balloons were launched representing nuclear fallout from a possible future accident at the proposed power station. One balloon landed in Eire, near to Carnsore Point, where a nuclear power station has since been built! This 'Balloon Day' raised much money for LAND.

During the winter there was a big campaign to get local support, and LAND members tramped round the parish delivering leaflets and letters in preparation for a referendum organised by the parish council. The referendum result showed that the majority of the parishioners were opposed to the nuclear power station. The farmers were preparing; they had 'bound' their land under Stannary Parliament laws. This would appear to make CEGB drilling illegal, although it would still be legal under Westminster laws.

In spite of all this, the CEGB moved onto some farms and started drilling and met with no real opposition until 19th February, when a drilling crew tried to get onto John Lawton's farm. John was one of the two farmers prepared to allow demonstrations on their lands. Demonstrators turned away the CEGB drilling crews. Later in February, the drilling crew arrived at Rex Searle's farm and the same thing happened.

Then, acting under Westminster Parliament laws, the CEGB applied for injunctions against Rex and John. The two farmers went to the High Court in London to plead their cases. They pointed out that eight acres of good farmland had already been ruined by CEGB vehicles and drilling. The judge expressed concern about the effect of drilling on farming and extended the hearing so he could get the full story from both sides. Nevertheless, the judge found in favour of the CEGB and granted them an injunction whereby they could require farmers neither to obstruct nor interfere with the drilling and they could require farmers to ask protesters to leave.

The CEGB were drilling at two other places in Cornwall: Nancekuke and Gwythian. At Gwythian, Farmer James would not allow demonstrators on his land, so 500 demonstrators on the CANA dem-onstration on 5th March kept to common land and a public footpath. A rally on 14th March, also organised by CANA at Gwythian, produced a pledge to do as much as possible to prevent the construction of a nuclear power station, with over 300 signatures.

The next move was made by the Stannary Parliament, when they brought into being the Chytan Cost Book Company. This acquired the rights to prospect for minerals, including tin, on Rex Searle's farm. Apparently this would prohibit the CEGB from drilling there. The Chytan Cost Book Company's first tinning operation took place on 11th April. They neither found tin nor did the CEGB appear for a confrontation.

On 14th April, 1981, LAND had its first annual general meeting, at a time when, although public resistance was strong and growing, all the farmers except Rex had given in to CEGB pressure and let drilling rigs onto their lands. Test drilling at Gwythian and Nancekuke had finished. Thus Lower Menadue Farm was the only site left to drill and all eyes were on it when, on Tuesday 12th May, the CEGB notified Rex that drilling was to start on his land on 13th May

Pam Maclean and Doreen Varcoe were told, and by 07.00 on 13th May they had a dozen volunteers blocking gateways with vehicles and farm implements. Chris Nicholls gave protesters a legal briefing. Soon, some had to leave to go work and others took their places. The day wore on. Nothing seemed to be happening at the four blockaded gates.

Then in the afternoon, the usual CEGB convoy of lorry mounted drill, tractor, compressor and police escort appeared. They stopped at one gate, blocking the narrow lane, and tried to move Pam's Mini. She objected and the police upheld her objection. They then tried a second gate, where Teddy Goldsmith was sitting on a farm roller working on his papers. He threatened to sue for assault if he was moved. Then the convoy surprised everyone by leaving the site.

At 06.00 on Wednesday the CEGB returned, only to find people still blockading the gates. They went away again and the farm was left in peace for a few days.

In all but name this was a peace camp. It is true that the protest was about the proposed construction of a nuclear power station and not a nuclear weapons base, but, if built, this nuclear power station would train technicians and produce materials to make nuclear weapons. People from peace camps at nuclear weapons bases have realised this connexion and have got involved in camps at nuclear power stations, whilst others from camps like Luxulyan have subsequently camped at nuclear weapons bases. The blockaders here were committed to peaceful protest and NVDA; they stayed at the site twenty-four hours a day; and they soon arranged temporary accommodation on site. Their first accommodation came in the form of a hired caravan, which was used as a HQ. Protesters' own cars were used for sitting and sleeping, but they also had to be used as transport and this meant that they could not be parked at Lower Menadue Farm all the time. David Southey lent some old cars, so that protesters' cars need not stay. Nobody knew at the time that they were at the beginning of a siege that was to last several months. One point where Luxulyan differed from pre-Heseltine Molesworth and every other peace camp was that one of the camp supporters, Rex Searle, owned the land in dispute. Had the MoD not owned Molesworth Airfield, things would have been very different there.

On 18th May, CEGB officials reminded Rex that there was an injunction in force, which required him to ask the blockaders to move. He asked them to go, at the same time making it clear he was not calling in the police to move them. The blockaders stayed.

The number of demonstrators at the farm was at its usual daily lowest at 15.00 on 19th May. Several mothers had left to feed children. Then two CEGB convoys appeared. One went towards Turnip Field, but found the gateway blocked by people sitting in a car, so they changed course and, after a brief scuffle in a gateway, managed to enter Rex's field across the road, where they had not been planning to drill. They set up the drill.

Meanwhile, the other drill had driven up the Luxulyan road and was attempting to enter a gateway which was not blockaded, at the top of the farm. Jimmy Combellack and David Southey bravely threw themselves in down in front of it, and the driver stopped in the nick of time. Quickly others arrived, and formed a human carpet under the machine. BBC TV filmed this demonstration and journalists scribbled furiously. The machine was stuck with its drill projecting over the road, and police asked the drilling crew to raise it so it would not obstruct the road, which they did.

That night a group of local young men dug a trench behind the drill stuck in the gateway to ensure no-body would sneak it into the field when the protesters were not looking. The young men hit the water main supplying the village, and for time Lower Menadue Farm sported the beginnings of a moat, complete with fountain.

There was a truce the following morning while the water board repaired the main. Then the drilling crew prepared to drill in the gateway, but demonstrators put shovels and pieces of iron under the drill, surrounded the machine and boarded the drill platform. After half-an-hour the drill's engine was stopped and the drill never even entered the ground. The attempt was over. Nobody got hurt or arrested and everyone was in good humour. Later, that drilling crew even donated £10 to the protesters' funds. That machine, registration number AWW 848S, neither moved nor did any drilling for five-and-a-half months. It served as a flagpole for the Flag of St. Piran that demonstrators mounted on it.

The CEGB had already criticised the police officer in command of policing the siege of Lower Menadue Farm, Chief Inspector Bradley, for not removing protesters, and now they complained to Chief Constable John Alderson, head of the Devon and Cornwall Police. He backed Bradley. The CEGB then applied to the High Court in London, which, on 26th May, issued injunctions against thirty-two named protesters. Although some prominent people had amazingly been missed, the list included most of the regular blockaders.

That evening, Malcolm Neill, Chairman of LAND, chaired an informal meeting at David Southey's home. Most of the regular blockaders were in a position where they could be imprisoned and thus rendered useless if they continued blockading, because of the injunctions. Should they be replaced by other people, the CEGB would just take out more injunctions, although this could cost the board much time and money. Reluctantly, the meeting decided to call off the blockade, remove the cars and farm implements from the gateways, fill in the trench and withdraw on the evening of Thursday 28th May. They would have to use other means of protest. John Bamford thought: "Their judgement was reasonable, but in the light of later events, wrong. It was unfortunate that LAND was so closely associated with this decision that some members felt later that it would be disloyal to their own organisation to support any further protest" (Quoted in *LAND Magazine*).

A press release was sent out immediately.

At 19.00 on Thursday, the protesters assembled

by the captured drilling rig on the road leading to Luxulyan. Led by the Lostwithiel Band, they marched off through a fine drizzle. Coincidentally, the drilling crew also left the site in their van at the same time and on the same route as the march. The van, waving Cornish and anti-nuclear flags, moved at a walking pace in the midst of the march! After a brief speech of thanks when they reached the village, the marchers dispersed.

The drilling crew returned to the site on Friday 29th May, only to find new protesters there – students from Dartington and people from neighbouring parishes mainly. The drilling crew withdrew. Immediately after the meeting at David Southey's, thirty protesters had got together and evolved a plan with which they could continue, and this was the result. The new blockaders, of course, were not bound by the injunctions. They dug in, helped by George Pritchard and David Lewis of CANA. A large caravan was donated, to use as a HQ and living accommodation. This was parked on the roadside at the turning to Menadue. It was home for the Butt family (Freda, Helen and Diana) who were not covered by injunctions, even though they had been active since the first day of the siege. They remained active to the end.

In early June the CEGB were unsuccessfully trying to remove groups of blockaders. They were having to think out new strategies, as the old ones were obviously not working.

On 10th June between eighty and one hundred people from all over Devon and Cornwall met at Rex's farm and made plans. Each twenty-four-hour shift would start at 20.00 and would require twelve people to guard the gateways. In order to keep people at the site seven days in every week, a rota was devised, with a different group responsible for each twenty-four-hour shift: one day would be Helston's turn, another would be Bude's, etc.

At 18.30 on 11th June, explosions started to shatter the evening quiet. Contractors working for the CEGB had walked across country carrying a small drill, had drilled holes in Caravan Field unobserved, had placed charges in the holes and exploded them to get seismic data.

Although on that occasion the protesters had been caught unawares and had arrived at the scene of the explosions too late to stop the contractors, they had done their homework and were ready for the contractors when they returned on the following morning. Immediately the holes were drilled, but before the charges were placed in them, they sat on the holes. The law requires the charges to be exploded after they are placed, so the holes had to be occupied before the charges were placed, if the seismic testing was to be stopped. The contractors gave up and left.

On 22nd June Rex Searle gathered in the last of his silage crop, which would have been much reduced if the CEGB had been able to drill freely. Demonstrators had dug trenches across some gateways to stop drilling rigs using them. They had to fill these trenches so that Rex could harvest his silage and decided not to replace them with new trenches. This meant that more people were needed to guard the gateways. Already the sneaky drilling of 11th June had taken place unhindered because not enough people were on guard, and blockaders were getting worried. Sadly, uneven performance by different groups meant that by the end of July the rota was working inefficiently, in spite of great efforts from John Spurr and Bude, Helston and Calstock groups. However, the school holidays arrived in the nick of time and this enabled new protesters to come and step into the gaps and those old protesters involved with education had more free time to give to the campaign. Another donated caravan was put behind the drilling rig. At about this time Jim and Anne Brewer brought their hut and children to the camp. They lived in the hut for long periods and helped enormously. Students on holiday also came to help from anti-nuclear groups in Scotland and Wales. Whilst people from outside Devon and Cornwall were welcomed in small numbers, large numbers were not invited, and there was no attempt to get a national demonstration at Luxulyan. LAND wanted to keep the protest mainly local because they believed that a local protest would have better chances of success and would avoid them being accused of calling in 'Rent-a-mob'. The visitors provided an invaluable source of information about anti-nuclear protests elsewhere and when they left took news of Luxulyan with them, so it would have been unwise to totally exclude them.

Now all had gone quiet down on the farm. The CEGB seemed to have given up trying to survey it. What was the point of guarding gates if nobody wanted to use them?

Unknown to all at Luxulyan, the CEGB had applied to the High Court in London for a writ of mandamus to compel Chief Constable John Alderson to evict the protesters when requested by the CEGB. At the end of July, this application was rejected, and the CEGB gave notice of appeal. The

High Court thought that this appeal raised such an important point of law, that they chose three judges, including none other that Lord Denning, Master of the Rolls himself, to hear it.

The case opened on 22nd September, 1981. Honnahan, the CEGB solicitor, gave a distorted account, calling the protesters 'Rent-a-mob' and trying to accuse them of violence. The judges apparently advised CEGB men to remove protesters, roughly if necessary, and then a breach of the peace could be provoked, which would give police cause to arrest and remove protesters if they persisted in getting in the way. Thus the site could be cleared. On the evening of the third day, counsel for the police had just started his case when the judges suggested that the court adjourn, while the police and the CEGB get together outside and talk things over, to see if they could reach a settlement. When the court reconvened on Friday morning, the police and the CEGB had not come to any arrangement, so the police side of the case was heard in full. As Chief Constable Alderson was in the USA, Chief Inspector Bradley was the senior police officer present. He was in charge of policing at Luxulyan, had visited the place, and knew something about the situation there. He maintained his neutral position under very heavy pressure and refused to side with the CEGB. Counsel for the police referred to the "impeccable behaviour" (Quoted in *LAND Magazine*) of protesters, praised their peaceful ways and referred to peaceful protest as a necessary part of a civilised society. This last theme was later taken up by John Alderson on TV. On 25th September the hearing ended. Lord Denning and his colleagues went to prepare their judgment.

Delivered on 20th October, the judgment was a consensus of three different opinions. The judges would not tell the police how to behave on their own patch, but they condemned the peaceful protests of the law-abiding people of Luxulyan and their friends. They did not actually order the police to move onto the site and clear it, but the judgment left no real alternative option, so they had not much choice but to do it if so ordered.

On the same evening, the protesters met at Luxulyan and, after two-and-a-half hours of argument, reluctantly decided to leave the site on 31st October. This was believed to be the last date on which they could leave before the CEGB might call in the police to move protesters, which could lead to violence and people getting hurt. LAND wanted no violence. Somebody asked, "If it takes six months to drill one hole, how long will it take to build a nuclear power station?" (Quoted in *LAND Magazine*)

John Alderson visited the campsite on 31st October, as the protesters were striking camp, and thanked them for their good behaviour. They, in their turn, thanked him for his fair policing. He let the mask of police neutrality slip a little as he walked happily back to his car holding an anti-nuclear balloon, with all the press and TV cameras on him.

After striking camp, the protesters went to a rally in the Village Hall, with hundreds of people and lots of journalists. There were even two MPs on the platform, who both wished the protesters success in their campaign. The mood was of victory, not retreat: significantly, none of the people involved in this campaign appear to have ever used the words, 'retreat' or 'defeat' in connexion with it. Perhaps this is a lesson for the rest of us.

Meanwhile, back at the farm, watched by about twenty protesters, the captured drilling rig was resurrected to life with some difficulty. A hole was drilled. Water appeared at the bottom – natural water from the water table, not a burst water main – and the CEGB took their test data. The job was quickly finished on 31st October. The CEGB and their contractors were able to take their equipment home now.

Although the camp had ended, the campaign against the building of the nuclear power station had not: on 17th December, LAND began a series of monthly meetings; they worked on the county council, winning a 'No' vote for the proposed power station; and their caravan, with an exhibition, toured shows, fairs and markets, recruiting many new 'Friends' for LAND.

Then in August 1982, the CEGB finally announced they were not going to build a nuclear power station at Luxulyan.

The flag of St. Piran that flew for so long over the drilling rig is now preserved in Truro Museum.

BUNKERS ARE BONKERS:

THE 57 DAYS OF MID-GLAMORGAN PEACE CAMP

In the wide central reservation of a dual carriageway road, between the Sony factory and a World War II building, converted into a factory and occupied by a firm called Richard Stump, on Bridgend Industrial Estate, sit two World War II bunkers owned by Mid-Glamorgan County Council. These form their County Civil Defence Wartime HQ, with its own special telephone links to Government Sub-Regional HQ 82, on Brackla Hill, about two miles to the north, behind a children's playground on the edge of a housing estate.

Neither SRHQ82 nor the bunkers were staffed in 1986. There was not even a security guard. Maintenance appeared to be carried out, as and when needed, by people from elsewhere. These establishments stood deserted, like relics of a bygone age when people fought and killed each other …

In March 1980, County Council Chief Executive Hugh Thomas told a council sub-committee that these two bunkers would have to be improved and enlarged to comply with the latest national government civil defence specifications. By June, plans had been drawn up for improvements, including a new block with a decontamination room; water tanks; recycling equipment; its own sewage system; and the whole lot was to be made into one huge bunker of interconnected rooms. The plans even included an underground dormitory to sleep forty. Home Office experts were consulted to make sure everything was to their satisfaction. Then the County Council Architect's Department was consulted. By March 1981,

they had produced a set of detailed plans for Job No. B6051, which were easily passed by the planning authority.

CND supporters and members on Mid-Glamorgan County Council had kept local CND groups informed. Photocopies, minutes and memos kept walking mysteriously out of County Hall and going to CND meetings. Local groups were thus in a position to mount a campaign against the new bunker, which they did.

At the start there were seven groups: Rhondda, Methyr, Pontypridd, Bridgend, Maesteg, Cynon and Rhymney Valleys. From May 1981, they began meeting regularly in a county-wide organisation, which became known as Mid-Glamorgan CND.

When the *South Wales Echo* headlined "£389,000 mystery of the super bunker", on 12th December, 1981, it was no mystery to Mid-Glamorgan CND!

On 17th December, jubilant CND members crowded into the council chamber at County Hall, to hear Phillip Squire, the Council Leader, declare Mid-Glamorgan a NFZ. Now Mid-Glamorgan could concentrate all its energies on preventing the construction of the new bunker, with the very important achievement of a NFZ behind it. It escaped the notice of most people that the NFZ resolution made no mention of civil defence at all. This was unfortunate, as the resolution could not be used as a tool in the campaign against the bunker, but only as a morale booster for campaigners.

Ironically, the final decision to approve the construction of the new bunker (which was designed to protect not the public, but about forty officials) was delegated to Mid-Glamorgan County Council's Public Protection Committee. On 3rd January a meeting of Mid-Glamorgan CND was told to expect this approval to be granted within forty-eight hours.

On 5th January, the press reported that the main contract to build the bunker had been placed with Fairclough Engineering. However, before work could start, snow started falling on the night of 7th/8th January. I was in Aberystwyth where the snow began to fall just after dawn on 8th January and continued to fall for over twenty-four hours until a full civil emergency was in operation with over 1,000 troops and RAF personnel involved. Roads were blocked all over the county – in many cases for more than a week – and thousands of vehicles were stranded, with their occupants, on the newly-completed M4; the railways and buses were in chaos; helicopters were the only aircraft that could take off and land; customers couldn't get to shops, nor workers to work, nor doctors to patients; pipes burst, with failure of water supplies and heating systems; and, just as the clearing-up operations were beginning to produce something, a spell of exceptionally severe temperatures, in which I saw moisture freezing in Newtown, brought road and rail traffic to a standstill once again. The construction and civil engineering industry could start no new outdoor work for weeks. Wales was paralysed.

The old bunkers, then standing on the site, were, of course, in working order, and an ideal HQ for controlling services and clearing-up operations. That is surely the job civil emergency bunkers should have been doing. This HQ was never used. The civil emergency was controlled from County Supplies Department at County Hall and the Fire Brigade HQ, as CND had already predicted would happen.

By Thursday 21st January, the worst was over and traffic was beginning to move freely again. Mid-Glamorgan CND held an emergency meeting at Bridgend. They agreed that, should work start on the bunker, direct action would be taken. Various ideas were discussed. They unanimously decided to mount an occupation of the site for the new bunker, in order to impede the contractors. The people working at the meeting passed the word round their groups and a telephone tree was prepared, so that as many folk as possible would be standing by to be ready to help with an occupation at short notice. CND members made discreet enquiries, which revealed

that, if the thaw continued, and it was possible to work, Faircloughs planned to move onto the bunker site on Monday 25th January. By 18.00 hours on 24th January, the weather reports for the next day being favourable and with the thaw continuing, it was obvious that Faircloughs would be moving in as planned. The wheels of CND began to roll.

At 19.00 on 24th January, several CND members and supporters, with a caravan borrowed from a local councillor, set up camp on the bunker site. A rota of people on a shift system, to ensure twenty-four-hours-a-day, seven-days-a-week occupation of the site had already been decided before the campers moved onto the site. The first shift, through that cold, wet, mid-winter night consisted of four women from Rhondda.

On the morning of 24th January, the workers arrived, to be met by an established peace camp. The contractors, county council and police did not seem to know what to do.

Fairclough's men eventually started work, and shortly after this, it became obvious to everyone that the caravan and tent were in a dangerous, awkward place. By agreement with police and contractors, the caravan and tent were moved to a safer place on another part of the site.

The media had been informed and soon the camp had good reports in the papers and on radio and TV. The Deputy Clerk to the County Council did not appear to be informed, however. He told people work was commencing as normal and he didn't know where the caravan was parked. Workers on the industrial estate and people who lived near it seemed to be favourably impressed by the publicity and by the campers. Factory workers provided access to telephones, toilets, water, tinder for the brazier and waste products to help with the manufacture of posters and placards. Visits from a local fish-and-chip van helped keep people fed.

On the evening of 26th January, Mid-Glamorgan CND met to assess what had happened so far and plan ahead. Originally, the seven groups had not been planning to co-ordinate, but had decided to co-ordinate their organisation when they saw the campaign required it, and now they were working closely together. They set up a travel fund to help people from outlying areas get to the bunker site, and an action sub-committee with a rota for a flying squad to reinforce pickets at the site at important times. The flying pickets, when they became practised, could respond very quickly indeed, and were to prove very useful.

At the end of the first week, on Sunday 31ˢᵗ January, people from Wales Against Nuclear Arms (WANA) and CND, along with three sympathetic county councillors, addressed a meeting of 250 to 300 people on the site. Most of the audience were from Bridgend. Many offers of support and help were received by the camp. This was the first of eight public meetings to be held on the site on Sundays.

Meanwhile, at County Hall, CND lobbying was paying dividends. A minute of a county council sub-committee meeting, held in March 1980, and a report of a council site meeting, in June 1980, were leaked to the press. On 1st February, the fifty-strong Public Protection Committee came to the site to meet peace campers and CND members. They were briefed by Hugh Thomas, who told them the police were worried about a possible confrontation between campers and councillors. There was none, even though campers were there in force, with banners, from a dozen or more towns. Councillors inspected the site and met with protesters in a bus shelter across the road. They agreed that a CND delegation should speak to councillors, but impossible conditions which would virtually end the campaign were imposed. Later the councillors backed down and agreed to a meeting on 18th February, without the conditions.

Quakers, United Reformed Church members and Welsh Congregationalists were among the religious groups and individuals helping with the lobbying of county councillors.

County Councillor Ray Davis, a staunch supporter of the campaign against the new bunker, was drafting a resolution to the council to get work stopped and CND made an unsuccessful attempt to get trades unions to black this non-union construction site. The camp had some support from trades unions: the Welsh TUC and the Fire Brigades Union gave moral support; the NUM sent £100, some miners to support the picket, free coal and a brazier. Other gifts included £200 from the Greenham Women, which was used to buy a caravan – the Mid-Glamorgan Peace Caravan, which later went to Caerwent and Llanishen.

Local MP Ray Powell saw a delegation who convinced him that the bunker was no good, and Ray became a keen supporter of the campaign. He asked questions in the House of Commons about the new bunker and the money being spent on it.

Welsh Labour Party leaders were approaching Labour Mid-Glamorgan county councillors privately and trying to persuade them to campaign against the bunker and get it stopped. Not all the Labour group on Mid-Glamorgan County Council were supporters of the peace camp's campaign at this time.

An enormous banner was now displayed at the bunker site, with the simple message: "Bunkers are Bonkers". This was visible in the press and TV coverage the camp was getting, which led to new CND groups being established all over South Wales. This good publicity was helping campers in getting the help they needed, and were always requesting, with all sorts of little things.

In preparation for meetings of the full Mid-Glamorgan County Council and its Public Protection Committee on 18th February, CND sent out information packs about the bunker to every councillor. Two Quakers in Bridgend CND paid for a copy of the book H-Bomb on Ogwr to be included in each information pack.

On the eve of the County Hall debates, a political storm appeared to be brewing. County councillors Jeff Jones and Morgan Chambers, who had supported CND and voted against the new bunker in the past, were sacked from the Labour group on the council. However, the storm failed to materialise and councillors debated the bunker peacefully in the full council meeting. Councillors were pushing for, and suggesting, modifications to, the bunker, to ensure it was built as a purely civil structure and seen to be one. They didn't want to see a bunker where the military and a few chosen councillors could hide and control the populace. It was clear councillors were being affected by the letters, lobbying, phone calls, visits, and other pressures from constituents opposed to the bunker. The public gallery was packed with CND members and supporters, both for the full council meeting and for the committee meeting which followed it. The Public Protection Committee meeting was enlarged by many councillors who were not on the committee and who just came to observe. This was the meeting with the campaigners against the bunker that had been originally agreed in the bus shelter on Bridgend Industrial Estate. Tony Simpson and Paul Llewellyn spoke against the bunker as CND delegates. Paul was a particularly sensible choice for this job, as he was not only chairman of Mid-Glamorgan CND, but also a practising lawyer.

Tony and Paul made the point about cuts in retained firemen adversely affecting civil emergency services (the council were trying to reduce the cost of their fire service at this time by making redundant some of their part-time firemen) and Paul asked several pertinent questions, including why it was necessary to accommodate forty people below four feet of earth for up to fourteen days for civil emergency work. When the committee argued that burying the bunker improved insulation and saved fuel, Paul asked if County Hall and other county council buildings were to be buried for the same reason. Some councillors joined in the cheering at this idea. Most councillors gave the CND case positive reception, but a storm was still brewing over the sacking of the two CND councillors from the Labour group. Chairperson Douglas MacDonald solved the problem by suspending discussion and calling on the council leader, Phillip Squire, who said he wished to make a statement. His statement was not very clear, but it seemed to make concessions to the protesters. The meeting ended, and the statement got a reserved welcome from CND, while in the peace camp's newsletter it was reported under the headline: "Victory in Sight". Perhaps this reveals an important aspect of this campaign: some people could see the possibility of winning a victory, all the time.

Work continued on the new bunker, without modifications. Then, as the daylight hours got longer and the weather warmer, the contractors appeared to speed up the work and introduced weekend working.

On the thirtieth day of the camp, 23rd February, campers celebrated not only the completion of their first whole month on the site, but also the announcement that day of a NFZ being declared in Clwyd. This was the last Welsh county to declare a NFZ, which made all of Wales a NFZ! There was a party on the campsite. Police squad cars arrived. The police thought the campers were burning down the bunker with their campfire, the smoke of which was visible for some distance. The fire was in the shape of a CND symbol and was on a high bank of earth and grass.

Faircloughs, whose men were working on the bunker during the party, sensed the feeling of jubilation in the campers and put their men on overtime, so that the last one did not leave the site until 21.00 hours. One or two of Fairclough's men stopped at the party on their way home and campers maintained friendly relations with them.

Some CND members were worried about the way Faircloughs were increasing the pace of work. Was the ruling cabal in the Labour-controlled county council trying the get the job done more quickly, in

case a future council meeting should decide to cancel the project? That night, Elizabeth Goffe, Chairperson of Bridgend CND, telegraphed Phillip Squire, protesting that the original contract was proceeding with increased speed and that modifications to comply with what appeared to have been decided on 18th February were not being included.

Within hours, County Clerk Hugh Thomas replied, saying there had been no instructions to the contractors to speed up or alter the work, and that the contractors decided on how fast they were to work. Obviously, the council leader had contacted his chief executive overnight, and this appeared to be a sign that the telegram had got Phillip Squire concerned. Normally he would have replied himself to a telegram like this, but this time he seemed worried enough to call in a second opinion. It was clear that no instructions to alter the bunker design had been issued. The bunker was being built as planned, in spite of all the discussion at the Public Protection Committee meeting on 18th February, and Phillip Squire's statement made at that meeting was now seen as just a smokescreen in the light of this statement from his chief executive.

On 26th February, an extraordinary meeting of the Public Protection Committee was held, and again CND lobbied councillors. CND gave them a document explaining the Campaign Committee's views and concern about the work on the bunker; and a letter warning that work had almost reached a stage where changes to convert the bunker to a purely civil structure would become prohibitively expensive, and calling for halt until modifications were made. Mid-Wales Peace Council, the Union of Welsh Congregationalists and CND Cymru wrote to councillors in support of CND's campaign and the Welsh NFZ. Councillors also received a 3,000 word report, from the Clerk (Hugh Thomas) and the Director of Lands and Buildings, on the bunker project, which dismissed CND's arguments against the bunkers, including arguments based on council documents. They also received copies of the government booklet *Civil Defence – Why We Need It*.

Councillors at the Public Protection Committee first discussed the Snow Emergency Report, and this report ended by saying that the now extended bunker would have been useful in the snow – although the existing bunkers weren't used. The timing of this item, before the Labour resolution to stop work on the bunker, appeared to be intended to make councillors consider the peacetime advantages, and possible peaceful uses of the bunker, instead of its proposed use as a government nuclear war control centre. Immediately before the bunker item on the agenda Hugh Thomas warned councillors that their votes would have to be individually recorded. He said councillors voting for the motion, to alter the bunker to one with a purely civil function as an emergency HQ, would risk loss of government grants and the government in Whitehall putting in a civil commissioner to run Civil Defence in Mid-Glamorgan. He warned that people voting for the motion would risk fines, disqualification from local government office and sequestration of their property, as they would be held to have committed wilful misconduct. The fines and other punishments would not, of course, apply to councillors who opposed the motion.

After a brief discussion, the committee by thirty-nine votes to one, voted to alter the bunker design to that of an emergency HQ for civil use only.

Tom Donne, Director of Lands and Buildings, told Mid-Glamorgan CND work would stop, but the *Western Mail* was not so sure, as the Public Protection Committee's vote still had to be confirmed by the full council in three weeks' time. Then CND issued a statement that it would be wasteful and foolish for work to continue. The Campaign Committee held an emergency meeting at the bunker site, which drew about 150 people. It was decided to continue the peace camp at least until the full council met, and to step up the already prodigious efforts directed at county councillors, so that the decision of the full council would, this time, be a clear and unequivocal one to stop building a government nuclear war control centre.

After a short halt, work resumed. Shuttering and reinforcing was erected for the bunker's concrete walls, the shuttering for the planned south wall being put up on St. David's Day. There was no provision for windows in the south wall and no modifications in the design were detected, which were clear indications that work was continuing as planned. The contractors were taking advantage of the lengthening daylight hours of March to work much overtime and work was progressing at a fast rate.

From its first meeting in March, Mid-Glamorgan CND sent a letter to the county council, seeking an urgent meeting with councillors and officials. They got no reply, so they sent another on 5th March, when, by coincidence, they received a strongly worded letter from Faircloughs, telling the peace campers to remove their flags from the radio towers on the bunker site and to take their caravan off the site. This letter seemed to confirm something that the campers had heard unofficially, which was that concrete was to come onto the site and be poured into the walls on 8th March.

CND called in Professor Alan Lipman, Professor of Architecture at the Welsh National School of Architecture in the University of Wales, to examine the bunker structure and what plans he could and prepare a report which would include mention of the possible uses of the bunker.

On Sunday 7th March, the Campaign Committee met briefly, before the public meeting, which was held on the site that day. They discussed what their next move should be and what to do if the concrete arrived to be poured into the shuttering on Monday, as they had unofficially been told it would. Supporting politicians had not been able to do all that had been expected of them. Faircloughs were outpacing the protesters. The first decision at the Campaign Committee was to ask for more mass action in the long-term. CND were to be asked to organise a big, all-Wales demonstration at the bunker site. The committee also decided to ask the protesters to step up the direct action at the bunker site, so that work was either stopped or seriously inhibited. Even with the excellent legal back-up that they had on this campaign, with at least one practising lawyer at the meeting, this was a grim prospect.

The public meeting assembled. The peace camp was presented with a copy of the *Declaration of a Nuclear Free Wales* by Peter Seggar and County Councillor Paul Flynn, members of WANA. They were taking the original of this document to the President of the European Parliament in Strasbourg. Paul Llewellyn told them all that had transpired at the meeting of the Campaign Committee and about its proposals for actions. The proposals were quietly accepted, without dissent.

The following day, Monday, was cold and wet. At 07.30 hours the workers arrived and went up to finish preparing the shuttering. News reached the campers that the concrete was expected to start arriving at 09.00. Although it was cold and wet, Faircloughs reckoned that a little rain was not going to ruin the mix of concrete. The main thing was that it was not freezing, so the concrete could be poured.

Suddenly a worker, high up on the top of the shuttering, cried out. He had found a lot of assorted debris in the shuttering, including enough old clothes to stock a church jumble sale. There was a delay while it was all removed, for the concrete could not be poured on top of it. Everything was kept humorous, with campers erecting a sign "Jumble Sale Today – Proceeds to P. Squire" and big macho workers standing on top of the shuttering holding up items of ladies lingerie they had pulled out of it.

Campers adjourned to the caravan to plan their next move.

Faircloughs cleared an area by the front entrance and at 09.30 a mobile concrete pump, with a long boom and flexible pipe capable of reaching the top of the shuttering, drove into this space. The pump was prepared for work. This was noted in the discussion in the caravan, where the jokes and humour had ceased, and the atmosphere had grown more tense that it had ever been throughout the campaign. They also noted the debris had nearly all been cleared from the shuttering by the workers, while the foreman was working at the far end of the shuttering.

The time had come. Quietly the campers filed out of the caravan and climbed onto the steel reinforcing rods and shuttering. About eight had got on top before the foreman turned and saw them. He gasped. He told them to leave. They did not. By 11.00 hours they had occupied thirty feet run of shuttering.

The police then became involved and, along with officials of Faircloughs, asked to speak to the leader of the activists. They had no leader. This annoyed the police, who then lectured them about the dangers of sitting and lying on top of walls under construction and told them they would achieve nothing by doing it. By an odd coincidence, Commander Squire, the local police chief, was the son of County Council leader, Phillip Squire.

The activists stayed on the shuttering, while more supporters arrived at the site. CND's telephone tree was working flat out. CND had lost no time in contacting the media, either, with the result that the first radio and TV reports to be broadcast brought in yet more supporters. Photographers from the press and *Rebecca* magazine were photographing everything in sight. Trade unionists, who had arrived to support the activists, complained about the working conditions on the bunker site and especially about the safety aspect.

The first concrete mixer lorries had arrived and one had backed up to the pump and coupled onto it. The pump started unloading the lorry and pushing the concrete through its giant hosepipe up towards the top of the shuttering. The boom of the pump was lowered onto the shuttering. The demonstrators lay down on top of the shuttering so that concrete could not be poured into it.

At 12.30 hours, Faircloughs' people went into action once again, this time dragging the heavy pipe from the pump over the activists. Eventually, one moved her legs slightly and the pump let some concrete into the shuttering. New people were coming up to replace activists who were getting tired, wet through, and cold by now. Tony lost his favourite Welsh tweed hat down the shuttering. When he came down, looking like death warned up and covered in setting concrete, he was smiling because he was thinking how his hat would weaken the concrete and hoping it would weaken it enough to make it unacceptable to the county council inspectors. The TV people interviewed him at the site and the interview was broadcast later that day, showing him still covered in concrete. Although the human barrier was

 Bunkers left at Bridgend.

catching some concrete and some was being spilt over the sides, some was getting into the shuttering.

Other campers and supporters were blockading the site, stopping the concrete mixer lorries, sitting around them and talking to the drivers. The police started forcing lorries through the blockade, by directing the drivers to reverse them into people, who had the choice of moving or being run over. One blockader narrowly avoided being crushed between a lorry and the pump, and some time later the driver of the lorry came to a CND meeting and apologised. He said he was obeying police instructions, reluctantly, and he had never been asked to reverse into people before.

In the afternoon a whole section of shuttering collapsed and wet concrete poured out. There was cheering. Fortunately nobody was hurt.

By 17.00 hours, a crowd of spectators had gathered, in addition to all the protesters, police, workers and media people. Everybody was cold and wet with the rain and the police and contractor's men were getting annoyed. By 18.00 a corner wall of the bunker was almost built, but had cost much more time and money than expected. There was no sign of the crowd of activists, demonstrators and spectators getting any smaller, and a possibility that they would increase considerably, when people who had finished work for the day and hurried their teas came to the site. By now the light was poor. Faircloughs packed up and went home.

The demonstrators and activists had not finished work for the day, however. By 19.00 the Campaign Committee had met and were assessing the situation so far. They called for an emergency, full county council meeting, and were to ask the council to make provision at County Hall for CND to put up a photographic exhibition showing what was happening at the site. They used the telephone tree to get supporters to lobby councillors about this meeting and exhibition. Requests for more help at particular times were also put out over the telephones. Bridgend CND, after this Campaign Committee meeting, sent ten telegrams to councillors and officials.

While all this was going on, Professor Lipman had agreed to his report being released to the public as well as to councillors. His report showed that the bunker, when finished, would be sufficiently blast resistant and equipped to resist a nuclear war, though it would not withstand a direct hit.

The next day the county council cancelled their eviction threat to campers, but the contractors continued working, hampered once again by activists. Police and the site foreman still continued to make casual visits to the caravan, but campers were not so keen to see them now, because the campers no longer thought of them as casual visitors, but as spies looking for information.

There were allegations that cables were criminally damaged and oil was said to be seeping into the new walls, ruining the new concrete, though no charges were ever brought. Throughout the period of the campaign at the bunker site, there appear to have been no charges and convictions for any crimes there. This contrasts with other direct action campaigns.

On 10th March, the county council announced it would hold a special meeting to discuss the bunker on 15th March. For the next few days, CND worked feverishly, lobbying councillors, preparing an exhibition and printing and distributing leaflets calling on everybody to visit, phone and lobby councillors.

The Western Mail then reported that a group calling itself 'Spanner in the Works' had announced that they had put oil and salt in the concrete used to pour the bunker walls. If true, this meant that the walls

Radio tower at Brackla Hill

could have been considerably weakened. The peace camp denied any connexion, but did not condemn 'Spanner in the Works'.

Demonstrators dressed in radiation suits and masks confronted councillors, as they arrived in County Hall for the 15th March meeting. Inside, the corridors were full with an exhibition of enlarged photographs of what was happening at the bunker site, and showing the real purpose of the bunker. CND Cymru gave councillors letters expressing concern about what was going on at the site, supporting the council's nuclear free policy, and reminding councillors of the peaceful uses of the bunker. The councillors discussed the recommendations of their Public Protection Committee. Once again, because their decision was linked to the Whitehall government's War Emergency Plan, councillors risked legal sanctions, so votes would have to be individually recorded. They voted in favour of the Public Protection Committee's recommendations sixty-three to four.

News reached the peace camp fast. Campers immediately converted the half-built bunker into a theatrical Welsh cottage by drawing windows, with cats and potted plants in them, on the walls – a reference, of course, to the windows that should have been put in to comply with the decision apparently made on 18th February. This sight greeted jubilant protesters returning from the County Hall victory. Even the sun joined in the celebrations, by making one of his extremely rare appearances over this peace camp!

That evening the Campaign Committee decided to end the occupation after seven more days, provided they had received proper assurances that this time the council would not again try to build a war emergency bunker in disguise. They started preparing their eighth and last newsletter for distribution to supporter and councillors.

The Campaign Committee received the assurances they wanted and on 21st March 1982, the peace camp ended, with a second victory celebration, fifty-seven days after it began.

Mid-Glamorgan CND's resources were now to be concentrated on the All-Wales Easter Demonstration, which was going to involve a march ending at Brackla Hill government bunker two miles from Bridgend Industrial Estate bunker.

At Easter, 1,000 people marched past the remains of the half built bunker on their way to Brackla Hill.

In May demolition workers flattened what was left of the new building, leaving the two original bunkers, established in their wartime blockhouses in 1961, still standing and with accessible doors, under mounds of earth upon which grass later grew. At the time of writing, Mid-Glamorgan County Council had not attempted to build another bunker.

Mid-Glamorgan CND had set themselves four objectives: to stop the war work; to expose the realities of civil defence plans; to further the council's NFZ policy; and to strengthen the peace movement. They achieved these goals. In doing so, they had received massive publicity in South Wales (but very little outside) and got a big boost for CND membership. By their campaigning and lobbying with councillors, they had not only got a county council decision altered by public pressure, but also had strengthened the links between county council decision makers and the general public, thus strengthening the very fabric of democracy in South Wales. Without the peace camp in occupation and their active co-operation in the campaign, as a secondary camp set up to serve the meetings, actions and demonstrations at the site, and as a place where people could maintain a twenty-four hour watch on the bunker, it is very doubtful if the campaign would have achieved anything other than the exposure of the civil defence plans. About 600 people helped at the campsite, and literally thousands more helped with letters, phone calls, transport, telegrams, supplies, and countless other things. The effort was worth it.

OUSTON
PEACE CAMP

Albemarle Barracks occupied an airfield on Ouston Moor, Northumbria, previously known as RAF Ouston. By 1982, Albemarle Barracks had become Northeast England's armed forces HQ for wartime use and was equipped with all the paraphernalia needed for a military HQ to survive a nuclear war – or the first few minutes of one, at any rate.

When I went to RAF Ouston, I lost quite some time searching for it, because there are two Oustons beside Newcastle. I might have had more success if I asked for Albemarle Barracks, but that name wasn't on my map and Ouston was. To find this airfield, follow A69 Westwards from Newcastle-upon-Tyne, and then take B6318 Military Road, signposted 'Wall'. After a mile or two, B6318 passes under a bridge carrying A69. The second turning on the right after this bridge leads across flat, open country, past a farm, to the main entrance to the base.

The Military Road got its name because it was used by Roman troops garrisoning Hadrian's Wall nearly two millennia ago. Now it is used by nuclear weapons convoys.

Exercise Hard Rock, in which Albemarle Barracks was taking part, took place in Autumn, 1982. The peace camp was a protest against this exercise and stayed outside the barracks for its duration.

On Sunday 18th September 1982, the campers first settled on land by the front entrance. This turned out to be MoD land and military police evicted them from it. The local farmer would not let them camp on

his field, so they camped on the grass verge of a lane on the Eastern side of the base, on land owned by the Department of Transport. This lane was the first turning on the right after the aforementioned bridge on Military Road.

Local disarmers countered Hard Rock with rock music in Stamfordham Village Hall, at a 'CND Show' held in support of the camp on 24th September.

Campers held vigils outside the gates, leafleted local villages and got nearly 200 replies to a questionnaire. Relations with local villagers were good, but the soldiers and their families had been ordered not to speak with the peace campers. Apparently nobody gave the camp any real aggro, throughout its three weeks in existence and there were no arrests. Ouston Peace Camp had over sixty visitors. Most of the work fell upon three people: Margaret Wright (who had been active at Hexham and Greenham Common) Andy Thurlow and Steve.

When Exercise Hard Rock ended on 9th October, the campers and supporters held a vigil at the front entrance. They presented the Commanding Officer with a cake decorated with a CND symbol and a book on nuclear disarmament, to show that they wanted the parting to be on friendly terms.

According to Andy Thurlow's report in *Peace News* on 29th October 1982: "The vast majority of local people had no idea of the significance of Albemarle Barracks, and a lot of local interest in peace issues was created by the camp."

FAST FOR LIFE VERSUS GERMS FOR DEATH, AND PORTON DOWN WOMEN'S CAMP FOR PEACE AND ANIMAL LIBERATION

The fifteen-mile long perimeter fence of the Porton Down Ranges enclosed an area of some 10,000 acres, and several secret establishments, including: The Nuclear, Biological, and Chemical Defence (NBC) School; the Chemical Defence Experimental Establishment (CDEE); the Microbiological Research Establishment (MRE); the Public Health Laboratory Service (PHLS) HQ; and Allington Farm, where animals were kept for vivisection experiments.

Documentary evidence existed that horrible experiments had been conducted on defenceless animals here. Often the experiments were done for military purposes, though results were usually made available within the constraints of the Official Secrets Acts to other interested parties. Chemical, gas and biological (germ) warfare experiments have been conducted at Porton. CS gas was invented here. Limited quantities of radioactive materials, along with germs and highly toxic chemicals have been stored here.

Porton Down had been in the hands of the military since World War I, and came under the Salisbury Plain Military By-laws.

The first protest took place at Porton in summer, 1963. I recall it well because it was my first demonstration at a military base. At the planning stage, several organisers, members of the Committee of 100, were arrested, charged, convicted and jailed under the Official Secrets Acts.

The first peace camp – although it was not then called a peace camp – began on 6th May 1967, when Guy Gladstone, a radio disc jockey from Devon, put up a tent beside one of the gates to Porton Down Ranges on A30. Before doing so, he announced, in a letter published in the *Salisbury Journal*, that he would be fasting there for one week. Originally two other people joined him in his 'Fast for Life v. Germs for Death', but he was alone in his tent one night when a firework was thrown into it from a passing car. Guy put out the resultant small fire. He then phoned supporters in Salisbury, and told them what had happened. It was decided that he would have to be rescued, but Salisbury supporters had no vehicle available. There was no bus either, so Guy had to stay the night. On the following morning, a *Southern Evening Echo* journalist heard of Guy's plight. He went in his van to the campsite and rescued Guy, in return for a story.

On 2nd April 1982 the largest of many Porton demonstrations took place. The British Union Against Vivisection estimated that there were 5,000 people on the march to the MRE Main Gate from Salisbury; the police estimated only 2,500. Several fences were torn down, five windows were broken and twenty-nine arrests made.

Porton Down Women's Camp for Peace and Animal Liberation was set up on the opposite side of A30 from Porton Down on 13the March 1983 at the unholy hour, for a Sunday, of 05.20. The camp was opposite a gated road that was normally open to the public and which led across the ranges past the MRE Main Gate. It lay on a piece of road verge reserved for a future road widening scheme at a junction between A30 and a minor road to Pitton. The new camp consisted of a small caravan and a tent or two. The campers were all women vegetarians and vegans and they planned to stay until September.

This camp's first big event was a march from Salisbury to the camp on Saturday 23rd April. Next, on 30th April, campers walked around the perimeter of Porton Down Ranges, leaving silver stars and moons on the fences in memory of the animals locked up in the laboratories. Unlike animals in fields, and in the wild, these animals may never see the stars and the moon.

On Mayday the women followed this up with a children's party at one of the gates. They climbed over an ordinary farm fence onto a MoD-owned field, and danced a traditional Maypole dance around a flagpole just inside. There were, apparently, no arrests.

On 24thMay, campers attended a vigil in Guildhall Square, Salisbury, in honour of Clara Haber, who tried, but failed to stop her husband from experimenting with nerve gas for the military.

In June, the Porton women, along with women on Greenham Common, about thirty miles away, began to make a giant cloth dragon, using pieces of cloth sent from all over the world. The manufacture of the dragon took months and it was reputed to be a mile or more long when it was finished.

Folk came to Porton Peace Camp for a women's batik workshop in early June; to a vigil at midsummer; and on a bicycle rally from Winchester on 30th June.

On Hiroshima Day, the Porton campers held a twenty-four-hour commemorative fast in Guildhall Square, Salisbury.

At about this time, a tent was set alight by two soldiers. Nobody was sleeping in it at the time, but the tent and contents were badly damaged. The soldiers, who also stole another tent, were arrested and charged with arson and theft.

On Saturday evening, 20th August, the last section of the giant dragon arrived at Porton Peace Camp, having been carried on a long march through Andover by thirty women from Greenham Common. They stayed the night at Porton and most of them left on the Sunday.

A few stayed on at Porton. These appear to have been the nucleus of the next action, when, on 22nd August, ten women were spotted on MoD land in CDEE. They were apparently setting up a new peace camp to replace the one beside A30, which would soon have to close because of road widening. When the modplods arrived, the women stood in a circle singing, and when they were asked to leave, seven refused. The seven were arrested and charged with remaining on military land without lawful authority or permission, in breach of the Salisbury Plain Military By-Laws.

On 27th August, about 250 people came to demonstrate at Allington Farm, on the other side of Porton Down from the peace camp. The Salisbury to Grateley railway line divides Allington Farm from a country road and civilian farmland. A public bridge across this railway leads to a gate to the farm. Before reaching the bridge, the minor road ran parallel to the railway for a few hundred yards. Some demonstrators took a shortcut across the railway and over the farm perimeter fence. The authorities claimed the railway had to be closed for forty-five minutes and when the 13.33 Exeter to Waterloo intercity train appeared, travelling very cautiously because the driver had been warned about demonstrators on the line, about 100 demonstrators sat down on the line, and forced it to stop. The demonstrators were then alleged to have swarmed over the engine and leafleted passengers in the coaches behind. About fifty demonstrators eventually got over the fence onto MoD land, some by means of the bridge and some by crossing the railway, but only two managed to reach and get among the buildings at Allington Farm.

This action was not entirely non-violent. *Salisbury Journal*, on 1st September 1983, reported Doug Read, a local man, as saying he saw another demonstrator punch a policeman who had repeatedly punched him; police dogs bit two women demonstrators, who had to go to hospital, along with four injured police personnel. None were kept in overnight. Amazingly, only two people were arrested and charged: Alex Mark Bywater and Rennie Stephen Rogers from Nottinghamshire. They were charged with trespassing on the railway and without authority or permission remaining on military land. Later, a special court sitting at Salisbury Police Station adjourned their cases because on the railway trespass charge both pleaded not guilty. After the big demonstration had ended, a small group continued the protest into the evening, at the gate to Allington Farm.

On Friday, 23rd September, at a special sitting of Salisbury magistrates in the Guildhall, the seven women peace campers arrested in CDEE, on 22nd August, were each fined £35, with £40 costs, for remaining on military land without permission. They were: Suzanne Woods, Julie Andrews, Lorna Richardson, Lucy Johns and Anne Turton of Greenham Common Peace Camp; Dorothea Shelly Annison of Birmingham and Marilyn Alice O'Brien of London. They pleaded not guilty and used the court to good advantage to explain why they were on military land and how they believed they had done the right thing in protesting there.

Bywater and Rogers appeared before Salisbury County Magistrates Bench on Tuesday 27th September. They maintained not guilty pleas on the railway trespass charges and were acquitted. They pleaded guilty to remaining on military land at Allington Farm without permission and were each fined £35 with £30 costs.

Also, in September, two soldiers charged with arson and theft appeared before the magistrates in the Guildhall. Both arson charges were dropped by the prosecution, but the soldiers were each convicted and fined £75 on the theft charges.

The peace camp ended about this time, and Wiltshire County Council started using the site to widen A30.

'Porton whitewash' had no connexion with 'Greenham porridge'. The former name originated in the way the Army tended to whitewash everything that didn't move, to make it look clean – 'a coat of paint can cover a multitude of sins', as the saying goes. Porton protesters gave this name early on to the method used by the authorities, which basically involved showing visitors and enquirers the nice things and blinding them with science, whilst endeavouring to stave off questions about the nasty bits, which are not shown. Misleading press releases were also part of this game.

Robert Key, the local Tory MP, visited Porton Down in October, after declaring himself an animal lover. He said he would ask awkward questions on his visit. They can't have been very awkward, for he completed his visit and he came out apparently satisfied with the way the animals were being treated there.

Although four campers – Mandy, Carolyn, Ruth and Margaret – had featured in a big write-up about the camp published in the *Salisbury Journal* on 30th June, and had followed it with two published letters to the editor, publicity was not this camp's strong point. Another weakness was its isolated location, six miles from Salisbury, and eleven miles from Andover, at least a half-an-hour's walk from the nearest village, with few buses passing nearby. Wiltshire is sparsely populated, and much of that population is military. For these reasons, local support was not good.

The Porton campers are to be commended for their brave efforts. Protests continue there with talk of another peace camp.

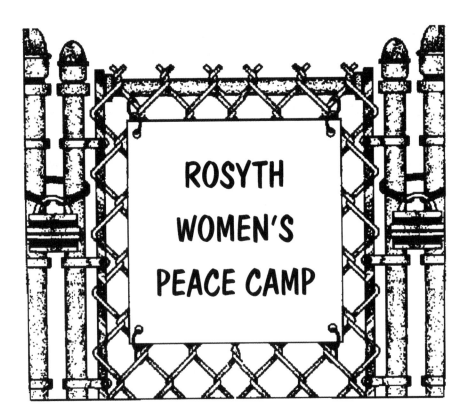

ROSYTH
WOMEN'S
PEACE CAMP

The Royal Naval Dockyard at Rosyth is where Britain's nuclear submarines are fitted out and repaired and there have been several demonstrations here, both before and after the peace camp.

On Sunday 22nd May 1983, Rosyth Women's Peace Camp was set up beside a roundabout running under the main road coming off the northern end of the Forth Bridge in Scotland. The camp was situated on wasteland between the roundabout and a sewage farm, about a mile from the dockyard gates.

On the first night fifteen women stayed at the camp.

The campers leafleted the local towns of Rosyth, North Queensferry and Inverkeithing in May and June.

The RN Dockyard held an open weekend on 9th and 10th July. On the Saturday, campers did street theatre and leafleted outside the dockyard, mostly at the Main Gate, which faced an enormous car park. On the Sunday, the campers went inside and as soon as the marines had finished a display, forty-two women moved onto the piece of ground they had just left and did an anti-war theatre act. The authorities broke it up and arrested one woman, who was charged with breach of the peace. The others refused to leave until the police released this woman. After charging her and detaining her for an hour, she was released and all the women left.

On the weekend of 24th-25th September, a vigil was held at the Main Gate and bulbs were planted at the campsite to flower in the spring. They were to be a reminder of the camp and why it was there. That Sunday the camp was laid down as planned, with neither eviction nor threat of eviction. While it had been there, Rosyth Women's Peace Camp had done much useful campaigning.

RAF
ST MAWGAN
FORGOTTEN,
FORLORN AND
WITHOUT A PROPER
PERIMETER FENCE

RAF St. Mawgan, in 1983, had no proper perimeter fence and looked forgotten and forlorn. It was nothing of the sort. In addition to being a vital airfield on the South-Western tip of the United Kingdom commanding the Channel and Irish Sea approaches and of great value to aircraft flying over the Atlantic, this was a USN forward operating base for anti-submarine aircraft capable of carrying nuclear depth charges. Up to November 1983, its remote location, just inland from Watergate Bay on the North Coast of Cornwall, far from any big cities, had protected it from protests.

In support of Greenham Women Against Cruise taking their fight against Cruise in Europe to the American courts, nuclear disarmers all over Britain organised actions at the local US bases for twenty-four hours over 8th and 9th November 1983. A peace camp was established on Tuesday 8th November, at RAF St. Mawgan.

On the morning of 9th November, after a group of women had camped the night, numbers increased to about seventy when people who had come for the day joined them. They all linked hands across the approach road in a circle, right in front of the entrance to the airfield. They then sang, and circled round and round in the road. Some women sat in the road and caused a traffic jam. Other women were then able to approach and talk to car drivers caught in the jam. Police appeared uncertain as to how to tackle this action. They neither removed nor arrested people, and the blockade broke up voluntarily. The campers broke camp, and left on Wednesday 9th No-

vember, as planned.

Over the weekend of 11th-12th December 1984, there was a vigil, peace camp and demonstration at the airfield. Local people organised these events to commemorate the fifth anniversary of the NATO decision to base Cruise missiles in Europe.

The third St. Mawgan Peace Camp took place over the weekend of 16th -17th March 1985. The organisers made a shrewd decision when choosing the campsite: just outside the offices of Radio Cornwall, not far from the airfield. This site virtually guaranteed them good radio and TV coverage! As well as raising the issue of nuclear weapons at RAF St. Mawgan, this camp raised £100 for Ethiopian famine relief. As at the previous camps, nobody was arrested and charged with any offence.

The campaign continued here, with several direct actions, but no more peace camps up to the time of writing. There were three arrests sat the first 'snowball' action here, in spring 1985. On 5th July, three more people were arrested, after spending an hour sunbathing on a flat roof inside the air base. At the same time, three other protesters lay padlocked to the gate until authorities released them. All six were released without charge. On 18th and 19th January 1986, as a result of another 'snowballing', twenty-five people were arrested and charged with criminal damage.

Clearly the protesters are not going to let us forget RAF St. Mawgan.

SHEFFIELD PEACE CENTRE

In a prime commercial site, at 94 Surrey Street, Sheffield, just across the road from the Central Library, stood an empty, disused Masonic hall, with electricity laid on and a telephone that worked. It was owned by Sheffield City Council. On 10th January 1983, it was taken over by squatters.

The squatters were members of Sheffield Peace Action, including Sheffield Poly students.

Disarmers in the city had been talking about a peace centre for years; the city council had been planning to start a peace shop for eighteen months. Now Sheffield Peace Centre was in being, with a library/workshop, crèche and exhibition hall. A vegetarian cafe, films, theatre and musical events were planned. Meetings of various organisations were being held there.

As the building was squatted, it could only be a temporary peace centre. To make it permanent, a lease for this building, or another like it, would have to be negotiated. Thousands of signatures were collected on a petition asking for a permanent peace centre, during the time that Sheffield Peace Centre was open.

Sheffield City Council were keen to welcome CND conferences to the NFZ, with all the money the visitors to these events brought, but they weren't so keen to encourage their local peace centre, because it occupied a prime commercial site from which the council wanted a fat profit. Immediately the centre was set up, the council applied for an order in possession. On the second day they arranged for the electricity and telephones to be disconnected.

The court hearing was set for 10.30 hours, on Monday 14th March 1983. The activists expected an eviction and arrived at court with plans for an alternative site to which they could move on 16th March, provided they could stay eviction until after that day. They found that the hearing had been held in camera at 10.00 hours and the council's order had been granted in their absence, without sufficient time being allowed to enable them to move to the other site as a centre. They were evicted and it seems were unable to restart on the other site. Sadly, this attempt to bring peace as a commodity to city centre shoppers failed after two months, during which it showed great promise.

At the time of writing 94 Surrey Street is part of a public house called 'The Surrey' selling 'Mansfield' beers.

THE CAMP FOR A SAFE FUTURE AT SNAPE AND SIZEWELL

The public enquiry for the Sizewell Pressurised Water Reactor Nuclear Power Station took place in a blaze of nation-wide publicity, at quiet, rural Snape Maltings, Suffolk, in 1983 and 1984.

During the enquiry, the Camp for a Safe Future stood across the river, on land owned by a sympathetic smallholder.

Set up in the spring of 1983, with a caravan borrowed from Molesworth, this camp soon established itself, with chickens and crops in the garden. The camp organisers, the Sizewell Non-violent Action Group, undertook various alternative technology projects. Sadly, reliable scientific reports of this aspect of their work do not seem to exist. The camp also provided support for anti-nuclear people attending the enquiry.

After a fast at Lakenheath Peace Camp and a night's rest, the 'Light for Life' march started on its seventy-mile walk to Sizewell, on New Year's Day, 1984. The march spent the night of 5ᵗ January at the Camp for a Safe Future. The campers by then had two buses and some other vehicles in which they lived. The marchers had performed street theatre in towns through which they passed. Now they sat in a circle, keening, in a hall at Snape Maltings, as the enquiry continued. Keening is an old American Indian custom, involving a kind of humming.

From Snape, the march went to Sizewell itself, where the marchers slept in a large marquee for the night of 6ᵗʰ January, before splitting. Sizewell Camp was thus only a one-night stand.

These peace camps were committed to positive non-violent opposition to the construction of a nuclear power station capable of producing materials and training technologists, for the manufacture of nuclear weapons.

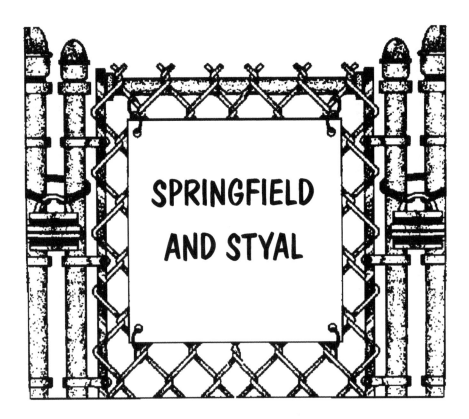

SPRINGFIELD AND STYAL

As tents were being pitched by twenty-five women outside the BNFL plant at Springfield, near Preston, Lancashire, on Saturday 24th August 1985, in preparation for a two-week peace camp, about fifty police arrived in five vehicles and ordered the women to leave the campsite within two minutes.

They had no eviction order; they did not say which law gave them the order to do what they were doing; but they did say all police leave in Lancashire had been cancelled that weekend so as to have enough policemen available to deal with Springfield Peace Camp. The police physically prevented some tents from being erected and harassed the women campers. There was a real danger of violence developing, which could lead to property damage, and people getting hurt. There was no way the women would tolerate anybody getting hurt, so after attempting to pitch camp, the women negotiated with police and were allowed to picket the gate provided they did not stop vehicles. They picketed the gate for a time, without incident.

It was clear that, after all that had happened at Capenhurst, BNFL was paranoid about peace camps and was not going to permit anything of the sort at Springfield. Although BNFL claims to be in the nuclear power business, its connexions with the manufacture and maintenance of nuclear weapons are well known – as also is the location of their Springfield plant, thanks to the publicity gained by the peace campers.

Over the years, many women peace campers had been imprisoned in Styal Women's Prison in Manchester. When all the women left Springfield later that Saturday, some went to Styal and finished the weekend with a brief uneventful camp outside the prison, in solidarity with sisters inside. Here they were allowed to set up a temporary peace camp without being evicted (see 'The Inside Story', by Sue Lamb and Lynn Fortt, *Radiator*, February 1983.).

Though short in duration, both these camps had received publicity, and had thus been able to publicise what was going on at Springfield in particular.

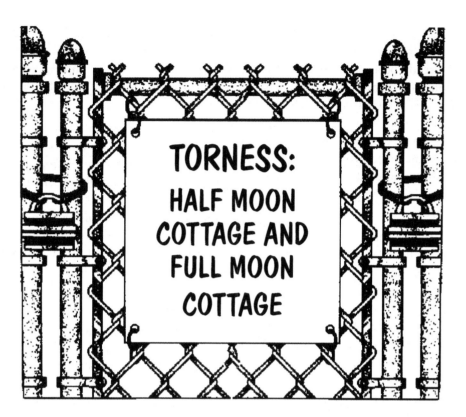

TORNESS:
HALF MOON COTTAGE AND FULL MOON COTTAGE

News of a plan to build a nuclear power station with an advanced gas-cooled reactor (the AGR type) and a private dock for the station's exclusive use, thirty miles from Edinburgh, Scotland, became public knowledge during 1977 and 1978.

At first local people on the whole accepted the plan, which promised well-paid jobs on the construction for some local workers. Construction was due to begin in October, 1978, after the farmers' leases on the land had expired on 30th September. The site chosen by the South of Scotland Electricity Board (SSEB) was farmland between A1 road and the sea at Torness, about seven miles south of Dunbar.

The SSEB went ahead with this plan to build a new power station to produce electricity, in spite of statistics based on their own figures, which said that, in 1978, Scotland already had an electricity generating capacity fifty per cent over demand, even after reducing this figure by twenty per cent to allow for possible equipment breakdowns.

After publicity all over Britain, the protests began with a march from Dunbar to the reactor site on Saturday 6th May 1978. Upon arrival at Torness, people set up the first camp at this site for the weekend, with the agreement of a farmer, who was still using land there. They held a rally, with the theme, 'Torness – Keep it Green'. Out of this grew the Torness Alliance. Only one arrest is reported to have taken place, apparently for a drugs offence.

Over the weekend of 1st-2nd July, the Torness Alliance held its first meeting in Edinburgh. This was an alliance of anti-nuclear groups from all over Scotland and from England as far south as Brighton. It was strongly supported by Lancashire and Cumbrian groups in particular. Consequently, the second meeting was in Colne, Lancashire, in August, by which time a plan for the second protest at Torness had been devised. This plan was to occupy the SSEB site in order to prevent, or at least delay, the start of construction in October. An occupying group was formed, with people from a dozen or so groups from all over the alliance area. The next meeting of the alliance was again in Lancashire, at the demonstration held against the new nuclear reactor at Heysham Power Station, on the weekend of 16th-17th September. This was not a full meeting. It involved just the occupying group, who met to discuss details of the plan and ascertain precisely who would be at Torness.

The action began in earnest when the occupying group assembled, along with other alliance people, in Edinburgh, at the offices of the Scottish Committee to Resist the Atomic Menace (SCRAM) on 22nd September. They were to be together from now until after they had moved into Half Moon Cottage.

On Sunday, 24th September, a person who lived in the Torness area told the occupiers all about the site and about its geography and topography as well. Included was information about the local people and up-to-date news of their opinions about the new power station. This was very useful, even to those who had already been to Torness. The group then prepared a fact sheet about the proposed power station, and arranged for 10,000 copies to be printed. They discussed details of tactics; liaison between the occupiers and their support group, who would be camped outside the fence; what to do if arrested; and many other things necessitated by the nature of an operation which had to be planned with military precision and secrecy.

On the Tuesday they went to the Base Camp, on land just outside the boundary of the area the SSEB was acquiring. Tents and a big bonfire were already there, having been put there by supporters who arrived early. Just to show that the camp wasn't against modern technology, they had a geodesic dome (a type of lightweight building only recently invented by Buckminster Fuller in the USA). This particular geodesic dome is believed to have subsequently been used in at least two other camps – the London Peace Camp in Jubilee Gardens and Upper Heyford Peace Camp – and was last heard of in the hands of a Campaign Atom member in Oxfordshire. The campers at Torness had access to a telephone in a local campaign supporter's home.

The campers then spent three days building up Base Camp and preparing the equipment, food and other supplies for their planned occupation, which was still being kept secret.

In spite of the campers' precautions, someone got wind of the proposed occupation,. On the Wednesday, a journalist from the East Lothian Courier visited the camp, and asked questions about it, and when it was to happen. He said SCRAM had told him there was to be an occupation, but had not given him details including the date and time. The campers pretended they knew nothing about the occupation. The next day the *Courier* announced that an occupation was planned, but gave no date. A *Courier* staff member phoned the camp's telephone contact and also spoke to SCRAM, saying the campers were hostile and obstructive to their reporter. SCRAM told the camp that the *Courier* had complained to them and also that nobody from SCRAM had told the *Courier* of the proposed occupation.

This put the occupiers in a spot. Would the authorities now bring in guards to prevent the occupation from starting? Originally they had planned to enter on the night of Saturday 30th September to be on site when midnight struck when the SSEB took over,

and then stay for a week before leaving. However, it was felt that, in view of the publicity, a start as soon as possible was imperative, so the incursion was brought forward twenty-four hours to the Friday evening.

In darkness and rain about seventeen occupiers moved in, and set up their tents around a roofless cottage standing where the reactor complex was to be built. Throughout the weekend, they worked on Half Moon Cottage, helped by a local builder, putting in floors, roof beams, a fireplace and a chimney. Most of the materials were donated by local farmers. It wasn't all work and no play, though! It was still warm enough weather for some workers to go down to the sea and bathe to wash off the dust and sweat from time to time.

Once the campers had entered, the media were informed. The local and national press were sympathetic with their first reports. Unfortunately, owing to there being no advance warning of the action because of the need for secrecy, no TV cameras could come and record the first day of the occupation. Now this problem of notice and TV cameras can be overcome. One method is that used to get the media to attend the direct action at Greenham Common on New Year's Day, 1983. (See '1983 Began Before Dawn on January 1') Another is to have a person with a cine camera in the group of activists, who can make a standing arrangement to supply a TV company with film, when their own people cannot film the action.

Some odd individuals got involved with the campers, though they were not part of either the support group, or of the occupying group. They soon left Torness itself, but stayed in the area, and caused some friction with local people, who thought they were part of the Torness Alliance. In spite of this, the locals, many of whom were not supporters in the beginning, were becoming sympathetic to the occupiers.

In the first week, the occupiers, working on the cottage, got many visits from reporters and TV people. Because there were so many visits, and there was so much work to be done, they decided to carry on working, and to talk to reporters as they worked. They spent much time explaining the Torness Alliance policy – as they worked, of course — to the media people. The TV people didn't like it, as they wanted people to pose for good camera shots, and needed timed interviews for their news bulletins.

At the end of the week, the occupiers decided to stay for a few more days. Half Moon Cottage was nearing completion and the SSEB was due to start work soon. The occupiers appeared to be the only people on the site, apart from their visitors. Some occupiers had to leave at the end of the first week, but others were prepared to stay much longer, especially after the support group from Base Camp joined the people at the cottage, in the middle of October.

A rumour was circulating locally at about this time, that the Communist Party was paying the campers £100 a week each. Unfortunately, (they could have done with the money) this was not true and the Communists paid them nothing.

The SSEB stated publicly that they would not evict the occupiers until after work started, and only then if they were in danger, or in the way of the work being done.

On 24th October, the Greenpeace boat *Rainbow Warrior* anchored offshore. The crew visited the occupiers and gave them food. This visit got the occupation still more publicity.

By the end of October, the cottage had been roofed and the SSEB had not even started construction. No matter – the cottage had no need of a nuclear power station! It had all the electric light it wanted from a wind generator, installed on the weekend of 28th -29th October. Torness was producing electricity, but not for the SSEB!

The cottage and tents around it now contained four women and twenty-five men. Throughout the occupation to date numbers had varied, up to around thirty, but seven people had lived there all the time.

Meanwhile, other members of the Torness Alliance were meeting in Nottingham, to hear a progress report from the occupiers – and a report of no progress by the SSEB – and plan future strategy.

At about this time, SCRAM did an 'Open Door' programme, which was broadcast by BBC TV. It included film of the occupation. Also, local and regional papers were giving sympathetic publicity to the occupation.

On Monday 13th November the occupiers, who had learned beforehand that they were coming, greeted the men who worked for Rodgers, the SSEB civil engineering contractors, when they arrived to start work, with a bonfire at the entrance to the site, and talked to them. The reporters and TV cameras arrived, and a local person read out a press statement to them, which had been prepared by the Lothians and Borders Anti-Nuclear Group. Two JCB diggers and a bulldozer arrived, but had to stay outside the site, as occupiers and local people had blocked their access with vans.

One of the JCBs attempted to knock down a field wall with its bucket, to gain entry to the site. Immediately three occupiers boarded the bucket. The driver jerked his bucket, causing one person to fall out, without sustaining serious injury. Rodgers' foreman then stopped work and called in the police. The activists got out of the bucket. By then the occupiers had started pulling out of the ground marker pegs left by the surveyors. When the police arrived, they saw them doing this and warned them that, if they continued, there would be arrests and malicious damage charges. Then a SCRAM activist sat in front of the bulldozer, which was about to go through the entrance, which police had cleared. He was arrested, charged with breach of the peace and released later that day. Not wanting any more arrests at this stage, the occupiers retreated to Half Moon Cottage.

On the Tuesday morning the police went to the cottage and removed all but three of the occupiers. The three were left sitting on the roof for a time, before they also were removed. By dusk on Tuesday 14th November, a total of fifteen occupiers had been arrested and Half Moon Cottage had been reduced to a heap of stones and rubble by Rodgers' machines.

Now men, materials and machines were on site ready to install a water main. Work began on digging the trench for it. The activists left.

The protesters began returning to Base Camp on 18th November, in preparation for a day of action to stop work on Monday 20th November.

On the Sunday morning, 400 people marched round the site and a local farmer returned to a field, which the SSEB had acquired from him and symbolically ploughed part of it. That evening activists met to plan tactics for the direct action. They were to organise into autonomous groups of about ten, each with its own back-up people and legal observers. Though autonomous, the groups would communicate and co-operate with each other.

At dawn on the Monday, the first groups went onto the SSEB land and lit fires. Some activists went to the ruins of Half Moon Cottage, where they built two low walls and a cairn. Rodgers' men arrived, to be greeted by the occupiers at the gate, who talked to them, gave them mugs of hot tea and let off balloons. Some machines were delayed getting onto the site. Shortly afterwards about fifty people occupied a pit that Rodgers' men were trying to enlarge, using two diggers. The men had a job to do, however, and in spite of the interruptions, they got on with it. Police were concentrating on helping to keep the work continuing, rather than arresting people. Nevertheless, they had to organise stops several times to remove occupiers from dangerous places and from machines left unguarded. Out of the hundreds of activists there, only thirty-eight were arrested. All were charged with breach of the peace. Then a policeman was hit and injured by a passing lorry on A1. Activists were not involved. However, because of this accident, they ceased the action early, met and issued a statement expressing sympathy with the injured man, and saying their campaign was against the SSEB, not the police. They then left.

A good supporting demonstration in Nottingham on 26th November was given much publicity by the media. This had one street theatre group trying to build a mock nuclear power station in several different places in the city, while another group of actors kept trying to stop them and trying to pull it down.

The 'Gathering' took place at a camp on Barns Ness, two miles up the coast from Torness towards Dunbar, on 5th-7th May, 1979. There was plenty of sea, sun and sand along with bands playing music, kites and a horse and cart giving rides for children – everything one could want for a good family holiday. There was good food available, plenty of information and the site was well signposted from A1. The weekend was not all fun, however; there was direct action too.

A briefing meeting for all the prospective participants was held on the Saturday night, with about 500 people present. Obviously getting any decision made was not easy with this large number. Some were in favour of the planned non-violence training outside the site during the Sunday, followed by an incursion on Sunday night, for NVDA when the workers arrived on the Monday. Others – the wreckers – wanted to go in on Sunday morning, as they could not stay for Monday. Unity was regarded as very important, even though people were organised into groups, so it was decided to cut short the non-violence training, and enter on Sunday morning.

Meanwhile, in the midst of the Saturday shopping crowds, some people climbed the 200 foot-high Walter Scott Memorial in the centre of Edinburgh and hung out a banner which read: STOP TORNESS. During this protest, a lorry carrying what appeared to be radioactive waste just happened to pass by. This lorry may have been a stunt arranged by the demonstrators.

During Saturday night the Torness fence was 'loosened' (Quoted by *Peace News* 22nd June 1979. More reports of this event are in *Peace News*, 18th May and 8th June.) and a few holes dug under it to assist entry. Though this had been agreed at the meeting, it was not part of the original plan.

On the Sunday morning a local farmer, as planned, produced a load of hay bales. Some were piled into a staircase up against the Torness boundary fence and others were dropped on the other side to make a staircase down. The incursion took place in three waves, the first being mainly composed of the wreckers, who wanted to leave early. Some of them made straight for the inner compound and started wrecking unguarded earth-moving machines, whilst others made for the main entrance and erected a barricade just inside it. Two more waves followed them and more NVDA took place all over the site. Messages, in felt-tip pen, were left on everything inside, telling the workers to stop building the nuclear power station. Other messages were made with stones, paint, flowers laid in a pattern and anything that came to hand. The surveyors' posts were moved, tyres were let down and a stream was diverted to make two big floods on the road through the site. About 3,000 activists were on the SSEB land. Although there was a hole in the fence and a couple dug under it nearby, most people entered by the staircase of bales. There was only a handful of police at the main gate and a similar number in the inner compound, so they did little to impede the action, the size of which seems to have come as a surprise to them, as even when reinforcements arrived at the main gate, there were only about sixty in that force, and they were unable to drive in because of the barrier. Already the police in the compound, in spite of their small number, had managed to make two arrests and were preparing to charge their prisoners with malicious damage, so their reinforcements could have arrested many more people. However, other activists managed to persuade the wreckers to leave the inner compound and cease wrecking before the reinforcements got to it and started arresting people. The press were expected to arrive in a helicopter, so the brilliant idea arose of forming the activists into a giant 'NO' for them. Although the press helicopter didn't come, the exercise was worth doing, because when it had been done, it was found to have eased an atmosphere that was getting tense in places, and helped to keep people together. Had the tense atmosphere erupted into a riot, people might have got hurt.

On the Sunday night, about 100 activists actually

stayed on the site in makeshift shelters and tents. The barrier had apparently been moved, police were coming and going as they pleased and more reinforcements may have come.

On Monday morning, more activists came onto the site in two waves. Rodgers' men also came on and began work. Vehicles were repaired, tyres inflated, shelters demolished and as many messages as possible were erased. Activists put a few more messages around, built a croft and an adventure playground and hindered operations a bit.

By Monday night only twenty-five were left on the site. These remaining activists had their morale boosted when police, in a hurry to leave the site, smashed some drainage pipes with their vehicle.

Whilst all this activity was taking place on the site, the young children were still camped on the seashore. They were being entertained by some of the older folk who had not wanted to be involved in the action.

A crowd of demonstrators formed outside the main gate on Tuesday morning and attempted to put an information hut there. Police would not allow it, so the trailer carrying the hut was towed off. Meanwhile, about fifty people started to leaflet the few workers who came to work. At this time the leafletters didn't know the authorities had diverted most of the workers by another gate. The leafletters then had a die-in and two people in white coats walked around with what appeared to be Geiger counters, checking the bodies for radioactivity and rearranging them. Then they all got up, and left, carrying a shrouded body, wearing a skull mask on a board. The people from inside the site apparently left with them.

On the weekend of 19th-20th May, the Torness Alliance met in York, and discussed this latest action. There was encouraging news about increasing local opposition to the power station. Lothian Regional Council was now opposed to the power station, and a local paper was campaigning against it. The information hut was stationed in a lay-by on A1 and the police had allowed it to stay there.

There was no camp at Torness for the next action, when, early on 29th October 1979, about twenty people from Severnside Anti-nuclear Alliance arrived and quickly erected a scaffold tower in the main entrance. They chained the main gate shut with their own chain and padlock. This did not worry the SSEB who just went to open the other two gates. Both had their padlocks glued up with 'Araldite'!

This delayed the start of work, while the SSEB brought a man with cutting gear to each gate in turn, and got him to cut the padlocks so that the gates could be opened. The main gates remained closed all day. All traffic had to enter and leave by roundabout routes through the other gates, and there were problems when large lorries could not get through them. Keith Wood reports: "As dusk fell an inspector intimated that we would be allowed to remain all night (and freeze)." (*Peace News*, 9th November 1979) Soon after dark, when the press had gone and activists' cameras had been put away, the police attacked the tower, and the activists chained to it, with bolt-cutters and oxy-acetylene. They brought down and arrested nine activists, and charged them with breach of the peace. The police then unchained the main gate and ensured it could be opened in the morning. The main gate was metal framed, with chain-link wire, opened from the centre and was about eight feet high. The tower was bedecked with banners and about four feet square and twenty high. At about this time the Severnside Alliance used a tower to stop a train carrying radioactive waste to docks on the River Severn. It may have been this same tower; at any rate the technique was the same.

By 1980, the Torness Alliance had evolved into the Torness Public Parks Department, with activists calling themselves park-keepers. On Friday 20th May 1980, about 150 park-keepers set up camp in a field near the reactor site, aiming to occupy the site, landscape some parts of it and do a little saboutage.

Around midnight a small advance party sneaked off to cut the fence to enable the park-keepers to just pull it aside and enter when the time came. Most of this group returned, somewhat shaken, after about half-an-hour. While they were at the fence, police with riot sticks and dogs had appeared and chased them. Within an hour, a crew that was already on site had repaired the fence. The strength of the forces behind that fence and their response times, meant that an incursion could not be contemplated lightly.

The rumour had got around in Dunbar that the activists were really armed terrorists, so on the Saturday many of them went into Dunbar to leaflet the town centre, and talk to shoppers to reassure them there were no armed terrorists at Torness.

Later on Saturday, a confrontation arose at the main gate. Some activists were yelling insults at police behind it. Police dogs were getting noisy and restless. Someone threw a stone from the back of the crowd over the heads and over the gate. The atmosphere was getting tense. Then one park-keeper threw a small black ball with the word bomb printed on it, over the fence. All hell was let loose. The police suddenly charged out of the gate and pursued him as he ran through the crowd. They caught him. Other activists then piled into the middle of the road, sat down, linked arms and blocked the road. The police waded in, kicking and shoving and eighteen more arrests were made, including a person at the side taking photos. Then a passage was cleared through the crowd. Shortly after, another park-keeper was arrested for painting on the road and three more were arrested for not getting up from the edge of the road when police executed a manoeuvre which succeeded in getting everyone off the tarmac. A few park-keepers were active elsewhere around the site at the time and four of these were also arrested, bringing the police score to twenty-seven. All were detained. The tough police action was not surprising, as there were about twice as many police as park-keepers and the police had a helicopter to help them with air cover and a launch to help them on the coast, as well as floodlights after dark.

For the rest of the weekend, everyone was making efforts to see that the detainees were fairly treated and trying to get them released. They were all going to be charged, and the police chief had said they would not be released on bail until the park-keepers broke camp and left Torness. Apparently the detainees were awkward customers inside the cells, and catering for such a large number of prisoners at the police station was inconvenient. Other park-keepers were constantly hanging around outside and hassling police about detainees. This all appeared to annoy the local police chief, and he probably found the activists in his cells more of a nuisance that they were worth. It appears that the charges he was threatening to use would not have stood up in court in many cases. He released the prisoners on Monday morning, and apparently all the charges were dropped. The park-keepers celebrated with street theatre in front of the police station before going home.

A week later, on Saturday, 10th May, 300 of the Students Against Nuclear Energy met near Torness and marched to the main gate where they left a coffin. Later that night, five of them were arrested cutting the perimeter fence. Some students camped that night, but no action appears to have taken place on the Sunday.

A week of action was planned for 9th-17th May 1981, for which a training weekend was held in Edinburgh on 25th-26th April.

At this time Edinburgh was a nuclear-free city, and had been the first NFZ in Britain (years before Manchester became one). Lothian Regional Council, however, was just leaning that way, although they had already come out against Torness after construction of the nuclear power station had started. Now, in the May local government elections, Lothian Council had acquired a Labour majority. Local anti-nuclear people had got a motion to declare Lothian a NFZ onto the council's agenda. This was coming up in early June and had a good chance of being passed.

On Saturday 9th May 1981, the week of action began in Edinburgh, with a picket of the SSEB showroom. Then the protesters organised a street theatre there. Some acted the parts of Rio Tinto Zinc prospectors drilling for uranium, while others attempted to stop them. Saturday shoppers were impressed.

Then eighteen gaily decorated vehicles left Edinburgh in a motorcade bound for Base Camp at Torness. They parked on the campsite and from there a group of women and children marched, with a group of women dressed in black carrying a coffin at the front, to the Main Gate of the reactor site. The coffin was laid outside the gate and covered in flowers. Some women started keening (an American Indian custom, where they make a sort of humming noise) and people stood around the coffin mourning the dead and dying who had been victims of nuclear power and weapons. They then went home.

On the Monday, the Consumer Campaign set up a stall outside the SSEB showroom and many people signed up to withhold the nuclear portions of their electricity bills. The stall stayed there for the rest of the week, although it closed while its staff joined about a thousand people who marched through Edinburgh campaigning for a nuclear-free Lothian on Friday, 15th May. Edinburgh was, of course, the principal city of the Lothian region.

The day after the march, forty cyclists rode from Edinburgh to Torness and were greeted by 300 activists at Main Gate, which was then blockaded for a short time. This was followed by a brief blockade on A1 Trunk Road. As yet the week of action had seen no arrests, but the activists were now sailing into dodgy waters. As all this was happening at the front gate, about a hundred people occupied three empty cottages close to Torness Western boundary fence at Skatteraw. They christened the cottages Full Moon Cottages, after Half Moon Cottage and announced a plan to turn them into a permanent peace centre. Out at sea, four more activists in a 'Zodiac' inflatable boat approached and boarded a dredger which was dredging a channel for a ship bringing in special equipment to the SSEB's private dock. They stayed on the dredger for two-and-a-half hours, talking and drinking tea with the Swedish crew.

Up to the night of Monday 18th May, the SSEB played it quietly, and the police arrested nobody. Then, after most of the weekenders and day-trippers had gone home and only a hard core of enthusiasts was left, forty police came and evicted everyone from Full Moon Cottages. At 04.30 hours on Tuesday morning, Rodgers' machines, driven by men getting a special overtime rate for the job, which they had been called in to do out of normal hours, started to demolish the little houses. This appears to be the end of the last camp at Torness.

In June 1982, about two dozen activists, some in fancy dress, chained themselves to the gates of Torness. Workers were unable to get through for about half-an-hour, during which time traffic jams formed for five miles along A1. Eventually the authorities cut the protesters' chains.

Subsequently the SSEB stated they had no plans for any more nuclear reactors in Scotland. A list compiled in 1979 by the Central Electricity Generating Board showed that the SSEB planned to build eleven more after Torness. Either the SSEB had changed its plans, or someone was lying. At the time of writing, it seems that the SSEB statement was what Sir Winston Churchill might have called a 'terminological inexactitude'.

> The occupation of the nuclear reactor site at Torness in May (1979) was the largest gathering for nonviolent direct action yet to take place in a rural area of Britain. The Torness Alliance is the first large mixed movement in Britain which had tried to develop libertarian and feminist modes of organisation *(Peace News,* 22nd June, 1979.).

It wasn't only the geodesic dome that Torness pioneered and passed on to other peace camps. Many ideas and techniques for NVDA against construction crews and dredgers, which were developed out of ideas from sources including Gandhi, Thoreau and the camp at Seabrook nuclear power station site in the USA, were tried for the first time in Europe at Torness. Some new ideas were developed there, too. Torness tactics frequently showed themselves at Greenham Common, Brambles Farm and other peace camps. Torness and Luxulyan, at opposite corners of Britain, though they were not called peace camps, in reality were. They showed the way for the big peace camps at the nuclear bases in the 1980s.

Throughout the campaign, the Torness Alliance and The Public Parks Department had the difficult job of maintaining friendly relations between the campaigners and the local people and police. They did this remarkably well, in spite of the fact that the campaigners were a nebulous body, from all over England and Scotland, some members of which did not espouse non-violence and some of whom were outside the law on counts other than those directly involved with the NVDA (i.e. smoking hash) on the demonstrations. The organisation was helped in countless ways by having the SCRAM offices only thirty miles away. These offices were completely involved in the demonstrations and supported them with full-time staff. The peace camps were necessary parts of most of the demonstrations because of the remoteness of Torness, several miles from the nearest village of any size, and a severe shortage of overnight accommodation in the immediate vicinity.

Though work wasn't stopped here, it was certainly delayed, and many new people were recruited into the anti-nuclear campaign. There were many temporary stoppages, but each time work restarted, and at the time of writing Torness sits, a great blot on a peaceful rural landscape beside A1 producing electricity.

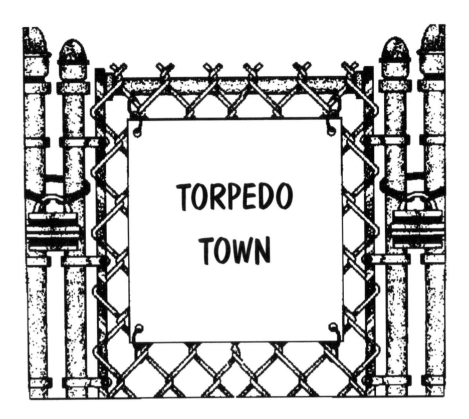

TORPEDO TOWN

Royal Naval Staff Requirement No. 7525 was for a heavyweight torpedo, with its own internal guidance system and a new type of warhead. This was to be a weapon for fighting a war, first and foremost, and not merely a deterrent.

Two firms were interested in the contract to make this torpedo: Gould Incorporated, of the USA, and Marconi Space and Defence Systems (MSDS) Limited in this country.

MSDS was a part of the GEC-Marconi group of companies and had a long record of work for the MoD. Marconi have made guidance systems for warships and took over the manufacture of the Sting Ray lightweight torpedo, after the MoD's own Admiralty Underwater Weapons Establishment (AUWE) had encountered difficulties with it. In 1976, MSDS had done a feasibility study for a heavyweight torpedo, Spearfish, followed by a project definition and experimental prototype vehicle trials. One prototype is understood to have set an underwater speed record of around eighty mph, which was the speed the Navy wanted on the production version. Spearfish was to be about twenty feet long and about one foot nine inches in diameter, with a Sundstrand gas turbine engine running on HAP/Otto fuel and seawater. This engine was much quieter, but gave more speed and range than the engine of the Mark 24 Tigerfish heavy torpedo also built for the MoD by MSDS, at their new assembly plant at Neston, near Capenhurst,

in Cheshire, which was opened by Prime Minister Margaret Thatcher in the spring of 1981. MSDS had several other establishments, some of them around Portsmouth, and they were looking for a site to build themselves a new HQ in the Portsmouth area.

Gould, who were already supplying their Type 48 torpedoes to the USN, were offering this torpedo to the MoD cheaper than Marconi were asking for their Spearfish. Because the USN had already paid for the research and development, Gould was able to price without charging any portion of these to the British Government, which gave them a price advantage. (Technical information extracted from *Jane's Defence Review*, Vol. 4, No. 6, 1983, and *The Observer*, 11th December 1983)

On 8th September, 1981, the contract was awarded to MSDS. To get round the cheaper price asked by Gould, the government had insisted MSDS meet certain financial conditions they had put in the contract. Apparently they were subsequently met.

At about this time, Tarmac, well known for their excellent civil engineering on Greenham Common and other RAF airfields, were negotiating with Havant Borough Council to buy Brambles Farm, Waterlooville. They obtained outline planning permission to build single story factory units on the thirty-seven acres and had offered, subject to them being able to sell in advance some factories, £3,600,000 for the land. However, at the time there was a glut of small factory units in South Hampshire, and there were not enough takers for their factories, so Tarmac withdrew their offer. It later transpired that, even as they withdrew the offer, Tarmac were talking to Marconi about building one big factory on part of the land, where Marconi could base its new HQ. Later Tarmac and Marconi went to Havant Council with a joint offer of £2,900,000 – £700,000 less than the earlier offer. The council had nobody else seriously interested in buying the land.

MSDS formed a new subsidiary, Marconi Underwater Systems Limited (MUSL) on April Fool's Day, 1982. The subsidiary company was to have the new purpose-built HQ which was planned for Brambles Farm, with an empty plot beside it, which would be kept vacant for two years, so that MUSL could use it to extend their HQ if necessary. They did not need to pay for it if they didn't use it.

On 12th May, Havant Council's district valuer presented a report to their policy and resources committee, which said he "certainly does not feel that this is a high price for the land," but the matter was "of some urgency in view of the imminent cessation of grant for this land." The grant was a central government grant to Havant Council. It would appear that central government were taking advantage of it to persuade Havant Council to sell the land cheaply to the firm making its torpedoes, so that Marconi got the building land cheap and passed on the savings in cheaper torpedoes. This may have had some connexion with the financial clauses in the contract, which required savings to be made. The report referred to MUSL only as a "major industrial company". (All three quotations come from *Radiator*, November/ December 1982) It mentioned a three-storey office block 500 feet long; a sixty-six-foot high chimney (though at the time there was no information about the possible emissions from this, it was later discovered to be a boiler chimney for the ingenious dual-fuel heating system) and four other large buildings on a fourteen acre site, surrounded by an eight-foot high fence with guard dogs

The plans were approved on 18th May, after the remarkably short time of three weeks from application, even though Marconi's public notice of application was just a piece of paper on a stick in a ditch at Brambles Farm, to satisfy the legal need to publicise the plans. Detailed plans were not available for public inspection at the Havant Council offices, which they should have been. When the information was brought out about the council approving the Tarmac/Marconi plans, the name Marconi was officially mentioned for the first time in public. On 27th May, Marconi announced the new factory would bring 250 new jobs to Waterlooville, but did not say how many of that 250 would be jobs done by people transferred in from other Marconi factories.

All this background information must have been known to Havant Council's development services committee when they met on 10th June and recommended the sale of Brambles Farm to the Tarmac/ Marconi partnership.

On 16th June, local people protested, and lobbied Havant councillors entering the full council meeting. Councillors refused even to delay the sale, agreeing to sell the land as soon as the legal formalities could be completed. One councillor in favour of the sale spoke at a CND rally in Gosport not long afterwards. So far as Waterlooville CND was concerned, there were no nuclear weapons involved, so they did not join the protest as a group. Apparently the CND chairman worked for Marconi.

Soon the productive farmland, which formed an attractive view from the parish church, would be gone forever in a jungle of concrete, metal and glass. The hedges and trees, with their striking autumn colours, would be grubbed out. The little river running through Brambles Farm had been the town's only public swimming bath for the local kids. Now this was to be its last summer open to the kids; it could well become a polluted, industrial sewer.

Some local residents, initially without support from CND and environmental groups, made plans carefully and at 20.30 hours on Friday 9th July 1982, a group of them took some tents onto a Brambles Farm field and set up camp. They had excellent local support and over the next few days got local and national publicity.

Although the deal was nearly complete, Havant Council could not now sell the land, because the buyer insisted on vacant possession.

On 29th July, a High Court judge in chambers, excluding press and public, granted the council an order in possession, so they could evict this peace camp.

Several eminent people spoke at two public meetings organised to enlist help for the protest against Marconi in Waterlooville. They included Professor George Hutchinson, sometime chairman of Southern Region CND, who led the campaign inside the National Trust over a new RAF bunker at Naphill. (See 'Peace Camps in the Chiltern Hills' elsewhere in this book.)

The camp grew larger and a big caravan joined it. There were frequent mentions in *Peace News* and there was talk of a TV documentary film. Campers were active in organising two petitions against the Marconi factory.

Then on Monday 6th September Hampshire Constabulary moved in, evicting the camp and towing the caravan off the site. As soon as this was done, representatives of the council and the Tarmac/Marconi consortium signed the deed of sale right outside the farm gate, on Hambledon Road. They left the scene contented. The police had acted beyond their jurisdiction; evicting the campers, who were charged with no crime, was a civil court affair and should have been done by council bailiffs.

That afternoon, the campers returned to the site, with others. Now there were about twice as many people as had stayed the previous night. For the next week the new peace camp stayed undisturbed on what was now Tarmac/Marconi land. A message of support came from Councillor Mrs. Barbara Barfoot, Mayor of Southampton, who was concerned that campers should stay within the law. Apparently, she had been approached by a member of Southampton CND, who suggested the message.

Early on the morning of Monday 13th September, earthmovers and mechanical diggers moved onto Brambles Farm at the request of Balfour Beatty, the firm that had won the contract to build the new Marconi factory. Building factories is not Tarmac's speciality, and they were probably too busy with airfield contracts for the MoD to do the job anyhow. There was no sign of a new order in possession, which would be necessary for the new owners to evict the campers legally.

Courageous peace campers sat down in front of the machines. A bulldozer actually ran over a man who refused to move from its path. Fortunately the blade was not involved and the vehicle had high ground clearance between its tracks, so the prostrate man was not hurt. Several other near misses occurred. The campers, who had not been legally evicted, intended to stay. The police on duty seemed to take it all casually, though campers noticed they were chatting with the workmen and site foreman and were in and out of the site canteen. It was obvious whose side the police took.

The workmen were digging holes, levelling ground, uprooting trees and demolishing the peace camp with their machines and hand tools as well. After at first taking no action, the police arrested three people and charged them. By the end of the day, when the contractors went home, the peace camp was still there, somewhat demolished, but not demoralised.

The following day the activists continued blockading the workmen and their machines, but things were quieter and there were no more arrests. Most of them went to the local magistrates court where the three arrested activists appeared, charged with breach of the peace, under the Justices of the Peace Act, 1361. They were each bound over to be of good behaviour for a year in the sum of £100.

During the court hearing Brian Burnell, secretary of Southampton CND, jumped up in the public gallery and announced that he believed that with the contractor's men working in a hurry, under pressure to get the job done, in the midst of protesters, someone was going to be hurt. The magistrates invited Brian to come down into the well of the court and make a statement, which he did. As a result, the contractors' site foreman, Ian Boiling, was charged with behaviour likely to lead to a breach of the peace, which was a more serious charge, under the same act, than that of causing an actual breach of the peace, with which the three campers had been charged. The summons was listed as taken out by Brian Burnell.

On 16th September, the campers continued obstructing and blockading the machines on Brambles Farm. The police did not wait long. After some fast moving direct action, they arrested eighteen and charged them all with breach of the peace.

It was clear the camp could not sustain this effort

The Marconi factory.

and stand these arrests indefinitely as there were not enough campers. When police removed the remaining campers on 17th September, without making any further arrests and charges, the peace camp came to an end. The campaign had not ended, however. A press statement was issued (see the end of this chapter.)

Most of the eighteen people arrested on 16th September were bound over on breach of the peace charges, but two who had broken binding-over orders set on 15th September, as a result of the earlier direct action arrests at Brambles Farm, had their cases adjourned to 8th October.

On Monday, 21st September, Ian Boiling and his solicitor, Michael Addison, appeared before Havant magistrates, who handled all the Brambles Farm cases, to answer Brian Burnell's summons. Brian was not there, but a CND person who knew him was and told the court that Brian had decided to drop the action, because the prosecution had made the contractor's men more careful, and therefore accidents and breaches of the peace were less likely. The magistrates were not advised soon enough for the case to be cancelled, and the defence had incurred considerable expense. Without conducting the case, they awarded costs of £732 against Brian. Then Anita Gulati and Matthew, two members of Southampton CND, set up a bust fund for Brian, who later told me he did not need the £732, as, when the courts chased up the costs, he refused to pay and being unemployed at the time, with no valuable possessions, he lost nothing to bailiffs who wanted to pay off the debt with his furniture and effects. The bust fund was later diverted to help other peace activists with fines and costs to pay. The fund passed into the hands of Carolyne Barnes, and then Carol Dukes, both of Southampton CND.

On the same day, twenty-five activists picketed Brambles Farm from 07.00 hours to 14.00 in blustery, wet weather, as the workmen struggled with the wet ground.

On Saturdays, for some weeks afterwards, there were pickets and demonstrations at Brambles Farm. It appears none were worth special mention and there were no more arrests. Then activity at the torpedo factory site died off for a while.

The two peace campers arrested on 16th September, each for a second breach of the peace, were, on 8th October, ordered by Havant magistrates to forfeit £50 each and remain bound over for a year.

Some of the peace campers came together for a |reunion to mark the end of their binding-over orders, on 17th September 1983, at Brambles Farm. At 16.00 hours eight of them entered the site where Balfour Beatty's men and the other contractors' men were working flat out. The activists climbed a ladder, already in place, to the top of the scaffolding on the three-storey main building. They sat down on the top deck of the scaffolding displaying their banners. When they told the workmen they intended staying until 18.00, the workers carried them all off, except for one woman. One activist's name and address was taken by police, and though not charged at the time, he was warned he could receive a summons for breach of the peace later. Nobody was arrested. The lone woman was allowed to stay on the top deck with a rainbow banner, while the others picketed outside. At 18.00 she came down, and they all left peacefully.

The authorities were taken by surprise on Saturday, 30th March, 1984, when thirty people walked onto a vacant plot next to the new MUSL HQ and erected a marquee. They knew there would be no chance of their being evicted until Monday at the earliest. Between twenty and thirty people camped there in the marquee, which stayed there for a whole week. The campers peacefully picketed the new factory,

Brambles Farm
PEACE FESTIVAL

Havant Borough Council hereby give notice that the holding of the above festival on Council owned land, (and also without necessary statutory licence) is unlawful and should not take place. The Council's Officers are authorised to take all steps through courts, and other action necessary to protect the council's interest.

Injunctions are being obtained to enforce the law. Any artist, performer or member of any organisation or group who attend the Festival will not only be liable for trespass, but to committal to prison for contempt and fees may be irrecoverable.

P.T. ADAMS, Borough Secretary. Havant Borough Council.

meeting the workers as they arrived each morning, offering them cups of tea and giving them leaflets. Both the workers and the campers gave each other friendly waves and greetings.

On Friday, 9th March, campers blockaded the gates for an hour and delayed people going in to work. The blockade was broken by the campers themselves, before the police started making arrests.

The campers had less luck with the police when, just before closing the peace camp, they held a die-in at Waterlooville Shopping Precinct. Here the police arrested seven and charged them with breach of the peace. While held in custody, as a result of these arrests, two of the campers apparently damaged their cell walls by writing over existing National Front graffiti and were subsequently charged with criminal damage. The fate of the National Front artists is not known.

On 16th March, the seven campers who had been held on breach of the peace charges were found guilty and bound over by Havant magistrates for twelve months, in sums ranging from £50 to £100. Each of the two with criminal damage charges apparently had thirty days imprisonment added because they refused to pay fines of £40 and £20 respectively.

Subsequently, I was told, nine demonstrators demonstrating against these arrests and imprisonments were violently arrested. These nine included two who only asked for the reasons for the arrests of the others and for policemen's numbers. Apparently, members of the public who saw this incident made over twenty complaints to the police, and as a result the demonstrators were released without charge.

For the summer event in 1984, the members of Waterlooville Area Campaign Against the Arms Race planned ambitiously. An eight-foot security fence now surrounded the new MUSL HQ and this prevented anything like a peace camp being set up there. The plot next door was still vacant so they decided to use that, and to hold a peace camp and festival. A programme of events was prepared and put on leaflets, which were widely distributed well in advance. Peace movement newspapers and the local media were briefed.

Needless to say, the festival of poetry and music with over a dozen bands and all their equipment met with opposition from the authorities. Local organisers, with determination, made it a success in spite of this. All the more credit to them, because this

was the first time Waterlooville had seen a festival of this kind and size. Over 1,000 people altogether came to the festival, and at one point in time a head count recorded over 800 on the site.

Meanwhile, Marconi announced export sales figures for its Stingray torpedoes – £15,000,000 to Egypt and £5,000,000 to Thailand. Needless to say, local Campaign Against the Arms Trade supporters (at one time there was an active group of them in the area) did not like these figures.

Much hard work went into planning the 1985 festival and peace camp. The date had been decided provisionally before the 1984 festival ended. In addition to the small group meetings, planning meetings with everyone involved taking part were held once every month on Tuesdays. Everyone except Havant Borough Council realised the festival had massive local support. Alan Rundle wrote to them giving assurances on safety, toilet provision, welfare, noise control, litter collection and other important aspects. Along with Rev. David Partridge, Chairman of South-East Hampshire Peace Council, he met with a group of councillors to try and arrange some form of co-operation on 25th July, but the talks broke down after about forty minutes. Havant Council then took out a court injunction to try and stop Alan Rundle from going onto any of their land at Brambles Farm, not all of which had been buried under factories yet. This, the first and only injunction, applied just to Alan Rundle. They hired a mechanical digger to dig trenches around Brambles Farm to prevent vehicles from entering. They put up notices around the area and more detailed ones appeared in the local papers, warning people not to go onto Brambles Farm, or they would risk legal action. Alan Rundle countered this by saying he

Entrance to Old Park Farm, the site of Torpedo Town Festival, August 1985. (The Portakabin was added after the festival had ended.)

306

would go to prison, rather than give up the festival. Not all the organisers were as keen! They sought an alternative site near Brambles Farm to enable the festival to take place without people being imprisoned, which could make organising more difficult for those left behind.

During the summer, leaflets were circulated advertising a Brambles Farm Peace Festival and naming some bands booked to perform. The leaflets announced that if it was impossible to use the site next door to the MUSL HQ, festival-goers would be directed to another site nearby.

By the end of July, local papers were giving the proposed festival much publicity, and Havant Council were criticised for their unsympathetic attitude. An editorial suggested: "Havant Council should rely on civil law, not direct action, to curb the nuisance and stop the trespass."(*The News* (Portsmouth) 1st August 1985.)

A suitable site had been found. Old Park Farm near Denmead, Hampshire, was only about a mile down the road from Brambles Farm, but was in Winchester District and therefore outside the jurisdiction of Havant Council. This farm was disused, with an empty bungalow, several derelict farm buildings and a water supply which had been turned off. A lane leading off Hambledon Road gave access. Only a handful of people lived near enough to be disturbed by the amplified music expected, and there were neither crops nor animals in the fields.

The organisers contacted both the owners of Old Park Farm and the water board, but neither wanted anything to do with the festival even though money was offered, so the water remained turned off. The organisers kept these negotiations secret and maintained public secrecy about the location of the new festival site, until the first vehicles drove onto it to set up the stage.

The morning of Nagasaki Day dawned pleasant and dry, and the festival began that evening as planned. Because of the new site, it had its name changed. It was now the Torpedo Town Festival of Peace.

Volunteers started digging trenches for long-drop toilets, to replace the hired waterless Portaloo. A local resident announced that campers could get water from a tap in her garden, on the other side of Hambledon Road. I was one of the many people grateful for this, though I remember it was a long trudge down the lane and Hambledon Road to reach the tap

That evening, Friday, 9th August, the first issue of the free festival newspaper, *Brambles Shambles,* was distributed, and the first of a big line-up of over thirty bands, singers and poets appeared on the main stage.

One group who came to the festival, Peace by Peace, set up a display and stall in Waterlooville shopping centre on the Friday, after getting permission from Havant Council. Peace by Peace was a group of people touring the country with literature from a wide range of organisations, including Peace Pledge Union, Greenpeace and Oxfam, trying to show the public how all these causes are related in their common opposition to violence in all forms. The reaction of a police sergeant to their exhibition showed how some – but by no means all – local people viewed the peace movement and proved that this work was necessary.

> The stall was hardly set up when a huge intimidating sergeant arrived with a bunch of uniformed cronies, and told them in no uncertain terms that they had one minute to leave. They eventually managed (to tell) this sergeant that he should check their claim to permission before he threw them out. First he contacted a council solicitor who said 'if anyone has given them permission, they need their head examined'. But eventually the sergeant found out, yes, they had got permission, and was suddenly all sweetness and light, apologising for the 'misunderstanding' and shaking hands with the peace people before he left. Waterlooville shoppers witnessed all this police aggro, and were firmly on the side of the peace stall. Most of them were interested in the things on display – peace once again showed itself more powerful than aggression. (Extracted from a report published by Linda Pierson of *Peace News*, and published in *Brambles Shambles*, number two. The words in brackets cover a misprint and are my own.)

The purpose of the festival was not only to commemorate the bombing of Hiroshima and Nagasaki in 1945, but also to publicise the weapons work of MUSL HQ. Hence Waterlooville's new name, Torpedo Town!

Entertainers included Roy Harper, who was appearing without pay. He took one look and listen to the festival's public address system and immediately made a return journey to London for his own, so it could be used for his own act and for others, free of charge. The sound quality improved. Not all the entertainers were free, though; one band cost £130. Admission was free, but a voluntary collection raised enough cash to cover costs and send money for food to starving Ethiopians. There was plenty of food and drink and vegetarians were especially well fed. On Friday and Saturday the weather stayed fine, but later continuous rain set in. As well as two stages, there were no less than twenty-one separate stalls selling – and doing – all sorts of things. I bought a good pair of boots off one stall for £2. Len Gibson brought the Peace Pledge Union Film Van from Yorkshire and was showing his peace films. Over a thousand people came on the Saturday alone, from several European countries, as well as all over England. One band came all the way from Trondheim, Norway.

As the festival began to wind down, on Monday 12th August, volunteers pulled one of the rubbish skips into a position where a lorry could get to it and began loading bags of litter into it.

After this a peace camp remained on Old Park Farm for a few months, but activity against the MUSL HQ died down as the new campers were promoting an alternative lifestyle, of which opposition to war was only one facet. The factory was now built, and working, and local support was insufficient to mount effective blockades.

I visited Brambles Farm several times, the first being in the summer of 1982, when only one youth was at the camp, which then consisted of a large caravan and one or two tents. I stayed and talked with him for about an hour until another camper returned from a visit to Waterlooville.

A trip I made to Brambles Farm in August, 1983, was one I would rather not have made. It upset me a lot. The MUSL factory was not the only one being built there. The main contractors building the MUSL HQ were Balfour Beatty and Tarmac was involved as the developer. I had agreed to deliver a lorry load of steel reinforcing to several construction sites in Southern England. When the lorry had been loaded and I was checking the delivery notes, I found I had a consignment aboard for a firm called Burke, on Brambles Farm. The ticket bore no mention of Tarmac, Balfour Beatty or Marconi and so I assumed the load was for one of the other factories being built. Here was a chance to see what was going on and get paid for doing it. I saw what was going on, Burkes got their steel, and I did the job honestly and efficiently. Unfortunately, the reinforcing rods were for the office block at the front of the Marconi factory!

I won't carry arms and ammunition, when I know they are on my lorry, and I have turned down Army work. It is not easy to refuse to deliver materials to places where they can be used in the creation of the war machine, but, when one has to deliver, one can always collect information, or put a spanner in the works, as French Resistance workers did in World War II.

This prophetic statement seems to sum up Brambles Farm. Brambles Farm Peace camp issued it to the media and the public on 17th September, 1982. That evening, *The News* in Portsmouth was the first paper to publish it in its report of the eviction.

This statement is written on the caterpillar track, which will eventually destroy Brambles Farm. We have done all we can. Marconi's consultation has been one piece of paper hidden on a ditch. Our consultation has been two public meetings, 10,000 leaflets and two petitions. We hope our struggle has made people ask themselves questions about what is happening around them. Brambles Farm is dead, but may the voice of peace grow louder.

Peace man warns 'I'll go to jail'

PEACE protester Alan Rundle is to go ahead with a controversial rally — even if it means he'll be thrown in jail.

This week Havant Borough Council won a High Court order to ban the three-day rally at Brambles Farm, Waterlooville, which it owns.

The decision leaves the way open for organisers to be put behind bars if they don't stop the rally. But Mr Rundle says the show must go on.

He says even if protesters are thrown off the land, the festival — which hopes to attract 5,000 — will be held "nearby".

Crime

"There is no way anyone is going to stop it. They think the rally is illegal. I think any build-up in nuclear arms is a much worse crime — a crime against mankind.

"We will go ahead with the festival even if they throw me in jail. They can't stop us. If

By JOURNAL REPORTER

they move us off land we'll go somewhere else. We won't just go away as they hope we will."

The council has warned it will take "steps" to stop the festival which will have over 30 groups "playing for peace".

The action includes moves to cut off the water supply to the site and public notices warning against the charge of trespass people face if they go.

A council spokesman said "Whatever steps are necessary to protect the council's interests will be taken."

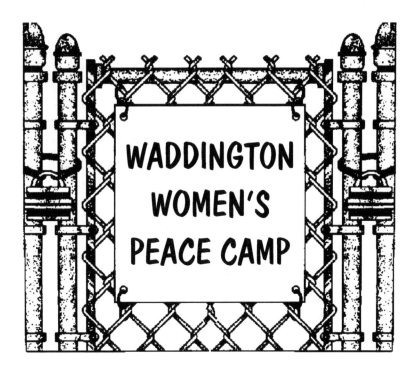

This airfield first came to the notice of the general public when the ear-splitting row of British V-bombers landing and taking off there shattered the peace of the countryside south of Lincoln. The V-bombers, of course, could carry both nuclear and conventional bombs, and RAF Waddington had storage space for all bomb types in RAF service. The airfield itself is about four miles south of Lincoln on a hilltop just off the Grantham Road (A607).

On Saturday, 30th May the public were invited to come and see Vulcan V-bombers flying at the airfield's open day. Nuclear disarmament groups from Lincolnshire, Yorkshire and Nottinghamshire went along. They met on South Common, Lincoln and, after a rousing speech from Bruce Kent, marched to one of the gates of RAF Waddington. When they arrived, four Vulcans took off, and one flew low over the demonstrators several times, probably with a cameraman aboard filming the demonstrators. After picketing the gate for a while, with a 'Danger: this is a nuclear war zone!' notice, the marchers returned to a peace festival on South Common.

By 1982 the Vulcans were being phased out, and Nimrod early warning planes were planned to replace them at Waddington. There was also talk of bringing in RAF Tornado nuclear bombers.

Some women set up a peace camp in protest at these plans, on Sunday 4th April 1982. RAF Waddington was their second choice for a women-only camp; their first was Burtonwood, (see elsewhere in this book) but a mixed camp got there first.

Ken Cole and Peter Baker of Basingstoke Organisation for Nuclear Disarmament, on their sponsored hitch around the peace camps, were given a warm welcome when they called at Waddington Women's Peace Camp on Wednesday, 23rd June . (See 'The First Greenham Common Peace Camp' elsewhere in this book.)

The parish council complained to Kesteven County Council, who owned the roadside verge where the camp lay. The County Council decided to take no action against the camp. The parish council then tried to get the camp declared a health hazard, but when the environmental health officer visited in June he gave the camp a clean bill of health.

On Hiroshima Day campers chained themselves to a nuclear bomb store. The authorities cut them free, arresting and charging five, who were told to appear before Lincoln magistrates in October.

The camp had no planning permission, and the authorities were preparing to prosecute the campers for breach of the planning laws. The campers decided they had done what they could in getting nuclear disarmament and the case against nuclear war preparations an airing. They left Waddington on 22nd August 1982.

ARTISTS AND GREENHAM WOMEN AT RAF WELFORD

The United States Air Forces in Europe Central Weapons Store is situated at RAF Welford on a hill overlooking the Kennet and Lambourn Valleys. The only entrance in use is on the Boxford to Chaddleworth road about five miles north-west of Newbury, Berkshire.

RAF Welford is about four minutes flying time by executive jet from Greenham Common, which is in the charge of the same RAF officer.

The War Department first acquired this place as an arsenal and airfield in 1942. It seems the USAF was involved right from the beginning. A railway was built to move armaments in and out of the base and was in use until its closure in 1973. The development of large freighter aircraft and their increasing availability, along with the completion of the motorway nearby, rendered the railway obsolete. Between Junctions 13 and 14 on the M4 a special junction was built to serve RAF Welford in the 1980s and the government swapped classifications between a B-class road and a C-class road near the base. By 1984 it had grown into a base which "… occupies just over 800 acres, and includes about 700,000 square feet of storage space. (Comparable figures for the real RAF Chilmark are about 350 acres and about 500,000 square feet)." (*Radiator*, April 1984. RAF Chilmark is the RAF's most important arsenal.) Although this arsenal at the time held a vast quantity of conventional weapons, there is no evidence of

nuclear weapons there.

The first known demonstration at Welford was a base visit by five members of Southampton CND on Easter Sunday, 1978.

In the spring of 1982 a Fairford peace camper drove two colleagues thirty-four miles from there to Welford and helped them to set up camp at the entrance to the base before returning to Fairford. The two left at Welford were artists and formed what was known as the Artists' Peace Camp. They were on a minor road, with no lay-by for parking, and little traffic, other than vehicles going in and out of the base, and so few people stopped to talk to them. They were in an isolated place – the nearest shop was five miles away and it was over an hour's walk to the nearest public telephone. They had no car of their own. Consequently, they weren't able to do much, other than keep alive, for the two weeks they were there. The artists left without getting arrested or evicted.

A twenty-four-hour peace camp, by campers from Greenham Common, took place at the entrance to RAF Welford on 8th-9th November, 1983, supporting Greenham Women Against Cruise in America.

Since 1982, Greenham women have also explored this base. They have painted and decorated weapons stored there.

A STAFFING ROTA THAT WORKED, AND ARSON AT WETHERSFIELD

Scene of some of the earliest NVDA by nuclear disarmers in Britain, RAF Wethersfield near Braintree, Essex and within an hour's drive of Central London, was constructed in a hurry for use in World War II.

In view of the hurry, it is not surprising that there were believed to be five public footpaths still crossing the airfield after it was first laid out. Apparently the authorities closed them later, without fuss, without obtaining closure orders and without providing diversions.

Although Wethersfield was not on the Spaatz-Tedder Agreement (see 'Peace Camps in the Fens' elsewhere in this book) it was one of the first British airfields to have USAF nuclear weapons and USAF nuclear bombers were stationed there in the 1950s and 1960s.

There were protests. Some of these involved NVDA, including the sit-downs that inspired the publication of *Beyond Counting Arses* by the Committee of 100 in 1962. (Out of print, but Housman's Bookshop may be able to locate a copy.)

What was probably the biggest protest ever held there, up to the time of writing, was due to take place the next day, when Helen Allegranza, Terry Chandler, Ian Dixon, Trevor Hatton, Pat Pottle and Michael Randle were all arrested on charges of conspiracy and incitement under Section One of the Official Secrets Act, 1911. They were arrested on 8th December 1961. In the following year the five men were sent to jail for eighteen months and Helen was sentenced to twelve months. Eric, an Upper Heyford

peace camper, who was involved with the Committee of 100 in 1961, told me that, sadly, Helen left jail broken in spirit and committed suicide not long after.

Despite these arrests, the big sit-down took place as planned. The publicity for them almost ensured that more folk came to it than would otherwise have done. About 600 people came on 9th December although not all were sitting down. Many who did sit down were arrested and charged with breach of the peace and obstruction of the highway. A large number, when convicted, refused to be bound over or pay fines in line with Committee of 100 practice, which was to try and jam up the courts and prisons with protesters in order to show the strength of the opposition to the nuclear weapons policies of what they called the 'war-fare state'. About forty women went to Holloway Prison for short sentences, the longest of which appeared to be two months for one woman who refused to be bound over. It is not known how many men were arrested.

USAF Phantom jets based at Wethersfield saw action in the Vietnam War. This was no great secret; US airmen openly talked about it in the neighbourhood. Surprisingly, this connexion didn't spark off any big protests.

When USAF involvement in Vietnam ended, RAF Wethersfield dropped in status from an active, operational airfield to a standby one, in 1970, and the Phantoms faded out.

Signs of activity that started appearing in 1980 suggested something was going on at RAF Wethersfield.

Many tipper and concrete mixer lorries were going in there; heavy freighter planes were landing and taking off at all times of the day and night – mainly at night; supplies were increasingly imported from Germany and the USA instead of being bought locally; there were muffled sounds of explosions; and both the MoD and the airbase commander were saying nothing.

In 1981, the suspicion arose of Wethersfield being the East Anglian base for Cruise missiles, possibly as a second choice if Molesworth was unsuitable. Although this never came about, the airfield almost certainly helped with the movement of men and materials necessary for the bringing of Cruise to Britain. The suspicion about Cruise led to a pre-emptive strike by Essex CND demonstrators, who attempted to enter the airfield and hold a 'families for peace picnic' on a green just inside the main gate. When they were prevented from entering, 700 or so activists sat down and blockaded the two entrances that led off the dead-end road for the rest of the afternoon. The authorities' tactics were different in 1981, probably because they wanted the airbase to appear unimportant, and they arrested nobody before the blockaders eventually left under their own steam. With this action, Essex CND had originally planned to enter the base and picnic there, so that the folk who lived on the base could meet them and share their picnic. Essex CND believed that, as residents of Essex, the folk who lived on the base – mainly families of USAF personnel – were entitled to be canvassed by CND people, as were any other Essex residents and should be able to join or support CND if they so wished.

At Easter a further demonstration was held.

Also in 1982, CND people went to the airfield's open days and demonstrated.

The USAF had set up the Rapid Emergency Deployable Heavy Operational Repair Squadron, Engineering – RED HORSE for short – at Wethersfield in 1979. This 400-strong squadron had the job of repairing bomb damage on runways. The idea was for them to fly directly to damaged airfields, land as best they could (using parachutes if necessary) and use emergency stocks of construction materials kept there to repair the runways and taxiways. In 1982, the British HQ of the USAF Office of Special Investigations was also at Wethersfield. This group, with the help of British Special Branch, collected and collated information about CND and other protesters. In addition to all this, Wethersfield was also used frequently for USAF exercises.

Essex CND had, for some time, been trying to contact the hundreds of USAF personnel and their families living on the airbase and talk to them about nuclear disarmament and Cruise missiles. It was thought a peace camp would help with this aim, so, after much careful planning, one was set up on 6th February 1983 – two years to the day before the big eviction at Molesworth just forty-five miles away.

Essex CND, which was a federation of about thirty groups from all over Essex and a few people from outside, got together on a march to Wethersfield on 6th February, which ended as a rally to set up the peace camp. Appalling weather kept the numbers down, but they put on a good show just the same. At the head of the march came Terry Dilliway, dressed as a hooded spectre, astride a dummy Cruise missile and flanked by other Brentwood CND members in fallout suits. A jazz band on the march gave it a vintage Aldermaston March atmosphere. A MoD barrier across the dead-end road leading up to the two main entrances to the airfield stopped the march from going right up to the gates. A group of opponents from Peace with Security were at the barrier, but gave no real trouble. The rally took place in front of the barrier and in a lay-by a few yards to the west along B1053 road. As there were no good campsites on the road up to the airfield and a site beside a through road used by other people as well as those entering the airfield had its advantages, the caravan and toilet tent were put in this lay-by. The police apparently agreed, provided the camp was temporary and did not normally accommodate people overnight. Had it not been so, the local council and police might well have acted against the peace camp and treated the caravan parked there as if it was illegally parked and moved it. The caravan did not comply with regulations that would normally be enforced on a commercial caravan site and didn't have planning permission.

The unique feature of this camp was the rota, which Essex CND drew up for staffing the caravan and which was continued and added to throughout the life of the camp. The rota worked well for nearly a year. The weekday rota involved four shifts each day and in order to maintain continuity and collect information, a peace camp logbook was started (An Essex CND member now has the logbook). This contained details of camp visitors, donations, road and air traffic in and out of the airfield and special events. It also told who had done their share of the rota and who had not! One person on each shift had to complete an entry in the camp logbook, even if nothing happened. There was a golden rule that each shift should leave the caravan tidy and they usually did. The rota system had a big advantage over the permanent resident system in that many people with limited spare time, including working folk, could come and fill specific slots and be useful parts of the camp, as 'time-share residents', when otherwise they would be only weekend visitors. Although people on the rota came from all over Essex, most lived nearby, as the cost in terms of time and money in travelling there regularly made it difficult for people far away. Many on the rota were retired people. The camp not being occupied throughout twenty-four hours every day was to prove a disadvantage later when camp wreckers began to attack at night.

The modplods soon developed paranoia, as is their custom, and over-reacted to things the peace campers did. Within a month of the camp starting, they had called out a vanload of civilian police from Braintree to investigate just one eighty-year-old woman walking along the road up towards the main gate. Essex police were friendly and less paranoid, and often popped in at the caravan for a friendly chat, though when an American called to talk with the campers, Essex Police were quick to inform the USAF. He visited the caravan a second time, but it is believed he was subsequently returned to the USA early. The authorities were security-conscious: Servicemen were not permitted to talk to peace campers and were threatened with being sent back to the USA if they were American and did so; British workmen there were not allowed to talk with the campers; and even the tea ladies were reminded of their obligations under the Official Secrets Act declarations they has signed.

The camp's first big event, after its launch, was a children's party on the afternoon of Easter Monday, 4th April, to which all children living on the airbase were invited. Alas, none came, though some families watched from a distance through the perimeter fence, until a USAF security patrol appeared and they went away, probably frightened off. The party was held on the approach road, outside the first of the two gates and lasted about ninety minutes. About 200 CND people were there, including many adults, who seemed to enjoy the party as much as the children. Apparently there was no blockade and there were no arrests.

In April, after untrue accusation that peace campers were uprooting young trees for firewood, good publicity was gained by the peace campers publicly

planting saplings in the verges in roadside lay-bys near the airfield. No intelligent peace camper would uproot young trees for firewood, because they are more difficult to burn than dry wood and the campers realised the value of young trees in the environment.

A petition against the camp was circulated through local villages and only collected twenty-four signatures.

On 30th July, RAF Wethersfield held an open day with civil and military aircraft on display. About 200 CND people, mostly from Essex, but with a few from further afield, were on the road to the base leafleting visitors and at the caravan. Some people who took leaflets gave encouraging responses, though there were a few whose remarks were not so pleasant. While this was going on, a separate group entered the base dressed as tourists, and spread out, mingling among the members of the public inside. They then began leafleting. As the authorities discovered them, they were removed, without being charged with any offences.

The camp wreckers usually struck under cover of darkness, as befitted their evil deeds and normally when the caravan was deserted. Extensive damage was done when a vehicle, probably a van, rammed the caravan in early August.

Also about this time local farmers, hostile to the camp, parked an opposing caravan in the lay-by. It did not stay long.

Some campers erected their own tents on the verge beside the lay-by, but had second thoughts when, on Thursday, 27th October, an arsonist destroyed the toilet tent.

> Between four and eight people were in the caravan for a shift change at 20.00 hours on 30th October. Someone smelt petrol, and opened the door to go and investigate. As the door opened, a man with long hair, about six feet tall, and wearing a donkey jacket, ran off towards Finchingfield. He appeared to have been messing about by the caravan. (One report mentioned people wearing black balaclavas running away, but the person who told me about them may have confused an earlier attempted attack by camp wreckers with this incident, as nobody else confirmed their presence and I saw no mention in press reports of it.) Near the caravan were bottles of inflammable gas, one of which was connected, and cars with petrol in their tanks. When the campers went outside, and found petrol had been spread around the caravan and a plastic bottle, apparently still containing petrol, to light

a conflagration. They became alarmed and called in the Essex Police, who came and inspected the scene. The police then took away the plastic bottle to analyse the contents and see if it could tell them anything about the person who put it under the caravan. They were treating it as attempted arson.

This was the latest in a whole series of attacks on the caravan within the past month. On Thursday the tent attached to the caravan was burned down. Following that was this quite horrific attack. This chap prepared what was in fact a little bomb. I think it is attempted murder. There were people in that caravan who could have been seriously injured or even killed. (Jimmy Johns, then a spokesman for Chelmsford CND, quoted in *Essex Chronicle*, 4th November 1983.)

Was it attempted arson, or attempted murder? We'll never know, for there was no trial, as apparently neither the long-haired man nor anyone in a balaclava was ever caught.

The last people to do rota duty in the caravan were apparently Helen Morse and Anne Gunn with a dog, Jabey, on Wednesday 2nd November 1983. That day the caravan was towed off, a month earlier than planned, for repairs and, as Anne said, "… because it is not safe to have it here, and we cannot risk lives." (Anne Gunn, quoted in *Essex Chronicle*, Braintree edition only, 4th November 1983.)

The caravan was due at Foulness Peace Camp in December.

An Essex CND member took a cinematograph film of the peace camp, and Essex CND still have it, along with the logbook, at the time of writing.

Without Essex CND's caravan but with their support, Chelmsford Women's Peace Group organised a twenty-four-hour vigil at Wethersfield in support of Greenham Women Against Cruise in the USA. Starting at 10.00 hours on 9th November, they decorated the airfield perimeter fence alongside the approach road with flowers and children's clothes and held a mock trial. The people's court, as it was called, was an interesting piece of street theatre. The case was Human Race against Arms Race. Black-hooded skeletons depicting death wandered through the crowd, and cigars, representing Cruise missiles, were handed round. Then a web of wool was woven across the main gate. Two coachloads of university students were there all day and a third coachload of students, this time from Essex University, arrived late in the afternoon and sat across the main gate. They were moved off by the police and warned that if they returned, they risked arrest and prosecution. They did not return and there were no arrests at all at this demonstration.

The problems faced by the caravan peace camp did not deter several people from setting up tents and camping the night on the grass verges beside the approach road as part of the vigil. This appears to have been the last peace camp at Wethersfield.

The Wethersfield campaign was conducted on a friendly basis, especially when Essex CND ran it in the 1980s because Essex CND wanted to befriend the people behind the fence. They concentrated on maintaining friendly relations with the authorities as well, and used techniques of friendly persuasion on them. This seems to have been a good policy here, though it hasn't yet succeeded in its ultimate aim of getting the USAF out of Wethersfield.

There was another demonstration at Wethersfield on 25th March 1984, and the campaign of friendly persuasion continues.

The last word must go to Chief Inspector Brian Tyrell of Braintree police, reported in the Braintree edition of the *Essex Chronicle* for 11th November 1983. He was commenting on the friendly relations during the 9th November vigil and demonstration, and spoke of "… a mutual respect between the police and protesters. I am pleased with the way the demonstration was carried out in the usual sensible and tolerable fashion."

Around 1950 Windscale was set up as Britain's – and the world's – first civil nuclear power station. In 1957 it had Britain's most serious nuclear accident to date when fallout precautions had to be taken over a wide area of northern England. Windscale lies on the coast of Cumbria, where it and the neighbouring nuclear establishments of Sellafield and Calder Hall are the main employers. The Irish Sea, off this coast, is reputed to be the most radioactive sea in the world, thanks to these three establishments. Just down the road is Barrow-in-Furness, famous not only as the port which handles radioactive materials going to and from these establishments, but also for the construction of nuclear submarines.

Women from Lancashire and Cumbria, including Jean Johnson, held a peace camp here from 8th to 10th October, 1985. They had an enormous bonfire and made a rainbow on the fence. There were no arrests and no eviction. The women only stayed the three days because they were frightened of radiation from the nuclear power station affecting them if they stayed longer.

THE YORKSHIRE MOORS CAMPS: FYLINGDALES AND MENWITH HILL

In July 1980, the *New Statesman* disclosed what was to be done with new equipment being installed at the US electronic surveillance base on Menwith Hill, a thousand feet up, on top of the Yorkshire Moors between Pateley Bridge and Harrogate. This new equipment, including four enormous spheres loooking like giant golf balls, which were visible for miles, gave Menwith Hill immense power. It was to become the biggest satellite signals communications terminal and intelligence centre in the whole of Europe, with a connexion to Hunter's Stones Tower, a British telephone microwave relay station five miles to the south. This connexion was to enable it to tap all the telephone calls relayed through Hunter's Stones Tower.

Menwith Hill was beyond the control of our Parliament or even the US Congress. It was controlled by the American National Security Agency, which was so secret even in the US, that it has earned the nickname 'No Such Agency'.

Only about fifty people turned up at the first protest outside the US base, on 24th July , 1980; but on the second, 7,000 marched to Menwith Hill, on 4th May 1981; and on 4th July 1982, 2,000 protesters held an Independence Day picnic outside the base. People were getting to know about No Such Agency.

On 30th April 1983, the first weekend peace camp began at Menwith Hill. These weekend peace camps, organised by the local Otley Peace Action Group, took place on several weekends in the summer of 1983.

In support of Greenham Women Against Cruise, who took the case against Cruise to the New York Federal Court in an attempt to get Cruise deployment in Europe declared illegal, there was a twenty-four-hour peace camp at Menwith Hill. This was on and around 9th November 1983. Two arrests for obstruction were reported.

At the same time, there was another peace camp at Fylingdales on the North Yorkshire Moors near Pickering.

Fylindales was the site of a radar station belonging to the US Distant Early Warning (DEW) Line of radar stations, set up in a rough ring around the North Pole, to give warning of attack with Soviet missiles or aircraft. It is Fylingdales which is supposed to give us the famous four-minute warning.

On 2nd July 1984 about forty people went to Menwith Hill and on 3rd July, about 100 handed in a letter to the RAF Duty Officer, complaining about the work Menwith Hill was doing. Curiously, the National Association for Freedom, a right-wing group, also handed in a letter to him. Then, on 4th July, a mixed sex peace camp was set up with support from several peace groups in the area. Folk may have camped there on 2nd and 3rd July, but reports say nothing about this.

The peace camp supported the Women's Weekend on 28th-29th July, when charges of conduct likely to lead to a breach of the peace and criminal damage were laid against six women arrested walking inside the base on 29th July. They were kept in Harrogate Police Station overnight, and in the morning were taken to Ripon Magistrates Court, where the magistrates were asked by police to remand them in custody for fingerprinting. The magistrates refused this request, and granted the women unconditional bail. They appeared again at Pateley Bridge Magistrates Court on 31st August 1984.

On 26th August a temporary peace camp outside the Fylingdales DEW Line Station ended. The camp had many visitors. The campers painted enormous signs on the road:

APPROACHING US BASE

THEIR WARS – OUR LIVES

and

NO MOOR WAR

This camp appears to have been popular with local folk.

From 31st August to September, thirty women stayed at Menwith Hill Peace Camp, to give it support, and to support the six women at their trials in Pateley Bridge. The cases were adjourned on 25th October, when all except one were dropped. On this occasion, Dee West defended herself before Pateley Bridge magistrates on a charge of criminal damage to a police station door and was acquitted. None of the women were, therefore, convicted.

Throughout the winter, support for the peace camp grew. It had many visitors at Winter Solstice, Christmas and New Year. Campers went carol singing to HMS Forest Moor. On New Year's Day, visitors found campers holding a silent vigil, and collecting for Oxfam.

In January 1985 three campers cut down part of the perimeter fence and were arrested.

On April Fools' Day, campers pulled off a marvelous publicity stunt. They spread the rumour that the MoD were selling Menwith Hill. Media folk believed them and made 'phone calls to the base to enquire the price!

In April, the big, new, thirty-seater bender was in use at the peace camp for meetings.

On 4th July, about 400 protestors came to the camp's First Birthday Party. On the same day, three campers arrested in January appeared before the Harrogate magistrates, and three more people were arrested at the base, one for obstructing a mayoral car taking its Very Important Passenger into the US Independence Day celebration in the base.

I am very grateful to Mike Holderness and *Peace News* for their permission to reprint Mike's account of a visit to Menwith Hill published in *Peace News* on 25th July.

A day in the life of a peace camp

It's not easy to report what goes on at a peace camp. Much of its energy goes simply into being there. News values have changed too; just five years ago six people invading a top-secret spy base would probably have had at least half a page in *PN*. Now such actions are so commonplace the actors often don't feel it's worth letting the outside world know. Those that get to hear, hear by gossip and visits. So, one sunny day two people want for a walk in the Yorkshire countryside …

"It's a quarter of a mile up the road left from the bus stop", the local CND contact had said. The road stretched at least two miles up the hill, with no sign of the base. So much for car-drivers' sense of distance. We passed the walk translating peace-camp visitors' all too predictable questions: "Where do you get your water from? (I'm thirsty), "How do you manage about, er, going to the toilet? (I'm dying for a crap), "How often do you get evicted?" (Will I see any action?) and how long have you been here" (I've run out of things to say).

"ISN'T IT BIG!"

Over the second summit, the base —a row of golf balls across the horizon. "Isn't it big!" "Well, it is the biggest spy base... oh, you mean the peace camp". An untidy row of benders and caravans stretched along the road to the base. Well away on the next hill, Hunter's Stones microwave tower and, on the crossroads by the camp, the access cover to the 32,000-line link that feeds telephone calls from all over Europe into the National Security Agency's computers. An ordinary battered concrete lid (what else?) over friends' voices, transatlantic affairs, dentists' appointments and shopping lists. At the camp, notebook out, get the routine facts dealt with. Menwith Hill Peace Camp has eight full time residents, one black kitten and a piano. The council aren't bothering them, but they're having to pay £40 a quarter for their standpipe.

BIG BROTHER IS WATCHING

The full time campers disappear into a caravan in a huddle. We go off for a wander along one of the public footpaths that runs across the base. I wander off the line of yellow markers to look at hardware across the hedge. Unnoticed, the television camera scanning the path swivels round, Mo"D" police hare up in a van... "Stop right there!" What are you doing?" Pull class: "Looking to see where the path goes onto. Now I am leaving your land by the shortest practicable route, of my own accord...", half remembered phrases from *Justices Manual*. Both retreat.

Back at the camp, a regular visitor has been asked to leave. I don't understand the reasons and they're none of my business. Half of me starts to feel sympathy for someone who obviously just doesn't fit in in straight society, and wants to offer help. Then I snap back to a more distanced judgment: a peace camp is a group trying to do a job, it has to be able to work together, and so many camps foundered through trying to take in just anyone who turned up.

Meanwhile another group has disappeared, and it's not hard to guess where. Even easier when a surly and embarrassed Mo"D" policeman strolls up to the campfire just happening to ask whether anyone's missing. Where's Sam today? Sam? What Sam?

So they're not giving their names. Sure enough, an hour later a couple of police vans pull up outside the camp and six very high people pour out, all talking at once. There's this massive new structure near the radomes (golf balls to you). Looks like the base for another one. Not sure quite how it's connected to the existing buildings ... but it was so easy to get in, no-one saw us, they even drove right past and didn't spot us, no we can't say much about the building, but it was vast, did we tell you about the time Simon and Alan went and ordered coffee in the flash restaurant inside the base, did you see the look on that Mod-plod's face, they just took us to the guardroom then brought us here...

LAST BUS TO OTLEY

Later, in a pub in Otley, we talk over the visit. The camp is far more thoughtful and (potentially) organised than we'd feared from second and third hand reports. If they had just proper support from people in Yorkshire, if they got stuff printed in Leeds instead of going to Nottingham. If someone helped them put together something explaining what Menwith's significance is, it's so easy to forget when you're having your breakfast next to the Nasty, that most of the world still doesn't have more than the vaguest idea about it...

And people in Yorkshire so obviously want

Menwith to be a focus. Is this a good idea? How could such a campaign be brought back into the places people live, from those windswept moortop fields? A campaign against Telecom for its role in military and spying communications? But it's so diffuse, so omnipresent; not like say, Tarmac, where there are relatively few manifestations and each target is a discovery, is News...

A TARGET FETISH

We start to question the whole idea of taking our campaigning to the Nasty. Does the movement have a technological fixation? A fetish with the point of delivery (why so little attention for Daws Hill, where cruise is controlled and programmed?) Isn't there something to be said for taking opposition to where the decisions are made: Whitehall, Washington even, Mildenhall?

But many people want Menwith as a focus, and so it will be, whatever we may discuss in a pub. We'll just have to see what comes up.

MIKE HOLDERNESS

(Peace News, 26th July 1985, p. 9)

On 17th August, campers strolled through the open gates, and wandered around in the base for some time, inspecting several installations, including the 'golf balls', before being asked to leave by mod-plods. They discovered that large areas of the base were deserted, and doors that should have been locked were open.

The locally organised peace walk from Fylingdales arrived on 26th August, after covering a route of some fifty miles. This acted as a catalyst to set off a series of actions. Early on Monday, 28th August,

Menwith Hill 1986

The first temporary two-day peace camp being set up on 30 April

riccade across the track, and they had to stop. They then left of their own accord, promising to return. Two of them returned that night, after donning dark clothes and blackening their faces. They met a soldier pointing a gun at them.

"Halt. Who goes there?" He repeated this two or three times.

The two activists walked on, giving silly answers like: "Rumble, rumble, I'm a tank." (Extracted from a report in *Peace News*, 20th September 1985.)

They then got nervous and sat down.

eight people got into the base, and five of them climbed a water tower. A diversion was created at the Main Gate, to distract the Modsquad from these people, so that they could climb the tower unseen. Once up the tower they unfurled a banner:

'US BASES GO HOME'

and were soon spotted. After four hours, they climbed down and were arrested and charged with an assortment of offences including attempting to breach the peace with noisy and turbulent behaviour, obstruction and "resisting a police officer on a USAF base(!)". (Exact words from *Peace News*, 6th September 1985). According to Janey Hulme in the "Roll Call" column in *New Statesman*, seven were charged and seven went before Pateley Bridge magistrates. Two arrests on the blockade and the first incursion, added to five, would make seven. Those charged were bailed to appear in Pateley Bridge on 27th September. A condition, that they reside at the address given on their bail application, meant three of them were ordered to live at the peace camp for one month. Then, at 14.00 hours, mass incursions into the base began. The police seemed happy with their tally of arrests, and apparently just picked people up in vans and drove them off the base.

On 3rd September, Menwith Hill had yet more excitement when three people were arrested on its first 'snowball' action.

Campers went to HMS Forest Moor, the Naval communications and radio station nearby, to make the 'Brave Defender' military exercise look silly. They made a daylight incursion. They carried on walking when ordered to stop by two armed soldiers taking part in the exercise, but when they reached an old farmhouse there were more soldiers manning a bar-

More soldiers came, and the campers were escorted off the base. As on the earlier incursion, they were neither arrested nor charged.

Although eight policemen gave evidence for the prosecution when the campers from the 28th August actions appeared before Pateley Bridge magistrates, all the cases were dismissed, because the prosecution evidence was useless. How peacefully climbing on a tower, then sitting or standing on it, and later peacefully descending, could be termed "violent and turbulent behaviour" was not adequately explained for one thing.

Late in Autumn there was a serious fire at the camp. Putting right the damage occupied much of the campers' time.

On 23rd November, about 150 protesters at the camp began a day of exciting actions by capturing and burning the base's US flag. There were incursions. Protesters were trying to kick an eight-foot diameter ball through the Main Gate and the Modplods kept sending it back. A camper climbed a radio mast and did some fire eating. Other campers started a fire, which was eating a fence. There was even a porridge fight with modplods in traditional Keystone Cops style. Although the ten-foot by ten-foot custody room was packed with activists for a time, nobody was charged. Each one was detained for about an hour, before being released.

In January, 1986, the base was brought under by-laws made under the Military Lands Act, 1892, which created many new offences, including interfering with the fences and trespass.

The 'snowball' action, planned to welcome the new by-laws on 19th January, appeared to be adversely affected by the rough winter weather, with gales and low temperatures, which set in about that time. The gales damaged tents in the camp. It must be remembered that this peace camp stood a thousand feet up, on top of a bleak moor, facing East, with no high ground to prevent the bitter East wind coming from Russia. This was the highest campsite and had a fair chance of beating Lossie and Fylingdales to the honour of having the coldest winters. Fylingdales Peace Camp only existed in summer and autumn, and campers would not stay a second winter at Lossie.

Sheffield Peace Action Network went to Menwith Hill on 24th March, when there were still several inches of snow lying. With careful planning and security, to prevent the Modsquad from learning exactly what their plans were in advance, they started at 07.30 hours with a running blockade of the main gate, helped by campers. They had already put extra padlocks on the other two gates, so these could not be opened straight away, and they lost the keys which meant that the keys would not be found by modplods

arresting and searching any of them. The blockade, with blockaders constantly getting up, running away, and returning to sit down, caused a queue of several hundred vehicles to form, and delayed folk going into work in the base.

Meanwhile, three Sheffield activists got inside (not by the Main Gate, of course!) and climbed eighty feet up one of the 'Raydome' dishes. They raised a banner. When they came down, they were arrested and detained for an hour. Even though they refused to give their names, and would not allow themselves to be photographed by police, they were all released without charge. Surprisingly, nobody was charged with an offence on this day. The camp got some good publicity out of these actions.

The campaign on Menwith Hill, at the time of writing, continues, with a big and vigorous camp publicising an extraordinary US base that belongs in the realms of science fiction.

PEACE CAMPS ABROAD

Here are brief notes of peace camps in twelve countries outside the United Kingdom of Great Britain and Northern Ireland. It is impossible to give full accounts, though some camps are also mentioned elsewhere in this book, in greater detail, as the notes will reveal. There may be other camps I have missed; certainly, I have seen inconclusive reports of others. However, I thought it wise to restrict the notes to information that is reasonably certain. Unfortunately, I have seen no reports of peace camps behind the Iron Curtain, so can't provide notes on any.

AUSTRALIA

COCKBURN SOUND, a port used by USN, hosted a women's peace camp, 1st -14th December 1984.

PINE GAP, a CIA communications centre in the desert in the centre of Australia, hosted a peace camp organised by Women for Survival. It was set up on 11th November, 1983, and closed about two weeks later.

SALISBURY PEACE CAMP was set up outside the Main Gate of the Weapons Research Establishment, at Salisbury, South Australia, about June 1984.

BELGIUM

DOEL nuclear power station construction site hosted a peace camp late one August, year unknown

CANADA

NORTHERN CAMP FOR ECOLOGY, near Key Lake, Northern Saskatchewan, was not strictly a peace camp, as it was set up in response to reports of spillages of radioactive water over a dam at Key Lake, but was near enough to a peace camp to count as our Northernmost camp. The radioactive water originated in a uranium mine that was supposed to be safe.

COLLINS BAY BLOCKADE AND CAMP, Northern Saskatchewan. More radioactive water from uranium mines was polluting Wollaston Lake and Rabbit Lake. Local residents blockaded Collins Bay mine HQ and camped by the entrance for about two weeks beginning 10th June, 1985. This was at about the same latitude as Key Lake Camp. To give some idea of the nature of this sparsely populated forest land, twelve local residents chartered a plane to fly to the four days of public meetings that preceded the blockade. Over there, you are still local even if you live 100 km away! Lady Humphrey lived only 20 miles (32 km) away from RAF Fairford, England, and people who lived there did not think she was local. The organisers were the Collins Bay Action Group.

PRIMROSE LAKE PEACE CAMP in protest at the test-firing of unarmed Cruise missiles on ranges nearby, was set up in October 1983.

DENMARK

THE INTERNATIONAL NON-VIOLENT MARCHES FOR DEMILITARISATION, which took place in Jutland in 1981, 1982, 1983, 1984 and 1985, were, in fact, peace camps organised by WRI, and the 1985 camp led to NVDA at Karup NATO base, where eighty people entered unofficially on Hiroshima Day. The arrests at this incursion inspired solidarity NVDA at Vandel Military base, and the courthouse in Vejle, where those arrested were tried. When these people, who had come from several countries for the international gathering, were released, WRI set up a camp to receive them on the Danish-German border at FLENSBERG, which lasted just a few days.

VIBORG PEACE CAMP was set up outside the NATO bunker near Ravnstrup, on 23rd June, 1984. It was on local council land at first, until asked to leave, when it moved to a sympathetic farmer's land. Closure date unknown.

EIRE

MOUNT GABRIEL unmanned, automatic radio and radar relay station was linked to the British air traffic control system, which made it part of the NATO information transmission network. Cork Youth CND set up weekend peace camps here on 27th August, 1983 and 17th-20th August, 1984.

PHOENIX PARK WOMEN'S PEACE CAMP was set up outside the US Ambassador's residence in Dublin, to protest against Cruise and other US nuclear weapons, on 10th June, 1985. Camp ended when all ten campers were arrested on 12th June. Guardai (police) could not charge them with anything, however, as they found Phoenix Park Act, 1925, which forbade many things in the park, did not forbid camping. The women were released, but did not return to the campsite. They later planned to sue the Guardai for wrongful arrest.

FRANCE

LARZAC PLATEAU, near Montpelier, the military, who owned a small area of ranges, were trying to expand this area by compulsory purchase, against the wishes of the local people and farmers, during the 1970s. Peace camps were used to occupy farmland, which the military had taken from local farmers, along with other tactics of NVDA. On 3rd June, 1981, the newly-elected French President, M. Miterand, as he had promised, ordered the military back to their original ranges, to stop taking farmland, and to return land they had already taken. The farmers had won.

Roger Rawlinson has written a book about this called *LARZAC: A non-violent campaign of the 1970s in Southern France,* published by Sessions of York.

HOLLAND

ALMELLO URENCO nuclear reprocessing plant possessed a centrifuge, and took in work from countries outside Holland. There was much protest action here, including a seventy-two-hour blockade, which, being continuous, was a de facto peace camp, in June, 1981.

MOERDIJK nuclear power plant construction site, South of Rotterdam, was occupied by about 700 people with a peace camp and festival, on 5th-7th October, 1985. The climax of their weekend camp was their demonstration of a nuclear accident, with hundreds of performers, sirens, and burning straw dummies.

SOESTERBURG USAF supply airfield had a women's peace camp outside it on International Women's Day, 1982.

VOLKEL AIRFIELD (USAF?) had a peace camp outside, which was evicted in June, 1984.

ITALY

COMISO PEACE CAMP was outside the Cruise missile base in Sicily, and was believed to be still there at the time of writing. It was a very big camp, and there were many large protest demonstrations and NVDAs. Right from the beginning, it had connexions with Greenham, with its campers visiting Greenham, and campers from England visiting Comiso. The camp was set up in Spring, 1982. In Summer, 1983, the camp bought 1.5 hectares of land near the base for 45,000,000 lire, in order to have their own permanent campsite free from the fear of eviction.

JAPAN

SHIBOKUSA WOMEN'S PEACE CAMP was on farmland that had been compulsorily purchased for military ranges. During the 'seventies' and 'eighties' women moved into some of the farmhouses, and lived there without any mains services – water, electricity, etc. They tried to continue farming the land, but evictions were frequent. (For a detailed account see *Women at the Wire* by Leonnie Caldecott and Lynne Jones, published by The Women's Press).

NEW ZEALAND

A peace camp was set up for a brief period at an international airport here, in September, 1984, in solidarity with the women's strike peace camps in Europe.

SWITZERLAND

GENEVA INTERNATIONAL PEACE CAMP was set up, in November 1983, on university land in La Place Des Nations, but was evicted on the orders of the Recteur, with eleven people arrested and detained, on 28th December, 1983. The last camper was released from prison 3rd January, 1984. The camp started again on another site nearby. Further activity included a fast, in August 1985. The camp was last reported active in October, 1985, nearly two years after it had been started.

UNITED STATES OF AMERICA

ALAMEDA U.S.N. AIR STATION: Weekend women's peace camps in late 1983 or 1984 apparently managed to contact the service personnel, and got growing support from within the base. The base is in California.

DAVIS MONTHAN U.S.A.F. Cruise missile training base had a peace camp in August, 1983.

GROUND ZERO CENTER FOR NONVIOLENT ACTION, 16159, Clear Creek Road, North-West Poulsco, Washington, WA98370, was set up on 3.8 acres of land adjoining a Trident submarine base, in 1977. In addition, a house was purchased by disarmers, directly outside the gate used by railway trains entering and leaving the base. As ownership of both properties was in the hands of disarmers, there were no problems with evictions. In December 1982, people observing from the house discovered the white train. This led to blockades, and American nuclear disarmers train-spotting all over the U.S.A. Later the White Train was painted in lots of different colours to try and make it look less conspicuous, but nuclear disarmers still had no difficulty in spotting it. At the time of writing, the house, which was bought in 1981, was still believed to be operating as a peace camp.

LIVERMORE LABORATORIES,

California, the US atomic weapons research centre, was reported to have had a peace camp outside it around 1984.

ROCKY FLATS

Jack Cohen-Joppa is co-editor of the *Nuclear Resister* (PO Box 43383, Tucson, Arizona, AZ 85733-3383 U.S.A.). He told me of a camp outside a nuclear installation at Rocky Flats, Montana, which existed for about a year around 1973.

Campers erected tents. Some tents were put on the railway line into the plant, which was used to transport nuclear material. Often trains carrying nuclear material were halted by these tents on the line. Although briefly mentioned in *Peace News* once, Rocky Flats Camp never achieved world fame. Jack told me he learned a lot about campaigning on this camp.

SAVANNAH RIVER nuclear power station complex manufactured nuclear weapons, and was in South Carolina. A peace camp was set up here on 21st October, 1983. Campers conducted several actions, including a one-hour blockade, which led to 105 arrests, and a fifteen-mile traffic jam. If this report is accurate, the Savannah River road traffic jam was more than twice as long as Faslane's record seven-mile jam, and would constitute a world record for a traffic jam arising out of a blockade by disarmers. This camp ended on 24th October after just four days.

SEABROOK, New Hampshire, was a site chosen for the construction of a nuclear power station. The site was occupied, in April and May 1977, by a number of groups who had combined into the Clamshell Alliance for this particular campaign. The organisers devised a system of affinity groups, for use in NVDAs, and this was almost certainly the first time affinity groups were used in a large protest of this kind. The idea has been copied all over the world.

SENECA arms dump in upper New York State is reported to have had a peace camp outside it in September 1985.

S.O.S. Peace Camp was the short title of Silence One Silo for Peace Camp, which was held outside missile silo number R29 in Montana, in June and July 1983.

WEST GERMANY

ALSFELD, FULDA, GREBENHEIM, HANAU and WILDFLECKEN

These NATO bases had peace camps during the

Women's Strike in September, 1984, as reported elsewhere in this book, under 'The Women's Strike".

GORLEBEN nuclear waste dump had a camp during May 1980, and another month-long camp in June and July 1983. Protests continue here.

GROSSENGSTINGEN U.S.A.F. Lance missile base suffered a 24-hour blockade in March 1981. As a result of this Tubingen, the local town, was made a NFZ. On 28th July, 1982, three peace camps were set up near Grossengstingen to operate a twenty-four-hour, seven day, continuous blockade from 1st to 8th August, with 600 people, organised in fifty-five affinity groups, in three shifts per day. Obviously this was a tremendous undertaking, especially as the people involved were volunteers. Apparently the blockade succeeded in closing the base for the whole week, and there were no arrests.

HALVETE PEACE CAMP was on a sympathetic farmer's land near a nuclear weapons store.

MULTLANGEN U.S.A.F. Pershing II missile base suffered many blockades of troop buses, Pershing vehicles, and supply trucks during 1983 and 1984. Campers chased convoys and individual military vehicles, as at Greenham Common. Mutlangen Peace Camp was linked with blockades at the future Pershing II missile base at Hasselbach and Waldheide Pershing I base. Mutlangen campers organised a 600km march to Bonn, with several small NVDAs taking place on the way. On 12th June, campers made a presentation to the UN Disarmament Commission.

ROCKERHAUSEN, near Hasselbach, was the site of a women's peace camp set up in opposition to Cruise and Pershing, and which lasted from 15th July to 15th August, 1983.

WACKERSDORF in Bavaria was the location of a site for a planned nuclear reprocessing plant, capable of making five tonnes of weapons-grade plutonium every year. At this time, West Germany was not bound by the Non-Proliferation Treaty. The peace camps here started with the Friendship House, on 15th August, 1985, which was evicted by police soon after being set up. On 7th December, a 40,000-strong rally took place here, and 2000 people set up a camp to occupy the construction site. They were evicted by police on 16th December. In early January 1986, a 10,000-strong rally here led to another camp on the site, this time with 400 people, who were brutally evicted by police. When 50,000 demonstrators assembled for a rally outside the site, on Easter Monday, 1986, police used water cannon and teargas to disperse them, and made about 300 arrests. There was no continuous camp at Wackersdorf, but the campaign was continuous, and was still being vigorously conducted at the time of writing.

WHYL became the location of the world's first peace camp at a site related to nuclear power, which was not a military base. This camp was actually at a nuclear power station construction site. It was started on 23rd February, 1975, long before Seabrook and Torness acquired their camps.

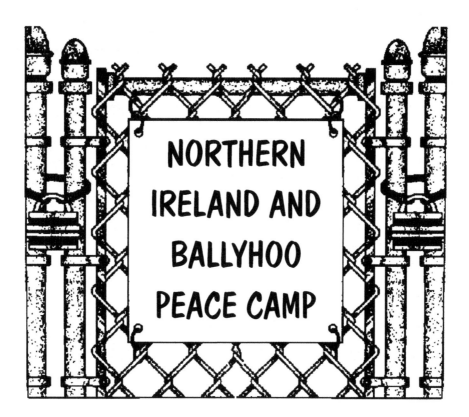

NORTHERN IRELAND AND BALLYHOO PEACE CAMP

Ballyhoo

Northern Ireland did not have any big nuclear bases like Greenham Common in 1983, but there was an early warning radar station linked into NATO's nuclear defence forces on the airfield at RAF Bishopscourt, near Downpatrick.

A peace camp was set up here. The area in which the peace camp was situated was known as Balyhouran, and this led to the nickname of Ballyhoo Peace Camp (believed to have been originally coined by a journalist). Ballyhoo seems to sum up the happy, friendly mood of campers, police and RAF security people here as one can see from this account by one of the peace campers, Peter Emerson. (I am grateful to Peter Emerson and *Peace News* for permission to reproduce this article from p. 12 of *Peace News* 8th July, 1983.)

Of Cabbage, Constables and Kettles: a diary of a peace camp, RAF Bishopscourt, Northern Ireland

December 1982: Dear Royal Ulster Constabulary, we're thinking about having a peace camp outside RAF Bishopscourt... CND, Greenham Common... okay?

—Oh, that's fine; just clear it with the Department of the Environment...

yours, Sergeant Campbell.

January: Dear DoE, we're thinking... and, as you know, Downpatrick Council voted against cruise last year... and, well, what do you think?

February: Silence. Not a murmur. Did the DoE think at all, we wondered.

March: And on the day Helen John addressed a public meeting in Belfast, one caravan set up camp

— Sergeant Campbell? Hallo. Here's OK, then, is it? We never did hear from the DoE. Extraordinary, isn't it?

— Extraordinary.

— Warrant Officer Cummings, I presume?

—Yes; how do you do?

— What's this new barricade for?

— Well...

— Now we always tell you everything we're going to do; the very least you could do is reciprocate.

— Well...

— Too late now. Can we have another water container please?

— Oh certainly.

And still there was silence from the DoE. Days passed. Plots were turned and potatoes were planted. And still there was the monthly demo outside the gates of the base. Plots were planned and ploys were planted: non-violent direct action.

April: Duncan. To you, he is still Warrant Officer Cummings, Officer in charge of security, RAF Bishopscourt, radar air defence station, Co Down. But, to us...

— Oh, call me Duncan, please.

— Cup o'tea?

— Thanks.

— Have a seat

— Ta. Now, this action...well, because of the security situation here we think it would be better if you didn't.

— Well, because of the security situation here we think it would be better if we did. After all, peaceful protest is part of 'normality' And you want 'normality' don't you Duncan?

— Yes of course! But … well, our boys are armed, and young, and they might make a mistake, and they shot a woman in Newry once who was only shaking a mop out of the window…

— OK. This is what we'll do. For as long as we live in a nuclear state 'normality' must involve climbing over fences, right?

— ... (he didn't say)

—But we will tell you what we're going to do and when we're going to do it. How's that?

— Fine, he said, a little reluctantly.

— OK. On Saturday, April 9, CND will, how shall we say, drop in.

And still there was silence from the DoE.

Thomas. To you, he is still Sergeant Campbell, Royal Ulster Constabulary, charged with keeping the Queen's Peace in rather a pleasant part of the world, somewhat unknown to that Queen.

— Morning: how are you?

— Och, shocking weather. Are you going in?

— Yeah.

— Over the top?

— Yeah.

— When?

— Saturday, April 9. D'you want to come in too?

April 9: Over a small barbed wire fence at 7.30 am, and five of us were strolling down the runway with our banner in front of us—there wasn't an airman to be seen—the world was ours. We approached the radar. Oh, there's the gate. My God; it's open; quick, sssssshh, quickly... A little head peeped round the corner of his sentrybox. O-oh was all he said to us, but I think I saw signs of a 'what the...?'to himself. We dashed inside and sat down.

The sun was now rising high over the Western Alliance, the sky was a beautiful NATO blue, and there wasn't a cloud or a Backfire bomber in sight.

— Gets a bit boring here doesn't it? we asked.

Soon, the screech of tyres, the bang of boots, the orders of sergeants, we were surrounded, and the officer in charge (why wasn't he Duncan?) spoke with authority:

— Will you come peacefully or do we have to arrest you?

— Both.

By the arm-pits we were led away, searched and questioned;

— Have you any excuse for this conduct?

— No: but we have a reason.

And we spoke just a little about Bishopscourt, about the UK nuclear war machine and about Greenham Common. Ten minutes later, we were enjoying that freedom which others wish to defend by restricting it and restrict by defending it.

Chief Inspector Thompson. To you and to us he was Chief Inspector Thompson, and he came to inspect, which was his job, just as we were putting the kettle on, which was ours.

— Well, he said, we haven't decided yet whether to charge you or not.

— Sugar?

— Thanks. The trouble is, of course, this: if we arrest you and charge you that will only give your cause more publicity, which is what you want. Right?

— Yes. Biscuit?

— Er, no thanks. But if we did arrest you, you'd probably refuse bail and so we'd have to release you without bail and you'd probably plead guilty so we'd have to fine you and you'd probably refuse the fine so we'd have to lock you up for a few weeks in the Crumlin Road or Armagh and you still wouldn't mind 'cos it would all help your cause wouldn't it?

— Absolutely; have some more tea.

* * *

And still there was silence from the DoE though of course things were still happening. In early April, we asked the DoE permission to pay rent. Later, our application to the Department of Finance to pay rates was accepted, our existence was officially acknowledged, and our address was recorded as 2A Lismore Road. The occasional press article showed a caravan or one, a cabbage plot or two, and even a goat. Now was it the application to pay rent, or was it the vision of cabbages on every roadside verge from here to Newtownwards? We don't know. But the raw nerve of the bureaucracy had twitched and on the 20th the DoE decided to answer our letter(s):

— Dear CND. Fuck off. Seven days or else .

— Dear DoE. We appeal.

DoE made no reply. Not even when we visited them. So, off to the RUC. Chief Inspector Thompson please; well, Charles to us of course.

— Och come in. How are you? Tea? No, don 't worry, we're not going to come in the middle of the night to tow you away. If anything, you will be given a court summons, a trial, the right of appeal... so it'll all take a little time yet. And even then the law the DoE's quoting talks of "reasonable excuses' so you might even win the case in court Changing the subject a little, are you going in again? We hadn't realised on April 9 that you were going to opt for 7am.

—Ah, but if you had, you'd have felt you had to be there to stop us, no?

— Yes.

— Well, in order to make sure you don't waste time chasing pacifists, we're not going to tell you the day next time. But we will be doing Greenham Common type stuff again, sometime, just sometime.

— And if we don't arrest you now for the little 9th escapade, you're just going to do something more spectacular later aren't you?

— Yes. Until cruise is cancelled. And we're sorry it puts you in the rather difficult position of having to decide whether to support the state no matter how nuclear that state (and no matter how many international laws and treaties it breaks) or whether to join the momentum for disarmament in whatever way you think fit.

— D'you want some more tea?

— Thanks.

May: The words flowed in letters and the letters flowed to the DoE; short curt replies came in return. And then with the seven days fully seven days old: "the matter is now in the hands of the police".

— Morning, Charles.

—Good morning to you. I must say your garden is coming on well.

— Your seven days are up then.

—Aye; but we've had no complaints about you at all. And the DoE should realise that here in Northern Ireland we've got bigger jobs to do than chasing pea-planting pacifists; the Provisional IRA still violent vandals burning down the town hall last week, Paisley threatening to march down Market Street on Saturday. There's one thing I must say, though.

— Go on.

— Well, you CND folk have already broken the law and you're likely to do it again and even after you've been tried and incarcerated you might well repeat the process...

— Certainly.

— I thought so; well this is the first time in my ca-reer that I the prosecutor have sat discussing which charges and whether bail and what procedures and all... with the accused!

— D'you want some more tea?

PETER EMERSON

On 25th June, just after the above was sent for publication, fifty cyclists rode from Belfast to Ballyhoo Peace Camp, on a ride to Germany organised through International Voluntary Service. They stayed the night, before proceeding via Dublin, Liverpool, Cambridge, High Wycombe, Greenham Common, Haslemere and a number of nuclear bases to Dover, where they embarked on a ferry for Ostende on 16th July.

At the time of writing, Ballyhoo held a world record with a most amazing achievement. History might have forgotten it, but for Peter Emerson, who wrote this account at the time. (I am grateful to Peter Emerson and *Peace News* for permission to reproduce this news item from p. 4 of *Peace News*, 14th October, 1983.)

Government-assisted peace camp!

"Lisburn five one double one."

"Hallo."

"Good morning Sir."

"Is that the British army community relations?"

"Just one minute, Sir. I'll try their extension."

Brrrr brrrr or tweep tweep depending on whether or not increased defence budgets allow brrrr to be a deleted and tweep to be inserted.

"Sir! Community relations branch; Sergeant Carruthers speaking."

"Oh hello. My name's only mister so you don't have to call me sir..."

"Very good Sir."

" ...and I'm speaking on behalf of the blankety-blank summer scheme in Belfast and... "

"You're one of those voluntary groups aren't you Sir?"

"Yes, that's right."

"And you're trying to bring the kids together during the summer holidays?"

"Yes, before the churches once more wrench them apart for another academic year."

"Terrible, Sir. Terrible. You'd think the churches would pull their fucking fingers out, wouldn't you ... oh pardon language, Sir."

"Well don't you think the fucking British government should stop funding the churches in such a system of state subsidised segregation?"

"Oh, that's politics Sir. Can't get into that. Not round 'ere. You'll be asking me about that nuclear stuff next. So —back to business —you're in the job of peace and reconciliation... what can we do to help?"

"Well, we're taking the kids away cycling and camping, to be at peace with themselves and their environment for a few days. Got any tents?"

"Of course, Sir; 'ow many would you like? Any camping gas, utensils, jerry cans … help yourself."

And so it was that girls and boy definitely, unionist and nationalist probably, and catholic and protestant mainly in name, went a-camping in the county of Down. And so it was that in a field outside RAF Bishopscourt a world record was broken; and a peace camp was equipped with three in number Ministry of Defence stores item mark nought dome tents bracket British army two men sleeping for the use of.

They fucking pardon my language leaked.

"Serve the so and so's right, Sir, Sergeant Carruthers might add if he too wrote articles for Peace News.

—PETER EMERSON

(*Peace News* 14ᵗʰ October 1983, p. 4)

On 9th November, 1983, peace campers here took action in support of Greenham Women Against Cruise, who were taking legal action in the USA to try and stop Cruise missiles coming to Britain. This was only a small event, but peace campers made up for it by organising a fine twenty-four-hour blockade the following weekend, on Saturday 12th November, when some traffic was turned away and some got through. The next day was Remembrance Sunday, the day when Britain remembers its war dead, which is particularly revered in Northern Ireland. On this Sunday, campers held a well-attended Alternative Remembrance Service in the open air.

In December the peace camp was still active, and on the weekend of 17ᵗʰ-18ᵗʰ December a twenty-four-hour blockade, similar to the one in November, surrounded RAF Bishopscourt. This was followed by a silent vigil on New Year's Eve and a walk onto the airfield on New Year's Day 1984. There were no

charges when the ten walkers were arrested and removed from the airfield.

17th March is the day of St. Patrick's Ireland's Patron Saint. The peace camp celebrated it with another twenty-four-hour blockade on the weekend of 17th-18th March.

The peace campers took over a nearby field, and on 19th-20th May weekend they held a Spring Festival, planting crops here and on the roadside verge to add to their Peace Garden. The caravan was painted so that it would act as an advertisement telling people why the camp was there.

During the Summer of 1985, numbers at the peace camp began dropping off, making it difficult to keep a human presence there all the time.

On 22nd-23rd June, in a rally at RAF Bishopscourt, speakers from Irish CND and British CND addressed about 250 people. After the rally, severe staffing problems set in, and for long periods there was nobody at the camp. The caravan still sat on the site, serving as an advertisement, and maintaining a presence … In April, 1986, the caravan was still there, staffed only occasionally, and an eviction notice was expected from the Department of the Environment.

At Least Cruise is Clean,

Written by 'Lynchcombe', who is believed to be a Newbury person, and published anonymously.

CND Story, The

Edited by J. Minion and P. Bosover; published by Alison and Busby, 44 Hill Street. London W1X 8BL.

Chronology of Upper Heyford Peace Camp

Written by Paul N. Rogers, never published, but several copies are believed to be in existence.

Faslane: Diary of a Peace Camp

Written by the campers, with a foreward by Kevin Dunion. Published by Polygon Books, Edinburgh University Press, 23 George Street, Edinburgh, EH8 9TJ.

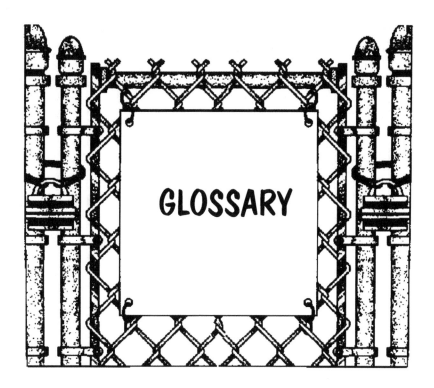

GLOSSARY

Some uncommon terms and abbreviations used in the text.

BNFL	British Nuclear Fules Limited
C100	Committee of One Hundred
CAAT	Campaign Against the Arms Trade
CEGB	Central Electricity Generating Board
CIA	Central Intellegence Agency (United States)
DHSS	Department of Health and Social Security
FAB	Families Against the Bomb
MoD	Ministry of Defence
modplod	Ministry of Defence policeman or policewoman
Modsquad	Ministry of Defence Police Force
MP	Member of Parliament or military policeman, depending on context
NCCL	National Council for Civil Liberties
NFZ	Nuclear-Free Zone
NVDA	Non-violent direct action
PC	Police Constable, sometimes followed by his name
RNAD	Royal Naval Armament Depot
ROF	Royal Ordnance Factory
SCCL	Scottish Council for Civil Liberties
USN	United States Navy
WRI	War Resisters International

BIBLIOGRAPHY

Larzac: a non-violent campaign of the 1970s in Southern France

Written by Roger Rawlinson. Published by Sessions of York, England. Obtainable from them direct or from good bookshops.

Molesworth Bulletin

Periodical, published and distributed by the camp

New Statesman

Weekly, 70 Great Turnstile Street, London WC1V 7HJ.

No Bunkers Here.

Written by Tony Simpson; published jointly by Mid-Glamorgan CND and Peace News, 5 Caledonian Road, London N1.

Peace News

Monthly; 5 Caledonian Road, London N1. Back issues can be obtained from this address, as can subscriptions for this monthly paper, which can be bought in some shops.

Radiator, The – renamed the Southern Resister.

Monthly; 37 Wordsworth Road, Salisbury, SP1 3BH. Has ceased publication.

ROF Burghfield: a nuclear weapons factory, as seen by the Burghfield Peace Camp.

Published by Acorn Books, 17 Chatham Street, Reading, Berks.

Sanity

No longer published but back issues can be inspected at CND Office, 162 Holloway Road, London N7 8DQ (Tel: 0171 700 2393)

Southern Resister, The

See *Radiator*.

Twenty-Four Hours at Greenham

Written by Rene Gill; illustrated by Richard Kennedy; published by Maidenhead CND.

Women at the Wire

Edited by Leonnie Caldecott and Lynne Jones; published by The Women's Press, 34 Great Sutton Street, London EC1V 0DX.

Women's Peace Camp

Published in February, 1983, by Greenham Common Peace Camp.

N.B. Some periodicals may have ceased publication and some books may be out of print by the time you read this. Housman's Bookshop, 5 Caledonian Road, London N1, can supply most – if not all – of the above items, and can suggest where to look for others. I regret I cannot supply them myself. Copies of newspapers mentioned in the text can be found in the relevant newspaper offices and public libraries near those offices. Public libraries often keep copies of national newspapers and periodicals, including back issues. Your local Friends' Meeting library or Friends' House library, tel 020 7663 1135 (173 Euston Road, London NW1 2BJ) or Woodbrooke library, tel 0121 472 5171 (1046 Bristol Road, Selly Oak, Birmingham B29 6LJ) may be able to help find a publication.

Lightning Source UK Ltd.
Milton Keynes UK
UKOW07f1127271117
313425UK00003B/90/P